GREAT BOOKS OF THE WEST

GREAT BOOKS
OF THE WESTERN WORLD

ROBERT MAYNARD HUTCHINS, *EDITOR IN CHIEF*

43.

AMERICAN STATE PAPERS

THE FEDERALIST

J. S. MILL

GREAT BOOKS
OF THE WESTERN WORLD

ROBERT MAYNARD HUTCHINS, EDITOR IN CHIEF

43.

AMERICAN STATE PAPERS
THE FEDERALIST
J. S. MILL

MORTIMER J. ADLER, Associate Editor

Members of the Advisory Board: STRINGFELLOW BARR, SCOTT BUCHANAN, JOHN ERSKINE,
CLARENCE H. FAUST, ALEXANDER MEIKLEJOHN, JOSEPH J. SCHWAB, MARK VAN DOREN.
Editorial Consultants: A. F. B. CLARK, F. L. LUCAS, WALTER MURDOCH.
WALLACE BROCKWAY, Executive Editor

AMERICAN STATE PAPERS

THE FEDERALIST
BY
ALEXANDER HAMILTON, JAMES MADISON, JOHN JAY

ON LIBERTY · REPRESENTATIVE GOVERNMENT · UTILITARIANISM
BY
JOHN STUART MILL

WILLIAM BENTON, *Publisher*

ENCYCLOPÆDIA BRITANNICA, INC.

CHICAGO · LONDON · TORONTO

THE UNIVERSITY OF CHICAGO

The Great Books
is published with the editorial advice of the faculties
of The University of Chicago

GENERAL CONTENTS

AMERICAN STATE PAPERS

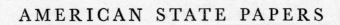

CONTENTS:

THE
DECLARATION OF INDEPENDENCE

[THOMAS JEFFERSON]

A DECLARATION BY THE REPRESENTATIVES OF THE UNITED STATES
OF AMERICA IN CONGRESS ASSEMBLED, JULY 4, 1776

WHEN, in the course of human events, it becomes necessary for one people
to dissolve the political bands which have connected them with another, and
to assume, among the powers of the earth, the separate and equal station to
which the laws of nature and of nature's God entitle them, a decent respect
to the opinions of mankind requires that they should declare the causes 5
which impel them to the separation.

We hold these truths to be self-evident, that all men are created equal;
that they are endowed by their Creator with certain unalienable rights;
that among these are life, liberty, and the pursuit of happiness. That, to secure these rights, governments are instituted among men, deriving their just 10
powers from the consent of the governed; that, whenever any form of government becomes destructive of these ends, it is the right of the people
to alter or to abolish it, and to institute a new government, laying its
foundation on such principles, and organizing its powers in such form, as
to them shall séem most likely to effect their safety and happiness. Prudence, 15
indeed, will dictate that governments long established should not be
changed for light and transient causes; and, accordingly, all experience hath
shown, that mankind are more disposed to suffer, while evils are sufferable,
than to right themselves by abolishing the forms to which they are accustomed. But, when a long train of abuses and usurpations, pursuing in- 20
variably the same object, evinces a design to reduce them under absolute
despotism, it is their right, it is their duty, to throw off such government, and
to provide new guards for their future security. Such has been the patient
sufferance of these colonies, and such is now the necessity which constrains
them to alter their former systems of government. The history of the present 25
King of Great Britain is a history of repeated injuries and usurpations, all
having, in direct object, the establishment of an absolute tyranny over these
states. To prove this, let facts be submitted to a candid world:

He has refused his assent to laws the most wholesome and necessary for
the public good. 30

He has forbidden his governors to pass laws of immediate and pressing
importance, unless suspended in their operation till his assent should be
obtained; and, when so suspended, he has utterly neglected to attend to
them.

He has refused to pass other laws for the accommodation of large districts of 35
people, unless those people would relinquish the right of representation in

the legislature; a right inestimable to them, and formidable to tyrants only.

He has called together legislative bodies at places unusual, uncomfortable, and distant from the depository of their public records, for the sole
40 purpose of fatiguing them into compliance with his measures.

He has dissolved representative houses repeatedly, for opposing, with manly firmness, his invasions on the rights of the people.

He has refused, for a long time after such dissolutions, to cause others to be elected; whereby the legislative powers, incapable of annihilation, have
45 returned to the people at large for their exercise; the state remaining, in the meantime, exposed to all the danger of invasion from without, and convulsions within.

He has endeavored to prevent the population of these States; for that purpose, obstructing the laws for naturalization of foreigners, refusing to pass
50 others to encourage their migration hither, and raising the conditions of new appropriations of lands.

He has obstructed the administration of justice, by refusing his assent to laws for establishing judiciary powers.

He has made judges dependent on his will alone, for the tenure of their
55 offices, and the amount and payment of their salaries.

He has erected a multitude of new offices, and sent hither swarms of officers to harass our people, and eat out their substance.

He has kept among us, in time of peace, standing armies, without the consent of our legislatures.
60 He has affected to render the military independent of, and superior to, the civil power.

He has combined, with others, to subject us to a jurisdiction foreign to our Constitution, and unacknowledged by our laws; giving his assent to their acts of pretended legislation:
65 For quartering large bodies of armed troops among us:

For protecting them by a mock trial, from punishment, for any murders which they should commit on the inhabitants of these States:

For cutting off our trade with all parts of the world:

For imposing taxes on us without our consent:
70 For depriving us, in many cases, of the benefit of trial by jury:

For transporting us beyond seas to be tried for pretended offenses:

For abolishing the free system of English laws in a neighboring province, establishing therein an arbitrary government, and enlarging its boundaries, so as to render it at once an example and fit instrument for introducing the
75 same absolute rule into these colonies:

For taking away our charters, abolishing our most valuable laws, and altering, fundamentally, the powers of our governments:

For suspending our own legislatures, and declaring themselves invested with power to legislate for us in all cases whatsoever.
80 He has abdicated government here, by declaring us out of his protection, and waging war against us.

He has plundered our seas, ravaged our coasts, burnt our towns, and destroyed the lives of our people.

He is, at this time, transporting large armies of foreign mercenaries to
85 complete the works of death, desolation, and tyranny, already begun, with circumstances of cruelty and perfidy scarcely paralleled in the most barbarous ages, and totally unworthy the head of a civilized nation.

He has constrained our fellow-citizens, taken captive on the high seas, to bear arms against their country, to become the executioners of their friends and brethren, or to fall themselves by their hands.   90

He has excited domestic insurrections amongst us, and has endeavored to bring on the inhabitants of our frontiers, the merciless Indian savages, whose known rule of warfare is an undistinguished destruction of all ages, sexes, and conditions.

In every stage of these oppressions, we have petitioned for redress, in the 95 most humble terms; our repeated petitions have been answered only by repeated injury. A prince, whose character is thus marked by every act which may define a tyrant, is unfit to be the ruler of a free people.

Nor have we been wanting in attention to our British brethren. We have warned them, from time to time, of attempts made by their legislature to 100 extend an unwarrantable jurisdiction over us. We have reminded them of the circumstances of our emigration and settlement here. We have appealed to their native justice and magnanimity, and we have conjured them, by the ties of our common kindred, to disavow these usurpations, which would inevitably interrupt our connections and correspondence. They, too, have 105 been deaf to the voice of justice and consanguinity. We must, therefore, acquiesce in the necessity which denounces our separation, and hold them, as we hold the rest of mankind, enemies in war, in peace, friends.

We, therefore, the representatives of the United States of America, in general Congress assembled, appealing to the Supreme Judge of the world 110 for the rectitude of our intentions, do, in the name, and by the authority of the good people of these colonies, solemnly publish and declare, that these united colonies are, and of right ought to be, free and independent states; that they are absolved from all allegiance to the British Crown, and that all political connection between them and the state of Great Britain 115 is, and ought to be, totally dissolved; and that, as free and independent states, they have full power to levy war, conclude peace, contract alliances, establish commerce, and to do all other acts and things which independent states may of right do. And, for the support of this declaration, with a firm reliance on the protection of Divine Providence, we mutually pledge to each 120 other our lives, our fortunes, and our sacred honour.

ARTICLES
OF CONFEDERATION

Articles of Confederation and perpetual Union between the States of New Hampshire, Massachusetts Bay, Rhode Island and Providence Plantations, Connecticut, New York, New Jersey, Pennsylvania, Delaware, Maryland, Virginia, North Carolina, South Carolina, and Georgia.

Article One

The style of this Confederacy shall be "The United States of America."

Article Two

Each State retains its sovereignty, freedom, and independence, and every power, jurisdiction, and right, which is not by this Confederation expressly delegated to the United States in Congress assembled.

Article Three

The said States hereby severally enter into a firm league of friendship with each other, for their common defence, the security of their liberties, and their mutual and general welfare, binding themselves to assist each other against all force offered to, or attacks made upon them, or any of them, on account of religion, sovereignty, trade, or any other pretence whatever.

Article Four

The better to secure and perpetuate mutual friendship and intercourse among the people of the different States in this Union, the free inhabitants of each of these States, paupers, vagabonds, and fugitives from justice excepted, shall be entitled to all the privileges and immunities of free citizens in the several States, and the people of each State shall have free ingress and regress to and from any other State, and shall enjoy therein all the privileges of trade and commerce, subject to the same duties, impositions, and restrictions as the inhabitants thereof respectively, provided that such restrictions shall not extend so far as to prevent the removal of property imported into any State, to any other State of which the owner is an inhabitant; provided also, that no imposition, duties, or restriction shall be laid by any State, on the property of the United States, or either of them.

If any person guilty of or charged with treason, felony, or other high misdemeanor in any State, shall flee from justice, and be found in any of the United States, he shall, upon demand of the governor or executive power of the State from which he fled, be delivered up and removed to the State having jurisdiction of his offence.

Full faith and credit shall be given in each of these States to the records, acts, and judicial proceedings of the courts and magistrates of every other State.

Article Five

For the more convenient management of the general interests of the United States, delegates shall be annually appointed in such manner as the legislature of each State shall direct, to meet in Congress on the first Monday in November, in every year, with a power reserved to each State to recall its delegates, or any of them, at any time within the year, and to send others in their stead, for the remainder of the year.

No State shall be represented in Congress by less than two, nor by more than seven members; and no person shall be capable of being a delegate for more than three years in any term of six years, nor shall any person, being a delegate, be capable of holding any office under the United States for which he or another for his benefit receives any salary, fees, or emolument of any kind.

Each State shall maintain its own delegates in a meeting of the States, and while they act as members of the committee of the States.

In determining questions in the United States, in Congress assembled, each State shall have one vote.

Freedom of speech and debate in Congress shall not be impeached or questioned in any court or place out of Congress, and the members of Congress shall be protected in their persons from arrests and imprisonments, during the time of their going to or from, and attendance on, Congress, except for treason, felony, or breach of the peace.

Article Six

No State, without the consent of the United States in Congress assembled, shall send any embassy to, or receive any embassy from, or enter into any conference, agreement, alliance, or treaty with, any king, prince, or state; nor shall any person holding any office of profit or trust under the United States, or any of them, accept of any present, emolument, office, or title of any kind whatever from any king, prince, or foreign state; nor shall the United States in Congress assembled, or any of them, grant any title of nobility.

No two or more States shall enter into any treaty, confederation, or alliance whatever between them, without the consent of the United States in Congress assembled, specifying accurately the purposes for which the same is to be entered into, and how long it shall continue.

No State shall lay any imposts or duties, which may interfere with any stipulations in treaties entered into by the United States in Congress assembled, with any king, prince, or state, in pursuance of any treaties already proposed by Congress, to the courts of France and Spain.

No vessels of war shall be kept in time of peace by any State, except such number only as shall be deemed necessary by the United States in Congress assembled, for the defence of such State or its trade; nor shall any body of forces be kept up by any State, in time of peace, except such number only as in the judgment of the United States in Congress assembled shall be deemed requisite to garrison the forts necessary for the defence of such State; but every State shall always keep up a well regulated and disciplined militia, sufficiently armed and accoutred, and shall provide and constantly have ready for use, in public stores, a due number of field-pieces and tents, and a proper quantity of arms, ammunition, and camp equipage.

No State shall engage in any war without the consent of the United States in Congress assembled, unless such State be actually invaded by enemies, or shall have received certain advice of a resolution being formed by some nation of Indians to invade such State, and the danger is so imminent as not to admit of a delay till the United States in Congress assembled can be consulted; nor shall any State grant commissions to any ships or vessels of war, nor letters of marque or reprisal, except it be after a declaration of war by the United States in Congress assembled, and then only against the kingdom or state, and the subjects thereof, against which war has been so declared, and under such regulations as shall be established by the United States in Congress assembled, unless such State be infested by pirates, in which case vessels of war may be fitted out for that occasion, and kept so long as the danger shall continue, or until the United States in Congress assembled shall determine otherwise.

Article Seven

WHEN land forces are raised by any State for the common defense, all officers of or under the rank of colonel shall be appointed by the legislature of each State respectively, by whom such forces shall be raised, or in such manner as such State shall direct; and all vacancies shall be filled up by the State which first made the appointment.

Article Eight

ALL charges of war and all other expenses that shall be incurred for the common defence or general welfare, and allowed by the United States in Congress assembled, shall be defrayed out of a common treasury, which shall be supplied by the several States, in proportion to the value of all land within each

State, granted to or surveyed for any person, and such land and the buildings and improvements thereon shall be estimated according to such mode as the United States in Congress assembled shall from time to time direct and appoint.

The taxes for paying that proportion shall be laid and levied by the authority and direction of the legislatures of the several States within the time agreed upon by the United States in Congress assembled.

Article Nine

THE United States in Congress assembled shall have the sole and exclusive right and power of determining on peace and war, except in the cases mentioned in the sixth article—of sending and receiving ambassadors—entering into treaties and alliances, provided that no treaty of commerce shall be made whereby the legislative power of the respective States shall be restrained from imposing such imposts and duties on foreigners as their own people are subjected to, or from prohibiting the exportation or importation of any species of goods or commodities whatsoever—of establishing rules for deciding, in all cases, what captures on land or water shall be legal, and in what manner prizes taken by land or naval forces in the service of the United States shall be divided or appropriated—of granting letters of marque and reprisal in times of peace —appointing courts for the trial of piracies and felonies committed on the high seas, and establishing courts for receiving and determining finally appeals in all cases of captures, provided that no member of Congress shall be appointed a judge of any of the said courts.

The United States in Congress assembled shall also be the last resort on appeal in all disputes and differences now subsisting or that hereafter may arise between two or more States concerning boundary, jurisdiction, or any other cause whatever; which authority shall always be exercised in the manner following:—Whenever the legislative or executive authority or lawful agent of any State in controversy with another shall present a petition to Congress stating the matter in question and praying for a hearing, notice thereof shall be given by order of Congress to the legislative or executive authority of the other State in controversy, and a day assigned for the appearance of the parties by their lawful agents, who shall then be directed to appoint, by joint consent, commissioners or judges to constitute a court for hearing and determining the matter in question; but if they cannot agree, Congress shall name three persons out of each of the United States, and from the list of such persons each party shall alternately strike out one, the petitioners beginning, until the number shall be reduced to thirteen; and from that number not less than seven nor more than nine names, as Congress shall direct, shall, in the presence of Congress, be drawn out by lot, and the persons whose names shall be so drawn, or any five of them, shall be commissioners or judges, to hear and finally determine the controversy, so always as a major part of the judges who shall hear the cause shall agree in the determination; and if either party shall neglect to attend at the day appointed, without showing reasons, which Congress shall judge sufficient, or, being present, shall refuse to strike, the Congress shall proceed to nominate three persons out of each State, and the Secretary of Congress shall strike in behalf of such party absent or refusing; and the judgment and sentence of the court to be appointed, in the manner before prescribed, shall be final and conclusive; and if any of the parties shall refuse to submit to the authority of such court, or to appear or defend their claim or cause, the court shall nevertheless proceed to pronounce sentence or judgment, which shall in like manner be final and decisive, the judgment or sentence and other proceedings being in either case transmitted to Congress, and lodged among the acts of Congress for the security of the parties concerned: provided that every commissioner, before he sits in judgment, shall take an oath, to be administered by one of the judges of the Supreme or Superior Court of the State where the cause shall be tried, "*well and truly to hear and determine the matter in question according to the best of his judgment, without favor, affection, or hope of reward,*" provided also that no State shall be deprived territory for the benefit of the United States.

All controversies concerning the private right of soil, claimed under different grants of two or more States, whose jurisdictions as they may respect such lands and the States which passed such grants are adjusted, the said grants or either of them being at the same time claimed to have originated antecedent to such settlement of jurisdiction, shall, on the petition of either party to the Congress of the

United States, be finally determined as near as may be in the same manner as is before prescribed for deciding disputes respecting territorial jurisdiction between different States.

275 The United States in Congress assembled shall also have the sole and exclusive right and power of regulating the alloy and value of coin struck by their own authority, or by that of the respective States—fixing the stand-

280 ard of weights and measures throughout the United States—regulating the trade and managing all affairs with the Indians, not members of any of the States, provided that the legislative right of any State within its own

285 limits be not infringed or violated—establishing and regulating post-offices from one State to another, throughout all the United States, and exacting such postage on the papers passing through the same as may be requisite to

290 defray the expenses of the said office—appointing all officers of the land forces in the service of the United States, excepting regimental officers—appointing all the officers of the naval forces, and commissioning all officers what-

295 ever in the service of the United States—making rules for the government and regulation of the said land and naval forces, and directing their operations.

The United States in Congress assembled

300 shall have authority to appoint a committee, to sit in the recess of Congress, to be denominated "A Committee of the States," and to consist of one delegate from each State; to appoint such other committees and civil of-

305 ficers as may be necessary for managing the general affairs of the United States under their direction; and to appoint one of their number to preside, provided that no person be allowed to serve in the office of president

310 more than one year in any term of three years —to ascertain the necessary sums of money to be raised for the service of the United States, and to appropriate and apply the same for defraying the public expenses—to borrow money,

315 or emit bills on the credit of the United States, transmitting every half-year to the respective States an account of the sums of money so borrowed or emitted—to build and equip a navy —to agree upon the number of land forces,

320 and to make requisitions from each State for its quota, in proportion to the number of white inhabitants in such State; which requisition shall be binding, and thereupon the legislature of each State shall appoint the reg-

325 imental officers, raise the men, and clothe, arm, and equip them in a soldier-like man-

ner, at the expense of the United States, and the officers and men so clothed, armed, and equipped shall march to the place appointed, and within the time agreed on by the United 33 States in Congress assembled; but if the United States in Congress assembled shall, on consideration of circumstances, judge proper that any State should not raise men, or should raise a smaller number than its quota, and 33 that any other State should raise a greater number of men than the quota thereof, such extra number shall be raised, officered, clothed, armed, and equipped in the same manner as the quota of such State, unless the legislature 34 of such State shall judge that such extra number cannot be safely spared out of the same, in which case they shall raise, officer, clothe, arm, and equip as many of such extra number as they judge can be safely spared: and 34 the officers and men, so clothed, armed, and equipped shall march to the place appointed, and within the time agreed on, by the United States in Congress assembled.

The United States in Congress assembled 35 shall never engage in a war, nor grant letters of marque and reprisal in time of peace, nor enter into any treaties or alliances, nor coin money, nor regulate the value thereof, nor ascertain the sums and expenses necessary for 35 the defence and welfare of the United States, or any of them, nor emit bills, nor borrow money on the credit of the United States, nor appropriate money, nor agree upon the number of vessels of war to be built or purchased, 36 or the number of land or sea forces to be raised, nor appoint a commander-in-chief of the army or navy, unless nine States assent to the same; nor shall a question on any other point, except for adjourning from day to day, 36 be determined, unless by the votes of a majority of the United States in Congress assembled.

The Congress of the United States shall have power to adjourn to any time within the year, and to any place within the United 37 States, so that no period of adjournment be for a longer duration than the space of six months, and shall publish the journal of their proceedings monthly, except such parts thereof relating to treaties, alliances, or mili- 37 tary operations, as in their judgment require secrecy, and the yeas and nays of the delegates of each State on any question shall be entered on the journal, when it is desired by any delegate; and the delegates of a State, or any of 38 them, at his or their request, shall be furnished with a transcript of the said journal, except such parts as are above excepted to lay before the legislatures of the several States.

Article Ten

35 THE Committee of the States, or any nine of them, shall be authorized to execute, in the recess of Congress, such of the powers of Congress as the United States in Congress assembled, by the consent of nine States, shall from 90 time to time think expedient to vest them with: provided that no power be delegated to the said Committee, for the exercise of which, by the Articles of Confederation, the voice of nine States in the Congress of the United 95 States assembled is requisite.

Article Eleven

CANADA, acceding to this Confederation, and joining in the measures of the United States, shall be admitted into and entitled to all the advantages of this Union; but no other colony oo shall be admitted into the same, unless such admission be agreed to by nine States.

Article Twelve

ALL bills of credit emitted, moneys borrowed, and debts contracted by or under the authority of Congress, before the assembling of the 05 United States in pursuance of the present Confederation, shall be deemed and considered as a charge against the United States, for payment and satisfaction whereof the said United States and the public faith are hereby 10 solemnly pledged.

Article Thirteen

EVERY State shall abide by the determinations of the United States in Congress assembled, on all questions which by this Confederation are submitted to them. And the Articles of this Confederation shall be invio- 415 lably observed by every State, and the Union shall be perpetual; nor shall any alteration at any time hereafter be made in any of them, unless such alteration be agreed to in a Congress of the United States, and be afterwards 420 confirmed by the legislatures of every State.

AND WHEREAS it hath pleased the Great Governor of the world to incline the hearts of the legislatures we respectfully represent in Congress to approve of and to authorize us to 425 ratify the said Articles of Confederation and perpetual Union, Know Ye, That we, the undersigned delegates, by virtue of the power and authority to us given for that purpose, do by these presents, in the name and in behalf 430 of our respective constituents, fully and entirely ratify and confirm each and every of the said Articles of Confederation and perpetual Union, and all and singular the matters and things therein contained: and we do further 435 solemnly plight and engage the faith of our respective constituents that they shall abide by the determinations of the United States in Congress assembled, on all questions which by the said Confederation are submitted to 440 them. And that the Articles thereof shall be inviolably observed by the States we respectively represent, and the Union shall be perpetual.

GEORGE WASHINGTON

THE CONSTITUTION
OF THE UNITED STATES
OF AMERICA

SEPTEMBER 17, 1787

WE, THE PEOPLE OF THE UNITED STATES, IN ORDER TO FORM A
MORE PERFECT UNION, ESTABLISH JUSTICE, INSURE DOMESTIC
TRANQUILLITY, PROVIDE FOR THE COMMON DEFENSE, PROMOTE
THE GENERAL WELFARE, AND SECURE THE BLESSINGS OF LIBERTY
TO OURSELVES AND OUR POSTERITY, DO ORDAIN AND ESTABLISH
THIS CONSTITUTION FOR THE UNITED STATES OF AMERICA.

Article One

SECTION 1. All legislative powers herein granted shall be vested in a Congress of the United States, which shall consist of a Senate and House of Representatives.

5 SECTION 2. The House of Representatives shall be composed of members chosen every second year by the people of the several States, and the electors in each State shall have the qualifications requisite for electors of the most

10 numerous branch of the State legislature.

No person shall be a Representative who shall not have attained the age of twenty-five years, and been seven years a citizen of the United States, and who shall not, when elect-

15 ed, be an inhabitant of that State in which he shall be chosen.

Representatives and direct taxes shall be apportioned among the several States which may be included within this Union, accord-

20 ing to their respective numbers, which shall be determined by adding to the whole number of free persons, including those bound to service for a term of years, and excluding Indians not taxed, three-fifths of all other per-

25 sons. The actual enumeration shall be made within three years after the first meeting of the Congress of the United States, and within every subsequent term of ten years, in such manner as they shall by law direct. The num-

ber of Representatives shall not exceed one 30 for every thirty thousand, but each State shall have at least one Representative; and until such enumeration shall be made, the State of *New Hampshire* shall be entitled to choose three, *Massachusetts* eight, *Rhode Island and* 35 *Providence Plantations* one, *Connecticut* five, *New York* six, *New Jersey* four, *Pennsylvania* eight, *Delaware* one, *Maryland* six, *Virginia* ten, *North Carolina* five, *South Carolina* five, and *Georgia* three. 4

When vacancies happen in the representation from any State, the executive authority thereof shall issue writs of election to fill such vacancies.

The House of Representatives shall choose 45 their Speaker and other officers, and shall have the sole power of impeachment.

SECTION 3. The Senate of the United States shall be composed of two Senators from each State, chosen by the legislature thereof, for six 50 years; and each Senator shall have one vote.

Immediately after they shall be assembled in consequence of the first election, they shall be divided as equally as may be into three classes. The seats of the Senators of the first 55 class shall be vacated at the expiration of the second year; of the second class, at the expiration of the fourth year, and of the third class, at the expiration of the sixth year, so that one-third may be chosen every second year; 60

and if vacancies happen by resignation or otherwise during the recess of the legislature of any State, the executive thereof may make temporary appointments until the next meet-
65 ing of the legislature, which shall then fill such vacancies.

No person shall be a Senator who shall not have attained to the age of thirty years, and been nine years a citizen of the United States,
70 and who shall not, when elected, be an inhabitant of that State for which he shall be chosen.

The Vice-President of the United States shall be President of the Senate, but shall
75 have no vote, unless they be equally divided.

The Senate shall choose their other officers, and also a President *pro tempore* in the absence of the Vice-President, or when he shall exercise the office of President of the United
80 States.

The Senate shall have the sole power to try all impeachments. When sitting for that purpose, they shall be on oath or affirmation. When the President of the United States is
85 tried, the Chief Justice shall preside: and no person shall be convicted without the concurrence of two-thirds of the members present.

Judgment in cases of impeachment shall not extend further than to removal from of-
90 fice, and disqualification to hold and enjoy any office of honor, trust, or profit under the United States; but the party convicted shall, nevertheless, be liable and subject to indictment, trial, judgment, and punishment, ac-
95 cording to law.

SECTION 4. The times, places, and manner of holding elections for Senators and Representatives shall be prescribed in each State by the legislature thereof; but the Congress
100 may at any time by law make or alter such regulations, except as to the places of choosing Senators.

The Congress shall assemble at least once in every year, and such meeting shall be on
105 the first Monday in December, unless they shall by law appoint a different day.

SECTION 5. Each house shall be the judge of the elections, returns, and qualifications of its own members, and a majority of each shall
110 constitute a quorum to do business; but a smaller number may adjourn from day to day, and may be authorized to compel the attendance of absent members, in such manner, and under such penalties, as each house
115 may provide.

Each house may determine the rules of its proceedings, punish its members for disorderly behavior, and, with the concurrence of two-thirds, expel a member.

Each house shall keep a journal of its proceedings, and from time to time publish the same, excepting such parts as may in their judgment require secrecy, and the yeas and nays of the members of either house on any question shall, at the desire of one-fifth of those present, be entered on the journal.

Neither house, during the session of Congress, shall, without the consent of the other, adjourn for more than three days, nor to any other place than that in which the two houses shall be sitting.

SECTION 6. The Senators and Representatives shall receive a compensation for their services, to be ascertained by law and paid out of the Treasury of the United States. They shall, in all cases except treason, felony, and breach of the peace, be privileged from arrest during their attendance at the session of their respective houses, and in going to and returning from the same; and for any speech or debate in either house they shall not be questioned in any other place.

No Senator or Representative shall, during the time for which he was elected, be appointed to any civil office under the authority of the United States, which shall have been created, or the emoluments whereof shall have been increased during such time; and no person holding any office under the United States shall be a member of either house during his continuance in office.

SECTION 7. All bills for raising revenue shall originate in the House of Representatives; but the Senate may propose or concur with amendments as on other bills.

Every bill which shall have passed the House of Representatives and the Senate shall, before it becomes a law, be presented to the President of the United States; if he approve he shall sign it, but if not he shall return it, with his objections, to that house in which it shall have originated, who shall enter the objections at large on their journal and proceed to reconsider it. If after such reconsideration two-thirds of that house shall agree to pass the bill, it shall be sent, together with the objections, to the other house, by which it shall likewise be reconsidered, and if approved by two-thirds of that house it shall become a law. But in all such cases the votes of both houses shall be determined by yeas and nays, and the names of the persons voting for and against the bill shall be entered on the journal of each house respectively. If any bill shall not be returned by the President within ten days (Sundays excepted) after it shall have been presented to him, the same shall be a law, in like manner as if he had signed it, unless the Congress by their adjournment prevent its return, in which case it shall not be a law.

Every order, resolution, or vote to which the concurrence of the Senate and House of Representatives may be necessary (except on a question of adjournment) shall be presented to the President of the United States; and before the same shall take effect, shall be approved by him, or being disapproved by him, shall be repassed by two-thirds of the Senate and House of Representatives, according to the rules and limitations prescribed in the case of a bill.

SECTION 8. The Congress shall have power to lay and collect taxes, duties, imposts, and excises, to pay the debts and provide for the common defense and general welfare of the United States; but all duties, imposts, and excises shall be uniform throughout the United States;

To borrow money on the credit of the United States;

To regulate commerce with foreign nations and among the several States, and with the Indian tribes;

To establish an uniform rule of naturalization, and uniform laws on the subject of bankruptcies throughout the United States;

To coin money, regulate the value thereof, and of foreign coin, and fix the standard of weights and measures;

To provide for the punishment of counterfeiting the securities and current coin of the United States;

To establish post-offices and post-roads;

To promote the progress of science and useful arts by securing for limited times to authors and inventors the exclusive right to their respective writings and discoveries;

To constitute tribunals inferior to the Supreme Court;

To define and punish piracies and felonies committed on the high seas and offenses against the law of nations;

To declare war, grant letters of marque and reprisal, and make rules concerning captures on land and water;

To raise and support armies, but no appropriation of money to that use shall be for a longer term than two years;

To provide and maintain a navy;

To make rules for the government and regulation of the land and naval forces;

To provide for calling forth the militia to execute the laws of the Union, suppress insurrections, and repel invasions;

To provide for organizing, arming, and disciplining the militia, and for governing such part of them as may be employed in the service of the United States, reserving to the States respectively the appointment of the officers, and the authority of training the militia according to the discipline prescribed by Congress;

To exercise exclusive legislation in all cases whatsoever over such district (not exceeding ten miles square) as may, by cession of particular States and the acceptance of Congress, become the seat of the Government of the United States, and to exercise like authority over all places purchased by the consent of the legislature of the State in which the same shall be, for the erection of forts, magazines, arsenals, dockyards, and other needful buildings; and

To make all laws which shall be necessary and proper for carrying into execution the foregoing powers, and all other powers vested by this Constitution in the Government of the United States, or in any department or officer thereof.

SECTION 9. The migration or importation of such persons as any of the States now existing shall think proper to admit shall not be prohibited by the Congress prior to the year one thousand eight hundred and eight, but a tax or duty may be imposed on such importation, not exceeding ten dollars for each person.

The privilege of the writ of habeas corpus shall not be suspended, unless when in cases of rebellion or invasion the public safety may require it.

No bill of attainder or ex post facto law shall be passed.

No capitation or other direct tax shall be laid, unless in proportion to the census or enumeration hereinbefore directed to be taken.

No tax or duty shall be laid on articles exported from any State.

No preference shall be given by any regulation of commerce or revenue to the ports of one State over those of another; nor shall vessels bound to or from one State be obliged to enter, clear, or pay duties in another.

No money shall be drawn from the Treasury but in consequence of appropriations

285 made by law; and a regular statement and account of the receipts and expenditures of all public money shall be published from time to time.

No title of nobility shall be granted by the 290 United States; and no person holding any office of profit or trust under them shall, without the consent of the Congress, accept of any present, emolument, office, or title, of any kind whatever, from any king, prince, or foreign 295 State.

SECTION 10. No State shall enter into any treaty, alliance, or confederation; grant letters of marque and reprisal; coin money; emit bills of credit; make anything but gold and 300 silver coin a tender in payment of debts; pass any bill of attainder, ex post facto law, or law impairing the obligation of contracts, or grant any title of nobility.

No State shall, without the consent of Con-305 gress, lay any imposts or duties on imports or exports, except what may be absolutely necessary for executing its inspection laws; and the net produce of all duties and imposts, laid by any State on imports or ex-310 ports, shall be for the use of the Treasury of the United States; and all such laws shall be subject to the revision and control of the Congress.

No State shall, without the consent of Con-315 gress, lay any duty of tonnage, keep troops or ships of war in time of peace, enter into any agreement or compact with another State or with a foreign power, or engage in war, unless actually invaded or in such imminent danger 320 as will not admit of delay.

Article Two

SECTION 1. The executive power shall be vested in a President of the United States of America. He shall hold his office during the term of four years, and together with the Vice-325 President, chosen for the same term, be elected as follows:

Each State shall appoint, in such manner as the legislature thereof may direct, a number of electors, equal to the whole number of Sen-330 ators and Representatives to which the State may be entitled in the Congress; but no Senator or Representative, or person holding an office of trust or profit under the United States, shall be appointed an elector.

335 [The electors shall meet in their respective States and vote by ballot for two persons, of whom one at least shall not be an inhabitant of the same State with themselves. And they shall make a list of all the persons voted for, and of the number of votes for each; which 340 list they shall sign and certify, and transmit sealed to the seat of government of the United States, directed to the President of the Senate. The President of the Senate shall, in the presence of the Senate and House of Representa-345 tives, open all the certificates, and the votes shall then be counted. The person having the greatest number of votes shall be the President, if such number be a majority of the whole number of electors appointed; and if 350 there be more than one who have such majority, and have an equal number of votes, then the House of Representatives shall immediately choose by ballot one of them for President; and if no person have a majority, then 355 from the five highest on the list the said House shall in like manner choose the President. But in choosing the President the votes shall be taken by States, the representation from each State having one vote; a quorum for this 360 purpose shall consist of a member or members from two-thirds of the States, and a majority of all the States shall be necessary to a choice. In every case, after the choice of the President, the person having the greatest num-365 ber of votes of the electors shall be the Vice-President. But if there should remain two or more who have equal votes, the Senate shall choose from them by ballot the Vice-President.]* 370

The Congress may determine the time of choosing the electors and the day on which they shall give their votes, which day shall be the same throughout the United States.

No person except a natural-born citizen, or 375 a citizen of the United States at the time of the adoption of this Constitution, shall be eligible to the office of President; neither shall any person be eligible to that office who shall not have attained to the age of thirty-five years, 380 and been fourteen years a resident within the United States.

In case of the removal of the President from office, or of his death, resignation, or inability to discharge the powers and duties of the said 385 office, the same shall devolve on the Vice-President, and the Congress may by law provide for the case of removal, death, resignation, or inability, both of the President and Vice-President, declaring what officer shall 390 then act as President, and such officer shall act

* This procedure was changed by the Twelfth Amendment.

accordingly until the disability be removed or a President shall be elected.

The President shall, at stated times, receive for his services a compensation, which shall neither be increased nor diminished during the period for which he may have been elected, and he shall not receive within that period any other emolument from the United States or any of them.

Before he enter on the execution of his office he shall take the following oath or affirmation:

"I do solemnly swear (or affirm) that I will faithfully execute the office of President of the United States, and will to the best of my ability preserve, protect, and defend the Constitution of the United States."

SECTION 2. The President shall be Commander-in-chief of the Army and Navy of the United States, and of the militia of the several States when called into the actual service of the United States; he may require the opinion, in writing, of the principal officer in each of the executive departments, upon any subject relating to the duties of their respective offices, and he shall have power to grant reprieves and pardons for offenses against the United States, except in cases of impeachment.

He shall have power, by and with the advice and consent of the Senate, to make treaties, provided two-thirds of the Senators present concur; and he shall nominate, and, by and with the advice and consent of the Senate, shall appoint ambassadors, other public ministers and consuls, judges of the Supreme Court, and all other officers of the United States, whose appointments are not herein otherwise provided for, and which shall be established by law; but the Congress may by law vest the appointment of such inferior officers, as they think proper, in the President alone, in the courts of law, or in the heads of departments.

The President shall have power to fill up vacancies that may happen during the recess of the Senate, by granting commissions which shall expire at the end of their next session.

SECTION 3. He shall from time to time give to the Congress information of the state of the Union, and recommend to their consideration such measures as he shall judge necessary and expedient; he may, on extraordinary occasions, convene both houses, or either of them, and in case of disagreement between them with respect to the time of adjournment, he may adjourn them to such time as he shall think proper; he shall receive ambassadors and other public ministers; he shall take care that the laws be faithfully executed, and shall commission all the officers of the United States.

SECTION 4. The President, Vice-President, and all civil officers of the United States shall be removed from office on impeachment for and conviction of treason, bribery, or other high crimes and misdemeanors.

Article Three

SECTION 1. The judicial power of the United States shall be vested in one Supreme Court, and in such inferior courts as the Congress may from time to time ordain and establish. The judges, both of the supreme and inferior courts, shall hold their offices during good behavior, and shall, at stated times, receive for their services a compensation which shall not be diminished during their continuance in office.

SECTION 2. The judicial power shall extend to all cases, in law and equity, arising under this Constitution, the laws of the United States, and treaties made, or which shall be made, under their authority; to all cases affecting ambassadors, other public ministers, and consuls; to all cases of admiralty and maritime jurisdiction; to controversies to which the United States shall be a party; to controversies between two or more States; between a State and citizens of another State; between citizens of different States; between citizens of the same State claiming lands under grants of different States, and between a State, or the citizens thereof, and foreign States, citizens, or subjects.

In all cases affecting ambassadors, other public ministers and consuls, and those in which a State shall be a party, the Supreme Court shall have original jurisdiction. In all the other cases before mentioned the Supreme Court shall have appellate jurisdiction, both as to law and fact, with such exceptions and under such regulations as the Congress shall make.

The trial of all crimes, except in cases of impeachment, shall be by jury; and such trial shall be held in the State where the said crimes shall have been committed; but when not committed within any State, the trial shall be at such place or places as the Congress may by law have directed.

SECTION 3. Treason against the United States

shall consist only in levying war against them, or in adhering to their enemies, giving them aid and comfort. No person shall be convicted of treason unless on the testimony of two wit-
505 nesses to the same overt act, or on confession in open court.

The Congress shall have power to declare the punishment of treason, but no attainder of treason shall work corruption of blood or
510 forfeiture except during the life of the person attainted.

Article Four

SECTION 1. Full faith and credit shall be given in each State to the public acts, records, and judicial proceedings of every other State.
515 And the Congress may by general laws prescribe the manner in which such acts, records, and proceedings shall be proved, and the effect thereof.

SECTION 2. The citizens of each State shall
520 be entitled to all privileges and immunities of citizens in the several States.

A person charged in any State with treason, felony, or other crime, who shall flee from justice, and be found in another State, shall,
525 on demand of the executive authority of the State from which he fled, be delivered up, to be removed to the State having jurisdiction of the crime.

No person held to service or labor in one
530 State, under the laws thereof, escaping into another, shall, in consequence of any law or regulation therein, be discharged from such service or labor, but shall be delivered up on claim of the party to whom such service or
535 labor may be due.

SECTION 3. New States may be admitted by the Congress into this Union; but no new State shall be formed or erected within the jurisdiction of any other State; nor any State
540 be formed by the junction of two or more States or parts of States, without the consent of the legislatures of the States concerned as well as of the Congress.

The Congress shall have power to dispose
545 of and make all needful rules and regulations respecting the territory or other property belonging to the United States; and nothing in this Constitution shall be so construed as to prejudice any claims of the United States or
550 of any particular State.

SECTION 4. The United States shall guarantee to every State in this Union a republican form of government, and shall protect each of them against invasion, and on application of the legislature, or of the executive (when 5 the legislature cannot be convened), against domestic violence.

Article Five

THE Congress, whenever two-thirds of both houses shall deem it necessary, shall propose amendments to this Constitution, or, on the 5 application of the Legislatures of two-thirds of the several States, shall call a convention for proposing amendments, which, in either case, shall be valid to all intents and purposes, as part of this Constitution, when 5 ratified by the Legislatures of three-fourths of the several States, or by conventions in three-fourths thereof, as the one or the other mode of ratification may be proposed by the Congress; provided that no amend- 5 ment which may be made prior to the Year One thousand eight hundred and eight shall in any manner affect the first and fourth Clauses in the Ninth Section of the first Article; and that no State, without its 5 consent, shall be deprived of its equal suffrage in the Senate.

Article Six

ALL debts contracted and engagements entered into, before the adoption of this Constitution, shall be as valid against the United 5 States under this Constitution, as under the Confederation.

This Constitution and the laws of the United States which shall be made in pursuance thereof and all treaties made, or which shall be made, 5 under the authority of the United States, shall be the supreme law of the land; and the judges in every State shall be bound thereby, anything in the Constitution or laws of any State to the contrary notwithstanding. 5

The Senators and Representatives before mentioned, and the members of the several State Legislatures, and all executive and judicial officers, both of the United States and of the several States, shall be bound by oath 5 or affirmation, to support this Constitution; but no religious test shall ever be required as a qualification to any office or public trust under the United States.

Article Seven

THE ratification of the Conventions of nine 6

States shall be sufficient for the establishment of this Constitution between the States so ratifying the same.

DONE in convention by the unanimous consent of the States present the seventeenth day of September in the year of our Lord one thousand seven hundred and eighty-seven and of the independence of the United States of America the twelfth, in witness whereof we have hereunto subscribed our names.

G̊ WASHINGTON—*Presid!*
and deputy from Virginia

Attest
WILLIAM JACKSON *Secretary*

AMENDMENTS

Article One

CONGRESS shall make no law respecting an establishment of religion, or prohibiting the free exercise thereof; or abridging the freedom of speech, or of the press; or the right of the people peaceably to assemble, and to petition the Government for a redress of grievances.

Article Two

A well-regulated militia being necessary to the security of a free State, the right of the people to keep and bear arms shall not be infringed.

Article Three

No soldier shall, in time of peace, be quartered in any house, without the consent of the owner, nor in time of war but in a manner to be prescribed by law.

Article Four

THE right of the people to be secure in their persons, houses, papers, and effects, against unreasonable searches and seizures, shall not be violated, and no warrants shall issue, but upon probable cause, supported by oath or affirmation, and particularly describing the place to be searched, and the person or things to be seized.

Article Five

No person shall be held to answer for a capital, or otherwise infamous crime, unless on a presentment or indictment of a Grand Jury, except in cases arising in the land or naval forces, or in the militia, when in actual service in time of war or public danger; nor shall any person be subject for the same offense to be twice put in jeopardy of life or limb; nor shall be compelled in any criminal case to be a witness against himself, nor be deprived of life, liberty, or property, without due process of law; nor shall private property be taken for public use, without just compensation.

Article Six

IN all criminal prosecutions the accused shall enjoy the right to a speedy and public trial, by an impartial jury of the State and district wherein the crime shall have been committed, which district shall have been previously ascertained by law, and to be informed of the nature and cause of the accusation; to be confronted with the witnesses against him; to have compulsory process for obtaining witnesses in his favor, and to have the assistance of counsel for his defense.

Article Seven

IN suits at common law, where the value of controversy shall exceed twenty dollars, the right of trial by jury shall be preserved, and no fact tried by a jury shall be otherwise reexamined in any court of the United States, than according to the rules of the common law.

Article Eight

EXCESSIVE bail shall not be required, nor excessive fines imposed, nor cruel and unusual punishments inflicted.

Article Nine

THE enumeration in the Constitution of certain rights shall not be construed to deny or disparage others retained by the people.

Article Ten

THE powers not delegated to the United States by the Constitution, nor prohibited by it to the States, are reserved to the States respectively or to the people.

Article Eleven

THE judicial power of the United States shall not be construed to extend to any suit in law or equity, commenced or prosecuted against one of the United States by citizens of another State, or by citizens or subjects of any foreign State.

Article Twelve

THE Electors shall meet in their respective States, and vote by ballot for President and Vice-President, one of whom, at least, shall not be an inhabitant of the same State with themselves; they shall name in their ballots the person voted for as President, and in distinct ballots the person voted for as Vice-President, and they shall make distinct lists of all persons voted for as President and of all persons voted for as Vice-President, and of the number of votes for each, which lists they shall sign and certify, and transmit sealed to the seat of the Government of the United States, directed to the President of the Senate; the President of the Senate shall, in the presence of the Senate and House of Representatives, open all the certificates and the votes shall then be counted; the person having the greatest number of votes for President shall be the President, if such number be a majority of the whole number of Electors appointed; and if no person have such majority, then from the persons having the highest numbers not exceeding three on the list of those voted for as President, the House of Representatives shall choose immediately, by ballot, the President. But in choosing the President the votes shall be taken by States, the representation from each State having one vote; a quorum for this purpose shall consist of a member or members from two-thirds of the States, and a majority of all the States shall be necessary to a choice. And if the House of Representatives shall not choose a President whenever the right of choice shall devolve upon them, before the fourth day of March next following, then the Vice-President shall act as President, as in the case of the death or other constitutional disability of the President. The person having the greatest number of votes as Vice-President shall be the Vice-President, if such number be a majority of the whole number of Electors appointed, and if no person have a majority, then from the two highest numbers on the list, the Senate shall choose the Vice-President; a quorum for the purpose shall consist of two-thirds of the whole number of Senators, and a majority of the whole number shall be necessary to a choice. But no person constitutionally ineligible to the office of President shall be eligible to that of Vice-President of the United States.

Article Thirteen

SECTION 1. Neither slavery nor involuntary servitude, except as a punishment for crime whereof the party shall have been duly convicted, shall exist within the United States, or any place subject to their jurisdiction.

SECTION 2. Congress shall have power to enforce this article by appropriate legislation.

Article Fourteen

SECTION 1. All persons born or naturalized in the United States, and subject to the jurisdiction thereof, are citizens of the United States and of the State wherein they reside. No State shall make or enforce any law which shall abridge the privileges or immunities of citizens of the United States; nor shall any State deprive any person of life, liberty, or property, without due process of law; nor deny to any person within its jurisdiction the equal protection of the laws.

SECTION 2. Representatives shall be apportioned among the several States according to their respective numbers, counting the whole number of persons in each State, excluding Indians not taxed. But when the right to vote at any election for the choice of Electors for President and Vice-President of the United States, Representatives in Congress, the executive and judicial officers of a State, or the members of the Legislature thereof, is denied to any of the male inhabitants of such State, being twenty-one years of age, and citizens of the United States, or in any way abridged, except for participation in rebellion, or other crime, the basis of representation therein shall be reduced in the proportion which the number of such male citizens shall bear to the whole number of male citizens twenty-one years of age in such State.

Section 3. No person shall be a Senator or Representative in Congress, or Elector of President and Vice-President, or hold any office, civil or military, under the United States, or under any State, who, having previously taken an oath as a member of Congress, or as an officer of the United States, or as a member of any State Legislature, or as an executive or judicial officer of any State, to support the Constitution of the United States, shall have engaged in insurrection or rebellion against the same, or given aid or comfort to the enemies thereof. But Congress may, by a vote of two-thirds of each House, remove such disability.

Section 4. The validity of the public debt of the United States, authorized by law, including debts incurred for payment of pensions and bounties for services in suppressing insurrection or rebellion, shall not be questioned. But neither the United States nor any State shall assume or pay any debt or obligation incurred in aid of insurrection or rebellion against the United States, or any claim for the loss or emancipation of any slave; but all such debts, obligations and claims shall be held illegal and void.

Section 5. The Congress shall have power to enforce, by appropriate legislation, the provisions of this article.

Article Fifteen

Section 1. The right of citizens of the United States to vote shall not be denied or abridged by the United States or by any State on account of race, color, or previous condition of servitude.

Section 2. The Congress shall have power to enforce this article by appropriate legislation.

Article Sixteen

THE Congress shall have power to lay and collect taxes on incomes, from whatever source derived, without apportionment among the several States, and without regard to any census or enumeration.

Article Seventeen

THE Senate of the United States shall be composed of two Senators from each State,

elected by the people thereof, for six years; and each Senator shall have one vote. The electors in each State shall have the qualifications requisite for electors of the most numerous branch of the State legislatures.

When vacancies happen in the representation of any State in the Senate, the executive authority of such State shall issue writs of election to fill such vacancies: *Provided,* That the Legislature of any State may empower the executive thereof to make temporary appointments until the people fill the vacancies by election as the legislature may direct.

This amendment shall not be so construed as to affect the election or term of any Senator chosen before it becomes valid as part of the Constitution.

Article Eighteen

Section 1. After one year from the ratification of this article the manufacture, sale, or transportation of intoxicating liquors within, the importation thereof into, or the exportation thereof from the United States and all territory subject to the jurisdiction thereof for beverage purposes is hereby prohibited.

Section 2. The Congress and the several States shall have concurrent power to enforce this article by appropriate legislation.

Section 3. This article shall be inoperative unless it shall have been ratified as an amendment to the Constitution by the legislatures of the several States, as provided in the Constitution, within seven years from the date of the submission hereof to the States by the Congress.

Article Nineteen

THE right of citizens of the United States to vote shall not be denied or abridged by the United States or by any State on account of sex.

Congress shall have power to enforce this article by appropriate legislation.

Article Twenty

Section 1. The terms of the President and Vice-President shall end at noon on the twentieth day of January, and the terms of Senators and Representatives at noon on the third day of January, of the years in which such terms would have ended if this article had not been ratified; and the terms of their successors shall then begin.

Section 2. The Congress shall assemble at

least once in every year, and such meeting shall begin at noon on the third day of January, unless they shall by law appoint a different day.

SECTION 3. If, at the time fixed for the beginning of the term of the President, the President elect shall have died, the Vice-President elect shall become President. If a President shall not have been chosen before the time fixed for the beginning of his term, or if the President elect shall have failed to qualify, then the Vice-President elect shall act as President until a President shall have qualified; and the Congress may by law provide for the case wherein neither a President elect nor a Vice-President elect shall have qualified, declaring who shall then act as President, or the manner in which one who is to act shall be selected, and such person shall act accordingly until a President or Vice-President shall have qualified.

SECTION 4. The Congress may by law provide for the case of the death of any of the persons from whom the House of Representatives may choose a President whenever the right of choice shall have devolved upon them, and for the case of the death of any of the persons from whom the Senate may choose a Vice-President whenever the right of choice shall have devolved upon them.

SECTION 5. Sections 1 and 2 shall take effect on the fifteenth day of October following the ratification of this article.

SECTION 6. This article shall be inoperative unless it shall have been ratified as an amendment to the Constitution by the legislatures of three-fourths of the several States within seven years from the date of its submission.

Article Twenty-one

SECTION 1. The eighteenth article of amendment to the Constitution of the United States is hereby repealed.

SECTION 2. The transportation or importation into any State, Territory, or possession of the United States for delivery or use therein of intoxicating liquors, in violation of the laws thereof, is hereby prohibited.

SECTION 3. This article shall be inoperative unless it shall have been ratified as an amendment to the Constitution by conventions in the several States, as provided in the Constitution, within seven years from the date of the submission hereof to the States by the Congress.

Article Twenty-two

SECTION 1. No person shall be elected to the office of the President more than twice, and no person who has held the office of President, or acted as President, for more than two years of a term to which some other person was elected President shall be elected to the office of the President more than once. But this Article shall not apply to any person holding the office of President when this Article was proposed by the Congress, and shall not prevent any person who may be holding the office of President, or acting as President, during the term within which this Article becomes operative from holding the office of President or acting as President during the remainder of such term.

SECTION 2. This article shall be inoperative unless it shall have been ratified as an amendment to the Constitution by the legislatures of three-fourths of the several States within seven years from the date of its submission to the States by the Congress.

THE FEDERALIST

BIOGRAPHICAL NOTE

Alexander Hamilton, 1757-1804   James Madison, 1751-1836
John Jay, 1745-1829

THE task for the *Federalist* authors was marked out for them the day the new Constitution for the United States was made known to the people of New York State. On the same day it was published, and immediately beside it in the papers, appeared an attack upon the Constitution, signed by Cato, who was known to be Governor Clinton. Thereafter, many of the most powerful figures in New York political life, writing under the name of renowned Romans, came out in opposition to the new instrument of government.

ALEXANDER HAMILTON, although only thirty years old and an immigrant, was the natural leader for the New York supporters of the new Constitution. Born illegitimately, of Scotch and French Huguenot stock, on the British Island of Nevis in the West Indies, his youthful talents at writing and commerce were so unusual that friends took up a collection and sent him to America in 1772 to complete his education. He used his writing talents to defend the cause of the Colonies during the events leading up to the Revolution, so successfully, in fact, that two of his pamphlets were thought to be the work of Jay. With a thirst for military glory that was to remain with him throughout his life, he took part in the New York campaign as an artillery captain and won a place on Washington's staff. Washington employed him, however, for his power with the pen, and for four years he was the General's private secretary. In this position he became acquainted with many of the most influential men in the states and learned at first hand the weakness of the Confederation. As early as 1780 he was writing men of influence and urging the calling of a convention to form a new government. As a lawyer in New York City, he took a prominent part in the events that finally resulted in the Constitutional Convention. One of the three New York delegates to the Convention, he argued for the establish-

ment of a strong national government based on the British model. He was the only New York member to sign the Constitution.

In the New York fight for ratification Hamilton at first took it upon himself to answer Clinton. Under the name of Cæsar he wrote two articles, bitterly personal and scornful of Cato's appeal to the "majesty of the multitude." But persuaded that such tactics would not win support for the new Constitution, he abandoned them. His next effort, written while returning on a Hudson sloop from legal duties in Albany, appeared under the signature of Publius. It was the first number of the *Federalist*. From late October 1787 until the following April a continuing stream of articles from the pen of Publius poured forth, sometimes as many as four in one week. They were printed by the newspapers throughout the states and issued in book form even before all the numbers had appeared in the papers. Although the articles appeared under the signature of Publius which Hamilton had used once before, they were soon known to be the work of several men. Their genesis as a joint work, however, is uncertain. Madison later reported that both Hamilton and Jay were agreed upon the work when Hamilton asked him to make a third in the undertaking. The combination was the strongest to be found in New York for an intellectual defense of the new Constitution.

JAMES MADISON was a representative of the Southern aristocracy, the eldest son of a Virginia planter. He gained his first political experience during the Revolution as a delegate to the Virginia Convention, which drew up a new state Constitution. After its establishment, he was a member of the Privy Council which advised the governor. In this capacity he served as Governor Patrick Henry's private secretary. Later as a delegate to the Continental Congress, he became acquainted with

Hamilton and Jay and with them was part of the group seeking to strengthen the national government. He was active in promoting the developments that led to the Constitutional Convention and, in the months immediately preceding the meeting, devoted his efforts to preparing for the establishment of a new government. He wrote an essay on the "Vices of the Political System of the United States," made an extensive study of ancient and modern confederacies, and drew up an outline for a new system of government. This was the basis for the Virginia plan which at Philadelphia led to the formation of the Constitution. With James Wilson of Pennsylvania, he shared the honors of being most responsible for its final form. September 1787 found him in New York serving for the second time as the Virginia Delegate to the Continental Congress.

JOHN JAY, at the time the *Federalist* appeared, enjoyed the greatest prestige of any of the three men. By some he was considered as second only to Washington in service to his country. The oldest of the three, he came from a well-to-do New York merchant family of Huguenot extraction. He served on the Continental Congress from its inception in 1774 and was later its president. In his own state he took a leading part in the Revolutionary political developments. He was the author of the first New York Constitution and, after its establishment, its first Chief Justice. His greatest fame at the time, however, came to him as a result of his role as a diplomat. His first venture into European diplomacy was to obtain a treaty with Spain. That proving a failure, he was sent on to Paris to act with John Adams and Franklin in negotiating the terms of peace with Great Britain. Described by Adams as "the Washington of the negotiations," he was instrumental in obtaining recognition of the independence of the United States which ended the Revolutionary War. He was rewarded for his role by being made the Secretary of Foreign Affairs for the Continental Congress, a post he continued to fill until Jefferson took over as Secretary of State under the new government. Because of his strongly national views, he was turned down as a delegate to the Constitutional Convention.

All three *Federalist* collaborators, in addition to their wide practical experience, were men of high intellectual culture, along very similar lines. Each began his schooling under a Christian minister and completed it with a college education. Hamilton and Jay attended King's College (now Columbia), Madison the College of New Jersey (now Princeton). They followed the standard curriculum of the time: the liberal arts program divided between the trivium and quadrivium and based on the ancient classics with considerable practice in scholastic disputation. The whole program was infused with religion and politics which were the primary ends of the program. The emphasis upon religion and politics is illustrated by the commencement exercises held at New Jersey while Madison was there in 1770. Among the many disputations there was a Latin syllogistic debate on the thesis: "Omnes Homines, Jure Naturæ, liberi sunt" (all men by the law of nature are free), and another in English on the topic: "The Different Religious Professions in any State if Maintained in their Liberty Serve it by Supplying the Place of a Censor Morum." Both Madison and Jay after completing their undergraduate course went on to do graduate work, thus being among the first graduate students in America. Jay received his master's degree in 1767 with a discourse on "The Usefulness of the Passions" and a debate on "Whether a man ought to engage in War without being persuaded of the Justness of his Cause." Madison remained an extra year at New Jersey, reading particularly in theology and Hebrew. Hamilton's college work was interrupted by the war, but he continued after the war to perfect himself in law, as had his other two collaborators. Hamilton, unlike them, depended upon the practice of law for his living, and, while not holding down a political office, earned the reputation of being the most brilliant lawyer in New York. Madison never practised law, nor did Jay except for the few years before he embarked upon his public life.

The actual writing of the *Federalist* and the authorship of the particular papers have been a matter of long and sometimes bitter dispute. They were done in a great hurry, and, as Madison later remarked, they often went directly from the writer to the printer without being seen by the other collaborators. One reason that Jay did so few is thought to be that he suffered from a serious illness soon after the series was begun. Hamilton was the busiest of the three men at the time. He was carrying on a full legal practice, attending the sessions of the state supreme court, and campaigning for election to the Continental Congress. Madison was called home before the papers were completed to take part in the battle for ratification in Virginia, which looked as bad for the Federalist cause as it did in New York.

The intellectual defense of the Constitution was put to practical use by the three collaborators in their state ratifying conventions. Madison led the Federalist forces in Virginia, and Hamilton and Jay in New York. Against what seemed hopeless odds, they won their fight, but not, in fact, until the new Constitution had already been ratified by the required nine states. Virginia was the tenth state to ratify and New York the eleventh, a month later.

The partnership which resulted in the *Federalist* was dissolved in the efforts to translate the Constitution from a paper document into a functioning government. Although all three men had expressed dissatisfaction with the Constitution as not providing a sufficiently strong national government, Madison parted company with Hamilton and Jay over the measures which they advocated for securing the supremacy of the national government.

Hamilton, as the first Secretary of the Treasury, had the task of placing the new government on a sound financial basis. He initiated this work by a series of three reports submitted to Congress. The first, on public credit, called for the full assumption by the national government of the war debts of the old Confederation and the states. The second provided for the establishment of a national bank. The third, on manufactures, called for government protection of manufactures by means of duties. Although this last proposal was defeated by Congress, it has been called the "first great revolt from Adam Smith."

Madison, elected a member of the House of Representatives, became the leader of the opposition in Congress against Hamilton's proposals. He led the move for a Bill of Rights, the lack of which had been one of the main issues in the fight for ratification. With his friend, Jefferson, who had been appointed the first Secretary of State, he advised the President that Hamilton's measures could not be reconciled with the Constitution. Difference over the interpretation of the Constitution was intensified by the conflict over foreign affairs that arose with the outbreak of war between England and Revolutionary France. Hamilton, in a series of letters published in the papers under the signature of Pacificus, defended England and the American policy of neutrality. Madison, at the instigation of Jefferson,

countered with a series of letters signed Helvidius.

Jay's activities during the opening years of the new government further embittered the relations of the former collaborators. As the first Chief Justice of the Supreme Court, he passed down decisions strongly supporting Hamilton's view of the national government. The decision in his greatest case, *Chisolm vs. Georgia,* caused a revolt in Congress over its emphasis on the supremacy of the national government over that of the states. This resulted in the passing of the eleventh amendment to the Constitution, asserting the sovereign irresponsibility of the states as regards private suits by citizens of another state. However, the greatest cause of division proved to be the treaty he negotiated with England which has since gone under his name. It was so bitterly attacked by the Jefferson and Madison groups, known as "Republicans," that in many places Jay was burnt in effigy. In defense of the treaty, Hamilton wrote his Camillus letters. Although Jefferson again appealed to Madison as the only one able to cope with Hamilton in debate, Madison did not respond.

The three *Federalist* authors, although divided by partisan strife, were brought together once again in Washington's Farewell Address. Washington appealed to all three for advice, and their suggestions, with most from Hamilton, went into the final draft of the message.

Hamilton's last years were rent by political strife. After retiring to the private practice of law, he continued to be the active leader of the Federalist Party. His influence was so great during the Adams administration that Cabinet members often consulted with him about official policy, even behind the President's back. This led to a break between the two men. Hamilton made the break irreparable by writing a pamphlet attacking Adams, which split the Federalist Party and led to its disintegration. His partisan battles reached a climax when he was challenged to a duel by Aaron Burr, then Vice President, with whom Hamilton had long been in political competition in the municipal, state, and national field. Hamilton died as a result of a shot received from Burr's pistol.

Jay, following the negotiation of the treaty with England, served two terms as governor of New York. His administration is noted among other things for the law commanding the gradual abolition of slavery in New York. (All three men looked upon slavery as a tragedy for America. Jay and Hamilton were active in the New York Society for the Manumission of Slaves, while Madison took a leading part in the movement for the colonization of negroes.) Jay, after completing his terms as governor, retired from public life to his farm in Bedford. He was often consulted for the early history of the Republic; his occasional reminiscences among other things, furnished Cooper with the material for his novel, *The Spy*. Known for his knowledge of the Bible, he was often asked by ministers for his interpretation of the prophecies and for the last years of his life was president of the American Bible Society.

Madison was Jefferson's Secretary of State for two terms and, as the chosen successor, followed him in the Presidency. He served for two terms and then, in 1817, retired to his home in Montpelier. His last years were spent in agricultural and literary pursuits. With Jefferson he gave much of his attention to the University of Virginia. At Jefferson's request, for instance, he prepared a list of theological works for the library, including, in addition to the Reformation theologians, the great Scholastics, Aquinas, Duns Scotus, Bellarmine. One of their last acts was to prescribe the curriculum in political philosophy with Locke and Sidney for political theory and the *Federalist* for the Constitution. He devoted much time to the preparation of his papers on Constitutional questions and to the editing of his monumental series of notes on the debates at the Federal Convention, the publication of which confirmed his fame as "Father of the Constitution."

CONTENTS

THE FEDERALIST

Number 1

[HAMILTON]

AFTER an unequivocal experience of the inefficiency of the subsisting federal government, you are called upon to deliberate on a new Constitution for the United States of America. The subject speaks its own importance; comprehending in its consequences nothing less than the existence of the UNION, the safety and welfare of the parts of which it is composed, the fate of an empire in many respects the most interesting in the world. It has been frequently remarked that it seems to have been reserved to the people of this country, by their conduct and example, to decide the important question, whether societies of men are really capable or not of establishing good government from reflection and choice, or whether they are forever destined to depend for their political constitutions on accident and force. If there be any truth in the remark, the crisis at which we are arrived may with propriety be regarded as the era in which that decision is to be made; and a wrong election of the part we shall act may, in this view, deserve to be considered as the general misfortune of mankind.

This idea will add the inducements of philanthropy to those of patriotism, to heighten the solicitude which all considerate and good men must feel for the event. Happy will it be if our choice should be directed by a judicious estimate of our true interests, unperplexed and unbiased by considerations not connected with the public good. But this is a thing more ardently to be wished than seriously to be expected. The plan offered to our deliberations affects too many particular interests, innovates upon too many local institutions, not to involve in its discussion a variety of objects foreign to its merits, and of views, passions and prejudices little favourable to the discovery of truth.

Among the most formidable of the obstacles which the new Constitution will have to encounter may readily be distinguished the obvious interest of a certain class of men in every State to resist all changes which may hazard a diminution of the power, emolument, and consequence of the offices they hold under the State establishments; and the perverted ambition of another class of men, who will either hope to aggrandise themselves by the confusions of their country, or will flatter themselves with fairer prospects of elevation from the subdivision of the empire into several partial confederacies than from its union under one government.

It is not, however, my design to dwell upon observations of this nature. I am well aware that it would be disingenuous to resolve indiscriminately the opposition of any set of men (merely because their situations might subject them to suspicion) into interested or ambitious views. Candour will oblige us to admit that even such men may be actuated by upright intentions; and it cannot be doubted that much of the opposition which has made its appearance, or may hereafter make its appearance, will spring from sources, blameless at least, if not respectable—the honest errors of minds led astray by preconceived jealousies and fears. So numerous indeed and so powerful are the causes which serve to give a false bias to the judgment, that we, upon many occasions, see wise and good men on the wrong as well as on the right side of questions of the first magnitude to society. This circumstance, if duly attended to, would furnish a lesson of moderation to those who are ever so much persuaded of their being in the right in any controversy. And a further reason for caution, in this respect, might be drawn from the reflection that we are not always sure that those who advocate the truth are influenced by purer principles than their antagonists. Ambition, avarice, personal animosity, party opposition, and many other motives not more laudable than these, are apt to operate as well upon those who support as those who oppose the right side of a question. Were there not even these inducements to moderation, nothing could be more ill-judged than that intolerant spirit which has, at all times, characterised political parties. For in politics, as in religion, it is equally absurd to aim at making proselytes by fire and sword. Heresies in either can rarely be cured by persecution.

And yet, however just these sentiments will be allowed to be, we have already sufficient indications that it will happen in this as in all former cases of great national discussion. A torrent of angry and malignant passions will be let loose. To judge from the conduct of the opposite parties, we shall be led to conclude that they will mutually hope to evince the justness of their opinions, and to increase the number of their converts by the loudness of their declamations and the bitterness of their invectives. An enlightened zeal for the energy and efficiency of government will be stigmatised as the offspring of a temper fond of despotic power and hostile to the principles of liberty. An over-scrupulous jealousy of danger to the rights of the people, which is more commonly the fault of the head than of the heart, will be represented as mere pretence and artifice, the stale bait for popularity at the expense of the public good. It will be forgotten, on the one hand, that jealousy is the usual concomitant of love, and that the noble enthusiasm of liberty is apt to be infected with a spirit of narrow and illiberal distrust. On the other hand, it will be equally forgotten that the vigour of government is essential to the security of liberty; that, in the contemplation of a sound and well-informed judgment, their interest can never be separated; and that a dangerous ambition more often lurks behind the specious mask of zeal for the rights of the people than under the forbidding appearance of zeal for the firmness and efficiency of government. History will teach us that the former has been found a much more certain road to the introduction of despotism than the latter, and that of those men who have overturned the liberties of republics, the greatest number have begun their career by paying an obsequious court to the people; commencing demagogues, and ending tyrants.

In the course of the preceding observations, I have had an eye, my fellow-citizens, to putting you upon your guard against all attempts, from whatever quarter, to influence your decision, in a matter of the utmost moment to your welfare, by any impressions other than those which may result from the evidence of truth. You will, no doubt, at the same time, have collected from the general scope of them, that they proceed from a source not unfriendly to the new Constitution. Yes, my countrymen, I own to you that, after having given it an attentive consideration, I am clearly of opinion it is your interest to adopt it. I am convinced that this is the safest course for your liberty, your dignity, and your happiness. I affect not reserves which I do not feel. I will not amuse you with an appearance of deliberation when I have decided. I frankly acknowledge to you my convictions, and I will freely lay before you the reasons on which they are founded. The consciousness of good intentions disdains ambiguity. I shall not, however, multiply professions on this head. My motives must remain in the depository of my own breast. My arguments will be open to all, and may be judged of by all. They shall at least be offered in a spirit which will not disgrace the cause of truth.

I propose, in a series of papers, to discuss the following interesting particulars:—*The utility of the UNION to your political prosperity— The insufficiency of the present Confederation to preserve that Union—The necessity of a government at least equally energetic with the one proposed, to the attainment of this object—The conformity of the proposed Constitution to the true principles of republican government—Its analogy to your own State constitution—and lastly, The additional security which its adoption will afford to the preservation of that species of government, to liberty, and to property.*

In the progress of this discussion I shall endeavour to give a satisfactory answer to all the objections which shall have made their appearance, that may seem to have any claim to your attention.

It may perhaps be thought superfluous to offer arguments to prove the utility of the UNION, a point, no doubt, deeply engraved on the hearts of the great body of the people in every State, and one which, it may be imagined, has no adversaries. But the fact is, that we already hear it whispered in the private circles of those who oppose the new Constitution, that the thirteen States are of too great extent for any general system, and that we must of necessity resort to separate confederacies of distinct portions of the whole.[1] This doctrine will, in all probability, be gradually propagated, till it has votaries enough to countenance an open avowal of it. For nothing can be more evident, to those who are able to take an enlarged view of the subject, than the alternative of an adoption of the new Constitution or a dismemberment of the Union. It will therefore be of use to begin by examining the advantages of that Union, the certain evils, and the probable dangers, to which every State will be exposed from its dissolution. This shall accordingly constitute the subject of my next address.   PUBLIUS

Number 2
[JAY]

WHEN the people of America reflect that they are now called upon to decide a question, which, in its consequences, must prove one of the most important that ever engaged their attention, the propriety of their taking a very comprehensive, as well as a very serious, view of it, will be evident.

Nothing is more certain than the indispensable necessity of government, and it is equally undeniable, that whenever and however it is instituted, the people must cede to it some of their natural rights, in order to vest it with requisite powers. It is well worthy of consideration, therefore, whether it would conduce more to the interest of the people of America that they should, to all general purposes, be one nation, under one federal government, or that they should divide themselves into separate confederacies, and give to the head of each the same kind of powers which they are advised to place in one national government.

It has until lately been a received and uncontradicted opinion, that the prosperity of the people of America depended on their continuing firmly united, and the wishes, prayers, and efforts of our best and wisest citizens have been constantly directed to that object. But politicians now appear, who insist that this opinion is erroneous, and that instead of looking for safety and happiness in union, we ought to seek it in a division of the States into distinct confederacies or sovereignties. However extraordinary this new doctrine may appear, it nevertheless has its advocates; and certain characters who were much opposed to it formerly, are at present of the number. Whatever may be the arguments or inducements which have wrought this change in the sentiments and declarations of these gentlemen, it certainly would not be wise in the people at large to adopt these new political tenets without being fully convinced that they are founded in truth and sound policy.

It has often given me pleasure to observe, that independent America was not composed of detached and distant territories, but that one connected, fertile, wide-spreading country was the portion of our western sons of liberty. Providence has in a particular manner blessed it with a variety of soils and productions, and watered it with innumerable streams, for the delight and accommodation of its inhabitants. A succession of navigable waters forms a kind of chain round its borders, as if to bind it together; while the most noble rivers in the world, running at convenient distances, present them with highways for the easy communication of friendly aids, and the mutual transportation and exchange of their various commodities.

With equal pleasure I have as often taken notice, that Providence has been pleased to give this one connected country to one united people—a people descended from the same ancestors, speaking the same language, professing the same religion, attached to the same principles of government, very similar in their manners and customs, and who, by their joint counsels, arms, and efforts, fighting side by side throughout a long and bloody war, have nobly established general liberty and independence.

This country and this people seem to have been made for each other, and it appears as if it was the design of Providence, that an inheritance so proper and convenient for a band of brethren, united to each other by the strongest ties, should never be split into a number of unsocial, jealous, and alien sovereignties.

Similar sentiments have hitherto prevailed among all orders and denominations of men among us. To all general purposes we have uniformly been one people; each individual citizen everywhere enjoying the same national rights, privileges, and protection. As a nation we have made peace and war; as a nation we have vanquished our common enemies; as a nation we have formed alliances, and made treaties, and entered into various compacts and conventions with foreign states.

[1] The same idea, tracing the arguments to their consequences, is held out in several of the late publications against the new Constitution.—PUBLIUS

A strong sense of the value and blessings of union induced the people, at a very early period, to institute a federal government to preserve and perpetuate it. They formed it almost as soon as they had a political existence; nay, at a time when their habitations were in flames, when many of their citizens were bleeding, and when the progress of hostility and desolation left little room for those calm and mature inquiries and reflections which must ever precede the formation of a wise and well-balanced government for a free people. It is not to be wondered at, that a government instituted in times so inauspicious, should on experiment be found greatly deficient and inadequate to the purpose it was intended to answer.

This intelligent people perceived and regretted these defects. Still continuing no less attached to union than enamoured of liberty, they observed the danger which immediately threatened the former and more remotely the latter; and being persuaded that ample security for both could only be found in a national government more wisely framed, they, as with one voice, convened the late convention at Philadelphia, to take that important subject under consideration.

This convention, composed of men who possessed the confidence of the people, and many of whom had become highly distinguished by their patriotism, virtue, and wisdom, in times which tried the minds and hearts of men, undertook the arduous task. In the mild season of peace, with minds unoccupied by other subjects, they passed many months in cool, uninterrupted, and daily consultation; and finally, without having been awed by power, or influenced by any passions except love for their country, they presented and recommended to the people the plan produced by their joint and very unanimous councils.

Admit, for so is the fact, that this plan is only *recommended*, not imposed, yet let it be remembered that it is neither recommended to *blind* approbation, nor to *blind* reprobation; but to that sedate and candid consideration which the magnitude and importance of the subject demand, and which it certainly ought to receive. But this (as was remarked in the foregoing number of this paper) is more to be wished than expected, that it may be so considered and examined. Experience on a former occasion teaches us not to be too sanguine in such hopes. It is not yet forgotten that well-grounded apprehensions of imminent danger induced the people of America to form the memorable Congress of 1774. That body recommended certain measures to their constituents, and the event proved their wisdom; yet it is fresh in our memories how soon the press began to teem with pamphlets and weekly papers against those very measures. Not only many of the officers of government, who obeyed the dictates of personal interest, but others, from a mistaken estimate of consequences, or the undue influence of former attachments, or whose ambition aimed at objects which did not correspond with the public good, were indefatigable in their efforts to persuade the people to reject the advice of that patriotic Congress. Many, indeed, were deceived and deluded, but the great majority of the people reasoned and decided judiciously; and happy they are in reflecting that they did so.

They considered that the Congress was composed of many wise and experienced men. That, being convened from different parts of the country, they brought with them and communicated to each other a variety of useful information. That, in the course of the time they passed together in inquiring into and discussing the true interests of their country, they must have acquired very accurate knowledge on that head. That they were individually interested in the public liberty and prosperity, and therefore that it was not less their inclination than their duty to recommend only such measures as, after the most mature deliberation, they really thought prudent and advisable.

These and similar considerations then induced the people to rely greatly on the judgment and integrity of the Congress; and they took their advice, notwithstanding the various arts and endeavours used to deter them from it. But if the people at large had reason to confide in the men of that Congress, few of whom had been fully tried or generally known, still greater reason have they now to respect the judgment and advice of the convention, for it is well known that some of the most distinguished members of that Congress, who have been since tried and justly approved for patriotism and abilities, and who have grown old in acquiring political information, were also members of this convention, and carried into it their accumulated knowledge and experience.

It is worthy of remark that not only the first, but every succeeding Congress, as well as the late convention, have invariably joined with the people in thinking that the prosperity of America depended on its Union. To preserve and perpetuate it was the great object of the people in forming that convention, and it is also the great object of the plan which the convention has advised them to adopt. With what propriety, therefore, or for what good purposes, are attempts at this particular period made by some men to depreciate the importance of the Union? Or why is it suggested that three or four confederacies would be better than one? I am persuaded in my own mind that the people have always thought right on this subject, and that their universal and uniform attachment to the cause of the Union rests on great and weighty reasons, which I shall endeavour to develop and explain in some ensuing papers. They who promote the idea of substituting a number of distinct confederacies in the room of the plan of the convention, seem clearly to foresee that the rejection of it would put the continuance of the Union in the utmost jeopardy. That certainly would be the case, and I sincerely wish that it may be as clearly foreseen by every good citizen, that whenever the dissolution of the Union arrives, America will have reason to exclaim, in the words of the poet: "FAREWELL! A LONG FAREWELL TO ALL MY GREATNESS."   PUBLIUS

Number 3
[JAY]

IT IS not a new observation that the people of any country (if, like the Americans, intelligent and well-informed) seldom adopt and steadily persevere for many years in an erroneous opinion respecting their interests. That consideration naturally tends to create great respect for the high opinion which the people of America have so long and uniformly entertained of the importance of their continuing firmly united under one federal government, vested with sufficient powers for all general and national purposes.

The more attentively I consider and investigate the reasons which appear to have given birth to this opinion, the more I become convinced that they are cogent and conclusive.

Among the many objects to which a wise and free people find it necessary to direct their attention, that of providing for their *safety* seems to be the first. The *safety* of the people doubtless has relation to a great variety of circumstances and considerations, and consequently affords great latitude to those who wish to define it precisely and comprehensively.

At present I mean only to consider it as it respects security for the preservation of peace and tranquillity, as well as against dangers from *foreign arms and influence,* as from dangers of the *like kind* arising from domestic causes. As the former of these comes first in order, it is proper it should be the first discussed. Let us therefore proceed to examine whether the people are not right in their opinion that a cordial Union, under an efficient national government, affords them the best security that can be devised against *hostilities* from abroad.

The number of wars which have happened or will happen in the world will always be found to be in proportion to the number and weight of the causes, whether *real* or *pretended,* which *provoke* or *invite* them. If this remark be just, it becomes useful to inquire whether so many *just* causes of war are likely to be given by *United America* as by *disunited* America; for if it should turn out that United America will probably give the fewest, then it will follow that in this respect the Union tends most to preserve the people in a state of peace with other nations.

The *just* causes of war, for the most part, arise either from violations of treaties or from direct violence. America has already formed treaties with no less than six foreign nations, and all of them, except Prussia, are maritime, and therefore able to annoy and injure us. She has also extensive commerce with Portugal, Spain, and Britain, and, with respect to the two latter, has, in addition, the circumstance of neighbourhood to attend to.

It is of high importance to the peace of America that she observe the laws of nations towards all these powers, and to me it appears evident that this will be more perfectly and punctually done by one national government than it could be either by thirteen separate States or by three or four distinct confederacies.

Because when once an efficient national government is established, the best men in the country will not only consent to serve, but also will generally be appointed to manage it; for, although town or country, or other contracted influence, may place men in State assemblies, or senates, or courts of justice, or executive departments, yet more general and extensive reputation for talents and other qualifications will be necessary to recommend men to offices under the national government —especially as it will have the widest field for choice, and never experience that want of proper persons which is not uncommon in some of the States. Hence, it will result that the administration, the political counsels, and the judicial decisions of the national government will be more wise, systematical, and judicious than those of individual States, and consequently more satisfactory with respect to other nations, as well as more *safe* with respect to us.

Because, under the national government, treaties and articles of treaties, as well as the laws of nations, will always be expounded in one sense and executed in the same manner— whereas adjudications on the same points and questions, in thirteen States, or in three or four confederacies, will not always accord or be consistent; and that, as well from the variety of independent courts and judges appointed by different and independent governments, as from the different local laws and interests which may affect and influence them. The wisdom of the convention, in committing such questions to the jurisdiction and judgment of courts appointed by and responsible only to one national government, cannot be too much commended.

Because the prospect of present loss or advantage may often tempt the governing party in one or two States to swerve from good faith and justice; but those temptations, not reaching the other States, and consequently having little or no influence on the national government, the temptation will be fruitless, and good faith and justice be preserved. The case of the treaty of peace with Britain adds great weight to this reasoning.

Because, even if the governing party in a State should be disposed to resist such temptations, yet, as such temptations may, and commonly do, result from circumstances peculiar to the State, and may affect a great number of the inhabitants, the governing party may not always be able, if willing, to prevent the injustice meditated, or to punish the aggressors. But the national government, not being affected by those local circumstances, will neither be induced to commit the wrong themselves, nor want power or inclination to prevent or punish its commission by others.

So far, therefore, as either designed or accidental violations of treaties and the laws of nations afford *just* causes of war, they are less

to be apprehended under one general government than under several lesser ones, and in that respect the former most favours the *safety* of the people.

As to those just causes of war which proceed from direct and unlawful violence, it appears equally clear to me that one good national government affords vastly more security against dangers of that sort than can be derived from any other quarter.

Because such violences are more frequently caused by the passions and interests of a part than of the whole; of one or two States than of the Union. Not a single Indian war has yet been occasioned by aggressions of the present federal government, feeble as it is; but there are several instances of Indian hostilities having been provoked by the improper conduct of individual States, who, either unable or unwilling to restrain or punish offences, have given occasion to the slaughter of many innocent inhabitants.

The neighbourhood of Spanish and British territories, bordering on some States and not on others, naturally confines the causes of quarrel more immediately to the borderers. The bordering States, if any, will be those who, under the impulse of sudden irritation, and a quick sense of apparent interest or injury, will be most likely, by direct violence, to excite war with these nations; and nothing can so effectually obviate that danger as a national government, whose wisdom and prudence will not be diminished by the passions which actuate the parties immediately interested.

But not only fewer just causes of war will be given by the national government, but it will also be more in their power to accommodate and settle them amicably. They will be more temperate and cool, and in that respect, as well as in others, will be more in capacity to act advisedly than the offending State. The pride of states, as well as of men, naturally disposes them to justify all their actions, and opposes their acknowledging, correcting, or repairing their errors and offences. The national government, in such cases, will not be affected by this pride, but will proceed with moderation and candour to consider and decide on the means most proper to extricate them from the difficulties which threaten them.

Besides, it is well known that acknowledgements, explanations, and compensations are often accepted as satisfactory from a strong united nation, which would be rejected as un-

satisfactory if offered by a State or confederacy of little consideration or power.

In the year 1685, the state of Genoa having
offended Louis XIV., endeavoured to appease
him. He demanded that they should send
their *Doge,* or chief magistrate, accompanied
by four of their senators, to *France,* to ask his
pardon and receive his terms. They were
obliged to submit to it for the sake of peace.
Would he on any occasion either have demanded or have received the like humiliation
from Spain. or Britain, or any other *powerful*
nation? PUBLIUS

Number 4

[JAY]

MY LAST paper assigned several reasons why
the safety of the people would be best secured
by union against the danger it may be exposed to by *just* causes of war given to other
nations; and those reasons show that such
causes would not only be more rarely given,
but would also be more easily accommodated,
by a national government than either by the
State governments or the proposed little confederacies.

But the safety of the people of America
against dangers from *foreign* force depends
not only on their forbearing to give *just* causes
of war to other nations, but also on their placing and continuing themselves in such a situation as not to *invite* hostility or insult; for it
need not be observed that there are *pretended*
as well as just causes of war.

It is too true, however disgraceful it may be
to human nature, that nations in general will
make war whenever they have a prospect of
getting anything by it; nay, absolute monarchs will often make war when their nations
are to get nothing by it, but for purposes and
objects merely personal, such as a thirst for
military glory, revenge for personal affronts,
ambition, or private compacts to aggrandise
or support their particular families or partisans. These and a variety of other motives, which
affect only the mind of the sovereign, often
lead him to engage in wars not sanctified by
justice or the voice and interests of his people. But, independent of these inducements
to war, which are more prevalent in absolute
monarchies, but which well deserve our attention, there are others which affect nations
as often as kings; and some of them will on
examination be found to grow out of our relative situation and circumstances.

With France and with Britain we are rivals
in the fisheries, and can supply their markets
cheaper than they can themselves, notwithstanding any efforts to prevent it by bounties
on their own duties on foreign fish.

With them and with most other European
nations we are rivals in navigation and the
carrying trade; and we shall deceive ourselves
if we suppose that any of them will rejoice to
see it flourish; for, as our carrying trade cannot increase without in some degree diminishing theirs, it is more their interest, and
will be more their policy, to restrain than to
promote it.

In the trade to China and India, we interfere with more than one nation, inasmuch as
it enables us to partake in advantages which
they had in a manner monopolised, and as
we thereby supply ourselves with commodities which we used to purchase from them.

The extension of our own commerce in our
own vessels cannot give pleasure to any nations who possess territories on or near this
continent, because the cheapness and excellence of our productions, added to the circumstance of vicinity, and the enterprise and
address of our merchants and navigators, will
give us a greater share in the advantages
which those territories afford, than consists
with the wishes or policy of their respective
sovereigns.

Spain thinks it convenient to shut the Mississippi against us on the one side, and Britain excludes us from the Saint Lawrence on
the other; nor will either of them permit the
other waters which are between them and us
to become the means of mutual intercourse
and traffic.

From these and such like considerations,
which might, if consistent with prudence, be
more amplified and detailed, it is easy to see
that jealousies and uneasinesses may gradually slide into the minds and cabinets of other
nations, and that we are not to expect that
they should regard our advancement in union,
in power and consequence by land and by
sea, with an eye of indifference and composure.

The people of America are aware that inducements to war may arise out of these circumstances, as well as from others not so
obvious at present, and that whenever such
inducements may find fit time and opportunity for operation, pretences to colour and
justify them will not be wanting. Wisely,
therefore, do they consider union and a good
national government as necessary to put and

keep them in *such a situation* as, instead of *inviting* war, will tend to repress and discourage it. That situation consists in the best possible state of defence, and necessarily depends on the government, the arms, and the resources of the country.

As the safety of the whole is the interest of the whole, and cannot be provided for without government, either one or more or many, let us inquire whether one good government is not, relative to the object in question, more competent than any other given number whatever.

One government can collect and avail itself of the talents and experience of the ablest men, in whatever part of the Union they may be found. It can move on uniform principles of policy. It can harmonise, assimilate, and protect the several parts and members, and extend the benefit of its foresight and precautions to each. In the formation of treaties, it will regard the interest of the whole, and the particular interests of the parts as connected with that of the whole. It can apply the resources and power of the whole to the defence of any particular part, and that more easily and expeditiously than State governments or separate confederacies can possibly do, for want of concert and unity of system. It can place the militia under one plan of discipline, and, by putting their officers in a proper line of subordination to the Chief Magistrate, will, as it were, consolidate them into one corps, and thereby render them more efficient than if divided into thirteen or into three or four distinct independent companies.

What would the militia of Britain be if the English militia obeyed the government of England, if the Scotch militia obeyed the government of Scotland, and if the Welsh militia obeyed the government of Wales? Suppose an invasion; would those three governments (if they agreed at all) be able, with all their respective forces, to operate against the enemy so effectually as the single government of Great Britain would?

We have heard much of the fleets of Britain, and the time may come, if we are wise, when the fleets of America may engage attention. But if one national government had not so regulated the navigation of Britain as to make it a nursery for seamen—if one national government had not called forth all the national means and materials for forming fleets, their prowess and their thunder would never have been celebrated. Let England have its naviga-

tion and fleet—let Scotland have its navigation and fleet—let Wales have its navigation and fleet—let Ireland have its navigation and fleet—let those four of the constituent parts of the British empire be under four independent governments, and it is easy to perceive how soon they would each dwindle into comparative insignificance.

Apply these facts to our own case. Leave America divided into thirteen or, if you please, into three or four independent governments—what armies could they raise and pay—what fleets could they ever hope to have? If one was attacked, would the others fly to its succour, and spend their blood and money in its defence? Would there be no danger of their being flattered into neutrality by its specious promises, or seduced by a too great fondness for peace to decline hazarding their tranquillity and present safety for the sake of neighbours, of whom perhaps they have been jealous, and whose importance they are content to see diminished. Although such conduct would not be wise, it would, nevertheless, be natural. The history of the states of Greece, and of other countries, abounds with such instances, and it is not improbable that what has so often happened would, under similar circumstances, happen again.

But admit that they might be willing to help the invaded State or confederacy. How, and when, and in what proportion shall aids of men and money be afforded? Who shall command the allied armies, and from which of them shall he receive his orders? Who shall settle the terms of peace, and in case of disputes what umpire shall decide between them and compel acquiescence? Various difficulties and inconveniences would be inseparable from such a situation; whereas one government, watching over the general and common interests, and combining and directing the powers and resources of the whole, would be free from all these embarrassments, and conduce far more to the safety of the people.

But whatever may be our situation, whether firmly united under one national government, or split into a number of confederacies, certain it is, that foreign nations will know and view it exactly as it is; and they will act towards us accordingly. If they see that our national government is efficient and well administered, our trade prudently regulated, our militia properly organised and disciplined, our resources and finances discreetly managed, our credit reestablished, our people free, contented, and united, they will be much more disposed to cultivate our friendship than provoke our resentment. If, on the other hand, they find us either destitute of an effectual government (each State doing right or wrong, as to its rulers may seem convenient), or split into three or four independent and probably discordant republics or confederacies, one inclining to Britain, another to France, and a third to Spain, and perhaps played off against each other by the three, what a poor, pitiful figure will America make in their eyes! How liable would she become not only to their contempt, but to their outrage; and how soon would dear-bought experience proclaim that when a people or family so divide, it never fails to be against themselves.   PUBLIUS

Number 5

[JAY]

QUEEN ANNE, in her letter of the 1st July 1706, to the Scotch Parliament, makes some observations on the importance of the *Union* then forming between England and Scotland, which merit our attention. I shall present the public with one or two extracts from it: "An entire and perfect union will be the solid foundation of lasting peace: It will secure your religion, liberty, and property; remove the animosities amongst yourselves, and the jealousies and differences betwixt our two kingdoms. It must increase your strength, riches and trade; and by this union the whole island, being joined in affection and free from all apprehensions of different interest, will be *enabled to resist all its enemies.*" "We most earnestly recommend to you calmness and unanimity in this great and weighty affair, that the union may be brought to a happy conclusion, being the only *effectual* way to secure our present and future happiness, and disappoint the designs of our and your enemies, who will doubtless, on this occasion, *use their utmost endeavours to prevent or delay this union.*"

It was remarked in the preceding paper, that weakness and divisions at home would invite dangers from abroad; and that nothing would tend more to secure us from them than union, strength, and good government within ourselves. This subject is copious and cannot easily be exhausted.

The history of Great Britain is the one with which we are in general the best acquainted, and it gives us many useful lessons. We may profit by their experience without paying the price which it cost them. Although it seems obvious to common sense that the people of such an island should be but one nation, yet we find that they were for ages divided into three, and that those three were almost constantly embroiled in quarrels and wars with one another. Notwithstanding their true interest with respect to the continental nations was really the same, yet by the arts and policy and practices of those nations, their mutual jealousies were perpetually kept inflamed, and for a long series of years they were far more inconvenient and troublesome than they were useful and assisting to each other.

Should the people of America divide themselves into three or four nations, would not the same thing happen? Would not similar jealousies arise, and be in like manner cherished? Instead of their being "joined in affection" and free from all apprehension of different "interests," envy and jealousy would soon extinguish confidence and affection, and the partial interests of each confederacy, instead of the general interests of all America, would be the only objects of their policy and pursuits. Hence, like most other *bordering* nations, they would always be either involved in disputes and war, or live in the constant apprehension of them.

The most sanguine advocates for three or four confederacies cannot reasonably suppose that they would long remain exactly on an equal footing in point of strength, even if it was possible to form them so at first; but, admitting that to be practicable, yet what human contrivance can secure the continuance of such equality? Independent of those local circumstances which tend to beget and increase power in one part and to impede its progress in another, we must advert to the effects of that superior policy and good management which would probably distinguish the government of one above the rest, and by which their relative equality in strength and consideration would be destroyed. For it cannot be presumed that the same degree of sound policy, prudence, and foresight, would uniformly be observed by each of these confederacies for a long succession of years.

Whenever, and from whatever causes, it might happen, and happen it would, that any one of these nations or confederacies should rise on the scale of political importance much above the degree of her neighbours, that moment would those neighbours behold her with envy and with fear. Both those passions would lead them to countenance, if not to promote, whatever might promise to diminish her importance; and would also restrain them from measures calculated to advance or even to secure her prosperity. Much time would not be necessary to enable her to discern these unfriendly dispositions. She would soon begin, not only to lose confidence in her neighbours, but also to feel a disposition equally unfavourable to them. Distrust naturally creates distrust, and by nothing is good-will and kind conduct more speedily changed than by invidious jealousies and uncandid imputations, whether expressed or implied.

The North is generally the region of strength, and many local circumstances render it probable that the most Northern of the proposed confederacies would, at a period not very distant, be unquestionably more formidable than any of the others. No sooner would this become evident than the *Northern Hive* would excite the same ideas and sensations in the more southern parts of America which it formerly did in the southern parts of Europe. Nor does it appear to be a rash conjecture that its young swarms might often be tempted to gather honey in the more blooming fields and milder air of their luxurious and more delicate neighbours.

They who well consider the history of similar divisions and confederacies will find abundant reason to apprehend that those in contemplation would in no other sense be neighbours than as they would be borderers; that they would neither love nor trust one another, but on the contrary would be a prey to discord, jealousy, and mutual injuries; in short, that they would place us exactly in the situations in which some nations doubtless wish to see us, viz., *formidable only to each other*.

From these considerations it appears that those gentlemen are greatly mistaken who suppose that alliances offensive and defensive might be formed between these confederacies, and would produce that combination and union of wills, of arms, and of resources, which would be necessary to put and keep them in a formidable state of defence against foreign enemies.

When did the independent states, into which Britain and Spain were formerly divided, combine in such alliance, or unite their forces against a foreign enemy? The proposed confederacies will be *distinct nations*. Each of them would have its commerce with foreigners to regulate by distinct treaties; and as their productions and commodities are different and proper for different markets, so would those treaties be essentially different. Different commercial concerns must create different interests, and of course different degrees of political attachment to and connection with different foreign nations. Hence it might and probably would happen that the foreign nation with whom the *Southern* confederacy might be at war would be the one with whom the *Northern* confederacy would be the most desirous of preserving peace and friendship. An alliance so contrary to their immediate interest would not therefore be easy to form, nor, if formed, would it be observed and fulfilled with perfect good faith.

Nay, it is far more probable that in America, as in Europe, neighbouring nations, acting under the impulse of opposite interests and unfriendly passions, would frequently be found taking different sides. Considering our distance from Europe, it would be more natural for these confederacies to apprehend danger from one another than from distant nations, and therefore that each of them should be more desirous to guard against the others by the aid of foreign alliances, than to guard against foreign dangers by alliances between themselves. And here let us not forget how much more easy it is to receive foreign fleets into our ports, and foreign armies into our country, than it is to persuade or compel them to depart. How many conquests did the Romans and others make in the characters of allies, and what innovations did they under the same character introduce into the governments of those whom they pretended to protect.

Let candid men judge, then, whether the division of America into any given number of independent sovereignties would tend to secure us against the hostilities and improper interference of foreign nations.   PUBLIUS

Number 6

[HAMILTON]

THE THREE last numbers of this paper have been dedicated to an enumeration of the dangers to which we should be exposed, in a state of disunion, from the arms and arts of foreign nations. I shall now proceed to delineate dangers of a different and, perhaps, still more alarming kind—those which will in all probability flow from dissensions between the States themselves, and from domestic factions and convulsions. These have been already in some instances slightly anticipated; but they deserve a more particular and more full investigation.

A man must be far gone in Utopian speculations who can seriously doubt that, if these States should either be wholly disunited, or only united in partial confederacies, the subdivisions into which they might be thrown would have frequent and violent contests with each other. To presume a want of motives for such contests as an argument against their existence, would be to forget that men are ambitious, vindictive, and rapacious. To look for a continuation of harmony between a number of independent, unconnected sovereignties in the same neighbourhood, would be to disregard the uniform course of human events, and to set at defiance the accumulated experience of ages.

The causes of hostility among nations are innumerable. There are some which have a general and almost constant operation upon the collective bodies of society. Of this description are the love of power or the desire of pre-eminence and dominion—the jealousy of power, or the desire of equality and safety. There are others which have a more circumscribed though an equally operative influence within their spheres. Such are the rivalships and competitions of commerce between commercial nations. And there are others, not less numerous than either of the former, which take their origin entirely in private passions; in the attachments, enmities, interests, hopes, and fears of leading individuals in the communities of which they are members. Men of this class, whether the favourites of a king or of a people, have in too many instances abused the confidence they possessed; and assuming the pretext of some public motive, have not scrupled to sacrifice the national tranquillity to personal advantage or personal gratification.

The celebrated Pericles, in compliance with the resentment of a prostitute,[1] at the expense of much of the blood and treasure of his countrymen, attacked, vanquished, and destroyed the city of the *Samnians*. The same man, stimulated by private pique against the *Megarensians*,[2] another nation of Greece, or to avoid a prosecution with which he was threatened as an accomplice in a supposed theft of the statuary Phidias,[3] or to get rid of the accusations prepared to be brought against him for dissipating the funds of the state in the purchase of popularity,[4] or from a combination of all these causes, was the primitive author of that famous and fatal war, distinguished in the Grecian annals by the name of the *Peloponnesian* war; which, after various vicissitudes, intermissions, and renewals, terminated in the ruin of the Athenian commonwealth.

The ambitious cardinal, who was prime minister to Henry VIII., permitting his vanity to aspire to the triple crown,[5] entertained hopes of succeeding in the acquisition of that splendid prize by the influence of the Emperor Charles V. To secure the favour and interest of this enterprising and powerful monarch, he precipitated England into a war with France, contrary to the plainest dictates of policy, and at the hazard of the safety and independence, as well of the kingdom over which he presided by his counsels, as of Europe in general. For if there ever was a sovereign who bid fair to realise the project of universal monarchy, it was the Emperor Charles V., of whose intrigues Wolsey was at once the instrument and the dupe.

The influence which the bigotry of one female,[6] the petulance of another,[7] and the cabals of a third,[8] had in the contemporary policy, ferments, and pacifications, of a considerable part of Europe, are topics that have been too often descanted upon not to be generally known.

To multiply examples of the agency of personal considerations in the production of great national events, either foreign or domestic, according to their direction, would be an unnecessary waste of time. Those who have but a superficial acquaintance with the sources from which they are to be drawn, will themselves recollect a variety of instances; and those who have a tolerable knowledge of human nature will not stand in need of such lights, to form their opinion either of the reality or extent of that agency. Perhaps, however, a reference, tending to illustrate the general principle, may with propriety be made to a case which has lately happened among ourselves.

---

[1] Aspasia, vide *Plutarch's Pericles.*—Publius
[2] *Ibid.*—Publius
[3] *Ibid.*—Publius
[4] *Ibid.* Phidias was supposed to have stolen some public gold, with the connivance of Pericles, for the embellishment of the statue of Minerva.—Publius
[5] Worn by the popes.—Publius
[6] Madame de Maintenon.—Publius
[7] Duchess of Marlborough.—Publius
[8] Madame de Pompadour.—Publius

If Shays had not been a *desperate debtor,* it is much to be doubted whether Massachusetts would have been plunged into a civil war.

But notwithstanding the concurring testimony of experience, in this particular, there are still to be found visionary or designing men, who stand ready to advocate the paradox of perpetual peace between the States, though dismembered and alienated from each other. The genius of republics (say they) is pacific; the spirit of commerce has a tendency to soften the manners of men, and to extinguish those inflammable humours which have so often kindled into wars. Commercial republics, like ours, will never be disposed to waste themselves in ruinous contentions with each other. They will be governed by mutual interest, and will cultivate a spirit of mutual amity and concord.

Is it not (we may ask these projectors in politics) the true interest of all nations to cultivate the same benevolent and philosophic spirit? If this be their true interest, have they in fact pursued it? Has it not, on the contrary, invariably been found that momentary passions, and immediate interests, have a more active and imperious control over human conduct than general and remote considerations of policy, utility, or justice? Have republics in practice been less addicted to war than monarchies? Are not the former administered by *men* as well as the latter? Are there not aversions, predilections, rivalships, and desires of unjust acquisitions, that affect nations as well as kings? Are not popular assemblies frequently subject to the impulses of rage, resentment, jealousy, avarice, and of other irregular and violent propensities? Is it not well known that their determinations are often governed by a few individuals in whom they place confidence, and are, of course, liable to be tinctured by the passions and views of those individuals? Has commerce hitherto done anything more than change the object of war? Is not the love of wealth as domineering and enterprising a passion as that of power or glory? Have there not been as many wars founded upon commercial motives since that has become the prevailing system of nations, as were before occasioned by the cupidity of territory or dominion? Has not the spirit of commerce, in many instances, administered new incentives to the appetite, both for the one and for the other? Let experience, the least fallible guide of human opinions, be appealed to for an answer to these inquiries.

Sparta, Athens, Rome, and Carthage were all republics; two of them, Athens and Carthage, of the commercial kind. Yet were they as often engaged in wars, offensive and defensive, as the neighbouring monarchies of the same times. Sparta was little better than a well-regulated camp; and Rome was never sated of carnage and conquest.

Carthage, though a commercial republic, was the aggressor in the very war that ended in her destruction. Hannibal had carried her arms into the heart of Italy, and to the gates of Rome, before Scipio, in turn, gave him an overthrow in the territories of Carthage, and made a conquest of the commonwealth.

Venice, in later times, figured more than once in wars of ambition, till, becoming an object to the other Italian states, Pope Julius II. found means to accomplish that formidable league,[1] which gave a deadly blow to the power and pride of this haughty republic.

The provinces of Holland, till they were overwhelmed in debts and taxes, took a leading and conspicuous part in the wars of Europe. They had furious contests with England for the dominion of the sea, and were among the most persevering and most implacable of the opponents of Louis XIV.

In the government of Britain the representatives of the people compose one branch of the national legislature. Commerce has been for ages the predominant pursuit of that country. Few nations, nevertheless, have been more frequently engaged in war; and the wars in which that kingdom has been engaged have, in numerous instances, proceeded from the people.

There have been, if I may so express it, almost as many popular as royal wars. The cries of the nation and the importunities of their representatives have, upon various occasions, dragged their monarchs into war, or continued them in it, contrary to their inclinations, and sometimes contrary to the real interests of the state. In that memorable struggle for superiority between the rival houses of *Austria* and *Bourbon,* which so long kept Europe in a flame, it is well known that the antipathies of the English against the French, seconding the ambition, or rather the avarice, of a favourite leader,[2] protracted the war beyond the limits marked out by sound policy, and for a con-

[1] The League of Cambray, comprehending the Emperor, the King of France, the King of Aragon, and most of the Italian princes and states.—PUBLIUS

[2] The Duke of Marlborough.—PUBLIUS

siderable time in opposition to the views of the court.

The wars of these two last-mentioned nations have in a great measure grown out of commercial considerations—the desire of supplanting and the fear of being supplanted, either in particular branches of traffic or in the general advantages of trade and navigation.[1]

From this summary of what has taken place in other countries, whose situations have borne the nearest resemblance to our own, what reason can we have to confide in those reveries which would seduce us into an expectation of peace and cordiality between the members of the present confederacy, in a state of separation? Have we not already seen enough of the fallacy and extravagance of those idle theories which have amused us with promises of an exemption from the imperfections, weaknesses, and evils incident to society in every shape? Is it not time to awake from the deceitful dream of a golden age, and to adopt as a practical maxim for the direction of our political conduct that we, as well as the other inhabitants of the globe, are yet remote from the happy empire of perfect wisdom and perfect virtue?

Let the point of extreme depression to which our national dignity and credit have sunk, let the inconveniences felt everywhere from a lax and ill administration of government, let the revolt of a part of the State of North Carolina, the late menacing disturb-

[1] In the text said to have been revised by Hamilton and Madison, and adopted by Mr. J. C. Hamilton, the following additional sentences occur at this point: "and sometimes even the more culpable desire of sharing in the commerce of other nations without their consent. The last war but two between Britain and Spain sprang from the attempts of the English merchants to prosecute an illicit trade with the Spanish main. These unjustifiable practices on their part produced severity on the part of the Spaniards towards the subjects of Great Britain which were not more justifiable, because they exceeded the bounds of a just retaliation and were chargeable with inhumanity and cruelty. Many of the English who were taken on the Spanish coast were sent to dig in the mines of Potosi; and by the usual progress of a spirit of resentment, the innocent were, after a while, confounded with the guilty in indiscriminate punishment. The complaints of the merchants kindled a violent flame throughout the nation, which soon after broke out in the House of Commons, and was communicated from that body to the ministry. Letters of reprisal were granted, and a war ensued, which in its consequences overthrew all the alliances that but twenty years before had been formed with sanguine expectations of the most beneficial fruits."

ances in Pennsylvania, and the actual insurrections and rebellions in Massachusetts, declare ——!

So far is the general sense of mankind from corresponding with the tenets of those who endeavour to lull asleep our apprehensions of discord and hostility between the States, in the event of disunion, that it has from long observation of the progress of society become a sort of axiom in politics, that vicinity, or nearness of situation, constitutes nations natural enemies. An intelligent writer expresses himself on this subject to this effect: "NEIGHBOURING NATIONS [says he] are naturally enemies of each other, unless their common weakness forces them to league in a CONFEDERATIVE REPUBLIC, and their constitution prevents the differences that neighbourhood occasions, extinguishing that secret jealousy which disposes all states to aggrandise themselves at the expense of their neighbours."[2] This passage, at the same time, points out the EVIL and suggests the REMEDY.

PUBLIUS

Number 7

[HAMILTON]

IT IS sometimes asked, with an air of seeming triumph, what inducements could the States have, if disunited, to make war upon each other? It would be a full answer to this question to say—precisely the same inducements which have, at different times, deluged in blood all the nations in the world. But, unfortunately for us, the question admits of a more particular answer. There are causes of differences within our immediate contemplation, of the tendency of which, even under the restraints of a federal constitution, we have had sufficient experience to enable us to form a judgment of what might be expected if those restraints were removed.

Territorial disputes have at all times been found one of the most fertile sources of hostility among nations. Perhaps the greatest proportion of wars that have desolated the earth have sprung from this origin. This cause would exist among us in full force. We have a vast tract of unsettled territory within the boundaries of the United States. There still are discordant and undecided claims between several of them, and the dissolution of the Union would lay a foundation for similar claims between them all. It is well known that they have

[2] Vide *Principes des Négociations,* par l'Abbé de Mably.—PUBLIUS

heretofore had serious and animated discussion concerning the rights to the lands which were ungranted at the time of the Revolution, and which usually went under the name of crown lands. The States within the limits of whose colonial governments they were comprised have claimed them as their property, the others have contended that the rights of the crown in this article devolved upon the Union; especially as to all that part of the Western territory which, either by actual possession, or through the submission of the Indian proprietors, was subjected to the jurisdiction of the king of Great Britain, till it was relinquished in the treaty of peace. This, it has been said, was at all events an acquisition to the Confederacy by compact with a foreign power. It has been the prudent policy of Congress to appease this controversy, by prevailing upon the States to make cessions to the United States for the benefit of the whole. This has been so far accomplished as, under a continuation of the Union, to afford a decided prospect of an amicable termination of the dispute. A dismemberment of the Confederacy, however, would revive this dispute, and would create others on the same subject. At present, a large part of the vacant Western territory is, by cession at least, if not by any anterior right, the common property of the Union. If that were at an end, the States which made the cession, on a principle of federal compromise, would be apt, when the motive of the grant had ceased, to reclaim the lands as a reversion. The other States would no doubt insist on a proportion, by right of representation. Their argument would be, that a grant, once made, could not be revoked; and that the justice of participating in territory acquired or secured by the joint efforts of the Confederacy, remained undiminished. If, contrary to probability, it should be admitted by all the States, that each had a right to a share of this common stock, there would still be a difficulty to be surmounted, as to a proper rule of apportionment. Different principles would be set up by different States for this purpose; and as they would affect the opposite interests of the parties, they might not easily be susceptible of a pacific adjustment.

In the wide field of Western territory, therefore, we perceive an ample theatre for hostile pretensions, without any umpire or common judge to interpose between the contending parties. To reason from the past to the future, we shall have good ground to apprehend that the sword would sometimes be appealed to as the arbiter of their differences. The circumstances of the dispute between Connecticut and Pennsylvania, respecting the land at Wyoming, admonish us not to be sanguine in expecting an easy accommodation of such differences. The articles of federation obliged the parties to submit the matter to the decision of a federal court. The submission was made, and the court decided in favour of Pennsylvania. But Connecticut gave strong indications of dissatisfaction with that determination; nor did she appear to be entirely resigned to it, till, by negotiation and management, something like an equivalent was found for the loss she supposed herself to have sustained. Nothing here said is intended to convey the slightest censure on the conduct of that State. She no doubt sincerely believed herself to have been injured by the decision; and States, like individuals, acquiesce with great reluctance in determinations to their disadvantage.

Those who had an opportunity of seeing the inside of the transactions which attended the progress of the controversy between this State and the district of Vermont, can vouch the opposition we experienced, as well from States not interested as from those which were interested in the claim; and can attest the danger to which the peace of the Confederacy might have been exposed, had this State attempted to assert its rights by force. Two motives preponderated in that opposition: one, a jealousy entertained of our future power; and the other, the interest of certain individuals of influence in the neighbouring States, who had obtained grants of lands under the actual government of that district. Even the States which brought forward claims, in contradiction to ours, seemed more solicitous to dismember this State than to establish their own pretensions. These were New Hampshire, Massachusetts, and Connecticut. New Jersey and Rhode Island, upon all occasions, discovered a warm zeal for the independence of Vermont; and Maryland, till alarmed by the appearance of a connection between Canada and that State, entered deeply into the same views. These being small States, saw with an unfriendly eye the perspective of our growing greatness. In a review of these transactions we may trace some of the causes which would be likely to embroil the States with each other, if it should be their unpropitious destiny to become disunited.

The competitions of commerce would be another fruitful source of contention. The States less favourably circumstanced would be desirous of escaping from the disadvantages of local situation, and of sharing in the advantages of their more fortunate neighbours. Each State, or separate confederacy, would pursue a system of commercial policy peculiar to itself. This would occasion distinctions, preferences, and exclusions, which would beget discontent. The habits of intercourse, on the basis of equal privileges, to which we have been accustomed since the earliest settlement of the country, would give a keener edge to those causes of discontent than they would naturally have independent of this circumstance. *We should be ready to denominate injuries those things which were in reality the justifiable acts of independent sovereignties consulting a distinct interest.* The spirit of enterprise, which characterises the commercial part of America, has left no occasion of displaying itself unimproved. It is not at all probable that this unbridled spirit would pay much respect to those regulations of trade by which particular States might endeavour to secure exclusive benefits to their own citizens. The infractions of these regulations, on one side, the efforts to prevent and repel them, on the other, would naturally lead to outrages, and these to reprisals and wars.

The opportunities which some States would have of rendering others tributary to them by commercial regulations would be impatiently submitted to by the tributary States. The relative situation of New York, Connecticut, and New Jersey, would afford an example of this kind. New York, from the necessities of revenue, must lay duties on her importations. A great part of these duties must be paid by the inhabitants of the two other states in the capacity of consumers of what we import. New York would neither be willing nor able to forego this advantage. Her citizens would not consent that a duty paid by them should be remitted in favour of the citizens of her neighbours; nor would it be practicable, if there were not this impediment in the way, to distinguish the customers in our own markets. Would Connecticut and New Jersey long submit to be taxed by New York for her exclusive benefit? Should we be long permitted to remain in the quiet and undisturbed enjoyment of a metropolis, from the possession of which we derived an advantage so odious to our neighbours, and, in their opinion, so oppressive? Should we be able to preserve it against the incumbent weight of Connecticut on the one side, and the co-operating pressure of New Jersey on the other? These are questions that temerity alone will answer in the affirmative.

The public debt of the Union would be a further cause of collision between the separate States or confederacies. The apportionment, in the first instance, and the progressive extinguishment afterward, would be alike productive of ill-humour and animosity. How would it be possible to agree upon a rule of apportionment satisfactory to all? There is scarcely any that can be proposed which is entirely free from real objections. These, as usual, would be exaggerated by the adverse interest of the parties. There are even dissimilar views among the States as to the general principle of discharging the public debt. Some of them, either less impressed with the importance of national credit, or because their citizens have little, if any, immediate interest in the question, feel an indifference, if not a repugnance, to the payment of the domestic debt at any rate. These would be inclined to magnify the difficulties of a distribution. Others of them, a numerous body of whose citizens are creditors to the public beyond the proportion of the State in the total amount of the national debt, would be strenuous for some equitable and effective provision. The procrastinations of the former would excite the resentments of the latter. The settlement of a rule would, in the meantime, be postponed by real differences of opinion and affected delays. The citizens of the States interested would clamour; foreign powers would urge for the satisfaction of their just demands, and the peace of the States would be hazarded to the double contingency of external invasion and internal contention.

Suppose the difficulties of agreeing upon a rule surmounted, and the apportionment made. Still there is great room to suppose that the rule agreed upon would, upon experiment, be found to bear harder upon some States than upon others. Those which were sufferers by it would naturally seek for a mitigation of the burden. The others would as naturally be disinclined to a revision, which was likely to end in an increase of their own incumbrances. Their refusal would be too plausible a pretext to the complaining States to withhold their contributions, not to be embraced with avidity; and the non-compliance of these States with their engagements would be a ground of bitter discussion and altercation. If even the rule adopted should in practice justify the equality of its principle, still delinquencies in payments on the part of some of the States would result from a diversity of other causes—the real deficiency of resources; the mismanagement of their finances; accidental disorders in the management of the government; and, in addition to the rest, the reluctance with which men commonly part with money for purposes that have outlived the exigencies which produced them, and interfere with the supply of immediate wants. Delinquencies, from whatever causes, would be productive of complaints, recriminations, and quarrels. There is, perhaps, nothing more likely to disturb the tranquillity of nations than their being bound to mutual contributions for any common object that does not yield an equal and coincident benefit. For it is an observation, as true as it is trite, that there is nothing men differ so readily about as the payment of money.

Laws in violation of private contracts, as they amount to aggressions on the rights of those States whose citizens are injured by them, may be considered as another probable source of hostility. We are not authorised to expect that a more liberal or more equitable spirit would preside over the legislations of the individual States hereafter, if unrestrained by any additional checks, than we have heretofore seen in too many instances disgracing their several codes. We have observed the disposition to retaliation excited in Connecticut, in consequence of the enormities perpetrated by the Legislature of Rhode Island; and we reasonably infer that, in similar cases under other circumstances, a war, not of *parchment,* but of the sword, would chastise such atrocious breaches of moral obligation and social justice.

The probability of incompatible alliances between the different States or confederacies and different foreign nations, and the effects of this situation upon the peace of the whole, have been sufficiently unfolded in some preceding papers. From the view they have exhibited of this part of the subject, this conclusion is to be drawn, that America, if not connected at all, or only by the feeble tie of a simple league, offensive and defensive, would, by the operation of such jarring alliances, be gradually entangled in all the pernicious labyrinths of European politics and wars; and by the destructive contentions of the parts into which she was divided, would be likely to become a prey to the artifices and machinations of powers equally the enemies of them all.

Divide et impera [1] must be the motto of every nation that either hates or fears us.[2]

PUBLIUS

Number 8

[HAMILTON]

ASSUMING IT therefore as an established truth that the several States, in case of disunion, or such combinations of them as might happen to be formed out of the wreck of the general Confederacy, would be subject to those vicissitudes of peace and war, of friendship and enmity with each other, which have fallen to the lot of all neighbouring nations not united under one government, let us enter into a concise detail of some of the consequences that would attend such a situation.

War between the States, in the first period of their separate existence, would be accompanied with much greater distresses than it commonly is in those countries where regular military establishments have long obtained. The disciplined armies always kept on foot on the continent of Europe, though they bear a malignant aspect to liberty and economy, have, notwithstanding, been productive of the signal advantage of rendering sudden conquests impracticable, and of preventing that rapid desolation which used to mark the progress of war prior to their introduction. The art of fortification has contributed to the same ends. The nations of Europe are encircled with chains of fortified places, which mutually obstruct invasion. Campaigns are wasted in reducing two or three frontier garrisons, to gain admittance into an enemy's country. Similar impediments occur at every step, to exhaust the strength and delay the progress of an invader. Formerly, an invading army would penetrate into the heart of a neighbouring country almost as soon as intelligence of its approach could be received; but now a comparatively small force of disciplined troops, acting on the defensive, with the aid of posts, is able to impede, and finally to frustrate, the enterprises of one much more considerable. The history of war, in that quarter of the globe, is no longer a history of nations subdued and empires overturned; but of towns taken and retaken; of battles that decide nothing, of re-

---

[1] Divide and command.—PUBLIUS
[2] In order that the whole subject of these papers may as soon as possible be laid before the public, it is proposed to publish them four times a week —on Tuesday in the *New York Packet* and on Thursday in the *Daily Advertiser.*—PUBLIUS

treats more beneficial than victories; of much effort and little acquisition.

In this country the scene would be altogether reversed. The jealousy of military establishments would postpone them as long as possible. The want of fortifications, leaving the frontiers of one State open to another, would facilitate inroads. The populous States would, with little difficulty, overrun their less populous neighbours. Conquests would be as easy to be made as difficult to be retained. War, therefore, would be desultory and predatory. PLUNDER and devastation ever march in the train of irregulars. The calamities of individuals would make the principal figure in the events which would characterise our military exploits.

This picture is not too highly wrought; though, I confess, it would not long remain a just one. Safety from external danger is the most powerful director of national conduct. Even the ardent love of liberty will, after a time, give way to its dictates. The violent destruction of life and property incident to war, the continual effort and alarm attendant on a state of continual danger, will compel nations the most attached to liberty to resort for repose and security to institutions which have a tendency to destroy their civil and political rights. To be more safe, they at length become willing to run the risk of being less free.

The institutions chiefly alluded to are STANDING ARMIES and the correspondent appendages of military establishments. Standing armies, it is said, are not provided against in the new Constitution; and it is therefore inferred that they may exist under it.[1] Their existence, however from the very terms of the proposition, is, at most, problematical and uncertain.[2] But standing armies, it may be replied, must inevitably result from a dissolution of the Confederacy. Frequent war and constant apprehension, which require a state of as constant preparation, will infallibly produce them. The weaker States or confederacies would first have recourse to them, to put themselves upon an equality with their more potent neighbours. They would endeavour to supply the inferiority of population and resources by a more regular and effective system of defence, by disciplined troops, and by fortifications. They would, at the same time, be necessitated to strengthen the executive arm of government, in doing which their constitutions would acquire a progressive direction towards monarchy. It is of the nature of war to increase the executive at the expense of the legislative authority.

The expedients which have been mentioned would soon give the States or confederacies that made use of them a superiority over their neighbours. Small states, or states of less natural strength, under vigorous governments, and with the assistance of disciplined armies, have often triumphed over large states, or states of greater natural strength, which have been destitute of these advantages. Neither the pride nor the safety of the more important States or confederacies would permit them long to submit to this mortifying and adventitious superiority. They would quickly resort to means similar to those by which it had been effected, to reinstate themselves in their lost pre-eminence. Thus we should, in a little time, see established in every part of this country the same engines of despotism which have been the scourge of the Old World. This, at least, would be the natural course of things; and our reasonings will be the more likely to be just, in proportion as they are accommodated to this standard.

These are not vague inferences drawn from supposed or speculative defects in a Constitution, the whole power of which is lodged in the hands of a people, or their representatives and delegates, but they are solid conclusions, drawn from the natural and necessary progress of human affairs.

It may, perhaps, be asked, by way of objection to this, why did not standing armies spring up out of the contentions which so often distracted the ancient republics of Greece? Different answers, equally satisfactory, may be given to this question. The industrious habits of the people of the present day, absorbed in the pursuits of gain, and devoted to the improvements of agriculture and commerce, are incompatible with the condition of a nation of soldiers, which was the true condition of the people of those republics. The means of revenue, which have been so greatly multiplied by the increase of gold and silver and of the arts of industry,

[1] This objection will be fully examined in its proper place, and it will be shown that the only natural precaution which could have been taken on this subject has been taken; and a much better one than is to be found in any constitution that has been heretofore framed in America, most of which contain no guard at all on this subject.—PUBLIUS

[2] In the revised text: "This inference, from the very form of the proposition, is, at best, problematical and uncertain."

and the science of finance, which is the off-spring of modern times, concurring with the habits of nations, have produced an entire revolution in the system of war, and have rendered disciplined armies, distinct from the body of the citizens, the inseparable companions of frequent hostility.

There is a wide difference, also, between military establishments in a country seldom exposed by its situation to internal invasions, and in one which is often subject to them, and always apprehensive of them. The rulers of the former can have no good pretext, if they are even so inclined, to keep on foot armies so numerous as must of necessity be maintained in the latter. These armies being, in the first case, rarely, if at all, called into activity for interior defence, the people are in no danger of being broken to military subordination. The laws are not accustomed to relaxations, in favour of military exigencies; the civil state remains in full vigour, neither corrupted, nor confounded with the principles or propensities of the other state. The smallness of the army renders the natural strength of the community an overmatch for it; and the citizens, not habituated to look up to the military power for protection, or to submit to its oppressions, neither love nor fear the soldiery; they view them with a spirit of jealous acquiescence in a necessary evil, and stand ready to resist a power which they suppose may be exerted to the prejudice of their rights. The army under such circumstances may usefully aid the magistrate to suppress a small faction, or an occasional mob, or insurrection; but it will be unable to enforce encroachments against the united efforts of the great body of the people.

In a country in the predicament last described, the contrary of all this happens. The perpetual menacings of danger oblige the government to be always prepared to repel it; its armies must be numerous enough for instant defence. The continual necessity for their services enhances the importance of the soldier, and proportionably degrades the condition of the citizen. The military state becomes elevated above the civil. The inhabitants of territories, often the theatre of war, are unavoidably subjected to frequent infringements on their rights, which serve to weaken their sense of those rights; and by degrees the people are brought to consider the soldiery not only as their protectors, but as their superiors. The transition from this disposition to that of considering them masters, is neither remote nor

difficult; but it is very difficult to prevail upon a people under such impressions, to make a bold or effectual resistance to usurpations supported by the military power.

The kingdom of Great Britain falls within the first description. An insular situation, and a powerful marine, guarding it in a great measure against the possibility of foreign invasion, supersede the necessity of a numerous army within the kingdom. A sufficient force to make head against a sudden descent, till the militia could have time to rally and embody, is all that has been deemed requisite. No motive of national policy has demanded, nor would public opinion have tolerated, a larger number of troops upon its domestic establishment. There has been, for a long time past, little room for the operation of the other causes, which have been enumerated as the consequences of internal war. This peculiar felicity of situation has, in a great degree, contributed to preserve the liberty which that country to this day enjoys, in spite of the prevalent venality and corruption. If, on the contrary, Britain had been situated on the continent, and had been compelled, as she would have been, by that situation, to make her military establishments at home co-extensive with those of the other great powers of Europe, she, like them, would in all probability be, at this day, a victim to the absolute power of a single man. 'Tis possible, though not easy, that the people of that island may be enslaved from other causes; but it cannot be by the prowess of an army so inconsiderable as that which has been usually kept up within the kingdom.

If we are wise enough to preserve the Union we may for ages enjoy an advantage similar to that of an insulated situation. Europe is at a great distance from us. Her colonies in our vicinity will be likely to continue too much disproportioned in strength to be able to give us any dangerous annoyance. Extensive military establishments cannot, in this position, be necessary to our security. But if we should be disunited, and the integral parts should either remain separated, or, which is most probable, should be drawn together into two or three confederacies, we should be, in a short course of time, in the predicament of the continental powers of Europe—our liberties would be a prey to the means of defending ourselves against the ambition and jealousy of each other.

This is an idea not superficial or futile, but solid and weighty. It deserves the most serious and mature consideration of every prudent and honest man of whatever party. If such men will make a firm and solemn pause, and meditate dispassionately on the importance of this interesting idea; if they will contemplate it in all its attitudes, and trace it to all its consequences, they will not hesitate to part with trivial objections to a Constitution, the rejection of which would in all probability put a final period to the Union. The airy phantoms that flit before the distempered imaginations of some of its adversaries would quickly give place to the more substantial forms of dangers, real, certain, and formidable.   PUBLIUS

Number 9

[HAMILTON]

A FIRM Union will be of the utmost moment to the peace and liberty of the States, as a barrier against domestic faction and insurrection. It is impossible to read the history of the petty republics of Greece and Italy without feeling sensations of horror and disgust at the distractions with which they were continually agitated, and at the rapid succession of revolutions by which they were kept in a state of perpetual vibration between the extremes of tyranny and anarchy. If they exhibit occasional calms, these only serve as short-lived contrasts to the furious storms that are to succeed. If now and then intervals of felicity open to view, we behold them with a mixture of regret, arising from the reflection that the pleasing scenes before us are soon to be overwhelmed by the tempestuous waves of sedition and party rage. If momentary rays of glory break forth from the gloom, while they dazzle us with a transient and fleeting brilliancy, they at the same time admonish us to lament that the vices of government should pervert the direction and tarnish the lustre of those bright talents and exalted endowments for which the favoured soils that produced them have been so justly celebrated.

From the disorders that disfigure the annals of those republics the advocates of despotism have drawn arguments, not only against the forms of republican government, but against the very principles of civil liberty. They have descried all free government as inconsistent with the order of society, and have indulged themselves in malicious exultation over its friends and partisans. Happily for mankind, stupendous fabrics reared on the basis of liberty, which have flourished for ages, have, in a few glorious instances, refuted their gloomy sophisms. And, I trust, America will be the broad and solid foundation of other edifices, not less magnificent, which will be equally permanent monuments of their errors.

But it is not to be denied that the portraits they have sketched of republican government were too just copies of the originals from which they were taken. If it had been found impracticable to have devised models of a more perfect structure, the enlightened friends to liberty would have been obliged to abandon the cause of that species of government as indefensible. The science of politics, however, like most other sciences, has received great improvement. The efficacy of various principles is now well understood, which were either not known at all, or imperfectly known to the ancients. The regular distribution of power into distinct departments; the introduction of legislative balances and checks; the institution of courts composed of judges holding their offices during good behaviour; the representation of the people in the legislature by deputies of their own election: these are wholly new discoveries, or have made their principal progress towards perfection in modern times. They are means, and powerful means, by which the excellences of republican government may be retained and its imperfections lessened or avoided. To this catalogue of circumstances that tend to the amelioration of popular systems of civil government, I shall venture, however novel it may appear to some, to add one more, on a principle which has been made the foundation of an objection to the new Constitution; I mean the ENLARGEMENT of the ORBIT within which such systems are to revolve, either in respect to the dimensions of a single State, or to the consolidation of several smaller States into one great Confederacy. The latter is that which immediately concerns the object under consideration. It will, however, be of use to examine the principle in its application to a single State, which shall be attended to in another place.

The utility of a Confederacy as well to suppress faction and to guard the internal tranquillity of states, as to increase their external force and security, is in reality not a new idea. It has been practised upon in different countries and ages, and has received the sanction of the most approved writers on the subjects of politics. The opponents of the plan proposed have, with great assiduity, cited and circulated the observations of Montesquieu on the necessity of contracted territory for a republican government. But they seem not to have been apprised of the sentiments of that great man expressed in another part of his work, nor to have adverted to the consequences of the principle to which they subscribe with such ready acquiescence.

When Montesquieu recommends a small extent for republics, the standards he had in view were of dimensions far short of the limits of almost every one of these States. Neither Virginia, Massachusetts, Pennsylvania, New York, North Carolina, nor Georgia can by any means be compared with the models from which he reasoned and to which the terms of his description apply. If we therefore take his ideas on this point as the criterion of truth, we shall be driven to the alternative either of taking refuge at once in the arms of monarchy, or of splitting ourselves into an infinity of little, jealous, clashing, tumultuous commonwealths, the wretched nurseries of unceasing discord, and the miserable objects of universal pity or contempt. Some of the writers who have come forward on the other side of the question seem to have been aware of the dilemma; and have even been bold enough to hint at the division of the larger States as a desirable thing. Such an infatuated policy, such a desperate expedient, might, by the multiplication of petty offices, answer the views of men who possess not qualifications to extend their influence beyond the narrow circles of personal intrigue, but it could never promote the greatness or happiness of the people of America.

Referring the examination of the principle itself to another place, as has been already mentioned, it will be sufficient to remark here that, in the sense of the author who has been most emphatically quoted upon the occasion, it would only dictate a reduction of the SIZE of the more considerable MEMBERS of the Union, but would not militate against their being all comprehended in one confederate government. And this is the true question, in the discussion of which we are at present interested.

So far are the suggestions of Montesquieu from standing in opposition to a general Union of the States, that he explicitly treats of a CONFEDERATE REPUBLIC as the expedient for extending the sphere of popular government, and reconciling the advantages of monarchy with those of republicanism.

"It is very probable" (says he [1]) "that mankind would have been obliged at length to live constantly under the government of a single person, had they not contrived a kind of constitution that has all the internal advantages of a republican, together with the external force of a monarchical, government. I mean a CONFEDERATE REPUBLIC.

"This form of government is a convention by which several smaller *states* agree to become members of a larger *one,* which they intend to form. It is a kind of assemblage of societies that constitute a new one, capable of increasing, by means of new associations, till they arrive to such a degree of power as to be able to provide for the security of the united body.

"A republic of this kind, able to withstand an external force, may support itself without any internal corruptions. The form of this society prevents all manner of inconveniences.

"If a single member should attempt to usurp the supreme authority, he could not be supposed to have an equal authority and credit in all the confederate states. Were he to have too great influence over one, this would alarm the rest. Were he to subdue a part, that which would still remain free might oppose him with forces independent of those which he had usurped, and overpower him before he could be settled in his usurpation.

"Should a popular insurrection happen in one of the confederate states, the others are able to quell it. Should abuses creep into one part, they are reformed by those that remain sound. The state may be destroyed on one side, and not on the other; the confederacy may be dissolved, and the confederates preserve their sovereignty.

"As this government is composed of small republics, it enjoys the internal happiness of each; and with respect to its external situation, it is possessed, by means of the association, of all the advantages of large monarchies."

I have thought it proper to quote at length these interesting passages, because they contain a luminous abridgment of the principal arguments in favour of the Union, and must effectually remove the false impressions which a misapplication of other parts of the work was calculated to make. They have, at the same time, an intimate connection with the more immediate design of this paper; which is, to illustrate the tendency of the Union to repress domestic faction and insurrection.

A distinction, more subtle than accurate, has been raised between a *confederacy* and a *con-*

[1] *Spirit of Laws,* book ix.—PUBLIUS

solidation of the States. The essential characteristic of the first is said to be the restriction of its authority to the members in their collective capacities, without reaching to the individuals of whom they are composed. It is contended that the national council ought to have no concern with any object of internal administration. An exact equality of suffrage between the members has also been insisted upon as a leading feature of a confederate government. These positions are, in the main, arbitrary; they are supported neither by principle nor precedent. It has indeed happened, that governments of this kind have generally operated in the manner which the distinction, taken notice of, supposes to be inherent in their nature; but there have been in most of them extensive exceptions to the practice, which serve to prove, as far as example will go, that there is no absolute rule on the subject. And it will be clearly shown, in the course of this investigation, that as far as the principle contended for has prevailed, it has been the cause of incurable disorder and imbecility in the government.

The definition of a *confederate republic* seems simply to be "an assemblage of societies," or an association of two or more states into one state. The extent, modifications, and objects of the federal authority, are mere matters of discretion. So long as the separate organisation of the members be not abolished; so long as it exists, by a constitutional necessity, for local purposes; though it should be in perfect subordination to the general authority of the union, it would still be, in fact and in theory, an association of states, or a confederacy. The proposed Constitution, so far from implying an abolition of the State governments, makes them constituent parts of the national sovereignty, by allowing them a direct representation in the Senate, and leaves in their possession certain exclusive and very important portions of sovereign power. This fully corresponds, in every rational import of the terms, with the idea of a federal government.

In the Lycian confederacy, which consisted of twenty-three CITIES or republics, the largest were entitled to *three* votes in the COMMON COUNCIL, those of the middle class to *two*, and the smallest to *one*. The COMMON COUNCIL had the appointment of all the judges and magistrates of the respective CITIES. This was certainly the most delicate species of interference in their internal administration; for if there

be anything that seems exclusively appropriated to the local jurisdictions, it is the appointment of their own officers. Yet Montesquieu, speaking of this association, says: "Were I to give a model of an excellent Confederate Republic, it would be that of Lycia." Thus we perceive that the distinctions insisted upon were not within the contemplation of this enlightened civilian; and we shall be led to conclude that they are the novel refinements of an erroneous theory.   PUBLIUS

Number 10

[MADISON]

AMONG THE numerous advantages promised by a well-constructed Union, none deserves to be more accurately developed than its tendency to break and control the violence of faction. The friend of popular governments never finds himself so much alarmed for their character and fate as when he contemplates their propensity to this dangerous vice. He will not fail, therefore, to set a due value on any plan which, without violating the principles to which he is attached, provides a proper cure for it. The instability, injustice, and confusion introduced into the public councils, have, in truth, been the mortal diseases under which popular governments have everywhere perished; as they continue to be the favourite and fruitful topics from which the adversaries to liberty derive their most specious declamations. The valuable improvements made by the American constitutions on the popular models, both ancient and modern, cannot certainly be too much admired; but it would be an unwarrantable partiality, to contend that they have as effectually obviated the danger on this side, as was wished and expected. Complaints are everywhere heard from our most considerate and virtuous citizens, equally the friends of public and private faith, and of public and personal liberty, that our governments are too unstable, that the public good is disregarded in the conflicts of rival parties, and that measures are too often decided, not according to the rules of justice and the rights of the minor party, but by the superior force of an interested and overbearing majority. However anxiously we may wish that these complaints had no foundation, the evidence of known facts will not permit us to deny that they are in some degree true. It will be found, indeed, on a candid review of our situation, that some of the distresses under which we labour have been erroneously charged on the operation of our governments; but it will be found, at the same time, that other causes will not alone account for many of our heaviest misfortunes; and, particularly, for that prevailing and increasing distrust of public engagements, and alarm for private rights, which are echoed from one end of the continent to the other. These must be chiefly, if not wholly, effects of the unsteadiness and injustice with which a factious spirit has tainted our public administrations.

By a faction, I understand a number of citizens, whether amounting to a majority or minority of the whole, who are united and actuated by some common impulse of passion, or of interest, adverse to the rights of other citizens, or to the permanent and aggregate interests of the community.

There are two methods of curing the mischiefs of faction: the one, by removing its causes; the other, by controlling its effects.

There are again two methods of removing the causes of faction: the one, by destroying the liberty which is essential to its existence; the other, by giving to every citizen the same opinions, the same passions, and the same interests.

It could never be more truly said than of the first remedy, that it was worse than the disease. Liberty is to faction what air is to fire, an aliment without which it instantly expires. But it could not be less folly to abolish liberty, which is essential to political life, because it nourishes faction, than it would be to wish the annihilation of air, which is essential to animal life, because it imparts to fire its destructive agency.

The second expedient is as impracticable as the first would be unwise. As long as the reason of man continues fallible, and he is at liberty to exercise it, different opinions will be formed. As long as the connection subsists between his reason and his self-love, his opinions and his passions will have a reciprocal influence on each other; and the former will be objects to which the latter will attach themselves. The diversity in the faculties of men, from which the rights of property originate, is not less an insuperable obstacle to a uniformity of interests. The protection of these faculties is the first object of government. From the protection of different and unequal faculties of acquiring property, the possession of different degrees and kinds of property immediately results; and from the influence of these on the sentiments and views of the respective proprietors, ensues a division of the society into different interests and parties.

The latent causes of faction are thus sown in the nature of man; and we see them everywhere brought into different degrees of activity, according to the different circumstances of civil society. A zeal for different opinions concerning religion, concerning government, and many other points, as well of speculation as of practice; an attachment of different leaders ambitiously contending for pre-eminence and power; or to persons of other descriptions whose fortunes have been interesting to the human passions, have, in turn, divided mankind into parties, inflamed them with mutual animosity, and rendered them much more disposed to vex and oppress each other than to cooperate for their common good. So strong is this propensity of mankind to fall into mutual animosities, that where no substantial occasion presents itself, the most frivolous and fanciful distinctions have been sufficient to kindle their unfriendly passions and excite their most violent conflicts. But the most common and durable source of factions has been the various and unequal distribution of property. Those who hold and those who are without property have ever formed distinct interests in society. Those who are creditors, and those who are debtors, fall under a like discrimination. A landed interest, a manufacturing interest, a mercantile interest, a moneyed interest, with many lesser interests, grow up of necessity in civilised nations, and divide them into different classes, actuated by different sentiments and views. The regulation of these various and interfering interests forms the principal task of modern legislation, and involves the spirit of party and faction in the necessary and ordinary operations of the government.

No man is allowed to be a judge in his own cause, because his interest would certainly bias his judgment, and, not improbably, corrupt his integrity. With equal, nay, with greater reason, a body of men are unfit to be both judges and parties at the same time; yet what are many of the most important acts of legislation but so many judicial determinations, not indeed concerning the rights of single persons, but concerning the rights of large bodies of citizens? And what are the different classes of legislators but advocates and parties to the causes which they determine? Is a law proposed concerning private debts? It is a question to which the creditors are parties on one side and the debtors on the other. Justice ought to hold the balance between them. Yet the parties are, and must be, themselves the judges; and the most numerous party, or, in other words, the most powerful faction must be expected to prevail. Shall domestic manufactures be encouraged, and in what degree, by restrictions on foreign manufactures? are questions which would be differently decided by the landed and the manufacturing classes, and probably by neither with a sole regard to justice and the public good. The apportionment of taxes on the various descriptions of property is an act which seems to require the most exact impartiality; yet there is, perhaps, no legislative act in which greater opportunity and temptation are given to a predominant party to trample on the rules of justice. Every shilling with which they overburden the inferior number is a shilling saved to their own pockets.

It is in vain to say that enlightened statesmen will be able to adjust these clashing interests, and render them all subservient to the public good. Enlightened statesmen will not always be at the helm. Nor, in many cases, can such an adjustment be made at all without taking into view indirect and remote considerations, which will rarely prevail over the immediate interest which one party may find in disregarding the rights of another or the good of the whole.

The inference to which we are brought is, that the *causes* of faction cannot be removed, and that relief is only to be sought in the means of controlling its *effects*.

If a faction consists of less than a majority, relief is supplied by the republican principle, which enables the majority to defeat its sinister views by regular vote. It may clog the administration, it may convulse the society; but it will be unable to execute and mask its violence under the forms of the Constitution. When a majority is included in a faction, the form of popular government, on the other hand, enables it to sacrifice to its ruling passion or interest both the public good and the rights of other citizens. To secure the public good and private rights against the danger of such a faction, and at the same time to preserve the spirit and the form of popular government, is then the great object to which our inquiries are directed. Let me add that it is the great desideratum by which this form of government can be rescued from the oppro-

brium under which it has so long laboured, and be recommended to the esteem and adoption of mankind.

By what means is this object obtainable? Evidently by one of two only. Either the existence of the same passion or interest in a majority at the same time must be prevented, or the majority, having such co-existent passion or interest, must be rendered, by their number and local situation, unable to concert and carry into effect schemes of oppression. If the impulse and the opportunity be suffered to coincide, we well know that neither moral nor religious motives can be relied on as an adequate control. They are not found to be such on the injustice and violence of individuals, and lose their efficacy in proportion to the number combined together, that is, in proportion as their efficacy becomes needful.

From this view of the subject it may be concluded that a pure democracy, by which I mean a society consisting of a small number of citizens, who assemble and administer the government in person, can admit of no cure for the mischiefs of faction. A common passion or interest will, in almost every case, be felt by a majority of the whole; a communication and concert result from the form of government itself; and there is nothing to check the inducements to sacrifice the weaker party or an obnoxious individual. Hence it is that such democracies have ever been spectacles of turbulence and contention; have ever been found incompatible with personal security or the rights of property; and have in general been as short in their lives as they have been violent in their deaths. Theoretic politicians, who have patronised this species of government, have erroneously supposed that by reducing mankind to a perfect equality in their political rights, they would, at the same time, be perfectly equalised and assimilated in their possessions, their opinions, and their passions.

A republic, by which I mean a government in which the scheme of representation takes place, opens a different prospect, and promises the cure for which we are seeking. Let us examine the points in which it varies from pure democracy, and we shall comprehend both the nature of the cure and the efficacy which it must derive from the Union.

The two great points of difference between a democracy and a republic are: first, the delegation of the government, in the latter, to a small number of citizens elected by the rest; secondly, the greater number of citizens, and greater sphere of country, over which the latter may be extended.

The effect of the first difference is, on the one hand, to refine and enlarge the public views, by passing them through the medium of a chosen body of citizens, whose wisdom may best discern the true interest of their country, and whose patriotism and love of justice will be least likely to sacrifice it to temporary or partial considerations. Under such a regulation, it may well happen that the public voice, pronounced by the representatives of the people, will be more consonant to the public good than if pronounced by the people themselves, convened for the purpose. On the other hand, the effect may be inverted. Men of factious tempers, of local prejudices, or of sinister designs, may, by intrigue, by corruption, or by other means, first obtain the suffrages, and then betray the interests, of the people. The question resulting is, whether small or extensive republics are more favourable to the election of proper guardians of the public weal; and it is clearly decided in favour of the latter by two obvious considerations:

In the first place, it is to be remarked that, however small the republic may be, the representatives must be raised to a certain number, in order to guard against the cabals of a few; and that, however large it may be, they must be limited to a certain number, in order to guard against the confusion of a multitude. Hence the number of representatives in the two cases not being in proportion to that of the two constituents, and being proportionally greater in the small republic, it follows that, if the proportion of fit characters be not less in the large than in the small republic, the former will present a greater option, and consequently a greater probability of a fit choice.

In the next place, as each representative will be chosen by a greater number of citizens in the large than in the small republic, it will be more difficult for unworthy candidates to practise with success the vicious arts by which elections are too often carried; and the suffrages of the people being more free, will be more likely to centre in men who possess the most attractive merit and the most diffusive and established character.

It must be confessed that in this, as in most other cases, there is a mean, on both sides of which inconveniences will be found to lie. By enlarging too much the number of electors, you render the representative too little acquainted with all their local circumstances and lesser interests; as by reducing it too much, you render him unduly attached to these, and too little fit to comprehend and pursue great and national objects. The federal Constitution forms a happy combination in this respect; the great and aggregate interests being referred to the national, the local and particular to the State legislatures.

The other point of difference is, the greater number of citizens and extent of territory which may be brought within the compass of republican than of democratic government; and it is this circumstance principally which renders factious combinations less to be dreaded in the former than in the latter. The smaller the society, the fewer probably will be the distinct parties and interests composing it; the fewer the distinct parties and interests, the more frequently will a majority be found of the same party; and the smaller the number of individuals composing a majority, and the smaller the compass within which they are placed, the more easily will they concert and execute their plans of oppression. Extend the sphere, and you take in a greater variety of parties and interests; you make it less probable that a majority of the whole will have a common motive to invade the rights of other citizens; or if such a common motive exists, it will be more difficult for all who feel it to discover their own strength, and to act in unison with each other. Besides other impediments, it may be remarked that, where there is a consciousness of unjust or dishonourable purposes, communication is always checked by distrust in proportion to the number whose concurrence is necessary.

Hence, it clearly appears, that the same advantage which a republic has over a democracy, in controlling the effects of faction, is enjoyed by a large over a small republic—is enjoyed by the Union over the States composing it. Does the advantage consist in the substitution of representatives whose enlightened views and virtuous sentiments render them superior to local prejudices and to schemes of injustice? It will not be denied that the representation of the Union will be most likely to possess these requisite endowments. Does it consist in the greater security afforded by a greater variety of parties, against the event of any one party being able to outnumber and oppress the rest? In an equal degree does the increased variety of parties comprised within the Union increase this security? Does it, in fine, consist in the greater obstacles opposed

to the concert and accomplishment of the secret wishes of an unjust and interested majority? Here, again, the extent of the Union gives
it the most palpable advantage.

The influence of factious leaders may kindle
a flame within their particular States, but will
be unable to spread a general conflagration
through the other States. A religious sect may
degenerate into a political faction in a part of
the Confederacy; but the variety of sects dispersed over the entire face of it must secure
the national councils against any danger from
that source. A rage for paper money, for an
abolition of debts, for an equal division of
property, or for any other improper or wicked
project, will be less apt to pervade the whole
body of the Union than a particular member
of it; in the same proportion as such a malady
is more likely to taint a particular county or
district, than an entire State.

In the extent and proper structure of the
Union, therefore, we behold a republican remedy for the diseases most incident to republican government. And according to the degree
of pleasure and pride we feel in being republicans, ought to be our zeal in cherishing the
spirit and supporting the character of Federal-
ists.   PUBLIUS

Number 11

[HAMILTON]

THE IMPORTANCE of the Union, in a commercial light, is one of those points about which
there is least room to entertain a difference of
opinion, and which has, in fact, commanded
the most general assent of men who have any
acquaintance with the subject. This applies as
well to our intercourse with foreign countries
as with each other.

There are appearances to authorise a supposition that the adventurous spirit, which distinguishes the commercial character of America, has already excited uneasy sensations in
several of the maritime powers of Europe.
They seem to be apprehensive of our too great
interference in that carrying trade which is
the support of their navigation and the foundation of their naval strength. Those of them
which have colonies in America look forward
to what this country is capable of becoming,
with painful solicitude. They foresee the dangers that may threaten their American dominions from the neighbourhood of States which
have all the dispositions, and would possess
all the means, requisite to the creation of a

powerful marine. Impressions of this kind will
naturally indicate the policy of fostering divisions among us, and of depriving us, as far
as possible, of an ACTIVE COMMERCE in our own
bottoms. This would answer the threefold purpose of preventing our interference in their
navigation, of monopolising the profits of our
trade, and of clipping the wings by which we
might soar to a dangerous greatness. Did not
prudence forbid the detail, it would not be
difficult to trace, by facts, the workings of this
policy to the cabinets of ministers.

If we continue united, we may counteract a
policy so unfriendly to our prosperity in a
variety of ways. By prohibitory regulations, extending, at the same time, throughout the
States, we may oblige foreign countries to bid
against each other, for the privileges of our
markets. This assertion will not appear chimerical to those who are able to appreciate the
importance of the markets of three millions
of people—increasing in rapid progression, for
the most part exclusively addicted to agriculture, and likely from local circumstances to
remain so—to any manufacturing nation; and
the immense difference there would be to the
trade and navigation of such a nation, between
a direct communication in its own ships, and
an indirect conveyance of its products and returns, to and from America, in the ships of
another country. Suppose, for instance, we
had a government in America, capable of excluding Great Britain (with whom we have at
present no treaty of commerce) from all our
ports; what would be the probable operation
of this step upon her politics? Would it not
enable us to negotiate, with the fairest prospect of success, for commercial privileges of
the most valuable and extensive kind, in the
dominions of that kingdom? When these questions have been asked, upon other occasions,
they have received a plausible, but not a solid
or satisfactory answer. It has been said that
prohibitions on our part would produce no
change in the system of Britain, because she
could prosecute her trade with us through the
medium of the Dutch, who would be her immediate customers and paymasters for those
articles which were wanted for the supply of
our markets. But would not her navigation be
materially injured by the loss of the important
advantage of being her own carrier in that
trade? Would not the principal part of its
profits be intercepted by the Dutch, as a compensation for their agency and risk? Would
not the mere circumstance of freight occasion

a considerable deduction? Would not so circuitous an intercourse facilitate the competitions of other nations, by enhancing the price of British commodities in our markets, and by transferring to other hands the management of this interesting branch of the British commerce?

A mature consideration of the objects suggested by these questions will justify a belief that the real disadvantages to Britain from such a state of things, conspiring with the prepossessions of a great part of the nation in favour of the American trade, and with the importunities of the West India Islands, would produce a relaxation in her present system, and would let us into the enjoyment of privileges in the markets of those islands and elsewhere, from which our trade would derive the most substantial benefits. Such a point gained from the British government, and which could not be expected without an equivalent in exemptions and immunities in our markets, would be likely to have a correspondent effect on the conduct of other nations, who would not be inclined to see themselves altogether supplanted in our trade.

A further resource for influencing the conduct of European nations toward us, in this respect, would arise from the establishment of a federal navy. There can be no doubt that the continuance of the Union under an efficient government, would put it in our power, at a period not very distant to create a navy which, if it could not vie with those of the great maritime powers, would at least be of respectable weight if thrown into the scale of either of two contending parties. This would be more peculiarly the case in relation to operations in the West Indies. A few ships of the line, sent opportunely to the reinforcement of either side, would often be sufficient to decide the fate of a campaign, on the event of which interests of the greatest magnitude were suspended. Our position is, in this respect, a most commanding one. And if to this consideration we add that of the usefulness of supplies from this country, in the prosecution of military operations in the West Indies, it will readily be perceived that a situation so favourable would enable us to bargain with great advantage for commercial privileges. A price would be set not only upon our friendship but upon our neutrality. By a steady adherence to the Union, we may hope, ere long, to become the arbiter of Europe in America, and to be able to incline the balance of European competitions in this part of the world as our interest may dictate.

But in the reverse of this eligible situation, we shall discover that the rivalships of the parts would make them checks upon each other, and would frustrate all the tempting advantages which nature has kindly placed within our reach. In a state so insignificant our commerce would be a prey to the wanton intermeddling of all nations at war with each other; who, having nothing to fear from us, would with little scruple or remorse supply their wants by depredations on our property as often as it fell in their way. The rights of neutrality will only be respected when they are defended by an adequate power. A nation, despicable by its weakness, forfeits even the privilege of being neutral.

Under a vigorous national government, the natural strength and resources of the country, directed to a common interest, would baffle all the combinations of European jealousy to restrain our growth. This situation would even take away the motive to such combinations, by inducing an impracticability of success. An active commerce, an extensive navigation, and a flourishing marine would then be the offspring of moral and physical necessity. We might defy the little arts of the little politicians to control or vary the irresistible and unchangeable course of nature.

But in a state of disunion, these combinations might exist and might operate with success. It would be in the power of the maritime nations, availing themselves of our universal impotence, to prescribe the conditions of our political existence; and as they have a common interest in being our carriers, and still more in preventing our becoming theirs, they would in all probability combine to embarrass our navigation in such a manner as would in effect destroy it, and confine us to a PASSIVE COMMERCE. We should then be compelled to content ourselves with the first price of our commodities, and to see the profits of our trade snatched from us to enrich our enemies and persecutors. That unequalled spirit of enterprise, which signalises the genius of the American merchants and navigators, and which is in itself an inexhaustible mine of national wealth, would be stifled and lost, and poverty and disgrace would overspread a country which, with wisdom, might make herself the admiration and envy of the world.

There are rights of great moment to the trade of America which are rights of the Union—I allude to the fisheries, to the navigation of the Western lakes, and to that of the Mississippi. The dissolution of the Confederacy would give room for delicate questions concerning the future existence of these rights; which the interest of more powerful partners would hardly fail to solve to our disadvantage. The disposition of Spain with regard to the Mississippi needs no comment. France and Britain are concerned with us in the fisheries, and view them as of the utmost moment to their navigation. They, of course, would hardly remain long indifferent to that decided mastery, of which experience has shown us to be possessed in this valuable branch of traffic, and by which we are able to undersell those nations in their own markets. What more natural than that they should be disposed to exclude from the lists such dangerous competitors?

This branch of trade ought not to be considered as a partial benefit. All the navigating States may, in different degrees, advantageously participate in it, and under circumstances of a greater extension of mercantile capital, would not be unlikely to do it. As a nursery of seamen, it now is, or, when time shall have more nearly assimilated the principles of navigation in the several States, will become, a universal resource. To the establishment of a navy, it must be indispensable.

To this great national object, a NAVY, union will contribute in various ways. Every institution will grow and flourish in proportion to the quantity and extent of the means concentred towards its formation and support. A navy of the United States, as it would embrace the resources of all, is an object far less remote than a navy of any single State or partial confederacy, which would only embrace the resources of a single part. It happens, indeed, that different portions of confederated America possess each some peculiar advantage for this essential establishment. The more southern States furnish in greater abundance certain kinds of naval stores—tar, pitch, and turpentine. Their wood for the construction of ships is also of a more solid and lasting texture. The difference in the duration of the ships of which the navy might be composed, if chiefly constructed of Southern wood, would be of signal importance, either in the view of naval strength or of national economy. Some of the Southern and of the Middle States yield a greater plenty of iron, and of better quality. Seamen must chiefly be drawn from the Northern hive. The necessity of naval protection to

external or maritime commerce does not require a particular elucidation, no more than the conduciveness of that species of commerce to the prosperity of a navy.

An unrestrained intercourse between the States themselves will advance the trade of each by an interchange of their respective productions, not only for the supply of reciprocal wants at home, but for exportation to foreign markets. The veins of commerce in every part will be replenished, and will require additional motion and vigour from a free circulation of the commodities of every part. Commercial enterprise will have much greater scope, from the diversity in the productions of different States. When the staple of one fails from a bad harvest or unproductive crop, it can call to its aid the staple of another. The variety, not less than the value, of products for exportation contributes to the activity of foreign commerce. It can be conducted upon much better terms with a large number of materials of a given value than with a small number of materials of the same value; arising from the competitions of trade and from the fluctuations of markets. Particular articles may be in great demand at certain periods, and unsaleable at others; but if there be a variety of articles, it can scarcely happen that they should all be at one time in the latter predicament, and on this account the operations of the merchant would be less liable to any considerable obstruction or stagnation. The speculative trader will at once perceive the force of these observations, and will acknowledge that the aggregate balance of the commerce of the United States would bid fair to be much more favourable than that of the thirteen States without union or with partial unions.

It may perhaps be replied to this, that whether the States are united or disunited, there would still be an intimate intercourse between them which would answer the same ends; but this intercourse would be fettered, interrupted, and narrowed by a multiplicity of causes, which in the course of these papers have been amply detailed. A unity of commercial, as well as political, interests, can only result from a unity of government.

There are other points of view in which this subject might be placed, of a striking and animating kind. But they would lead us too far into the regions of futurity, and would involve topics not proper for a newspaper discussion. I shall briefly observe, that our situation invites and our interests prompt us to aim at an ascendant in the system of American affairs. The world may politically, as well as geographically, be divided into four parts, each having a distinct set of interests. Unhappily for the other three, Europe, by her arms and by her negotiations, by force and by fraud, has, in different degrees, extended her dominion over them all. Africa, Asia, and America, have successively felt her domination. The superiority she has long maintained has tempted her to plume herself as the Mistress of the World, and to consider the rest of mankind as created for her benefit. Men admired as profound philosophers have, in direct terms, attributed to her inhabitants a physical superiority, and have gravely asserted that all animals, and with them the human species, degenerate in America—that even dogs cease to bark after having breathed awhile in our atmosphere.[1] Facts have too long supported these arrogant pretensions of the Europeans. It belongs to us to vindicate the honour of the human race, and to teach that assuming brother, moderation. Union will enable us to do it. Disunion will add another victim to his triumphs. Let Americans disdain to be the instruments of European greatness! Let the thirteen States, bound together in a strict and indissoluble Union, concur in erecting one great American system, superior to the control of all transatlantic force or influence, and able to dictate the terms of the connection between the old and the new world!   PUBLIUS

Number 12

[HAMILTON]

THE EFFECTS of Union upon the commercial prosperity of the States have been sufficiently delineated. Its tendency to promote the interests of revenue will be the subject of our present inquiry.

The prosperity of commerce is now perceived and acknowledged by all enlightened statesmen to be the most useful as well as the most productive source of national wealth, and has accordingly become a primary object of their political cares. By multiplying the means of gratification, by promoting the introduction and circulation of the precious metals, those darling objects of human avarice and enterprise, it serves to vivify and invigorate the channels of industry, and to make them

[1] *Recherches philosophiques sur les Americans.*
—PUBLIUS

flow with greater activity and copiousness. The assiduous merchant, the laborious husbandman, the active mechanic, and the industrious manufacturer—all orders of men, look forward with eager expectation and growing alacrity to this pleasing reward of their toils. The often-agitated question between agriculture and commerce has, from indubitable experience, received a decision which has silenced the rivalship that once subsisted between them, and has proved, to the satisfaction of their friends, that their interests are intimately blended and interwoven. It has been found in various countries that, in proportion as commerce has flourished, land has risen in value. And how could it have happened otherwise? Could that which procures a freer vent for the products of the earth, which furnishes new incitements to the cultivation of land, which is the most powerful instrument in increasing the quantity of money in a state —could that, in fine, which is the faithful handmaid of labour and industry, in every shape, fail to augment that article, which is the prolific parent of far the greatest part of the objects upon which they are exerted? It is astonishing that so simple a truth should ever have had an adversary; and it is one, among a multitude of proofs, how apt a spirit of ill-formed jealousy, or of too great abstraction and refinement, is to lead men astray from the plainest truths of reason and conviction.

The ability of a country to pay taxes must always be proportioned, in a great degree, to the quantity of money in circulation, and to the celerity with which it circulates. Commerce, contributing to both these objects, must of necessity render the payment of taxes easier, and facilitate the requisite supplies to the treasury. The hereditary dominions of the Emperor of Germany contain a great extent of fertile, cultivated, and populous territory, a large proportion of which is situated in mild and luxuriant climates. In some parts of this territory are to be found the best gold and silver mines in Europe. And yet, from the want of the fostering influence of commerce, that monarch can boast but slender revenues. He has several times been compelled to owe obligations to the pecuniary succours of other nations for the preservation of his essential interests, and is unable, upon the strength of his own resources, to sustain a long or continued war.

But it is not in this aspect of the subject

alone that Union will be seen to conduce to the purpose of revenue. There are other points of view, in which its influence will appear more immediate and decisive. It is evident from the state of the country, from the habits of the people, from the experience we have had on the point itself, that it is impracticable to raise any very considerable sums by direct taxation. Tax laws have in vain been multiplied; new methods to enforce the collection have in vain been tried; the public expectation has been uniformly disappointed, and the treasuries of the States have remained empty. The popular system of administration inherent in the nature of popular government, coinciding with the real scarcity of money incident to a languid and mutilated state of trade, has hitherto defeated every experiment for extensive collections, and has at length taught the different legislatures the folly of attempting them.

No person acquainted with what happens in other countries will be surprised at this circumstance. In so opulent a nation as that of Britain, where direct taxes from superior wealth must be much more tolerable, and, from the vigour of the government, much more practicable, than in America, far the greatest part of the national revenue is derived from taxes of the indirect kind, from imposts, and from excises. Duties on imported articles form a large branch of this latter description.

In America, it is evident that we must a long time depend for the means of revenue chiefly on such duties. In most parts of it, excises must be confined within a narrow compass. The genius of the people will ill brook the inquisitive and peremptory spirit of excise laws. The pockets of the farmers, on the other hand, will reluctantly yield but scanty supplies, in the unwelcome shape of impositions on their houses and lands; and personal property is too precarious and invisible a fund to be laid hold of in any other way than by the imperceptible agency of taxes on consumption.

If these remarks have any foundation, that state of things which will best enable us to improve and extend so valuable a resource must be best adapted to our political welfare. And it cannot admit of a serious doubt, that this state of things must rest on the basis of a general Union. As far as this would be conducive to the interests of commerce, so far it must tend to the extension of the revenue to be drawn from that source. As far as it would

contribute to rendering regulations for the collection of the duties more simple and efficacious, so far it must serve to answer the purposes of making the same rate of duties more productive, and of putting it into the power of the government to increase the rate without prejudice to trade.

The relative situation of these States; the number of rivers with which they are intersected, and of bays that wash their shores; the facility of communication in every direction; the affinity of language and manners; the familiar habits of intercourse;—all these are circumstances that would conspire to render an illicit trade between them a matter of little difficulty, and would insure frequent evasions of the commercial regulations of each other. The separate States or confederacies would be necessitated by mutual jealousy to avoid the temptations to that kind of trade by the lowness of their duties. The temper of our governments, for a long time to come, would not permit those rigorous precautions by which the European nations guard the avenues into their respective countries, as well by land as by water; and which, even there, are found insufficient obstacles to the adventurous stratagems of avarice.

In France, there is an army of patrols (as they are called) constantly employed to secure their fiscal regulations against the inroads of the dealers in contraband trade. Mr. Neckar computes the number of these patrols at upwards of twenty thousand. This shows the immense difficulty in preventing that species of traffic, where there is an inland communication, and places in a strong light the disadvantages with which the collection of duties in this country would be encumbered, if by disunion the States should be placed in a situation, with respect to each other, resembling that of France with respect to her neighbours. The arbitrary and vexatious powers with which the patrols are necessarily armed, would be intolerable in a free country.

If, on the contrary, there be but one government pervading all the States, there will be, as to the principal part of our commerce, but ONE SIDE to guard—the ATLANTIC COAST. Vessels arriving directly from foreign countries, laden with valuable cargoes, would rarely choose to hazard themselves to the complicated and critical perils which would attend attempts to unlade prior to their coming into port. They would have to dread both the dangers of the coast, and of detection, as well after as before their arrival at the places of their final destination. An ordinary degree of vigilance would be competent to the prevention of any material infractions upon the rights of the revenue. A few armed vessels, judiciously stationed at the entrances of our ports, might at a small expense be made useful sentinels of the laws. And the government having the same interest to provide against violations everywhere, the co-operation of its measures in each State would have a powerful tendency to render them effectual. Here also we should preserve, by Union, an advantage which nature holds out to us, and which would be relinquished by separation. The United States lie at a great distance from Europe, and at a considerable distance from all other places with which they would have extensive connections of foreign trade. The passage from them to us, in a few hours, or in a single night, as between the coasts of France and Britain, and of other neighbouring nations, would be impracticable. This is a prodigious security against a direct contraband with foreign countries; but a circuitous contraband to one State, through the medium of another, would be both easy and safe. The difference between a direct importation from abroad, and an indirect importation through the channel of a neighbouring State, in small parcels, according to time and opportunity, with the additional facilities of inland communication, must be palpable to every man of discernment.

It is therefore evident, that one national government would be able, at much less expense, to extend the duties on imports, beyond comparison, further than would be practicable to the States separately, or to any partial confederacies. Hitherto, I believe, it may safely be asserted, that these duties have not upon an average exceeded in any State three per cent. In France they are estimated to be about fifteen per cent., and in Britain they exceed this proportion.[1] There seems to be nothing to hinder their being increased in this country to at least treble their present amount. The single article of ardent spirits, under federal regulation, might be made to furnish a considerable revenue. Upon a ratio to the importation into this State, the whole quantity imported into the United States may be estimated at four millions of gallons; which, at a shilling per gallon, would produce two hundred thousand

pounds. That article would well bear this rate of duty; and if it should tend to diminish the consumption of it, such an effort would be equally favourable to the agriculture, to the economy, to the morals, and to the health of the society. There is, perhaps, nothing so much a subject of national extravagance as these spirits.

What will be the consequence, if we are not able to avail ourselves of the resource in question in its full extent? A nation cannot long exist without revenues. Destitute of this essential support, it must resign its independence, and sink into the degraded condition of a province. This is an extremity to which no government will of choice accede. Revenue, therefore, must be had at all events. In this country, if the principal part be not drawn from commerce, it must fall with oppressive weight upon land. It has been already intimated that excises, in their true signification, are too little in unison with the feelings of the people to admit of great use being made of that mode of taxation; nor, indeed, in the States where almost the sole employment is agriculture, are the objects proper for excise sufficiently numerous to permit very ample collections in that way. Personal estate (as has been before remarked), from the difficulty in tracing it, cannot be subjected to large contributions by any other means than by taxes on consumption. In populous cities, it may be enough the subject of conjecture to occasion the oppression of individuals without much aggregate benefit to the State; but beyond these circles, it must, in a great measure, escape the eye and the hand of the tax-gatherer. As the necessities of the State, nevertheless, must be satisfied in some mode or other, the defect of other resources must throw the principal weight of public burdens on the possessors of land. And as, on the other hand, the wants of the government can never obtain an adequate supply, unless all the sources of revenue are open to its demands, the finances of the community, under such embarrassments, cannot be put into a situation consistent with its respectability or its security. Thus we shall not even have the consolations of a full treasury to atone for the oppression of that valuable class of the citizens who are employed in the cultivation of the soil. But public and private distress will keep pace with each other in gloomy concert; and unite in deploring the infatuation of those counsels which led to disunion.   PUBLIUS

[1] If my memory be right they amount to twenty per cent.—PUBLIUS

Number *13*

[HAMILTON]

As CONNECTED with the subject of revenue, we may with propriety consider that of economy. The money saved from one object may be usefully applied to another, and there will be so much the less to be drawn from the pockets of the people. If the States are united under one government, there will be but one national civil list to support; if they are divided into several confederacies, there will be as many different national civil lists to be provided for—and each of them, as to the principal departments, coextensive with that which would be necessary for a government of the whole. The entire separation of the States into thirteen unconnected sovereignties is a project too extravagant and too replete with danger to have many advocates. The ideas of men who speculate upon the dismemberment of the empire seemed generally turned towards three confederacies—one consisting of the four Northern, another of the four Middle, and a third of the five Southern States. There is little probability that there would be a greater number. According to this distribution, each confederacy would comprise an extent of territory larger than that of the kingdom of Great Britain. No well-informed man will suppose that the affairs of such a confederacy can be properly regulated by a government less comprehensive in its organs or institutions than that which has been proposed by the convention. When the dimensions of a State attain to a certain magnitude, it requires the same energy of government and the same forms of administration which are requisite in one of much greater extent. This idea admits not of precise demonstration, because there is no rule by which we can measure the momentum of civil power necessary to the government of any given number of individuals; but when we consider that the island of Britain, nearly commensurate with each of the supposed confederacies, contains about eight millions of people, and when we reflect upon the degree of authority required to direct the passions of so large a society to the public good, we shall see no reason to doubt that the like portion of power would be sufficient to perform the same task in a society far more numerous. Civil power, properly organised and exerted, is capable of diffusing its force to a very great extent; and can, in a manner, reproduce itself in every part of a great empire by a judicious arrangement of subordinate institutions.

The supposition that each confederacy into which the States would be likely to be divided would require a government not less comprehensive than the one proposed, will be strengthened by another supposition more probable than that which presents us with three confederacies as the alternative to a general Union. If we attend carefully to geographical and commercial considerations, in conjunction with the habits and prejudices of the different States, we shall be led to conclude that in cases of disunion they will most naturally league themselves under two governments. The four Eastern States, from all the causes that form the links of national sympathy and connection, may with certainty be expected to unite. New York, situated as she is, would never be unwise enough to oppose a feeble and unsupported flank to the weight of that confederacy. There are other obvious reasons that would facilitate her accession to it. New Jersey is too small a State to think of being a frontier, in opposition to this still more powerful combination; nor do there appear to be any obstacles to her admission into it. Even Pennsylvania would have strong inducements to join the Northern league. An active foreign commerce, on the basis of her own navigation, is her true policy, and coincides with the opinions and dispositions of her citizens. The more Southern States, from various circumstances, may not think themselves much interested in the encouragement of navigation. They may prefer a system which would give unlimited scope to all nations to be the carriers as well as the purchasers of their commodities. Pennsylvania may not choose to confound her interests in a connection so adverse to her policy. As she must at all events be a frontier, she may deem it most consistent with her safety to have her exposed side turned towards the weaker power of the Southern, rather than towards the stronger power of the Northern, Confederacy. This would give her the fairest chance to avoid being the Flanders of America. Whatever may be the determination of Pennsylvania, if the Northern Confederacy includes New Jersey, there is no likelihood of more than one confederacy to the south of that State.

Nothing can be more evident than that the thirteen States will be able to support a national government better than one half, or one third, or any number less than the whole. This reflection must have great weight in obviating that objection to the proposed plan, which is founded on the principle of expense; an objection, however, which, when we come to take a nearer view of it, will appear in every light to stand on mistaken ground.

If, in addition to the consideration of a plurality of civil lists, we take into view the number of persons who must necessarily be employed to guard the inland communication between the different confederacies against illicit trade, and who in time will infallibly spring up out of the necessities of revenue; and if we also take into view the military establishments which it has been shown would unavoidably result from the jealousies and conflicts of the several nations into which the States would be divided, we shall clearly discover that a separation would be not less injurious to the economy, than to the tranquillity, commerce, revenue, and liberty of every part.   PUBLIUS

Number 14

[MADISON]

WE HAVE seen the necessity of the Union, as our bulwark against foreign danger, as the conservator of peace among ourselves, as the guardian of our commerce, and other common interests, as the only substitute for those military establishments which have subverted the liberties of the Old World, and as the proper antidote for the diseases of faction, which have proved fatal to other popular governments, and of which alarming symptoms have been betrayed by our own. All that remains, within this branch of our inquiries, is to take notice of an objection that may be drawn from the great extent of country which the Union embraces. A few observations on this subject will be the more proper, as it is perceived that the adversaries of the new Constitution are availing themselves of the prevailing prejudice with regard to the practicable sphere of republican administration, in order to supply, by imaginary difficulties, the want of those solid objections which they endeavour in vain to find.

The error which limits republican government to a narrow district has been unfolded and refuted in preceding papers. I remark here only that it seems to owe its rise and prevalence chiefly to the confounding of a republic with a democracy, applying to the former reasonings drawn from the nature of the latter. The true distinction between these forms was also adverted to on a former occasion. It

is, that in a democracy the people meet and exercise the government in person; in a republic, they assemble and administer it by their representatives and agents. A democracy, consequently, will be confined to a small spot. A republic may be extended over a large region.

To this accidental source of the error may be added the artifice of some celebrated authors, whose writings have had a great share in forming the modern standard of political opinions. Being subjects either of an absolute or limited monarchy, they have endeavoured to heighten the advantages, or palliate the evils of those forms, by placing in comparison the vices and defects of the republican, and by citing as specimens of the latter the turbulent democracies of ancient Greece and modern Italy. Under the confusion of names, it has been an easy task to transfer to a republic observations applicable to a democracy only; and among others, the observation that it can never be established but among a small number of people, living within a small compass of territory.

Such a fallacy may have been the less perceived, as most of the popular governments of antiquity were of the democratic species; and even in modern Europe, to which we owe the great principle of representation, no example is seen of a government wholly popular, and founded, at the same time, wholly on that principle. If Europe has the merit of discovering this great mechanical power in government, by the simple agency of which the will of the largest political body may be concentred, and its force directed to any object which the public good requires, America can claim the merit of making the discovery the basis of unmixed and extensive republics. It is only to be lamented that any of her citizens should wish to deprive her of the additional merit of displaying its full efficacy in the establishment of the comprehensive system now under her consideration.

As the natural limit of a democracy is that distance from the central point which will just permit the most remote citizens to assemble as often as their public functions demand, and will include no greater number than can join in those functions; so the natural limit of a republic is that distance from the centre which will barely allow the representatives to meet as often as may be necessary for the administration of public affairs. Can it be said that the limits of the United States exceed this distance? It will not be said by those who recollect that the Atlantic coast is the longest side of the Union, that during the term of thirteen years the representatives of the States have been almost continually assembled, and that the members from the most distant States are not chargeable with greater intermissions of attendance than those from the States in the neighbourhood of Congress.

That we may form a juster estimate with regard to this interesting subject, let us resort to the actual dimensions of the Union. The limits, as fixed by the treaty of peace, are: on the east the Atlantic, on the south the latitude of thirty-one degrees, on the west the Mississippi, and on the north an irregular line running in some instances beyond the forty-fifth degree, in others falling as low as the forty-second. The southern shore of Lake Erie lies below that latitude. Computing the distance between the thirty-first and forty-fifth degrees, it amounts to nine hundred and seventy-three common miles; computing it from thirty-one to forty-two degrees, to seven hundred and sixty-four miles and a half. Taking the mean for the distance, the amount will be eight hundred and sixty-eight miles and three fourths. The mean distance from the Atlantic to the Mississippi does not probably exceed seven hundred and fifty miles. On a comparison of this extent with that of several countries in Europe, the practicability of rendering our system commensurate to it appears to be demonstrable. It is not a great deal larger than Germany, where a diet representing the whole empire is continually assembled; or than Poland before the late dismemberment, where another national diet was the depositary of the supreme power. Passing by France and Spain, we find that in Great Britain, inferior as it may be in size, the representatives of the northern extremity of the island have as far to travel to the national council as will be required of those of the most remote parts of the Union.

Favourable as this view of the subject may be, some observations remain which will place it in a light still more satisfactory.

In the first place it is to be remembered that the general government is not to be charged with the whole power of making and administering laws. Its jurisdiction is limited to certain enumerated objects, which concern all the members of the republic, but which are not to be attained by the separate provisions of any. The subordinate governments, which can extend their care to all those other objects which can be separately provided for, will retain their due authority and activity. Were it proposed by the plan of the convention to abolish the governments of the particular States, its adversaries would have some ground for their objection; though it would not be difficult to show that if they were abolished the general government would be compelled, by the principle of self-preservation, to reinstate them in their proper jurisdiction.

A second observation to be made is that the immediate object of the federal Constitution is to secure the union of the thirteen primitive States, which we know to be practicable; and to add to them such other States as may arise in their own bosoms, or in their neighbourhoods, which we cannot doubt to be equally practicable. The arrangements that may be necessary for those angles and fractions of our territory which lie on our north-western frontier, must be left to those whom further discoveries and experience will render more equal to the task.

Let it be remarked, in the third place, that the intercourse throughout the Union will be facilitated by new improvements. Roads will everywhere be shortened, and kept in better order; accommodations for travellers will be multiplied and meliorated; an interior navigation on our eastern side will be opened throughout, or nearly throughout, the whole extent of the thirteen States. The communication between the Western and Atlantic districts, and between different parts of each, will be rendered more and more easy by those numerous canals with which the beneficence of nature has intersected our country, and which art finds it so little difficult to connect and complete.

A fourth and still more important consideration is, that as almost every State will, on one side or other, be a frontier, and will thus find, in a regard to its safety, an inducement to make some sacrifices for the sake of the general protection; so the States which lie at the greatest distance from the heart of the Union, and which, of course, may partake least of the ordinary circulation of its benefits, will be at the same time immediately contiguous to foreign nations, and will consequently stand, on particular occasions, in greatest need of its strength and resources. It may be inconvenient for Georgia, or the States forming our western or north-eastern borders, to send their representatives to the seat of government; but they would find it more so to struggle alone against an invading enemy, or even to support alone the whole expense of those precautions which may be dictated by the neighbourhood of continual danger. If they should derive less benefit, therefore, from the Union in some respects than the less distant States, they will derive greater benefit from it in other respects, and thus the proper equilibrium will be maintained throughout.

I submit to you, my fellow-citizens, these considerations, in full confidence that the good sense which has so often marked your decisions will allow them their due weight and effect; and that you will never suffer difficulties, however formidable in appearance, or however fashionable the error on which they may be founded, to drive you into the gloomy and perilous scene into which the advocates for disunion would conduct you. Hearken not to the unnatural voice which tells you that the people of America, knit together as they are by so many cords of affection, can no longer live together as members of the same family; can no longer continue the mutual guardians of their mutual happiness; can no longer be fellow-citizens of one great, respectable, and flourishing empire. Hearken not to the voice which petulantly tells you that the form of government recommended for your adoption is a novelty in the political world; that it has never yet had a place in the theories of the wildest projectors; that it rashly attempts what it is impossible to accomplish. No, my countrymen, shut your ears against this unhallowed language. Shut your hearts against the poison which it conveys; the kindred blood which flows in the veins of American citizens, the mingled blood which they have shed in defence of their sacred rights, consecrate their Union, and excite horror at the idea of their becoming aliens, rivals, enemies. And if novelties are to be shunned, believe me, the most alarming of all novelties, the most wild of all projects, the most rash of all attempts, is that of rending us in pieces, in order to preserve our liberties and promote our happiness. But why is the experiment of an extended republic to be rejected, merely because it may comprise what is new? Is it not the glory of the people of America, that, whilst they have paid a decent regard to the opinions of former times and other nations, they have not suffered a blind veneration for antiquity, for custom, or for names, to overrule the suggestions of their own good sense, the knowledge of their own situation, and the lessons of their own experience? To this manly spirit, posterity will be indebted for the possession, and the world for the example, of the numerous innovations displayed on the American theatre, in favour of private rights and public happiness. Had no important step been taken by the leaders of the Revolution for which a precedent could not be discovered, no government established of which an exact model did not present itself, the people of the United States might, at this moment, have been numbered among the melancholy victims of misguided councils, must at best have been labouring under the weight of some of those forms which have crushed the liberties of the rest of mankind. Happily for America, happily, we trust, for the whole human race, they pursued a new and more noble course. They accomplished a revolution which has no parallel in the annals of human society. They reared the fabrics of governments which have no model on the face of the globe. They formed the design of a great Confederacy, which it is incumbent on their successors to improve and perpetuate. If their works betray imperfections, we wonder at the fewness of them. If they erred most in the structure of the Union, this was the work most difficult to be executed; this is the work which has been new modelled by the act of your convention, and it is that act on which you are now to deliberate and to decide.   PUBLIUS

Number 15

[HAMILTON]

IN THE course of the preceding papers, I have endeavoured, my fellow-citizens, to place before you, in a clear and convincing light, the importance of Union to your political safety and happiness. I have unfolded to you a complication of dangers to which you would be exposed, should you permit that sacred knot which binds the people of America together to be severed or dissolved by ambition or by avarice, by jealousy or by misrepresentation. In the sequel of the inquiry through which I propose to accompany you, the truths intended to be inculcated will receive further confirmation from facts and arguments hitherto unnoticed. If the road over which you will still have to pass should in some places appear to you tedious or irksome, you will recollect that you are in quest of information on a subject the most momentous which can engage the attention of a free people, that the field through which you have to travel is in itself spacious, and that the difficulties of the journey have been unnecessarily increased by the mazes with which sophistry has beset the way. It will be my aim to remove the obstacles from your progress in as compendious a manner as it can be done, without sacrificing utility to despatch.

In pursuance of the plan which I have laid down for the discussion of the subject, the point next in order to be examined is the "insufficiency of the present Confederation to the preservation of the Union." It may perhaps be asked what need there is of reasoning or proof to illustrate a position which is not either controverted or doubted, to which the understandings and feelings of all classes of men assent, and which in substance is admitted by the opponents as well as by the friends of the new Constitution. It must in truth be acknowledged that, however these may differ in other respects, they in general appear to harmonise in this sentiment, at least, that there are material imperfections in our national system, and that something is necessary to be done to rescue us from impending anarchy. The facts that support this opinion are no longer objects of speculation. They have forced themselves upon the sensibility of the people at large, and have at length extorted from those, whose mistaken policy has had the principal share in precipitating the extremity at which we are arrived, a reluctant confession of the reality of those defects in the scheme of our federal government, which have been long pointed out and regretted by the intelligent friends of the Union.

We may indeed with propriety be said to have reached almost the last stage of national humiliation. There is scarcely anything that can wound the pride or degrade the character of an independent nation which we do not experience. Are there engagements to the performance of which we are held by every tie respectable among men? These are the subjects of constant and unblushing violation. Do we owe debts to foreigners and to our own citizens contracted in a time of imminent peril for the preservation of our political existence? These remain without any proper or satisfactory provision for their discharge. Have we valuable territories and important posts in the possession of a foreign power which, by express stipulations, ought long since to have been surrendered? These are still retained, to the prejudice of our interests, not less than of our rights. Are we in a condition to resent or to repel the aggression? We have neither troops, nor treasury, nor government.[1] Are we even in a condition to remonstrate with dignity? The just imputations on our own faith, in respect to the same treaty, ought first to be removed. Are we entitled by nature and compact to a free participation in the navigation of the Mississippi? Spain excludes us from it. Is public credit an indispensable resource in time of public danger? We seem to have abandoned its cause as desperate and irretrievable. Is commerce of importance to national wealth? Ours is at the lowest point of declension. Is respectability in the eyes of foreign powers a safeguard against foreign encroachments? The imbecility of our government even forbids them to treat with us. Our ambassadors abroad are the mere pageants of mimic sovereignty. Is a violent and unnatural decrease in the value of land a symptom of national distress? The price of improved land in most parts of the country is much lower than can be accounted for by the quantity of waste land at market, and can only be fully explained by that want of private and public confidence which are so alarmingly prevalent among all ranks, and which have a direct tendency to depreciate property of every kind. Is private credit the friend and patron of industry. That most useful kind which relates to borrowing and lending is reduced within the narrowest limits, and this still more from an opinion of insecurity than from the scarcity of money. To shorten an enumeration of particulars which can afford neither pleasure nor instruction, it may in general be demanded, what indication is there of national disorder, poverty, and insignificance that could befall a community so peculiarly blessed with natural advantages as we are, which does not form a part of the dark catalogue of our public misfortunes?

This is the melancholy situation to which we have been brought by those very maxims and councils which would now deter us from adopting the proposed Constitution; and which, not content with having conducted us to the brink of a precipice, seem resolved to plunge us into the abyss that awaits us below. Here, my countrymen, impelled by every motive that ought to influence an enlightened people, let us make a firm stand for our safety, our tranquillity, our dignity, our reputation. Let us at last break the fatal charm which has too long seduced us from the paths of felicity and prosperity.

It is true, as has been before observed, that

[1] "I mean for the Union."—PUBLIUS

facts, too stubborn to be resisted, have produced a species of general assent to the abstract proposition that there exist material defects in our national system; but the usefulness of the concession, on the part of the old adversaries of federal measures, is destroyed by a strenuous opposition to a remedy, upon the only principles that can give it a chance of success. While they admit that the government of the United States is destitute of energy, they contend against conferring upon it those powers which are requisite to supply that energy. They seem still to aim at things repugnant and irreconcilable! at an augmentation of federal authority, without a diminution of State authority; at sovereignty in the Union, and complete independence in the members. They still, in fine, seem to cherish with blind devotion the political monster of an *imperium in imperio.* This renders a full display of the principal defects of the Confederation necessary, in order to show that the evils we experience do not proceed from minute or partial imperfections, but from fundamental errors in the structure of the building, which cannot be amended otherwise than by an alteration in the first principles and main pillars of the fabric.

The great and radical vice in the construction of the existing Confederation is in the principle of LEGISLATION for STATES or GOVERNMENTS, in their CORPORATE or COLLECTIVE CAPACITIES, and as contradistinguished from the INDIVIDUALS of which they consist. Though this principle does not run through all the powers delegated to the Union, yet it pervades and governs those on which the efficacy of the rest depends. Except as to the rule of apportionment, the United States has an indefinite discretion to make requisitions for men and money; but they have no authority to raise either, by regulations extending to the individual citizens of America. The consequence of this is, that though in theory their resolutions concerning those objects are laws, constitutionally binding on the members of the Union, yet in practice they are mere recommendations which the States observe or disregard at their option.

It is a singular instance of the capriciousness of the human mind, that, after all the admonitions we have had from experience on this head, there should still be found men who object to the new Constitution for deviating from a principle which has been found the bane of the old, and which is in itself evidently incompatible with the idea of GOVERNMENT; a principle, in short, which, if it is to be executed at all, must substitute the violent and sanguinary agency of the sword to the mild influence of the magistracy.

There is nothing absurd or impracticable in the idea of a league or alliance between independent nations for certain defined purposes precisely stated in a treaty regulating all the details of time, place, circumstance, and quantity; leaving nothing to future discretion; and depending for its execution on the good faith of the parties. Compacts of this kind exist among all civilised nations, subject to the usual vicissitudes of peace and war, of observance and non-observance, as the interests or passions of the contracting powers dictate. In the early part of the present century there was an epidemical rage in Europe for this species of compacts, from which the politicians of the times fondly hoped for benefits which were never realised. With a view to establishing the equilibrium of power and the peace of that part of the world, all the resources of negotiation were exhausted, and triple and quadruple alliances were formed; but they were scarcely formed before they were broken, giving an instructive but afflicting lesson to mankind, how little dependence is to be placed on treaties which have no other sanction than the obligations of good faith, and which oppose general considerations of peace and justice to the impulse of any immediate interest or passion.

If the particular States in this country are disposed to stand in a similar relation to each other, and to drop the project of a general DISCRETIONARY SUPERINTENDENCE, the scheme would indeed be pernicious, and would entail upon us all the mischiefs which have been enumerated under the first head; but it would have the merit of being, at least, consistent and practicable. Abandoning all views towards a confederate government, this would bring us to a simple alliance offensive and defensive; and would place us in a situation to be alternate friends and enemies of each other, as our mutual jealousies and rivalships, nourished by the intrigues of foreign nations, should prescribe to us.

But if we are unwilling to be placed in this perilous situation; if we still will adhere to the design of a national government, or, which is the same thing, of a superintending power, under the direction of a common council, we must resolve to incorporate into our plan those ingredients which may be considered as forming the characteristic difference between a league and a government; we must extend the authority of the Union to the persons of the citizens—the only proper objects of government.

Government implies the power of making laws. It is essential to the idea of a law, that it be attended with a sanction; or, in other words, a penalty or punishment for disobedience. If there be no penalty annexed to disobedience, the resolutions or commands which pretend to be laws will, in fact, amount to nothing more than advice or recommendation. This penalty, whatever it may be, can only be inflicted in two ways: by the agency of the courts and ministers of justice, or by military force; by the COERCION of the magistracy, or by the COERCION of arms. The first kind can evidently apply only to men; the last kind must of necessity be employed against bodies politic, or communities, or States. It is evident that there is no process of a court by which the observance of the laws can, in the last resort, be enforced. Sentences may be denounced against them for violations of their duty; but these sentences can only be carried into execution by the sword. In an association where the general authority is confined to the collective bodies of the communities that compose it, every breach of the laws must involve a state of war; and military execution must become the only instrument of civil obedience. Such a state of things can certainly not deserve the name of government, nor would any prudent man choose to commit his happiness to it.

There was a time when we were told that breaches, by the States, of the regulations of the federal authority were not to be expected; that a sense of common interest would preside over the conduct of the respective members, and would beget a full compliance with all the constitutional requisitions of the Union. This language, at the present day, would appear as wild as a great part of what we now hear from the same quarter will be thought, when we shall have received further lessons from that best oracle of wisdom, experience. It at all times betrayed an ignorance of the true springs by which human conduct is actuated, and belied the original inducements to the establishment of civil power. Why has government been instituted at all? Because the passions of men will not conform to the dictates of reason and justice, without constraint. Has it been found that bodies of men act with more rectitude or greater disinterestedness than individuals? The contrary of this has been inferred by all accurate observers of the conduct of mankind; and the inference is founded upon obvious reasons. Regard to reputation has a less active influence, when the infamy of a bad action is to be divided among a number, than when it is to fall singly upon one. A spirit of faction, which is apt to mingle its poison in the deliberations of all bodies of men, will often hurry the persons of whom they are composed into improprieties and excesses, for which they would blush in a private capacity.

In addition to all this, there is, in the nature of sovereign power, an impatience of control, that disposes those who are invested with the exercise of it, to look with an evil eye upon all external attempts to restrain or direct its operations. From this spirit it happens, that in every political association which is formed upon the principle of uniting in a common interest a number of lesser sovereignties, there will be found a kind of eccentric tendency in the subordinate or inferior orbs, by the operation of which there will be a perpetual effort in each to fly off from the common centre. This tendency is not difficult to be accounted for. It has its origin in the love of power. Power controlled or abridged is almost always the rival and enemy of that power by which it is controlled or abridged. This simple proposition will teach us how little reason there is to expect that the persons intrusted with the administration of the affairs of the particular members of a confederacy will at all times be ready, with perfect good humour, and an unbiased regard to the public weal, to execute the resolutions or decrees of the general authority. The reverse of this results from the constitution of human nature.

If, therefore, the measures of the Confederacy cannot be executed without the intervention of the particular administrations, there will be little prospect of their being executed at all. The rulers of the respective members, whether they have a constitutional right to do it or not, will undertake to judge of the propriety of the measures themselves. They will consider the conformity of the thing proposed or required to their immediate interests or aims; the momentary conveniences or inconveniences that would attend its adoption. All this will be done; and in a spirit of interested and suspicious scrutiny, without that knowledge of national circumstances and reasons of state, which is essential to a right judgment, and with that strong predilection in favour of local objects, which can hardly fail to mislead the decision. The same process must be repeated in every member of which the body is constituted; and the execution of the plans, framed by the councils of the whole, will always fluctuate on the discretion of the ill-informed and prejudiced opinion of every part. Those who have been conversant in the proceedings of popular assemblies; who have seen how difficult it often is, where there is no exterior pressure of circumstances, to bring them to harmonious resolutions on important points, will readily conceive how impossible it must be to induce a number of such assemblies, deliberating at a distance from each other, at different times, and under different impressions, long to cooperate in the same views and pursuits.

In our case, the concurrence of thirteen distinct sovereign wills is requisite, under the Confederation, to the complete execution of every important measure that proceeds from the Union. It has happened as was to have been foreseen. The measures of the Union have not been executed; the delinquencies of the States have, step by step, matured themselves to an extreme, which has, at length, arrested all the wheels of the national government, and brought them to an awful stand. Congress at this time scarcely possess the means of keeping up the forms of administration, till the States can have time to agree upon a more substantial substitute for the present shadow of a federal government. Things did not come to this desperate extremity at once. The causes which have been specified produced at first only unequal and disproportionate degrees of compliance with the requisitions of the Union. The greater deficiencies of some States furnished the pretext of example and the temptation of interest to the complying, or to the least delinquent States. Why should we do more in proportion than those who are embarked with us in the same political voyage? Why should we consent to bear more than our proper share of the common burden? These were suggestions which human selfishness could not withstand, and which even speculative men, who looked forward to remote consequences, could not, without hesitation, combat. Each State, yielding to the persuasive voice of immediate interest or convenience, has successively withdrawn its support, till the frail and tottering edifice seems ready to fall upon our heads, and to crush us beneath its ruins.

PUBLIUS

Number 16

[HAMILTON]

THE TENDENCY of the principle of legislation for States, or communities, in their political capacities, as it has been exemplified by the experiment we have made of it, is equally attested by the events which have befallen all other governments of the confederate kind, of which we have any account, in exact proportion to its prevalence in those systems. The confirmations of this fact will be worthy of a distinct and particular examination. I shall content myself with barely observing here, that of all the confederacies of antiquity, which history has handed down to us, the Lycian and Achæan leagues, as far as there remain vestiges of them, appear to have been most free from the fetters of that mistaken principle, and were accordingly those which have best deserved, and have most liberally received, the applauding suffrages of political writers.

This exceptional principle may, as truly as emphatically, be styled the parent of anarchy: It has been seen that delinquencies in the members of the Union are its natural and necessary offspring; and that whenever they happen, the only constitutional remedy is force, and the immediate effect of the use of it, civil war.

It remains to inquire how far so odious an engine of government, in its application to us, would even be capable of answering its end. If there should not be a large army constantly at the disposal of the national government it would either not be able to employ force at all, or, when this could be done, it would amount to a war between parts of the Confederacy concerning the infractions of a league, in which the strongest combination would be most likely to prevail, whether it consisted of those who supported or of those who resisted the general authority. It would rarely happen that the delinquency to be redressed would be confined to a single member, and if there were more than one who had neglected their duty, similarity of situation would induce them to unite for common defence. Independent of this motive of sympathy, if a large and influential State should happen to be the aggressing member, it would commonly have weight enough with its neighbours to win over some of them as associates to its cause. Specious arguments of danger to the common liberty could easily be contrived; plausible excuses for the deficiencies of the party could, without difficulty, be invented to alarm the apprehensions, inflame the passions, and conciliate the good-will, even of those States which were not chargeable with any violation or omission of duty. This would be the more likely to take place, as the delinquencies of the larger members might be expected sometimes to proceed from an ambitious premeditation in their rulers, with a view to getting rid of all external control upon their designs of personal aggrandisement; the better to effect which it is presumable they would tamper beforehand with leading individuals in the adjacent States. If associates could not be found at home, recourse would be had to the aid of foreign powers, who would seldom be disinclined to encouraging the dissensions of a Confederacy, from the firm union of which they had so much to fear. When the sword is once drawn, the passions of men observe no bounds of moderation. The suggestions of wounded pride, the instigations of irritated resentment, would be apt to carry the States against which the arms of the Union were exerted, to any extremes necessary to avenge the affront or to avoid the disgrace of submission. The first war of this kind would probably terminate in a dissolution of the Union.

This may be considered as the violent death of the Confederacy. Its more natural death is what we now seem to be on the point of experiencing, if the federal system be not speedily renovated in a more substantial form. It is not probable, considering the genius of this country, that the complying States would often be inclined to support the authority of the Union by engaging in a war against the non-complying States. They would always be more ready to pursue the milder course of putting themselves upon an equal footing with the delinquent members by an imitation of their example. And the guilt of all would thus become the security of all. Our past experience has exhibited the operation of this spirit in its full light. There would, in fact, be an insuperable difficulty in ascertaining when force could with propriety be employed. In the article of pecuniary contribution, which would be the most usual source of delinquency, it would often be impossible to decide whether it had proceeded from disinclination or inability. The pretence of the latter would always be at hand. And the case must be very flagrant in which its fallacy could be detected with sufficient certainty to justify the harsh expedient of compulsion. It is easy to see that this problem alone, as often as it should occur, would open a wide field for the exercise of factious views, of partiality, and of oppression, in the majority that happened to prevail in the national council.

It seems to require no pains to prove that the States ought not to prefer a national Constitution which could only be kept in motion by the instrumentality of a large army continually on foot to execute the ordinary requisitions or decrees of the government. And yet this is the plain alternative involved by those who wish to deny it the power of extending its operations to individuals. Such a scheme, if practicable at all, would instantly degenerate into a military despotism; but it will be found in every light impracticable. The resources of the Union would not be equal to the maintenance of an army considerable enough to confine the larger States within the limits of their duty; nor would the means ever be furnished of forming such an army in the first instance. Whoever considers the populousness and strength of several of these States singly at the present juncture, and looks forward to what they will become, even at the distance of half a century, will at once dismiss as idle and visionary any scheme which aims at regulating their movements by laws to operate upon them in their collective capacities, and to be executed by a coercion applicable to them in the same capacities. A project of this kind is little less romantic than the monster-taming spirit which is attributed to the fabulous heroes and demigods of antiquity.

Even in those confederacies which have been composed of members smaller than many of our countries, the principle of legislation for sovereign States, supported by military coercion, has never been found effectual. It has rarely been attempted to be employed, but against the weaker members; and in most instances attempts to coerce the refractory and disobedient have been the signals of bloody wars, in which one half of the confederacy has displayed its banners against the other half.

The result of these observations to an intelligent mind must be clearly this, that if it be possible at any rate to construct a federal government capable of regulating the common concerns and preserving the general tranquility, it must be founded, as to the objects committed to its care, upon the reverse of the principle contended for by the opponents of the proposed Constitution. It must carry its agency to the persons of the citizens. It must stand in need of no intermediate legislations; but must itself be empowered to employ the arm of the ordinary magistrate to execute its own resolutions. The majesty of the national authority must be manifested through the medium of the courts of justice. The government of the Union, like that of each State, must be able to address itself immediately to the hopes and fears of individuals; and to attract to its support those passions which have the strongest influence upon the human heart. It must, in short, possess all the means, and have a right to resort to all the methods, of executing the powers with which it is intrusted, that are possessed and exercised by the governments of the particular States.

To this reasoning it may perhaps be objected, that if any State should be disaffected to the authority of the Union, it could at any time obstruct the execution of its laws, and bring the matter to the same issue of force, with the necessity of which the opposite scheme is reproached.

The plausibility of this objection will vanish the moment we advert to the essential difference between a mere NON-COMPLIANCE and a DIRECT and ACTIVE RESISTANCE. If the interposition of the State legislatures be necessary to give effect to a measure of the Union, they have only NOT TO ACT, or to ACT EVASIVELY, and the measure is defeated. This neglect of duty may be disguised under affected but unsubstantial provisions, so as not to appear, and of course not to excite any alarm in the people for the safety of the Constitution. The State leaders may even make a merit of their surreptitious invasions of it on the ground of some temporary convenience, exemption, or advantage.

But if the execution of the laws of the national government should not require the intervention of the State legislatures, if they were to pass into immediate operation upon the citizens themselves, the particular governments could not interrupt their progress without an open and violent exertion of an unconstitutional power. No omissions nor evasions would answer the end. They would be obliged to act, and in such a manner as would leave no doubt that they had encroached on the national rights. An experiment of this nature would always be hazardous in the face of a constitution in any degree competent to its own defence, and of a people enlightened enough to distinguish between a legal exercise and an illegal usurpation of authority. The success of it would require not merely a factious majority in the legislature, but the concurrence of the courts of justice and of the body of the people. If the judges were not embarked in a conspiracy with the legislature, they would pronounce the resolutions of such a majority to be contrary to the supreme law of the land, unconstitutional, and void. If the people were not tainted with the spirit of their State representatives, they, as the natural guardians of the Constitution, would throw their weight into the national scale and give it a decided preponderancy in the contest. Attempts of this kind would not often be made with levity or rashness, because they could seldom be made without danger to the authors, unless in cases of a tyrannical exercise of the federal authority.

If opposition to the national government should arise from the disorderly conduct of refractory or seditious individuals, it could be overcome by the same means which are daily employed against the same evil under the State governments. The magistracy, being equally the ministers of the law of the land, from whatever source it might emanate, would doubtless be as ready to guard the national as the local regulations from the inroads of private licentiousness. As to those partial commotions and insurrections, which sometimes disquiet society, from the intrigues of an inconsiderable faction, or from sudden or occasional ill-humours that do not infect the great body of the community, the general government could command more extensive resources for the suppression of disturbances of that kind than would be in the power of any single member. And as to those mortal feuds which, in certain conjunctures, spread a conflagration through a whole nation, or through a very large proportion of it, proceeding either from weighty causes of discontent given by the government or from the contagion of some violent popular paroxysm, they do not fall within any ordinary rules of calculation. When they happen, they commonly amount to revolutions and dismemberments of empire. No form of government can always either avoid or control them. It is in vain to hope to guard against events too mighty for human foresight or precaution, and it would be idle to object to a government because it could not perform impossibilities.

PUBLIUS

Number 17

[HAMILTON]

AN OBJECTION, of a nature different from that which has been stated and answered, in my last address, may perhaps be likewise urged against the principle of legislation for the individual citizens of America. It may be said that it would tend to render the government of the Union too powerful, and to enable it to absorb those residuary authorities, which it might be judged proper to leave with the States for local purposes. Allowing the utmost latitude to the love of power which any reasonable man can require, I confess I am at a loss to discover what temptation the persons intrusted with the administration of the general government could ever feel to divest the States of the authorities of that description. The regulation of the mere domestic police of a State appears to me to hold out slender allurements to ambition. Commerce, finance, negotiation, and war seem to comprehend all the objects which have charms for minds governed by that passion; and all the powers necessary to those objects ought, in the first instance, to be lodged in the national depository. The administration of private justice between the citizens of the same State, the supervision of agriculture and of other concerns of a similar nature, all those things, in short, which are proper to be provided for by local legislation, can never be desirable cares of a general jurisdiction. It is therefore improbable that there should exist a disposition in the federal councils to usurp the powers with which they are connected; because the attempt to exercise those powers would be as troublesome as it would be nugatory; and the possession of them, for that reason, would contribute nothing to the dignity, to the importance, or to the splendour of the national government.

But let it be admitted, for argument's sake, that mere wantonness and lust of domination would be sufficient to beget that disposition; still it may be safely affirmed, that the sense of the constituent body of the national representatives, or, in other words, the people of the several States, would control the indulgence of so extravagant an appetite. It will always be far more easy for the State governments to encroach upon the national authorities, than for the national government to encroach upon the State authorities. The proof of this proposition turns upon the greater degree of influence which the State governments, if they administer their affairs with uprightness and prudence, will generally possess over the people; a circumstance which at the same time teaches us that there is an inherent and intrinsic weakness in all federal constitutions; and that too much pains cannot be taken in their organisation, to give them all the force which is compatible with the principles of liberty.

The superiority of influence in favour of the particular governments would result partly from the diffusive construction of the national government, but chiefly from the nature of the objects to which the attention of the State administrations would be directed.

It is a known fact in human nature, that its affections are commonly weak in proportion to the distance or diffusiveness of the object. Upon the same principle that a man is more attached to his family than to his neighbourhood, to his neighbourhood than to the community at large, the people of each State would be apt to feel a stronger bias towards their local governments than towards the government of the Union; unless the force of that principle should be destroyed by a much better administration of the latter.

This strong propensity of the human heart would find powerful auxiliaries in the objects of State regulation.

The variety of more minute interests, which will necessarily fall under the superintendence of the local administrations, and which will form so many rivulets of influence, running through every part of the society, cannot be particularised, without involving a detail too tedious and uninteresting to compensate for the instruction it might afford.

There is one transcendent advantage belonging to the province of the State governments, which alone suffices to place the matter in a clear and satisfactory light,—I mean the ordinary administration of criminal and civil justice. This, of all others, is the most powerful, most universal, and most attractive source of popular obedience and attachment. It is that which, being the immediate and visible guardian of life and property, having its benefits and its terrors in constant activity before the public eye, regulating all those personal interests and familiar concerns to which the sensibility of individuals is more immediately awake, contributes, more than any other circumstance, to impressing upon the minds of the people, affection, esteem, and reverence towards the government. This great cement of society, which will diffuse itself almost wholly through the channels of the particular governments, independent of all other causes of influence, would insure them so decided an empire over their respective citizens as to render them at all times a complete counterpoise, and, not unfrequently, dangerous rivals to the power of the Union.

The operations of the national government, on the other hand, falling less immediately under the observation of the mass of the citizens, the benefits derived from it will chiefly be perceived, and attended to by speculative men. Relating to more general interests, they will be less apt to come home to the feelings of the people; and, in proportion, less likely to inspire an habitual sense of obligation, and an active sentiment of attachment.

The reasoning on this head has been abundantly exemplified by the experience of all federal constitutions with which we are acquainted, and of all others which have borne the least analogy to them.

Though the ancient feudal systems were not, strictly speaking, confederacies, yet they partook of the nature of that species of association. There was a common head, chieftain, or sovereign, whose authority extended over the whole nation; and a number of subordinate vassals, or feudatories, who had large portions of land allotted to them, and numerous trains of *inferior* vassals or retainers, who occupied and cultivated that land upon the tenure of fealty or obedience to the persons of whom they held it. Each principal vassal was a kind of sovereign within his particular demesnes. The consequences of this situation were a continual opposition to authority of the sovereign, and frequent wars between the great barons or chief feudatories themselves. The power of the head of the nation was commonly too weak, either to preserve the public peace, or to protect the people against the oppressions of their immediate lords. This period of European affairs is emphatically styled by historians the times of feudal anarchy.

When the sovereign happened to be a man of vigorous and warlike temper and of superior abilities, he would acquire a personal weight and influence, which answered, for the time, the purposes of a more regular authority. But in general, the power of the barons triumphed over that of the prince; and in many instances his dominion was entirely thrown off, and the great fiefs were erected into independent principalities or States. In those instances in which the monarch finally prevailed over his vassals, his success was chiefly owing to the tyranny of those vassals over their dependents. The barons, or nobles, equally the enemies of the sovereign and the oppressors of the common people, were dreaded and detested by both; till mutual danger and mutual interest affected a union between them fatal to the power of the aristocracy. Had the nobles, by a conduct of clemency and justice, preserved the fidelity and devotion of their retainers and followers, the contests between them and the prince must almost always have ended in their favour, and in the abridgment or subversion of the royal authority.

This is not an assertion founded merely in speculation or conjecture. Among other illustrations of its truth which might be cited, Scotland will furnish a cogent example. The spirit of clanship which was, at an early day, introduced into that kingdom, uniting the nobles and their dependants by ties equivalent to those of kindred, rendered the aristocracy a constant overmatch for the power of the monarch, till the incorporation with England subdued its fierce and ungovernable spirit, and reduced it within those rules of subordination which a more rational and more energetic system of civil polity had previously established in the latter kingdom.

The separate governments in a confederacy may aptly be compared with the feudal baronies; with this advantage in their favour, that from the reasons already explained, they will generally possess the confidence and good-will of the people, and with so important a support, will be able effectually to oppose all encroachments of the national government. It will be well if they are not able to counteract its legitimate and necessary authority. The points of similitude consist in the rivalship of power, applicable to both, and in the CONCENTRATION of large portions of the strength of the community into particular DEPOSITS, in one case at the disposal of individuals, in the other case at the disposal of political bodies.

A concise review of the events that have attended confederate governments will further illustrate this important doctrine; an inattention to which has been the great source of our political mistakes, and has given our jealousy a direction to the wrong side. This review shall form the subject of some ensuing papers.

PUBLIUS

Number 18

[HAMILTON AND MADISON]

AMONG THE confederacies of antiquity, the most considerable was that of the Grecian republics, associated under the Amphictyonic council. From the best accounts transmitted of this celebrated institution, it bore a very instructive analogy to the present Confederation of the American States.

The members retained the character of independent and sovereign states, and had equal votes in the federal council. This council had a general authority to propose and resolve whatever it judged necessary for the common welfare of Greece; to declare and carry on war; to decide, in the last resort, all controversies between the members; to fine the aggressing party; to employ the whole force of the confederacy against the disobedient; to admit new members. The Amphictyons were the guardians of religion, and of the immense riches belonging to the temple of Delphos, where they had the right of jurisdiction in controversies between the inhabitants and those who came to consult the oracle. As a further provision for the efficacy of the federal powers, they took an oath mutually to defend and protect the united cities, to punish the violators of this oath, and to inflict vengeance on sacrilegious despoilers of the temple.

In theory, and upon paper, this apparatus of powers seems amply sufficient for all general purposes. In several material instances they exceed the powers enumerated in the articles of confederation. The Amphictyons had in their hands the superstition of the times, one of the principal engines by which government was then maintained; they had a declared authority to use coercion against refractory cities, and were bound by oath to exert this authority on the necessary occasions.

Very different, nevertheless, was the experiment from the theory. The powers, like those of the present Congress, were administered by deputies appointed wholly by the cities in their political capacities; and exercised over them in the same capacities. Hence the weakness, the disorders, and finally the destruction of the confederacy. The more powerful members, instead of being kept in awe and subordination, tyrannised successively over all the rest. Athens, as we learn from Demosthenes, was the arbiter of Greece seventy-three years. The Lacedæmonians next governed it twenty-nine years; at a subsequent period, after the battle of Leuctra, the Thebans had their turn of domination.

It happened but too often, according to Plutarch, that the deputies of the strongest cities awed and corrupted those of the weaker; and that judgment went in favour of the most powerful party.

Even in the midst of defensive and dangerous wars with Persia and Macedon, the members never acted in concert, and were, more or fewer of them, eternally the dupes or the hirelings of the common enemy. The intervals of foreign war were filled up by domestic vicissitudes, convulsions, and carnage.

After the conclusion of the war with Xerxes, it appears that the Lacedæmonians required that a number of the cities should be turned out of the confederacy for the unfaithful part they had acted. The Athenians, finding that the Lacedæmonians would lose fewer partisans by such a measure than themselves, and would become masters of the public deliberations, vigorously opposed and defeated the attempt. This piece of history proves at once the inefficiency of the union, the ambition and jealousy of its most powerful members, and the dependent and degraded condition of the rest. The smaller members, though entitled by the theory of their system to revolve in equal pride and majesty around the common centre, had become, in fact, satellites of the orbs of primary magnitude.

Had the Greeks, says the Abbé Milot, been as wise as they were courageous, they would have been admonished by experience of the necessity of a closer union, and would have availed themselves of the peace which followed their success against the Persian arms, to establish such a reformation. Instead of this obvious policy, Athens and Sparta, inflated with the victories and the glory they had acquired, became first rivals and then enemies; and did each other infinitely more mischief than they had suffered from Xerxes. Their mutual jealousies, fears, hatreds, and injuries ended in the celebrated Peloponnesian war; which itself ended in the ruin and slavery of the Athenians who had begun it.

As a weak government, when not at war, is ever agitated by internal dissensions, so these never fail to bring on fresh calamities from abroad. The Phocians having ploughed up some consecrated ground belonging to the temple of Apollo, the Amphictyonic council, according to the superstition of the age, imposed a fine on the sacrilegious offenders. The

Phocians, abetted by Athens and Sparta, refused to submit to the decree. The Thebans, with others of the cities, undertook to maintain the authority of the Amphictyons, and to avenge the violated god. The latter, being the weaker party, invited the assistance of Philip of Macedon, who had secretly fostered the contest. Philip gladly seized the opportunity of executing the designs he had long planned against the liberties of Greece. By his intrigues and bribes he won over to his interests the popular leaders of several cities; by their influence and votes, gained admission into the Amphictyonic council; and by his arts and his arms made himself master of the confederacy.

Such were the consequences of the fallacious principle on which this interesting establishment was founded. Had Greece, says a judicious observer on her fate, been united by a stricter confederation, and persevered in her union, she would never have worn the chains of Macedon; and might have proved a barrier to the vast projects of Rome.

The Achæan league, as it is called, was another society of Grecian republics, which supplies us with valuable instruction.

The Union here was far more intimate, and its organisation much wiser, than in the preceding instance. It will accordingly appear, that though not exempt from a similar catastrophe, it by no means equally deserved it.

The cities composing this league retained their municipal jurisdiction, appointed their own officers, and enjoyed a perfect equality. The senate, in which they were represented, had the sole and exclusive right of peace and war; of sending and receiving ambassadors; of entering into treaties and alliances; of appointing a chief magistrate or prætor, as he was called, who commanded their armies, and who, with the advice and consent of ten of the senators, not only administered the government in the recess of the senate, but had a great share in its deliberations, when assembled. According to the primitive constitution, there were two prætors associated in the administration; but on trial a single one was preferred.

It appears that the cities had all the same laws and customs, the same weights and measures, and the same money. But how far this effect proceeded from the authority of the federal council is left in uncertainty. It is said only that the cities were in a manner compelled to receive the same laws and usages. When Lacedæmon was brought into the league by Philopœmen, it was attended with an abolition of the institutions and laws of Lycurgus, and an adoption of those of the Achæans. The Amphictyonic confederacy, of which she had been a member, left her in the full exercise of her government and her legislation. This circumstance alone proves a very material difference in the genius of the two systems.

It is much to be regretted that such imperfect monuments remain of this curious political fabric. Could its interior structure and regular operation be ascertained, it is probable that more light would be thrown by it on the science of federal government, than by any of the like experiments with which we are acquainted.

One important fact seems to be witnessed by all the historians who take notice of Achæan affairs. It is, that as well after the renovation of the league by Aratus, as before its dissolution by the arts of Macedon, there was infinitely more of moderation and justice in the administration of its government, and less of violence and sedition in the people, than were to be found in any of the cities exercising *singly* all the prerogatives of sovereignty. The Abbé Mably, in his observations on Greece, says that the popular government, which was so tempestuous elsewhere, caused no disorders in the members of the Achæan republic, *because it was there tempered by the general authority and laws of the confederacy.*

We are not to conclude too hastily, however, that faction did not, in a certain degree, agitate the particular cities; much less that a due subordination and harmony reigned in the general system. The contrary is sufficiently displayed in the vicissitudes and fate of the republic.

Whilst the Amphictyonic confederacy remained, that of the Achæans, which comprehended the less important cities only, made little figure on the theatre of Greece. When the former became a victim to Macedon, the latter was spared by the policy of Philip and Alexander. Under the successors of these princes, however, a different policy prevailed. The arts of division were practised among the Achæans. Each city was seduced into a separate interest; the union was dissolved. Some of the cities fell under the tyranny of Macedonian garrisons; others under that of usurpers springing out of their own confusions. Shame and oppression ere long awakened their love of liberty. A few cities reunited. Their example was followed by others, as opportunities were found of cutting off their tyrants. The league soon embraced almost the whole Peloponnesus.

Macedon saw its progress; but was hindered by internal dissensions from stopping it. All Greece caught the enthusiasm and seemed ready to unite in one confederacy, when the jealousy and envy in Sparta and Athens, of the rising glory of the Achæans, threw a fatal damp on the enterprise. The dread of the Macedonian power induced the league to court the alliance of the kings of Egypt and Syria, who, as successors of Alexander, were rivals of the king of Macedon. This policy was defeated by Cleomenes, king of Sparta, who was led by his ambition to make an unprovoked attack on his neighbours, the Achæans, and who, as an enemy to Macedon, had interest enough with the Egyptian and Syrian princes to effect a breach of their engagements with the league. The Achæans were now reduced to the dilemma of submitting to Cleomenes, or of supplicating the aid of Macedon, its former oppressor. The latter expedient was adopted. The contests of the Greeks always afforded a pleasing opportunity to that powerful neighbour of intermeddling in their affairs. A Macedonian army quickly appeared. Cleomenes was vanquished. The Achæans soon experienced, as often happens, that a victorious and powerful ally is but another name for a master. All that their most abject compliances could obtain from him was a toleration of the exercise of their laws. Philip, who was now on the throne of Macedon, soon provoked by his tyrannies, fresh combinations among the Greeks. The Achæans, though weakened by internal dissensions and by the revolt of Messene, one of its members, being joined by the Ætolians and Athenians, erected the standard of opposition. Finding themselves, though thus supported, unequal to the undertaking, they once more had recourse to the dangerous expedient of introducing the succour of foreign arms. The Romans, to whom the invitation was made, eagerly embraced it. Philip was conquered; Macedon subdued. A new crisis ensued to the league. Dissensions broke out among its members. These the Romans fostered. Callicrates and other popular leaders became mercenary instruments for inveigling their countrymen. The more effectually to nourish discord and disorder the Romans had, to the astonishment of those who confided in their sincerity, already proclaimed universal liberty[1] throughout Greece. With the same

[1]This was but another name more specious for the independence of the members on the federal head.—PUBLIUS

insidious views, they now seduced the members from the league, by representing to their pride the violation it committed on their sovereignty. By these arts this union, the last hope of Greece, the last hope of ancient liberty, was torn into pieces; and such imbecility and distraction introduced that the arms of Rome found little difficulty in completing the ruin which their arts had commenced. The Achæans were cut to pieces, and Achaia loaded with chains, under which it is groaning at this hour.

I have thought it not superfluous to give the outlines of this important portion of history; both because it teaches more than one lesson, and because, as a supplement to the outlines of the Achæan constitution, it emphatically illustrates the tendency of federal bodies rather to anarchy among the members, than to tyranny in the head.   PUBLIUS

Number 19
[HAMILTON AND MADISON]

THE EXAMPLES of ancient confederacies, cited in my last paper, have not exhausted the source of experimental instruction on the subject. There are existing institutions, founded on a similar principle, which merit particular consideration. The first which presents itself is the Germanic body.

In the early ages of Christianity, Germany was occupied by seven distinct nations, who had no common chief. The Franks, one of the number, having conquered the Gauls, established the kingdom which has taken its name from them. In the ninth century Charlemagne, its warlike monarch, carried his victorious arms in every direction; and Germany became a part of his vast dominions. On the dismemberment, which took place under his sons, this part was erected into a separate and independent empire. Charlemagne and his immediate descendants possessed the reality, as well as the ensigns and dignity of imperial power. But the principal vassals, whose fiefs had become hereditary, and who composed the national diets which Charlemagne had not abolished, gradually threw off the yoke and advanced to sovereign jurisdiction and independence. The force of imperial sovereignty was insufficient to restrain such powerful dependants; or to preserve the unity and tranquillity of the empire. The most furious private wars, accompanied with every species of calamity, were carried on between the different princes and states. The imperial authority, unable to maintain the public order, declined by degrees till it was almost extinct in the anarchy which agitated the long interval between the death of the last emperor of the Suabian and the accession of the first emperor of the Austrian lines. In the eleventh century the emperors enjoyed full sovereignty: In the fifteenth they had little more than the symbols and decorations of power.

Out of this feudal system, which has itself many of the important features of a confederacy, has grown the federal system which constitutes the Germanic empire. Its powers are vested in a diet representing the component members of the confederacy; in the emperor, who is the executive magistrate, with a negative on the decrees of the diet; and in the imperial chamber and the aulic council, two judiciary tribunals having supreme jurisdiction in controversies which concern the empire, or which happen among its members.

The diet possesses the general power of legislating for the empire; of making war and peace; contracting alliances; assessing quotas of troops and money; constructing fortresses; regulating coin; admitting new members; and subjecting disobedient members to the ban of the empire, by which the party is degraded from his sovereign rights and his possessions forfeited. The members of the confederacy are expressly restricted from entering into compacts prejudicial to the empire; from imposing tolls and duties on their mutual intercourse, without the consent of the emperor and diet; from altering the value of money; from doing injustice to one another; or from affording assistance or retreat to disturbers of the public peace. And the ban is denounced against such as shall violate any of these restrictions. The members of the diet, as such, are subject in all cases to be judged by the emperor and diet, and in their private capacities by the aulic council and imperial chamber.

The prerogatives of the emperor are numerous. The most important of them are: his exclusive right to make propositions to the diet; to negative its resolutions; to name ambassadors; to confer dignities and titles; to fill vacant electorates; to found universities; to grant privileges not injurious to the states of the empire; to receive and apply the public revenues; and generally to watch over the public safety. In certain cases, the electors form a council to him. In quality of emperor, he possesses no territory within the empire, nor receives any revenue for his support. But his revenue and dominions, in other qualities, constitute him one of the most powerful princes in Europe.

From such a parade of constitutional powers, in the representatives and head of this confederacy, the natural supposition would be, that it must form an exception to the general character which belongs to its kindred systems. Nothing would be further from the reality. The fundamental principle on which it rests, that the empire is a community of sovereigns, that the diet is a representation of sovereigns, and that the laws are addressed to sovereigns, renders the empire a nerveless body, incapable of regulating its own members, insecure against external dangers, and agitated with unceasing fermentations in its own bowels.

The history of Germany is a history of wars between the emperor and the princes and states; of wars among the princes and states themselves; of the licentiousness of the strong, and the oppression of the weak; of foreign intrusions, and foreign intrigues; of requisitions of men and money disregarded, or partially complied with; of attempts to enforce them, altogether abortive, or attended with slaughter and desolation, involving the innocent with the guilty; of general imbecility, confusion, and misery.

In the sixteenth century, the emperor, with one part of the empire on his side, was seen engaged against the other princes and states. In one of the conflicts, the emperor himself was put to flight, and very near being made prisoner by the Elector of Saxony. The late king of Prussia was more than once pitted against his imperial sovereign; and commonly proved an overmatch for him. Controversies and wars among the members themselves have been so common, that the German annals are crowded with the bloody pages which describe them. Previous to the peace of Westphalia, Germany was desolated by a war of thirty years, in which the emperor, with one half of the empire, was on one side, and Sweden, with the other half, on the opposite side. Peace was at length negotiated, and dictated by foreign powers; and the articles of it, to which foreign powers are parties, made a fundamental part of the Germanic constitution.

If the nation happens, on any emergency, to be more united by the necessity of self-defence, its situation is still deplorable. Military preparations must be preceded by so many tedious discussions, arising from the jealousies, pride, separate views, and clashing pretensions of sovereign bodies, that before the diet can settle the arrangements, the enemy are in the field; and before the federal troops are ready to take it, are retiring into winter quarters.

The small body of national troops, which has been judged necessary in time of peace, is defectively kept up, badly paid, infected with local prejudices, and supported by irregular and disproportionate contributions to the treasury.

The impossibility of maintaining order and dispensing justice among these sovereign subjects, produced the experiment of dividing the empire into nine or ten circles or districts; of giving them an interior organisation, and of charging them with the military execution of the laws against delinquent and contumacious members. This experiment has only served to demonstrate more fully the radical vice of the constitution. Each circle is the miniature picture of the deformities of this political monster. They either fail to execute their commissions, or they do it with all the devastation and carnage of civil war. Sometimes whole circles are defaulters; and then they increase the mischief which they were instituted to remedy.

We may form some judgment of this scheme of military coercion from a sample given by Thuanus. In Donawerth, a free and imperial city of the circle of Suabia, the Abbé de St. Croix enjoyed certain immunities which had been reserved to him. In the exercise of these, on some public occasions, outrages were committed on him by the people of the city. The consequence was that the city was put under the ban of the empire, and the Duke of Bavaria, though director of another circle, obtained an appointment to enforce it. He soon appeared before the city with a corps of ten thousand troops, and finding it a fit occasion, as he had secretly intended from the beginning, to revive an antiquated claim, on the pretext that his ancestors had suffered the place to be dismembered from his territory,[1] he took possession of it in his own name, disarmed, and punished the inhabitants, and reannexed the city to his domains.

It may be asked, perhaps, what has so long kept this disjointed machine from falling entirely to pieces? The answer is obvious: The weakness of most of the members, who are unwilling to expose themselves to the mercy of

[1] Pfeffel, *Nouvel Abrég. Chronol. de l'Hist.*, etc., *d'Allemagne*, says the pretext was to indemnify himself for the expense of the expedition.— PUBLIUS

foreign powers; the weakness of most of the principal members, compared with the formidable powers all around them; the vast weight and influence which the emperor derives from his separate and hereditary dominions; and the interest he feels in preserving a system with which his family pride is connected, and which constitutes him the first prince in Europe;—these causes support a feeble and precarious Union; whilst the repellent quality, incident to the nature of sovereignty, and which time continually strengthens, prevents any reform whatever, founded on a proper consolidation. Nor is it to be imagined, if this obstacle could be surmounted, that the neighbouring powers would suffer a revolution to take place, which would give to the empire the force and pre-eminence to which it is entitled. Foreign nations have long considered themselves as interested in the changes made by events in this constitution; and have, on various occasions, betrayed their policy of perpetuating its anarchy and weakness.

If more direct examples were wanting, Poland, as a government over local sovereigns, might not improperly be taken notice of. Nor could any proof more striking be given of the calamities flowing from such institutions. Equally unfit for self-government and self-defence, it has long been at the mercy of its powerful neighbours; who have lately had the mercy to disburden it of one-third of its people and territories.

The connection among the Swiss cantons scarcely amounts to a confederacy; though it is sometimes cited as an instance of the stability of such institutions.

They have no common treasury; no common troops even in war; no common coin; no common judicatory; nor any other common mark of sovereignty.

They are kept together by the peculiarity of their topographical position; by their individual weakness and insignificancy; by the fear of powerful neighbours, to one of which they were formerly subject; by the few sources of contention among a people of such simple and homogeneous manners; by their joint interest in their dependent possessions; by the mutual aid they stand in need of, for suppressing insurrections and rebellions, an aid expressly stipulated, and often required and afforded; and by the necessity of some regular and permanent provision for accommodating disputes among the cantons. The provision is, that the parties at variance shall each choose four judges out of the neutral cantons, who, in case of disagreement, choose an umpire. This tribunal, under an oath of impartiality, pronounces definitive sentence, which all the cantons are bound to enforce. The competency of this regulation may be estimated by a clause in their treaty of 1683, with Victor Amadeus of Savoy; in which he obliges himself to interpose as mediator in disputes between the cantons, and to employ force, if necessary, against the contumacious party.

So far as the peculiarity of their case will admit of comparison with that of the United States, it serves to confirm the principle intended to be established. Whatever efficacy the union may have had in ordinary cases, it appears that the moment a cause of difference sprang up, capable of trying its strength, it failed. The controversies on the subject of religion, which in three instances have kindled violent and bloody contests, may be said, in fact, to have severed the league. The Protestant and Catholic cantons have since had their separate diets, where all the most important concerns are adjusted, and which have left the general diet little other business than to take care of the common bailages.

That separation had another consequence, which merits attention. It produced opposite alliances with foreign powers: of Berne, at the head of the Protestant association, with the United Provinces; and of Luzerne, at the head of the Catholic association, with France.

PUBLIUS

Number 20

[HAMILTON AND MADISON]

THE UNITED NETHERLANDS are a confederacy of republics, or rather of aristocracies of a very remarkable texture, yet confirming all the lessons derived from those which we have already reviewed.

The union is composed of seven coequal and sovereign states, and each state or province is a composition of equal and independent cities. In all important cases, not only the provinces but the cities must be unanimous.

The sovereignty of the Union is represented by the States-General, consisting usually of about fifty deputies appointed by the provinces. They hold their seats, some for life, some for six, three, and one years; from two provinces they continue in appointment during pleasure.

The States-General have authority to enter into treaties and alliances; to make war and peace; to raise armies and equip fleets; to ascertain quotas and demand contributions. In all these cases, however, unanimity and the sanction of their constituents are requisite. They have authority to appoint and receive ambassadors; to execute treaties and alliances already formed; to provide for the collection of duties on imports and exports; to regulate the mint, with a saving to the provincial rights; to govern as sovereigns the dependent territories. The provinces are restrained, unless with the general consent, from entering into foreign treaties; from establishing imposts injurious to others, or charging their neighbours with higher duties than their own subjects. A council of state, a chamber of accounts, with five colleges of admiralty, aid and fortify the federal administration.

The executive magistrate of the union is the stadtholder, who is now an hereditary prince. His principal weight and influence in the republic are derived from this independent title; from his great patrimonial estates; from his family connections with some of the chief potentates of Europe; and, more than all, perhaps, from his being stadtholder in the several provinces, as well as for the union; in which provincial quality he has the appointment of town magistrates under certain regulations, executes provincial decrees, presides when he pleases in the provincial tribunals, and has throughout the power of pardon.

As stadtholder of the union, he has, however, considerable prerogatives.

In his political capacity, he has authority to settle disputes between the provinces, when other methods fail; to assist at the deliberations of the States-General, and at their particular conferences; to give audiences to foreign ambassadors, and to keep agents for his particular affairs at foreign courts.

In his military capacity he commands the federal troops, provides for garrisons, and in general regulates military affairs; disposes of all appointments, from colonels to ensigns, and of the governments and posts of fortified towns.

In his marine capacity he is admiral-general, and superintends and directs everything relative to naval forces and other naval affairs; presides in the admiralties in person or by proxy; appoints lieutenant-admirals and other officers; and establishes councils of war, whose sentences are not executed till he approves them.

His revenue, exclusive of his private income, amounts to three hundred thousand florins.

The standing army which he commands consists of about forty thousand men.

Such is the nature of the celebrated Belgic confederacy, as delineated on parchment. What are the characters which practice has stamped upon it? Imbecility in the government; discord among the provinces; foreign influence and indignities; a precarious existence in peace, and peculiar calamities from war.

It was long ago remarked by Grotius, that nothing but the hatred of his countrymen to the house of Austria kept them from being ruined by the vices of their constitution.

The union of Utrecht, says another respectable writer, reposes an authority in the States-General, seemingly sufficient to secure harmony, but the jealousy in each province renders the practice very different from the theory.

The same instrument, says another, obliges each province to levy certain contributions; but this article never could, and probably never will, be executed; because the inland provinces, who have little commerce, cannot pay an equal quota.

In matters of contribution, it is the practice to waive the articles of the constitution. The danger of delay obliges the consenting provinces to furnish their quota, without waiting for the others; and then to obtain reimbursement from the others, by deputations, which are frequent, or otherwise, as they can. The great wealth and influence of the province of Holland enable her to effect both these purposes.

It has more than once happened that the deficiencies had to be ultimately collected at the point of the bayonet; a thing practicable, though dreadful, in a confederacy where one of the members exceeds in force all the rest, and where several of them are too small to meditate resistance, but utterly impracticable in one composed of members, several of which are equal to each other in strength and resources, and equal singly to a vigorous and persevering defence.

Foreign ministers, says Sir William Temple, who was himself a foreign minister, elude matters taken *ad referendum,* by tampering with the provinces and cities. In 1726, the treaty of Hanover was delayed by these means a whole year. Instances of a like nature are numerous and notorious.

In critical emergencies, the States-General are often compelled to overleap their constitutional bounds. In 1688, they concluded a treaty of themselves at the risk of their heads. The treaty of Westphalia, in 1648, by which their independence was formally and finally recognised, was concluded without the consent of Zealand. Even as recently as the last treaty of peace with Great Britain, the constitutional principle of unanimity was departed from. A weak constitution must necessarily terminate in dissolution, for want of proper powers, or the usurpation of powers requisite for the public safety. Whether the usurpation, when once begun, will stop at the salutary point, or go forward to the dangerous extreme, must depend on the contingencies of the moment. Tyranny has perhaps oftener grown out of the assumptions of power, called for, on pressing exigencies, by a defective constitution, than out of the full exercise of the largest constitutional authorities.

Notwithstanding the calamities produced by the stadtholdership, it has been supposed that without his influence in the individual provinces, the causes of anarchy manifest in the confederacy would long ago have dissolved it. "Under such a government," says the Abbé Mably, "the Union could never have subsisted, if the provinces had not a spring within themselves, capable of quickening their tardiness, and compelling them to the same way of thinking. This spring is the stadtholder." It is remarked by Sir William Temple, "that in the intermissions of the stadtholdership, Holland, by her riches and her authority, which drew the others into a sort of dependence, supplied the place."

These are not the only circumstances which have controlled the tendency to anarchy and dissolution. The surrounding powers impose an absolute necessity of union to a certain degree, at the same time that they nourish by their intrigues the constitutional vices which keep the republic in some degree always at their mercy.

The true patriots have long bewailed the fatal tendency of these vices, and have made no less than four regular experiments by *extraordinary assemblies,* convened for the special purpose, to apply a remedy. As many times has their laudable zeal found it impossible to *unite the public councils* in reforming the known, the acknowledged, the fatal evils of the existing constitution. Let us pause, my fellow-citizens, for one moment, over this melancholy and monitory lesson of history; and with the tear that drops for the calamities brought on mankind by their adverse opinions and selfish passions, let our gratitude mingle an ejaculation to Heaven, for the propitious concord which has distinguished the consultations for our political happiness.

A design was also conceived of establishing a general tax to be administered by the federal authority. This also had its adversaries and failed.

This unhappy people seem to be now suffering from popular convulsions, from dissensions among the states, and from the actual invasion of foreign arms, the crisis of their destiny. All nations have their eyes fixed on the awful spectacle. The first wish prompted by humanity is, that this severe trial may issue in such a revolution of their government as will establish their union, and render it the parent of tranquillity, freedom, and happiness: The next, that the asylum under which, we trust, the enjoyment of these blessings will speedily be secured in this country, may receive and console them for the catastrophe of their own.

I make no apology for having dwelt so long on the contemplation of these federal precedents. Experience is the oracle of truth; and where its responses are unequivocal, they ought to be conclusive and sacred. The important truth, which it unequivocally pronounces in the present case, is that a sovereignty over sovereigns, a government over governments, a legislation for communities, as contradistinguished from individuals, as it is a solecism in theory, so in practice it is subversive of the order and ends of civil polity, by substituting *violence* in place of *law,* or the destructive *coercion* of the *sword* in place of the mild and salutary *coercion* of the *magistracy.*

PUBLIUS

Number 21

[HAMILTON]

HAVING IN the three last numbers taken a summary review of the principal circumstances and events which have depicted the genius and fate of other confederate governments, I shall now proceed in the enumeration of the most important of those defects which have hitherto disappointed our hopes from the system established among ourselves. To form a safe and satisfactory judgment of the proper remedy, it is absolutely necessary that we should be well acquainted with the extent and malignity of the disease.

The next most palpable defect of the sub-sisting Confederation is the total want of a SANCTION to its laws. The United States, as now composed, have no powers to exact obedience, or punish disobedience to their resolutions, either by pecuniary mulcts, by a suspension or divestiture of privileges, or by any other constitutional mode. There is no express delegation of authority to them to use force against delinquent members; and if such a right should be ascribed to the federal head, as resulting from the nature of the social compact between the States, it must be by inference and construction, in the face of that part of the second article, by which it is declared, "that each State shall retain every power, jurisdiction, and right, not *expressly* delegated to the United States in Congress assembled." There is, doubtless, a striking absurdity in supposing that a right of this kind does not exist, but we are reduced to the dilemma either of embracing that supposition, preposterous as it may seem, or of contravening or explaining away a provision, which has been of late a repeated theme of the eulogies of those who oppose the new Constitution; and the want of which, in that plan, has been the subject of much plausible animadversion and severe criticism. If we are unwilling to impair the force of this applauded provision, we shall be obliged to conclude, that the United States afford the extraordinary spectacle of a government destitute even of the shadow of constitutional power to enforce the execution of its own laws. It will appear, from the specimens which have been cited, that the American Confederacy, in this particular, stands discriminated from every other institution of a similar kind, and exhibits a new and unexampled phenomenon in the political world.

The want of a mutual guaranty of the State governments is another capital imperfection in the federal plan. There is nothing of this kind declared in the articles that compose it; and to imply a tacit guaranty from considerations of utility, would be a still more flagrant departure from the clause which has been mentioned, than to imply a tacit power of coercion from the like considerations. The want of a guaranty, though it might in its consequences endanger the Union, does not so immediately attack its existence as the want of a constitutional sanction to its laws.

Without a guaranty the assistance to be derived from the Union in repelling those domestic dangers which may sometimes threaten the existence of the State constitutions, must be renounced. Usurpation may rear its crest in each State, and trample upon the liberties of the people, while the national government could legally do nothing more than behold its encroachments with indignation and regret. A successful faction may erect a tyranny on the ruins of order and law, while no succour could constitutionally be afforded by the Union to the friends and supporters of the government. The tempestuous situation from which Massachusetts has scarcely emerged, evinces that dangers of this kind are not merely speculative. Who can determine what might have been the issue of her late convulsions, if the malcontents had been headed by a Cæsar or by a Cromwell? Who can predict what effect a despotism, established in Massachusetts, would have upon the liberties of New Hampshire or Rhode Island, of Connecticut or New York?

The inordinate pride of State importance has suggested to some minds an objection to the principle of a guaranty in the federal government, as involving an officious interference in the domestic concerns of the members. A scruple of this kind would deprive us of one of the principal advantages to be expected from union, and can only flow from a misapprehension of the nature of the provision itself. It could be no impediment to reforms of the State constitutions by a majority of the people in a legal and peaceable mode. This right would remain undiminished. The guaranty could only operate against changes to be effected by violence. Towards the preventions of calamities of this kind, too many checks cannot be provided. The peace of society and the stability of government depend absolutely on the efficacy of the precautions adopted on this head. Where the whole power of the government is in the hands of the people, there is the less pretence for the use of violent remedies in partial or occasional distempers of the State. The natural cure for an ill-administration, in a popular or representative constitution, is a change of men. A guaranty by the national authority would be as much levelled against the usurpations of rulers as against the ferments and outrages of faction and sedition in the community.

The principle of regulating the contributions of the States to the common treasury by QUOTAS is another fundamental error in the Confederation. Its repugnancy to an adequate supply of the national exigencies has been already pointed out, and has sufficiently appeared from the trial which has been made of it. I speak of it now solely with a view to equality among the States. Those who have been accustomed to contemplate the circumstances which produce and constitute national wealth, must be satisfied that there is no common standard or barometer by which the degrees of it can be ascertained. Neither the value of lands, nor the numbers of the people, which have been successively proposed as the rule of State contributions, has any pretension to being a just representative. If we compare the wealth of the United Netherlands with that of Russia or Germany, or even of France, and if we at the same time compare the total value of the lands and the aggregate population of that contracted district with the total value of the lands and the aggregate population of the immense regions of either of the three last-mentioned countries, we shall at once discover that there is no comparison between the proportion of either of these two objects and that of the relative wealth of those nations. If the like parallel were to be run between several of the American States, it would furnish a like result. Let Virginia be contrasted with North Carolina, Pennsylvania with Connecticut, or Maryland with New Jersey, and we shall be convinced that the respective abilities of those States, in relation to revenue, bear little or no analogy to their comparative stock in lands or to their comparative population. The position may be equally illustrated by a similar process between the counties of the same State. No man who is acquainted with the State of New York will doubt that the active wealth of King's County bears a much greater proportion to that of Montgomery than it would appear to be if we should take either the total value of the lands or the total number of the people as a criterion!

The wealth of nations depends upon an infinite variety of causes. Situation, soil, climate, the nature of the productions, the nature of the government, the genius of the citizens, the degree of information they possess, the state of commerce, of arts, of industry,—these circumstances and many more, too complex, minute, or adventitious to admit of a particular specification, occasion differences hardly conceivable in the relative opulence and riches of different countries. The consequence clearly is that there can be no common measure of national wealth, and, of course, no general or stationary rule by which the ability of a state to pay taxes can be determined. The attempt, therefore, to regulate the contributions of the members of a confederacy by any such rule, cannot fail to be productive of glaring inequality and extreme oppression.

This inequality would of itself be sufficient in America to work the eventual destruction of the Union, if any mode of enforcing a compliance with its requisitions could be devised. The suffering States would not long consent to remain associated upon a principle which distributes the public burdens with so unequal a hand, and which was calculated to impoverish and oppress the citizens of some States, while those of others would scarcely be conscious of the small proportion of the weight they were required to sustain. This, however, is an evil inseparable from the principle of quotas and requisitions.

There is no method of steering clear of this inconvenience, but by authorising the national government to raise its own revenues in its own way. Imposts, excises, and, in general, all duties upon articles of consumption, may be compared to a fluid, which will, in time, find its level with the means of paying them. The amount to be contributed by each citizen will in a degree be at his own option, and can be regulated by an attention to his resources. The rich may be extravagant, the poor can be frugal; and private oppression may always be avoided by a judicious selection of objects proper for such impositions. If inequalities should arise in some States from duties on particular objects, these will, in all probability, be counterbalanced by proportional inequalities in other States, from the duties on other objects. In the course of time and things, an equilibrium, as far as it is attainable in so complicated a subject, will be established everywhere. Or, if inequalities should still exist, they would neither be so great in their degree, so uniform in their operation, nor so odious in their appearance, as those which would necessarily spring from quotas, upon any scale that can possibly be devised.

It is a signal advantage of taxes on articles of consumption, that they contain in their own nature a security against excess. They prescribe their own limit; which cannot be exceeded without defeating the end proposed,— that is, an extension of the revenue. When applied to this object, the saying is as just as it is witty, that, "in political arithmetic, two and two do not always make four." If duties are too high, they lessen the consumption; the collection is eluded; and the product to the treasury is not so great as when they are confined within proper and moderate bounds. This forms a complete barrier against any material oppression of the citizens by taxes of this class, and is itself a natural limitation of the power of imposing them.

Impositions of this kind usually fall under the denomination of indirect taxes, and must for a long time constitute the chief part of the revenue raised in this country. Those of the direct kind, which principally relate to land and buildings, may admit of a rule of apportionment. Either the value of land, or the number of the people, may serve as a standard. The state of agriculture and the populousness of a country have been considered as nearly connected with each other. And, as a rule, for the purpose intended, numbers, in the view of simplicity and certainty, are entitled to a preference. In every country it is a herculean task to obtain a valuation of the land; in a country imperfectly settled and progressive in improvement, the difficulties are increased almost to impracticability. The expense of an accurate valuation is, in all situations, a formidable objection. In a branch of taxation where no limits to the discretion of the government are to be found in the nature of things, the establishment of a fixed rule, not incompatible with the end, may be attended with fewer inconveniences than to leave that discretion altogether at large.   PUBLIUS

Number 22

[HAMILTON]

IN ADDITION to the defects already enumerated in the existing federal system, there are others of not less importance, which concur in rendering it altogether unfit for the administration of the affairs of the Union.

The want of a power to regulate commerce is by all parties allowed to be of the number. The utility of such a power has been anticipated under the first head of our inquiries; and for this reason, as well as from the universal conviction entertained upon the subject, little need be added in this place. It is indeed evident, on the most superficial view, that there is no object, either as it respects the interests of trade or finance, that more strongly demands a federal superintendence. The want of it has already operated as a bar to the formation of beneficial treaties with foreign powers, and has given occasions of dissatisfaction between the States. No nation acquainted with the nature of our political association would be unwise enough to enter into stipulations with the United States, by which they conceded privileges of any importance to them, while they were apprised that the engagements on the part of the Union might at any moment be violated by its members, and while they found from experience that they might enjoy every advantage they desired in our markets, without granting us any return but such as their momentary convenience might suggest. It is not, therefore, to be wondered at that Mr. Jenkinson, in ushering into the House of Commons a bill for regulating the temporary intercourse between the two countries, should preface its introduction by a declaration that similar provisions in former bills had been found to answer every purpose to the commerce of Great Britain, and that it would be prudent to persist in the plan until it should appear whether the American government was likely or not to acquire greater consistency.[1]

Several States have endeavoured, by separate prohibitions, restrictions, and exclusions, to influence the conduct of that kingdom in this particular, but the want of concert, arising from the want of a general authority and from clashing and dissimilar views in the State, has hitherto frustrated every experiment of the kind, and will continue to do so as long as the same obstacles to a uniformity of measures continue to exist.

The interfering and unneighbourly regulations of some States, contrary to the true spirit of the Union, have, in different instances, given just cause of umbrage and complaint to others, and it is to be feared that examples of this nature, if not restrained by a national control, would be multiplied and extended till they became not less serious sources of animosity and discord than injurious impediments to the intercourse between the different parts of the Confederacy. "The commerce of the German empire[2] is in continual trammels from the multiplicity of the duties which the several princes and states exact upon the merchandises passing through their territories, by means of which the fine streams and navigable rivers with which Germany is so happily watered are rendered almost useless." Though the genius of the people of this country might never permit this description to be strictly applicable to us, yet we may reasonably expect, from the gradual conflicts of State regulations, that the

citizens of each would at length come to be considered and treated by the others in no better light than that of foreigners and aliens.

The power of raising armies, by the most obvious construction of the articles of the Confederation, is merely a power of making requisitions upon the States for quotas of men. This practice, in the course of the late war, was found replete with obstructions to a vigorous and to an economical system of defence. It gave birth to a competition between the States which created a kind of auction for men. In order to furnish the quotas required of them, they outbid each other till bounties grew to an enormous and insupportable size. The hope of a still further increase afforded an inducement to those who were disposed to serve to procrastinate their enlistment, and disinclined them from engaging for any considerable periods. Hence, slow and scanty levies of men, in the most critical emergencies of our affairs; short enlistments at an unparalleled expense; continual fluctuations in the troops, ruinous to their discipline and subjecting the public safety frequently to the perilous crisis of a disbanded army. Hence, also, those oppressive expedients for raising men which were upon several occasions practised, and which nothing but the enthusiasm of liberty would have induced the people to endure.

This method of raising troops is not more unfriendly to economy and vigour than it is to an equal distribution of the burden. The States near the seat of war, influenced by motives of self-preservation, made efforts to furnish their quotas, which even exceeded their abilities; while those at a distance from danger were, for the most part, as remiss as the others were diligent, in their exertions. The immediate pressure of this inequality was not in this case, as in that of the contributions of money, alleviated by the hope of a final liquidation. The States which did not pay their proportions of money might at least be charged with their deficiencies; but no account could be formed of the deficiencies in the supplies of men. We shall not, however, see much reason to regret the want of this hope, when we consider how little prospect there is, that the most delinquent States will ever be able to make compensation for their pecuniary failures. The system of quotas and requisitions, whether it be applied to men or money, is, in every view, a system of imbecility in the Union, and of inequality and injustice among the members.

---

[1] This, as nearly as I can recollect, was the sense of his speech on introducing the last bill.—PUBLIUS

[2] Encyclopaedia, article "Empire."—PUBLIUS

The right of equal suffrage among the States is another exceptionable part of the Confederation. Every idea of proportion and every rule of fair representation conspire to condemn a principle, which gives to Rhode Island an equal weight in the scale of power with Massachusetts, or Connecticut, or New York; and to Delaware an equal voice in the national deliberations with Pennsylvania, or Virginia, or North Carolina. Its operation contradicts the fundamental maxim of republican government, which requires that the sense of the majority should prevail. Sophistry may reply, that sovereigns are equal, and that a majority of the votes of the States will be a majority of confederated America. But this kind of logical legerdemain will never counteract the plain suggestions of justice and commonsense. It may happen that this majority of States is a small minority of the people of America;[1] and two thirds of the people of America could not long be persuaded, upon the credit of artificial distinctions and syllogistic subtleties, to submit their interests to the management and disposal of one third. The larger States would after a while revolt from the idea of receiving the law from the smaller. To acquiesce in such a privation of their due importance in the political scale, would be not merely to be insensible to the love of power, but even to sacrifice the desire of equality. It is neither rational to expect the first, nor just to require the last. The smaller States, considering how peculiarly their safety and welfare depend on union, ought readily to renounce a pretension which, if not relinquished, would prove fatal to its duration.

It may be objected to this, that not seven but nine States, or two-thirds of the whole number, must consent to the most important resolutions; and it may be thence inferred, that nine States would always comprehend a majority of the Union. But this does not obviate the impropriety of an equal vote between States of the most unequal dimensions and populousness; nor is the inference accurate in point of fact; for we can enumerate nine States which contain less than a majority of the people;[2] and it is constitutionally possi-

ble that these nine may give the vote. Besides, there are matters of considerable moment determinable by a bare majority; and there are others, concerning which doubts have been entertained, which, if interpreted in favour of the sufficiency of a vote of seven States, would extend its operation to interests of the first magnitude. In addition to this, it is to be observed that there is a probability of an increase in the number of States, and no provision for a proportional augmentation of the ratio of votes.

But this is not all: what at first sight may seem a remedy, is, in reality, a poison. To give a minority a negative upon the majority (which is always the case where more than a majority is requisite to a decision), is, in its tendency, to subject the sense of the greater number to that of the lesser. Congress, from the non-attendance of a few States, have been frequently in the situation of a Polish diet, where a single VOTE has been sufficient to put a stop to all their movements. A sixtieth part of the Union, which is about the proportion of Delaware and Rhode Island, has several times been able to oppose an entire bar to its operations. This is one of those refinements which, in practice, has an effect the reverse of what is expected from it in theory. The necessity of unanimity in public bodies, or of something approaching towards it, has been founded upon a supposition that it would contribute to security. But its real operation is to embarrass the administration, to destroy the energy of the government, and to substitute the pleasure, caprice, or artifices of an insignificant, turbulent, or corrupt junto, to the regular deliberations and decisions of a respectable majority. In those emergencies of a nation, in which the goodness or badness, the weakness or strength of its government, is of the greatest importance, there is commonly a necessity for action. The public business must, in some way or other, go forward. If a pertinacious minority can control the opinion of a majority respecting the best mode of conducting it, the majority, in order that something may be done, must conform to the views of the minority; and thus the sense of the smaller number will overrule that of the greater, and give a tone to the national proceedings. Hence, tedious delays; continual negotiation and intrigue; contemptible compromises of the public good. And yet, in such a system, it is even happy when such compromises can take place: for upon some occasions things will not admit

[1] New Hampshire, Rhode Island, New Jersey, Delaware, Georgia, South Carolina, and Maryland are a majority of the whole number of the States, but they do not contain one third of the people.— PUBLIUS

[2] Add New York and Connecticut to the foregoing seven, and they will be less than a majority. —PUBLIUS

of accommodation; and then the measures of government must be injuriously suspended, or fatally defeated. It is often, by the impracticability of obtaining the concurrence of the necessary number of votes, kept in a state of inaction. Its situation must always savour of weakness, sometimes border upon anarchy.

It is not difficult to discover, that a principle of this kind gives greater scope to foreign corruption, as well as to domestic faction, than that which permits the sense of the majority to decide; though the contrary of this has been presumed. The mistake has proceeded from not attending with due care to the mischiefs that may be occasioned by obstructing the progress of government at certain critical seasons. When the concurrence of a large number is required by the Constitution to the doing of any national act, we are apt to rest satisfied that all is safe, because nothing improper will be likely *to be done;* but we forget how much good may be prevented, and how much ill may be produced, by the power of hindering the doing what may be necessary, and of keeping affairs in the same unfavourable posture in which they may happen to stand at particular periods.

Suppose, for instance, we were engaged in a war, in conjunction with one foreign nation, against another. Suppose the necessity of our situation demanded peace, and the interest or ambition of our ally led him to seek the prosecution of the war, with views that might justify us in making separate terms. In such a state of things, this ally of ours would evidently find it much easier, by his bribes and intrigues, to tie up the hands of government from making peace, where two-thirds of all the votes were requisite to that object, than where a simple majority would suffice. In the first case, he would have to corrupt a smaller number; in the last, a greater number. Upon the same principle, it would be much easier for a foreign power with which we were at war to perplex our councils, and embarrass our exertions. And, in a commercial view, we may be subjected to similar inconveniences. A nation, with which we might have a treaty of commerce, could with much greater facility prevent our forming a connection with her competitor in trade, though such a connection should be ever so beneficial to ourselves.

Evils of this description ought not to be regarded as imaginary. One of the weak sides of republics, among their numerous advantages, is that they afford too easy an inlet to foreign corruption. An hereditary monarch, though often disposed to sacrifice his subjects to his ambition, has so great a personal interest in the government and in the external glory of the nation, that it is not easy for a foreign power to give him an equivalent for what he would sacrifice by treachery to the state. The world has accordingly been witness to few examples of this species of royal prostitution, though there have been abundant specimens of every other kind.

In republics, persons elevated from the mass of the community, by the suffrages of their fellow-citizens, to stations of great pre-eminence and power, may find compensations for betraying their trust, which, to any but minds animated and guided by superior virtue, may appear to exceed the proportion of interest they have in the common stock, and to overbalance the obligations of duty. Hence it is that history furnishes us with so many mortifying examples of the prevalency of foreign corruption in republican governments. How much this contributed to the ruin of the ancient commonwealths has been already delineated. It is well known that the deputies of the United Provinces have, in various instances, been purchased by the emissaries of the neighbouring kingdoms. The Earl of Chesterfield (if my memory serves me right), in a letter to his court, intimates that his success in an important negotiation must depend on his obtaining a major's commission for one of those deputies. And in Sweden the parties were alternately bought by France and England in so barefaced and notorious a manner that it excited universal disgust in the nation, and was a principal cause that the most limited monarch in Europe, in a single day, without tumult, violence, or opposition, became one of the most absolute and uncontrolled.

A circumstance which crowns the defects of the Confederation remains yet to be mentioned—the want of a judiciary power. Laws are a dead letter without courts to expound and define their true meaning and operation. The treaties of the United States, to have any force at all, must be considered as part of the law of the land. Their true import, as far as respects individuals, must, like all other laws, be ascertained by judicial determinations. To produce uniformity in these determinations, they ought to be submitted, in the last resort, to one SUPREME TRIBUNAL. And this tribunal ought to be instituted under the same authority which forms the treaties themselves. These ingredients are both indispensable. If there is in each State a court of final jurisdiction, there there may be as many different final determinations on the same point as there are courts. There are endless diversities in the opinions of men. We often see not only different courts but the judges of the same court differing from each other. To avoid the confusion which would unavoidably result from the contradictory decisions of a number of independent judicatories, all nations have found it necessary to establish one court paramount to the rest, possessing a general superintendence, and authorised to settle and declare in the last resort a uniform rule of civil justice.

This is the more necessary where the frame of the government is so compounded that the laws of the whole are in danger of being contravened by the laws of the parts. In this case, if the particular tribunals are invested with a right of ultimate jurisdiction, besides the contradictions to be expected from difference of opinion, there will be much to fear from the bias of local views and prejudices, and from the interference of local regulations. As often as such an interference was to happen, there would be reason to apprehend that the provisions of the particular laws might be preferred to those of the general laws; for nothing is more natural to men in office than to look with peculiar deference towards that authority to which they owe their official existence. The treaties of the United States, under the present Constitution, are liable to the infractions of thirteen different legislatures, and as many different courts of final jurisdiction, acting under the authority of those legislatures. The faith, the reputation, the peace of the whole Union, are thus continually at the mercy of the prejudices, the passions, and the interests of every member of which it is composed. Is it possible that foreign nations can either respect or confide in such a government? Is it possible that the people of America will longer consent to trust their honour, their happiness, their safety, on so precarious a foundation?

In this review of the Confederation, I have confined myself to the exhibition of its most material defects; passing over those imperfections in its details by which even a great part of the power intended to be conferred upon it has been in a great measure rendered abortive. It must be by this time evident to all men of reflection, who can divest themselves of the prepossessions of preconceived opinions that it is a system so radically vicious and unsound,

as to admit not of amendment but by an entire change in its leading features and characters.

The organisation of Congress is itself utterly improper for the exercise of those powers which are necessary to be deposited in the Union. A single assembly may be a proper receptacle of those slender, or rather fettered, authorities, which have been heretofore delegated to the federal head; but it would be inconsistent with all the principles of good government, to intrust it with those additional powers which, even the moderate and more rational adversaries of the proposed Constitution admit, ought to reside in the United States. If that plan should not be adopted, and if the necessity of the Union should be able to withstand the ambitious aims of those men who may indulge magnificent schemes of personal aggrandisement from its dissolution, the probability would be, that we should run into the project of conferring supplementary powers upon Congress, as they are now constituted; and either the machine, from the intrinsic feebleness of its structure, will moulder into pieces, in spite of our ill-judged efforts to prop it; or, by successive augmentations of its force and energy, as necessity might prompt, we shall finally accumulate, in a single body, all the most important prerogatives of sovereignty, and thus entail upon our posterity one of the most execrable forms of government that human infatuation ever contrived. Thus we should create in reality that very tyranny which the adversaries of the new Constitution either are, or effect to be, solicitous to avert.

It has not a little contributed to the infirmities of the existing federal system, that it never had a ratification by the PEOPLE. Resting on no better foundation than the consent of the several legislatures, it has been exposed to frequent and intricate questions concerning the validity of its powers, and has, in some instances, given birth to the enormous doctrine of a right of legislative repeal. Owing its ratification to the law of a State, it has been contended that the same authority might repeal the law by which it was ratified. However gross a heresy it may be to maintain that a *party* to a *compact* has a right to revoke that *compact,* the doctrine itself has had respectable advocates. The possibility of a question of this nature proves the necessity of laying the foundations of our national government deeper than in the mere sanction of delegated authority. The fabric of American empire ought to rest on the solid basis of THE CONSENT OF THE

PEOPLE. The streams of national power ought to flow immediately from that pure, original fountain of all legitimate authority.

PUBLIUS

Number 23

[HAMILTON]

THE NECESSITY of a Constitution, at least equally energetic with the one proposed, to the preservation of the Union, is the point at the examination of which we are now arrived.

This inquiry will naturally divide itself into three branches—the objects to be provided for by the federal government, the quantity of power necessary to the accomplishment of those objects, the persons upon whom that power ought to operate. Its distribution and organisation will more properly claim our attention under the succeeding head.

The principal purposes to be answered by union are these—the common defence of the members; the preservation of the public peace, as well against internal convulsions as external attacks; the regulation of commerce with other nations and between the States; the superintendence of our intercourse, political and commercial, with foreign countries.

The authorities essential to the common defence are these: to raise armies; to build and equip fleets; to prescribe rules for the government of both; to direct their operations; to provide for their support. These powers ought to exist without limitation, *because it is impossible to foresee or define the extent and variety of national exigencies, or the correspondent extent and variety of the means which may be necessary to satisfy them.* The circumstances that endanger the safety of nations are infinite, and for this reason no constitutional shackles can wisely be imposed on the power to which the care of it is committed. This power ought to be co-extensive with all the possible combinations of such circumstances; and ought to be under the direction of the same councils which are appointed to preside over the common defence.

This is one of those truths which, to a correct and unprejudiced mind, carries its own evidence along with it; and may be obscured, but cannot be made plainer by argument or reasoning. It rests upon axioms as simple as they are universal; the *means* ought to be proportioned to the *end;* the persons, from whose agency the attainment of any *end* is expected, ought to possess the *means* by which it is to be attained.

Whether there ought to be a federal government intrusted with the care of the common defence, is a question in the first instance open for discussion; but the moment it is decided in the affirmative, it will follow, that that government ought to be clothed with all the powers requisite to complete execution of its trust. And unless it can be shown that the circumstances which may affect the public safety are reducible within certain determinate limits; unless the contrary of this position can be fairly and rationally disputed, it must be admitted, as a necessary consequence, that there can be no limitation of that authority which is to provide for the defence and protection of the community, in any matter essential to its efficacy—that is, in any matter essential to the *formation, direction,* or *support* of the NATIONAL FORCES.

Defective as the present Confederation has been proved to be, this principle appears to have been fully recognised by the framers of it; though they have not made proper or adequate provision for its exercise. Congress have an unlimited discretion to make requisitions of men and money; to govern the army and navy; to direct their operations. As their requisitions are made constitutionally binding upon the States, who are in fact under the most solemn obligation to furnish the supplies required of them, the intention evidently was, that the United States should command whatever resources were by them judged requisite to the "common defence and general welfare." It was presumed that a sense of their true interests, and a regard to the dictates of good faith, would be found sufficient pledges for the punctual performance of the duty of the members to the federal head.

The experiment has, however, demonstrated that this expectation was ill-founded and illusory; and the observations, made under the last head, will, I imagine, have sufficed to convince the impartial and discerning, that there is an absolute necessity for an entire change in the first principles of the system; that if we are in earnest about giving the Union energy and duration, we must abandon the vain project of legislating upon the States in their collective capacities; we must extend the laws of the federal government to the individual citizens of America; we must discard the fallacious scheme of quotas and requisitions, as equally impracticable and unjust. The result from all this is that the Union ought to be invested with full power to levy troops; to build and equip fleets; and to raise the revenues which will be required for the formation and support of an army and navy, in the customary and ordinary modes practised in other governments.

If the circumstances of our country are such as to demand a compound instead of a simple, a confederate instead of a sole, government, the essential point which will remain to be adjusted will be to discriminate the OBJECTS, as far as it can be done, which shall appertain to the different provinces or departments of power; allowing to each the most ample authority for fulfilling the objects committed to its charge. Shall the Union be constituted the guardian of the common safety? Are fleets and armies and revenues necessary to this purpose? The government of the Union must be empowered to pass all laws, and to make all regulations which have relation to them. The same must be the case in respect to commerce, and to every other matter to which its jurisdiction is permitted to extend. Is the administration of justice between the citizens of the same State the proper department of the local governments? These must possess all the authorities which are connected with this object, and with every other that may be allotted to their particular cognisance and direction. Not to confer in each case a degree of power commensurate to the end, would be to violate the most obvious rules of prudence and propriety, and improvidently to trust the great interests of the nation to hands which are disabled from managing them with vigour and success.

Who so likely to make suitable provisions for the public defence as that body to which the guardianship of the public safety is confided; which, as the centre of information, will best understand the extent and urgency of the dangers that threaten; as the representative of the WHOLE, will feel itself most deeply interested in the preservation of every part; which, from the responsibility implied in the duty assigned to it, will be most sensibly impressed with the necessity of proper exertions; and which, by the extension of its authority throughout the States, can alone establish uniformity and concert in the plans and measures by which the common safety is to be secured? Is there not a manifest inconsistency in devolving upon the federal government the care of the general defence, and leaving in the State governments the *effective* powers by which it is to be provided for? Is not a want of co-operation the infallible consequence of such a system? And will not weakness, disorder, an undue distribution of the burdens and calamities of war, an unnecessary and intolerable increase of expense, be its natural and inevitable concomitants? Have we not had unequivocal experience of its effects in the course of the revolution which we have just accomplished?

Every view we may take of the subject, as candid inquirers after truth, will serve to convince us, that it is both unwise and dangerous to deny the federal government an unconfined authority, as to all those objects which are intrusted to its management. It will indeed deserve the most vigilant and careful attention of the people, to see that it be modelled in such a manner as to admit of its being safely vested with the requisite powers. If any plan which has been, or may be, offered to our consideration, should not, upon a dispassionate inspection, be found to answer this description, it ought to be rejected. A government, the constitution of which renders it unfit to be trusted with all the powers which a free people *ought to delegate to any government,* would be an unsafe and improper depositary of the NATIONAL INTERESTS. Wherever THESE can with propriety be confided, the coincident powers may safely accompany them. This is the true result of all just reasoning upon the subject. And the adversaries of the plan promulgated by the convention ought to have confined themselves to showing that the internal structure of the proposed government was such as to render it unworthy of the confidence of the people. They ought not to have wandered into inflammatory declamations and unmeaning cavils about the extent of the powers. The POWERS are not too extensive for the OBJECTS of federal administration, or, in other words, for the management of our NATIONAL INTERESTS; nor can any satisfactory argument be framed to show that they are chargeable with such an excess. If it be true, as has been insinuated by some of the writers on the other side, that the difficulty arises from the nature of the thing, and that the extent of the country will not permit us to form a government in which such ample powers can safely be reposed, it would prove that we ought to contract our views, and resort to the expedient of separate confederacies, which will move within more practicable spheres. For the absurdity must continually stare us in the face of confiding to a government the direction of the most essential national interests, without daring to trust it to the authorities which are indispensable to their proper and efficient management. Let us not attempt to reconcile contradictions, but firmly embrace a rational alternative.

I trust, however, that the impracticability of one general system cannot be shown. I am greatly mistaken, if anything of weight has yet been advanced of this tendency; and I flatter myself that the observations which have been made in the course of these papers have served to place the reverse of that position in as clear a light as any matter still in the womb of time and experience can be susceptible of. This, at all events, must be evident, that the very difficulty itself, drawn from the extent of the country, is the strongest argument in favour of an energetic government; for any other can certainly never preserve the Union of so large an empire. If we embrace the tenets of those who oppose the adoption of the proposed Constitution, as the standard of our political creed, we cannot fail to verify the gloomy doctrines which predict the impracticability of a national system pervading entire limits of the present Confederacy.   PUBLIUS

Number 24

[HAMILTON]

To THE powers proposed to be conferred upon the federal government, in respect to the creation and direction of the national forces, I have met with but one specific objection, which, if I understand it right, is this—that proper provision has not been made against the existence of standing armies in time of peace; an objection which, I shall now endeavour to show, rests on weak and unsubstantial foundations.

It has indeed been brought forward in the most vague and general form, supported only by bold assertions, without the appearance of argument; without even the sanction of theoretical opinions; in contradiction to the practice of other free nations, and to the general sense of America, as expressed in most of the existing constitutions. The propriety of this remark will appear the moment it is recollected that the objection under consideration turns upon a supposed necessity of restraining the LEGISLATIVE authority of the nation, in the article of military establishments; a principle unheard of, except in one or two of our State constitutions, and rejected in all the rest.

A stranger to our politics, who was to read

our newspapers at the present juncture, without having previously inspected the plan reported by the convention, would be naturally led to one of two conclusions: either that it contained a positive injunction, that standing armies should be kept up in time of peace; or that it vested in the EXECUTIVE the whole power of levying troops, without subjecting his discretion, in any shape, to the control of the legislature.

If he came afterwards to peruse the plan itself, he would be surprised to discover that neither the one nor the other was the case; that the whole power of raising armies was lodged in the *Legislature,* not in the *Executive;* that this legislature was to be a popular body, consisting of the representatives of the people periodically elected; and that instead of the provision he had supposed in favour of standing armies, there was to be found, in respect to this object, an important qualification even of the legislative discretion, in that clause which forbids the appropriation of money for the support of an army for any longer period than two years—a precaution which, upon a nearer view of it, will appear to be a great and real security against the keeping up of troops without evident necessity.

Disappointed in his first surmise, the person I have supposed would be apt to pursue his conjectures a little further. He would naturally say to himself, it is impossible that all this vehement and pathetic declamation can be without some colourable pretext. It must needs be that this people, so jealous of their liberties, have, in all the preceding models of the constitutions which they have established, inserted the most precise and rigid precautions on this point, the omission of which, in the new plan, has given birth to all this apprehension and clamour.

If, under this impression, he proceeded to pass in review the several State constitutions, how great would be his disappointment to find that *two only* of them[1] contained an interdic-

---

[1] This statement of the matter is taken from the printed collection of State constitutions. Pennsylvania and North Carolina are the two which contain the interdiction in these words: "As standing armies in time of peace are dangerous to liberty, THEY OUGHT NOT to be kept up." This is, in truth, rather a CAUTION than a PROHIBITION. New Hampshire, Massachusetts, Delaware, and Maryland have, in each of their bills of rights, a clause to this effect: "Standing armies are dangerous to liberty, and ought not to be raised or kept up WITHOUT THE CONSENT OF THE LEGISLATURE"; which is a formal admission of the authority of the Legisla-

tion of standing armies in time of peace; that the other eleven had either observed a profound silence on the subject, or had in express terms admitted the right of the legislature to authorise their existence.

Still, however, he would be persuaded that there must be some plausible foundation for the cry raised on this head. He would never be able to imagine, while any source of information remained unexplored, that it was nothing more than an experiment upon the public credulity, dictated either by a deliberate intention to deceive, or by the overflowings of a zeal too intemperate to be ingenuous. It would probably occur to him, that he would be likely to find the precautions he was in search of in the primitive compact between the States. Here, at length, he would expect to meet with a solution of the enigma. No doubt, he would observe to himself, the existing Confederation must contain the most explicit provisions against military establishments in time of peace; and a departure from this model, in a favourite point, has occasioned the discontent which appears to influence these political champions.

If he should now apply himself to a careful and critical survey of the articles of Confederation, his astonishment would not only be increased, but would acquire a mixture of indignation, at the unexpected discovery that these articles, instead of containing the prohibition he looked for, and though they had, with jealous circumspection, restricted the authority of the State legislatures in this particular, had not imposed a single restraint on that of the United States. If he happened to be a man of quick sensibility, or ardent temper, he could now no longer refrain from regarding these clamours as the dishonest artifices of a sinister and unprincipled opposition to a plan which ought at least to receive a fair and candid examination from all sincere lovers of their country! How else, he would say, could the authors of them have been tempted to vent such loud censures upon that plan, about a point in which it seems to have conformed itself to the general sense of America as declared

in its different forms of government, and in which it has even superadded a new and powerful guard unknown to any of them? If, on the contrary, he happened to be a man of calm and dispassionate feelings, he would indulge a sigh for the frailty of human nature, and would lament that in a matter so interesting to the happiness of millions, the true merits of the question should be perplexed and entangled by expedients so unfriendly to an impartial and right determination. Even such a man could hardly forbear remarking, that a conduct of this kind has too much the appearance of an intention to mislead the people by alarming their passions, rather than to convince them by arguments addressed to their understandings.

But however little this objection may be countenanced, even by precedents among ourselves, it may be satisfactory to take a nearer view of its intrinsic merits. From a close examination it will appear that restraints upon the discretion of the legislature in respect to military establishments in time of peace, would be improper to be imposed, and if imposed, from the necessities of society, would be unlikely to be observed.

Though a wide ocean separates the United States from Europe, yet there are various considerations that warn us against an excess of confidence or security. On one side of us, and stretching far into our rear, are growing settlements subject to the dominion of Britain. On the other side, and extending to meet the British settlements, are colonies and establishments subject to the dominion of Spain. This situation, and the vicinity of the West India Islands, belonging to these two powers, create between them, in respect to their American possessions and in relation to us, a common interest. The savage tribes on our Western frontier ought to be regarded as our natural enemies, their natural allies, because they have most to fear from us, and most to hope from them. The improvements in the art of navigation have, as to the facility of communication, rendered distant nations, in a great measure, neighbours. Britain and Spain are among the principal maritime powers of Europe. A future concert of views between these nations ought not to be regarded as improbable. The increasing remoteness of consanguinity is every day diminishing the force of the family compact between France and Spain. And politicians have ever with great reason considered the ties of blood as feeble and precarious links of

---

ture. New York has no bills of rights, and her constitution says not a word about the matter. No bills of rights appear annexed to the constitutions of the other States, except the foregoing, and their constitutions are equally silent. I am told, however, that one or two States have bills of rights which do not appear in this collection; but that those also recognise the right of the legislative authority in this respect.—PUBLIUS

political connection. These circumstances combined, admonish us not to be too sanguine in considering ourselves as entirely out of the reach of danger.

Previous to the Revolution, and ever since the peace, there has been a constant necessity for keeping small garrisons on our Western frontier. No person can doubt that these will continue to be indispensable, if it should only be against the ravages and depredations of the Indians. These garrisons must either be furnished by occasional detachments from the militia, or by permanent corps in the pay of the government. The first is impracticable; and if practicable, would be pernicious. The militia would not long, if at all, submit to be dragged from their occupations and families to perform that most disagreeable duty in times of profound peace. And if they could be prevailed upon or compelled to do it, the increased expense of a frequent rotation of service, and the loss of labour and disconcertion of the industrious pursuits of individuals, would form conclusive objections to the scheme. It would be as burdensome and injurious to the public as ruinous to private citizens. The latter resource of permanent corps in the pay of the government amounts to a standing army in time of peace; a small one, indeed, but not the less real for being small. Here is a simple view of the subject that shows us at once the impropriety of a constitutional interdiction of such establishments, and the necessity of leaving the matter to the discretion and prudence of the legislature.

In proportion to our increase in strength, it is probable, nay, it may be said certain, that Britain and Spain would augment their military establishments in our neighbourhood. If we should not be willing to be exposed, in a naked and defenceless condition, to their insults and encroachments, we should find it expedient to increase our frontier garrison in some ratio to the force by which our Western settlements might be annoyed. There are, and will be, particular posts, the possession of which will include the command of large districts of territory, and facilitate future invasions of the remainder. It may be added that some of those posts will be keys to the trade with the Indian nations. Can any man think it would be wise to leave such posts in a situation to be at any instant seized by one or the other of two neighbouring and formidable powers? To act this part would be to desert all the usual maxims of prudence and policy.

If we mean to be a commercial people, or even to be secure on our Atlantic side, we must endeavour, as soon as possible, to have a navy. To this purpose there must be dockyards and arsenals; and for the defence of these, fortifications, and probably garrisons. When a nation has become so powerful by sea that it can protect its dockyards by its fleets, this supersedes the necessity of garrisons for that purpose; but where naval establishments are in their infancy, moderate garrisons will, in all likelihood, be found an indispensable security against descents for the destruction of the arsenals and dockyards, and sometimes of the fleet itself.   PUBLIUS

Number 25

[HAMILTON]

IT MAY perhaps be urged that the objects enumerated in the preceding number ought to be provided for by the State governments, under the direction of the Union. But this would be, in reality, an inversion of the primary principle of our political association, as it would in practice transfer the care of the common defence from the federal head to the individual members: a project oppressive to some States, dangerous to all, and baneful to the Confederacy.

The territories of Britain, Spain, and of the Indian nations in our neighbourhood do not border on particular States, but encircle the Union from Maine to Georgia. The danger, though in different degrees, is therefore common. And the means of guarding against it ought, in like manner, to be the objects of common councils and of a common treasury. It happens that some States, from local situation, are more directly exposed. New York is of this class. Upon the plan of separate provisions, New York would have to sustain the whole weight of the establishments requisite to her immediate safety, and to the mediate or ultimate protection of her neighbours. This would neither be equitable as it respected New York nor safe as it respected the other States. Various inconveniences would attend such a system. The States, to whose lot it might fall to support the necessary establishments, would be as little able as willing, for a considerable time to come, to bear the burden of competent provisions. The security of all would thus be subjected to the parsimony, improvidence, or inability of a part. If the resources of such part becoming more abundant and extensive, its provisions should be proportionally enlarged, the other States would quickly take the alarm at seeing the whole military force of the Union in the hands of two or three of its members, and those probably amongst the most powerful. They would each choose to have some counterpoise, and pretences could easily be contrived. In this situation, military establishments, nourished by mutual jealousy, would be apt to swell beyond their natural or proper size; and being at the separate disposal of the members, they would be engines for the abridgment or demolition of the national authority.

Reasons have been already given to induce a supposition that the State governments will too naturally be prone to a rivalship with that of the Union, the foundation of which will be the love of power; and that in any contest between the federal head and one of its members the people will be most apt to unite with their local government. If, in addition to this immense advantage, the ambition of the members should be stimulated by the separate and independent possession of military forces, it would afford too strong a temptation and too great a facility to them to make enterprises upon, and finally to subvert, the constitutional authority of the Union. On the other hand, the liberty of the people would be less safe in this state of things than in that which left the national forces in the hands of the national government. As far as an army may be considered as a dangerous weapon of power, it had better be in those hands of which the people are most likely to be jealous than in those of which they are least likely to be jealous. For it is a truth, which the experience of ages has attested, that the people are always most in danger when the means of injuring their rights are in the possession of those of whom they entertain the least suspicion.

The framers of the existing Confederation, fully aware of the danger to the Union from the separate possession of military forces by the States, have, in express terms, prohibited them from having either ships or troops, unless with the consent of Congress. The truth is, that the existence of a federal government and military establishments under State authority are not less at variance with each other than a due supply of the federal treasury and the system of quotas and requisitions.

There are other lights besides those already taken notice of, in which the impropriety of restraints on the discretion of the national legislature will be equally manifest. The design of the objection, which has been mentioned, is to preclude standing armies in time of peace, though we have never been informed how far it is designed the prohibition should extend: whether to raising armies as well as to *keeping them up* in a season of tranquillity or not. If it be confined to the latter it will have no precise signification, and it will be ineffectual for the purpose intended. When armies are once raised what shall be denominated "keeping them up," contrary to the sense of the Constitution? What time shall be requisite to ascertain the violation? Shall it be a week, a month, a year? Or shall we say they may be continued as long as the danger which occasioned their being raised continues? This would be to admit that they might be kept up *in time of peace,* against threatening or impending danger, which would be at once to deviate from the literal meaning of the prohibition, and to introduce an extensive latitude of construction. Who shall judge of the continuance of the danger? This must undoubtedly be submitted to the national government, and the matter would then be brought to this issue, that the national government, to provide against apprehended danger, might in the first instance raise troops, and might afterwards keep them on foot as long as they supposed the peace or safety of the community was in any degree of jeopardy. It is easy to perceive that a discretion so latitudinary as this would afford ample room for eluding the force of the provision.

The supposed utility of a provision of this kind can only be founded on the supposed probability, or at least possibility, of a combination between the executive and the legislative, in some scheme of usurpation. Should this at any time happen, how easy would it be to fabricate pretences of approaching danger! Indian hostilities, instigated by Spain or Britain, would always be at hand. Provocations to produce the desired appearances might even be given to some foreign power, and appeased again by timely concessions. If we can reasonably presume such a combination to have been formed, and that the enterprise is warranted by a sufficient prospect of success, the army, when once raised, from whatever cause, or on whatever pretext, may be applied to the execution of the project.

If, to obviate this consequence, it should be resolved to extend the prohibition to the *raising* of armies in time of peace, the United States would then exhibit the most extraordinary spectacle which the world has yet seen— that of a nation incapacitated by its Constitution to prepare for defence, before it was actually invaded. As the ceremony of a formal denunciation of war has of late fallen into disuse, the presence of an enemy within our territories must be waited for, as the legal warrant to the government to begin its levies of men for the protection of the State. We must receive the blow, before we could even prepare to return it. All that kind of policy by which nations anticipate distant danger, and meet the gathering storm, must be abstained from, as contrary to the genuine maxims of a free government. We must expose our property and liberty to the mercy of foreign invaders, and invite them by our weakness to seize the naked and defenceless prey, because we are afraid that rulers, created by our choice, dependent on our will, might endanger that liberty, by an abuse of the means necessary to its preservation.

Here I expect we shall be told that the militia of the country is its natural bulwark, and would be at all times equal to the national defence. This doctrine, in substance, had like to have lost us our independence. It costs millions to the United States that might have been saved. The facts which, from our own experience, forbid a reliance of this kind, are too recent to permit us to be the dupes of such a suggestion. The steady operations of war against a regular and disciplined army can only be successfully conducted by a force of the same kind. Considerations of economy, not less than of stability and vigour, confirm this position. The American militia, in the course of the late war, have, by their valour on numerous occasions, erected eternal monuments to their fame; but the bravest of them feel and know that the liberty of their country could not have been established by their efforts alone, however great and valuable they were. War, like most other things, is a science to be acquired and perfected by diligence, by perseverance, by time, and by practice.

All violent policy, as it is contrary to the natural and experienced course of human affairs, defeats itself. Pennsylvania, at this instant, affords an example of the truth of this remark. The Bill of Rights of that State declares that standing armies are dangerous to liberty, and ought not to be kept up in time of peace. Pennsylvania, nevertheless, in a time of profound peace, from the existence of partial disorders in one or two of her counties, has resolved to raise a body of troops; and in all probability will keep them up as long as there is any appearance of danger to the public peace. The conduct of Massachusetts affords a lesson on the same subject, though on different ground. That State (without waiting for the sanction of Congress, as the articles of the Confederation require) was compelled to raise troops to quell a domestic insurrection, and still keeps a corps in pay to prevent a revival of the spirit of revolt. The particular constitution of Massachusetts opposed no obstacle to the measure; but the instance is still of use to instruct us that cases are likely to occur under our government, as well as under those of other nations, which will sometimes render a military force in time of peace essential to the security of the society, and that it is therefore improper in this respect to control the legislative discretion. It also teaches us, in its application to the United States, how little the rights of a feeble government are likely to be respected, even by its own constituents. And it teaches us, in addition to the rest, how unequal parchment provisions are to a struggle with public necessity.

It was a fundamental maxim of the Lacedæmonian commonwealth, that the post of admiral should not be conferred twice on the same person. The Peloponnesian confederates, having suffered a severe defeat at sea from the Athenians, demanded Lysander, who had before served with success in that capacity, to command the combined fleets. The Lacedæmonians, to gratify their allies, and yet preserve the semblance of an adherence to their ancient institutions, had recourse to the flimsy subterfuge of investing Lysander with the real power of admiral under the nominal title of vice-admiral. This instance is selected from among a multitude that might be cited to confirm the truth already advanced and illustrated by domestic examples; which is, that nations pay little regard to rules and maxims calculated in their very nature to run counter to the necessities of society. Wise politicians will be cautious about fettering the government with restrictions that cannot be observed, because they know that every breach of the fundamental laws, though dictated by necessity, impairs that sacred reverence which ought to be maintained in the breast of rulers towards the constitution of a country, and forms a precedent for other breaches where the same plea of necessity does not exist at all, or is less urgent and palpable. PUBLIUS

Number 26

[HAMILTON]

IT WAS a thing hardly to be expected that in a popular revolution the minds of men should stop at that happy mean which marks the salutary boundary between POWER and PRIVILEGE, and combines the energy of government with the security of private rights. A failure in this delicate and important point is the great source of the inconveniences we experience, and if we are not cautious to avoid a repetition of the error, in our future attempts to rectify and ameliorate our system, we may travel from one chimerical project to another; we may try change after change; but we shall never be likely to make any material change for the better.

The idea of restraining the legislative authority, in the means of providing for the national defence, is one of those refinements which owe their origin to a zeal for liberty more ardent than enlightened. We have seen, however, that it has not had thus far an extensive prevalency; that even in this country, where it made its first appearance, Pennsylvania and North Carolina are the only two States by which it has been in any degree patronised; and that all the others have refused to give it the least countenance; wisely judging that confidence must be placed somewhere; that the necessity of doing it is implied in the very act of delegating power; and that it is better to hazard the abuse of that confidence than to embarrass the government and endanger the public safety by impolitic restrictions on the legislative authority. The opponents of the proposed Constitution combat, in this respect, the general decision of America; and instead of being taught by experience the propriety of correcting any extremes into which we may have heretofore run, they appear disposed to conduct us into others still more dangerous, and more extravagant. As if the tone of government had been found too high, or too rigid, the doctrines they teach are calculated to induce us to depress or to relax it, by expedients which, upon other occasions, have been condemned or forborne. It may be affirmed without the imputation of invective, that if the principles they inculcate, on various points, could so far obtain as to become the popular creed, they would utterly unfit the people of this country for any species of government whatever. But a danger of this kind is not to be apprehended. The citizens of America have too much discernment to be argued into anarchy. And I am much mistaken if experience has not wrought a deep and solemn conviction in the public mind, that greater energy of government is essential to the welfare and prosperity of the community.

It may not be amiss in this place concisely to remark the origin and progress of the idea, which aims at the exclusion of military establishments in time of peace. Though in speculative minds it may arise from a contemplation of the nature and tendency of such institutions, fortified by the events that have happened in other ages and countries, yet as a national sentiment, it must be traced to those habits of thinking which we derive from the nation from whom the inhabitants of these States have in general sprung.

In England, for a long time after the Norman Conquest, the authority of the monarch was almost unlimited. Inroads were gradually made upon the prerogative, in favour of liberty, first by the barons, and afterwards by the people, till the greatest part of its most formidable pretensions became extinct. But it was not till the revolution in 1688, which elevated the Prince of Orange to the throne of Great Britain, that English liberty was completely triumphant. As incident to the undefined power of making war, an acknowledged prerogative of the crown, Charles II. had, by his own authority, kept on foot in time of peace a body of 5,000 regular troops. And this number James II. increased to 30,000; who were paid out of his civil list. At the revolution, to abolish the exercise of so dangerous an authority, it became an article of the Bill of Rights then framed, that "the raising or keeping a standing army within the kingdom in time of peace, *unless with the consent of Parliament,* was against law."

In that kingdom, when the pulse of liberty was at its highest pitch, no security against the danger of standing armies was thought requisite, beyond a prohibition of their being raised or kept up by the mere authority of the executive magistrate. The patriots, who effected that memorable revolution, were too temperate, too well-informed, to think of any restraint on the legislative discretion. They were aware that a certain number of troops for guards and garrisons were indispensable; that no precise bounds could be set to the national exigencies; that a power equal to every possible contingency must exist somewhere in the government: and that when they referred the exercise of that power to the judgment of the legislature, they had arrived at the ultimate point of precaution which was reconcilable with the safety of the community.

From the same source, the people of America may be said to have derived an hereditary impression of danger to liberty, from standing armies in time of peace. The circumstances of a revolution quickened the public sensibility on every point connected with the security of popular rights, and in some instances raised the warmth of our zeal beyond the degree which consisted with the due temperature of the body politic. The attempts of two of the States to restrict the authority of the legislature in the article of military establishments, are of the number of these instances. The principles which had taught us to be jealous of the power of an hereditary monarch were by an injudicious excess extended to the representatives of the people in their popular assemblies. Even in some of the States where this error was not adopted, we find unnecessary declarations that standing armies ought not to be kept up, in time of peace, WITHOUT THE CONSENT OF THE LEGISLATURE. I call them unnecessary, because the reason which had introduced a similar provision into the English Bill of Rights is not applicable to any of the State constitutions. The power of raising armies at all, under those constitutions, can by no construction be deemed to reside anywhere else than in the legislatures themselves; and it was superfluous, if not absurd, to declare that a matter should not be done without the consent of a body which alone had the power of doing it. Accordingly, in some of those constitutions, and among others in that of this State of New York, which has been justly celebrated, both in Europe and America, as one of the best of the forms of government established in this country, there is a total silence upon the subject.

It is remarkable, that even in the two States which seem to have meditated an interdiction of military establishments in time of peace, the mode of expression made use of is rather cautionary than prohibitory. It is not said, that standing armies *shall not be* kept up, but that they *ought not* to be kept up, in time of peace. This ambiguity of terms appears to have been the result of a conflict between jealousy and conviction; between the desire of excluding such establishments at all events, and the persuasion that an absolute exclusion would be unwise and unsafe.

Can it be doubted that such a provision, whenever the situation of public affairs was understood to require a departure from it, would be interpreted by the legislature into a mere admonition and would be made to yield to the necessities or supposed necessities of the State? Let the fact already mentioned, with respect to Pennsylvania, decide. What then (it may be asked) is the use of such a provision, if it cease to operate the moment there is an inclination to disregard it?

Let us examine whether there be any comparison, in point of efficacy, between the provision alluded to and that which is contained in the new Constitution, for restraining the appropriations of money for military purposes to the period of two years. The former, by aiming at too much, is calculated to effect nothing; the latter, by steering clear of an imprudent extreme, and by being perfectly compatible with a proper provision for the exigencies of the nation, will have a salutary and powerful operation.

The legislature of the United States will be *obliged,* by this provision, once at least in every two years, to deliberate upon the propriety of keeping a military force on foot; to come to a new resolution on the point; and to declare their sense of the matter, by a formal vote in the face of their constituents. They are not *at liberty* to vest in the executive department permanent funds for the support of an army, if they were even incautious enough to be willing to repose in it so improper a confidence. As the spirit of party, in different degrees, must be expected to infect all political bodies, there will be, no doubt, persons in the national legislature willing enough to arraign the measures and criminate the views of the majority. The provision for the support of a military force will always be a favourable topic for declamation. As often as the question comes forward, the public attention will be roused and attracted to the subject by the party in opposition; and if the majority should be really disposed to exceed the proper limits, the community will be warned of the danger, and will have an opportunity of taking measures to guard against it. Independent of parties in the national legislature itself, as often as the period of discussion arrived, the State legislatures, who will always be not only vigilant but suspicious and jealous guardians of the rights of the citizens against encroachments from the federal government, will constantly have their attention awake to the conduct of the national rulers, and will be ready enough, if anything improper appears, to sound the alarm to the people, and not only to be the VOICE, but, if necessary, the ARM of their discontent.

Schemes to subvert the liberties of a great community *require time* to mature them for execution. An army, so large as seriously to menace those liberties, could only be formed by progressive augmentations; which would suppose, not merely a temporary combination between the legislature and executive, but a continued conspiracy for a series of time. Is it probable that such a combination would exist at all? Is it probable that it would be persevered in, and transmitted along through all the successive variations in a representative body, which biennial elections would naturally produce in both houses? Is it presumable that every man, the instant he took his seat in the national Senate or House of Representatives, would commence a traitor to his constituents and to his country? Can it be supposed that there would not be found one man discerning enough to detect so atrocious a conspiracy, or bold or honest enough to apprise his constituents of their danger? If such presumptions can fairly be made, there ought at once to be an end of all delegated authority. The people should resolve to recall all the powers they have heretofore parted with out of their own hands, and to divide themselves into as many States as there are counties, in order that they may be able to manage their own concerns in person.

If such suppositions could even be reasonably made, still the concealment of the design, for any duration, would be impracticable. It would be announced, by the very circumstance of augmenting the army to so great an extent in time of profound peace. What colourable reason could be assigned, in a country so situated, for such vast augmentations of the military force? It is impossible that the people could be long deceived; and the destruction of the project, and of the projectors, would quickly follow the discovery.

It has been said that the provision which limits the appropriation of money for the support of an army to the period of two years would be unavailing, because the Executive, when once possessed of a force large enough to awe the people into submission, would find resources in that very force sufficient to enable him to dispense with supplies from the acts of the legislature. But the question again recurs, upon what pretence could he be put in possession of a force of that magnitude in time of peace? If we suppose it to have been created in consequence of some domestic insurrection or

foreign war, then it becomes a case not within the principles of the objection; for this is levelled against the power of keeping up troops in time of peace. Few persons will be so visionary as seriously to contend that military forces ought not to be raised to quell a rebellion or resist an invasion; and if the defence of the community under such circumstances should make it necessary to have an army so numerous as to hazard its liberty, this is one of those calamities for which there is neither preventative nor cure. It cannot be provided against by any possible form of government; it might even result from a simple league offensive and defensive, if it should ever be necessary for the confederates or allies to form an army for common defence.

But it is an evil infinitely less likely to attend us in a united than in a disunited state; nay, it may be safely asserted that it is an evil altogether unlikely to attend us in the latter situation. It is not easy to conceive a possibility that dangers so formidable can assail the whole Union as to demand a force considerable enough to place our liberties in the least jeopardy, especially if we take into our view the aid to be derived from the militia, which ought always to be counted upon as a valuable and powerful auxiliary. But in a state of disunion (as has been fully shown in another place), the contrary of this supposition would become not only probable, but almost unavoidable. PUBLIUS

Number 27
[HAMILTON]

IT HAS been urged, in different shapes, that a Constitution of the kind proposed by the convention cannot operate without the aid of a military force to execute its laws. This, however, like most other things that have been alleged on that side, rests on mere general assertion, unsupported by any precise or intelligible designation of the reasons upon which it is founded. As far as I have been able to divine the latent meaning of the objectors, it seems to originate in a presupposition that the people will be disinclined to the exercise of federal authority in any matter of an internal nature. Waiving any exception that might be taken to the inaccuracy or inexplicitness of the distinction between internal and external, let us inquire what ground there is to presuppose that disinclination in the people. Unless we presume at the same time that the powers of the general government will be worse administered than those of the State government, there seems to be no room for the presumption of ill-will, disaffection, or opposition in the people. I believe it may be laid down as a general rule that their confidence in and obedience to a government will commonly be proportioned to the goodness or badness of its administration. It must be admitted that there are exceptions to this rule; but these exceptions depend so entirely on accidental causes, that they cannot be considered as having any relation to the intrinsic merits or demerits of a constitution. These can only be judged of by general principles and maxims.

Various reasons have been suggested, in the course of these papers, to induce a probability that the general government will be better administered than the particular governments: the principal of which reasons are that the extension of the spheres of election will present a greater option, or latitude of choice, to the people; that through the medium of the State legislatures—which are select bodies of men, and which are to appoint the members of the national Senate—there is reason to expect that this branch will generally be composed with peculiar care and judgment; that these circumstances promise greater knowledge and more extensive information in the national councils, and that they will be less apt to be tainted by the spirit of faction, and more out of the reach of those occasional ill-humours, or temporary prejudices and propensities, which, in smaller societies, frequently contaminate the public councils, beget injustice and oppression of a part of the community, and engender schemes which, though they gratify a momentary inclination or desire, terminate in general distress, dissatisfaction, and disgust. Several additional reasons of considerable force, to fortify that probability, will occur when we come to survey, with a more critical eye, the interior structure of the edifice which we are invited to erect. It will be sufficient here to remark, that until satisfactory reasons can be assigned to justify an opinion, that the federal government is likely to be administered in such a manner as to render it odious or contemptible to the people, there can be no reasonable foundation for the supposition that the laws of the Union will meet with any greater obstruction from them, or will stand in need of any other methods to enforce their execution, than the laws of the particular members.

The hope of impunity is a strong incitement to sedition; the dread of punishment, a proportionably strong discouragement to it. Will not the government of the Union which, if possessed of a due degree of power, can call to its aid the collective resources of the whole Confederacy be more likely to repress the *former* sentiment and to inspire the *latter,* than that of a single State, which can only command the resources within itself? A turbulent faction in a State may easily suppose itself able to contend with the friends to the government in that State; but it can hardly be so infatuated as to imagine itself a match for the combined efforts of the Union. If this reflection be just, there is less danger of resistance from irregular combinations of individuals to the authority of the Confederacy than to that of a single member.

I will, in this place, hazard an observation, which will not be the less just because to some it may appear new; which is, that the more the operations of the national authority are intermingled in the ordinary exercise of government, the more the citizens are accustomed to meet with it in the common occurrences of their political life, the more it is familiarised to their sight and to their feelings, the further it enters into those objects which touch the most sensible chords and put in motion the most active springs of the human heart, the greater will be the probability that it will conciliate the respect and attachment of the community. Man is very much a creature of habit. A thing that rarely strikes his senses will generally have but little influence upon his mind. A government continually at a distance and out of sight can hardly be expected to interest the sensations of the people. The inference is, that the authority of the Union, and the affections of the citizens towards it, will be strengthened, rather than weakened, by its extension to what are called matters of internal concern; and will have less occasion to recur to force, in proportion to the familiarity and comprehensiveness of its agency. The more it circulates through those channels and currents in which the passions of mankind naturally flow, the less will it require the aid of the violent and perilous expedients of compulsion.

One thing, at all events, must be evident, that a government like the one proposed would bid much fairer to avoid the necessity of using force, than that species of league contended for by most of its opponents; the authority of which should only operate upon the States in their political or collective capacities. It has been shown that in such a Confederacy there can be no sanction for the laws but force; that frequent delinquencies in the members are the natural offspring of the very frame of the government; and that as often as these happen, they can only be redressed, if at all, by war and violence.

The plan reported by the convention, by extending the authority of the federal head to the individual citizens of the several States, will enable the government to employ the ordinary magistracy of each, in the execution of its laws. It is easy to perceive that this will tend to destroy, in the common apprehension, all distinction between the sources from which they might proceed; and will give the federal government the same advantage for securing a due obedience to its authority which is enjoyed by the government of each State, in addition to the influence on public opinion which will result from the important consideration of its having power to call to its assistance and support the resources of the whole Union. It merits particular attention in this place, that the laws of the Confederacy, as to the *enumerated* and *legitimate* objects of its jurisdiction, will become the SUPREME LAW of the land; to the observance of which all officers, legislative, executive, and judicial, in each State, will be bound by the sanctity of an oath. Thus the legislatures, courts, and magistrates, of the respective members, will be incorporated into the operations of the national government *as far as its just and constitutional authority extends;* and will be rendered auxiliary to the enforcement of its laws.[1] Any man who will pursue, by his own reflections, the consequences of this situation, will perceive that there is good ground to calculate upon a regular and peaceable execution of the laws of the Union, if its powers are administered with a common share of prudence. If we will arbitrarily suppose the contrary, we may deduce any inferences we please from the supposition; for it is certainly possible, by an injudicious exercise of the authorities of the best government that ever was, or ever can be instituted, to provoke and precipitate the people into the wildest excesses. But though the adversaries of the proposed Constitution should presume that the national rulers would be insensible to the motives of public good, or to the obligations of duty, I would still ask them how the interests of ambition, or

the views of encroachment, can be promoted by such a conduct? PUBLIUS

Number 28

[HAMILTON]

THAT THERE may happen cases in which the national government may be necessitated to resort to force, cannot be denied. Our own experience has corroborated the lessons taught by the examples of other nations; that emergencies of this sort will sometimes arise in all societies, however constituted; that seditions and insurrections are, unhappily, maladies as inseparable from the body politic as tumours and eruptions from the natural body; that the idea of governing at all times by the simple force of law (which we have been told is the only admissible principle of republican government) has no place but in the reveries of those political doctors whose sagacity disdains the admonitions of experimental instruction.

Should such emergencies at any time happen under the national government, there could be no remedy but force. The means to be employed must be proportioned to the extent of the mischief. If it should be a slight commotion in a small part of a State, the militia of the residue would be adequate to its suppression! and the natural presumption is that they would be ready to do their duty. An insurrection, whatever may be its immediate cause, eventually endangers all government. Regard to the public peace, if not to the rights of the Union, would engage the citizens to whom the contagion had not communicated itself to oppose the insurgents; and if the general government should be found in practice conducive to the prosperity and felicity of the people, it were irrational to believe that they would be disinclined to its support.

If, on the contrary, the insurrection should pervade a whole State, or a principal part of it, the employment of a different kind of force might become unavoidable. It appears that Massachusetts found it necessary to raise troops for repressing the disorders within that State; that Pennsylvania, from the mere apprehension of commotions among a part of her citizens, has thought proper to have recourse to the same measure. Suppose the State of New York had been inclined to re-establish her lost jurisdiction over the inhabitants of Vermont, could she have hoped for success in such an

[1] The sophistry which has been employed, to show that this will tend to the destruction of the State governments, will, in its proper place, be fully detected.—PUBLIUS

enterprise from the efforts of the militia alone? Would she not have been compelled to raise and to maintain a more regular force for the execution of her design? If it must then be admitted that the necessity of recurring to a force different from the militia, in cases of this extraordinary nature, is applicable to the State governments themselves, why should the possibility that the national government might be under a like necessity, in similar extremities, be made an objection to its existence? Is it not surprising that men who declare an attachment to the Union in the abstract, should urge as an objection to the proposed Constitution what applies with tenfold weight to the plan for which they contend; and what, as far as it has any foundation in truth, is an inevitable consequence of civil society upon an enlarged scale? Who would not prefer that possibility to the unceasing agitations and frequent revolutions which are the continual scourges of petty republics?

Let us pursue this examination in another light. Suppose, in lieu of one general system, two, or three, or even four Confederacies were to be formed, would not the same difficulty oppose itself to the operations of either of these Confederacies? Would not each of them be exposed to the same casualties; and when these happened, be obliged to have recourse to the same expedients for upholding its authority which are objected to in a government for all the States? Would the militia, in this supposition, be more ready or more able to support the federal authority than in the case of a general union? All candid and intelligent men must, upon due consideration, acknowledge that the principle of the objection is equally applicable to either of the two cases; and that whether we have one government for all the States, or different governments for different parcels of them, or even if there should be an entire separation of the States,[1] there might sometimes be a necessity to make use of a force constituted differently from the militia, to preserve the peace of the community and to maintain the just authority of the laws against those violent invasions of them which amount to insurrections and rebellions.

Independent of all other reasonings upon the subject, it is a full answer to those who require a more peremptory provision against military establishments in time of peace, to say that the whole power of the proposed government is to be in the hands of the representatives of the people. This is the essential, and, after all, only efficacious security for the rights and privileges of the people, which is attainable in civil society.[2]

If the representatives of the people betray their constituents, there is then no resource left but in the exertion of that original right of self-defence which is paramount to all positive forms of government, and which against the usurpations of the national rulers, may be exerted with infinitely better prospect of success than against those of the rulers of an individual State. In a single State, if the persons intrusted with supreme power become usurpers, the different parcels, subdivisions, or districts of which it consists, having no distinct government in each, can take no regular measures for defence. The citizens must rush tumultuously to arms, without concert, without system, without resource; except in their courage and despair. The usurpers, clothed with the forms of legal authority, can too often crush the opposition in embryo. The smaller the extent of the territory, the more difficult will it be for the people to form a regular or systematic plan of opposition, and the more easy will it be to defeat their early efforts. Intelligence can be more speedily obtained of their preparations and movements, and the military force in the possession of the usurpers can be more rapidly directed against the part where the opposition has begun. In this situation there must be a peculiar coincidence of circumstances to insure success to the popular resistance.

The obstacles to usurpation and the facilities of resistance increase with the increased extent of the state, provided the citizens understand their rights and are disposed to defend them. The natural strength of the people in a large community, in proportion to the artificial strength of the government, is greater than in a small, and of course more competent to a struggle with the attempts of the government to establish a tyranny. But in a confederacy the people, without exaggeration, may be said to be entirely the masters of their own fate. Power being almost always the rival of power, the general government will at all times stand ready to check the usurpations of the state governments, and these will have the same disposition towards the general government. The people, by throwing themselves into either scale, will infallibly make it preponderate. If their

[1] In the revised text, "or if there should be as many unconnected governments as there are States."

[2] Its full efficacy will be examined hereafter.—PUBLIUS

rights are invaded by either, they can make use of the other as the instrument of redress. How wise will it be in them by cherishing the union to preserve to themselves an advantage which can never be too highly prized!

It may safely be received as an axiom in our political system, that the State governments will, in all possible contingencies, afford complete security against invasions of the public liberty by the national authority. Projects of usurpation cannot be masked under pretences so likely to escape the penetration of select bodies of men, as of the people at large. The legislatures will have better means of information. They can discover the danger at a distance; and possessing all the organs of civil power and the confidence of the people, they can at once adopt a regular plan of opposition, in which they can combine all the resources of the community. They can readily communicate with each other in the different States, and unite their common forces for the protection of their common liberty.

The great extent of the country is a further security. We have already experienced its utility against the attacks of a foreign power. And it would have precisely the same effect against the enterprises of ambitious rulers in the national councils. If the federal army should be able to quell the resistance of one State, the distant States would have it in their power to make head with fresh forces. The advantages obtained in one place must be abandoned to subdue the opposition in others; and the moment the part which had been reduced to submission was left to itself, its efforts would be renewed, and its resistance revive.

We should recollect that the extent of the military force must, at all events, be regulated by the resources of the country. For a long time to come, it will not be possible to maintain a large army; and as the means of doing this increase, the population and natural strength of the community will proportionably increase. When will the time arrive that the federal government can raise and maintain an army capable of erecting a despotism over the great body of the people of an immense empire, who are in a situation, through the medium of their State governments, to take measures for their own defence, with all the celerity, regularity, and system of independent nations? The apprehension may be considered as a disease, for which there can be found no cure in the resources of argument and reasoning.

PUBLIUS

Number 29[1]

[HAMILTON]

THE POWER of regulating the militia, and of commanding its services in times of insurrection and invasion are natural incidents to the duties of superintending the common defence, and of watching over the internal peace of the Confederacy.

It requires no skill in the science of war to discern that uniformity in the organisation and discipline of the militia would be attended with the most beneficial effects, whenever they were called into service for the public defence. It would enable them to discharge the duties of the camp and of the field with mutual intelligence and concert—an advantage of peculiar moment in the operations of an army; and it would fit them much sooner to acquire the degree of proficiency in military functions which would be essential to their usefulness. This desirable uniformity can only be accomplished by confiding the regulation of the militia to the direction of the national authority. It is, therefore, with the most evident propriety, that the plan of the convention proposes to empower the Union "to provide for organising, arming, and disciplining the militia, and for governing such part of them as may be employed in the service of the United States, *reserving to the States respectively the appointment of the officers, and the authority of training the militia according to the discipline prescribed by Congress.*"

Of the different grounds which have been taken in opposition to the plan of the convention, there is none that was so little to have been expected, or is so untenable in itself, as the one from which this particular provision has been attacked. If a well-regulated militia be the most natural defence of a free country, it ought certainly to be under the regulation and at the disposal of that body which is constituted the guardian of the national security. If standing armies are dangerous to liberty, an efficacious power over the militia, in the body to whose care the protection of the State is committed, ought, as far as possible, to take away the inducement and the pretext to such unfriendly institutions. If the federal govern-

[1] This essay appeared as Number 35 in the original publication in the newspapers, and is therefore here misplaced chronologically. In the first edition of 1788, however, it is printed as Number 29, which gives it its proper place according to subject, and for this reason the order of the first edition has been followed.

ment can command the aid of the militia in those emergencies which call for the military arm in support of the civil magistrate, it can the better dispense with the employment of a different kind of force. If it cannot avail itself of the former, it will be obliged to recur to the latter. To render an army unnecessary, will be a more certain method of preventing its existence than a thousand prohibitions upon paper.

In order to cast an odium upon the power of calling forth the militia to execute the laws of the Union, it has been remarked that there is nowhere any provision in the proposed Constitution for calling out the POSSE COMITATUS to assist the magistrate in the execution of his duty; whence it has been inferred that military force was intended to be his only auxiliary. There is a striking incoherence in the objections which have appeared, and sometimes even from the same quarter, not much calculated to inspire a very favourable opinion of the sincerity or fair dealing of their authors. The same persons who tell us in one breath that the powers of the federal government will be despotic and unlimited, inform us in the next that it has not authority sufficient even to call out the POSSE COMITATUS. The latter, fortunately, is as much short of the truth as the former exceeds it. It would be as absurd to doubt that a right to pass all laws *necessary and proper* to execute its declared powers, would include that of requiring the assistance of the citizens to the officers who may be intrusted with the execution of those laws, as it would be to believe that a right to enact laws necessary and proper for the imposition and collection of taxes would involve that of varying the rules of descent and of the alienation of landed property, or of abolishing the trial by jury in cases relating to it. It being therefore evident that the supposition of a want of power to require the aid of the POSSE COMITATUS is entirely destitute of colour, it will follow that the conclusion which has been drawn from it, in its application to the authority of the federal government over the militia, is as uncandid as it is illogical. What reason could there be to infer that force was intended to be the sole instrument of authority, merely because there is a power to make use of it when necessary? What shall we think of the motives which could induce men of sense to reason in this manner? How shall we prevent a conflict between charity and judgment?

By a curious refinement upon the spirit of republican jealousy, we are even taught to ap-

prehend danger from the militia itself, in the hands of the federal government. It is observed that select corps may be formed, composed of the young and ardent, who may be rendered subservient to the views of arbitrary power. What plan for the regulation of the militia may be pursued by the national government is impossible to be foreseen. But so far from viewing the matter in the same light with those who object to select corps as dangerous, were the Constitution ratified, and were I to deliver my sentiments to a member of the federal legislature from the State on the subject of a militia establishment, I should hold to him, in substance, the following discourse:

"The project of disciplining all the militia of the United States is as futile as it would be injurious, if it were capable of being carried into execution. A tolerable expertness in military movements is a business that requires time and practice. It is not a day, or even a week, that will suffice for the attainment of it. To oblige the great body of the yeomanry, and of the other classes of the citizens, to be under arms for the purpose of going through military exercises and evolutions, as often as might be necessary to acquire the degree of perfection which would entitle them to the character of a well-regulated militia, would be a real grievance to the people, and a serious public inconvenience and loss. It would form an annual deduction from the productive labour of the country, to an amount which, calculating upon the present numbers of the people, would not fall far short of the whole expense of the civil establishments of all the States. To attempt a thing which would abridge the mass of labour and industry to so considerable an extent, would be unwise: and the experiment, if made, could not succeed, because it would not long be endured. Little more can reasonably be aimed at, with respect to the people at large, than to have them properly armed and equipped; and in order to see that this be not neglected, it will be necessary to assemble them once or twice in the course of a year.

"But though the scheme of disciplining the whole nation must be abandoned as mischievous or impracticable; yet it is a matter of the utmost importance that a well-digested plan should, as soon as possible, be adopted for the proper establishment of the militia. The attention of the government ought particularly to be directed to the formation of a select corps of moderate extent, upon such principles as will really fit them for service in case of need.

By thus circumscribing the plan, it will be possible to have an excellent body of well-trained militia ready to take the field whenever the defence of the State shall require it. This will not only lessen the call for military establishments, but if circumstances should at any time oblige the government to form an army of any magnitude, that army can never be formidable to the liberties of the people while there is a large body of citizens, little, if at all, inferior to them in discipline and the use of arms, who stand ready to defend their own rights and those of their fellow-citizens. This appears to me the only substitute that can be devised for a standing army, and the best possible security against it, if it should exist."

Thus differently from the adversaries of the proposed Constitution should I reason on the same subject, deducing arguments of safety from the very sources which they represent as fraught with danger and perdition. But how the national legislature may reason on the point is a thing which neither they nor I can foresee.

There is something so far-fetched and so extravagant in the idea of danger to liberty from the militia, that one is at a loss whether to treat it with gravity or with raillery; whether to consider it as a mere trial of skill, like the paradoxes of rhetoricians; as a disingenuous artifice to instil prejudices at any price; or as the serious offspring of political fanaticism. Where, in the name of common sense, are our fears to end if we may not trust our sons, our brothers, our neighbours, our fellow-citizens? What shadow of danger can there be from men who are daily mingling with the rest of their countrymen, and who participate with them in the same feelings, sentiments, habits, and interests? What reasonable cause of apprehension can be inferred from a power in the Union to prescribe regulations for the militia, and to command its services when necessary, while the particular States are to have the *sole and exclusive appointment of the officers?* If it were possible seriously to indulge a jealousy of the militia upon any conceivable establishment under the federal government, the circumstance of the officers being in the appointment of the States ought at once to extinguish it. There can be no doubt that this circumstance will always secure to them a preponderating influence over the militia.

In reading many of the publications against the Constitution, a man is apt to imagine that he is perusing some ill-written tale or romance, which, instead of natural and agreeable images, exhibits to the mind nothing but frightful and distorted shapes—

Gorgons, hydras, and chimeras dire;

discolouring and disfiguring whatever it represents, and transforming everything it touches into a monster.

A sample of this is to be observed in the exaggerated and improbable suggestions which have taken place respecting the power of calling for the services of the militia. That of New Hampshire is to be marched to Georgia, of Georgia to New Hampshire, of New York to Kentucky, and of Kentucky to Lake Champlain. Nay, the debts due to the French and Dutch are to be paid in militiamen instead of louis d'ors and ducats. At one moment there is to be a large army to lay prostrate the liberties of the people; at another moment the militia of Virginia are to be dragged from their homes five or six hundred miles to tame the republican contumacy of Massachusetts; and that of Massachusetts is to be transported an equal distance to subdue the refractory haughtiness of the aristocratic Virginians. Do the persons who rave at this rate imagine that their art or their eloquence can impose any conceits or absurdities upon the people of America for infallible truths?

If there should be an army to be made use of as the engine of despotism, what need of the militia? If there should be no army, whither would the militia, irritated by being called upon to undertake a distant and hopeless expedition for the purpose of riveting the chains of slavery upon a part of their countrymen, direct their course, but to the seat of the tyrants, who had meditated so foolish as well as so wicked a project, to crush them in their imagined intrenchments of power, and to make them an example of the just vengeance of an abused and incensed people? Is this the way in which usurpers stride to dominion over a numerous and enlightened nation? Do they begin by exciting the detestation of the very instruments of their intended usurpations? Do they usually commence their career by wanton and disgustful acts of power, calculated to answer no end, but to draw upon themselves universal hatred and execration? Are suppositions of this sort the sober admonitions of discerning patriots to a discerning people? Or are they the inflammatory ravings of incendiaries or distempered enthusiasts? If we were even to suppose the national rulers actuated by the most ungovernable ambition, it is impossible to believe that they would employ such preposterous means to accomplish their designs.

In times of insurrection, or invasion, it would be natural and proper that the militia of a neighbouring State should be marched into another, to resist a common enemy, or to guard the republic against the violence of faction or sedition. This was frequently the case, in respect to the first object, in the course of the late war; and this mutual succour is, indeed, a principal end of our political association. If the power of affording it be placed under the direction of the Union, there will be no danger of a supine and listless inattention to the dangers of a neighbour, till its near approach had superadded the incitements of self-preservation to the too feeble impulses of duty and sympathy. PUBLIUS

Number 30

[HAMILTON]

IT HAS been already observed that the federal government ought to possess the power of providing for the support of the national forces; in which proposition was intended to be included the expense of raising troops, of building and equipping fleets, and all other expenses in any wise connected with military arrangements and operations. But these are not the only objects to which the jurisdiction of the Union, in respect to revenue, must necessarily be empowered to extend. It must embrace a provision for the support of the national civil list; for the payment of the national debts contracted, or that may be contracted; and, in general, for all those matters which will call for disbursements out of the national treasury. The conclusion is, that there must be interwoven, in the frame of the government, a general power of taxation, in one shape or another.

Money is, with propriety, considered as the vital principle of the body politic; as that which sustains its life and motion, and enables it to perform its most essential functions. A complete power, therefore, to procure a regular and adequate supply of it, as far as the resources of the community will permit, may be regarded as an indispensable ingredient in every constitution. From a deficiency in this particular, one of two evils must ensue; either the people must be subjected to continual plunder, as a substitute for a more eligible mode of supplying the public wants, or the government must sink into a fatal atrophy, and, in a short course of time, perish.

In the Ottoman or Turkish empire, the sovereign, though in other respects absolute master of the lives and fortunes of his subjects, has no right to impose a new tax. The consequence is that he permits the bashaws or governors of provinces to pillage the people without mercy; and, in turn, squeezes out of them the sums of which he stands in need, to satisfy his own exigencies and those of the state. In America, from a like cause, the government of the Union has gradually dwindled into a state of decay, approaching nearly to annihilation. Who can doubt that the happiness of the people in both countries would be promoted by competent authorities in the proper hands, to provide the revenues which the necessities of the public might require?

The present Confederation, feeble as it is, intended to repose in the United States an unlimited power of providing for the pecuniary wants of the Union. But proceeding upon an erroneous principle, it has been done in such a manner as entirely to have frustrated the intention. Congress, by the articles which compose that compact (as has already been stated), are authorised to ascertain and call for any sums of money necessary, in their judgment, to the service of the United States; and their requisitions, if conformable to the rule of apportionment, are in every constitutional sense obligatory upon the States. These have no right to question the propriety of the demand; no discretion beyond that of devising the ways and means of furnishing the sums demanded. But though this be strictly and truly the case; though the assumption of such a right would be an infringement of the articles of Union; though it may seldom or never have been avowedly claimed, yet in practice it has been constantly exercised, and would continue to be so, as long as the revenues of the Confederacy should remain dependent on the intermediate agency of its members. What the consequences of this system have been, is within the knowledge of every man the least conversant in our public affairs, and has been amply unfolded in different parts of these inquiries. It is this which has chiefly contributed to reduce us to a situation which affords ample cause both of mortification to ourselves, and of triumph to our enemies.

What remedy can there be for this situation, but in a change of the system which has produced it—in a change of the fallacious and delusive system of quotas and requisitions? What substitute can there be imagined for this *ignis fatuus* in finance, but that of permitting the national government to raise its own revenues by the ordinary methods of taxation authorised in every well-ordered constitution of civil government? Ingenious men may declaim with plausibility on any subject; but no human ingenuity can point out any other expedient to rescue us from the inconveniences and embarrassments naturally resulting from defective supplies of the public treasury.

The more intelligent adversaries of the new Constitution admit the force of this reasoning; but they qualify their admission by a distinction between what they call *internal* and *external* taxation. The former they would reserve to the State governments; the latter, which they explain into commercial imposts, or rather duties on imported articles, they declare themselves willing to concede to the federal head. This distinction, however, would violate the maxim of good sense and sound policy, which dictates that every POWER ought to be in proportion to its OBJECT; and would still leave the general government in a kind of tutelage to the State governments, inconsistent with every idea of vigour or efficiency. Who can pretend that commercial imposts are, or would be, alone equal to the present and future exigencies of the Union? Taking into the account the existing debt, foreign and domestic, upon any plan of extinguishment which a man moderately impressed with the importance of public justice and public credit could approve, in addition to the establishments which all parties will acknowledge to be necessary, we could not reasonably flatter ourselves that this resource alone, upon the most improved scale, would even suffice for its present necessities. Its future necessities admit not of calculation or limitation; and upon the principle, more than once adverted to, the power of making provision for them as they arise ought to be equally unconfined. I believe it may be regarded as a position warranted by the history of mankind, that, *in the usual progress of things, the necessities of a nation, in every stage of its existence, will be found at least equal to its resources.*

To say that deficiencies may be provided for by requisitions upon the States is on the one hand to acknowledge that this system cannot be depended upon, and on the other hand to depend upon it for everything beyond a certain limit. Those who have carefully attended to its vices and deformities as they have been exhibited by experience or delineated in the course of these papers, must feel invincible repugnancy to trusting the national interests in any degree to its operation. Its inevitable tendency, whenever it is brought into activity, must be to enfeeble the Union, and sow the seeds of discord and contention between the federal head and its members, and between the members themselves. Can it be expected that the deficiencies would be better supplied in this mode than the total wants of the Union have heretofore been supplied in the same mode? It ought to be recollected that if less will be required from the States, they will have proportionably less means to answer the demand. If the opinions of those who contend for the distinction which has been mentioned were to be received as evidence of truth, one would be led to conclude that there was some known point in the economy of national affairs at which it would be safe to stop and to say: Thus far the ends of public happiness will be promoted by supplying the wants of government, and all beyond this is unworthy of our care or anxiety. How is it possible that a government half supplied and always necessitous, can fulfil the purposes of its institution, can provide for the security, advance the prosperity, or support the reputation of the commonwealth? How can it ever possess either energy or stability, dignity or credit, confidence at home or respectability abroad? How can its administration be anything else than a succession of expedients temporising, impotent, disgraceful? How will it be able to avoid a frequent sacrifice of its engagements to immediate necessity? How can it undertake or execute any liberal or enlarged plans of public good?

Let us attend to what would be the effects of this situation in the very first war in which we should happen to be engaged. We will presume, for argument's sake, that the revenue arising from the impost duties answers the purposes of a provision for the public debt and of a peace establishment for the Union. Thus circumstanced, a war breaks out. What would be the probable conduct of the government in such an emergency? Taught by experience that proper dependence could not be placed on the success of requisitions, unable by its own authority to lay hold of fresh resources, and urged by considerations of national danger, would it not be driven to the expedient of diverting the funds already appropriated from their proper objects to the defence of the State? It is not easy to see how a step of this kind could be avoided; and if it should be taken, it is evident that it would prove the destruction of public credit at the very moment that it was becoming essential to the public safety. To imagine that at such a crisis credit might be dispensed with, would be the extreme of infatuation. In the modern system of war, nations the most wealthy are obliged to have recourse to large loans. A country so little opulent as ours must feel this necessity in a much stronger degree. But who would lend to a government that prefaced its overtures for borrowing by an act which demonstrated that no reliance could be placed on the steadiness of its measures for paying? The loans it might be able to procure would be as limited in their extent as burdensome in their conditions. They would be made upon the same principles that usurers commonly lend to bankrupt and fraudulent debtors—with a sparing hand and at enormous premiums.

It may perhaps be imagined that, from the scantiness of the resources of the country, the necessity of diverting the established funds in the case supposed would exist, though the national government should possess an unrestrained power of taxation. But two considerations will serve to quiet all apprehension on this head: one is, that we are sure the resources of the community, in their full extent, will be brought into activity for the benefit of the Union; the other is, that whatever deficiencies there may be, can without difficulty be supplied by loans.

The power of creating new funds upon new objects of taxation, by its own authority, would enable the national government to borrow as far as its necessities might require. Foreigners, as well as the citizens of America, could then reasonably repose confidence in its engagements; but to depend upon a government that must itself depend upon thirteen other governments for the means of fulfilling its contracts, when once its situation is clearly understood, would require a degree of credulity not often to be met with in the pecuniary transactions of mankind, and little reconcilable with the usual sharp-sightedness of avarice.

Reflections of this kind may have trifling weight with men who hope to see realised in America the halcyon scenes of the poetic or fabulous age; but to those who believe we are likely to experience a common portion of the vicissitudes and calamities which have fallen to the lot of other nations, they must appear entitled to serious attention. Such men must behold the actual situation of their country with painful solicitude, and deprecate the evils which

ambition or revenge might, with too much facility, inflict upon it.   PUBLIUS

Number 31

[HAMILTON]

IN DISQUISITIONS of every kind, there are certain primary truths, or first principles, upon which all subsequent reasonings must depend. These contain an internal evidence which, antecedent to all reflection or combination, commands the assent of the mind. Where it produces not this effect, it must proceed either from some defect or disorder in the organs of perception, or from the influence of some strong interest, or passion, or prejudice. Of this nature are the maxims in geometry, that "the whole is greater than its part; things equal to the same are equal to one another; two straight lines cannot enclose a space; and all right angles are equal to each other." Of the same nature are these other maxims in ethics and politics, that there cannot be an effect without a cause; that the means ought to be proportioned to the end; that every power ought to be commensurate with its object; that there ought to be no limitation of a power destined to effect a purpose which is itself incapable of limitation. And there are other truths in the two latter sciences which, if they cannot pretend to rank in the class of axioms, are yet such direct inferences from them, and so obvious in themselves, and so agreeable to the natural and unsophisticated dictates of common sense, that they challenge the assent of a sound and unbiased mind, with a degree of force and conviction almost equally irresistible.

The objects of geometrical inquiry are so entirely abstracted from those pursuits which stir up and put in motion the unruly passions of the human heart, that mankind, without difficulty, adopt not only the more simple theorems of the science, but even those abstruse paradoxes which, however they may appear susceptible of demonstration, are at variance with the natural conceptions which the mind, without the aid of philosophy, would be led to entertain upon the subject. The INFINITE DIVISIBILITY of matter, or, in other words, the INFINITE divisibility of a FINITE thing, extending even to the minutest atom, is a point agreed among geometricians, though not less incomprehensible to common sense than any of those mysteries in religion against which the batteries of infidelity have been so industriously levelled.

But in the sciences of morals and politics, men are found far less tractable. To a certain degree, it is right and useful that this should be the case. Caution and investigation are a necessary armour against error and imposition. But this untractableness may be carried too far, and may degenerate into obstinacy, perverseness, or disingenuity. Though it cannot be pretended that the principles of moral and political knowledge have, in general, the same degree of certainty with those of the mathematics, yet they have much better claims in this respect than, to judge from the conduct of men in particular situations, we should be disposed to allow them. The obscurity is much oftener in the passions and prejudices of the reasoner than in the subject. Men, upon too many occasions, do not give their own understandings fair play; but, yielding to some untoward bias, they entangle themselves in words and confound themselves in subtleties.

How else could it happen (if we admit the objectors to be sincere in their opposition) that positions so clear as those which manifest the necessity of a general power of taxation in the government of the Union, should have to encounter any adversaries among men of discernment? Though these positions have been elsewhere fully stated, they will perhaps not be improperly recapitulated in this place, as introductory to an examination of what may have been offered by way of objection to them. They are in substance as follows:

A government ought to contain in itself every power requisite to the full accomplishment of the objects committed to its care, and to the complete execution of the trusts for which it is responsible, free from every other control but a regard to the public good and to the sense of the people.

As the duties of superintending the national defence and of securing the public peace against foreign or domestic violence involve a provision for casualties and dangers to which no possible limits can be assigned, the power of making that provision ought to know no other bounds than the exigencies of the nation and the resources of the community.

As revenue is the essential engine by which the means of answering the national exigencies must be procured, the power of procuring that article in its full extent must necessarily be comprehended in that of providing for those exigencies.

As theory and practice conspire to prove that the power of procuring revenue is una-vailing when exercised over the States in their collective capacities, the federal government must of necessity be invested with an unqualified power of taxation in the ordinary modes.

Did not experience evince the contrary, it would be natural to conclude that the propriety of a general power of taxation in the national government might safely be permitted to rest on the evidence of these propositions, unassisted by any additional arguments or illustrations. But we find, in fact, that the antagonists of the proposed Constitution, so far from acquiescing in their justness or truth, seem to make their principal and most zealous effort against this part of the plan. It may therefore be satisfactory to analyse the arguments with which they combat it.

Those of them which have been most laboured with that view, seem in substance to amount to this: "It is not true, because the exigencies of the Union may not be susceptible of limitation, that its power of laying taxes ought to be unconfined. Revenue is as requisite to the purposes of the local administrations as to those of the Union; and the former are at least of equal importance with the latter to the happiness of the people. It is, therefore, as necessary that the State governments should be able to command the means of supplying their wants, as that the national government should possess the like faculty in respect to the wants of the Union. But an indefinite power of taxation in the *latter* might, and probably would in time, deprive the *former* of the means of providing for their own necessities; and would subject them entirely to the mercy of the national legislature. As the laws of the Union are to become the supreme law of the land, as it is to have power to pass all laws that may be NECESSARY for carrying into execution the authorities with which it is proposed to vest it, the national government might at any time abolish the taxes imposed for State objects upon the pretence of an interference with its own. It might allege a necessity of doing this in order to give efficacy to the national revenues. And thus all the resources of taxation might by degrees become the subjects of federal monopoly, to the entire exclusion and destruction of the State governments."

This mode of reasoning appears sometimes to turn upon the supposition of usurpation in the national government; at other times it seems to be designed only as a deduction from the constitutional operation of its intended powers. It is only in the latter light that it can be admitted to have any pretensions to fairness. The moment we launch into conjectures about the usurpations of the federal government, we get into an unfathomable abyss, and fairly put ourselves out of the reach of all reasoning. Imagination may range at pleasure till it gets bewildered amidst the labyrinths of an enchanted castle, and knows not on which side to turn to extricate itself from the perplexities into which it has so rashly adventured. Whatever may be then limits or modifications of the powers of the Union, it is easy to imagine an endless train of possible dangers; and by indulging an excess of jealousy and timidity, we may bring ourselves to a state of absolute scepticism and irresolution. I repeat here what I have observed in substance in another place, that all observations founded upon the danger of usurpation ought to be referred to the composition and structure of the government, not to the nature or extent of its powers. The State governments, by their original constitutions, are invested with complete sovereignty. In what does our security consist against usurpation from that quarter? Doubtless in the manner of their formation, and in a due dependence of those who are to administer them upon the people. If the proposed construction of the federal government be found, upon an impartial examination of it, to be such as to afford, to a proper extent, the same species of security, all apprehensions on the score of usurpation ought to be discarded.

It should not be forgotten that a disposition in the State governments to encroach upon the rights of the Union is quite as probable as a disposition in the Union to encroach upon the rights of the State governments. What side would be likely to prevail in such a conflict must depend on the means which the contending parties could employ towards insuring success. As in republics strength is always on the side of the people, and as there are weighty reasons to induce a belief that the State governments will commonly possess most influence over them, the natural conclusion is that such contests will be most apt to end to the disadvantage of the Union; and that there is greater probability of encroachments by the members upon the federal head, than by the federal head upon the members. But it is evident that all conjectures of this kind must be extremely vague and fallible: and that it is by far the safest course to lay them altogether aside, and to confine our attention wholly to the nature and extent of the powers as they are delineated in the Constitution. Everything beyond this must be left to the prudence and firmness of the people; who, as they will hold the scales in their own hands, it is to be hoped, will always take care to preserve the constitutional equilibrium between the general and the State governments. Upon this ground, which is evidently the true one, it will not be difficult to obviate the objections which have been made to an indefinite power of taxation in the United States. PUBLIUS

Number 32

[HAMILTON]

ALTHOUGH I am of opinion that there would be no real danger of the consequences which seem to be apprehended to the State governments from a power in the Union to control them in the levies of money, because I am persuaded that the sense of the people, the extreme hazard of provoking the resentments of the State governments, and a conviction of the utility and necessity of local administrations for local purposes, would be a complete barrier against the oppressive use of such a power; yet I am willing here to allow, in its full extent, the justness of the reasoning which requires that the individual States should possess an independent and uncontrollable authority to raise their own revenues for the supply of their own wants. And making this concession, I affirm that (with the sole exception of duties on imports and exports) they would, under the plan of the convention, retain that authority in the most absolute and unqualified sense; and that an attempt on the part of the national government to abridge them in the exercise of it, would be a violent assumption of power, unwarranted by any article or clause of its Constitution.

An entire consolidation of the States into one complete national sovereignty would imply an entire subordination of the parts; and whatever powers might remain in them, would be altogether dependent on the general will. But as the plan of the convention aims only at a partial union or consolidation, the State governments would clearly retain all the rights of sovereignty which they before had, and which were not, by that act, *exclusively* delegated to the United States. This exclusive delegation, or rather this alienation, of State sovereignty, would only exist in three cases: where the Constitution in express terms granted an exclusive authority to the Union; where it granted in one instance an authority to the Union, and in another prohibited the States from exercising the like authority; and where it granted an authority to the Union, to which a similar authority in the States would be absolutely and totally *contradictory* and *repugnant*. I use these terms to distinguish this last case from another which might appear to resemble it, but which would, in fact, be essentially different; I mean where the exercise of a concurrent jurisdiction might be productive of occasional interferences in the *policy* of any branch of administration, but would not imply any direct contradiction of repugnancy in point of constitutional authority. These three cases of exclusive jurisdiction in the federal government may be exemplified by the following instances: The last clause but one in the eighth section of the first article provides expressly that Congress shall exercise *"exclusive legislation"* over the district to be appropriated as the seat of government. This answers to the first case. The first clause of the same section empowers Congress *"to lay and collect taxes, duties, imposts, and excises"*; and the second clause of the tenth section of the same article declares that, *"no State shall,* without the consent of Congress, *lay any imposts or duties on imports or exports,* except for the purpose of executing its inspection laws." Hence would result an exclusive power in the Union to lay duties on imports and exports, with the particular exception mentioned; but this power is abridged by another clause, which declares that no tax or duty shall be laid on articles exported from any State; in consequence of which qualification, it now only extends to the *duties on imports*. This answers to the second case. The third will be found in that clause which declares that Congress shall have power "to establish an UNIFORM RULE of naturalisation throughout the United States." This must necessarily be exclusive; because if each State had power to prescribe a DISTINCT RULE, there could not be a UNIFORM RULE.

A case which may perhaps be thought to resemble the latter, but which is in fact widely different, affects the question immediately under consideration. I mean the power of imposing taxes on all articles other than exports and imports. This, I contend, is manifestly a concurrent and coequal authority in the United States and in the individual States. There is plainly no expression in the granting clause which makes that power *exclusive* in the Union. There is no independent clause or sentence which prohibits the States from exercis-

ing it. So far is this from being the case that a plain and conclusive argument to the contrary is to be deduced from the restraint laid upon the States in relation to duties on imports and exports. This restriction implies an admission that, if it were not inserted, the States would possess the power it excludes; and it implies a further admission, that as to all other taxes, the authority of the States remains undiminished. In any other view it would be both unnecessary and dangerous; it would be unnecessary, because if the grant to the Union of the power of laying such duties implied the exclusion of the States, or even their subordination in this particular, there could be no need of such a restriction; it would be dangerous, because the introduction of it leads directly to the conclusion which has been mentioned, and which, if the reasoning of the objectors be just, could not have been intended; I mean that the States, in all cases to which the restriction did not apply, would have a concurrent power of taxation with the Union. The restriction in question amounts to what lawyers call a NEGATIVE PREGNANT—that is, a *negation* of one thing, and an *affirmance* of another; a negation of the authority of the States to impose taxes on imports and exports, and an affirmance of their authority to impose them on all other articles. It would be mere sophistry to argue that it was meant to exclude them *absolutely* from the imposition of taxes of the former kind, and to leave them at liberty to lay others *subject to the control* of the national legislature. The restraining or prohibitory clause only says, that they shall not, *without the consent of Congress,* lay such duties; and if we are to understand this in the sense last mentioned, the Constitution would then be made to introduce a formal provision for the sake of a very absurd conclusion; which is, that the States, *with the consent* of the national legislature, might tax imports and exports; and that they might tax every other article, *unless controlled* by the same body. If this was the intention, why not leave it, in the first instance, to what is alleged to be the natural operation of the original clause, conferring a general power of taxation upon the Union? It is evident that this could not have been the intention, and that it will not bear a construction of the kind.

As to a supposition of repugnancy between the power of taxation in the States and in the Union, it cannot be supported in that sense which would be requisite to work an exclusion of the States. It is, indeed, possible that a tax might be laid on a particular article by a State which might render it *inexpedient* that thus a further tax should be laid on the same article by the Union; but it would not imply a constitutional inability to impose a further tax. The quantity of the imposition, the expediency or inexpediency of an increase on either side, would be mutually questions of prudence; but there would be involved no direct contradiction of power. The particular policy of the national and of the State systems of finance might now and then not exactly coincide, and might require reciprocal forbearances. It is not, however, a mere possibility of inconvenience in the exercise of powers, but an immediate constitutional repugnancy that can by implication alienate and extinguish a pre-existing right of sovereignty.

The necessity of a concurrent jurisdiction in certain cases results from the division of the sovereign power; and the rule that all authorities, of which the States are not explicitly divested in favour of the Union, remain with them in full vigour, is not a theoretical consequence of that division, but is clearly admitted by the whole tenor of the instrument which contains the articles of the proposed Constitution. We there find that, notwithstanding the affirmative grants of general authorities, there has been the most pointed care in those cases where it was deemed improper that the like authorities should reside in the States, to insert negative clauses prohibiting the exercise of them by the States. The tenth section of the first article consists altogether of such provisions. This circumstance is a clear indication of the sense of the convention, and furnishes a rule of interpretation out of the body of the act, which justifies the position I have advanced and refutes every hypothesis to the contrary.

PUBLIUS

Number 33

[HAMILTON]

THE RESIDUE of the argument against the provisions of the Constitution in respect to taxation is ingrafted upon the following clause.[1] The last clause of the eighth section of the first article of the plan under consideration authorises the national legislature "to make all laws which shall be *necessary* and *proper* for carry-

[1] This was the point at which No. XXXI. of the original newspaper essays was divided, and this opening sentence appeared in the McLean edition of 1788.

ing into execution *the powers* by that Constitution vested in the government of the United States, or in any department or officer thereof"; and the second clause of the sixth article declares, "that the Constitution and the laws of the United States made in *pursuance thereof*, and the treaties made by their authority shall be the *supreme law* of the land, anything in the constitution or laws of any State to the contrary notwithstanding."

These two clauses have been the source of much virulent invective and petulant declamation against the proposed Constitution. They have been held up to the people in all the exaggerated colours of misrepresentation as the pernicious engines by which their local governments were to be destroyed and their liberties exterminated; as the hideous monster whose devouring jaws would spare neither sex nor age, nor high nor low, nor sacred nor profane; and yet, strange as it may appear, after all this clamour, to those who may not have happened to contemplate them in the same light, it may be affirmed with perfect confidence that the constitutional operation of the intended government would be precisely the same if these clauses were entirely obliterated as if they were repeated in every article. They are only declaratory of a truth which would have resulted by necessary and unavoidable implication from the very act of constituting a federal government, and vesting it with certain specified powers. This is so clear a proposition, that moderation itself can scarcely listen to the railings which have been so copiously vented against this part of the plan, without emotions that disturb its equanimity.

What is a power, but the ability or faculty of doing a thing? What is the ability to do a thing but the power of employing the *means* necessary to its execution? What is a LEGISLATIVE power but a power of making LAWS? What are the *means* to execute a LEGISLATIVE power but LAWS? What is the power of laying and collecting taxes, but a *legislative power,* or a power of *making laws,* to lay and collect taxes? What are the proper means of executing such a power but *necessary* and *proper* laws?

This simple train of inquiry furnishes us at once with a test by which to judge of the true nature of the clause complained of. It conducts us to this palpable truth, that a power to lay and collect taxes must be a power to pass all laws *necessary* and *proper* for the execution of that power; and what does the unfortunate and calumniated provision in question do more than declare the same truth, to wit, that the national legislature, to whom the power of laying and collecting taxes had been previously given, might, in the execution of that power, pass all laws *necessary* and *proper* to carry it into effect? I have applied these observations thus particularly to the power of taxation, because it is the immediate subject under consideration, and because it is the most important of the authorities proposed to be conferred upon the Union. But the same process will lead to the same result in relation to all other powers declared in the Constitution. And it is *expressly* to execute these powers that the sweeping clause, as it has been affectedly called, authorises the national legislature to pass all *necessary* and *proper* laws. If there is any thing exceptionable, it must be sought for in the specific powers upon which this general declaration is predicated. The declaration itself, though it may be chargeable with tautology or redundancy, is at least perfectly harmless.

But SUSPICION may ask, Why then was it introduced? The answer is, that it could only have been done for greater caution, and to guard against all cavilling refinements in those who might hereafter feel a disposition to curtail and evade the legitimate authorities of the Union. The Convention probably foresaw, what it has been a principal aim of these papers to inculcate, that the danger which most threatens our political welfare is that the State governments will finally sap the foundations of the Union; and might therefore think it necessary, in so cardinal a point, to leave nothing to construction. Whatever may have been the inducement to it, the wisdom of the precaution is evident from the cry which has been raised against it; as that very cry betrays a disposition to question the great and essential truth which it is manifestly the object of that provision to declare.

But it may be again asked, Who is to judge of the *necessity* and *propriety* of the laws to be passed for executing the powers of the Union? I answer, first, that this question arises as well and as fully upon the simple grant of those powers as upon the declaratory clause; and I answer, in the second place, that the national government, like every other, must judge, in the first instance, of the proper exercise of its powers, and its constituents in the last. If the federal government should overpass the just bounds of its authority and make a tyrannical use of its powers, the people, whose creature it is, must appeal to the standard they have formed, and take such measures to redress the injury done to the Constitution as the exigency may suggest and prudence justify. The propriety of a law, in a constitutional light, must always be determined by the nature of the powers upon which it is founded. Suppose, by some forced constructions of its authority (which, indeed, cannot easily be imagined), the Federal legislature should attempt to vary the law of descent in any State, would it not be evident that, in making such an attempt, it had exceeded its jurisdiction and infringed upon that of the State? Suppose, again, that upon the pretence of an interference with its revenues, it should undertake to abrogate a land-tax imposed by the authority of a State; would it not be equally evident that this was an invasion of that concurrent jurisdiction in respect to this species of tax, which its Constitution plainly supposes to exist in the State governments? If there ever should be a doubt on this head, the credit of it will be entirely due to those reasoners who, in the imprudent zeal of their animosity to the plan of the convention, have laboured to envelop it in a cloud calculated to obscure the plainest and simplest truths.

But it is said that the laws of the Union are to be the *supreme law* of the land. But what inference can be drawn from this, or what would they amount to, if they were not to be supreme? It is evident they would amount to nothing. A LAW, by the very meaning of the term, includes supremacy. It is a rule which those to whom it is prescribed are bound to observe. This results from every political association. If individuals enter into a state of society, the laws of that society must be the supreme regulator of their conduct. If a number of political societies enter into a larger political society, the laws which the latter may enact, pursuant to the powers intrusted to it by its constitution, must necessarily be supreme over those societies, and the individuals of whom they are composed. It would otherwise be a mere treaty, dependent on the good faith of the parties, and not a government, which is only another word for POLITICAL POWER AND SUPREMACY. But it will not follow from this doctrine that acts of the larger society which are *not pursuant* to its constitutional powers, but which are invasions of the residuary authorities of the smaller societies, will become the supreme law of the land. These will be merely acts of usurpation, and will deserve to be treated as such. Hence we perceive that the clause which declares the supremacy of the laws of the Union, like the one we have just before considered, only declares a truth, which flows immediately and necessarily from the institution of a federal government. It will not, I presume, have escaped observation, that it *expressly* confines this supremacy to laws made *pursuant to the Constitution;* which I mention merely as an instance of caution in the convention; since that limitation would have been to be understood, though it had not been expressed.

Though a law, therefore, laying a tax for the use of the United States would be supreme in its nature, and could not legally be opposed or controlled, yet a law for abrogating or preventing the collection of a tax laid by the authority of the State (unless upon imports and exports), would not be the supreme law of the land, but a usurpation of power not granted by the Constitution. As far as an improper accumulation of taxes on the same object might tend to render the collection difficult or precarious, this would be a mutual inconvenience, not arising from a superiority or defect of power on either side, but from an injudicious exercise of power by one or the other, in a manner equally disadvantageous to both. It is to be hoped and presumed, however, that mutual interest would dictate a concert in this respect which would avoid any material inconvenience. The inference from the whole is, that the individual States would, under the proposed Constitution, retain an independent and uncontrollable authority to raise revenue to any extent of which they may stand in need, by every kind of taxation, except duties on imports and exports. It will be shown in the next paper that this CONCURRENT JURISDICTION in the article of taxation was the only admissible substitute for an entire subordination, in respect to this branch of power, of the State authority to that of the Union.   PUBLIUS

Number 34

[HAMILTON]

I FLATTER myself it has been clearly shown in my last number that the particular States, under the proposed Constitution, would have CO-EQUAL authority with the Union in the article of revenue, except as to duties on imports. As this leaves open to the States far the greatest part of the resources of the community there can be no colour for the assertion that they would not possess means as abundant as could be desired for the supply of their own wants,

independent of all external control. That the field is sufficiently wide will more fully appear when we come to advert to the inconsiderable share of the public expenses for which it will fall to the lot of the State governments to provide.

To argue upon abstract principles that this co-ordinate authority cannot exist, is to set up supposition and theory against fact and reality. However proper such reasonings might be to show that a thing *ought not to exist,* they are wholly to be rejected when they are made use of to prove that it does not exist contrary to the evidence of the fact itself. It is well known that in the Roman republic the legislative authority, in the last resort, resided for ages in two different political bodies—not as branches of the same legislature, but as distinct and independent legislatures, in each of which an opposite interest prevailed: in one the patrician; in the other, the plebeian. Many arguments might have been adduced to prove the unfitness of two such seemingly contradictory authorities, each having power to *annul* or *repeal* the acts of the other. But a man would have been regarded as frantic who should have attempted at Rome to disprove their existence. It will be readily understood that I allude to the COMITIA CENTURIATA and the COMITIA TRIBUTA. The former, in which the people voted by centuries, were so arranged as to give a superiority to the patrician interest; in the latter, in which numbers prevailed, the plebeian interest had an entire predominancy. And yet these two legislatures co-existed for ages, and the Roman republic attained to the utmost height of human greatness.

In the case particularly under consideration, there is no such contradiction as appears in the example cited; there is no power on either side to annul the acts of the other. And in practice there is little reason to apprehend any inconvenience; because, in a short course of time, the wants of the States will naturally reduce themselves within *a very narrow compass;* and in the interim, the United States will, in all probability, find it convenient to abstain wholly from those objects to which the particular States would be inclined to resort.

To form a more precise judgment of the true merits of this question, it will be well to advert to the proportion between the objects that will require a federal provision in respect to revenue, and those which will require a State provision. We shall discover that the former are altogether unlimited, and that the latter are circumscribed within very moderate bounds. In pursuing this inquiry, we must bear in mind that we are not to confine our view to the present period, but to look forward to remote futurity. Constitutions of civil government are not to be framed upon a calculation of existing exigencies, but upon a combination of these with the probable exigencies of ages, according to the natural and tried course of human affairs. Nothing, therefore, can be more fallacious than to infer the extent of any power, proper to be lodged in the national government, from an estimate of its immediate necessities. There ought to be a CAPACITY to provide for future contingencies as they may happen, and as these are illimitable in their nature, it is impossible safely to limit that capacity. It is true, perhaps, that a computation might be made with sufficient accuracy to answer the purpose of the quantity of revenue requisite to discharge the subsisting engagements of the Union, and to maintain those establishments which, for some time to come, would suffice in time of peace. But would it be wise, or would it not rather be the extreme of folly, to stop at this point, and to leave the government intrusted with the care of the national defence in a state of absolute incapacity to provide for the protection of the community against future invasions of the public peace by foreign war or domestic convulsions? If, on the contrary, we ought to exceed this point, where can we stop, short of an indefinite power of providing for emergencies as they may arise? Though it is easy to assert, in general terms, the possibility of forming a rational judgment of a due provision against probable dangers, yet we may safely challenge those who make the assertion to bring forward their data, and may affirm that they would be found as vague and uncertain as any that could be produced to establish the probable duration of the world. Observations confined to the mere prospect of internal attacks can deserve no weight; though even these will admit of no satisfactory calculation: but if we mean to be a commercial people, it must form a part of our policy to be able one day to defend that commerce. The support of a navy and of naval wars would involve contingencies that must baffle all the efforts of political arithmetic.

Admitting that we ought to try the novel and absurd experiment in politics of tying up the hands of government from offensive war founded upon reasons of State, yet certainly we ought not to disable it from guarding the community against the ambition or enmity of other nations. A cloud has been for some time hanging over the European world. If it should break forth into a storm, who can insure us that in its progress a part of its fury would not be spent upon us? No reasonable man would hastily pronounce that we are entirely out of its reach. Or if the combustible materials that now seem to be collecting should be dissipated without coming to maturity, or if a flame should be kindled without extending to us, what security can we have that our tranquillity will long remain undisturbed from some other cause or from some other quarter? Let us recollect that peace or war will not always be left to our option; that however moderate or unambitious we may be, we cannot count upon the moderation, or hope to extinguish the ambition of others. Who could have imagined at the conclusion of the last war that France and Britain, wearied and exhausted as they both were, would so soon have looked with so hostile an aspect upon each other? To judge from the history of mankind, we shall be compelled to conclude that the fiery and destructive passions of war reign in the human breast with much more powerful sway than the mild and beneficent sentiments of peace; and that to model our political systems upon speculations of lasting tranquillity is to calculate on the weaker springs of the human character.

What are the chief sources of expense in every government? What has occasioned that enormous accumulation of debts with which several of the European nations are oppressed? The answer plainly is, wars and rebellions; the support of those institutions which are necessary to guard the body politic against these two most mortal diseases of society. The expenses arising from those institutions which are relative to the mere domestic police of a State, to the support of its legislative, executive, and judicial departments, with their different appendages, and to the encouragement of agriculture and manufactures (which will comprehend almost all the objects of state expenditure), are insignificant in comparison with those which relate to the national defence.

In the kingdom of Great Britain, where all the ostentatious apparatus of monarchy is to be provided for, not above a fifteenth part of the annual income of the nation is appropriated to the class of expenses last mentioned; the other fourteen fifteenths are absorbed in the payment of the interest of debts contracted for carrying on the wars in which that country has been engaged, and in the maintenance of fleets and armies. If, on the one hand, it should be observed that the expenses incurred in the prosecution of the ambitious enterprises and vainglorious pursuits of a monarchy are not a proper standard by which to judge of those which might be necessary in a republic, it ought, on the other hand, to be remarked that there should be as great a disproportion between the profusion and extravagance of a wealthy kingdom in its domestic administration, and the frugality and economy which in that particular become the modest simplicity of republican government. If we balance a proper deduction from one side against that which it is supposed ought to be made from the other, the proportion may still be considered as holding good.

But let us advert to the large debt which we have ourselves contracted in a single war, and let us only calculate on a common share of the events which disturb the peace of nations, and we shall instantly perceive, without the aid of any elaborate illustration, that there must always be an immense disproportion between the objects of federal and state expenditures. It is true that several of the States, separately, are encumbered with considerable debts, which are an excrescence of the late war. But this cannot happen again, if the proposed system be adopted; and when these debts are discharged, the only call for revenue of any consequence, which the State governments will continue to experience, will be for the mere support of their respective civil lists; to which, if we add all contingencies, the total amount in every State ought to fall considerably short of two hundred thousand pounds.

In framing a government for posterity as well as ourselves, we ought, in those provisions which are designed to be permanent, to calculate, not on temporary, but on permanent causes of expense. If this principle be a just one, our attention would be directed to a provision in favour of the State governments for an annual sum of about two hundred thousand pounds; while the exigencies of the Union could be susceptible of no limits, even in imagination. In this view of the subject, by what logic can it be maintained that the local governments ought to command, in perpetuity, an EXCLUSIVE source of revenue for any sum beyond the extent of two hundred thousand pounds? To extend its power further, in *exclusion* of the authority of the Union, would

be to take the resources of the community out of those hands which stood in need of them for the public welfare, in order to put them into other hands which could have no just or proper occasion for them.

Suppose, then, the convention had been inclined to proceed upon the principle of a repartition of the objects of revenue, between the Union and its members, in *proportion* to their comparative necessities; what particular fund could have been selected for the use of the States that would not either have been too much or too little—too little for their present, too much for their future wants? As to the line of separation between external and internal taxes, this would leave to the States, at a rough computation, the command of two thirds of the resources of the community to defray from a tenth to a twentieth part of its expenses; and to the Union, one third of the resources of the community, to defray from nine tenths to nineteen twentieths of its expenses. If we desert this boundary and content ourselves with leaving to the States an exclusive power of taxing houses and lands, there would still be a great disproportion between the *means* and the *end;* the possession of one third of the resources of the community to supply, at most, one tenth of its wants. If any fund could have been selected and appropriated, equal to and not greater than the object, it would have been inadequate to the discharge of the existing debts of the particular States, and would have left them dependent on the Union for a provision for this purpose.

The preceding train of observation will justify the position which has been elsewhere laid down, that "A CONCURRENT JURISDICTION in the article of taxation was the only admissible substitute for an entire subordination, in respect to this branch of power, of State authority to that of the Union." Any separation of the objects of revenue that could have been fallen upon would have amounted to a sacrifice of the great INTERESTS of the Union to the power of the individual States. The convention thought the concurrent jurisdiction preferable to that subordination; and it is evident that it has at least the merit of reconciling an indefinite constitutional power of taxation in the Federal government with an adequate and independent power in the States to provide for their own necessities. There remain a few other lights, in which this important subject of taxation will claim a further consideration.

PUBLIUS

Number 35

[HAMILTON]

BEFORE WE proceed to examine any other objections to an indefinite power of taxation in the Union, I shall make one general remark; which is, that if the jurisdiction of the national government, in the article of revenue, should be restricted to particular objects, it would naturally occasion an undue proportion of the public burdens to fall upon those objects. Two evils would spring from this source: the oppression of particular branches of industry; and an unequal distribution of the taxes, as well among the several States as among the citizens of the same State.

Suppose, as has been contended for, the federal power of taxation were to be confined to duties on imports, it is evident that the government, for want of being able to command other resources, would frequently be tempted to extend these duties to an injurious excess. There are persons who imagine that they can never be carried to too great a length; since the higher they are the more it is alleged they will tend to discourage an extravagant consumption, to produce a favourable balance of trade, and to promote domestic manufactures. But all extremes are pernicious in various ways. Exorbitant duties on imported articles would beget a general spirit of smuggling; which is always prejudicial to the fair trader, and eventually to the revenue itself: they tend to render other classes of the community tributary, in an improper degree, to the manufacturing classes, to whom they give a premature monopoly of the markets; they sometimes force industry out of its more natural channels into others in which it flows with less advantage; and in the last place, they oppress the merchant, who is often obliged to pay them himself without any retribution from the consumer. When the demand is equal to the quantity of goods at market, the consumer generally pays the duty; but when the markets happen to be overstocked, a great proportion falls upon the merchant, and sometimes not only exhausts his profits, but breaks in upon his capital. I am apt to think that a division of the duty, between the seller and the buyer, more often happens than is commonly imagined. It is not always possible to raise the price of a commodity in exact proportion to every additional imposition laid upon it. The merchant, especially in a country of small commercial capital, is often under a necessity of keeping prices down in order to a more expeditious sale.

The maxim that the consumer is the payer, is so much oftener true than the reverse of the proposition, that it is far more equitable that the duties on imports should go into a common stock, than that they should redound to the exclusive benefit of the importing States. But it is not so generally true as to render it equitable, that those duties should form the only national fund. When they are paid by the merchant they operate as an additional tax upon the importing State, whose citizens pay their proportion of them in the character of consumers. In this view they are productive of inequality among the States; which inequality would be increased with the increased extent of the duties. The confinement of the national revenues to this species of imposts would be attended with inequality, from a different cause, between the manufacturing and the non-manufacturing States. The States which can go farthest towards the supply of their own wants, by their own manufactures, will not, according to their numbers or wealth, consume so great a proportion of imported articles as those States which are not in the same favourable situation. They would not, therefore, in this mode alone contribute to the public treasury in a ratio to their abilities. To make them do this it is necessary that recourse be had to excises, the proper objects of which are particular kinds of manufactures. New York is more deeply interested in these considerations than such of her citizens as contend for limiting the power of the Union to external taxation may be aware of. New York is an importing State, and is not likely speedily to be, to any great extent,[1] a manufacturing State. She would, of course, suffer in a double light from restraining the jurisdiction of the Union to commercial imposts.

So far as these observations tend to inculcate a danger of the import duties being extended to an injurious extreme it may be observed, conformably to a remark made in another part of these papers, that the interest of the revenue itself would be a sufficient guard against such an extreme. I readily admit that this would be the case, as long as other resources were open; but if the avenues to them were closed, HOPE, stimulated by necessity, would beget experiments, fortified by rigorous precautions and additional penalties, which, for a time, would have the intended effect, till there had been

[1] In the revised text, "and from a greater disproportion between her population and territory is unlikely speedily to be, to any great extent."

leisure to contrive expedients to elude these new precautions. The first success would be apt to inspire false opinions, which it might require a long course of subsequent experience to correct. Necessity, especially in politics, often occasions false hopes, false reasonings, and a system of measures correspondingly erroneous. But even if this supposed excess should not be a consequence of the limitation of the federal power of taxation, the inequalities spoken of would still ensue, though not in the same degree, from the other causes that have been noticed. Let us now return to the examination of objections.

One which, if we may judge from the frequency of its repetition, seems most to be relied on, is, that the House of Representatives is not sufficiently numerous for the reception of all the different classes of citizens, in order to combine the interests and feelings of every part of the community, and to produce a due sympathy between the representative body and its constituents. This argument presents itself under a very specious and seducing form; and is well calculated to lay hold of the prejudices of those to whom it is addressed. But when we come to dissect it with attention, it will appear to be made up of nothing but fair-sounding words. The object it seems to aim at is, in the first place, impracticable, and in the sense in which it is contended for, is unnecessary. I reserve for another place the discussion of the question which relates to the sufficiency of the representative body in respect to numbers, and shall content myself with examining here the particular use which has been made of a contrary supposition, in reference to the immediate subject of our inquiries.

The idea of an actual representation of all classes of the people, by persons of each class, is altogether visionary. Unless it were expressly provided in the Constitution, that each different occupation should send one or more members, the thing would never take place in practice. Mechanics and manufacturers will always be inclined, with few exceptions, to give their votes to merchants, in preference to persons of their own professions or trades. Those discerning citizens are well aware that the mechanic and manufacturing arts furnish the materials of mercantile enterprise and industry. Many of them, indeed, are immediately connected with the operations of commerce. They know that the merchant is their natural patron and friend; and they are aware, that however great the confidence they may justly feel

in their own good sense, their interests can be more effectually promoted by the merchant than by themselves. They are sensible that their habits in life have not been such as to give them those acquired endowments, without which, in a deliberative assembly, the greatest natural abilities are for the most part useless; and that the influence and weight, and superior acquirements of the merchants render them more equal to a contest with any spirit which might happen to infuse itself into the public councils, unfriendly to the manufacturing and trading interests. These considerations, and many others that might be mentioned, prove, and experience confirms it, that artisans and manufacturers will commonly be disposed to bestow their votes upon merchants and those whom they recommend. We must therefore consider merchants as the natural representatives of all these classes of the community.

With regard to the learned professions, little need be observed; they truly form no distinct interest in society, and according to their situation and talents, will be indiscriminately the objects of the confidence and choice of each other, and of other parts of the community.

Nothing remains but the landed interest; and this, in a political view, and particularly in relation to taxes, I take to be perfectly united, from the wealthiest landlord down to the poorest tenant. No tax can be laid on land which will not affect the proprietor of millions of acres as well as the proprietor of a single acre. Every landholder will therefore have a common interest to keep the taxes on land as low as possible; and common interest may always be reckoned upon as the surest bond of sympathy. But if we even could suppose a distinction of interest between the opulent landholder and the middling farmer, what reason is there to conclude, that the first would stand a better chance of being deputed to the national legislature than the last? If we take fact as our guide, and look into our own senate and assembly, we shall find that moderate proprietors of land prevail in both; nor is this less the case in the senate which consists of a smaller number than in the assembly which is composed of a greater number. Where the qualifications of the electors are the same, whether they have to choose a small or a large number, their votes will fall upon those in whom they have most confidence; whether these happen to be men of large fortunes, or of moderate property, or of no property at all.

It is said to be necessary, that all classes of

citizens should have some of their own number in the representative body, in order that their feelings and interests may be the better understood and attended to. But we have seen that this will never happen under any arrangement that leaves the votes of the people free. Where this is the case, the representative body, with too few exceptions to have any influence on the spirit of the government, will be composed of landholders, merchants, and men of the learned professions. But where is the danger that the interests and feelings of the different classes of citizens will not be understood or attended to by these three descriptions of men? Will not the landholder know and feel whatever will promote or insure the interest of landed property? And will he not, from his own interest in that species of property, be sufficiently prone to resist every attempt to prejudice or encumber it? Will not the merchant understand and be disposed to cultivate, as far as may be proper, the interests of the mechanic and manufacturing arts, to which his commerce is so nearly allied? Will not the man of the learned profession, who will feel a neutrality to the rivalships between the different branches of industry, be likely to prove an impartial arbiter between them, ready to promote either, so far as it shall appear to him conducive to the general interests of the society?

If we take into the account the momentary humours or dispositions which may happen to prevail in particular parts of the society, and to which a wise administration will never be inattentive, is the man whose situation leads to extensive inquiry and information less likely to be a competent judge of their nature, extent, and foundation than one whose observation does not travel beyond the circle of his neighbours and acquaintances? Is it not natural that a man who is a candidate for the favour of the people, and who is dependent on the suffrages of his fellow-citizens for the continuance of his public honours, should take care to inform himself of their dispositions and inclinations, and should be willing to allow them their proper degree of influence upon his conduct? This dependence, and the necessity of being bound himself, and his posterity, by the laws to which he gives his assent, are the true, and they are the strong chords of sympathy between the representative and the constituent.

There is no part of the administration of government that requires extensive information and a thorough knowledge of the principles of political economy, so much as the business of taxation. The man who understands those principles best will be least likely to resort to oppressive expedients, or to sacrifice any particular class of citizens to the procurement of revenue. It might be demonstrated that the most productive system of finance will always be the least burdensome. There can be no doubt that in order to [obtain] a judicious exercise of the power of taxation, it is necessary that the person in whose hands it is should be acquainted with the general genius, habits, and modes of thinking of the people at large, and with the resources of the country. And this is all that can be reasonably meant by a knowledge of the interests and feelings of the people. In any other sense the proposition has either no meaning, or an absurd one. And in that sense let every considerate citizen judge for himself where the requisite qualification is most likely to be found.   PUBLIUS

Number 36

[HAMILTON]

WE HAVE seen that the result of the observations, to which the foregoing number has been principally devoted, is, that from the natural operation of the different interests and views of the various classes of the community, whether the representation of the people be more or less numerous, it will consist almost entirely of proprietors of land, of merchants, and of members of the learned professions, who will truly represent all those different interests and views. If it should be objected that we have seen other descriptions of men in the local legislatures, I answer that it is admitted there are exceptions to the rule, but not in sufficient number to influence the general complexion or character of the government. There are strong minds in every walk of life that will rise superior to the disadvantages of situation, and will command the tribute due to their merit, not only from the classes to which they particularly belong, but from the society in general. The door ought to be equally open to all; and I trust, for the credit of human nature, that we shall see examples of such vigorous plants flourishing in the soil of federal as well as of State legislation; but occasional instances of this sort will not render the reasoning, founded upon the general course of things, less conclusive.

The subject might be placed in several other lights that would all lead to the same result; and in particular it might be asked, What greater affinity or relation of interest can be conceived between the carpenter and blacksmith, and the linen manufacturer or stockingweaver, than between the merchant and either of them? It is notorious that there are often as great rivalships between different branches of the mechanic or manufacturing arts as there are between any of the departments of labour and industry; so that, unless the representative body were to be far more numerous than would be consistent with any idea of regularity or wisdom in its deliberations, it is impossible that what seems to be the spirit of the objection we have been considering should ever be realised in practice. But I forbear to dwell any longer on a matter which has hitherto worn too loose a garb to admit even of an accurate inspection of its real shape or tendency.

There is another objection of a somewhat more precise nature that claims our attention. It has been asserted that a power of internal taxation in the national legislature could never be exercised with advantage, as well from the want of a sufficient knowledge of local circumstances, as from an interference between the revenue laws of the Union and of the particular States. The supposition of a want of proper knowledge seems to be entirely destitute of foundation. If any question is depending in a State legislature respecting one of the counties, which demands a knowledge of local details, how is it acquired? No doubt from the information of the members of the county. Cannot the like knowledge be obtained in the national legislature from the representatives of each State? And is it not to be presumed that the men who will generally be sent there will be possessed of the necessary degree of intelligence to be able to communicate that information? Is the knowledge of local circumstances, as applied to taxation, a minute topographical acquaintance with all the mountains, rivers, streams, highways, and by-paths in each State; or is it a general acquaintance with its situation and resources, with the state of its agriculture, commerce, manufactures, with the nature of its products and consumptions, with the different degrees and kinds of its wealth, property, and industry?

Nations in general, even under governments of the more popular kind, usually commit the administration of their finances to single men or to boards composed of a few individuals, who digest and prepare, in the first instance, the plans of taxation, which are afterwards passed into laws by the authority of the sovereign or legislature.

Inquisitive and enlightened statesmen are deemed everywhere best qualified to make a judicious selection of the objects proper for revenue; which is a clear indication, as far as the sense of mankind can have weight in the question, of the species of knowledge of local circumstances requisite to the purposes of taxation.

The taxes intended to be comprised under the general denomination of internal taxes may be subdivided into those of the *direct* and those of the *indirect* kind. Though the objection be made to both, yet the reasoning upon it seems to be confined to the former branch. And indeed, as to the latter, by which must be understood duties and excises on articles of consumption, one is at a loss to conceive what can be the nature of the difficulties apprehended. The knowledge relating to them must evidently be of a kind that will either be suggested by the nature of the article itself, or can easily be procured from any well-informed man, especially of the mercantile class. The circumstances that may distinguish its situation in one State from its situation in another must be few, simple, and easy to be comprehended. The principal thing to be attended to would be to avoid those articles which had been previously appropriated to the use of a particular State; and there could be no difficulty in ascertaining the revenue system of each. This could always be known from the respective codes of laws, as well as from the information of the members from the several States.

The objection, when applied to real property or to houses and lands, appears to have, at first sight, more foundation, but even in this view it will not bear a close examination. Land-taxes are commonly laid in one of two modes, either by *actual* valuations, permanent or periodical, or by *occasional* assessments, at the discretion, or according to the best judgment, of certain officers whose duty it is to make them. In either case, the EXECUTION of the business, which alone requires the knowledge of local details, must be devolved upon discreet persons in the character of commissioners or assessors, elected by the people or appointed by the government for the purpose. All that the law can do must be to name the persons or to prescribe the manner of their election or appointment, to fix their numbers and qualifications and to draw the general outlines of their powers and duties. And what is there in all this that cannot as well be performed by the national legislature as by a State legislature? The attention of either can only reach to general principles; local details, as already observed, must be referred to those who are to execute the plan.

But there is a simple point of view in which this matter may be placed that must be altogether satisfactory. The national legislature can make use of the *system of each State within that State*. The method of laying and collecting this species of taxes in each State can, in all its parts, be adopted and employed by the federal government.

Let it be recollected that the proportion of these taxes is not to be left to the discretion of the national legislature, but is to be determined by the numbers of each State, as described in the second section of the first article. An actual census or enumeration of the people must furnish the rule, a circumstance which effectually shuts the door to partiality or oppression. The abuse of this power of taxation seems to have been provided against with guarded circumspection. In addition to the precaution just mentioned, there is a provision that "all duties, imposts, and excises shall be UNIFORM throughout the United States."

It has been very properly observed by different speakers and writers on the side of the Constitution, that if the exercise of the power of internal taxation by the Union should be discovered on experiment to be really inconvenient, the federal government may then forbear the use of it, and have recourse to requisitions in its stead. By way of answer to this, it has been triumphantly asked, Why not in the first instance omit that ambiguous power, and rely upon the latter resource? Two solid answers may be given. The first is, that the exercise of that power, if convenient, will be preferable, because it will be more effectual; and it is impossible to prove in theory, or otherwise than by the experiment, that it cannot be advantageously exercised. The contrary, indeed, appears most probable. The second answer is, that the existence of such a power in the Constitution will have a strong influence in giving efficacy to requisitions. When the States know that the Union can apply itself without their agency, it will be a powerful motive for exertion on their part.

As to the interference of the revenue laws of the Union, and of its members, we have already seen that there can be no clashing or repugnancy of authority. The laws cannot, therefore, in a legal sense, interfere with each other;

and it is far from impossible to avoid an interference even in the policy of their different systems. An effectual expedient for this purpose will be mutually to abstain from those objects which either side may have first had recourse to. As neither can *control* the other, each will have an obvious and sensible interest in this reciprocal forbearance. And where there is an immediate common interest, we may safely count upon its operation. When the particular debts of the States are done away, and their expenses come to be limited within their natural compass, the possibility almost of interference will vanish. A small land-tax will answer the purpose of the States, and will be their most simple and most fit resource.

Many spectres have been raised out of this power of internal taxation, to excite the apprehensions of the people: double sets of revenue officers, a duplication of their burdens by double taxations, and the frightful forms of odious and oppressive poll-taxes, have been played off with all the ingenious dexterity of political legerdemain.

As to the first point there are two cases in which there can be no room for double sets of officers: one, where the right of imposing the tax is exclusively vested in the Union, which applies to the duties on imports; the other, where the object has not fallen under any State regulation or provision, which may be applicable to a variety of objects. In other cases, the probability is that the United States will either wholly abstain from the objects preoccupied for local purposes, or will make use of the State officers and State regulations for collecting the additional imposition. This will best answer the views of revenue, because it will save expense in the collection, and will best avoid any occasion of disgust to the State governments and to the people. At all events, here is a practicable expedient for avoiding such an inconvenience; and nothing more can be required than to show that evils predicted do not necessarily result from the plan.

As to any argument derived from a supposed system of influence, it is a sufficient answer to say that it ought not to be presumed; but the supposition is susceptible of a more precise answer. If such a spirit should infest the councils of the Union, the most certain road to the accomplishment of its aim would be to employ the State officers as much as possible, and to attach them to the Union by an accumulation of their emoluments. This would serve to turn the tide of State influence into the channels of the national government, instead of making federal influence flow in an opposite and adverse current. But all suppositions of this kind are invidious, and ought to be banished from the consideration of the great question before the people. They can answer no other end than to cast a mist over the truth.

As to the suggestion of double taxation, the answer is plain. The wants of the Union are to be supplied in one way or another; if to be done by the authority of the federal government, it will not be to be done by that of the State government. The quantity of taxes to be paid by the community must be the same in either case; with this advantage, if the provision is to be made by the Union—that the capital resource of commercial imposts, which is the most convenient branch of revenue, can be prudently improved to a much greater extent under federal than under State regulation, and of course will render it less necessary to recur to more inconvenient methods; and with this further advantage, that as far as there may be any real difficulty in the exercise of the power of internal taxation, it will impose a disposition to greater care in the choice and arrangement of the means; and must naturally tend to make it a fixed point of policy in the national administration to go as far as may be practicable in making the luxury of the rich tributary to the public treasury, in order to diminish the necessity of those impositions which might create dissatisfaction in the poorer and most numerous classes of the society. Happy it is when the interest which the government has in the preservation of its own power, coincides with a proper distribution of the public burdens, and tends to guard the least wealthy part of the community from oppression!

As to poll-taxes, I, without scruple, confess my disapprobation of them; and though they have prevailed from an early period in those States[1] which have uniformly been the most tenacious of their rights, I should lament to see them introduced into practice under the national government. But does it follow because there is a power to lay them, that they will actually be laid? Every State in the Union has power to impose taxes of this kind; and yet in several of them they are unknown in practice. Are the State governments to be stigmatised as tyrannies because they possess this power? If they are not, with what propriety can the like power justify such a charge against the na-

tional government, or even be urged as an obstacle to its adoption? As little friendly as I am to the species of imposition, I still feel a thorough conviction that the power of having recourse to it ought to exist in the federal government. There are certain emergencies of nations in which expedients, that in the ordinary state of things ought to be forborne, become essential to the public weal. And the government, from the possibility of such emergencies, ought ever to have the option of making use of them. The real scarcity of objects in this country, which may be considered as productive sources of revenue, is a reason peculiar to itself, for not abridging the discretion of the national councils in this respect. There may exist certain critical and tempestuous conjunctures of the State, in which a poll-tax may become an inestimable resource. And as I know nothing to exempt this portion of the globe from the common calamities that have befallen other parts of it, I acknowledge my aversion to every project that is calculated to disarm the government of a single weapon, which in any possible contingency might be usefully employed for the general defence and security.

I have now gone through the examination of such of the powers proposed to be vested in the United States, which may be considered as having an immediate relation to the energy of the government; and have endeavoured to answer the principal objections which have been made to them. I have passed over in silence those minor authorities, which are either too inconsiderable to have been thought worthy of the hostilities of the opponents of the Constitution, or of too manifest propriety to admit of controversy. The mass of judiciary power, however, might have claimed an investigation under this head, had it not been for the consideration that its organisation and its extent may be more advantageously considered in connection. This has determined me to refer it to the branch of our inquiries upon which we shall next enter.   PUBLIUS

[1] The New England States.—PUBLIUS

Number 37

[MADISON]

IN REVIEWING the defects of the existing Confederation, and showing that they cannot be supplied by a government of less energy than that before the public, several of the most important principles of the latter fell of course under consideration. But as the ultimate object of these papers is to determine clearly and fully the merits of this Constitution, and the expediency of adopting it, our plan cannot be complete without taking a more critical and thorough survey of the work of the convention, without examining it in all its sides, comparing it in all its parts, and calculating its probable effects.

That this remaining task may be executed under impressions conducive to a just and fair result, some reflections must in this place be indulged, which candour previously suggests.

It is a misfortune, inseparable from human affairs, that public measures are rarely investigated with that spirit of moderation which is essential to a just estimate of their real tendency to advance or obstruct the public good; and that this spirit is more apt to be diminished than promoted by those occasions which require an unusual exercise of it. To those who have been led by experience to attend to this consideration, it could not appear surprising that the act of the convention, which recommends so many important changes and innovations, which may be viewed in so many lights and relations, and which touches the springs of so many passions and interests, should find or excite dispositions unfriendly, both on one side and on the other, to a fair discussion and accurate judgment of its merits. In some, it has been too evident from their own publications, that they have scanned the proposed Constitution, not only with a predisposition to censure, but with a predetermination to condemn; as the language held by others betrays an opposite predetermination or bias, which must render their opinions also of little moment in the question. In placing, however, these different characters on a level, with respect to the weight of their opinions, I wish not to insinuate that there may not be a material difference in the purity of their intentions. It is but just to remark in favour of the latter description, that as our situation is universally admitted to be peculiarly critical, and to require indispensably that something should be done for our relief, the predetermined patron of what has been actually done may have taken his bias from the weight of these considerations, as well as from considerations of a sinister nature. The predetermined adversary, on the other hand, can have been governed by no venial motive whatever. The intentions of the first may be upright, as they may on the contrary be culpable. The views of the last cannot be upright, and must be cul-

pable. But the truth is, that these papers are not addressed to persons falling under either of these characters. They solicit the attention of those only who add to a sincere zeal for the happiness of their country a temper favourable to a just estimate of the means of promoting it.

Persons of this character will proceed to an examination of the plan submitted by the convention, not only without a disposition to find or to magnify faults; but will see the propriety of reflecting that a faultless plan was not to be expected. Nor will they barely make allowances for the errors which may be chargeable on the fallibility to which the convention, as a body of men, were liable; but will keep in mind that they themselves also are but men, and ought not to assume an infallibility in rejudging the fallible opinions of others.

With equal readiness will it be perceived, that besides these inducements to candour, many allowances ought to be made for the difficulties inherent in the very nature of the undertaking referred to the convention.

The novelty of the undertaking immediately strikes us. It has been shown in the course of these papers, that the existing Confederation is founded on principles which are fallacious; that we must consequently change this first foundation, and with it the superstructure resting upon it. It has been shown that the other confederacies which could be consulted as precedents have been vitiated by the same erroneous principles, and can therefore furnish no other light than that of beacons which give warning of the course to be shunned, without pointing out that which ought to be pursued. The most that the convention could do in such a situation, was to avoid the errors suggested by the past experience of other countries, as well as of our own; and to provide a convenient mode of rectifying their own errors, as future experience may unfold them.

Among the difficulties encountered by the convention, a very important one must have lain in combining the requisite stability and energy in government with the inviolable attention due to liberty and to the republican form. Without substantially accomplishing this part of their undertaking, they would have very imperfectly fulfilled the object of their appointment, or the expectation of the public; yet that it could not be easily accomplished will be denied by no one who is unwilling to betray his ignorance of the subject. Energy in government is essential to that security against external and internal danger, and to that prompt and salutary execution of the laws which enter into the very definition of good government. Stability in government is essential to national character and to the advantages annexed to it, as well as to that repose and confidence in the minds of the people, which are among the chief blessings of civil society. An irregular and mutable legislation is not more an evil in itself than it is odious to the people; and it may be pronounced with assurance that the people of this country, enlightened as they are with regard to the nature, and interested, as the great body of them are, in the effects of good government, will never be satisfied till some remedy be applied to the vicissitudes and uncertainties which characterise the State administrations. On comparing, however, these valuable ingredients with the vital principles of liberty, we must perceive at once the difficulty of mingling them together in their due proportions. The genius of republican liberty seems to demand on one side not only that all power should be derived from the people, but that those intrusted with it should be kept in dependence on the people, by a short duration of their appointments; and that even during this short period the trust should be placed not in a few, but a number of hands. Stability, on the contrary, requires that the hands in which power is lodged should continue for a length of time the same. A frequent change of men will result from a frequent return of elections; and a frequent change of measures from a frequent change of men: whilst energy in government requires not only a certain duration of power, but the execution of it by a single hand.

How far the convention may have succeeded in this part of their work, will better appear on a more accurate view of it. From the cursory view here taken, it must clearly appear to have been an arduous part.

Not less arduous must have been the task of marking the proper line of partition between the authority of the general and that of the State governments. Every man will be sensible of this difficulty, in proportion as he has been accustomed to contemplate and discriminate objects extensive and complicated in their nature. The faculties of the mind itself have never yet been distinguished and defined, with satisfactory precision, by all the efforts of the most acute and metaphysical philosophers. Sense, perception, judgment, desire, volition, memory, imagination, are found to be separated by such delicate shades and minute gradations that their boundaries have eluded the most subtle investigations, and remain a pregnant source of ingenious disquisition and controversy. The boundaries between the great kingdom of nature, and, still more, between the various provinces and lesser portions into which they are subdivided, afford another illustration of the same important truth. The most sagacious and laborious naturalists have never yet succeeded in tracing with certainty the line which separates the district of vegetable life from the neighbouring region of unorganised matter, or which marks the termination of the former and the commencement of the animal empire. A still greater obscurity lies in the distinctive characters by which the objects in each of these great departments of nature have been arranged and assorted.

When we pass from the works of nature, in which all the delineations are perfectly accurate, and appear to be otherwise only from the imperfection of the eye which surveys them, to the institutions of man, in which the obscurity arises as well from the object itself as from the organ by which it is contemplated, we must perceive the necessity of moderating still further our expectations and hopes from the efforts of human sagacity. Experience has instructed us that no skill in the science of government has yet been able to discriminate and define, with sufficient certainty, its three great provinces—the legislative, executive, and judiciary; or even the privileges and powers of the different legislative branches. Questions daily occur in the course of practice which prove the obscurity which reigns in these subjects, and which puzzle the greatest adepts in political science.

The experience of ages, with the continued and combined labours of the most enlightened legislators and jurists, has been equally unsuccessful in delineating the several objects and limits of different codes of laws and different tribunals of justice. The precise extent of the common law, and the statute law, the maritime law, the ecclesiastical law, the law of corporations, and other local laws and customs, remains still to be clearly and finally established in Great Britain, where accuracy in such subjects has been more industriously pursued than in any other part of the world. The jurisdiction of her several courts, general and local, of law, of equity, of admiralty, etc., is not less a source of frequent and intricate discussions, sufficiently denoting the indeterminate limits by which they are respectively circumscribed. All new laws, though penned with the greatest technical skill, and passed on the fullest and most mature deliberation, are considered as more or less obscure and equivocal, until their meaning be liquidated and ascertained by a series of particular discussions and adjudications. Besides the obscurity arising from the complexity of objects, and the imperfection of the human faculties, the medium through which the conceptions of men are conveyed to each other adds a fresh embarrassment. The use of words is to express ideas. Perspicuity, therefore, requires not only that the ideas should be distinctly formed, but that they should be expressed by words distinctly and exclusively appropriate to them. But no language is so copious as to supply words and phrases for every complex idea, or so correct as not to include many equivocally denoting different ideas. Hence it must happen that however accurately objects may be discriminated in themselves, and however accurately the discrimination may be considered, the definition of them may be rendered inaccurate by the inaccuracy of the terms in which it is delivered. And this unavoidable inaccuracy must be greater or less, according to the complexity and novelty of the objects defined. When the Almighty himself condescends to address mankind in their own language, his meaning, luminous as it must be, is rendered dim and doubtful by the cloudy medium through which it is communicated.

Here, then, are three sources of vague and incorrect definitions: indistinctness of the object, imperfection of the organ of conception, inadequateness of the vehicle of ideas. Any one of these must produce a certain degree of obscurity. The convention, in delineating the boundary between the federal and State jurisdictions, must have experienced the full effect of them all.

To the difficulties already mentioned may be added the interfering pretensions of the larger and smaller States. We cannot err in supposing that the former would contend for a participation in the government, fully proportioned to their superior wealth and importance; and that the latter would not be less tenacious of the equality at present enjoyed by them. We may well suppose that neither side would entirely yield to the other, and consequently that the struggle could be terminated only by compromise. It is extremely probable, also, that after the ratio of representation had been adjusted, this very compromise must have produced a fresh struggle between the same parties, to give such a turn to the organisation of the government, and to the distribution of its powers, as would increase the importance of the branches, in forming which they had respectively obtained the greatest share of influence. There are features in the Constitution which warrant each of these suppositions; and as far as either of them is well founded, it shows that the convention must have been compelled to sacrifice theoretical propriety to the force of extraneous considerations.

Nor could it have been the large and small States only, which would marshal themselves in opposition to each other on various points. Other combinations, resulting from a difference of local position and policy, must have created additional difficulties. As every State may be divided into different districts, and its citizens into different classes, which give birth to contending interests and local jealousies, so the different parts of the United States are distinguished from each other by a variety of circumstances which produce a like effect on a larger scale. And although this variety of interests, for reasons sufficiently explained in a former paper, may have a salutary influence on the administration of the government when formed, yet every one must be sensible of the contrary influence which must have been experienced in the task of forming it.

Would it be wonderful if, under the pressure of all these difficulties, the convention should have been forced into some deviations from that artificial structure and regular symmetry which an abstract view of the subject might lead an ingenious theorist to bestow on a Constitution planned in his closet or in his imagination? The real wonder is that so many difficulties should have been surmounted, and surmounted with a unanimity almost as unprecedented as it must have been unexpected. It is impossible for any man of candour to reflect on this circumstance without partaking of the astonishment. It is impossible for the man of pious reflection not to perceive in it a finger of that Almighty hand which has been so frequently and signally extended to our relief in the critical stages of the revolution.

We had occasion, in a former paper, to take notice of the repeated trials which have been unsuccessfully made in the United Netherlands for reforming the baneful and notorious vices of their constitution. The history of almost all the great councils and consultations held among mankind for reconciling their discordant opinions, assuaging their mutual jealousies, and adjusting their respective interests, is a history of factions, contentions, and disappointments, and may be classed among the most dark and degraded pictures which display the infirmities and depravities of the human character. If, in a few scattered instances, a brighter aspect is presented, they serve only as exceptions to admonish us of the general truth; and by their lustre to darken the gloom of the adverse prospect to which they are contrasted. In revolving the causes from which these exceptions result, and applying them to the particular instances before us, we are necessarily led to two important conclusions. The first is, that the convention must have enjoyed, in a very singular degree, an exemption from the pestilential influence of party animosities—the disease most incident to deliberative bodies, and most apt to contaminate their proceedings. The second conclusion is that all the deputations composing the convention were satisfactorily accommodated by the final act, or were induced to accede to it by a deep conviction of the necessity of sacrificing private opinions and partial interests to the public good, and by a despair of seeing this necessity diminished by delays or by new experiments.

PUBLIUS

Number 38

[MADISON]

IT IS not a little remarkable that in every case reported by ancient history, in which government has been established with deliberation and consent, the task of framing it has not been committed to an assembly of men, but has been performed by some individual citizen of pre-eminent wisdom and approved integrity.

Minos, we learn, was the primitive founder of the government of Crete, as Zaleucus was of that of the Locrians. Theseus first, and after him Draco and Solon, instituted the government of Athens. Lycurgus was the lawgiver of Sparta. The foundation of the original government of Rome was laid by Romulus, and the work completed by two of his elective successors, Numa and Tullius Hostilius. On the abolition of royalty the consular administration was substituted by Brutus, who stepped forward with a project for such a reform, which, he alleged, had been prepared by Tullius Hos-

tilius, and to which his address obtained the assent and ratification of the senate and people. This remark is applicable to confederate governments also. Amphictyon, we are told, was the author of that which bore his name. The Achæan league received its first birth from Achæus, and its second from Aratus.

What degree of agency these reputed lawgivers might have in their respective establishments, or how far they might be clothed with the legitimate authority of the people, cannot in every instance be ascertained. In some, however, the proceeding was strictly regular. Draco appears to have been intrusted by the people of Athens with indefinite powers to reform its government and laws. And Solon, according to Plutarch, was in a manner compelled, by the universal suffrage of his fellow-citizens, to take upon him the sole and absolute power of new-modelling the constitution. The proceedings under Lycurgus were less regular; but as far as the advocates for a regular reform could prevail, they all turned their eyes towards the single efforts of that celebrated patriot and sage, instead of seeking to bring about a revolution by the intervention of a deliberative body of citizens.

Whence could it have proceeded that a people, jealous as the Greeks were of their liberty, should so far abandon the rules of caution as to place their destiny in the hands of a single citizen? Whence could it have proceeded that the Athenians, a people who would not suffer an army to be commanded by fewer than ten generals, and who required no other proof of danger to their liberties than the illustrious merit of a fellow-citizen, should consider one illustrious citizen as a more eligible depositary of the fortunes of themselves and their posterity than a select body of citizens from whose common deliberations more wisdom, as well as more safety, might have been expected? These questions cannot be fully answered without supposing that the fears of discord and disunion among a number of counsellors exceeded the apprehension of treachery or incapacity in a single individual. History informs us, likewise, of the difficulties with which these celebrated reformers had to contend, as well as the expedients which they were obliged to employ in order to carry their reforms into effect. Solon, who seems to have indulged a more temporising policy, confessed that he had not given to his countrymen the government best suited to their happiness, but most tolerable to their prejudices. And Lycurgus, more true to his object, was under the necessity of mixing a portion of violence with the authority of superstition, and of securing his final success by a voluntary renunciation, first of his country, and then of his life. If these lessons teach us, on one hand, to admire the improvement made by America on the ancient mode of preparing and establishing regular plans of government, they serve not less, on the other, to admonish us of the hazards and difficulties incident to such experiments, and of the great imprudence of unnecessarily multiplying them.

Is it an unreasonable conjecture that the errors which may be contained in the plan of the convention are such as have resulted rather from the defect of antecedent experience on this complicated and difficult subject, than from a want of accuracy or care in the investigation of it; and, consequently, such as will not be ascertained until an actual trial shall have pointed them out? This conjecture is rendered probable, not only by many considerations of a general nature, but by the particular case of the Articles of Confederation. It is observable that among the numerous objections and amendments suggested by the several States, when these articles were submitted for their ratification, not one is found which alludes to the great and radical error which on actual trial has discovered itself. And if we except the observations which New Jersey was led to make, rather by her local situation than by her peculiar foresight, may be questioned whether a single suggestion was of sufficient moment to justify a revision of the system. There is abundant reason, nevertheless, to suppose that immaterial as these objections were, they would have been adhered to with a very dangerous inflexibility, in some States, had not a zeal for their opinions and supposed interest been stifled by the more powerful sentiment of self-preservation. One State, we may remember, persisted for several years in refusing her concurrence, although the enemy remained the whole period at our gates, or rather in the very bowels of our country. Nor was her pliancy in the end effected by a less motive than the fear of being chargeable with protracting the public calamities, and endangering the event of the contest. Every candid reader will make the proper reflections on these important facts.

A patient who finds his disorder daily growing worse, and that an efficacious remedy can no longer be delayed without extreme danger, after coolly revolving his situation, and the characters of different physicians, selects and calls in such of them as he judges most capable of administering relief, and best entitled to his confidence. The physicians attend; the case of the patient is carefully examined; a consultation is held; they are unanimously agreed that the symptoms are critical, but that the case, with proper and timely relief, so far from being desperate, that it may be made to issue in an improvement of his constitution. They are equally unanimous in prescribing the remedy, by which this happy effect is to be produced. The prescription is no sooner made known, however, than a number of persons interpose, and, without denying the reality or danger of the disorder, assure the patient that the prescription will be poison to his constitution, and forbid him, under pain of certain death, to make use of it. Might not the patient reasonably demand, before he ventured to follow this advice, that the authors of it should at least agree among themselves on some other remedy to be substituted? And if he found them differing as much from one another as from his first counsellors, would he not act prudently in trying the experiment unanimously recommended by the latter, rather than be hearkening to those who could neither deny the necessity of a speedy remedy, nor agree in proposing one?

Such a patient and in such a situation is America at this moment. She has been sensible of her malady. She has obtained a regular and unanimous advice from men of her own deliberate choice. And she is warned by others against following this advice under pain of the most fatal consequences. Do the monitors deny the reality of her danger? No. Do they deny the necessity of some speedy and powerful remedy? No. Are they agreed, are any two of them agreed, in their objections to the remedy proposed, or in the proper one to be substituted? Let them speak for themselves. This one tells us that the proposed Constitution ought to be rejected, because it is not a confederation of the States, but a government over individuals. Another admits that it ought to be a government over individuals to a certain extent, but by no means to the extent proposed. A third does not object to the government over individuals, or to the extent proposed, but to the want of a bill of rights. A fourth concurs in the absolute necessity of a bill of rights, but contends that it ought to be declaratory, not of the personal rights of individuals, but of the rights reserved to the

States in their political capacity. A fifth is of opinion that a bill of rights of any sort would be superfluous and misplaced, and that the plan would be unexceptionable but for the fatal power of regulating the times and places of election. An objector in a large State exclaims loudly against the unreasonable equality of representation in the Senate. An objector in a small State is equally loud against the dangerous inequality in the House of Representatives. From this quarter, we are alarmed with the amazing expense, from the number of persons who are to administer the new government. From another quarter, and sometimes from the same quarter, on another occasion, the cry is that the Congress will be but a shadow of a representation, and that the government would be far less objectionable if the number and the expense were doubled. A patriot in a State that does not import or export discerns insuperable objections against the power of direct taxation. The patriotic adversary in a State of great exports and imports is not less dissatisfied that the whole burden of taxes may be thrown on consumption. This politician discovers in the Constitution a direct and irresistible tendency to monarchy; that is equally sure it will end in aristocracy. Another is puzzled to say which of these shapes it will ultimately assume, but sees clearly it must be one or other of them; whilst a fourth is not wanting, who with no less confidence affirms that the Constitution is so far from having a bias towards either of these dangers, that the weight on that side will not be sufficient to keep it upright and firm against its opposite propensities. With another class of adversaries to the Constitution the language is that the legislative, executive, and judiciary departments are intermixed in such a manner as to contradict all the ideas of regular government and all the requisite precautions in favour of liberty. Whilst this objection circulates in vague and general expressions, there are but a few who lend their sanction to it. Let each one come forward with his particular explanation, and scarce any two are exactly agreed upon the subject. In the eyes of one the junction of the Senate with the President in the responsible function of appointing to offices, instead of vesting this executive power in the Executive alone, is the vicious part of the organisation. To another, the exclusion of the House of Representatives, whose numbers alone could be a due security against corruption and partiality in the exercise of such a power, is equally obnoxious. With another, the admission of the President into any share of a power which must ever be a dangerous engine in the hands of the executive magistrate, is an unpardonable violation of the maxims of republican jealousy. No part of the arrangement, according to some, is more inadmissible than the trial of impeachments by the Senate, which is alternately a member both of the legislative and executive departments, when this power so evidently belonged to the judiciary department. "We concur fully," reply others, "in the objection to this part of the plan, but we can never agree that a reference of impeachments to the judiciary authority would be an amendment of the error. Our principal dislike to the organisation arises from the extensive powers already lodged in that department." Even among the zealous patrons of a council of state the most irreconcilable variance is discovered concerning the mode in which it ought to be constituted. The demand of one gentleman is, that the council should consist of a small number to be appointed by the most numerous branch of the legislature. Another would prefer a larger number, and considers it as a fundamental condition that the appointment should be made by the President himself.

As it can give no umbrage to the writers against the plan of the federal Constitution, let us suppose that as they are the most zealous, so they are also the most sagacious of those who think the late convention were unequal to the task assigned them, and that a wiser and better plan might and ought to be substituted. Let us further suppose that their country should concur, both in this favourable opinion of their merits, and in their unfavourable opinion of the convention; and should accordingly proceed to form them into a second convention, with full powers, and for the express purpose of revising and remoulding the work of the first. Were the experiment to be seriously made, though it required some effort to view it seriously even in fiction, I leave it to be decided by the sample of opinions just exhibited, whether, with all their enmity to their predecessors, they would, in any one point, depart so widely from their example, as in the discord and ferment that would mark their own deliberations; and whether the Constitution now before the public would not stand as fair a chance for immortality as Lycurgus gave to that of Sparta, by making its change to depend on his own return from exile and death, if it were to be immediately adopted, and were to continue in force, not until a BETTER, but until ANOTHER should be agreed upon by this new assembly of lawgivers.

It is a matter both of wonder and regret that those who raise so many objections against the new Constitution should never call to mind the defects of that which is to be exchanged for it. It is not necessary that the former should be perfect: it is sufficient that the latter is more imperfect. No man would refuse to give brass for silver or gold, because the latter had some alloy in it. No man would refuse to quit a shattered and tottering habitation for a firm and commodious building, because the latter had not a porch to it, or because some of the rooms might be a little larger or smaller, or the ceiling a little higher or lower than his fancy would have planned them. But waiving illustrations of this sort, is it not manifest that most of the capital objections urged against the new system lie with tenfold weight against the existing Confederation? Is an indefinite power to raise money dangerous in the hands of the federal government? The present Congress can make requisitions to any amount they please, and the States are constitutionally bound to furnish them; they can emit bills of credit as long as they will pay for the paper; they can borrow, both abroad and at home, as long as a shilling will be lent. Is an indefinite power to raise troops dangerous? The Confederation gives to Congress that power also; and they have already begun to make use of it. Is it improper and unsafe to intermix the different powers of government in the same body of men? Congress, a single body of men, are the sole depositary of all the federal powers. Is it particularly dangerous to give the keys of the treasury, and the command of the army, into the same hands? The Confederation places them both in the hands of Congress. Is a bill of rights essential to liberty? The Confederation has no bill of rights. Is it an objection against the new Constitution that it empowers the Senate, with the concurrence of the Executive, to make treaties which are to be the laws of the land? The existing Congress, without any such control, can make treaties which they themselves have declared, and most of the States have recognized, to be the supreme law of the land. Is the importation of slaves permitted by the new Constitution for twenty years? By the old it is permitted for ever.

I shall be told that however dangerous this mixture of powers may be in theory, it is rendered harmless by the dependence of Congress on the States for the means of carrying them into practice; that however large the mass of powers may be, it is in fact a lifeless mass. Then, say I, in the first place, that the Confederation is chargeable with the still greater folly of declaring certain powers in the federal government to be absolutely necessary, and at the same time rendering them absolutely nugatory; and, in the next place, that if the Union is to continue, and no better government be substituted, effective powers must either be granted to, or assumed by, the existing Congress; in either of which events, the contrast just stated will hold good. But this is not all. Out of this lifeless mass has already grown an excrescent power, which tends to realise all the dangers that can be apprehended from a defective construction of the supreme government of the Union. It is now no longer a point of speculation and hope that the Western territory is a mine of vast wealth to the United States; and although it is not of such a nature as to extricate them from their present distresses, or, for some time to come, to yield any regular supplies for the public expenses, yet must it hereafter be able, under proper management, both to effect a gradual discharge of the domestic debt, and to furnish, for a certain period, liberal tributes to the federal treasury. A very large proportion of this fund has been already surrendered by individual States; and it may with reason be expected that the remaining States will not persist in withholding similar proofs of their equity and generosity. We may calculate, therefore, that a rich and fertile country, of an area equal to the inhabited extent of the United States, will soon become a national stock. Congress have assumed the administration of this stock. They have begun to render it productive. Congress have undertaken to do more: they have proceeded to form new States, to erect temporary governments, to appoint officers for them, and to prescribe the conditions on which such States shall be admitted into the Confederacy. All this has been done; and done without the least colour of constitutional authority. Yet no blame has been whispered; no alarm has been sounded. A GREAT and INDEPENDENT fund of revenue is passing into the hands of a SINGLE BODY of men, who can RAISE TROOPS to an INDEFINITE NUMBER, and appropriate money to their support for an INDEFINITE PERIOD OF TIME. And yet there are men who have not only been silent spectators of this prospect, but who are advocates for the system which exhibits it; and, at the same time, urge against the new system the objections which we have heard. Would they not act with more consistency, in urging the establishment of the latter, as no less necessary to guard the Union against the future powers and resources of a body constructed like the existing Congress, than to save it from the dangers threatened by the present impotency of that Assembly?

I mean not, by anything here said, to throw censure on the measures which have been pursued by Congress. I am sensible they could not have done otherwise. The public interest, the necessity of the case, imposed upon them the task of overleaping their constitutional limits. But is not the fact an alarming proof of the danger resulting from a government which does not possess regular powers commensurate to its objects? A dissolution or usurpation is the dreadful dilemma to which it is continually exposed. PUBLIUS

Number *39*

[MADISON]

THE LAST paper having concluded the observations which were meant to introduce a candid survey of the plan of government reported by the convention, we now proceed to the execution of that part of our undertaking.

The first question that offers itself is, whether the general form and aspect of the government be strictly republican. It is evident that no other form would be reconcilable with the genius of the people of America; with the fundamental principles of the Revolution; or with that honourable determination which animates every votary of freedom, to rest all our political experiments on the capacity of mankind for self-government. If the plan of the convention, therefore, be found to depart from the republican character, its advocates must abandon it as no longer defensible.

What, then, are the distinctive characters of the republican form? Were an answer to this question to be sought, not by recurring to principles, but in the application of the term by political writers, to the constitutions of different States, no satisfactory one would ever be found. Holland, in which no particle of the supreme authority is derived from the people, has passed almost universally under the denomination of a republic. The same title has been bestowed on Venice, where absolute power over the great body of the people is exercised, in the most absolute manner, by a small body of hereditary nobles. Poland, which is a mixture of aristocracy and of monarchy in their worst forms, has been dignified with the same appellation. The government of England, which has one republican branch only, combined with an hereditary aristocracy and monarchy, has, with equal impropriety, been frequently placed on the list of republics. These examples, which are nearly as dissimilar to each other as to a genuine republic, show the extreme inaccuracy with which the term has been used in political disquisitions.

If we resort for a criterion to the different principles on which different forms of government are established, we may define a republic to be, or at least may bestow that name on, a government which derives all its powers directly or indirectly from the great body of the people, and is administered by persons holding their offices during pleasure, for a limited period, or during good behaviour. It is *essential* to such a government that it be derived from the great body of the society, not from an inconsiderable proportion, or a favoured class of it; otherwise a handful of tyrannical nobles, exercising their oppressions by a delegation of their powers, might aspire to the rank of republicans, and claim for their government the honourable title of republic. It is *sufficient* for such a government that the persons administering it be appointed, either directly or indirectly, by the people; and that they hold their appointments by either of the tenures just specified; otherwise every government in the United States, as well as every other popular government that has been or can be well organised or well executed, would be degraded from the republican character. According to the constitution of every State in the Union, some one or other of the officers of government are appointed indirectly only by the people. According to most of them, the chief magistrate himself is so appointed. And according to one, this mode of appointment is extended to one of the co-ordinate branches of the legislature. According to all the constitutions, also, the tenure of the highest offices is extended to a definite period, and in many instances, both within the legislative and executive departments, to a period of years. According to the provisions of most of the constitutions, again, as well as according to the most respectable and received opinions on the subject, the members of the judiciary department are to retain their offices by the firm tenure of good behaviour.

On comparing the Constitution planned by the convention with the standard here fixed, we perceive at once that it is, in the most rigid sense, conformable to it. The House of Representatives, like that of one branch at least of all the State legislatures, is elected immediately by the great body of the people. The Senate, like the present Congress, and the Senate of Maryland, derives its appointment indirectly from the people. The President is indirectly derived from the choice of the people, according to the example in most of the States. Even the judges, with all other officers of the Union, will, as in the several States, be the choice, though a remote choice, of the people themselves. The duration of the appointments is equally conformable to the republican standard, and to the model of State constitutions. The House of Representatives is periodically elective, as in all the States; and for the period of two years, as in the State of South Carolina. The Senate is elective, for the period of six years; which is but one year more than the period of the Senate of Maryland, and but two more than that of the Senates of New York and Virginia. The President is to continue in office for the period of four years; as in New York and Delaware the chief magistrate is elected for three years, and in South Carolina for two years. In the other States the election is annual. In several of the States, however, no constitutional provision is made for the impeachment of the chief magistrate. And in Delaware and Virginia he is not impeachable till out of office. The President of the United States is impeachable at any time during his continuance in office. The tenure by which the judges are to hold their places is, as it unquestionably ought to be, that of good behaviour. The tenure of the ministerial offices generally will be a subject of legal regulation, conformably to the reason of the case and the example of the State constitutions.

Could any further proof be required of the republican complexion of this system, the most decisive one might be found in its absolute prohibition of titles of nobility, both under the federal and the State governments; and in its express guarantee of the republican form to each of the latter.

"But it was not sufficient," say the adversaries of the proposed Constitution, "for the convention to adhere to the republican form. They ought, with equal care, to have preserved the *federal* form, which regards the Union as a *Confederacy* of sovereign states; instead of which, they have framed a *national* government, which regards the Union as a *consolidation* of the States." And it is asked by what authority this bold and radical innovation was undertaken? The handle which has been made of this objection requires that it should be examined with some precision.

Without inquiring into the accuracy of the distinction on which the objection is founded, it will be necessary to a just estimate of its force, first, to ascertain the real character of the government in question; secondly, to inquire how far the convention were authorised to propose such a government; and thirdly, how far the duty they owed to their country could supply any defect of regular authority.

First.—In order to ascertain the real character of the government, it may be considered in relation to the foundation on which it is to be established; to the sources from which its ordinary powers are to be drawn; to the operation of those powers; to the extent of them; and to the authority by which future changes in the government are to be introduced.

On examining the first relation, it appears, on one hand, that the Constitution is to be founded on the assent and ratification of the people of America, given by deputies elected for the special purpose; but, on the other, that this assent and ratification is to be given by the people, not as individuals composing one entire nation, but as composing the distinct and independent States to which they respectively belong. It is to be the assent and ratification of the several States, derived from the supreme authority in each State,—the authority of the people themselves. The act, therefore, establishing the Constitution, will not be a *national*, but a *federal* act.

That it will be a federal and not a national act, as these terms are understood by the objectors; the act of the people, as forming so many independent States, not as forming one aggregate nation, is obvious from this single consideration, that it is to result neither from the decision of a *majority* of the people of the Union, nor from that of a *majority* of the States. It must result from the *unanimous* assent of the several States that are parties to it, differing no otherwise from their ordinary assent than in its being expressed, not by the legislative authority, but by that of the people themselves. Were the people regarded in this transaction as forming one nation, the will of the majority of the whole people of the United States would bind the minority, in the same manner as the majority in each State must bind the minority; and the will of the majority must be determined either by a comparison of the individual votes, or by considering the will of the majority of the States as evidence of the will of a majority of the people of the United States. Neither of these rules has been adopted. Each State, in ratifying the Constitution, is considered as a sovereign body, independent of all others, and only to be bound by its own voluntary act. In this relation, then, the new Constitution will, if established, be a *federal,* and not a *national,* constitution.

The next relation is to the sources from which the ordinary powers of government are to be derived. The House of Representatives will derive its powers from the people of America; and the people will be represented in the same proportion, and on the same principle, as they are in the legislature of a particular State. So far the government is *national,* not *federal.* The Senate, on the other hand, will derive its powers from the States, as political and coequal societies; and these will be represented on the principle of equality in the Senate, as they now are in the existing Congress. So far the government is *federal,* not *national.* The executive power will be derived from a very compound source. The immediate election of the President is to be made by the States in their political characters. The votes allotted to them are in a compound ratio, which considers them partly as distinct and coequal societies, partly as unequal members of the same society. The eventual election, again, is to be made by that branch of the legislature which consists of the national representatives; but in this particular act they are to be thrown into the form of individual delegations, from so many distinct and coequal bodies politic. From this aspect of the government, it appears to be of a mixed character, presenting at least as many *federal* as *national* features.

The difference between a federal and national government, as it relates to the *operation of the government,* is supposed to consist in this, that in the former the powers operate on the political bodies composing the Confederacy, in their political capacities; in the latter, on the individual citizens composing the nation, in their individual capacities. On trying the Constitution by this criterion, it falls under the *national,* not the *federal* character; though perhaps not so completely as has been understood. In several cases, and particularly in the trial of controversies to which States may be parties, they must be viewed and proceeded against in their collective and political capacities only. So far the national countenance of the government on this side seems to be disfigured by a few federal features. But this blemish is perhaps unavoidable in any plan; and the operation of the government on the people, in their individual capacities, in its ordinary and most essential proceedings, may, on the whole, designate it, in this relation, a *national* government.

But if the government be national with regard to the *operation* of its powers, it changes its aspect again when we contemplate it in relation to the *extent* of its powers. The idea of a national government involves in it, not only an authority over the individual citizens, but an indefinite supremacy over all persons and things, so far as they are objects of lawful government. Among a people consolidated into one nation, this supremacy is completely vested in the national legislature. Among communities united for particular purposes, it is vested partly in the general and partly in the municipal legislatures. In the former case, all local authorities are subordinate to the supreme; and may be controlled, directed, or abolished by it at pleasure. In the latter, the local or municipal authorities form distinct and independent portions of the supremacy, no more subject, within their respective spheres, to the general authority than the general authority is subject to them within its own sphere. In this relation, then, the proposed government cannot be deemed a *national* one; since its jurisdiction extends to certain enumerated objects only, and leaves to the several states a residuary and inviolable sovereignty over all other objects. It is true that in controversies relating to the boundary between the two jurisdictions, the tribunal which is ultimately to decide, is to be established under the general government. But this does not change the principle of the case. The decision is to be impartially made, according to the rules of the Constitution; and all the usual and most effectual precautions are taken to secure this impartiality. Some such tribunal is clearly essential to prevent an appeal to the sword and a dissolution of the compact; and that it ought to be established under the general rather than under the local governments, or, to speak more properly, that it could be safely established under the first alone, is a position not likely to be combated.

If we try the Constitution by its last relation to the authority by which amendments are to be made, we find it neither wholly *national* nor wholly *federal*. Were it wholly national, the supreme and ultimate authority would reside in the *majority* of the people of the Union; and this authority would be competent at all times, like that of a majority of every national society, to alter, or abolish its established government. Were it wholly federal, on the other hand, the concurrence of each State in the Union would be essential to every alteration that would be binding on all. The mode provided by the plan of the convention is not founded on either of these principles. In requiring more than a majority, and particularly in computing the proportion by *States,* not by *citizens,* it departs from the *national* and advances towards the *federal* character; in rendering the concurrence of less than the whole number of States sufficient, it loses again the *federal* and partakes of the *national* character.

The proposed Constitution, therefore, is, in strictness, neither a national nor a federal Constitution, but a composition of both. In its foundation it is federal, not national; in the sources from which the ordinary powers of the government are drawn, it is partly federal and partly national; in the operation of these powers, it is national, not federal; in the extent of them, again, it is federal, not national; and, finally, in the authoritative mode of introducing amendments, it is neither wholly federal nor wholly national.   PUBLIUS

Number 40

[MADISON]

THE *second* point to be examined is, whether the convention were authorised to frame and propose this mixed Constitution.

The powers of the convention ought, in strictness, to be determined by an inspection of the commissions given to the members by their respective constituents. As all of these, however, had reference, either to the recommendation from the meeting at Annapolis, in September 1786, or to that from Congress, in February 1787, it will be sufficient to recur to these particular acts.

The act from Annapolis recommends the "appointment of commissioners to take into consideration the situation of the United States; to devise *such further provisions* as shall appear to them necessary to render the Constitution of the federal government *adequate*

to the exigencies of the Union; and to report such an act for that purpose, to the United States in Congress assembled, as when agreed to by them, and afterwards confirmed by the legislature of every State, will effectually provide for the same."

The recommendatory act of Congress is in the words following: "Whereas, there is provision in the articles of Confederation and perpetual Union, for making alterations therein, by the assent of a Congress of the United States, and of the legislatures of the several States; and whereas experience hath evinced that there are defects in the present Confederation; as a mean to remedy which, several of the States, and *particularly the State of New York,* by express instructions to their delegates in Congress, have suggested a convention for the purposes expressed in the following resolution; and such convention appearing to be the most probable mean of establishing in these States *a firm national government:*

"*Resolved,*—That in the opinion of Congress it is expedient, that on the second Monday of May next a convention of delegates who shall have been appointed by the several States, be held at Philadelphia, for the sole and express purpose *of revising the articles of Confederation,* and reporting to Congress and the several legislatures such *alterations and provisions therein,* as shall, when agreed to in Congress, and confirmed by the States, render the federal Constitution *adequate to the exigencies of government and the preservation of the Union.*"

From these two acts, it appears, 1st, that the object of the convention was to establish, in these States, *a firm national government;* 2nd, that this government was to be such as would be *adequate to the exigencies of government* and *the preservation of the Union;* 3rd, that these purposes were to be effected by *alterations and provisions in the articles of Confederation,* as it is expressed in the act of Congress, or by *such further provisions as should appear necessary,* as it stands in the recommendatory act from Annapolis; 4th, that the alterations and provisions were to be reported to Congress, and to the States, in order to be agreed to by the former and confirmed by the latter.

From a comparison and fair construction of these several modes of expression is to be deduced the authority under which the convention acted. They were to frame a *national government,* adequate to the *exigencies of gov-*

ernment, and *of the Union;* and to reduce the articles of Confederation into such form as to accomplish these purposes.

There are two rules of construction, dictated by plain reason, as well as founded on legal axioms. The one is, that every part of the expression ought, if possible, to be allowed some meaning, and be made to conspire to some common end. The other is, that where the several parts cannot be made to coincide, the less important should give way to the more important part; the means should be sacrificed to the end, rather than the end to the means.

Suppose, then, that the expressions defining the authority of the convention were irreconcilably at variance with each other; that a *national* and *adequate government* could not possibly, in the judgment of the convention, be effected by *alterations* and *provisions* in the *articles of Confederation;* which part of the definition ought to have been embraced, and which rejected? Which was the more important, which the less important part? Which the end; which the means? Let the most scrupulous expositors of delegated powers; let the most inveterate objector against those exercised by the convention, answer these questions. Let them declare, whether it was of most importance to the happiness of the people of America, that the articles of Confederation should be disregarded, and an adequate government be provided, and the Union preserved; or that an adequate government should be omitted, and the articles of Confederation preserved. Let them declare whether the preservation of these articles was the end for securing which a reform of the government was to be introduced as the means; or whether the establishment of a government, adequate to the national happiness, was the end at which these articles themselves originally aimed, and to which they ought, as insufficient means, to have been sacrificed.

But is it necessary to suppose that these expressions are absolutely irreconcilable to each other; that no *alterations* or *provisions* in *the articles of the Confederation* could possibly mould them into a national and adequate government; into such a government as has been proposed by the convention?

No stress, it is presumed, will, in this case, be laid on the *title;* a change of that could never be deemed an exercise of ungranted power. *Alterations* in the body of the instrument are expressly authorised. *New provisions* therein are also expressly authorised. Here then is a power to change the title; to insert new articles; to alter old ones. Must it of necessity be admitted that this power is infringed, so long as a part of the old articles remain? Those who maintain the affirmative ought at least to mark the boundary between authorised and usurped innovations; between that degree of change which lies within the compass of *alterations and further provisions,* and that which amounts to a *transmutation* of the government. Will it be said that the alterations ought not to have touched the substance of the Confederation? The States would never have appointed a convention with so much solemnity, nor described its objects with so much latitude, if some *substantial* reform had not been in contemplation. Will it be said that the *fundamental principles* of the Confederation were not within the purview of the convention, and ought not to have been varied? I ask, What are these principles? Do they require that, in the establishment of the Constitution, the States should be regarded as distinct and independent sovereigns? They are so regarded by the Constitution proposed. Do they require that the members of the government should derive their appointment from the legislatures, not from the people of the States? One branch of the new government is to be appointed by these legislatures; and under the Confederation, the delegates to Congress *may all* be appointed immediately by the people, and in two States[1] are actually so appointed. Do they require that the powers of the government should act on the States, and not immediately on individuals? In some instances, as has been shown, the powers of the new government will act on the States in their collective characters. In some instances, also, those of the existing government act immediately on individuals. In cases of capture; of piracy; of the post-office; of coins, weights, and measures; of trade with the Indians; of claims under grants of land by different States; and, above all, in the case of trials by courts-martial in the army and navy, by which death may be inflicted without the intervention of a jury, or even of a civil magistrate;—in all these cases the powers of the Confederation operate immediately on the persons and interests of individual citizens. Do these fundamental principles require, particularly, that no tax should be levied without the intermediate agency of the States? The Confederation itself author-

[1] Connecticut and Rhode Island.—PUBLIUS

ises a direct tax, to a certain extent, on the post-office. The power of coinage has been so construed by Congress as to levy a tribute immediately from that source also. But pretermitting these instances, was it not an acknowledged object of the convention and the universal expectation of the people that the regulation of trade should be submitted to the general government in such a form as would render it an immediate source of general revenue? Had not Congress repeatedly recommended this measure as not inconsistent with the fundamental principles of the Confederation? Had not every State but one; had not New York herself, so far complied with the plan of Congress as to recognise the *principle* of the innovation? Do these principles, in fine, require that the powers of the general government should be limited, and that, beyond this limit, the States should be left in possession of their sovereignty and independence? We have seen that in the new government, as in the old, the general powers are limited; and that the States, in all unenumerated cases, are left in the enjoyment of their sovereign and independent jurisdiction.

The truth is, that the great principles of the Constitution proposed by the convention may be considered less as absolutely new, than as the expansion of principles which are found in the articles of Confederation. The misfortune under the latter system has been, that these principles are so feeble and confined as to justify all the charges of inefficiency which have been urged against it, and to require a degree of enlargement which gives to the new system the aspect of an entire transformation of the old.

In one particular it is admitted that the convention have departed from the tenor of their commission. Instead of reporting a plan requiring the confirmation *of the legislatures of all the States,* they have reported a plan which is to be confirmed by the *people,* and may be carried into effect by *nine States only.* It is worthy of remark that this objection, though the most plausible, has been the least urged in the publications which have swarmed against the convention. The forbearance can only have proceeded from an irresistible conviction of the absurdity of subjecting the fate of twelve States to the perverseness or corruption of a thirteenth; from the example of inflexible opposition given by a *majority* of one sixtieth of the people of America to a measure approved and called for by the voice of twelve

States, comprising fifty-nine sixtieths of the people—an example still fresh in the memory and indignation of every citizen who has felt for the wounded honour and prosperity of his country. As this objection, therefore, has been in a manner waived by those who have criticised the powers of the convention, I dismiss it without further observation.

The *third* point to be inquired into is, how far considerations of duty arising out of the case itself could have supplied any defect of regular authority.

In the preceding inquiries the powers of the convention have been analysed and tried with the same rigour, and by the same rules, as if they had been real and final powers for the establishment of a Constitution for the United States. We have seen in what manner they have borne the trial even on that supposition. It is time now to recollect that the powers were merely advisory and recommendatory; that they were so meant by the States, and so understood by the convention; and that the latter have accordingly planned and proposed a Constitution which is to be of no more consequence than the paper on which it is written, unless it be stamped with the approbation of those to whom it is addressed. This reflection places the subject in a point of view altogether different, and will enable us to judge with propriety of the course taken by the convention.

Let us view the ground on which the convention stood. It may be collected from their proceedings, that they were deeply and unanimously impressed with the crisis which had led their country almost with one voice to make so singular and solemn an experiment for correcting the errors of a system by which this crisis had been produced; that they were no less deeply and unanimously convinced that such a reform as they have proposed was absolutely necessary to effect the purposes of their appointment. It could not be unknown to them that the hopes and expectations of the great body of citizens, throughout this great empire, were turned with the keenest anxiety to the event of their deliberations. They had every reason to believe that the contrary sentiments agitated the minds and bosoms of every external and internal foe to the liberty and prosperity of the United States. They had seen in the origin and progress of the experiment, the alacrity with which the *proposition,* made by a single State (Virginia), towards a partial amendment of the Confederation, had been attended to and promoted. They had seen the *liberty assumed* by a *very few* deputies from a *very few* States, convened at Annapolis, of recommending a great and critical object, wholly foreign to their commission, not only justified by the public opinion, but actually carried into effect by twelve out of the thirteen States. They had seen, in a variety of instances, assumptions by Congress, not only of recommendatory, but of operative, powers, warranted, in the public estimation, by occasions and objects infinitely less urgent than those by which their conduct was to be governed. They must have reflected, that in all great changes of established governments, forms ought to give way to substance; that a rigid adherence in such cases to the former, would render nominal and nugatory the transcendent and precious right of the people to "abolish or alter their governments as to them shall seem most likely to effect their safety and happiness,"[1] since it is impossible for the people spontaneously and universally to move in concert towards their object; and it is therefore essential that such changes be instituted by some *informal and unauthorised propositions,* made by some patriotic and respectable citizen or number of citizens. They must have recollected that it was by this irregular and assumed privilege of proposing to the people plans for their safety and happiness, that the States were first united against the danger with which they were threatened by their ancient government; that committees and congresses were formed for concentrating their efforts and defending their rights; and that *conventions* were *elected* in *the several States* for establishing the constitutions under which they are now governed; nor could it have been forgotten that no little ill-timed scruples, no zeal for adhering to ordinary forms, were anywhere seen, except in those who wished to indulge, under these masks, their secret enmity to the substance contended for. They must have borne in mind that as the plan to be framed and proposed was to be submitted *to the people themselves,* the disapprobation of this supreme authority would destroy it for ever; its approbation blot out antecedent errors and irregularities. It might even have occurred to them, that where a disposition to cavil prevailed, their neglect to execute the degree of power vested in them, and still more their recommendation of any measure whatever, not warranted by their commission, would not less excite animadversion,

[1] Declaration of Independence.—PUBLIUS

than a recommendation at once of a measure fully commensurate to the national exigencies.

Had the convention, under all these impressions, and in the midst of all these considerations, instead of exercising a manly confidence in their country, by whose confidence they had been so peculiarly distinguished, and of pointing out a system capable, in their judgment, of securing its happiness, taken the cold and sullen resolution of disappointing its ardent hopes, of sacrificing substance to forms, of committing the dearest interest of their country to the uncertainties of delay and the hazard of events, let me ask the man who can raise his mind to one elevated conception, who can awaken in his bosom one patriotic emotion, what judgment ought to have been pronounced by the impartial world, by the friends of mankind, by every virtuous citizen, on the conduct and character of this assembly? Or if there be a man whose propensity to condemn is susceptible of no control, let me then ask what sentence he has in reserve for the twelve States who *usurped the power* of sending deputies to the convention, a body utterly unknown to their constitutions; for Congress, who recommended the appointment of this body, equally unknown to the Confederation; and for the State of New York, in particular, which first urged and then complied with this unauthorised interposition?

But that the objectors may be disarmed of every pretext, it shall be granted for a moment that the convention were neither authorised by their commission, nor justified by circumstances in proposing a Constitution for their country: does it follow that the Constitution ought, for that reason alone, to be rejected? If, according to the noble precept, it be lawful to accept good advice even from an enemy, shall we set the ignoble example of refusing such advice even when it is offered by our friends? The prudent inquiry, in all cases, ought surely to be, not so much *from whom* the advice comes, as whether the advice be *good.*

The sum of what has been here advanced and proved is, that the charge against the convention of exceeding their powers, except in one instance little urged by the objectors, has no foundation to support it; that if they had exceeded their powers, they were not only warranted, but required, as the confidential servants of their country, by the circumstances in which they were placed, to exercise the liberty which they assumed; and that finally, if they had violated both their powers and their obligations, in proposing a Constitution, this ought nevertheless to be embraced, if it be calculated to accomplish the views and happiness of the people of America. How far this character is due to the Constitution, is the subject under investigation.   PUBLIUS

Number 41

[MADISON]

THE CONSTITUTION proposed by the convention may be considered under two general points of view. The FIRST relates to the sum or quantity of power which it vests in the government, including the restraints imposed on the States. The SECOND, to the particular structure of the government, and the distribution of this power among its several branches.

Under the *first* view of the subject, two important questions arise: 1. Whether any part of the powers transferred to the general government be unnecessary or improper? 2. Whether the entire mass of them be dangerous to the portion of jurisdiction left in the several States?

Is the aggregate power of the general government greater than ought to have been vested in it? This is the *first* question.

It cannot have escaped those who have attended with candour to the arguments employed against the extensive powers of the government, that the authors of them have very little considered how far these powers were necessary means of attaining a necessary end. They have chosen rather to dwell on the inconveniences which must be unavoidably blended with all political advantages; and on the possible abuses which must be incident to every power or trust, of which a beneficial use can be made. This method of handling the subject cannot impose on the good sense of the people of America. It may display the subtlety of the writer; it may open a boundless field for rhetoric and declamation; it may inflame the passions of the unthinking, and may confirm the prejudices of the misthinking: but cool and candid people will at once reflect, that the purest of human blessings must have a portion of alloy in them; that the choice must always be made, if not of the lesser evil, at least of the GREATER, not the PERFECT, good; and that in every political institution, a power to advance the public happiness involves a discretion which may be misapplied and abused. They will see, therefore, that in all cases where power is to be conferred, the point first to be decided is, whether such a power be necessary to the public good; as the next will be, in case of an affirmative decision, to guard as effectually as possible against a perversion of the power to the public detriment.

That we may form a correct judgment on this subject, it will be proper to review the several powers conferred on the government of the Union; and that this may be the more conveniently done they may be reduced into different classes as they relate to the following different objects: 1. Security against foreign danger; 2. Regulation of the intercourse with foreign nations; 3. Maintenance of harmony and proper intercourse among the States; 4. Certain miscellaneous objects of general utility; 5. Restraint of the States from certain injurious acts; 6. Provisions for giving due efficacy to all these powers.

The powers falling within the *first* class are those of declaring war and granting letters of marque; of providing armies and fleets; of regulating and calling forth the militia; of levying and borrowing money.

Security against foreign danger is one of the primitive objects of civil society. It is an avowed and essential object of the American Union. The powers requisite for attaining it must be effectually confided to the federal councils.

Is the power of declaring war necessary? No man will answer this question in the negative. It would be superfluous, therefore, to enter into a proof of the affirmative. The existing Confederation establishes this power in the most ample form.

Is the power of raising armies and equipping fleets necessary? This is involved in the foregoing power. It is involved in the power of self-defence.

But was it necessary to give an INDEFINITE POWER of raising TROOPS, as well as providing fleets; and of maintaining both in PEACE, as well as in war?

The answer to these questions has been too far anticipated in another place to admit an extensive discussion of them in this place. The answer indeed seems to be so obvious and conclusive as scarcely to justify such a discussion in any place. With what colour of propriety could the force necessary for defence be limited by those who cannot limit the force of offence? If a federal Constitution could chain the ambition or set bounds to the exertions of all other nations, then indeed might it prudently chain the discretion of its own government, and set bounds to the exertions for its own safety.

How could a readiness for war in time of peace be safely prohibited, unless we could prohibit, in like manner, the preparations and establishments of every hostile nation? The means of security can only be regulated by the means and the danger of attack. They will, in fact, be ever determined by these rules, and by no others. It is in vain to oppose constitutional barriers to the impulse of self-preservation. It is worse than in vain; because it plants in the Constitution itself necessary usurpations of power, every precedent of which is a germ of unnecessary and multiplied repetitions. If one nation maintains constantly a disciplined army, ready for the service of ambition or revenge, it obliges the most pacific nations who may be within the reach of its enterprises to take corresponding precautions. The fifteenth century was the unhappy epoch of military establishments in the time of peace. They were introduced by Charles VII. of France. All Europe has followed, or been forced into, the example. Had the example not been followed by other nations all Europe must long ago have worn the chains of a universal monarch. Were every nation except France now to disband its peace establishments, the same event might follow. The veteran legions of Rome were an overmatch for the undisciplined valour of all other nations, and rendered her the mistress of the world.

Not the less true is it, that the liberties of Rome proved the final victim to her military triumphs; and that the liberties of Europe, as far as they ever existed, have, with few exceptions, been the price of her military establishments. A standing force, therefore, is a dangerous, at the same time that it may be a necessary, provision. On the smallest scale it has its inconveniences. On an extensive scale its consequences may be fatal. On any scale it is an object of laudable circumspection and precaution. A wise nation will combine all these considerations; and, whilst it does not rashly preclude itself from any resource which may become essential to its safety, will exert all its prudence in diminishing both the necessity and the danger of resorting to one which may be inauspicious to its liberties.

The clearest marks of this prudence are stamped on the proposed Constitution. The Union itself, which it cements and secures, destroys every pretext for a military establishment which could be dangerous. America

united, with a handful of troops, or without a single soldier, exhibits a more forbidding posture to foreign ambition than America disunited, with a hundred thousand veterans ready for combat. It was remarked on a former occasion, that the want of this pretext had saved the liberties of one nation in Europe. Being rendered by her insular situation and her maritime resources impregnable to the armies of her neighbours, the rulers of Great Britain have never been able, by real or artificial dangers, to cheat the public into an extensive peace establishment. The distance of the United States from the powerful nations of the world gives them the same happy security. A dangerous establishment can never be necessary or plausible, so long as they continue a united people. But let it never, for a moment, be forgotten that they are indebted for this advantage to the Union alone. The moment of its dissolution will be the date of a new order of things. The fears of the weaker, or the ambition of the stronger States, or Confederacies, will set the same example in the New as Charles VII. did in the Old World. The example will be followed here from the same motives which produced universal imitation there. Instead of deriving from our situation the precious advantage which Great Britain has derived from hers, the face of America will be but a copy of that of the continent of Europe. It will present liberty everywhere crushed between standing armies and perpetual taxes. The fortunes of disunited America will be even more disastrous than those of Europe. The sources of evil in the latter are confined to her own limits. No superior powers of another quarter of the globe intrigue among her rival nations, inflame their mutual animosities, and render them the instruments of foreign ambition, jealousy, and revenge. In America the miseries springing from her internal jealousies, contentions, and wars, would form a part only of her lot. A plentiful addition of evils would have their source in that relation in which Europe stands to this quarter of the earth, and which no other quarter of the earth bears to Europe.

This picture of the consequences of disunion cannot be too highly coloured, or too often exhibited. Every man who loves peace, every man who loves his country, every man who loves liberty, ought to have it ever before his eyes, that he may cherish in his heart a due attachment to the Union of America, and be able to set a due value on the means of preserving it.

Next to the effectual establishment of the Union, the best possible precaution against danger from standing armies is a limitation of the term for which revenue may be appropriated to their support. This precaution the Constitution has prudently added. I will not repeat here the observations which I flatter myself have placed this subject in a just and satisfactory light. But it may not be improper to take notice of an argument against this part of the Constitution which has been drawn from the policy and practice of Great Britain. It is said that the continuance of an army in that kingdom requires an annual vote of the legislature; whereas the American Constitution has lengthened this critical period to two years. This is the form in which the comparison is usually stated to the public: but is it a just form? Is it a fair comparison? Does the British Constitution restrain the parliamentary discretion to one year? Does the American impose on the Congress appropriations for two years? On the contrary, it cannot be unknown to the authors of the fallacy themselves, that the British Constitution fixes no limit whatever to the discretion of the legislature, and that the American ties down the legislature to two years, as the longest admissible term.

Had the argument from the British example been truly stated, it would have stood thus: The term for which supplies may be appropriated to the army establishment, though unlimited by the British Constitution, has nevertheless, in practice, been limited by parliamentary discretion to a single year. Now, if in Great Britain, where the House of Commons is elected for seven years; where so great a proportion of the members are elected by so small a proportion of the people; where the electors are so corrupted by the representatives, and the representatives so corrupted by the Crown, the representative body can possess a power to make appropriations to the army for an indefinite term, without desiring, or without daring, to extend the term beyond a single year, ought not suspicion herself to blush, in pretending that the representatives of the United States, elected FREELY by the WHOLE BODY of the people, every SECOND YEAR, cannot be safely intrusted with the discretion over such appropriations, expressly limited to the short period of TWO YEARS?

A bad cause seldom fails to betray itself. Of this truth, the management of the opposition to the federal government is an unvaried exemplification. But among all the blunders which have been committed, none is more striking than the attempt to enlist on that side the prudent jealousy entertained by the people of standing armies. The attempt has awakened fully the public attention to that important subject; and has led to investigations which must terminate in a thorough and universal conviction, not only that the Constitution has provided the most effectual guards against danger from that quarter, but that nothing short of a Constitution fully adequate to the national defence and the preservation of the Union can save America from as many standing armies as it may be split into States or Confederacies, and from such a progressive augmentation of these establishments in each as will render them as burdensome to the properties and ominous to the liberties of the people as any establishment that can become necessary, under a united and efficient government, must be tolerable to the former and safe to the latter.

The palpable necessity of the power to provide and maintain a navy has protected that part of the Constitution against a spirit of censure, which has spared few other parts. It must, indeed, be numbered among the greatest blessings of America, that as her Union will be the only source of her maritime strength, so this will be a principal source of her security against danger from abroad. In this respect our situation bears another likeness to the insular advantage of Great Britain. The batteries most capable of repelling foreign enterprises on our safety are happily such as can never be turned by a perfidious government against our liberties.

The inhabitants of the Atlantic frontier are all of them deeply interested in this provision for naval protection, and if they have hitherto been suffered to sleep quietly in their beds; if their property has remained safe against the predatory spirit of licentious adventurers; if their maritime towns have not yet been compelled to ransom themselves from the terrors of a conflagration, by yielding to the exactions of daring and sudden invaders, these instances of good fortune are not to be ascribed to the capacity of the existing government for the protection of those from whom it claims allegiance, but to causes that are fugitive and fallacious. If we except perhaps Virginia and Maryland, which are peculiarly vulnerable on their eastern frontiers, no part of the Union ought to feel more anxiety on this subject than New York. Her sea-coast is extensive. A very important district of the State is an island. The State itself is penetrated by a large navigable river for more than fifty leagues. The great emporium of its commerce, the great reservoir of its wealth, lies every moment at the mercy of events, and may almost be regarded as a hostage for ignominious compliances with the dictates of a foreign enemy, or even with the rapacious demands of pirates and barbarians. Should a war be the result of the precarious situation of European affairs, and all the unruly passions attending it be let loose on the ocean, our escape from insults and depredations, not only on that element, but every part of the other bordering on it, will be truly miraculous. In the present condition of America, the States more immediately exposed to these calamities have nothing to hope from the phantom of a general government which now exists; and if their single resources were equal to the task of fortifying themselves against the danger, the object to be protected would be almost consumed by the means of protecting them.

The power of regulating and calling forth the militia has been already sufficiently vindicated and explained.

The power of levying and borrowing money, being the sinew of that which is to be exerted in the national defence, is properly thrown into the same class with it. This power, also, has been examined already with much attention, and has, I trust, been clearly shown to be necessary, both in the extent and form given to it by the Constitution. I will address one additional reflection only to those who contend that the power ought to have been restrained to external taxation—by which they mean taxes on articles imported from other countries. It cannot be doubted that this will always be a valuable source of revenue; that for a considerable time it must be a principal source; that at this moment it is an essential one. But we may form very mistaken ideas on this subject if we do not call to mind in our calculations that the extent of revenue drawn from foreign commerce must vary with the variations, both in the extent and the kind of imports; and that these variations do not correspond with the progress of population, which must be the general measure of the public wants. As long as agriculture continues the sole field of labour, the importation of manufactures must increase as the consumers multiply. As soon as domestic manufactures are begun by the hands not called for by agriculture, the imported manufactures will decrease as the numbers of people increase. In a more remote stage, the imports may consist in a considerable part of raw materials, which will be wrought into articles for exportation, and will, therefore, require rather the encouragement of bounties than to be loaded with discouraging duties. A system of government, meant for duration, ought to contemplate these revolutions, and be able to accommodate itself to them.

Some, who have not denied the necessity of the power of taxation, have grounded a very fierce attack against the Constitution on the language in which it is defined. It has been urged and echoed that the power "to lay and collect taxes, duties, imposts, and excises, to pay the debts, and provide for the common defence and general welfare of the United States," amounts to an unlimited commission to exercise every power which may be alleged to be necessary for the common defence or general welfare. No stronger proof could be given of the distress under which these writers labour for objections, than their stooping to such a misconstruction.

Had no other enumeration or definition of the powers of the Congress been found in the Constitution than the general expressions just cited, the authors of the objection might have had some colour for it; though it would have been difficult to find a reason for so awkward a form of describing an authority to legislate in all possible cases. A power to destroy the freedom of the press, the trial by jury, or even to regulate the course of descents, or the forms of conveyances, must be very singularly expressed by the terms "to raise money for the general welfare."

But what colour can the objection have when a specification of the objects alluded to by these general terms immediately follows, and is not even separated by a longer pause than a semicolon? If the different parts of the same instrument ought to be so expounded, as to give meaning to every part which will bear it, shall one part of the same sentence be excluded altogether from a share in the meaning; and shall the more doubtful and indefinite terms be retained in their full extent, and the clear and precise expressions be denied any signification whatsoever? For what purpose could the enumeration of particular powers be inserted, if these and all others were meant to be included in the preceding general power? Nothing is more natural nor common than first to use a general phrase, and then to explain and qualify it by a recital of particulars. But the idea of an enumeration of particulars which neither explain nor qualify the general meaning, and can have no other effect than to confound and mislead, is an absurdity, which, as we are reduced to the dilemma of charging either on the authors of the objection or on the authors of the Constitution, we must take the liberty of supposing, had not its origin with the latter.

The objection here is the more extraordinary, as it appears that the language used by the convention is a copy from the articles of Confederation. The objects of the Union among the States, as described in article third, are, "their common defence, security of their liberties, and mutual and general welfare." The terms of article eighth are still more identical: "All charges of war and all other expenses that shall be incurred for the common defence or general welfare, and allowed by the United States in Congress, shall be defrayed out of a common treasury," etc. A similar language again occurs in article ninth. Construe either of these articles by the rules which would justify the construction put on the new Constitution, and they vest in the existing Congress a power to legislate in all cases whatsoever. But what would have been thought of that assembly, if, attaching themselves to these general expressions, and disregarding the specifications which ascertain and limit their import, they had exercised an unlimited power of providing for the common defence and general welfare? I appeal to the objectors themselves, whether they would in that case have employed the same reasoning in justification of Congress as they now make use of against the convention. How difficult it is for error to escape its own condemnation!

PUBLIUS

Number 42

[MADISON]

THE *second* class of powers, lodged in the general government, consist of those which regulate the intercourse with foreign nations, to wit: to make treaties; to send and receive ambassadors, other public ministers, and consuls; to define and punish piracies and felonies committed on the high seas, and offences against the law of nations; to regulate foreign commerce, including a power to prohibit, after the year 1808, the importation of slaves, and to lay an intermediate duty of ten dollars per head, as a discouragement to such importations.

This class of powers forms an obvious and essential branch of the federal administration. If we are to be one nation in any respect, it clearly ought to be in respect to other nations.

The powers to make treaties and to send and receive ambassadors speak their own propriety. Both of them are comprised in the articles of Confederation, with this difference only, that the former is disembarrassed, by the plan of the convention, of an exception, under which treaties might be substantially frustrated by regulations of the States; and that a power of appointing and receiving "other public ministers and consuls," is expressly and very properly added to the former provision concerning ambassadors. The term ambassador, if taken strictly, as seems to be required by the second of the articles of Confederation, comprehends the highest grade only of public ministers, and excludes the grades which the United States will be most likely to prefer, where foreign embassies may be necessary. And under no latitude of construction will the term comprehend consuls. Yet it has been found expedient, and has been the practice of Congress, to employ the inferior grades of public ministers, and to send and receive consuls.

It is true that where treaties of commerce stipulate for the mutual appointment of consuls, whose functions are connected with commerce, the admission of foreign consuls may fall within the power of making commercial treaties; and that where no such treaties exist, the mission of American consuls into foreign countries may *perhaps* be covered under the authority, given by the ninth article of the Confederation, to appoint all such civil officers as may be necessary for managing the general affairs of the United States. But the admission of consuls into the United States, where no previous treaty has stipulated it, seems to have been nowhere provided for. A supply of the omission is one of the lesser instances in which the convention have improved on the model before them. But the most minute provisions become important when they tend to obviate the necessity or the pretext for gradual and unobserved usurpations of power. A list of the cases in which Congress have been betrayed, or forced by the defects of the Confederation, into violations of their chartered authorities, would not a little surprise those who have paid no attention to the subject; and would be no inconsiderable argument in favour of the new Constitution, which seems to have provided no less studiously for the lesser, than the more obvious and striking defects of the old.

The power to define and punish piracies and felonies committed on the high seas, and offences against the law of nations, belongs with equal propriety to the general government, and is a still greater improvement on the articles of Confederation. These articles contain no provision for the case of offences against the law of nations; and consequently leave it in the power of any indiscreet member to embroil the Confederacy with foreign nations. The provision of the federal articles on the subject of piracies and felonies extends no further than to the establishment of courts for the trial of these offences. The definition of piracies might, perhaps, without inconveniency, be left to the law of nations; though a legislative definition of them is found in most municipal codes. A definition of felonies on the high seas is evidently requisite. Felony is a term of loose signification, even in the common law of England; and of various import in the statute law of that kingdom. But neither the common nor the statute law of that, or of any other nation, ought to be a standard for the proceedings of this, unless previously made its own by legislative adoption. The meaning of the term, as defined in the codes of the several States, would be as impracticable as the former would be a dishonourable and illegitimate guide. It is not precisely the same in any two of the States; and varies in each with every revision of its criminal laws. For the sake of certainty and uniformity, therefore, the power of defining felonies in this case was in every respect necessary and proper.

The regulation of foreign commerce, having fallen within several views which have been taken of this subject, has been too fully discussed to need additional proofs here of its being properly submitted to the federal administration.

It were doubtless to be wished that the power of prohibiting the importation of slaves had not been postponed until the year 1808, or rather that it had been suffered to have immediate operation. But it is not difficult to account, either for this restriction on the general government, or for the manner in which the whole clause is expressed. It ought to be considered as a great point gained in favour of humanity, that a period of twenty years may terminate for ever, within these States, a traffic which has so long and so loudly upbraided the barbarism of modern policy; that within that period it will receive a considerable discouragement from the federal government, and may be totally abolished by a concurrence of the few States which continue the unnatural traffic in the prohibitory example which has been given by so great a majority of the Union. Happy would it be for the unfortunate Africans, if an equal prospect lay before them of being redeemed from the oppressions of their European brethren!

Attempts have been made to pervert this clause into an objection against the Constitution, by representing it on one side as a criminal toleration of an illicit practice, and on another as calculated to prevent voluntary and beneficial emigrations from Europe to America. I mention these misconstructions, not with a view to give them an answer, for they deserve none, but as specimens of the manner and spirit in which some have thought fit to conduct their opposition to the proposed government.

The powers included in the *third* class are those which provide for the harmony and proper intercourse among the States.

Under this head might be included the particular restraints imposed on the authority of the States, and certain powers of the judicial department; but the former are reserved for a distinct class, and the latter will be particularly examined when we arrive at the structure and organisation of the government. I shall confine myself to a cursory review of the remaining powers comprehended under this third description, to wit: to regulate commerce among the several States and the Indian tribes; to coin money, regulate the value thereof, and of foreign coin; to provide for the punishment of counterfeiting the current coin and securities of the United States; to fix the standard of weights and measures; to establish a uniform rule of naturalisation, and uniform laws of bankruptcy; to prescribe the manner in which the public acts, records, and judicial proceedings of each State shall be proved, and the effect they shall have in other States; and to establish post-offices and post-roads.

The defect of power in the existing Confederacy to regulate the commerce between its several members is in the number of those which have been clearly pointed out by experience. To the proofs and remarks which former papers have brought into view on this subject, it may be added that, without this supplemental provision, the great and essential power of regulating foreign commerce would have been incomplete and ineffectual. A very material object of this power was the relief of the States which import and export through other States from the improper contributions levied on them by the latter. Were these at liberty to regulate the trade between State and State, it must be foreseen that ways would be found out to load the articles of import and export, during the passage through their jurisdiction, with duties which would fall on the makers of the latter and the consumers of the former. We may be assured by past experience, that such a practice would be introduced by future contrivances; and both by that and a common knowledge of human affairs, that it would nourish unceasing animosities and not improbably terminate in serious interruptions of the public tranquillity. To those who do not view the question through the medium of passion or of interest, the desire of the commercial States to collect, in any form, an indirect revenue from their uncommercial neighbours, must appear not less impolitic than it is unfair; since it would stimulate the injured party, by resentment as well as interest, to resort to less convenient channels for their foreign trade. But the mild voice of reason, pleading the cause of an enlarged and permanent interest, is but too often drowned, before public bodies as well as individuals, by the clamours of an impatient avidity for immediate and immoderate gain.

The necessity of a superintending authority over the reciprocal trade of confederated States has been illustrated by other examples as well as our own. In Switzerland, where the Union is so very slight, each canton is obliged to allow to merchandises a passage through its jurisdiction into other cantons, without an augmentation of the tolls. In Germany it is a law of the empire that the princes and states shall not lay tolls or customs on bridges, rivers, or passages, without the consent of the emperor and the diet; though it appears from a quotation in an antecedent paper that the practice in this, as in many other instances in that confederacy, has not followed the law, and has produced there the mischiefs which have been foreseen here. Among the restraints imposed by the Union of the Netherlands on its members, one is, that they shall not establish imposts disadvantageous to their neighbours, without the general permission.

The regulation of commerce with the Indian tribes is very properly unfettered from two limitations in the articles of Confederation, which render the provision obscure and contradictory. The power is there restrained to Indians, not members of any of the States, and is not to violate or infringe the legislative right of any State within its own limits. What description of Indians are to be deemed members of a State is not yet settled, and has been a question of frequent perplexity and contention in the federal councils. And how the trade with Indians, though not members of a State, yet residing within its legislative jurisdiction, can be regulated by an external authority, without so far intruding on the internal rights of legislation, is absolutely incomprehensible. This is not the only case in which the articles of Confederation have inconsiderately endeavoured to accomplish impossibilities; to reconcile a partial sovereignty in the Union, with complete sovereignty in the States; to subvert a mathematical axiom, by taking away a part, and letting the whole remain.

All that need be remarked on the power to coin money, regulate the value thereof, and of foreign coin, is, that by providing for this last case, the Constitution has supplied a material omission in the articles of Confederation. The authority of the existing Congress is restrained to the regulation of coin *struck* by their own authority, or that of the respective States. It must be seen at once that the proposed uniformity in the *value* of the current coin might be destroyed by subjecting that of foreign coin to the different regulations of the different States.

The punishment of counterfeiting the public securities, as well as the current coin, is submitted of course to that authority which is to secure the value of both.

The regulation of weights and measures is transferred from the articles of Confederation, and is founded on like considerations with the preceding power of regulating coin.

The dissimilarity in the rules of naturalisation has long been remarked as a fault in our system, and as laying a foundation for intricate and delicate questions. In the fourth article of the Confederation it is declared "that the *free inhabitants* of each of these States, paupers, vagabonds, and fugitives from justice excepted, shall be entitled to all privileges and immunities of *free citizens* in the several States; and *the people* of each State shall, in every other, enjoy all the privileges of trade and commerce," etc. There is a confusion of language here which is remarkable. Why the terms *free inhabitants* are used in one part of the article, *free citizens* in another, and *people* in another; or what was meant by superadding to "all privileges and immunities of free citizens," "all the privileges of trade and commerce," cannot easily be determined. It seems to be a construction scarcely avoidable, however, that those who come under the denomination of *free inhabitants* of a State, although not citizens of such State, are entitled, in every other State, to all the privileges of *free citizens* of the latter; that is, to greater privileges than they may be entitled to in their own State: so that it may be in the power of a particular State, or rather every State is laid under a necessity, not only to confer the rights of citizenship in other States upon any whom it may admit to such rights within itself, but upon any whom it may allow to become inhabitants within its jurisdiction. But were an exposition of the term "inhabitants" to be admitted which would confine the stipulated privileges to citizens alone, the difficulty is diminished only, not removed. The very improper power would still be retained by each State of naturalising aliens in every other State. In one State residence for a short term confirms all the rights of citizenship: in another, qualifications of greater importance are required. An alien, therefore, legally incapacitated for certain rights in the latter, may, by previous residence only in the former, elude his incapacity; and thus the law of one State be preposterously rendered paramount to the law of another, within the jurisdiction of the other. We owe it to mere casualty, that very serious embarrassments on this subject have been hitherto escaped. By the laws of several States, certain descriptions of aliens, who had rendered themselves obnoxious, were laid under interdicts inconsistent not only with the rights of citizenship but with the privilege of residence. What would have been the consequence, if such persons, by residence or otherwise, had acquired the character of citizens under the laws of another State, and then asserted their rights as such, both to residence and citizenship, within the State proscribing them? Whatever the legal consequences might have been, other consequences would probably have resulted of too serious a nature not to be provided against. The new Constitution has accordingly, with great propriety, made pro-

vision against them, and all others proceeding from the defect of the Confederation on this head, by authorising the general government to establish a uniform rule of naturalisation throughout the United States.

The power of establishing uniform laws of bankruptcy is so intimately connected with the regulation of commerce, and will prevent so many frauds where the parties or their property may lie or be removed into different States, that the expediency of it seems not likely to be drawn into question.

The power of prescribing by general laws, the manner in which the public acts, records, and judicial proceedings of each State shall be proved, and the effect they shall have in other States, is an evident and valuable improvement on the clause relating to this subject in the articles of Confederation. The meaning of the latter is extremely indeterminate, and can be of little importance under any interpretation which it will bear. The power here established may be rendered a very convenient instrument of justice, and be particularly beneficial on the borders of contiguous States, where the effects liable to justice may be suddenly and secretly translated, in any stage of the process, within a foreign jurisdiction.

The power of establishing post-roads must, in every view, be a harmless power, and may, perhaps, by judicious management, become productive of great public conveniency. Nothing which tends to facilitate the intercourse between the States can be deemed unworthy of the public care.   PUBLIUS

Number 43

[MADISON]

THE *fourth* class comprises the following miscellaneous powers:

1. A power "to promote the progress of science and useful arts, by securing, for a limited time, to authors and inventors, the exclusive right to their respective writings and discoveries."

The utility of this power will scarcely be questioned. The copyright of authors has been solemnly adjudged, in Great Britain, to be a right of common law. The right to useful inventions seems with equal reason to belong to the inventors. The public good fully coincides in both cases with the claims of individuals. The States cannot separately make effectual provision for either of the cases, and most of them have anticipated the decision of this point, by laws passed at the instance of Congress.

2. "To exercise exclusive legislation, in all cases whatsoever, over such district (not exceeding ten miles square) as may, by cession of particular States and the acceptance of Congress, become the seat of the government of the United States; and to exercise like authority over all places purchased by the consent of the legislatures of the States in which the same shall be, for the erection of forts, magazines, arsenals, dockyards, and other needful buildings."

The indispensable necessity of complete authority at the seat of government carries its own evidence with it. It is a power exercised by every legislature of the Union, I might say of the world, by virtue of its general supremacy. Without it, not only the public authority might be insulted and its proceedings interrupted with impunity; but a dependence of the members of the general government on the State comprehending the seat of the government, for protection in the exercise of their duty, might bring on the national councils an imputation of awe or influence, equally dishonourable to the government and dissatisfactory to the other members of the Confederacy. This consideration has the more weight, as the gradual accumulation of public improvements at the stationary residence of the government would be both too great a public pledge to be left in the hands of a single State, and would create so many obstacles to a removal of the government, as still further to abridge its necessary independence. The extent of this federal district is sufficiently circumscribed to satisfy every jealousy of an opposite nature. And as it is to be appropriated to this use with the consent of the State ceding it; as the State will no doubt provide in the compact for the rights and the consent of the citizens inhabiting it; as the inhabitants will find sufficient inducements of interest to become willing parties to the cession; as they will have had their voice in the election of the government which is to exercise authority over them; as a municipal legislature for local purposes, derived from their own suffrages, will of course be allowed them; and as the authority of the legislature of the State, and of the inhabitants of the ceded part of it, to concur in the cession, will be derived from the whole people of the State, in their adoption of the Con-

stitution, every imaginable objection seems to be obviated.

The necessity of a like authority over forts, magazines, etc., established by the general government, is not less evident. The public money expended on such places, and the public property deposited in them, require that they should be exempt from the authority of the particular State. Nor would it be proper for the places on which the security of the entire Union may depend to be in any degree dependent on a particular member of it. All objections and scruples are here also obviated, by requiring the concurrence of the States concerned in every such establishment.

3. "To declare the punishment of treason, but no attainder of treason shall work corruption of blood, or forfeiture, except during the life of the person attainted."

As treason may be committed against the United States, the authority of the United States ought to be enabled to punish it. But as new-fangled and artificial treasons have been the great engines by which violent factions, the natural offspring of free government, have usually wreaked their alternate malignity on each other, the convention have, with great judgment, opposed a barrier to this peculiar danger, by inserting a constitutional definition of the crime, fixing the proof necessary for conviction of it, and restraining the Congress, even in punishing it, from extending the consequences of guilt beyond the person of its author.

4. "To admit new States into the Union; but no new State shall be formed or erected within the jurisdiction of any other State; nor any State be formed by the junction of two or more States, or parts of States, without the consent of the legislatures of the States concerned, as well as of the Congress."

In the articles of Confederation, no provision is found on this important subject. Canada was to be admitted of right, on her joining in the measures of the United States; and the other *colonies,* by which were evidently meant the other British colonies, at the discretion of nine States. The eventual establishment of *new States* seems to have been overlooked by the compilers of that instrument. We have seen the inconvenience of this omission, and the assumption of power into which Congress have been led by it. With great propriety, therefore, has the new system supplied the defect. The general precaution, that no new States shall be formed without the concurrence of the federal authority, and that of the States concerned, is consonant to the principles which ought to govern such transactions. The particular precaution against the erection of new States, by the partition of a State without its consent, quiets the jealousy of the larger States; as that of the smaller is quieted by a like precaution, against a junction of States without their consent.

5. "To dispose of and make all needful rules and regulations respecting the territory or other property belonging to the United States, with a proviso that nothing in the Constitution shall be so construed as to prejudice any claims of the United States, or of any particular State."

This is a power of very great importance, and required by considerations similar to those which show the propriety of the former. The proviso annexed is proper in itself, and was probably rendered absolutely necessary by jealousies and questions concerning the Western territory sufficiently known to the public.

6. "To guarantee to every State in the Union a republican form of government; to protect each of them against invasion; and on application of the legislature, or of the executive (when the legislature cannot be convened), against domestic violence."

In a confederacy founded on republican principles, and composed of republican members, the superintending government ought clearly to possess authority to defend the system against aristocratic or monarchical innovations. The more intimate the nature of such a union may be, the greater interest have the members in the political institutions of each other; and the greater right to insist that the forms of government under which the compact was entered into should be *substantially* maintained. But a right implies a remedy; and where else could the remedy be deposited than where it is deposited by the Constitution? Governments of dissimilar principles and forms have been found less adapted to a federal coalition of any sort than those of a kindred nature. "As the confederate republic of Germany," says Montesquieu, "consists of free cities and petty states, subject to different princes, experience shows us that it is more imperfect than that of Holland and Switzerland." "Greece was undone," he adds, "as soon as the king of Macedon obtained a seat among the Amphictyons." In the latter case, no doubt, the disproportionate force, as well as the monarchical form, of the new confederate, had its share of influence on the events. It may pos-

sibly be asked, what need there could be of such a precaution, and whether it may not become a pretext for alterations in the State governments, without the concurrence of the States themselves. These questions admit of ready answers. If the interposition of the general government should not be needed, the provision for such an event will be a harmless superfluity only in the Constitution. But who can say what experiments may be produced by the caprice of particular States, by the ambition of enterprising leaders, or by the intrigues and influence of foreign powers? To the second question it may be answered, that if the general government should interpose by virtue of this constitutional authority, it will be, of course, bound to pursue the authority. But the authority extends no further than to a *guarantee* of a republican form of government, which supposes a pre-existing government of the form which is to be guaranteed. As long, therefore, as the existing republican forms are continued by the States, they are guaranteed by the federal Constitution. Whenever the States may choose to substitute other republican forms, they have a right to do so, and to claim the federal guarantee for the latter. The only restriction imposed on them is, that they shall not exchange republican for anti-republican Constitutions; a restriction which, it is presumed, will hardly be considered as a grievance.

A protection against invasion is due from every society to the parts composing it. The latitude of the expression here used seems to secure each State, not only against foreign hostility, but against ambitious or vindictive enterprises of its more powerful neighbours. The history, both of ancient and modern confederacies, proves that the weaker members of the union ought not to be insensible to the policy of this article.

Protection against domestic violence is added with equal propriety. It has been remarked that even among the Swiss cantons, which, properly speaking, are not under one government, provision is made for this object; and the history of that league informs us that mutual aid is frequently claimed and afforded; and as well by the most democratic as the other cantons. A recent and well-known event among ourselves has warned us to be prepared for emergencies of a like nature.

At first view, it might seem not to square with the republican theory, to suppose either that a majority have not the right, or that a minority will have the force, to subvert a government; and consequently, that the federal interposition can never be required but when it would be improper. But theoretic reasoning, in this as in most other cases, must be qualified by the lessons of practice. Why may not illicit combinations, for purposes of violence, be formed as well by a majority of a State, especially a small State, as by a majority of a county, or a district of the same State; and if the authority of the State ought, in the latter case, to protect the local magistracy, ought not the federal authority, in the former, to support the State authority? Besides, there are certain parts of the State constitutions which are so interwoven with the federal Constitution, that a violent blow cannot be given to the one without communicating the wound to the other. Insurrections in a State will rarely induce a federal interposition, unless the number concerned in them bear some proportion to the friends of government. It will be much better that the violence in such cases should be repressed by the superintending power than that the majority should be left to maintain their cause by a bloody and obstinate contest. The existence of a right to interpose will generally prevent the necessity of exerting it.

Is it true that force and right are necessarily on the same side in republican governments? May not the minor party possess such a superiority of pecuniary resources, of military talents and experience, or of secret succours from foreign powers, as will render it superior also in an appeal to the sword? May not a more compact and advantageous position turn the scale on the same side, against a superior number, so situated as to be less capable of a prompt and collected exertion of its strength? Nothing can be more chimerical than to imagine that in a trial of actual force, victory may be calculated by the rules which prevail in a census of the inhabitants, or which determine the event of an election! May it not happen, in fine, that the minority of CITIZENS may become a majority of PERSONS, by the accession of alien residents, of a casual concourse of adventurers, or of those whom the constitution of the State has not admitted to the rights of suffrage? I take no notice of an unhappy species of population abounding in some of the States, who, during the calm of regular government, are sunk below the level of men; but who, in the tempestuous scenes of civil violence, may emerge into the human character, and give a superiority of strength to any party with which they may associate themselves.

In cases where it may be doubtful on which side justice lies, what better umpires could be desired by two violent factions, flying to arms and tearing a State to pieces, than the representatives of confederate States not heated by the local flame? To the impartiality of judges they would unite the affection of friends. Happy would it be if such a remedy for its infirmities could be enjoyed by all free governments; if a project equally effectual could be established for the universal peace of mankind!

Should it be asked, what is to be the redress for an insurrection pervading all the States, and comprising a superiority of the entire force, though not a constitutional right? the answer must be, that such a case, as it would be without the compass of human remedies, so it is fortunately not within the compass of human probability; and that it is a sufficient recommendation of the federal Constitution, that it diminishes the risk of a calamity for which no possible constitution can provide a cure.

Among the advantages of a confederate republic enumerated by Montesquieu, an important one is, "that should a popular insurrection happen in one of the States, the others are able to quell it. Should abuses creep into one part, they are reformed by those that remain sound."

7. "To consider all debts contracted, and engagements entered into, before the adoption of this Constitution, as being no less valid against the United States, under this Constitution, than under the Confederation."

This can only be considered as a declaratory proposition; and may have been inserted, among other reasons, for the satisfaction of the foreign creditors of the United States, who cannot be strangers to the pretended doctrine, that a change in the political form of civil society has the magical effect of dissolving its moral obligations.

Among the lesser criticisms which have been exercised on the Constitution, it has been remarked that the validity of engagements ought to have been asserted in favour of the United States, as well as against them; and in the spirit which usually characterises little critics, the omission has been transformed and magnified into a plot against the national rights. The authors of this discovery may be told, what few others need to be informed of, that as engagements are in their nature reciprocal, an assertion of their validity on one side, necessarily involves a validity on the other side; and that as the article is merely declaratory, the establishment of the principle in one case is sufficient for every case. They may be further told that every constitution must limit its precautions to dangers that are not altogether imaginary; and that no real danger can exist that the government would DARE, with, or even without, this constitutional declaration before it, to remit the debts justly due to the public, on the pretext here condemned.

8. "To provide for amendments to be ratified by three fourths of the States, under two exceptions only."

That useful alterations will be suggested by experience could not but be foreseen. It was requisite, therefore, that a mode for introducing them should be provided. The mode preferred by the convention seems to be stamped with every mark of propriety. It guards equally against that extreme facility which would render the Constitution too mutable; and that extreme difficulty, which might perpetuate its discovered faults. It, moreover, equally enables the general and the State governments to originate the amendment of errors, as they may be pointed out by the experience on one side or on the other. The exception in favour of the equality of suffrage in the Senate, was probably meant as a palladium to the residuary sovereignty of the States, implied and secured by that principle of representation in one branch of the legislature; and was probably insisted on by the States particularly attached to that equality. The other exception must have been admitted on the same considerations which produced the privilege defended by it.

9. "The ratification of the conventions of nine States shall be sufficient for the establishment of this Constitution between the States ratifying the same."

This article speaks for itself. The express authority of the people alone could give due validity to the Constitution. To have required the unanimous ratification of the thirteen States would have subjected the essential interests of the whole to the caprice or corruption of a single member. It would have marked a want of foresight in the convention which our own experience would have rendered inexcusable.

Two questions of a very delicate nature present themselves on this occasion: 1. On what principle the Confederation, which stands in the solemn form of a compact among the States, can be superseded without the unanimous consent of the parties to it? 2. What relation is to subsist between the nine or more States ratifying the Constitution, and the remaining few who do not become parties to it?

The first question is answered at once by recurring to the absolute necessity of the case; to the great principle of self-preservation; to the transcendent law of nature and of nature's God, which declares that the safety and happiness of society are the objects at which all political institutions aim, and to which all such institutions must be sacrificed. PERHAPS, also, an answer may be found without searching beyond the principles of the compact itself. It has been heretofore noted among the defects of the Confederation that in many of the States it had received no higher sanction than a mere legislative ratification. The principle of reciprocality seems to require that its obligation on the other States should be reduced to the same standard. A compact between independent sovereigns, founded on ordinary acts of legislative authority, can pretend to no higher validity than a league or treaty between the parties. It is an established doctrine on the subject of treaties, that all the articles are mutually conditions of each other; that a breach of any one article is a breach of the whole treaty; and that a breach, committed by either of the parties, absolves the others, and authorises them, if they please, to pronounce the compact violated and void. Should it unhappily be necessary to appeal to these delicate truths for a justification for dispensing with the consent of particular States to a dissolution of the federal pact, will not the complaining parties find it a difficult task to answer the MULTIPLIED and IMPORTANT infractions with which they may be confronted? The time has been when it was incumbent on us all to veil the ideas which this paragraph exhibits. The scene is now changed, and with it the part which the same motives dictate.

The second question is not less delicate; and the flattering prospect of its being merely hypothetical forbids an over-curious discussion of it. It is one of those cases which must be left to provide for itself. In general, it may be observed, that although no political relation can subsist between the assenting and dissenting States, yet the moral relations will remain uncancelled. The claims of justice, both on one side and on the other, will be in force, and must be fulfilled; the rights of humanity must in all cases be duly and mutually respected; whilst considerations of a common interest, and, above all, the remembrance of the endearing scenes which are past, and the anticipation of a speedy triumph over the obstacles to reunion, will, it is hoped, not urge in vain MODERATION on one side, and PRUDENCE on the other. PUBLIUS

Number 44

[MADISON]

A *fifth* class of provisions in favour of the federal authority consists of the following restrictions on the authority of the several States:

1. "No State shall enter into any treaty, alliance, or confederation; grant letters of marque and reprisal; coin money; emit bills of credit; make anything but gold and silver a legal tender in payment of debts; pass any bill of attainder, *ex post facto* law, or law impairing the obligation of contracts; or grant any title of nobility."

The prohibition against treaties, alliances, and confederations makes a part of the existing articles of Union; and for reasons which need no explanation is copied into the new Constitution. The prohibition of letters of marque is another part of the old system, but is somewhat extended in the new. According to the former, letters of marque could be granted by the States after a declaration of war; according to the latter, these licenses must be obtained, as well during war as previous to its declaration, from the government of the United States. This alteration is fully justified by the advantage of uniformity in all points which relate to foreign powers; and of immediate responsibility to the nation in all those for whose conduct the nation itself is to be responsible.

The right of coining money, which is here taken from the States, was left in their hands by the Confederation, as a concurrent right with that of Congress, under an exception in favour of the exclusive right of Congress to regulate the alloy and value. In this instance, also, the new provision is an improvement on the old. Whilst the alloy and value depended on the general authority, a right of coinage in the particular States could have no other effect than to multiply expensive mints and diversify the forms and weights of the circulating pieces. The latter inconveniency defeats one purpose for which the power was originally submitted to the federal head; and as far as the former might prevent an inconvenient remittance of gold and silver to the central mint for recoinage, the end can be as well attained by local mints established under the general authority.

The extension of the prohibition to bills of credit must give pleasure to every citizen, in proportion to his love of justice and his knowledge of the true springs of public prosperity. The loss which America has sustained since the peace from the pestilent effects of paper money on the necessary confidence between man and man, on the necessary confidence in the public councils, on the industry and morals of the people and on the character of republican government, constitutes an enormous debt against the States chargeable with this unadvised measure, which must long remain unsatisfied; or rather an accumulation of guilt, which can be expiated no otherwise than by a voluntary sacrifice on the altar of justice of the power which has been the instrument of it. In addition to these persuasive considerations, it may be observed that the same reasons which show the necessity of denying to the States the power of regulating coin, prove with equal force that they ought not to be at liberty to substitute a paper medium in the place of coin. Had every State a right to regulate the value of its coin, there might be as many different currencies as States, and thus the intercourse among them would be impeded; retrospective alterations in its value might be made, and thus the citizens of other States be injured, and animosities be kindled among the States themselves. The subjects of foreign powers might suffer from the same cause, and hence the Union be discredited and embroiled by the indiscretion of a single member. No one of these mischiefs is less incident to a power in the States to emit paper money, than to coin gold or silver. The power to make anything but gold and silver a tender in payment of debts is withdrawn from the States, on the same principle with that of issuing a paper currency.

Bills of attainder, *ex post facto* laws, and laws impairing the obligation of contracts, are contrary to the first principles of the social compact, and to every principle of sound legislation. The two former are expressly prohibited by the declarations prefixed to some of the State constitutions, and all of them are prohibited by the spirit and scope of these fundamental charters. Our own experience has taught us, nevertheless, that additional fences against these dangers ought not to be omitted.

Very properly, therefore, have the convention added this constitutional bulwark in favour of personal security and private rights; and I am much deceived if they have not, in so doing, as faithfully consulted the genuine sentiments as the undoubted interests of their constituents. The sober people of America are weary of the fluctuating policy which has directed the public councils. They have seen with regret and indignation that sudden changes and legislative interferences, in cases affecting personal rights, become jobs in the hands of enterprising and influential speculators, and snares to the more-industrious and less-informed part of the community. They have seen, too, that one legislative interference is but the first link of a long chain of repetitions, every subsequent interference being naturally produced by the effects of the preceding. They very rightly infer, therefore, that some thorough reform is wanting, which will banish speculations on public measures, inspire a general prudence and industry, and give a regular course to the business of society. The prohibition with respect to titles of nobility is copied from the articles of Confederation, and needs no comment.

2. "No State shall, without the consent of the Congress, lay any imposts or duties on imports or exports, except what may be absolutely necessary for executing its inspection laws, and the net produce of all its duties and imposts laid by any State on imports or exports, shall be for the use of the treasury of the United States; and all such laws shall be subject to the revision and control of the Congress. No State shall, without the consent of Congress, lay any duty on tonnage, keep troops or ships of war in time of peace, enter into any agreement or compact with another State, or with a foreign power, or engage in war unless actually invaded, or in such imminent danger as will not admit of delay."

The restraint on the power of the States over imports and exports is enforced by all the arguments which prove the necessity of submitting the regulation of trade to the federal councils. It is needless, therefore, to remark further on this head, than that the manner in which the restraint is qualified seems well calculated at once to secure to the States a reasonable discretion in providing for the conveniency of their imports and exports, and to the United States a reasonable check against the abuse of this discretion. The remaining particulars of this clause fall within reasonings which are either so obvious, or have been so fully developed, that they may be passed over without remark.

The *sixth* and last class consists of the several powers and provisions by which efficacy is given to all the rest.

1. Of these the first is, the "power to make all laws which shall be necessary and proper for carrying into execution the foregoing powers, and all other powers vested by this Constitution in the government of the United States, or in any department or officer thereof."

Few parts of the Constitution have been assailed with more intemperance than this; yet on a fair investigation of it, no part can appear more completely invulnerable. Without the *substance* of this power, the whole Constitution would be a dead letter. Those who object to the article, therefore, as a part of the Constitution, can only mean that the *form* of the provision is improper. But have they considered whether a better form could have been substituted?

There are four other possible methods which the Constitution might have taken on this subject. They might have copied the second article of the existing Confederation, which would have prohibited the exercise of any power not *expressly* delegated; they might have attempted a positive enumeration of the powers comprehended under the general terms "necessary and proper"; they might have attempted a negative enumeration of them, by specifying the powers excepted from the general definition; they might have been altogether silent on the subject, leaving these necessary and proper powers to construction and inference.

Had the convention taken the first method of adopting the second article of Confederation, it is evident that the new Congress would be continually exposed, as their predecessors have been, to the alternative of construing the term *"expressly"* with so much rigour, as to disarm the government of all real authority whatever, or with so much latitude as to destroy altogether the force of the restriction. It would be easy to show, if it were necessary, that no important power delegated by the articles of Confederation has been or can be executed by Congress without recurring more or less to the doctrine of *construction* or *implication*. As the powers delegated under the new system are more extensive, the government which is to administer it would find itself still more distressed with the alternative of betraying the public interests by doing nothing, or of violating the Constitution by exercising powers indispensably necessary and proper, but, at the same time, not *expressly* granted.

Had the convention attempted a positive enumeration of the powers necessary and proper for carrying their other powers into effect, the attempt would have involved a complete digest of laws on every subject to which the Constitution relates; accommodated too, not only to the existing state of things, but to all the possible changes which futurity may produce; for in every new application of a general power, the *particular powers,* which are the means of attaining the *object* of the general power, must always necessarily vary with that object, and be often properly varied whilst the object remains the same.

Had they attempted to enumerate the particular powers or means not necessary or proper for carrying the general powers into execution, the task would have been no less chimerical; and would have been liable to this further objection, that every defect in the enumeration would have been equivalent to a positive grant of authority. If, to avoid this consequence, they had attempted a partial enumeration of the exceptions, and described the residue by the general terms, *not necessary or proper,* it must have happened that the enumeration would comprehend a few of the excepted powers only; that these would be such as would be least likely to be assumed or tolerated, because the enumeration would of course select such as would be least necessary or proper; and that the unnecessary and improper powers included in the residuum would be less forcibly excepted than if no partial enumeration had been made.

Had the Constitution been silent on this head, there can be no doubt that all the particular powers requisite as means of executing the general powers would have resulted to the government, by unavoidable implication. No axiom is more clearly established in law, or in reason, than that wherever the end is required, the means are authorised; wherever a general power to do a thing is given, every particular power necessary for doing it is included. Had this last method, therefore, been pursued by the convention, every objection now urged against their plan would remain in all its plausibility; and the real inconveniency would be incurred of not removing a pretext which may be seized on critical occasions for drawing into question the essential powers of the Union.

If it be asked what is to be the consequence, in case the Congress shall misconstrue this part of the Constitution, and exercise powers not warranted by its true meaning, I answer, the same as if they should misconstrue or enlarge any other power vested in them; as if the general power had been reduced to particulars, and any one of these were to be violated; the same, in short, as if the State legislatures should violate their respective constitutional authorities. In the first instance, the success of the usurpation will depend on the executive and judiciary departments, which are to expound and give effect to the legislative acts; and in the last resort a remedy must be obtained from the people, who can, by the election of more faithful representatives, annul the acts of the usurpers. The truth is, that this ultimate redress may be more confided in against unconstitutional acts of the federal than of the State legislatures, for this plain reason, that as every such act of the former will be an invasion of the rights of the latter, these will be ever ready to mark the innovation, to sound the alarm to the people, and to exert their local influence in effecting a change of federal representatives. There being no such intermediate body between the State legislatures and the people interested in watching the conduct of the former, violations of the State constitutions are more likely to remain unnoticed and unredressed.

2. "This Constitution and the laws of the United States which shall be made in pursuance thereof, and all treaties made, or which shall be made, under the authority of the United States, shall be the supreme law of the land, and the judges in every State shall be bound thereby, anything in the constitution or laws of any State to the contrary notwithstanding."

The indiscreet zeal of the adversaries to the Constitution has betrayed them into an attack on this part of it also, without which it would have been evidently and radically defective. To be fully sensible of this, we need only suppose for a moment that the supremacy of the State constitutions had been left complete by a saving clause in their favour.

In the first place, as these constitutions invest the State legislatures with absolute sovereignty, in all cases not excepted by the existing articles of Confederation, all the authorities contained in the proposed Constitution, so far as they exceed those enumerated in the Confederation, would have been annulled, and the new Congress would have been reduced to the same impotent condition with their predecessors.

In the next place, as the constitutions of some of the States do not even expressly and fully recognise the existing powers of the Confederacy, an express saving of the supremacy of the former would, in such States, have brought into question every power contained in the proposed Constitution.

In the third place, as the constitutions of the States differ much from each other, it might happen that a treaty or national law, of great and equal importance to the States, would interfere with some and not with other constitutions, and would consequently be valid in some of the States, at the same time that it would have no effect in others.

In fine, the world would have seen, for the first time, a system of government founded on an inversion of the fundamental principles of all government; it would have seen the authority of the whole society everywhere subordinate to the authority of the parts; it would have seen a monster in which the head was under the direction of the members.

3. "The Senators and Representatives, and the members of the several State legislatures, and all executive and judicial officers, both of the United States and the several States, shall be bound by oath or affirmation to support this Constitution."

It has been asked why it was thought necessary that the State magistracy should be bound to support the federal Constitution, and unnecessary that a like oath should be imposed on the officers of the United States, in favour of the State constitutions.

Several reasons might be assigned for the distinction. I content myself with one, which is obvious and conclusive. The members of the federal government will have no agency in carrying the State constitutions into effect. The members and officers of the State governments, on the contrary, will have an essential agency in giving effect to the federal Constitution. The election of the President and Senate will depend, in all cases, on the legislatures of the several States. And the election of the House of Representatives will equally depend on the same authority in the first instance; and will, probably, for ever be conducted by the officers, and according to the laws, of the States.

4. Among the provisions for giving efficacy to the federal powers might be added those which belong to the executive and judiciary departments: but as these are reserved for particular examination in another place, I pass them over in this.

We have now reviewed, in detail, all the articles composing the sum or quantity of power delegated by the proposed Constitution to the federal government, and are brought to this undeniable conclusion, that no part of the power is unnecessary or improper for accomplishing the necessary objects of the Union. The question, therefore, whether this amount of power shall be granted or not, resolves itself into another question, whether or not a government commensurate to the exigencies of the Union shall be established; or, in other words, whether the Union itself shall be preserved.

PUBLIUS

Number 45
[MADISON]

HAVING SHOWN that no one of the powers transferred to the federal government is unnecessary or improper, the next question to be considered is, whether the whole mass of them will be dangerous to the portion of authority left in the several States.

The adversaries to the plan of the convention, instead of considering in the first place what degree of power was absolutely necessary for the purposes of the federal government, have exhausted themselves in a secondary inquiry into the possible consequences of the proposed degree of power to the governments of the particular States. But if the Union, as has been shown, be essential to the security of the people of America against foreign danger; if it be essential to their security against contentions and wars among the different States; if it be essential to guard them against those violent and oppressive factions which embitter the blessings of liberty, and against those military establishments which must gradually poison its very fountain; if, in a word, the Union be essential to the happiness of the people of America, is it not preposterous to urge as an objection to a government, without which the objects of the Union cannot be attained, that such a government may derogate from the importance of the governments of the individual States? Was, then, the American Revolution effected, was the American Confederacy formed, was the precious blood of thousands spilt, and the hardearned substance of millions lavished, not that the people of America should enjoy peace, liberty, and safety, but that the government of the individual States, that particular municipal establishments, might enjoy a certain extent of power, and be arrayed with certain dignities and attributes of sovereignty? We have heard of the impious doctrine in the Old World, that the people were made for kings, not kings for the people. Is the same doctrine to be revived in the New in another shape—that the solid happiness of the people is to be sacrificed to the views of political institutions of a different form? It is too early for politicians to presume on our forgetting that the public good, the real welfare of the great body of the people, is the supreme object to be pursued; and that no form of government whatever has any other value than as it may be fitted for the attainment of this object. Were the plan of the convention adverse to the public happiness, my voice would be, Reject the plan. Were the Union itself inconsistent with the public happiness, it would be, Abolish the Union. In like manner, as far as the sovereignty of the States cannot be reconciled to the happiness of the people, the voice of every good citizen must be, Let the former be sacrificed to the latter. How far the sacrifice is necessary, has been shown. How far the unsacrificed residue will be endangered, is the question before us.

Several important considerations have been touched in the course of these papers, which discountenance the supposition that the operation of the federal government will by degrees prove fatal to the State governments. The more I revolve the subject, the more fully I am persuaded that the balance is much more likely to be disturbed by the preponderancy of the last than of the first scale.

We have seen, in all the examples of ancient and modern confederacies, the strongest tendency continually betraying itself in the members to despoil the general government of its authority with a very ineffectual capacity in the latter to defend itself against the encroachments. Although, in most of these examples, the system has been so dissimilar from that under consideration as greatly to weaken any inference concerning the latter from the fate of the former, yet, as the States will retain, under the proposed Constitution, a very extensive portion of active sovereignty, the inference ought not to be wholly disregarded. In the Achæan league it is probable that the federal head had a degree and species of power which gave it a considerable likeness to the government framed by the convention. The Lycian Confederacy, as far as its principles and form are transmitted, must have borne a still greater analogy to it. Yet history does not inform us that either of them ever degenerated, or tended to degenerate, into one consolidated government. On the contrary, we know that the ruin of one of them proceeded from the incapacity of the federal authority to prevent the dissensions, and finally the disunion, of the subordinate authorities. These cases are the more worthy of our attention, as the external causes by which the component parts were pressed together were much more numerous and powerful than in our case; and consequently less powerful ligaments within would be sufficient to bind the members to the head, and to each other.

In the feudal system, we have seen a similar propensity exemplified. Notwithstanding the want of proper sympathy in every instance between the local sovereigns and the people, and the sympathy in some instances between the general sovereign and the latter, it usually happened that the local sovereigns prevailed in the rivalship for encroachments. Had no external dangers enforced internal harmony and subordination, and, particularly, had the local sovereigns possessed the affections of the people, the great kingdoms in Europe would at this time consist of as many independent princes as there were formerly feudatory barons.

The State governments will have the advantage of the Federal government, whether we compare them in respect to the immediate dependence of the one on the other; to the weight of personal influence which each side will possess; to the powers respectively vested in them; to the predilection and probable support of the people; to the disposition and faculty of resisting and frustrating the measures of each other.

The State governments may be regarded as constituent and essential parts of the federal government; whilst the latter is nowise essential to the operation or organisation of the former. Without the intervention of the State legislatures, the President of the United States cannot be elected at all. They must in all cases have a great share in his appointment, and will, perhaps, in most cases, of themselves determine it. The Senate will be elected absolutely and exclusively by the State legislatures. Even the House of Representatives, though drawn immediately from the people, will be chosen very much under the influence of that class of men, whose influence over the people obtains for themselves an election into the State legislatures. Thus, each of the principal branches of the federal government will owe its existence more or less to the favour of the State governments, and must consequently feel a dependence, which is much more likely to beget a disposition too obsequious than too overbearing towards them. On the other side, the component parts of the State governments will in no instance be indebted for their appointment to the direct agency of the federal government, and very little, if at all, to the local influence of its members.

The number of individuals employed under the Constitution of the United States will be much smaller than the number employed under the particular States. There will consequently be less of personal influence on the side of the former than of the latter. The members of the legislative, executive, and judiciary departments of thirteen and more States, the justices of peace, officers of militia, ministerial officers of justice, with all the county, corporation, and town officers, for three millions and more of people, intermixed, and having particular acquaintance with every class and circle of people, must exceed, beyond all proportion, both in number and influence, those of every description who will be employed in the administration of the federal system. Compare the members of the three great departments of the thirteen States, excluding from the judiciary department the justices of peace, with the members of the corresponding departments of the single government of the Union; compare the militia officers of three millions of people with the military and marine officers of any establishment which is within the compass of probability, or, I may add, of possibility, and in this view alone, we may pronounce the advantage of the States to be decisive. If the federal government is to have collectors of revenue, the State governments will have theirs also. And as those of the former will be principally on the sea-coast, and not very numerous, whilst those of the latter will be spread over the face of the country, and will be very numerous, the advantage in this view also lies on the same side. It is true, that the Confederacy is to possess, and may exercise, the power of collecting internal as well as external taxes throughout the States; but it is probable that this power will not be resorted to except for supplemental purposes of revenue; that an op-

tion will then be given to the States to supply their quotas by previous collections of their own; and that the eventual collection, under the immediate authority of the Union, will generally be made by the officers, and according to the rules, appointed by the several States. Indeed it is extremely probable that in other instances, particularly in the organisation of the judicial power, the officers of the States will be clothed with the correspondent authority of the Union. Should it happen, however, that separate collectors of internal revenue should be appointed under the federal government, the influence of the whole number would not bear a comparison with that of the multitude of State officers in the opposite scale. Within every district to which a federal collector would be allotted, there would not be less than thirty or forty, or even more, officers of different descriptions, and many of them persons of character and weight, whose influence would lie on the side of the State.

The powers delegated by the proposed Constitution to the federal government are few and defined. Those which are to remain in the State governments are numerous and indefinite. The former will be exercised principally on external objects, as war, peace, negotiation, and foreign commerce; with which last the power of taxation will, for the most part, be connected. The powers reserved to the several States will extend to all the objects which, in the ordinary course of affairs, concern the lives, liberties, and properties of the people, and the internal order, improvement, and prosperity of the State.

The operations of the federal government will be most extensive and important in times of war and danger; those of the State governments, in times of peace and security. As the former periods will probably bear a small proportion to the latter, the State governments will here enjoy another advantage over the federal government. The more adequate, indeed, the federal powers may be rendered to the national defence, the less frequent will be those scenes of danger which might favour their ascendancy over the governments of the particular States.

If the new Constitution be examined with accuracy and candour, it will be found that the change which it proposes consists much less in the addition of NEW POWERS to the Union, than in the invigoration of its ORIGINAL POWERS. The regulation of commerce, it is true, is a new power; but that seems to be an addition which few oppose, and from which no apprehensions are entertained. The powers relating to war and peace, armies and fleets, treaties and finance, with the other more considerable powers, are all vested in the existing Congress by the articles of Confederation. The proposed change does not enlarge these powers; it only substitutes a more effectual mode of administering them. The change relating to taxation may be regarded as the most important; and yet the present Congress have as complete authority to REQUIRE of the States indefinite supplies of money for the common defence and general welfare as the future Congress will have to require them of individual citizens; and the latter will be no more bound than the States themselves have been to pay the quotas respectively taxed on them. Had the States complied punctually with the articles of Confederation, or could their compliance have been enforced by as peaceable means as may be used with success towards single persons, our past experience is very far from countenancing an opinion that the State governments would have lost their constitutional powers, and have gradually undergone an entire consolidation. To maintain that such an event would have ensued, would be to say at once that the existence of the State governments is incompatible with any system whatever that accomplishes the essential purposes of the Union. PUBLIUS

Number 46

[MADISON]

RESUMING the subject of the last paper, I proceed to inquire whether the federal government or the State governments will have the advantage with regard to the predilection and support of the people. Notwithstanding the different modes in which they are appointed, we must consider both of them as substantially dependent on the great body of the citizens of the United States. I assume this position here as it respects the first, reserving the proofs for another place. The federal and State governments are in fact but different agents and trustees of the people, constituted with different powers, and designed for different purposes. The adversaries of the Constitution seem to have lost sight of the people altogether in their reasonings on this subject; and to have viewed these different establishments, not only as mutual rivals and enemies, but as uncontrolled by any common superior in their efforts to usurp the authorities of each other. These gentlemen must here be reminded of their error. They must be told that the ultimate authority, wherever the derivative may be found, resides in the people alone, and that it will not depend merely on the comparative ambition or address of the different governments, whether either, or which of them, will be able to enlarge its sphere of jurisdiction at the expense of the other. Truth, no less than decency, requires that the event in every case should be supposed to depend on the sentiments and sanction of their common constituents.

Many considerations, besides those suggested on a former occasion, seem to place it beyond doubt that the first and most natural attachment of the people will be to the governments of their respective States. Into the administration of these a greater number of individuals will expect to rise. From the gift of these a greater number of offices and emoluments will flow. By the superintending care of these, all the more domestic and personal interests of the people will be regulated and provided for. With the affairs of these, the people will be more familiarly and minutely conversant. And with the members of these will a greater proportion of the people have the ties of personal acquaintance and friendship, and of family and party attachments; on the side of these, therefore, the popular bias may well be expected most strongly to incline.

Experience speaks the same language in this case. The federal administration, though hitherto very defective in comparison with what may be hoped under a better system, had, during the war, and particularly whilst the independent fund of paper emissions was in credit, an activity and importance as great as it can well have in any future circumstances whatever. It was engaged, too, in a course of measures which had for their object the protection of everything that was dear, and the acquisition of everything that could be desirable to the people at large. It was, nevertheless, invariably found, after the transient enthusiasm for the early Congresses was over, that the attention and attachment of the people were turned anew to their own particular governments; that the federal council was at no time the idol of popular favour; and that opposition to proposed enlargements of its powers and importance was the side usually taken by the men who wished to build their political consequence on the prepossessions of their fellow-citizens.

If, therefore, as has been elsewhere remarked, the people should in future become more partial to the federal than to the State governments, the change can only result from such manifest and irresistible proofs of a better administration, as will overcome all their antecedent propensities. And in that case, the people ought not surely to be precluded from giving most of their confidence where they may discover it to be most due; but even in that case the State governments could have little to apprehend, because it is only within a certain sphere that the federal power can, in the nature of things, be advantageously administered.

The remaining points on which I propose to compare the federal and State governments, are the disposition and the faculty they may respectively possess to resist and frustrate the measures of each other.

It has been already proved that the members of the federal will be more dependent on the members of the State governments, than the latter will be on the former. It has appeared also, that the prepossessions of the people, on whom both will depend, will be more on the side of the State governments than of the federal government. So far as the disposition of each towards the other may be influenced by these causes, the State governments must clearly have the advantage. But in a distinct and very important point of view, the advantage will lie on the same side. The prepossessions, which the members themselves will carry into the federal government, will generally be favourable to the States; whilst it will rarely happen, that the members of the State governments will carry into the public councils a bias in favour of the general government. A local spirit will infallibly prevail much more in the members of Congress than a national spirit will prevail in the legislatures of the particular States. Every one knows that a great proportion of the errors committed by the State legislatures proceeds from the disposition of the members to sacrifice the comprehensive and permanent interest of the State, to the particular and separate views of the counties or districts in which they reside. And if they do not sufficiently enlarge their policy to embrace the collective welfare of their particular State, how can it be imagined that they will make the aggregate prosperity of the Union, and the dignity and respectability of its government, the objects of their affections

and consultations? For the same reason that the members of the State legislatures will be unlikely to attach themselves sufficiently to national objects, the members of the federal legislature will be likely to attach themselves too much to local objects. The States will be to the latter what counties and towns are to the former. Measures will too often be decided according to their probable effect, not on the national prosperity and happiness, but on the prejudices, interests, and pursuits of the governments and people of the individual States. What is the spirit that has in general characterised the proceedings of Congress? A perusal of their journals, as well as the candid acknowledgments of such as have had a seat in that assembly, will inform us, that the members have but too frequently displayed the character, rather of partisans of their respective States than of impartial guardians of a common interest; that where on one occasion improper sacrifices have been made of local considerations, to the aggrandisement of the federal government, the great interests of the nation have suffered on a hundred, from an undue attention to the local prejudices, interests, and views of the particular States. I mean not by these reflections to insinuate, that the new federal government will not embrace a more enlarged plan of policy than the existing government may have pursued; much less, that its views will be as confined as those of the State legislatures; but only that it will partake sufficiently of the spirit of both to be disinclined to invade the rights of the individual States, or the prerogatives of their governments. The motives on the part of the State governments, to augment their prerogatives by defalcations from the federal government, will be overruled by no reciprocal predispositions in the members.

Were it admitted, however, that the Federal government may feel an equal disposition with the State governments to extend its power beyond the due limits, the latter would still have the advantage in the means of defeating such encroachments. If an act of a particular State, though unfriendly to the national government, be generally popular in that State, and should not too grossly violate the oaths of the state officers, it is executed immediately and, of course, by means on the spot and depending on the State alone. The opposition of the federal government, or the interposition of federal officers, would but inflame the zeal of all parties on the side of the State, and the evil could not be prevented or repaired, if at all, without the employment of means which must always be resorted to with reluctance and difficulty. On the other hand, should an unwarrantable measure of the federal government be unpopular in particular States, which would seldom fail to be the case, or even a warrantable measure be so, which may sometimes be the case, the means of opposition to it are powerful and at hand. The disquietude of the people; their repugnance and, perhaps, refusal to co-operate with the officers of the Union; the frowns of the executive magistracy of the State; the embarrassments created by legislative devices, which would often be added on such occasions, would oppose, in any State, difficulties not to be despised; would form, in a large State, very serious impediments; and where the sentiments of several adjoining States happened to be in unison, would present obstructions which the federal government would hardly be willing to encounter.

But ambitious encroachments of the federal government, on the authority of the State governments, would not excite the opposition of a single State, or of a few States only. They would be signals of general alarm. Every government would espouse the common cause. A correspondence would be opened. Plans of resistance would be concerted. One spirit would animate and conduct the whole. The same combinations, in short, would result from an apprehension of the federal, as was produced by the dread of a foreign, yoke; and unless the projected innovations should be voluntarily renounced, the same appeal to a trial of force would be made in the one case as was made in the other. But what degree of madness could ever drive the federal government to such an extremity. In the contest with Great Britain, one part of the empire was employed against the other. The more numerous part invaded the rights of the less numerous part. The attempt was unjust and unwise; but it was not in speculation absolutely chimerical. But what would be the contest in the case we are supposing? Who would be the parties? A few representatives of the people would be opposed to the people themselves; or rather one set of representatives would be contending against thirteen sets of representatives, with the whole body of their common constituents on the side of the latter.

The only refuge left for those who prophesy the downfall of the State governments is the visionary supposition that the federal government may previously accumulate a military force for the projects of ambition. The reasonings contained in these papers must have been employed to little purpose indeed, if it could be necessary now to disprove the reality of this danger. That the people and the States should, for a sufficient period of time, elect an uninterrupted succession of men ready to betray both; that the traitors should, throughout this period, uniformly and systematically pursue some fixed plan for the extension of the military establishment; that the governments and the people of the States should silently and patiently behold the gathering storm, and continue to supply the materials, until it should be prepared to burst on their own heads, must appear to every one more like the incoherent dreams of a delirious jealousy, or the misjudged exaggerations of a counterfeit zeal, than like the sober apprehensions of genuine patriotism. Extravagant as the supposition is, let it however be made. Let a regular army, fully equal to the resources of the country, be formed; and let it be entirely at the devotion of the federal government; still it would not be going too far to say, that the State governments, with the people on their side, would be able to repel the danger. The highest number to which, according to the best computation, a standing army can be carried in any country, does not exceed one hundreth part of the whole number of souls; or one twenty-fifth part of the number able to bear arms. This proportion would not yield, in the United States, an army of more than twenty-five or thirty thousand men. To these would be opposed a militia amounting to near half a million of citizens with arms in their hands, officered by men chosen from among themselves, fighting for their common liberties, and united and conducted by governments possessing their affections and confidence. It may well be doubted, whether a militia thus circumstanced could ever be conquered by such a proportion of regular troops. Those who are best acquainted with the last successful resistance of this country against the British arms will be most inclined to deny the possibility of it. Besides the advantage of being armed, which the Americans possess over the people of almost every other nation, the existence of subordinate governments, to which the people are attached, and by which the militia officers are appointed, forms a barrier against the enterprises of ambition, more insurmountable than any which a simple government of any form can admit of. Notwithstanding the military establishments in the several kingdoms of Europe, which are carried as far as the public resources will bear, the governments are afraid to trust the people with arms. And it is not certain that with this aid alone they would not be able to shake off their yokes. But were the people to possess the additional advantages of local governments chosen by themselves, who could collect the national will and direct the national force, and of officers appointed out of the militia, by these governments, and attached both to them and to the militia, it may be affirmed with the greatest assurance, that the throne of every tyranny in Europe would be speedily overturned in spite of the legions which surround it. Let us not insult the free and gallant citizens of America with the suspicion, that they would be less able to defend the rights of which they would be in actual possession, than the debased subjects of arbitrary power would be to rescue theirs from the hands of their oppressors. Let us rather no longer insult them with the supposition that they can ever reduce themselves to the necessity of making the experiment, by a blind and tame submission to the long train of insidious measures which must precede and produce it.

The argument under the present head may be put into a very concise form, which appears altogether conclusive. Either the mode in which the federal government is to be constructed will render it sufficiently dependent on the people, or it will not. On the first supposition, it will be restrained by that dependence from forming schemes obnoxious to their constituents. On the other supposition, it will not possess the confidence of the people, and its schemes of usurpation will be easily defeated by the State governments, who will be supported by the people.

On summing up the considerations stated in this and the last paper, they seem to amount to the most convincing evidence, that the powers proposed to be lodged in the federal government are as little formidable to those reserved to the individual States, as they are indispensably necessary to accomplish the purposes of the Union; and that all those alarms which have been sounded, of a meditated and consequential annihilation of the State governments, must, on the most favourable interpretation, be ascribed to the chimerical fears of the authors of them.

PUBLIUS

Number 47
[MADISON]

HAVING REVIEWED the general form of the proposed government and the general mass of power allotted to it, I proceed to examine the particular structure of this government, and the distribution of this mass of power among its constituent parts.

One of the principal objections inculcated by the more respectable adversaries to the Constitution is its supposed violation of the political maxim, that the legislative, executive, and judiciary departments ought to be separate and distinct. In the structure of the federal government, no regard, it is said, seems to have been paid to this essential precaution in favour of liberty. The several departments of power are distributed and blended in such a manner as at once to destroy all symmetry and beauty of form, and to expose some of the essential parts of the edifice to the danger of being crushed by the disproportionate weight of other parts.

No political truth is certainly of greater intrinsic value, or is stamped with the authority of more enlightened patrons of liberty, than that on which the objection is founded. The accumulation of all powers, legislative, executive, and judiciary, in the same hands, whether of one, a few, or many, and whether hereditary, self-appointed, or elective, may justly be pronounced the very definition of tyranny. Were the federal Constitution, therefore, really chargeable with the accumulation of power, or with a mixture of powers, having a dangerous tendency to such an accumulation, no further arguments would be necessary to inspire a universal reprobation of the system. I persuade myself, however, that it will be made apparent to every one that the charge cannot be supported, and that the maxim on which it relies has been totally misconceived and misapplied. In order to form correct ideas on this important subject, it will be proper to investigate the sense in which the preservation of liberty requires that the three great departments of power should be separate and distinct.

The oracle who is always consulted and cited on this subject is the celebrated Montesquieu. If he be not the author of this invaluable precept in the science of politics, he has the merit at least of displaying and recommending it most effectually to the attention of mankind. Let us endeavour, in the first place, to ascertain his meaning on this point.

The British Constitution was to Montesquieu what Homer has been to the didactic writers on epic poetry. As the latter have considered the work of the immortal bard as the perfect model from which the principles and rules of the epic art were to be drawn, and by which all similar works were to be judged, so this great political critic appears to have viewed the Constitution of England as the standard, or to use his own expression, as the mirror of political liberty; and to have delivered, in the form of elementary truths, the several characteristic principles of that particular system. That we may be sure, then, not to mistake his meaning in this case, let us recur to the source from which the maxim was drawn.

On the slightest view of the British Constitution, we must perceive that the legislative, executive, and judiciary departments are by no means totally separate and distinct from each other. The executive magistrate forms an integral part of the legislative authority. He alone has the prerogative of making treaties with foreign sovereigns, which, when made, have, under certain limitations, the force of legislative acts. All the members of the judiciary department are appointed by him, can be removed by him on the address of the two Houses of Parliament, and form, when he pleases to consult them, one of his constitutional councils. One branch of the legislative department forms also a great constitutional council to the executive chief, as, on another hand, it is the sole depositary of judicial power in cases of impeachment, and is invested with the supreme appellate jurisdiction in all other cases. The judges, again, are so far connected with the legislative department as often to attend and participate in its deliberations, though not admitted to a legislative vote.

From these facts, by which Montesquieu was guided, it may clearly be inferred that, in saying "There can be no liberty where the legislative and executive powers are united in the same person, or body of magistrates," or, "if the power of judging be not separated from the legislative and executive powers," he did not mean that these departments ought to have no *partial agency* in, or no *control* over, the acts of each other. His meaning, as his own words import, and still more conclusively as illustrated by the example in his eye, can amount to no more than this, that where the *whole* power of one department is exercised by the same hands which possess the *whole* power of another department, the fundamental principles of a free constitution are subverted. This would have been the case in the constitution examined by him, if the king, who is the sole executive magistrate, had possessed also the complete legislative power, or the supreme administration of justice; or if the entire legislative body had possessed the supreme judiciary, or the supreme executive authority. This, however, is not among the vices of that constitution. The magistrate in whom the whole executive power resides cannot of himself make a law, though he can put a negative on every law; nor administer justice in person, though he has the appointment of those who do administer it. The judges can exercise no executive prerogative, though they are shoots from the executive stock; nor any legislative function, though they may be advised with by the legislative councils. The entire legislature can perform no judiciary act, though by the joint act of two of its branches the judges may be removed from their offices, and though one of its branches is possessed of the judicial power in the last resort. The entire legislature, again, can exercise no executive prerogative, though one of its branches constitutes the supreme executive magistracy, and another, on the impeachment of a third, can try and condemn all the subordinate officers in the executive department.

The reasons on which Montesquieu grounds his maxim are a further demonstration of his meaning. "When the legislative and executive powers are united in the same person or body," says he, "there can be no liberty, because apprehensions may arise lest *the same* monarch or senate should *enact* tyrannical laws to *execute* them in a tyrannical manner." Again: "Were the power of judging joined with the legislative, the life and liberty of the subject would be exposed to arbitrary control, for *the judge* would then be *the legislator*. Were it joined to the executive power, *the judge* might behave with all the violence of *an oppressor*." Some of these reasons are more fully explained in other passages; but briefly stated as they are here, they sufficiently establish the meaning which we have put on this celebrated maxim of this celebrated author.

If we look into the constitutions of the several States, we find that, notwithstanding the emphatical and, in some instances, the unqualified terms in which this axiom has been laid down, there is not a single instance in which the several departments of power have been kept absolutely separate and distinct. New Hampshire, whose constitution was the last formed, seems to have been fully aware of the impossibility and inexpediency of avoiding any mixture whatever of these departments, and has qualified the doctrine by declaring "that the legislative, executive, and judiciary powers ought to be kept as separate from, and independent of, each other *as the nature of a free government will admit; or as is consistent with that chain of connection that binds the whole fabric of the constitution in one indissoluble bond of unity and amity."* Her constitution accordingly mixes these departments in several respects. The Senate, which is a branch of the legislative department, is also a judicial tribunal for the trial of impeachments. The president, who is the head of the executive department, is the presiding member also of the Senate; and, besides an equal vote in all cases, has a casting vote in case of a tie. The executive head is himself eventually elective every year by the legislative department and his council is every year chosen by and from the members of the same department. Several of the officers of state are also appointed by the legislature. And the members of the judiciary department are appointed by the executive department.

The constitution of Massachusetts has observed a sufficient though less pointed caution, in expressing this fundamental article of liberty. It declares "that the legislative department shall never exercise the executive and judicial powers, or either of them; the executive shall never exercise the legislative and judicial powers, or either of them; the judicial shall never exercise the legislative and executive powers, or either of them." This declaration corresponds precisely with the doctrine of Montesquieu, as it has been explained, and is not in a single point violated by the plan of the convention. It goes no farther than to prohibit any one of the entire departments from exercising the powers of another department. In the very Constitution to which it is prefixed, a partial mixture of powers has been admitted. The executive magistrate has a qualified negative on the legislative body, and the Senate, which is a part of the legislature, is a court of impeachment for members both of the executive and judiciary departments. The members of the judiciary department, again, are appointable by the executive department, and removable by the same authority on the address of the two legislative branches. Lastly, a

number of the officers of government are annually appointed by the legislative department. As the appointment to offices, particularly executive offices, is in its nature an executive function, the compilers of the Constitution have, in this last point at least, violated the rule established by themselves.

I pass over the constitutions of Rhode Island and Connecticut, because they were formed prior to the Revolution, and even before the principle under examination had become an object of political attention.

The constitution of New York contains no declaration on this subject; but appears very clearly to have been framed with an eye to the danger of improperly blending the different departments. It gives, nevertheless, to the executive magistrate, a partial control over the legislative department; and, what is more, gives a like control to the judiciary department; and even blends the executive and judiciary departments in the exercise of this control. In its council of appointment, members of the legislative are associated with the executive authority, in the appointment of officers, both executive and judiciary. And its court for the trial of impeachments and correction of errors is to consist of one branch of the legislature and the principal members of the judiciary department.

The constitution of New Jersey has blended the different powers of government more than any of the preceding. The governor, who is the executive magistrate, is appointed by the legislature; is chancellor and ordinary, or surrogate of the State; is a member of the Supreme Court of Appeals, and president, with a casting vote, of one of the legislative branches. The same legislative branch acts again as executive council of the governor, and with him constitutes the Court of Appeals. The members of the judiciary department are appointed by the legislative department, and removable by one branch of it on the impeachment of the other.

According to the constitution of Pennsylvania, the president, who is the head of the executive department, is annually elected by a vote in which the legislative department predominates. In conjunction with an executive council, he appoints the members of the judiciary department, and forms a court of impeachment for trial of all officers, judiciary as well as executive. The judges of the Supreme Court and justices of the peace seem also to be removable by the legislature; and the executive power of pardoning in certain cases to be referred to the same department. The members of the executive council are made EX-OFFICIO justices of peace throughout the State.

In Delaware, the chief executive magistrate is annually elected by the legislative department. The speakers of the two legislative branches are vice-presidents in the executive department. The executive chief, with six others, appointed, three by each of the legislative branches, constitutes the Supreme Court of Appeals; he is joined with the legislative department in the appointment of the other judges. Throughout the States, it appears that the members of the legislature may at the same time be justices of the peace; in this State, the members of one branch of it are EX-OFFICIO justices of the peace; as are also the members of the executive council. The principal officers of the executive department are appointed by the legislative; and one branch of the latter forms a court of impeachments. All officers may be removed on address of the legislature.

Maryland has adopted the maxim in the most unqualified terms; declaring that the legislative, executive, and judicial powers of government ought to be for ever separate and distinct from each other. Her constitution, notwithstanding, makes the executive magistrate appointable by the legislative department; and the members of the judiciary by the executive department.

The language of Virginia is still more pointed on this subject. Her constitution declares, "that the legislative, executive, and judiciary departments shall be separate and distinct; so that neither exercise the powers properly belonging to the other; nor shall any person exercise the powers of more than one of them at the same time, except that the justices of county courts shall be eligible to either House of Assembly." Yet we find not only this express exception, with respect to the members of the inferior courts, but that the chief magistrate, with his executive council, are appointable by the legislature; that two members of the latter are triennially displaced at the pleasure of the legislature; and that all the principal offices, both executive and judiciary, are filled by the same department. The executive prerogative of pardon, also, is in one case vested in the legislative department.

The constitution of North Carolina, which declares "that the legislative, executive, and supreme judicial powers of government ought to be for ever separate and distinct from each

other," refers, at the same time, to the legislative department, the appointment not only of the executive chief, but all the principal officers within both that and the judiciary department.

In South Carolina, the constitution makes the executive magistracy eligible by the legislative department. It gives to the latter, also, the appointment of the members of the judiciary department, including even justices of the peace and sheriffs; and the appointment of officers in the executive department, down to captains in the army and navy of the State.

In the constitution of Georgia, where it is declared "that the legislative, executive, and judiciary departments shall be separate and distinct, so that neither exercise the powers properly belonging to the other," we find that the executive department is to be filled by appointments of the legislature; and the executive prerogative of pardon to be finally exercised by the same authority. Even justices of the peace are to be appointed by the legislature.

In citing these cases, in which the legislative, executive, and judiciary departments have not been kept totally separate and distinct, I wish not to be regarded as an advocate for the particular organisations of the several State governments. I am fully aware that among the many excellent principles which they exemplify, they carry strong marks of the haste, and still stronger of the inexperience, under which they were framed. It is but too obvious that in some instances the fundamental principle under consideration has been violated by too great a mixture, and even an actual consolidation, of the different powers; and that in no instance has a competent provision been made for maintaining in practice the separation delineated on paper. What I have wished to evince is, that the charge brought against the proposed Constitution, of violating the sacred maxim of free government, is warranted neither by the real meaning annexed to that maxim by its author, nor by the sense in which it has hitherto been understood in America. This interesting subject will be resumed in the ensuing paper.   PUBLIUS

Number 48
[MADISON]

IT WAS shown in the last paper that the political apothegm there examined does not require that the legislative, executive, and judiciary departments should be wholly unconnected with each other. I shall undertake, in the next place, to show that unless these departments be so far connected and blended as to give to each a constitutional control over the others, the degree of separation which the maxim requires, as essential to a free government, can never in practice be duly maintained.

It is agreed on all sides, that the powers properly belonging to one of the departments ought not to be directly and completely administered by either of the other departments. It is equally evident, that none of them ought to possess, directly or indirectly, an overruling influence over the others, in the administration of their respective powers. It will not be denied that power is of an encroaching nature, and that it ought to be effectually restrained from passing the limits assigned to it. After discriminating, therefore, in theory, the several classes of power, as they may in their nature be legislative, executive, or judiciary, the next and most difficult task is to provide some practical security for each, against the invasion of the others. What this security ought to be is the great problem to be solved.

Will it be sufficient to mark, with precision, the boundaries of these departments, in the constitution of the government, and to trust to these parchment barriers against the encroaching spirit of power? This is the security which appears to have been principally relied on by the compilers of most of the American constitutions. But experience assures us, that the efficacy of the provision has been greatly overrated; and that some more adequate defence is indispensably necessary for the more feeble, against the more powerful, members of the government. The legislative department is everywhere extending the sphere of its activity, and drawing all power into its impetuous vortex.

The founders of our republics have so much merit for the wisdom which they have displayed, that no task can be less pleasing than that of pointing out the errors into which they have fallen. A respect for truth, however, obliges us to remark that they seem never for a moment to have turned their eyes from the danger to liberty from the overgrown and all-grasping prerogative of an hereditary magistrate, supported and fortified by an hereditary branch of the legislative authority. They seem never to have recollected the danger from legislative usurpations, which, by assembling all power in the same hands, must lead to the same tyranny as is threatened by executive usurpations.

In a government where numerous and extensive prerogatives are placed in the hands of an hereditary monarch, the executive department is very justly regarded as the source of danger, and watched with all the jealousy which a zeal for liberty ought to inspire. In a democracy, where a multitude of people exercise in person the legislative functions, and are continually exposed, by their incapacity for regular deliberation and concerted measures, to the ambitious intrigues of their executive magistrates, tyranny may well be apprehended, on some favourable emergency, to start up in the same quarter. But in a representative republic, where the executive magistracy is carefully limited, both in the extent and the duration of its power; and where the legislative power is exercised by an assembly which is inspired, by a supposed influence over the people, with an intrepid confidence in its own strength; which is sufficiently numerous to feel all the passions which actuate a multitude, yet not so numerous as to be incapable of pursuing the objects of its passions, by means which reason prescribes; it is against the enterprising ambition of this department that the people ought to indulge all their jealousy and exhaust all their precautions.

The legislative department derives a superiority in our governments from other circumstances. Its constitutional powers being at once more extensive, and less susceptible of precise limits, it can, with the greater facility, mask, under complicated and indirect measures, the encroachments which it makes on the co-ordinate departments. It is not unfrequently a question of real nicety in legislative bodies, whether the operation of a particular measure will, or will not, extend beyond the legislative sphere. On the other side, the executive power being restrained within a narrower compass, and being more simple in its nature, and the judiciary being described by landmarks still less uncertain, projects of usurpation by either of these departments would immediately betray and defeat themselves. Nor is this all: as the legislative department alone has access to the pockets of the people, and has in some constitutions full discretion, and in all a prevailing influence, over the pecuniary rewards of those who fill the other departments, a dependence is thus created in the latter, which gives still greater facility to encroachments of the former.

I have appealed to our own experience for the truth of what I advance on this subject.

Were it necessary to verify this experience by particular proofs, they might be multiplied without end. I might find a witness in every citizen who has shared in, or been attentive to, the course of public administrations. I might collect vouchers in abundance from the records and archives of every State in the Union. But as a more concise, and at the same time equally satisfactory, evidence, I will refer to the example of two States, attested by two unexceptionable authorities.

The first example is that of Virginia, a State which, as we have seen, has expressly declared in its constitution, that the three great departments ought not to be intermixed. The authority in support of it is Mr. Jefferson, who, besides his other advantages for remarking the operation of the government, was himself the chief magistrate of it. In order to convey fully the ideas with which his experience had impressed him on this subject, it will be necessary to quote a passage of some length from his very interesting *Notes on the State of Virginia*, p. 195. "All the powers of government, legislative, executive, and judiciary, result to the legislative body. The concentrating these in the same hands is precisely the definition of despotic government. It will be no alleviation, that these powers will be exercised by a plurality of hands, and not by a single one. One hundred and seventy-three despots would surely be as oppressive as one. Let those who doubt it turn their eyes on the republic of Venice. As little will it avail us that they are chosen by ourselves. An *elective despotism* was not the government we fought for; but one which should not only be founded on free principles, but in which the powers of government should be so divided and balanced among several bodies of magistracy, as that no one could transcend their legal limit, without being effectually checked and restrained by the others. For this reason, that convention which passed the ordinance of government, laid its foundation on this basis, that the legislative, executive, and judiciary departments should be separate and distinct, so that no person should exercise the powers of more than one of them at the same time. *But no barrier was provided between these several powers.* The judiciary and the executive members were left dependent on the legislative for their subsistence in office, and some of them for their continuance in it. If, therefore, the legislature assumes executive and judiciary powers, no opposition is likely to be made; nor, if made, can be effec-

tual; because in that case they may put their proceedings into the form of acts of Assembly, which will render them obligatory on the other branches. They have accordingly, in *many* instances, *decided rights* which should have been left to *judiciary controversy*, and *the direction of the executive, during the whole time of their session, is becoming habitual and familiar."*

The other State which I shall take for an example is Pennsylvania; and the other authority, the Council of Censors, which assembled in the years 1783 and 1784. A part of the duty of this body, as marked out by the constitution, was "to inquire whether the constitution had been preserved inviolate in every part, and whether the legislative and executive branches of government had performed their duty as guardians of the people, or assumed to themselves, or exercised, other or greater powers than they are entitled to by the constitution." In the execution of this trust, the council were necessarily led to a comparison of both the legislative and executive proceedings with the constitutional powers of these departments; and from the facts enumerated, and to the truth of most of which both sides in the council subscribed, it appears that the constitution had been flagrantly violated by the legislature in a variety of important instances.

A great number of laws had been passed, violating, without any apparent necessity, the rule requiring that all bills of a public nature shall be previously printed for the consideration of the people; although this is one of the precautions chiefly relied on by the constitution against improper acts of the legislature.

The constitutional trial by jury had been violated, and powers assumed which had not been delegated by the constitution.

Executive powers had been usurped.

The salaries of the judges, which the constitution expressly requires to be fixed, had been occasionally varied; and cases belonging to the judiciary department frequently drawn within legislative cognisance and determination.

Those who wish to see the several particulars falling under each of these heads may consult the journals of the council, which are in print. Some of them, it will be found, may be imputable to peculiar circumstances connected with the war; but the greater part of them may be considered as the spontaneous shoots of an ill-constituted government.

It appears, also, that the executive department had not been innocent of frequent breaches of the constitution. There are three observations, however, which ought to be made on this head; *first,* a great proportion of the instances were either immediately produced by the necessities of the war, or recommended by Congress or the commander-in-chief; *secondly,* in most of the other instances, they conformed either to the declared or the known sentiments of the legislative department; *thirdly,* the executive department of Pennsylvania is distinguished from that of the other States by the number of members composing it. In this respect it has as much affinity to a legislative assembly as to an executive council. And being at once exempt from the restraint of an individual responsibility for the acts of the body, and deriving confidence from mutual example and joint influence, unauthorised measures would, of course, be more freely hazarded than where the executive department is administered by a single hand, or by a few hands.

The conclusion which I am warranted in drawing from these observations is, that a mere demarcation on parchment of the constitutional limits of the several departments is not a sufficient guard against those encroachments which lead to a tyrannical concentration of all the powers of government in the same hands.

PUBLIUS

Number 49

[HAMILTON OR MADISON]

THE AUTHOR of the *Notes on the State of Virginia,* quoted in the last paper, has subjoined to that valuable work the draught of a constitution, which had been prepared in order to be laid before a convention expected to be called in 1783 by the legislature for the establishment of a constitution for that commonwealth. The plan, like everything from the same pen, marks a turn of thinking, original, comprehensive, and accurate; and is the more worthy of attention as it equally displays a fervent attachment to republican government and an enlightened view of the dangerous propensities against which it ought to be guarded. One of the precautions which he proposes, and on which he appears ultimately to rely as a palladium to the weaker departments of power against the invasions of the stronger, is perhaps altogether his own, and as it immediately relates to the subject of our present inquiry, ought not to be overlooked.

His proposition is, "that whenever any two of the three branches of government shall concur in opinion, each by the voices of two thirds of their whole number, that a convention is necessary for altering the constitution, or *correcting breaches of it,* a convention shall be called for the purpose."

As the people are the only legitimate fountain of power, and it is from them that the constitutional charter, under which the several branches of government hold their power, is derived, it seems strictly consonant to the republican theory, to recur to the same original authority, not only whenever it may be necessary to enlarge, diminish, or new-model the powers of the government, but also whenever any one of the departments may commit encroachments on the chartered authorities of the others. The several departments being perfectly co-ordinate by the terms of their common commission, none of them, it is evident, can pretend to an exclusive or superior right of settling the boundaries between their respective powers; and how are the encroachments of the stronger to be prevented, or the wrongs of the weaker to be redressed, without an appeal to the people themselves, who, as the grantors of the commission, can alone declare its true meaning, and enforce its observance?

There is certainly great force in this reasoning, and it must be allowed to prove that a constitutional road to the decision of the people ought to be marked out and kept open, for certain great and extraordinary occasions. But there appear to be insuperable objections against the proposed recurrence to the people, as a provision in all cases for keeping the several departments of power within their constitutional limits.

In the first place the provision does not reach the case of a combination of two of the departments against the third. If the legislative authority, which possesses so many means of operating on the motives of the other departments, should be able to gain to its interest either of the others, or even one third of its members, the remaining department could derive no advantage from its remedial provision. I do not dwell, however, on this objection, because it may be thought to be rather against the modification of the principle, than against the principle itself.

In the next place, it may be considered as an objection inherent in the principle, that as every appeal to the people would carry an implication of some defect in the government, frequent appeals would, in a great measure, deprive the government of that veneration which time bestows on everything, and without which perhaps the wisest and freest governments would not possess the requisite stability. If it be true that all governments rest on opinion, it is no less true that the strength of opinion in each individual, and its practical influence on his conduct, depend much on the number which he supposes to have entertained the same opinion. The reason of man, like man himself, is timid and cautious when left alone, and acquires firmness and confidence in proportion to the number with which it is associated. When the examples which fortify opinion are *ancient* as well as *numerous*, they are known to have a double effect. In a nation of philosophers, this consideration ought to be disregarded. A reverence for the laws would be sufficiently inculcated by the voice of an enlightened reason. But a nation of philosophers is as little to be expected as the philosophical race of kings wished for by Plato. And in every other nation, the most rational government will not find it a superfluous advantage to have the prejudices of the community on its side.

The danger of disturbing the public tranquillity by interesting too strongly the public passions, is a still more serious objection against a frequent reference of constitutional questions to the decision of the whole society. Notwithstanding the success which has attended the revisions of our established forms of government, and which does so much honour to the virtue and intelligence of the people of America, it must be confessed that the experiments are of too ticklish a nature to be unnecessarily multiplied. We are to recollect that all the existing constitutions were formed in the midst of a danger which repressed the passions most unfriendly to order and concord; of an enthusiastic confidence of the people in their patriotic leaders, which stifled the ordinary diversity of opinions on great national questions; of a universal ardour for new and opposite forms, produced by a universal resentment and indignation against the ancient government; and whilst no spirit of party connected with the changes to be made, or the abuses to be reformed, could mingle its leaven in the operation. The future situations in which we must expect to be usually placed, do not present any equivalent security against the danger which is apprehended.

But the greatest objection of all is, that the decisions which would probably result from such appeals would not answer the purpose of maintaining the constitutional equilibrium of the government. We have seen that the tendency of republican governments is to an aggrandisement of the legislative at the expense of the other departments. The appeals to the people, therefore, would usually be made by the executive and judiciary departments. But whether made by one side or the other, would each side enjoy equal advantages on the trial? Let us view their different situations. The members of the executive and judiciary departments are few in number, and can be personally known to a small part only of the people. The latter, by the mode of their appointment, as well as by the nature and permanency of it, are too far removed from the people to share much in their prepossessions. The former are generally the objects of jealousy, and their administration is always liable to be discoloured and rendered unpopular. The members of the legislative department, on the other hand, are numerous. They are distributed and dwell among the people at large. Their connections of blood, of friendship, and of acquaintance embrace a great proportion of the most influential part of the society. The nature of their public trust implies a personal influence among the people, and that they are more immediately the confidential guardians of the rights and liberties of the people. With these advantages, it can hardly be supposed that the adverse party would have an equal chance for a favourable issue.

But the legislative party would not only be able to plead their cause most successfully with the people. They would probably be constituted themselves the judges. The same influence which had gained them an election into the legislature would gain them a seat in the convention. If this should not be the case with all, it would probably be the case with many, and pretty certainly with those leading characters on whom everything depends in such bodies. The convention, in short, would be composed chiefly of men who had been, who actually were, or who expected to be, members of the department whose conduct was arraigned. They would consequently be parties to the very question to be decided by them.

It might, however, sometimes happen that appeals would be made under circumstances less adverse to the executive and judiciary departments. The usurpations of the legislature might be so flagrant and so sudden as to admit of no specious colouring. A strong party among themselves might take side with the other branches. The executive power might be in the hands of a peculiar favourite of the people. In such a posture of things, the public decision might be less swayed by prepossessions in favour of the legislative party. But still it could never be expected to turn on the true merits of the question. It would inevitably be connected with the spirit of pre-existing parties, or of parties springing out of the question itself. It would be connected with persons of distinguished character and extensive influence in the community. It would be pronounced by the very men who had been agents in, or opponents of, the measures to which the decision would relate. The *passions,* therefore, not the *reason,* of the public would sit in judgment. But it is the reason, alone, of the public that ought to control and regulate the government. The passions ought to be controlled and regulated by the government.

We found in the last paper, that mere declarations in the written constitution are not sufficient to restrain the several departments within their legal rights. It appears in this, that occasional appeals to the people would be neither a proper nor an effectual provision for that purpose. How far the provisions of a different nature contained in the plan above quoted might be adequate, I do not examine. Some of them are unquestionably founded on sound political principles, and all of them are framed with singular ingenuity and precision. PUBLIUS

Number 50

[HAMILTON OR MADISON]

It MAY be contended, perhaps, that instead of *occasional* appeals to the people, which are liable to the objections urged against them, *periodical* appeals are the proper and adequate means of *preventing and correcting infractions of the Constitution.*

It will be attended to, that in the examination of these expedients, I confine myself to their aptitude for *enforcing* the Constitution, by keeping the several departments of power within their due bounds, without particularly considering them as provisions for *altering* the Constitution itself. In the first view, appeals to the people at fixed periods appear to be nearly as ineligible as appeals on particular

occasions as they emerge. If the periods be separated by short intervals, the measures to be reviewed and rectified will have been of recent date, and will be connected with all the circumstances which tend to vitiate and pervert the result of occasional revisions. If the periods be distant from each other, the same remark will be applicable to all recent measures; and in proportion as the remoteness of the others may favour a dispassionate review of them, this advantage is inseparable from inconveniences which seem to counterbalance it. In the first place, a distant prospect of public censure would be a very feeble restraint on power from those excesses to which it might be urged by the force of present motives. Is it to be imagined that a legislative assembly, consisting of a hundred or two hundred members, eagerly bent on some favourite object, and breaking through the restraints of the Constitution in pursuit of it, would be arrested in their career, by considerations drawn from a censorial revision of their conduct at the future distance of ten, fifteen, or twenty years? In the next place, the abuses would often have completed their mischievous effects before the remedial provision would be applied. And in the last place, where this might not be the case, they would be of long standing, would have taken deep root, and would not easily be extirpated.

The scheme of revising the constitution, in order to correct recent breaches of it, as well as for other purposes, has been actually tried in one of the States. One of the objects of the Council of Censors which met in Pennsylvania in 1783 and 1784, was, as we have seen, to inquire, "whether the constitution had been violated, and whether the legislative and executive departments had encroached on each other." This important and novel experiment in politics merits, in several points of view, very particular attention. In some of them it may, perhaps, as a single experiment, made under circumstances somewhat peculiar, be thought to be not absolutely conclusive. But as applied to the case under consideration, it involves some facts which I venture to remark as a complete and satisfactory illustration of the reasoning which I have employed.

First. It appears, from the names of the gentlemen who composed the council, that some, at least, of its most active and leading members had also been active and leading characters in the parties which pre-existed in the State.

Secondly. It appears that the same active and leading members of the council had been active and influential members of the legislative and executive branches within the period to be reviewed; and even patrons or opponents of the very measures to be thus brought to the test of the constitution. Two of the members had been vice-presidents of the State, and several other members of the executive council, within the seven preceding years. One of them had been speaker, and a number of others distinguished members, of the legislative assembly within the same period.

Thirdly. Every page of their proceedings witnesses the effect of all these circumstances on the temper of their deliberations. Throughout the continuance of the council, it was split into two fixed and violent parties. The fact is acknowledged and lamented by themselves. Had this not been the case, the face of their proceedings exhibits a proof equally satisfactory. In all questions, however unimportant in themselves, or unconnected with each other, the same names stand invariably contrasted on the opposite columns. Every unbiased observer may infer, without danger of mistake, and at the same time without meaning to reflect on either party, or any individuals of either party, that, unfortunately, *passion,* not *reason,* must have presided over their decisions. When men exercise their reason coolly and freely on a variety of distinct questions, they inevitably fall into different opinions on some of them. When they are governed by a common passion, their opinions, if they are so to be called, will be the same.

Fourthly. It is at least problematical, whether the decisions of this body do not, in several instances, misconstrue the limits prescribed for the legislative and executive departments, instead of reducing and limiting them within their constitutional places.

Fifthly. I have never understood that the decisions of the council on constitutional questions, whether rightly or erroneously formed, have had any effect in varying the practice founded on legislative constructions. It even appears, if I mistake not, that in one instance the contemporary legislature denied the constructions of the council, and actually prevailed in the contest.

This censorial body, therefore, proves at the same time, by its researches, the existence of the disease, and by its example, the inefficacy of the remedy.

This conclusion cannot be invalidated by alleging that the State in which the experiment was made was at that crisis, and had been for a long time before, violently heated and distracted by the rage of party. Is it to be presumed that at any future septennial epoch the same State will be free from parties? Is it to be presumed that any other State, at the same or any other given period, will be exempt from them? Such an event ought to be neither presumed nor desired; because an extinction of parties necessarily implies either a universal alarm for the public safety, or an absolute extinction of liberty.

Were the precaution taken of excluding from the assemblies elected by the people, to revise the preceding administration of the government, all persons who should have been concerned with the government within the given period, the difficulties would not be obviated. The important task would probably devolve on men, who, with inferior capacities, would in other respects be little better qualified. Although they might not have been personally concerned in the administration, and therefore not immediately agents in the measures to be examined, they would probably have been involved in the parties connected with these measures, and have been elected under their auspices.   PUBLIUS

Number 51

[HAMILTON OR MADISON]

TO WHAT expedient, then, shall we finally resort, for maintaining in practice the necessary partition of power among the several departments, as laid down in the Constitution? The only answer that can be given is, that as all these exterior provisions are found to be inadequate, the defect must be supplied, by so contriving the interior structure of the government as that its several constituent parts may, by their mutual relations, be the means of keeping each other in their proper places. Without presuming to undertake a full development of this important idea, I will hazard a few general observations, which may perhaps place it in a clearer light, and enable us to form a more correct judgment of the principles and structure of the government planned by the convention.

In order to lay a due foundation for that separate and distinct exercise of the different powers of government, which to a certain extent is admitted on all hands to be essential to the preservation of liberty, it is evident that each department should have a will of its own; and consequently should be so constituted that the members of each should have as little agency as possible in the appointment of the members of the others. Were this principle rigorously adhered to, it would require that all the appointments for the supreme executive, legislative, and judiciary magistracies should be drawn from the same fountain of authority, the people, through channels having no communication whatever with one another. Perhaps such a plan of constructing the several departments would be less difficult in practice than it may in contemplation appear. Some difficulties, however, and some additional expense would attend the execution of it. Some deviations, therefore, from the principle must be admitted. In the constitution of the judiciary department in particular, it might be inexpedient to insist rigorously on the principle: first, because peculiar qualifications being essential in the members, the primary consideration ought to be to select that mode of choice which best secures these qualifications; secondly, because the permanent tenure by which the appointments are held in that department must soon destroy all sense of dependence on the authority conferring them.

It is equally evident, that the members of each department should be as little dependent as possible on those of the others, for the emoluments annexed to their offices. Were the executive magistrate, or the judges, not independent of the legislature in this particular, their independence in every other would be merely nominal.

But the great security against a gradual concentration of the several powers in the same department, consists in giving to those who administer each department the necessary constitutional means and personal motives to resist encroachments of the others. The provision for defence must in this, as in all other cases, be made commensurate to the danger of attack. Ambition must be made to counteract ambition. The interest of the man must be connected with the constitutional rights of the place. It may be a reflection on human nature that such devices should be necessary to control the abuses of government. But what is government itself but the greatest of all reflections on human nature? If men were angels, no government would be necessary. If angels were to govern men, neither external nor internal controls on government would be neces-

sary. In framing a government which is to be administered by men over men, the great difficulty lies in this: you must first enable the government to control the governed; and in the next place oblige it to control itself. A dependence on the people is, no doubt, the primary control on the government; but experience has taught mankind the necessity of auxiliary precautions.

This policy of supplying, by opposite and rival interests, the defect of better motives, might be traced through the whole system of human affairs, private as well as public. We see it particularly displayed in all the subordinate distributions of power, where the constant aim is to divide and arrange the several offices in such a manner as that each may be a check on the other—that the private interest of every individual may be a sentinel over the public rights. These inventions of prudence cannot be less requisite in the distribution of the supreme powers of the State.

But it is not possible to give to each department an equal power of self-defence. In republican government, the legislative authority necessarily predominates. The remedy for this inconveniency is to divide the legislature into different branches; and to render them, by different modes of election and different principles of action, as little connected with each other as the nature of their common functions and their common dependence on the society will admit. It may even be necessary to guard against dangerous encroachments by still further precautions. As the weight of the legislative authority requires that it should be thus divided, the weakness of the executive may require, on the other hand, that it should be fortified. An absolute negative on the legislature appears, at first view, to be the natural defence with which the executive magistrate should be armed. But perhaps it would be neither altogether safe nor alone sufficient. On ordinary occasions it might not be exerted with the requisite firmness, and on extraordinary occasions it might be perfidiously abused. May not this defect of an absolute negative be supplied by some qualified connection between this weaker department and the weaker branch of the stronger department, by which the latter may be led to support the constitutional rights of the former, without being too much detached from the rights of its own department?

If the principles on which these observations are founded be just, as I persuade myself they are, and they be applied as a criterion to the several State constitutions, and to the federal Constitution, it will be found that if the latter does not perfectly correspond with them, the former are infinitely less able to bear such a test.

There are, moreover, two considerations particularly applicable to the federal system of America, which place that system in a very interesting point of view.

First. In a single republic all the power surrendered by the people is submitted to the administration of a single government; and the usurpations are guarded against by a division of the government into distinct and separate departments. In the compound republic of America, the power surrendered by the people is first divided between two distinct governments, and then the portion allotted to each subdivided among distinct and separate departments. Hence a double security arises to the rights of the people. The different governments will control each other, at the same time that each will be controlled by itself.

Second. It is of great importance in a republic not only to guard the society against the oppression of its rulers, but to guard one part of the society against the injustice of the other part. Different interests necessarily exist in different classes of citizens. If a majority be united by a common interest, the rights of the minority will be insecure. There are but two methods of providing against this evil: the one by creating a will in the community independent of the majority—that is, of the society itself; the other, by comprehending in the society so many separate descriptions of citizens as will render an unjust combination of a majority of the whole very improbable, if not impracticable. The first method prevails in all governments possessing an hereditary or self-appointed authority. This, at best, is but a precarious security; because a power independent of the society may as well espouse the unjust views of the major, as the rightful interests of the minor party, and may possibly be turned against both parties. The second method will be exemplified in the federal republic of the United States. Whilst all authority in it will be derived from and dependent on the society, the society itself will be broken into so many parts, interests, and classes of citizens, that the rights of individuals, or of the minority, will be in little danger from interested combinations of the majority. In a free government the security for civil rights must be the same as that for religious rights. It consists in the one case in the multiplicity of interests, and in the other in the multiplicity of sects. The degree of security in both cases will depend on the number of interests and sects; and this may be presumed to depend on the extent of country and number of people comprehended under the same government. This view of the subject must particularly recommend a proper federal system to all the sincere and considerate friends of republican government, since it shows that in exact proportion as the territory of the Union may be formed into more circumscribed Confederacies, or States, oppressive combination of a majority will be facilitated; the best security, under the republican forms, for the rights of every class of citizens will be diminished; and consequently the stability and independence of some member of the government, the only other security, must be proportionally increased. Justice is the end of government. It is the end of civil society. It ever has been and ever will be pursued until it be obtained, or until liberty be lost in the pursuit. In a society under the forms of which the stronger faction can readily unite and oppress the weaker, anarchy may as truly be said to reign as in a state of nature, where the weaker individual is not secured against the violence of the stronger; and as, in the latter state, even the stronger individuals are prompted, by the uncertainty of their condition, to submit to a government which may protect the weak as well as themselves; so, in the former state, will the more powerful factions or parties be gradually induced, by a like motive, to wish for a government which will protect all parties, the weaker as well as the more powerful. It can be little doubted that if the State of Rhode Island was separated from the Confederacy and left to itself, the insecurity of rights under the popular form of government within such narrow limits would be displayed by such reiterated oppressions of factious majorities that some power altogether independent of the people would soon be called for by the voice of the very factions whose misrule had proved the necessity of it. In the extended republic of the United States, and among the great variety of interests, parties, and sects which it embraces, a coalition of a majority of the whole society could seldom take place on any other principles than those of justice and the general good; whilst there being thus less danger to a minor from the will of a major party, there must be less pretext, also, to provide for the security of the former, by introducing into the government a will not dependent on the latter, or, in other words, a will independent of the society itself. It is no less certain than it is important, notwithstanding the contrary opinions which have been entertained, that the larger the society, provided it lie within a practical sphere, the more duly capable it will be of self-government. And happily for the *republican cause,* the practicable sphere may be carried to a very great extent by a judicious modification and mixture of the *federal principle.*   PUBLIUS

Number 52

[HAMILTON OR MADISON]

FROM THE more general inquiries pursued in the four last papers, I pass on to a more particular examination of the several parts of the government. I shall begin with the House of Representatives.

The first view to be taken of this part of the government relates to the qualifications of the electors and the elected.

Those of the former are to be the same with those of the electors of the most numerous branch of the State legislatures. The definition of the right of suffrage is very justly regarded as a fundamental article of republican government. It was incumbent on the convention, therefore, to define and establish this right in the Constitution. To have left it open for the occasional regulation of the Congress would have been improper for the reason just mentioned. To have submitted it to the legislative discretion of the States would have been improper for the same reason; and for the additional reason that it would have rendered too dependent on the State governments that branch of the federal government which ought to be dependent on the people alone. To have reduced the different qualifications in the different States to one uniform rule would probably have been as dissatisfactory to some of the States as it would have been difficult to the convention. The provision made by the convention appears, therefore, to be the best that lay within their option. It must be satisfactory to every State, because it is conformable to the standard already established, or which may be established, by the State itself. It will be safe to the United States, because, being fixed by the State constitutions, it is not alterable by the State governments, and it cannot be feared that the people of the States will

alter this part of their constitutions in such a manner as to abridge the rights secured to them by the federal Constitution.

The qualifications of the elected, being less carefully and properly defined by the State constitutions, and being at the same time more susceptible of uniformity, have been very properly considered and regulated by the convention. A representative of the United States must be of the age of twenty-five years; must have been seven years a citizen of the United States; must, at the time of his election, be an inhabitant of the State he is to represent; and, during the time of his service, must be in no office under the United States. Under these reasonable limitations, the door of this part of the federal government is open to merit of every description, whether native or adoptive, whether young or old, and without regard to poverty or wealth, or to any particular profession of religious faith.

The term for which the representatives are to be elected falls under a second view which may be taken of this branch. In order to decide on the propriety of this article, two questions must be considered: first, whether biennial elections will, in this case, be safe; secondly, whether they be necessary or useful.

As it is essential to liberty that the government in general should have a common interest with the people, so it is particularly essential that the branch of it under consideration should have an immediate dependence on, and an intimate sympathy with, the people. Frequent elections are unquestionably the only policy by which this dependence and sympathy can be effectually secured. But what particular degree of frequency may be absolutely necessary for the purpose does not appear to be susceptible of any precise calculation, and must depend on a variety of circumstances with which it may be connected. Let us consult experience, the guide that ought always to be followed whenever it can be found.

The scheme of representation, as a substitute for a meeting of the citizens in person, being at most but very imperfectly known to ancient polity, it is in more modern times only that we are to expect instructive examples. And even here, in order to avoid a research too vague and diffusive, it will be proper to confine ourselves to the few examples which are best known, and which bear the greatest analogy to our particular case. The first to which this character ought to be applied is the House of Commons in Great Britain. The history of this branch of the English Constitution, anterior to the date of Magna Charta, is too obscure to yield instruction. The very existence of it has been made a question among political antiquaries. The earliest records of subsequent date prove that parliaments were to *sit* only every year; not that they were to be *elected* every year. And even these annual sessions were left so much at the discretion of the monarch, that, under various pretexts, very long and dangerous intermissions were often contrived by royal ambition. To remedy this grievance, it was provided by a statute in the reign of Charles II. that the intermissions should not be protracted beyond a period of three years. On the accession of William III., when a revolution took place in the government, the subject was still more seriously resumed, and it was declared to be among the fundamental rights of the people, that parliaments ought to be held *frequently*. By another statute, which passed a few years later in the same reign, the term "frequently," which had alluded to the triennial period settled in the time of Charles II., is reduced to a precise meaning, it being expressly enacted that a new parliament shall be called within three years after the termination of the former. The last change, from three to seven years, is well known to have been introduced pretty early in the present century, under an alarm for the Hanoverian succession. From these facts it appears that the greatest frequency of elections which has been deemed necessary in that kingdom, for binding the representatives to their constituents, does not exceed a triennial return of them. And if we may argue from the degree of liberty retained even under septennial elections, and all the other vicious ingredients in the parliamentary constitution, we cannot doubt that a reduction of the period from seven to three years, with the other necessary reforms, would so far extend the influence of the people over their representatives as to satisfy us that biennial elections, under the federal system, cannot possibly be dangerous to the requisite dependence of the House of Representatives on their constituents.

Elections in Ireland, till of late, were regulated entirely by the discretion of the crown, and were seldom repeated, except on the accession of a new prince, or some other contingent event. The parliament which commenced with George II. was continued throughout his whole reign, a period of about thirty-five years. The only dependence of the representatives on the people consisted in the right of the latter to supply occasional vacancies, by the election of new members, and in the chance of some event which might produce a general new election. The ability also of the Irish parliament to maintain the rights of their constituents, so far as the disposition might exist, was extremely shackled by the control of the crown over the subjects of their deliberation. Of late, these shackles, if I mistake not, have been broken; and octennial parliaments have besides been established. What effect may be produced by this partial reform must be left to further experience. The example of Ireland, from this view of it, can throw but little light on the subject. As far as we can draw any conclusion from it, it must be that if the people of that country have been able under all these disadvantages to retain any liberty whatever, the advantage of biennial elections would secure to them every degree of liberty, which might depend on a due connection between their representatives and themselves.

Let us bring our inquiries nearer home. The example of these States, when British colonies, claims particular attention, at the same time that it is so well known as to require little to be said on it. The principle of representation, in one branch of the legislature at least, was established in all of them. But the periods of election were different. They varied from one to seven years. Have we any reason to infer, from the spirit and conduct of the representatives of the people, prior to the Revolution, that biennial elections would have been dangerous to the public liberties? The spirit which everywhere displayed itself at the commencement of the struggle, and which vanquished the obstacles to independence, is the best of proofs that a sufficient portion of liberty had been everywhere enjoyed to inspire both a sense of its worth and a zeal for its proper enlargement. This remark holds good, as well with regard to the then colonies whose elections were least frequent, as to those whose elections were most frequent. Virginia was the colony which stood first in resisting the parliamentary usurpations of Great Britain; it was the first also in espousing, by public act, the resolution of independence. In Virginia, nevertheless, if I have not been misinformed, elections under the former government were septennial. This particular example is brought into view, not as a proof of any peculiar merit, for the priority in those instances was probably accidental; and still less of any advantage in *septennial* elections, for when compared with a greater frequency they are inadmissible; but merely as a proof, and I conceive it to be a very substantial proof, that the liberties of the people can be in no danger from *biennial* elections.

The conclusion resulting from these examples will be not a little strengthened by recollecting three circumstances. The first is, that the federal legislature will possess a part only of that supreme legislative authority which is vested completely in the British Parliament; and which, with a few exceptions, was exercised by the colonial assemblies and the Irish legislature. It is a received and well-founded maxim, that where no other circumstances affect the case, the greater the power is, the shorter ought to be its duration; and, conversely, the smaller the power, the more safely may its duration be protracted. In the second place, it has, on another occasion, been shown that the federal legislature will not only be restrained by its dependence on the people, as other legislative bodies are, but that it will be, moreover, watched and controlled by the several collateral legislatures, which other legislative bodies are not. And in the third place, no comparison can be made between the means that will be possessed by the more permanent branches of the federal government for seducing, if they should be disposed to seduce, the House of Representatives from their duty to the people, and the means of influence over the popular branch possessed by the other branches of the government above cited. With less power, therefore, to abuse, the federal representatives can be less tempted on one side, and will be doubly watched on the other.

PUBLIUS

Number 53

[HAMILTON OR MADISON]

I SHALL here, perhaps, be reminded of a current observation, "that where annual elections end, tyranny begins." If it be true, as has often been remarked, that sayings which become proverbial are generally founded in reason, it is not less true that when once established they are often applied to cases to which the reason of them does not extend. I need not look for a proof beyond the case before us. What is the reason on which this proverbial observation is founded? No man will subject himself to the ridicule of pretending that any natural connection subsists between the sun or the seasons, and the period within which human virtue can bear the temptations of power. Happily for mankind, liberty is not, in this respect, confined to any single point of time; but lies within extremes, which afford sufficient latitude for all the variations which may be required by the various situations and circumstances of civil society. The election of magistrates might be, if it were found expedient, as in some instances it actually has been, daily, weekly, or monthly, as well as annual; and if circumstances may require a deviation from the rule on one side, why not also on the other side? Turning our attention to the periods established among ourselves, for the election of the most numerous branches of the State legislatures, we find them by no means coinciding any more in this instance than in the elections of other civil magistrates. In Connecticut and Rhode Island the periods are half-yearly. In the other States, South Carolina excepted, they are annual. In South Carolina they are biennial—as is proposed in the federal government. Here is a difference, as four to one, between the longest and shortest periods; and yet it would not be easy to show that Connecticut or Rhode Island is better governed, or enjoys a greater share of rational liberty, than South Carolina; or that either the one or the other of these States is distinguished in these respects, and by these causes, from the States whose elections are different from both.

In searching for the grounds of this doctrine, I can discover but one, and that is wholly inapplicable to our case. The important distinction so well understood in America, between a Constitution established by the people and unalterable by the government, and a law established by the government and alterable by the government, seems to have been little understood and less observed in any other country. Wherever the supreme power of legislation has resided, has been supposed to reside also a full power to change the form of the government. Even in Great Britain, where the principles of political and civil liberty have been most discussed, and where we hear most of the rights of the Constitution, it is maintained that the authority of the Parliament is transcendent and uncontrollable, as well with regard to the Constitution as the ordinary objects of legislative provision. They have accordingly, in several instances, actually changed, by legislative acts some of the most fundamental articles of the government. They have in particular, on several occasions, changed the period of election; and, on the last occasion, not only introduced septennial in place of triennial elections, but by the same act continued themselves in place four years beyond the term for which they were elected by the people. An attention to these dangerous practices has produced a very natural alarm in the votaries of free government, of which frequency of elections is the corner-stone; and has led them to seek for some security to liberty, against the danger to which it is exposed. Where no Constitution, paramount to the government, either existed or could be obtained, no constitutional security, similar to that established in the United States, was to be attempted. Some other security, therefore, was to be sought for; and what better security would the case admit than that of selecting and appealing to some simple and familiar portion of time, as a standard for measuring the danger of innovations, for fixing the national sentiment, and for uniting the patriotic exertions? The most simple and familiar portion of time, applicable to the subject, was that of a year; and hence the doctrine has been inculcated by a laudable zeal, to erect some barrier against the gradual innovations of an unlimited government, that the advance towards tyranny was to be calculated by the distance of departure from the fixed point of annual elections. But what necessity can there be of applying this expedient to a government limited, as the federal government will be, by the authority of a paramount Constitution? Or who will pretend that the liberties of the people of America will not be more secure under biennial elections, unalterably fixed by such a Constitution, than those of any other nation would be where elections were annual, or even more frequent, but subject to alterations by the ordinary power of the government?

The second question stated is, whether biennial elections be necessary or useful. The propriety of answering this question in the affirmative will appear from several very obvious considerations.

No man can be a competent legislator who does not add to an upright intention and a sound judgment a certain degree of knowledge of the subjects on which he is to legislate. A part of this knowledge may be acquired by means of information which lie within the compass of men in private as well as public stations. Another part can only be attained, or at least thoroughly attained, by actual experience in the station which requires the use of it. The period of service ought, therefore, in all such cases, to bear some proportion to the extent of practical knowledge requisite to the due performance of the service. The period of legislative service established in most of the States for the more numerous branch is, as we have seen, one year. The question then may be put into this simple form: does the period of two years bear no greater proportion to the knowledge requisite for federal legislation than one year does to the knowledge requisite for State legislation? The very statement of the question, in this form, suggests the answer that ought to be given to it.

In a single State, the requisite knowledge relates to the existing laws, which are uniform throughout the State, and with which all the citizens are more or less conversant; and to the general affairs of the State, which lie within a small compass, are not very diversified, and occupy much of the attention and conversation of every class of people. The great theatre of the United States presents a very different scene. The laws are so far from being uniform that they vary in every State; whilst the public affairs of the Union are spread throughout a very extensive region, and are extremely diversified by the local affairs connected with them, and can with difficulty be correctly learnt in any other place than in the central councils, to which a knowledge of them will be brought by the representatives of every part of the empire. Yet some knowledge of the affairs, and even of the laws, of all the States ought to be possessed by the members from each of the States. How can foreign trade be properly regulated by uniform laws without some acquaintance with the commerce, the ports, the usages, and the regulations of the different States? How can the trade between the different States be duly regulated without some knowledge of their relative situations in these and other respects? How can taxes be judiciously imposed and effectually collected if they be not accommodated to the different laws and local circumstances relating to these objects in the different States? How can uniform regulations for the militia be duly provided without a similar knowledge of many internal circumstances by which the States are distinguished from each other? These are the principal objects of federal legislation, and suggest most forcibly the extensive information which the representatives ought to acquire.

The other interior objects will require a proportional degree of information with regard to them.

It is true that all these difficulties will, by degrees, be very much diminished. The most laborious task will be the proper inauguration of the government and the primeval formation of a federal code. Improvements on the first draughts will every year become both easier and fewer. Past transactions of the government will be a ready and accurate source of information to new members. The affairs of the Union will become more and more objects of curiosity and conversation among the citizens at large. And the increased intercourse among those of different States will contribute not a little to diffuse a mutual knowledge of their affairs, as this again will contribute to a general assimilation of their manners and laws. But with all these abatements, the business of federal legislation must continue so far to exceed, both in novelty and difficulty, the legislative business of a single State, as to justify the longer period of service assigned to those who are to transact it.

A branch of knowledge which belongs to the acquirements of a federal representative, and which has not been mentioned, is that of foreign affairs. In regulating our own commerce, he ought to be not only acquainted with the treaties between the United States and other nations, but also with the commercial policy and laws of other nations. He ought not to be altogether ignorant of the law of nations; for that, as far as it is a proper object of municipal legislation, is submitted to the federal government. And although the House of Representatives is not immediately to participate in foreign negotiations and arrangements, yet from the necessary connection between the several branches of public affairs, those particular branches will frequently deserve attention in the ordinary course of legislation, and will sometimes demand particular legislative sanction and co-operation. Some portion of this knowledge may, no doubt, be acquired in a man's closet; but some of it also can only be derived from the public sources of information; and all of it will be acquired to best effect by a practical attention to the subject during the period of actual service in the legislature.

There are other considerations of less importance, perhaps, but which are not unworthy of notice. The distance which many of the representatives will be obliged to travel, and the arrangements rendered necessary by that circumstance, might be much more serious objections with fit men to this service, if limited to a single year, than if extended to two years. No argument can be drawn on this subject from the case of the delegates to the existing Congress. They are elected annually, it is true; but their re-election is considered by the legislative assemblies almost as a matter of course. The election of the representatives by the people would not be governed by the same principle.

A few of the members, as happens in all such assemblies, will possess superior talents; will, by frequent re-elections, become members of long standing; will be thoroughly masters of the public business, and perhaps not unwilling to avail themselves of those advantages. The greater the proportion of new members, and the less the information of the bulk of the members, the more apt will they be to fall into the snares that may be laid for them. This remark is no less applicable to the relation which will subsist between the House of Representatives and the Senate.

It is an inconvenience mingled with the advantages of our frequent elections, even in single States, where they are large, and hold but one legislative session in a year, that spurious elections cannot be investigated and annulled in time for the decision to have its due effect. If a return can be obtained, no matter by what unlawful means, the irregular member, who takes his seat of course, is sure of holding it a sufficient time to answer his purposes. Hence a very pernicious encouragement is given to the use of unlawful means for obtaining irregular returns. Were elections for the federal legislature to be annual, this practice might become a very serious abuse, particularly in the more distant States. Each house is, as it necessarily must be, the judge of the elections, qualifications, and returns of its members; and whatever improvements may be suggested by experience, for simplifying and accelerating the process in disputed cases, so great a portion of a year would unavoidably elapse before an illegitimate member could be dispossessed of his seat, that the prospect of such an event would be little check to unfair and illicit means of obtaining a seat.

All these considerations taken together warrant us in affirming that biennial elections will be as useful to the affairs of the public as we have seen that they will be safe to the liberty of the people.   PUBLIUS

Number 54

THE NEXT view which I shall take of the House of Representatives relates to the appointment of its members to the several States, which is to be determined by the same rule with that of direct taxes.

It is not contended that the number of people in each State ought not to be the standard for regulating the proportion of those who are to represent the people of each State. The establishment of the same rule for the appointment of taxes will probably be as little contested; though the rule itself, in this case, is by no means founded on the same principle. In the former case, the rule is understood to refer to the personal rights of the people, with which it has a natural and universal connection. In the latter, it has reference to the proportion of wealth, of which it is in no case a precise measure, and in ordinary cases a very unfit one. But notwithstanding the imperfection of the rule as applied to the relative wealth and contributions of the States, it is evidently the least objectionable among the practicable rules, and had too recently obtained the general sanction of America, not to have found a ready preference with the convention.

All this is admitted, it will perhaps be said; but does it follow, from an admission of numbers for the measure of representation, or of slaves combined with free citizens as a ratio of taxation, that slaves ought to be included in the numerical rule of representation? Slaves are considered as property, not as persons. They ought therefore to be comprehended in estimates of taxation which are founded on property, and to be excluded from representation which is regulated by a census of persons. This is the objection, as I understand it, stated in its full force. I shall be equally candid in stating the reasoning which may be offered on the opposite side.

"We subscribe to the doctrine," might one of our Southern brethren observe, "that representation relates more immediately to persons, and taxation more immediately to property, and we join in the application of this distinction to the case of our slaves. But we must deny the fact that slaves are considered merely as property, and in no respect whatever as persons. The true state of the case is, that they partake of both these qualities: being considered by our laws, in some respects, as persons, and in other respects as property. In being compelled to labour, not for himself, but for a master; in being vendible by one master to another master; and in being subject at all times to be restrained in his liberty and chastised in his body, by the capricious will of another,—the slave may appear to be degraded from the human rank, and classed with those irrational animals which fall under the legal denomination of property. In being protected, on the other hand, in his life and in his limbs, against the violence of all others, even the master of his labour and his liberty; and in being punishable himself for all violence committed against others,—the slave is no less evidently regarded by the law as a member of the society, not as a part of the irrational creation; as a moral person, not as a mere article of property. The federal Constitution, therefore, decides with great propriety on the case of our slaves, when it views them in the mixed character of persons and of property. This is in fact their true character. It is the character bestowed on them by the laws under which they live; and it will not be denied that these are the proper criterion; because it is only under the pretext that the laws have transformed the negroes into subjects of property that a place is disputed them in the computation of numbers; and it is admitted, that if the laws were to restore the rights which have been taken away, the negroes could no longer be refused an equal share of representation with the other inhabitants.

"This question may be placed in another light. It is agreed on all sides, that numbers are the best scale of wealth and taxation, as they are the only proper scale of representation. Would the convention have been impartial or consistent, if they had rejected the slaves from the list of inhabitants when the shares of representation were to be calculated, and inserted them on the lists when the tariff of contributions was to be adjusted? Could it be reasonably expected that the Southern States would concur in a system which considered their slaves in some degree as men when burdens were to be imposed, but refused to consider them in the same light when advantages were to be conferred? Might not some surprise also be expressed, that those who reproach the Southern States with the barbarous policy of considering as property a part of their human brethren, should themselves contend that the government to which all the States are to be parties, ought to consider this unfortunate race more completely in the un-natural light of property than the very laws of which they complain?

"It may be replied, perhaps, that slaves are not included in the estimate of representatives in any of the States possessing them. They neither vote themselves nor increase the votes of their masters. Upon what principle, then, ought they to be taken into the federal esti-mate of representation? In rejecting them al-together, the Constitution would, in this re-spect, have followed the very laws which have been appealed to as the proper guide.

"This objection is repelled by a single ob-servation. It is a fundamental principle of the proposed Constitution, that as the aggre-gate number of representatives allotted to the several States is to be determined by a federal rule, founded on the aggregate number of inhabitants, so the right of choosing this al-lotted number in each State is to be exercised by such part of the inhabitants as the State itself may designate. The qualifications on which the right of suffrage depend are not, perhaps, the same in any two States. In some of the States the difference is very material. In every State, a certain proportion of inhabi-tants are deprived of this right by the consti-tution of the State, who will be included in the census by which the federal Constitution apportions the representatives. In this point of view the Southern States might retort the complaint, by insisting that the principle laid down by the convention required that no re-gard should be had to the policy of particular States towards their own inhabitants; and consequently, that the slaves, as inhabitants, should have been admitted into the census according to their full number, in like manner with other inhabitants, who, by the policy of other States, are not admitted to all the rights of citizens. A rigorous adherence, however, to this principle, is waived by those who would be gainers by it. All that they ask is that equal moderation be shown on the other side. Let the case of the slaves be considered, as it is in truth, a peculiar one. Let the compromising expedient of the Constitution be mutually adopted, which regards them as inhabitants, but as debased by servitude below the equal level of free inhabitants; which regards the *slave* as divested of two-fifths of the *man*.

"After all, may not another ground be taken on which this article of the Constitution will admit of a still more ready defence? We have hitherto proceeded on the idea that represen-tation related to persons only, and not at all to property. But is it a just idea? Government is instituted no less for protection of the prop-erty, than of the persons, of individuals. The one as well as the other, therefore, may be considered as represented by those who are charged with the government. Upon this prin-ciple it is that in several of the States, and particularly in the State of New York, one branch of the government is intended more especially to be the guardian of property, and is accordingly elected by that part of the society which is most interested in this object of government. In the federal Constitution this policy does not prevail. The rights of property are committed into the same hands with the personal rights. Some attention ought, therefore, to be paid to property in the choice of those hands.

"For another reason, the votes allowed in the federal legislature to the people of each State ought to bear some proportion to the comparative wealth of the States. States have not, like individuals, an influence over each other, arising from superior advantages of fortune. If the law allows an opulent citizen but a single vote in the choice of his represen-tative, the respect and consequence which he derives from his fortunate situation very fre-quently guide the votes of others to the objects of his choice; and through this imperceptible channel the rights of property are conveyed into the public representation. A State pos-sesses no such influence over other States. It is not probable that the richest State in the Con-federacy will ever influence the choice of a single representative in any other State. Nor will the representatives of the larger and richer States possess any other advantage in the fed-eral legislature, over the representatives of other States, than what may result from their superior number alone. As far, therefore, as their superior wealth and weight may justly entitle them to any advantage, it ought to be secured to them by a superior share of repre-sentation. The new Constitution is, in this respect, materially different from the existing Confederation, as well as from that of the United Netherlands, and other similar con-federacies. In each of the latter, the efficacy of the federal resolutions depends on the sub-sequent and voluntary resolutions of the states composing the union. Hence the states, though possessing an equal vote in the public coun-cils, have an unequal influence, corresponding with the unequal importance of these subsequent and voluntary resolutions. Under the proposed Constitution, the federal acts will take effect without the necessary intervention of the individual States. They will depend merely on the majority of votes in the federal legislature, and consequently each vote, whether proceeding from a larger or smaller State, or a State more or less wealthy or powerful, will have an equal weight and efficacy: in the same manner as the votes individually given in a State legislature, by the representatives of unequal counties or other districts, have each a precise equality of value and effect; or if there be any difference in the case, it proceeds from the difference in the personal character of the individual representative, rather than from any regard to the extent of the district from which he comes."

Such is the reasoning which an advocate for the Southern interests might employ on this subject; and although it may appear to be a little strained in some points, yet, on the whole, I must confess that it fully reconciles me to the scale of representation which the convention have established.

In one respect, the establishment of a common measure for representation and taxation will have a very salutary effect. As the accuracy of the census to be obtained by the Congress will necessarily depend, in a considerable degree, on the disposition, if not on the co-operation, of the States, it is of great importance that the States should feel as little bias as possible to swell or to reduce the amount of their numbers. Were their share of representation alone to be governed by this rule, they would have an interest in exaggerating their inhabitants. Were the rule to decide their share of taxation alone, a contrary temptation would prevail. By extending the rule to both objects, the States will have opposite interests, which will control and balance each other, and produce the requisite impartiality.

PUBLIUS

Number 55

[HAMILTON OR MADISON]

THE NUMBER of which the House of Representatives is to consist forms another and a very interesting point of view under which this branch of the federal legislature may be contemplated. Scarce any article, indeed, in the whole Constitution seems to be rendered more worthy of attention, by the weight of character and the apparent force of argument with which it has been assailed. The charges exhibited against it are, first, that so small a number of representatives will be an unsafe depository of the public interests; secondly, that they will not possess a proper knowledge of the local circumstances of their numerous constituents; thirdly, that they will be taken from that class of citizens which will sympathise least with the feelings of the mass of the people, and be most likely to aim at a permanent elevation of the few on the depression of the many; fourthly, that defective as the number will be in the first instance, it will be more and more disproportionate, by the increase of the people, and the obstacles which will prevent a correspondent increase of the representatives.

In general it may be remarked on this subject, that no political problem is less susceptible of a precise solution than that which relates to the number most convenient for a representative legislature; nor is there any point on which the policy of the several States is more at variance, whether we compare their legislative assemblies directly with each other, or consider the proportions which they respectively bear to the number of their constituents. Passing over the difference between the smallest and largest States, as Delaware, whose most numerous branch consists of twenty-one representatives, and Massachusetts, where it amounts to between three and four hundred, a very considerable difference is observable among States nearly equal in population. The number of representatives in Pennsylvania is not more than one-fifth of that in the State last mentioned. New York, whose population is to that of South Carolina as six to five, has little more than one-third of the number of representatives. As great a disparity prevails between the States of Georgia and Delaware or Rhode Island. In Pennsylvania the representatives do not bear a greater proportion to their constituents than of one for every four or five thousand. In Rhode Island they bear a proportion of at least one for every thousand. And according to the constitution of Georgia, the proportion may be carried to one to every ten electors; and must unavoidably far exceed the proportion in any of the other States.

Another general remark to be made is, that the ratio between the representatives and the people ought not to be the same where the latter are very numerous as where they are very few. Were the representatives in Virginia to be regulated by the standard in Rhode Island, they would, at this time, amount to between four and five hundred; and twenty or thirty years hence, to a thousand. On the other hand, the ratio of Pennsylvania, if applied to the State of Delaware, would reduce the representative assembly of the latter to seven or eight members. Nothing can be more fallacious than to found our political calculations on arithmetical principles. Sixty or seventy men may be more properly trusted with a given degree of power than six or seven. But it does not follow that six or seven hundred would be proportionably a better depositary. And if we carry on the supposition to six or seven thousand, the whole reasoning ought to be reversed. The truth is, that in all cases a certain number at least seems to be necessary to secure the benefits of free consultation and discussion, and to guard against too easy a combination for improper purposes; as, on the other hand, the number ought at most to be kept within a certain limit, in order to avoid the confusion and intemperance of a multitude. In all very numerous assemblies, of whatever character composed, passion never fails to wrest the sceptre from reason. Had every Athenian citizen been a Socrates, every Athenian assembly would still have been a mob.

It is necessary also to recollect here the observations which were applied to the case of biennial elections. For the same reason that the limited powers of the Congress, and the control of the State legislatures, justify less frequent elections than the public safety might otherwise require, the members of the Congress need be less numerous than if they possessed the whole power of legislation, and were under no other than the ordinary restraints of other legislative bodies.

With these general ideas in our minds, let us weigh the objections which have been stated against the number of members proposed for the House of Representatives. It is said, in the first place, that so small a number cannot be safely trusted with so much power.

The number of which this branch of the legislature is to consist, at the outset of the government, will be sixty-five. Within three years a census is to be taken, when the number may be augmented to one for every thirty thousand inhabitants; and within every successive period of ten years the census is to be renewed, and augmentations may continue to be made under the above limitation. It will

not be thought an extravagant conjecture that the first census will, at the rate of one for every thirty thousand, raise the number of representatives to at least one hundred. Estimating the negroes in the proportion of three-fifths, it can scarcely be doubted that the population of the United States will by that time, if it does not already, amount to three millions. At the expiration of twenty-five years, according to the computed rate of increase, the number of representatives will amount to two hundred; and of fifty years, to four hundred. This is a number which, I presume, will put an end to all fears arising from the smallness of the body. I take for granted here what I shall, in answering the fourth objection, hereafter show, that the number of representatives will be augmented from time to time in the manner provided by the Constitution. On a contrary supposition, I should admit the objection to have very great weight indeed.

The true question to be decided then is, whether the smallness of the number, as a temporary regulation, be dangerous to the public liberty? Whether sixty-five members for a few years, and a hundred or two hundred for a few more, be a safe depositary for a limited and well-guarded power of legislating for the United States? I must own that I could not give a negative answer to this question without first obliterating every impression which I have received with regard to the present genius of the people of America, the spirit which actuates the State legislatures, and the principles which are incorporated with the political character of every class of citizens. I am unable to conceive that the people of America, in their present temper, or under any circumstances which can speedily happen, will choose, and every second year repeat the choice of, sixty-five or a hundred men who would be disposed to form and pursue a scheme of tyranny or treachery. I am unable to conceive that the State legislatures, which must feel so many motives to watch, and which possess so many means of counteracting, the federal legislature, would fail either to detect or to defeat a conspiracy of the latter against the liberties of their common constituents. I am equally unable to conceive that there are at this time, or can be in any short time, in the United States, any sixty-five or a hundred men capable of recommending themselves to the choice of the people at large, who would either desire or dare, within the short space of two years, to betray the solemn trust committed to them. What change of circumstances, time, and a fuller population of our country may produce, requires a prophetic spirit to declare, which makes no part of my pretensions. But judging from the circumstances now before us, and from the probable state of them within a moderate period of time, I must pronounce that the liberties of America cannot be unsafe in the number of hands proposed by the federal Constitution.

From what quarter can the danger proceed? Are we afraid of foreign gold? If foreign gold could so easily corrupt our federal rulers and enable them to ensnare and betray their constituents, how has it happened that we are at this time a free and independent nation? The congress which conducted us through the Revolution was a less numerous body than their successors will be; they were not chosen by, nor responsible to, their fellow-citizens at large; though appointed from year to year, and recallable at pleasure, they were generally continued for three years, and, prior to the ratification of the federal articles, for a still longer term. They held their consultations always under the veil of secrecy; they had the sole transaction of our affairs with foreign nations; through the whole course of the war they had the fate of their country more in their hands than it is to be hoped will ever be the case with our future representatives; and from the greatness of the prize at stake, and the eagerness of the party which lost it, it may well be supposed that the use of other means than force would not have been scrupled. Yet we know by happy experience that the public trust was not betrayed; nor has the purity of our public councils in this particular ever suffered, even from the whispers of calumny.

Is the danger apprehended from the other branches of the federal government? But where are the means to be found by the President, or the Senate, or both? Their emoluments of office, it is to be presumed, will not, and without a previous corruption of the House of Representatives cannot, more than suffice for very different purposes; their private fortunes, as they must all be American citizens, cannot possibly be sources of danger. The only means, then, which they can possess will be in the dispensation of appointments. Is it here that suspicion rests her charge? Sometimes we are told that this fund of corruption is to be exhausted by the President in subduing the virtue of the Senate. Now, the fidelity of the other

House is to be the victim. The improbability of such a mercenary and perfidious combination of the several members of government, standing on as different foundations as republican principles will well admit, and at the same time accountable to the society over which they are placed, ought alone to quiet this apprehension. But, fortunately, the Constitution has provided a still further safeguard. The members of the Congress are rendered ineligible to any civil offices that may be created, or of which the emoluments may be increased, during the term of their election. No offices therefore can be dealt out to the existing members but such as may become vacant by ordinary casualties: and to suppose that these would be sufficient to purchase the guardians of the people, selected by the people themselves, is to renounce every rule by which events ought to be calculated, and to substitute an indiscriminate and unbounded jealousy, with which all reasoning must be vain. The sincere friends of liberty, who give themselves up to the extravagancies of this passion, are not aware of the injury they do their own cause. As there is a degree of depravity in mankind which requires a certain degree of circumspection and distrust, so there are other qualities in human nature which justify a certain portion of esteem and confidence. Republican government presupposes the existence of these qualities in a higher degree than any other form. Were the pictures which have been drawn by the political jealousy of some among us faithful likenesses of the human character, the inference would be that there is not sufficient virtue among men for self-government; and that nothing less than the chains of despotism can restrain them from destroying and devouring one another.

PUBLIUS

Number 56

[HAMILTON OR MADISON]

THE *second* charge against the House of Representatives is, that it will be too small to possess a due knowledge of the interests of its constituents.

As this objection evidently proceeds from a comparison of the proposed number of representatives with the great extent of the United States, the number of their inhabitants, and the diversity of their interests, without taking into view at the same time the circumstances which will distinguish the Congress from other legislative bodies, the best answer that can be given to it will be a brief explanation of these peculiarities.

It is a sound and important principle that the representative ought to be acquainted with the interests and circumstances of his constituents. But this principle can extend no further than to those circumstances and interests to which the authority and care of the representative relate. An ignorance of a variety of minute and particular objects, which do not lie within the compass of legislation, is consistent with every attribute necessary to a due performance of the legislative trust. In determining the extent of information required in the exercise of a particular authority, recourse then must be had to the objects within the purview of that authority.

What are to be the objects of federal legislation? Those which are of most importance, and which seem most to require local knowledge, are commerce, taxation, and the militia.

A proper regulation of commerce requires much information, as has been elsewhere remarked; but as far as this information relates to the laws and local situation of each individual State, a very few representatives would be very sufficient vehicles of it to the federal councils.

Taxation will consist, in a great measure, of duties which will be involved in the regulation of commerce. So far the preceding remark is applicable to this object. As far as it may consist of internal collections, a more diffusive knowledge of the circumstances of the State may be necessary. But will not this also be possessed in sufficient degree by a very few intelligent men, diffusively elected within the State? Divide the largest State into ten or twelve districts, and it will be found that there will be no peculiar local interests in either which will not be within the knowledge of the representative of the district. Besides this source of information, the laws of the State, framed by representatives from every part of it, will be almost of themselves a sufficient guide. In every State there have been made, and must continue to be made, regulations on this subject which will, in many cases, leave little more to be done by the federal legislature than to review the different laws, and reduce them in one general act. A skilful individual in his closet, with all the local codes before him, might compile a law on some subjects of taxation for the whole Union without any aid from oral information, and it may

be expected that whenever internal taxes may be necessary, and particularly in cases requiring uniformity throughout the States, the more simple objects will be preferred. To be fully sensible of the facility which will be given to this branch of federal legislation by the assistance of the State codes, we need only suppose for a moment that this or any other State were divided into a number of parts, each having and exercising within itself a power of local legislation. Is it not evident that a degree of local information and preparatory labour would be found in the several volumes of their proceedings which would very much shorten the labours of the general legislature, and render a much smaller number of members sufficient for it?

The federal councils will derive great advantage from another circumstance. The representatives of each State will not only bring with them a considerable knowledge of its laws, and a local knowledge of their respective districts, but will probably in all cases have been members, and may even at the very time be members, of the State legislature, where all the local information and interests of the State are assembled, and from whence they may easily be conveyed by a very few hands into the legislature of the United States.

The observations made on the subject of taxation apply with greater force to the case of the militia. For however different the rules of discipline may be in different States, they are the same throughout each particular State; and depend on circumstances which can differ but little in different parts of the same State.

The attentive reader will discern that the reasoning here used, to prove the sufficiency of a moderate number of representatives, does not in any respect contradict what was urged on another occasion with regard to the extensive information which the representatives ought to possess, and the time that might be necessary for acquiring it. This information, so far as it may relate to local objects, is rendered necessary and difficult, not by a difference of laws and local circumstances within a single State, but of those among different States. Taking each State by itself, its laws are the same, and its interests but little diversified. A few men, therefore, will possess all the knowledge requisite for a proper representation of them. Were the interests and affairs of each individual State perfectly simple and uniform, a knowledge of them in one part would involve a knowledge of them in every other, and the whole State might be competently represented by a single member taken from any part of it. On a comparison of the different States together, we find a great dissimilarity in their laws, and in many other circumstances connected with the objects of federal legislation, with all of which the federal representatives ought to have some acquaintance. Whilst a few representatives, therefore, from each State may bring with them a due knowledge of their own State, every representative will have much information to acquire concerning all the other States. The changes of time, as was formerly remarked, on the comparative situation of the different States, will have an assimilating effect. The effect of time on the internal affairs of the States, taken singly, will be just the contrary. At present some of the States are little more than a society of husbandmen. Few of them have made much progress in those branches of industry which give a variety and complexity to the affairs of a nation. These, however, will in all of them be the fruits of a more advanced population; and will require, on the part of each State, a fuller representation. The foresight of the convention has accordingly taken care that the progress of population may be accompanied with a proper increase of the representative branch of the government.

The experience of Great Britain, which presents to mankind so many political lessons, both of the monitory and exemplary kind, and which has been frequently consulted in the course of these inquiries, corroborates the result of the reflections which we have just made. The number of inhabitants in the two kingdoms of England and Scotland cannot be stated at less than eight millions. The representatives of these eight millions in the House of Commons amount to five hundred and fifty-eight. Of this number, one ninth are elected by three hundred and sixty-four persons, and one half by five thousand seven hundred and twenty-three persons.[1] It cannot be supposed that the half thus elected, and who do not even reside among the people at large, can add anything either to the security of the people against the government, or to the knowledge of their circumstances and interests in the legislative councils. On the contrary, it is notorious that they are more frequently the representatives and instruments of the executive magistrate than the guardians and advocates

[1] Burgh's *Political Disquisitions.*—PUBLIUS

of the popular rights. They might, therefore, with great propriety, be considered as something more than a mere deduction from the real representatives of the nation. We will, however, consider them in this light alone, and will not extend the deduction to a considerable number of others, who do not reside among their constituents, are very faintly connected with them, and have very little particular knowledge of their affairs. With all these concessions two hundred and seventy-nine persons only will be the depositary of the safety, interest, and happiness of eight millions—that is to say, there will be one representative only to maintain the rights and explain the situation *of twenty-eight thousand six hundred and seventy* constituents, in an assembly exposed to the whole force of executive influence, and extending its authority to every other object of legislation within a nation whose affairs are in the highest degree diversified and complicated. Yet it is very certain, not only that a valuable portion of freedom has been preserved under all these circumstances, but that the defects in the British code are chargeable, in a very small proportion, on the ignorance of the legislature concerning the circumstances of the people. Allowing to this case the weight which is due to it, and comparing it with that of the House of Representatives as above explained, it seems to give the fullest assurance that a representative for every *thirty thousand inhabitants* will render the latter both a safe and competent guardian of the interests which will be confided to it.   PUBLIUS

Number 57

[HAMILTON OR MADISON]

THE *third* charge against the House of Representatives is, that it will be taken from that class of citizens which will have least sympathy with the mass of the people, and be most likely to aim at an ambitious sacrifice of the many to the aggrandisement of the few.

Of all the objections which have been framed against the federal Constitution, this is perhaps the most extraordinary. Whilst the objection itself is levelled against a pretended oligarchy, the principle of it strikes at the very root of republican government.

The aim of every political constitution is, or ought to be, first to obtain for rulers men who possess most wisdom to discern, and most virtue to pursue, the common good of the society; and in the next place, to take the most effectual precautions for keeping them virtuous whilst they continue to hold their public trust. The elective mode of obtaining rulers is the characteristic policy of republican government. The means relied on in this form of government for preventing their degeneracy are numerous and various. The most effectual one is such a limitation of the term of appointments as will maintain a proper responsibility to the people.

Let me now ask what circumstance there is in the constitution of the House of Representatives that violates the principles of republican government, or favours the elevation of the few on the ruins of the many? Let me ask whether every circumstance is not, on the contrary, strictly conformable to these principles, and scrupulously impartial to the rights and pretensions of every class and description of citizens?

Who are to be the electors of the federal representatives? Not the rich, more than the poor; not the learned, more than the ignorant; not the haughty heirs of distinguished names, more than the humble sons of obscurity and unpropitious fortune. The electors are to be the great body of the people of the United States. They are to be the same who exercise the right in every State of electing the corresponding branch of the legislature of the State.

Who are to be the objects of popular choice? Every citizen whose merit may recommend him to the esteem and confidence of his country. No qualification of wealth, of birth, of religious faith, or of civil profession is permitted to fetter the judgment or disappoint the inclination of the people.

If we consider the situation of the men on whom the free suffrages of their fellow-citizens may confer the representative trust, we shall find it involving every security which can be devised or desired for their fidelity to their constituents.

In the first place, as they will have been distinguished by the preference of their fellow-citizens, we are to presume that in general they will be somewhat distinguished also by those qualities which entitle them to it, and which promise a sincere and scrupulous regard to the nature of their engagements.

In the second place, they will enter into the public service under circumstances which cannot fail to produce a temporary affection at least to their constituents. There is in every breast a sensibility to marks of honour, of favour, of esteem, and of confidence, which, apart from all considerations of interest, is some pledge for grateful and benevolent returns. Ingratitude is a common topic of declamation against human nature; and it must be confessed that instances of it are but too frequent and flagrant, both in public and in private life. But the universal and extreme indignation which it inspires is itself a proof of the energy and prevalence of the contrary sentiment.

In the third place, those ties which bind the representative to his constituents are strengthened by motives of a more selfish nature. His pride and vanity attach him to a form of government which favours his pretensions and give him a share in its honours and distinctions. Whatever hopes or projects might be entertained by a few aspiring characters, it must generally happen that a great proportion of the men deriving their advancement from their influence with the people, would have more to hope from a preservation of the favour, than from innovations in the government subversive of the authority of the people.

All these securities, however, would be found very insufficient without the restraint of frequent elections. Hence, in the fourth place, the House of Representatives is so constituted as to support in the members an habitual recollection to their dependence on the people. Before the sentiments impressed on their minds by the mode of their elevation can be effaced by the exercise of power, they will be compelled to anticipate the moment when their power is to cease, when their exercise of it is to be reviewed, and when they must descend to the level from which they were raised: there for ever to remain unless a faithful discharge of their trust shall have established their true title to a renewal of it.

I will add, as a fifth circumstance in the situation of the House of Representatives, restraining them from oppressive measures, that they can make no law which will not have its full operation on themselves and their friends, as well as on the great mass of the society. This has always been deemed one of the strongest bonds by which human policy can connect the rulers and the people together. It creates between them that communion of interests and sympathy of sentiments of which few governments have furnished examples; but without which every government degenerates into tyranny. If it be asked what is to restrain the House of Representatives from making legal discriminations in favour of themselves and a particular class of the society? I answer: the genius of the whole system; the nature of just and constitutional laws; and above all, the vigilant, and manly spirit which actuates the people of America—a spirit which nourishes freedom, and in return is nourished by it.

If this spirit shall ever be so far debased as to tolerate a law not obligatory on the legislature, as well as on the people, the people will be prepared to tolerate anything but liberty.

Such will be the relation between the House of Representatives and their constituents. Duty, gratitude, interest, ambition itself, are the chords by which they will be bound to fidelity and sympathy with the great mass of the people. It is possible that these may all be insufficient to control the caprice and wickedness of man. But are they not all that government will admit, and that human prudence can devise? Are they not the genuine and the characteristic means by which republican government provides for the liberty and happiness of the people? Are they not the identical means on which every State government in the Union relies for the attainment of these important ends? What then are we to understand by the objection which this paper has combated? What are we to say to the men who profess the most flaming zeal for republican government, yet boldly impeach the fundamental principle of it; who pretend to be champions for the right and the capacity of the people to choose their own rulers, yet maintain that they will prefer those only who will immediately and infallibly betray the trust committed to them?

Were the objection to be read by one who had not seen the mode prescribed by the Constitution for the choice of representatives, he could suppose nothing less than that some unreasonable qualification of property was annexed to the right of suffrage; or that the right of eligibility was limited to persons of particular families or fortunes; or at least that the mode prescribed by the State constitutions was, in some respect or other, very grossly departed from. We have seen how far such a supposition would err, as to the two first points. Nor would it, in fact, be less erroneous as to the last. The only difference discoverable between the two cases is, that each representative of the United States will be elected by five or six thousand citizens; whilst in the individual States, the election of a representative is left to about as many hundreds. Will it be pretended that this difference is sufficient to justify an attachment to the State governments, and an abhorrence to the federal government? If this be the point on which the objection turns, it deserves to be examined.

Is it supported by *reason*? This cannot be said, without maintaining that five or six thousand citizens are less capable of choosing a fit representative, or more liable to be corrupted by an unfit one, than five or six hundred. Reason, on the contrary, assures us, that as in so great a number a fit representative would be most likely to be found, so the choice would be less likely to be diverted from him by the intrigues of the ambitious or the bribes of the rich.

Is the *consequence* from this doctrine admissible? If we say that five or six hundred citizens are as many as can jointly exercise their right of suffrage, must we not deprive the people of the immediate choice of their public servants, in every instance where the administration of the government does not require as many of them as will amount to one for that number of citizens?

Is the doctrine warranted by *facts*? It was shown in the last paper that the real representation in the British House of Commons very little exceeds the proportion of one for every thirty thousand inhabitants. Besides a variety of powerful causes not existing here, and which favour in that country the pretensions of rank and wealth, no person is eligible as a representative of a county, unless he possess real estate of the clear value of six hundred pounds sterling per year; nor of a city or borough, unless he possess a like estate of half that annual value. To this qualification on the part of the county representatives is added another on the part of the county electors, which restrains the right of suffrage to persons having a freehold estate of the annual value of more than twenty pounds sterling, according to the present rate of money. Notwithstanding these unfavourable circumstances, and notwithstanding some very unequal laws in the British code, it cannot be said that the representatives of the nation have elevated the few on the ruins of the many.

But we need not resort to foreign experience on this subject. Our own is explicit and decisive. The districts in New Hampshire in which the senators are chosen immediately by the people are nearly as large as will be necessary for her representatives in the Congress. Those of Massachusetts are larger than will be necessary for that purpose; and those of New York still more so. In the last State the members of Assembly for the cities and counties of New York and Albany are elected by very nearly as many voters as will be entitled to a representative in the Congress, calculating on the number of sixty-five representatives only. It makes no difference that in these senatorial districts and counties a number of representatives are voted for by each elector at the same time. If the same electors at the same time are capable of choosing four or five representatives, they cannot be incapable of choosing one. Pennsylvania is an additional example. Some of her counties, which elect her State representatives, are almost as large as her districts will be by which her federal representatives will be elected. The city of Philadelphia is supposed to contain between fifty and sixty thousand souls. It will therefore form nearly two districts for the choice of federal representatives. It forms, however, but one county, in which every elector votes for each of its representatives in the State legislature. And what may appear to be still more directly to our purpose, the whole city actually elects a *single member* for the executive council. This is the case in all the other counties of the State.

Are not these facts the most satisfactory proofs of the fallacy which has been employed against the branch of the federal government under consideration? Has it appeared on trial that the senators of New Hampshire, Massachusetts, and New York, or the executive council of Pennsylvania, or the members of the Assembly in the two last States, have betrayed any peculiar disposition to sacrifice the many to the few, or are in any respect less worthy of their places than the representatives and magistrates appointed in other States by very small divisions of the people?

But there are cases of a stronger complexion than any which I have yet quoted. One branch of the legislature of Connecticut is so constituted that each member of it is elected by the whole State. So is the governor of that State, of Massachusetts, and of this State, and the president of New Hampshire. I leave every man to decide whether the result of any one of these experiments can be said to countenance a suspicion, that a diffusive mode of choosing representatives of the people tends to elevate traitors and to undermine the public liberty.

PUBLIUS

Number 58

[HAMILTON OR MADISON]

THE REMAINING charge against the House of Representatives, which I am to examine, is grounded on a supposition that the number of members will not be augmented from time to time, as the progress of population may demand.

It has been admitted that this objection, if well supported, would have great weight. The following observations will show that, like most other objections against the Constitution, it can only proceed from a partial view of the subject, or from a jealousy which discolours and disfigures every object which is beheld.

1. Those who urge the objection seem not to have recollected that the federal Constitution will not suffer by a comparison with the State constitutions, in the security provided for a gradual augmentation of the number of representatives. The number which is to prevail in the first instance is declared to be temporary. Its duration is limited to the short term of three years. Within every successive term of ten years a census of inhabitants is to be repeated. The unequivocal objects of these regulations are, first, to readjust, from time to time, the apportionment of representatives to the number of inhabitants, under the single exception that each State shall have one representative at least; secondly, to augment the number of representatives at the same periods, under the sole limitation that the whole number shall not exceed one for every thirty thousand inhabitants. If we review the constitutions of the several States, we shall find that some of them contain no determinate regulations on this subject, that others correspond pretty much on this point with the federal Constitution, and that the most effectual security in any of them is resolvable into a mere directory provision.

2. As far as experience has taken place on this subject, a gradual increase of representatives under the State constitutions, has at least kept pace with that of the constituents, and it appears that the former have been as ready to concur in such measures as the latter have been to call for them.

3. There is a peculiarity in the federal Constitution which insures a watchful attention in a majority both of the people and of their representatives to a constitutional augmentation of the latter. The peculiarity lies in this,

that one branch of the legislature is a representation of citizens, the other of the States: in the former, consequently, the larger States will have most weight; in the latter, the advantage will be in favour of the smaller States. From this circumstance it may with certainty be inferred that the larger States will be strenuous advocates for increasing the number and weight of that part of the legislature in which their influence predominates. And it so happens that four only of the largest will have a majority of the whole votes in the House of Representatives. Should the representatives or people, therefore, of the smaller States oppose at any time a reasonable addition of members, a coalition of a very few States will be sufficient to overrule the opposition; a coalition which, notwithstanding the rivalship and local prejudices which might prevent it on ordinary occasions, would not fail to take place, when not merely prompted by common interest, but justified by equity and the principles of the Constitution.

It may be alleged, perhaps, that the Senate would be prompted by like motives to an adverse coalition; and as their concurrence would be indispensable, the just and constitutional views of the other branch might be defeated. This is the difficulty which has probably created the most serious apprehensions in the jealous friends of a numerous representation. Fortunately it is among the difficulties which, existing only in appearance, vanish on a close and accurate inspection. The following reflections will, if I mistake not, be admitted to be conclusive and satisfactory on this point.

Notwithstanding the equal authority which will subsist between the two houses on all legislative subjects, except the originating of money bills, it cannot be doubted that the House, composed of the greater number of members, when supported by the more powerful States, and speaking the known and determined sense of a majority of the people, will have no small advantage in a question depending on the comparative firmness of the two houses.

This advantage must be increased by the consciousness, felt by the same side, of being supported in its demands by right, by reason, and by the Constitution; and the consciousness, on the opposite side, of contending against the force of all these solemn considerations.

It is farther to be considered, that in the gradation between the smallest and largest States, there are several which, though most likely in general to arrange themselves among the former, are too little removed in extent and population from the latter, to second an opposition to their just and legitimate pretensions. Hence it is by no means certain that a majority of votes, even in the Senate, would be unfriendly to proper augmentations in the number of representatives.

It will not be looking too far to add, that the senators from all the new States may be gained over to the just views of the House of Representatives, by an expedient too obvious to be overlooked. As these States will, for a great length of time, advance in population with peculiar rapidity, they will be interested in frequent reapportionments of the representatives to the number of inhabitants. The large States, therefore, who will prevail in the House of Representatives, will have nothing to do but to make reapportionments and augmentations mutually conditions of each other; and the senators from all the most growing States will be bound to contend for the latter, by the interest which their States will feel in the former.

These considerations seem to afford ample security on this subject, and ought alone to satisfy all the doubts and fears which have been indulged with regard to it. Admitting, however, that they should all be insufficient to subdue the unjust policy of the smaller States, or their predominant influence in the councils of the Senate, a constitutional and infallible resource still remains with the larger States, by which they will be able at all times to accomplish their just purposes. The House of Representatives cannot only refuse, but they alone can propose, the supplies requisite for the support of government. They, in a word, hold the purse—that powerful instrument by which we behold, in the history of the British Constitution, an infant and humble representative of the people gradually enlarging the sphere of its activity and importance, and finally reducing, as far as it seems to have wished, all the overgrown prerogatives of the other branches of the government. This power over the purse may, in fact, be regarded as the most complete and effectual weapon with which any constitution can arm the immediate representatives of the people, for obtaining a redress of every grievance, and for carrying into effect every just and salutary measure.

But will not the House of Representatives be as much interested as the Senate in maintaining the government in its proper functions, and will they not therefore be unwilling to stake its existence or its reputation on the pliancy of the Senate? Or, if such a trial of firmness between the two branches were hazarded, would not the one be as likely first to yield as the other? These questions will create no difficulty with those who reflect that in all cases the smaller the number, and the more permanent and conspicuous the station, of men in power, the stronger must be the interest which they will individually feel in whatever concerns the government. Those who represent the dignity of their country in the eyes of other nations will be particularly sensible to every prospect of public danger, or of dishonourable stagnation in public affairs. To those causes we are to ascribe the continual triumph of the British House of Commons over the other branches of the government, whenever the engine of a money bill has been employed. An absolute inflexibility on the side of the latter, although it could not have failed to involve every department of the state in the general confusion, has neither been apprehended nor experienced. The utmost degree of firmness that can be displayed by the federal Senate or President, will not be more than equal to a resistance in which they will be supported by constitutional and patriotic principles.

In this review of the Constitution of the House of Representatives, I have passed over the circumstances of economy which, in the present state of affairs, might have had some effect in lessening the temporary number of representatives, and a disregard of which would probably have been as rich a theme of declamation against the Constitution as has been shown by the smallness of the number proposed. I omit also any remarks on the difficulty which might be found, under present circumstances, in engaging in the federal service a large number of such characters as the people will probably elect. One observation, however, I must be permitted to add on this subject as claiming, in my judgment, a very serious attention. It is, that in all legislative assemblies the greater the number composing them may be, the fewer will be the men who will in fact direct their proceedings. In the first place, the more numerous an assembly may be, of whatever characters composed, the greater is known to be the ascendancy of passion over reason. In the next place, the larger the number, the greater will be the proportion of members of limited information and of weak capacities.

Now, it is precisely on characters of this description that the eloquence and address of the few are known to act with all their force. In the ancient republics, where the whole body of the people assembled in person, a single orator, or an artful statesman, was generally seen to rule with as complete a sway as if a sceptre had been placed in his single hand. On the same principle, the more multitudinous a representative assembly may be rendered, the more it will partake of the infirmities incident to collective meetings of the people. Ignorance will be the dupe of cunning, and passion the slave of sophistry and declamation. The people can never err more than in supposing that by multiplying their representatives beyond a certain limit, they strengthen the barrier against the government of a few. Experience will for ever admonish them that, on the contrary, *after securing a sufficient number for the purposes of safety, of local information, and of diffusive sympathy with the whole society,* they will counteract their own views by every addition to their representatives. The countenance of the government may become more democratic, but the soul that animates it will be more oligarchic. The machine will be enlarged, but the fewer, and often the more secret, will be the springs by which its motions are directed.

As connected with the objection against the number of representatives, may properly be here noticed, that which has been suggested against the number made competent for legislative business. It has been said that more than a majority ought to have been required for a quorum; and in particular cases, if not in all, more than a majority of a quorum for a decision. That some advantages might have resulted from such a precaution cannot be denied. It might have been an additional shield to some particular interests, and another obstacle generally to hasty and partial measures. But these considerations are outweighed by the inconveniences in the opposite scale. In all cases where justice or the general good might require new laws to be passed, or active measures to be pursued, the fundamental principle of free government would be reversed. It would be no longer the majority that would rule: the power would be transferred to the minority. Were the defensive privilege limited to particular cases, an interested minority might take advantage of it to screen themselves from equitable sacrifices to the general weal, or, in particular emergencies, to extort unreasonable indulgences. Lastly it would facilitate and foster the baneful practice of secessions; a practice which has shown itself even in States where a majority only is required; a practice subversive of all the principles of order and regular government; a practice which leads more directly to public convulsions, and the ruin of popular governments than any other which has yet been displayed among us.

PUBLIUS

Number 59

[HAMILTON]

THE NATURAL order of the subject leads us to consider, in this place, that provision of the Constitution which authorises the national legislature to regulate, in the last resort, the election of its own members.

It is in these words: "The *times, places,* and *manner* of holding elections for senators and representatives shall be prescribed in each State by the legislature thereof; but the Congress may, at any time, by law, make or alter *such regulations,* except as to the *places* of choosing senators." [1] This provision has not only been declaimed against by those who condemn the Constitution in the gross; but it has been censured by those who have objected with less latitude and greater moderation; and, in one instance, it has been thought exceptionable by a gentleman who has declared himself the advocate of every other part of the system.

I am greatly mistaken, notwithstanding, if there be any article in the whole plan more completely defensible than this. Its propriety rests upon the evidence of this plain proposition, that *every government ought to contain in itself the means of its own preservation.* Every just reasoner will, at first sight, approve an adherence to this rule, in the work of the convention; and will disapprove every deviation from it which may not appear to have been dictated by the necessity of incorporating into the work some particular ingredient, which with a rigid conformity to the rule was incompatible. Even in this case, though he may acquiesce in the necessity, yet he will not cease to regard and to regret a departure from so fundamental a principle as a portion of imperfection in the system which may prove the seed of future weakness, and perhaps anarchy.

It will not be alleged that an election law could have been framed and inserted in the Constitution which would have been always applicable to every probable change in the situation of the country; and it will therefore not be denied, that a discretionary power over elections ought to exist somewhere. It will, I presume, be as readily conceded that there were only three ways in which this power could have been reasonably modified and disposed: that it must either have been lodged wholly in the national legislature, or wholly in the State legislatures, or primarily in the latter and ultimately in the former. The last mode has, with reason, been preferred by the convention. They have submitted the regulation of elections for the federal government, in the first instance, to the local administrations; which, in ordinary cases, and when no improper views prevail, may be both more convenient and more satisfactory; but they have reserved to the national authority a right to interpose, whenever extraordinary circumstances might render that interposition necessary to its safety.

Nothing can be more evident than that an exclusive power of regulating elections for the national government, in the hands of the State legislatures, would leave the existence of the Union entirely at their mercy. They could at any moment annihilate it, by neglecting to provide for the choice of persons to administer its affairs. It is to little purpose to say that a neglect or omission of this kind would not be likely to take place. The constitutional possibility of the thing, without an equivalent for the risk, is an unanswerable objection. Nor has any satisfactory reason been yet assigned for incurring that risk. The extravagant surmises of a distempered jealousy can never be dignified with that character. If we are in a humour to presume abuses of power, it is as fair to presume them on the part of the State governments as on the part of the general government. And as it is more consonant to the rules of a just theory, to trust the Union with the care of its own existence, than to transfer that care to any other hands, if abuses of power are to be hazarded on the one side or on the other, it is more rational to hazard them where the power would naturally be placed, than where it would unnaturally be placed.

Suppose an article had been introduced into the Constitution, empowering the United States to regulate the elections for the particular States, would any man have hesitated to condemn it, both as an unwarrantable transposition of power, and as a premeditated en-

---

[1] 1st clause, 4th section, of the 1st article.— PUBLIUS

gine for the destruction of the State governments? The violation of principle, in this case, would have required no comment; and, to an unbiased observer, it will not be less apparent in the project of subjecting the existence of the national government, in a similar respect, to the pleasure of the State governments. An impartial view of the matter cannot fail to result in a conviction, that each, as far as possible, ought to depend on itself for its own preservation.

As an objection to this position, it may be remarked that the constitution of the national Senate would involve, in its full extent, the danger which it is suggested might flow from an exclusive power in the State legislatures to regulate the federal elections. It may be alleged that, by declining the appointment of senators, they might at any time give a fatal blow to the Union; and from this it may be inferred that as its existence would be thus rendered dependent upon them in so essential a point, there can be no objection to intrusting them with it in the particular case under consideration. The interest of each State, it may be added, to maintain its representation in the national councils, would be a complete security against an abuse of the trust.

This argument, though specious, will not, upon examination, be found solid. It is certainly true that the State legislatures, by forbearing the appointment of senators, may destroy the national government. But it will not follow that, because they have the power to do this in one instance, they ought to have it in every other. There are cases in which the pernicious tendency of such a power may be far more decisive, without any motive equally cogent with that which must have regulated the conduct of the convention in respect to the formation of the Senate, to recommend their admission into the system. So far as that construction may expose the Union to the possibility of injury from the State legislatures, it is an evil; but it is an evil which could not have been avoided without excluding the States, in their political capacities, wholly from a place in the organisation of the national government. If this had been done, it would doubtless have been interpreted into an entire dereliction of the federal principle; and would certainly have deprived the State governments of that absolute safeguard which they will enjoy under this provision. But however wise it may have been to have submitted in this instance to an inconvenience, for the attainment

of a necessary advantage or a greater good, no inference can be drawn from thence to favour an accumulation of the evil, where no necessity urges, nor any greater good invites.

It may be easily discerned also that the national government would run a much greater risk from a power in the State legislatures over the elections of its House of Representatives, than from their power of appointing the members of its Senate. The senators are to be chosen for the period of six years; there is to be a rotation, by which the seats of a third part of them are to be vacated and replenished every two years; and no State is to be entitled to more than two senators; a quorum of the body is to consist of sixteen members. The joint result of these circumstances would be, that a temporary combination of a few States to intermit the appointment of senators, could neither annul the existence nor impair the activity of the body; and it is not from a general and permanent combination of the States that we can have anything to fear. The first might proceed from sinister designs in the leading members of a few of the State legislatures; the last would suppose a fixed and rooted disaffectation in the great body of the people, which will either never exist at all, or will, in all probability, proceed from an experience of the inaptitude of the general government to the advancement of their happiness—in which event no good citizen could desire its continuance.

But with regard to the federal House of Representatives, there is intended to be a general election of members once in two years. If the State legislatures were to be invested with an exclusive power of regulating these elections, every period of making them would be a delicate crisis in the national situation, which might issue in a dissolution of the Union, if the leaders of a few of the most important States should have entered into a previous conspiracy to prevent an election.

I shall not deny that there is a degree of weight in the observation, that the interests of each State, to be represented in the federal councils, will be a security against the abuse of a power over its elections in the hands of the State legislatures. But the security will not be considered as complete by those who attend to the force of an obvious distinction between the interest of the people in the public felicity and the interest of their local rulers in the power and consequence of their offices. The people of America may be warmly attached to the government of the Union, at times when the particular rulers of particular States, stimulated by the natural rivalship of power, and by the hopes of personal aggrandisement, and supported by a strong faction in each of those States, may be in a very opposite temper. This diversity of sentiment between a majority of the people and the individuals who have the greatest credit in their councils is exemplified in some of the States at the present moment, on the present question. The scheme of separate confederacies, which will always multiply the chances of ambition, will be a never failing bait to all such influential characters in the State administrations as are capable of preferring their own emolument and advancement to the public weal. With so effectual a weapon in their hands as the exclusive power of regulating elections for the national government, a combination of a few such men, in a few of the most considerable States, where the temptation will always be the strongest, might accomplish the destruction of the Union, by seizing the opportunity of some casual dissatisfaction among the people (and which perhaps they may themselves have excited), to discontinue the choice of members for the federal House of Representatives. It ought never to be forgotten that a firm union of this country, under an efficient government, will probably be an increasing object of jealousy to more than one nation of Europe; and that enterprises to subvert it will sometimes originate in the intrigues of foreign powers, and will seldom fail to be patronised and abetted by some of them. Its preservation therefore ought, in no case that can be avoided, to be committed to the guardianship of any but those whose situation will uniformly beget an immediate interest in the faithful and vigilant performance of the trust. PUBLIUS

Number 60

[HAMILTON]

WE HAVE seen that an uncontrollable power over the elections to the federal government could not, without hazard, be committed to the State legislatures. Let us now see what would be the danger on the other side; that is, from confiding the ultimate right of regulating its own elections to the Union itself. It is not pretended that this right would ever be used for the exclusion of any State from its share in the representation. The interest of all would, in this respect at least, be the security

of all. But it is alleged that it might be employed in such a manner as to promote the election of some favourite class of men in exclusion of others, by confining the places of election to particular districts, and rendering it impracticable to the citizens at large to partake in the choice. Of all chimerical suppositions, this seems to be the most chimerical. On the one hand, no rational calculation of probabilities would lead us to imagine that the disposition which a conduct so violent and extraordinary would imply, could ever find its way into the national councils; and on the other, it may be concluded with certainty, that if so improper a spirit should ever gain admittance into them, it would display itself in a form altogether different and far more decisive.

The improbability of the attempt may be satisfactorily inferred from this single reflection, that it could never be made without causing an immediate revolt of the great body of the people, headed and directed by the State governments. It is not difficult to conceive that this characteristic right of freedom may, in certain turbulent and factious seasons, be violated, in respect to a particular class of citizens, by a victorious and overbearing majority; but that so fundamental a privilege, in a country so situated and enlightened, should be invaded to the prejudice of the great mass of the people, by the deliberate policy of the government, without occasioning a popular revolution, is altogether inconceivable and incredible.

In addition to this general reflection, there are considerations of a more precise nature, which forbid all apprehension on the subject. The dissimilarity in the ingredients which will compose the national government, and still more in the manner in which they will be brought into action in its various branches, must form a powerful obstacle to a concert of views in any partial scheme of elections. There is sufficient diversity in the state of property, in the genius, manners, and habits of the people of the different parts of the Union, to occasion a material diversity of disposition in their representatives towards the different ranks and conditions in society. And though an intimate intercourse under the same government will promote a gradual assimilation in some of these respects, yet there are causes, as well physical as moral, which may, in a greater or less degree, permanently nourish different propensities and inclinations in this respect. But the circumstance which will be likely to have the greatest influence in the matter will be the dissimilar modes of constituting the several component parts of the government. The House of Representatives being to be elected immediately by the people, the Senate by the State legislatures, the President by electors chosen for that purpose by the people, there would be little probability of a common interest to cement these different branches in a predilection for any particular class of electors.

As to the Senate, it is impossible that any regulation of "time and manner," which is all that is proposed to be submitted to the national government in respect to that body, can affect the spirit which will direct the choice of its members. The collective sense of the State legislatures can never be influenced by extraneous circumstances of that sort; a consideration which alone ought to satisfy us that the discrimination apprehended would never be attempted. For what inducement could the Senate have to concur in a preference in which itself would not be included? Or to what purpose would it be established, in reference to one branch of the legislature, if it could not be extended to the other. The composition of the one would in this case counteract that of the other. And we can never suppose that it would embrace the appointments to the Senate, unless we can at the same time suppose the voluntary co-operation of the State legislatures. If we make the latter supposition, it then becomes immaterial where the power in question is placed—whether in their hands or in those of the Union.

But what is to be the object of this capricious partiality in the national councils? Is it to be exercised in a discrimination between the different departments of industry, or between the different kinds of property, or between the different degrees of property? Will it lean in favour of the landed interest, or the moneyed interest, or the mercantile interest, or the manufacturing interest? Or, to speak in the fashionable language of the adversaries to the Constitution, will it court the elevation of "the wealthy and the well-born," to the exclusion and debasement of all the rest of the society?

If this partiality is to be exerted in favour of those who are concerned in any particular description of industry or property, I presume it will readily be admitted that the competition for it will lie between landed men and merchants. And I scruple not to affirm that it

is infinitely less likely that either of them should gain an ascendant in the national councils, than that the one or the other of them should predominate in all the local councils. The inference will be, that a conduct tending to give an undue preference to either is much less to be dreaded from the former than from the latter.

The several States are in various degrees addicted to agriculture and commerce. In most, if not all of them, agriculture is predominant. In a few of them, however, commerce nearly divides its empire, and in most of them has a considerable share of influence. In proportion as either prevails, it will be conveyed into the national representation; and for the very reason that this will be an emanation from a greater variety of interests, and in much more various proportions than are to be found in any single State, it will be much less apt to espouse either of them with a decided partiality than the representation of any single State.

In a country consisting chiefly of the cultivators of land, where the rules of an equal representation obtain, the landed interest must, upon the whole, preponderate in the government. As long as this interest prevails in most of the State legislatures, so long it must maintain a correspondent superiority in the national Senate which will generally be a faithful copy of the majorities of those assemblies. It cannot therefore be presumed that a sacrifice of the landed to the mercantile class will ever be a favourite object of this branch of the federal legislature. In applying thus particularly to the Senate a general observation suggested by the situation of the country, I am governed by the consideration that the credulous votaries of State power cannot, upon their own principles, suspect that the State legislatures would be warped from their duty by any external influence. But in reality the same situation must have the same effect, in the primitive composition at least of the federal House of Representatives: an improper bias towards the mercantile class is as little to be expected from this quarter as from the other.

In order, perhaps, to give countenance to the objection at any rate, it may be asked, is there not danger of an opposite bias in the national government which may dispose it to endeavour to secure a monopoly of the federal administration to the landed class? As there is little likelihood that the supposition of such a bias will have any terrors for those who would be immediately injured by it, a laboured answer to this question will be dispensed with. It will be sufficient to remark, first, that for the reasons elsewhere assigned, it is less likely that any decided partiality should prevail in the councils of the Union than in those of any of its members. Secondly, that there would be no temptation to violate the Constitution in favour of the landed class, because that class would, in the natural course of things, enjoy as great a preponderancy as itself could desire. And thirdly, that men accustomed to investigate the sources of public prosperity upon a large scale must be too well convinced of the utility of commerce to be inclined to inflict upon it so deep a wound as would result from the entire exclusion of those who would best understand its interest from a share in the management of them. The importance of commerce, in the view of revenue alone, must effectually guard it against the enmity of a body which would be continually importuned in its favour by the urgent calls of public necessity.

I the rather consult brevity in discussing the probability of a preference founded upon a discrimination between the different kinds of industry and property, because, as far as I understand the meaning of the objectors, they contemplate a discrimination of another kind. They appear to have in view, as the objects of the preference with which they endeavour to alarm us, those whom they designate by the description of "the wealthy and the well-born." These, it seems, are to be exalted to an odious pre-eminence over the rest of their fellow-citizens. At one time, however, their elevation is to be a necessary consequence of the smallness of the representative body; at another time it is to be effected by depriving the people at large of the opportunity of exercising their right of suffrage in the choice of that body.

But upon what principle is the discrimination of the places of election to be made, in order to answer the purpose of the meditated preference? Are "the wealthy and the well-born," as they are called, confined to particular spots in the several States? Have they, by some miraculous instinct or foresight, set apart in each of them a common place of residence? Are they only to be met with in the towns or cities? Or are they, on the contrary, scattered over the face of the country as avarice or chance may have happened to cast their own lot or that of their predecessors? If the latter is the case (as every intelligent man knows it

to be,[1]) is it not evident that the policy of confining the places of election to particular districts would be as subversive of its own aim as it would be exceptionable on every other account? The truth is, that there is no method of securing to the rich the preference apprehended, but by prescribing qualifications of property either for those who may elect or be elected. But this forms no part of the power to be conferred upon the national government. Its authority would be expressly restricted to the regulation of the *times*, the *places*, the *manner* of elections. The qualifications of the persons who may choose or be chosen, as has been remarked upon other occasions, are defined and fixed in the Constitution, and are unalterable by the legislature.

Let it, however, be admitted, for argument sake, that the expedient suggested might be successful; and let it at the same time be equally taken for granted that all the scruples which a sense of duty or an apprehension of the danger of the experiment might inspire, were overcome in the breasts of the national rulers, still I imagine it will hardly be pretended that they could ever hope to carry such an enterprise into execution without the aid of a military force sufficient to subdue the resistance of the great body of the people. The improbability of the existence of a force equal to that object has been discussed and demonstrated in different parts of these papers; but that the futility of the objection under consideration may appear in the strongest light, it shall be conceded for a moment that such a force might exist, and the national government shall be supposed to be in the actual possession of it. What will be the conclusion? With a disposition to invade the essential rights of the community, and with the means of gratifying that disposition, is it presumable that the persons who were actuated by it would amuse themselves in the ridiculous task of fabricating election laws for securing a preference to a favourite class of men? Would they not be likely to prefer a conduct better adapted to their own immediate aggrandisement? Would they not rather boldly resolve to perpetuate themselves in office by one decisive act of usurpation, than to trust to precarious expedients which, in spite of all the precautions that might accompany them, might terminate in the dismission, disgrace, and ruin of their authors? Would they not fear that citizens,

[1] Particularly in the Southern States and in this state.—PUBLIUS

not less tenacious than conscious of their rights, would flock from the remote extremes of their respective States to the places of election, to overthrow their tyrants, and to substitute men who would be disposed to avenge the violated majesty of the people? PUBLIUS

Number 61

[HAMILTON]

THE MORE candid opposers of the provision respecting elections, contained in the plan of the convention, when pressed in argument, will sometimes concede the propriety of that provision; with this qualification, however, that it ought to have been accompanied with a declaration that all elections should be had in the counties where the electors resided. This, say they, was a necessary precaution against an abuse of the power. A declaration of this nature would certainly have been harmless; so far as it would have had the effect of quieting apprehensions, it might not have been undesirable. But it would, in fact, have afforded little or no additional security against the danger apprehended; and the want of it will never be considered, by an impartial and judicious examiner, as a serious, still less as an insuperable, objection to the plan. The different views taken of the subject in the two preceding papers must be sufficient to satisfy all dispassionate and discerning men that if the public liberty should ever be the victim of the ambition of the national rulers, the power under examination, at least, will be guiltless of the sacrifice.

If those who are inclined to consult their jealousy only would exercise it in a careful inspection of the several State constitutions, they would find little less room for disquietude and alarm from the latitude which most of them allow in respect to elections than from the latitude which is proposed to be allowed to the national government in the same respect. A review of their situation, in this particular, would tend greatly to remove any ill impressions which may remain in regard to this matter. But as that view would lead into long and tedious details, I shall content myself with the single example of the State in which I write. The constitution of New York makes no other provision for *locality* of elections than that the members of the Assembly shall be elected in the *counties;* those of the Senate, in the great districts into which the State is or may be divided: these at present are

four in number, and comprehend each from two to six counties. It may readily be perceived that it would not be more difficult to the legislature of New York to defeat the suffrages of the citizens of New York, by confining elections to particular places, than for the legislature of the United States to defeat the suffrages of the citizens of the Union, by the like expedient. Suppose, for instance, the city of Albany was to be appointed the sole place of election for the county and district of which it is a part, would not the inhabitants of that city speedily become the only electors of the members both of the Senate and Assembly for that county and district? Can we imagine that the electors who reside in the remote subdivisions of the counties of Albany, Saratoga, Cambridge, etc., or in any part of the county of Montgomery, would take the trouble to come to the city of Albany, to give their votes for members of the Assembly or Senate, sooner than they would repair to the city of New York, to participate in the choice of the members of the federal House of Representatives? The alarming indifference discoverable in the exercise of so invaluable a privilege under the existing laws, which afford every facility to it, furnishes a ready answer to this question. And, abstracted from any experience on the subject, we can be at no loss to determine that when the place of election is at an *inconvenient distance* from the elector, the effect upon his conduct will be the same whether that distance be twenty miles or twenty thousand miles. Hence it must appear that objections to the particular modification of the federal power of regulating elections will, in substance, apply with equal force to the modification of the like power in the constitution of this State; and for this reason it will be impossible to acquit the one and to condemn the other. A similar comparison would lead to the same conclusion in respect to the constitutions of most of the other States.

If it should be said that defects in the State constitutions furnish no apology for those which are to be found in the plan proposed, I answer, that as the former have never been thought chargeable with inattention to the security of liberty, where the imputations thrown on the latter can be shown to be applicable to them also, the presumption is that they are rather the cavilling refinements of a predetermined opposition than the well-founded inferences of a candid research after truth. To those who are disposed to consider as innocent omissions in the State constitutions what they regard as unpardonable blemishes in the plan of the convention, nothing can be said; or at most, they can only be asked to assign some substantial reason why the representatives of the people in a single State should be more impregnable to the lust of power, or other sinister motives, than the representatives of the people of the United States? If they cannot do this, they ought at least to prove to us that it is easier to subvert the liberties of three millions of people, with the advantage of local governments to head their opposition, than of two hundred thousand people who are destitute of that advantage. And in relation to the point immediately under consideration, they ought to convince us that it is less probable that a predominant faction in a single State should, in order to maintain its superiority, incline to a preference of a particular class of electors, than that a similar spirit should take possession of the representatives of thirteen States, spread over a vast region, and in several respects distinguishable from each other by a diversity of local circumstances, prejudices, and interests.

Hitherto my observations have only aimed at a vindication of the provision in question, on the ground of theoretic propriety, on that of the danger of placing the power elsewhere, and on that of the safety of placing it in the manner proposed. But there remains to be mentioned a positive advantage which will result from this disposition, and which could not as well have been obtained from any other: I allude to the circumstance of uniformity in the time of elections for the federal House of Representatives. It is more than possible that this uniformity may be found by experience to be of great importance to the public welfare, both as a security against the perpetuation of the same spirit in the body, and as a cure for the diseases of faction. If each State may choose its own time of election, it is possible there may be at least as many different periods as there are months in the year. The times of election in the several States, as they are now established for local purposes, vary between extremes as wide as March and November. The consequence of this diversity would be that there could never happen a total dissolution or renovation of the body at one time. If an improper spirit of any kind should happen to prevail in it, that spirit would be apt to infuse itself into the new members, as they come forward in succession. The mass would be likely to remain nearly the same, assimilating constantly to itself its gradual accretions. There is a contagion in example which few men have sufficient force of mind to resist. I am inclined to think that treble the duration in office, with the condition of a total dissolution of the body at the same time, might be less formidable to liberty than one third of that duration subject to gradual and successive alterations.

Uniformity in the time of elections seems not less requisite for executing the idea of a regular rotation in the Senate, and for conveniently assembling the legislature at a stated period in each year.

It may be asked, Why, then, could not a time have been fixed in the Constitution? As the most zealous adversaries of the plan of the convention in this State are, in general, not less zealous admirers of the constitution of the State, the question may be retorted, and it may be asked, Why was not a time for the like purpose fixed in the constitution of this State? No better answer can be given than that it was a matter which might safely be entrusted to legislative discretion; and that if a time had been appointed, it might, upon experiment, have been found less convenient than some other time. The same answer may be given to the question put on the other side. And it may be added that the supposed danger of a gradual change being merely speculative, it would have been hardly advisable upon that speculation to establish, as a fundamental point, what would deprive several States of the convenience of having the elections for their own government and for the national government at the same epochs.　　PUBLIUS

Number 62
[HAMILTON OR MADISON]

HAVING examined the constitution of the House of Representatives, and answered such of the objections against it as seemed to merit notice, I enter next on the examination of the Senate.

The heads into which this member of the government may be considered are: I. The qualification of senators; II. The appointment of them by the State legislatures; III. The equality of representation in the Senate; IV. The number of senators, and the term for which they are to be elected; V. The powers vested in the Senate.

I. The qualifications proposed for senators, as distinguished from those of representatives, consist in a more advanced age and a longer period of citizenship. A senator must be thirty years of age at least; as a representative must be twenty-five. And the former must have been a citizen nine years; as seven years are required for the latter. The propriety of these distinctions is explained by the nature of the senatorial trust, which, requiring greater extent of information and stability of character, requires at the same time that the senator should have reached a period of life most likely to supply these advantages; and which, participating immediately in transactions with foreign nations, ought to be exercised by none who are not thoroughly weaned from the prepossessions and habits incident to foreign birth and education. The term of nine years appears to be a prudent mediocrity between a total exclusion of adopted citizens, whose merits and talents may claim a share in the public confidence, and an indiscriminate and hasty admission of them, which might create a channel for foreign influence on the national councils.

II. It is equally unnecessary to dilate on the appointment of senators by the State legislatures. Among the various modes which might have been devised for constituting this branch of the government, that which has been proposed by the convention is probably the most congenial with the public opinion. It is recommended by the double advantage of favouring a select appointment, and of giving to the State governments such an agency in the formation of the federal government as must secure the authority of the former, and may form a convenient link between the two systems.

III. The equality of representation in the Senate is another point, which, being evidently the result of compromise between the opposite pretensions of the large and the small States, does not call for much discussion. If indeed it be right, that among a people thoroughly incorporated into one nation, every district ought to have a *proportional* share in the government, and that among independent and sovereign States, bound together by a simple league, the parties, however unequal in size, ought to have an *equal* share in the common councils, it does not appear to be without some reason that in a compound republic, partaking both of the national and federal character, the government ought to be founded on a mixture of the principles of proportional and equal representation. But it is superfluous to try, by the standard of theory, a part of the

Constitution which is allowed on all hands to be the result, not of theory, but "of a spirit of amity, and that mutual deference and concession which the peculiarity of our political situation rendered indispensable." A common government, with powers equal to its objects, is called for by the voice, and still more loudly by the political situation, of America. A government founded on principles more consonant to the wishes of the larger States is not likely to be obtained from the smaller States. The only option, then, for the former, lies between the proposed government and a government still more objectionable. Under this alternative, the advice of prudence must be to embrace the lesser evil; and, instead of indulging a fruitless anticipation of the possible mischiefs which may ensue, to contemplate rather the advantageous consequences which may qualify the sacrifice.

In this spirit it may be remarked, that the equal vote allowed to each State is at once a constitutional recognition of the portion of sovereignty remaining in the individual States, and an instrument for preserving that residuary sovereignty. So far the equality ought to be no less acceptable to the large than to the small States; since they are not less solicitous to guard, by every possible expedient, against an improper consolidation of the States into one simple republic.

Another advantage accruing from this ingredient in the constitution of the Senate is the additional impediment it must prove against improper acts of legislation. No law or resolution can now be passed without the concurrence, first, of a majority of the people, and then, of a majority of the States. It must be acknowledged that this complicated check on legislation may in some instances be injurious as well as beneficial; and that the peculiar defence which it involves in favour of the smaller States would be more rational, if any interests common to them, and distinct from those of the other States, would otherwise be exposed to peculiar danger. But as the larger States will always be able, by their power over the supplies, to defeat unreasonable exertions of this prerogative of the lesser States, and as the facility and excess of law-making seem to be the diseases to which our governments are most liable, it is not impossible that this part of the Constitution may be more convenient in practice than it appears to many in contemplation.

IV. The number of senators, and the duration of their appointment, come next to be considered. In order to form an accurate judgment on both these points, it will be proper to inquire into the purposes which are to be answered by a senate; and in order to ascertain these, it will be necessary to review the inconveniences which a republic must suffer from the want of such an institution.

First. It is a misfortune incident to republican government, though in a less degree than to other governments, that those who administer it may forget their obligations to their constituents, and prove unfaithful to their important trust. In this point of view, a senate, as a second branch of the legislative assembly, distinct from, and dividing the power with, a first, must be in all cases a salutary check on the government. It doubles the security to the people, by requiring the concurrence of two distinct bodies in schemes of usurpation or perfidy, where the ambition or corruption of one would otherwise be sufficient. This is a precaution founded on such clear principles, and now so well understood in the United States, that it would be more than superfluous to enlarge on it. I will barely remark, that as the improbability of sinister combinations will be in proportion to the dissimilarity in the genius of the two bodies, it must be politic to distinguish them from each other by every circumstance which will consist with a due harmony in all proper measures, and with the genuine principles of republican government.

Secondly. The necessity of a senate is not less indicated by the propensity of all single and numerous assemblies to yield to the impulse of sudden and violent passions, and to be seduced by factious leaders into intemperate and pernicious resolutions. Examples on this subject might be cited without number; and from proceedings within the United States, as well as from the history of other nations. But a position that will not be contradicted need not be proved. All that need be remarked is, that a body which is to correct this infirmity ought itself to be free from it, and consequently ought to be less numerous. It ought, moreover, to possess great firmness, and consequently ought to hold its authority by a tenure of considerable duration.

Thirdly. Another defect to be supplied by a senate lies in a want of due acquaintance with the objects and principles of legislation. It is not possible that an assembly of men called for the most part from pursuits of a private nature, continued in appointment for a short time, and led by no permanent motive to devote the intervals of public occupation to a study of the laws, the affairs, and the comprehensive interests of their country, should, if left wholly to themselves, escape a variety of important errors in the exercise of their legislative trust. It may be affirmed, on the best grounds, that no small share of the present embarrassments of America is to be charged on the blunders of our governments; and that these have proceeded from the heads rather than the hearts of most of the authors of them. What indeed are all the repealing, explaining, and amending laws, which fill and disgrace our voluminous codes, but so many monuments of deficient wisdom; so many impeachments exhibited by each succeeding against each preceding session; so many admonitions to the people of the value of those aids which may be expected from a well-constituted senate?

A good government implies two things: first, fidelity to the object of government, which is the happiness of the people; secondly, a knowledge of the means by which that object can be best attained. Some governments are deficient in both these qualities; most governments are deficient in the first. I scruple not to assert that in American governments too little attention has been paid to the last. The federal Constitution avoids this error; and what merits particular notice, it provides for the last in a mode which increases the security for the first.

Fourthly. The mutability in the public councils arising from a rapid succession of new members, however qualified they may be, points out, in the strongest manner, the necessity of some stable institution in the government. Every new election in the States is found to change one half of the representatives. From this change of men must proceed a change of opinions; and from a change of opinions, a change of measures. But a continual change even of good measures is inconsistent with every rule of prudence and every prospect of success. The remark is verified in private life, and becomes more just, as well as more important, in national transactions.

To trace the mischievous effects of a mutable government would fill a volume. I will hint a few only, each of which will be perceived to be a source of innumerable others.

In the first place, it forfeits the respect and confidence of other nations, and all the advantages connected with national character. An individual who is observed to be inconstant to his plans, or perhaps to carry on his affairs without any plan at all, is marked at once, by all prudent people, as a speedy victim to his own unsteadiness and folly. His more friendly neighbours may pity him, but all will decline to connect their fortunes with his; and not a few will seize the opportunity of making their fortunes out of his. One nation is to another what one individual is to another; with this melancholy distinction perhaps, that the former, with fewer of the benevolent emotions than the latter, are under fewer restraints also from taking undue advantage from the indiscretions of each other. Every nation, consequently, whose affairs betray a want of wisdom and stability, may calculate on every loss which can be sustained from the more systematic policy of their wiser neighbours. But the best instruction on this subject is unhappily conveyed to America by the example of her own situation. She finds that she is held in no respect by her friends; that she is the derision of her enemies; and that she is a prey to every nation which has an interest in speculating on her fluctuating councils and embarrassed affairs.

The internal effects of a mutable policy are still more calamitous. It poisons the blessing of liberty itself. It will be of little avail to the people that the laws are made by men of their own choice, if the laws be so voluminous that they cannot be read, or so incoherent that they cannot be understood; if they be repealed or revised before they are promulgated, or undergo such incessant changes that no man, who knows what the law is to-day, can guess what it will be to-morrow. Law is defined to be a rule of action; but how can that be a rule which is little known and less fixed?

Another effect of public instability is the unreasonable advantage it gives to the sagacious, the enterprising, and the moneyed few over the industrious and uninformed mass of the people. Every new regulation concerning commerce or revenue, or in any manner affecting the value of the different species of property, presents a new harvest to those who watch the change and can trace its consequences; a harvest, reared not by themselves, but by the toils and cares of the great body of their fellow-citizens. This is a state of things in which it may be said with some truth that laws are made for the *few*, not for the *many*.

In another point of view, great injury results from an unstable government. The want of confidence in the public councils damps every useful undertaking, the success and profit of which may depend on a continuance of existing arrangements. What prudent merchant will hazard his fortunes in any new branch of commerce when he knows not but that his plans may be rendered unlawful before they can be executed? What farmer or manufacturer will lay himself out for the encouragement given to any particular cultivation or establishment when he can have no assurance that his preparatory labours and advances will not render him a victim to an inconstant government? In a word, no great improvement or laudable enterprise can go forward which requires the auspices of a steady system of national policy.

But the most deplorable effect of all is that diminution of attachment and reverence which steals into the hearts of the people towards a political system which betrays so many marks of infirmity, and disappoints so many of their flattering hopes. No government, any more than an individual, will long be respected without being truly respectable; nor be truly respectable without possessing a certain portion of order and stability.   PUBLIUS

Number 63

[HAMILTON OR MADISON]

A *fifth* desideratum, illustrating the utility of a senate, is the want of a due sense of national character. Without a select and stable member of the government, the esteem of foreign powers will not only be forfeited by an unenlightened and variable policy, proceeding from the causes already mentioned, but the national councils will not possess that sensibility to the opinion of the world which is perhaps not less necessary in order to merit, than it is to obtain, its respect and confidence.

An attention to the judgment of other nations is important to every government for two reasons: the one is, that, independently of the merits of any particular plan or measure, it is desirable, on various accounts, that it should appear to other nations as the offspring of a wise and honourable policy; the second is, that in doubtful cases, particularly where the national councils may be warped by some strong passion or momentary interest, the presumed or known opinion of the impartial world may be the best guide that can be followed. What has not America lost by her want of character with foreign nations; and how many errors and follies would she not have avoided, if the justice and propriety of her measures had, in every instance, been previously tried by the light in which they would probably appear to the unbiased part of mankind?

Yet however requisite a sense of national character may be, it is evident that it can never be sufficiently possessed by a numerous and changeable body. It can only be found in a number so small that a sensible degree of the praise and blame of public measures may be the portion of each individual; or in an assembly so durably invested with public trust, that the pride and consequence of its members may be sensibly incorporated with the reputation and prosperity of the community. The half-yearly representatives of Rhode Island would probably have been little affected in their deliberations on the iniquitous measures of that State by arguments drawn from the light in which such measures would be viewed by foreign nations, or even by the sister States; whilst it can scarcely be doubted that if the concurrence of a select and stable body had been necessary, a regard to national character alone would have prevented the calamities under which that misguided people is now labouring.

I add, as a *sixth* defect, the want, in some important cases, of a due responsibility in the government to the people, arising from that frequency of elections which in other cases produces this responsibility. This remark will, perhaps, appear not only new, but paradoxical. It must nevertheless be acknowledged, when explained, to be as undeniable as it is important.

Responsibility, in order to be reasonable, must be limited to objects within the power of the responsible party, and in order to be effectual, must relate to operations of that power, of which a ready and proper judgment can be formed by the constituents. The objects of government may be divided into two general classes: the one depending on measures which have singly an immediate and sensible operation; the other depending on a succession of well-chosen and well-connected measures, which have a gradual and perhaps unobserved operation. The importance of the latter description to the collective and permanent welfare of every country needs no explanation. And yet it is evident that an assembly elected for so short a term as to be unable to provide more than one or two links in a chain of measures, on which the general welfare may essentially depend, ought not to be answerable for

the final result, any more than a steward or tenant, engaged for one year, could be justly made to answer for places or improvements which could not be accomplished in less than half a dozen years. Nor is it possible for the people to estimate the *share* of influence which their annual assemblies may respectively have on events resulting from the mixed transactions of several years. It is sufficiently difficult to preserve a personal responsibility in the members of a *numerous* body for such acts of the body as have an immediate, detached, and palpable operation on its constituents.

The proper remedy for this defect must be an additional body in the legislative department, which, having sufficient permanency to provide for such objects as require a continued attention and a train of measures, may be justly and effectually answerable for the attainment of those objects.

Thus far I have considered the circumstances which point out the necessity of a well-constructed Senate only as they relate to the representatives of the people. To a people as little blinded by prejudice or corrupted by flattery as those whom I address, I shall not scruple to add that such an institution may be sometimes necessary as a defence to the people against their own temporary errors and delusions. As the cool and deliberate sense of the community ought, in all governments, and actually will, in all free governments, ultimately prevail over the views of its rulers; so there are particular moments in public affairs when the people, stimulated by some irregular passion, or some illicit advantage, or misled by the artful misrepresentations of interested men, may call for measures which they themselves will afterwards be the most ready to lament and condemn. In these critical moments, how salutary will be the interference of some temperate and respectable body of citizens in order to check the misguided career, and to suspend the blow meditated by the people against themselves, until reason, justice, and truth can regain their authority over the public mind? What bitter anguish would not the people of Athens have often escaped if their government had contained so provident a safeguard against the tyranny of their own passions? Popular liberty might then have escaped the indelible reproach of decreeing to the same citizens the hemlock on one day and statues on the next.

It may be suggested that a people spread over an extensive region cannot, like the crowded inhabitants of a small district, be subject to the infection of violent passions, or to the danger of combining in pursuit of unjust measures. I am far from denying that this is a distinction of peculiar importance. I have, on the contrary, endeavoured in a former paper to show that it is one of the principal recommendations of a confederated republic. At the same time, this advantage ought not to be considered as superseding the use of auxiliary precautions. It may even be remarked that the same extended situation, which will exempt the people of America from some of the dangers incident to lesser republics, will expose them to the inconveniency of remaining for a longer time under the influence of those misrepresentations which the combined industry of interested men may succeed in distributing among them.

It adds no small weight to all these considerations to recollect that history informs us of no long-lived republic which had not a senate. Sparta, Rome, and Carthage are, in fact, the only states to whom that character can be applied. In each of the two first there was a senate for life. The constitution of the senate in the last is less known. Circumstantial evidence makes it probable that it was not different in this particular from the two others. It is at least certain that it had some quality or other which rendered it an anchor against popular fluctuations; and that a smaller council, drawn out of the senate, was appointed not only for life, but filled up vacancies itself. These examples, though as unfit for the imitation, as they are repugnant to the genius, of America, are, notwithstanding, when compared with the fugitive and turbulent existence of other ancient republics, very instructive proofs of the necessity of some institution that will blend stability with liberty. I am not unaware of the circumstances which distinguish the American from other popular governments, as well ancient as modern; and which render extreme circumspection necessary in reasoning from the one case to the other. But after allowing due weight to this consideration, it may still be maintained that there are many points of similitude which render these examples not unworthy of our attention. Many of the defects, as we have seen, which can only be supplied by a senatorial institution, are common to a numerous assembly frequently elected by the people, and to the people themselves. There are others peculiar to the former, which require the control of such an institu-

tion. The people can never wilfully betray their own interests; but they may possibly be betrayed by the representatives of the people; and the danger will be evidently greater where the whole legislative trust is lodged in the hands of one body of men, than where the concurrence of separate and dissimilar bodies is required in every public act.

The difference most relied on between the American and other republics consists in the principle of representation; which is the pivot on which the former move, and which is supposed to have been unknown to the latter, or at least to the ancient part of them. The use which has been made of this difference, in reasonings contained in former papers, will have shown that I am disposed neither to deny its existence nor to undervalue its importance. I feel the less restraint, therefore, in observing that the position concerning the ignorance of the ancient governments on the subject of representation is by no means precisely true in the latitude commonly given to it. Without entering into a disquisition which here would be misplaced, I will refer to a few known facts in support of what I advance.

In the most pure democracies of Greece many of the executive functions were performed, not by the people themselves, but by officers elected by the people, and *representing* the people in their *executive* capacity.

Prior to the reform of Solon, Athens was governed by nine Archons, annually *elected by the people at large*. The degree of power delegated to them seems to be left in great obscurity. Subsequent to that period, we find an assembly, first of four, and afterwards of six hundred members, annually *elected by the people;* and *partially* representing them in their *legislative* capacity, since they were not only associated with the people in the function of making laws, but had the exclusive right of originating legislative propositions to the people. The senate of Carthage, also, whatever might be its power or the duration of its appointment, appears to have been *elective* by the suffrages of the people. Similar instances might be traced in most, if not all, the popular governments of antiquity.

Lastly, in Sparta we meet with the Ephori, and in Rome with the Tribunes; two bodies, small indeed in numbers, but annually *elected by the whole body of the people*, and considered as the *representatives* of the people, almost in their *plenipotentiary* capacity. The Cosmi of Crete were also annually *elected by the people,* and have been considered by some authors as an institution analogous to those of Sparta and Rome, with this difference only, that in the election of that representative body the right of suffrage was communicated to a part only of the people.

From these facts, to which many others might be added, it is clear that the principle of representation was neither unknown to the ancients nor wholly overlooked in their political constitutions. The true distinction between these and the American governments lies *in the total exclusion of the people, in their collective capacity,* from any share in the *latter,* and not in the *total exclusion of the representatives of the people* from the administration of the *former.* The distinction, however, thus qualified, must be admitted to leave a most advantageous superiority in favour of the United States. But to insure to this advantage its full effect, we must be careful not to separate it from the other advantage of an extensive territory. For it cannot be believed that any form of representative government could have succeeded within the narrow limits occupied by the democracies of Greece.

In answer to all these arguments, suggested by reason, illustrated by examples, and enforced by our own experience, the jealous adversary of the Constitution will probably content himself with repeating that a senate appointed not immediately by the people, and for the term of six years, must gradually acquire a dangerous pre-eminence in the government, and finally transform it into a tyrannical aristocracy.

To this general answer, the general reply ought to be sufficient, that liberty may be endangered by the abuses of liberty as well as by the abuses of power; that there are numerous instances of the former as well as of the latter; and that the former, rather than the latter, are apparently most to be apprehended by the United States. But a more particular reply may be given.

Before such a revolution can be effected, the Senate, it is to be observed, must in the first place corrupt itself; must next corrupt the State legislatures; must then corrupt the House of Representatives and must finally corrupt the people at large. It is evident that the Senate must be first corrupted before it can attempt an establishment of tyranny. Without corrupting the State legislatures it cannot prosecute the attempt, because the periodical change of members would otherwise regener-

ate the whole body. Without exerting the means of corruption with equal success on the House of Representatives, the opposition of that coequal branch of the government would inevitably defeat the attempt; and without corrupting the people themselves, a succession of new representatives would speedily restore all things to their pristine order. Is there any man who can seriously persuade himself that the proposed Senate can, by any possible means within the compass of human address, arrive at the object of a lawless ambition through all these obstructions?

If reason condemns the suspicion, the same sentence is pronounced by experience. The constitution of Maryland furnishes the most opposite example. The Senate of that State is elected, as the federal Senate will be, indirectly by the people and for a term less by one year only than the federal Senate. It is distinguished, also, by the remarkable prerogative of filling up its own vacancies within the term of its appointment, and, at the same time, is not under the control of any such rotation as is provided for the federal Senate. There are some other lesser distinctions which would expose the former to colourable objections that do not lie against the latter. If the federal Senate, therefore, really contained the danger which has been so loudly proclaimed, some symptoms at least of a like danger ought by this time to have been betrayed by the Senate of Maryland, but no such symptoms have appeared. On the contrary, the jealousies at first entertained by men of the same description with those who view with terror the correspondent part of the federal Constitution, have been gradually extinguished by the progress of the experiment; and the Maryland constitution is daily deriving, from the salutary operation of this part of it, a reputation in which it will probably not be rivalled by that of any State in the Union.

But if anything could silence the jealousies on this subject it ought to be the British example. The Senate there, instead of being elected for a term of six years and of being unconfined to particular families or fortunes, is an hereditary assembly of opulent nobles. The House of Representatives, instead of being elected for two years, and by the whole body of the people, is elected for seven years and, in very great proportion, by a very small proportion of the people. Here, unquestionably, ought to be seen in full display the aristocratic usurpations and tyranny which are at some future period to be exemplified in the United States. Unfortunately, however, for the anti-federal argument, the British history informs us that this hereditary assembly has not been able to defend itself against the continual encroachments of the House of Representatives; and that it no sooner lost the support of the monarch than it was actually crushed by the weight of the popular branch.

As far as antiquity can instruct us on this subject, its examples support the reasoning which we have employed. In Sparta, the Ephori, the annual representatives of the people, were found an overmatch for the senate for life, continually gained on its authority, and finally drew all power into their own hands. The Tribunes of Rome, who were the representatives of the people, prevailed, it is well known, in almost every contest with the senate for life, and in the end gained the most complete triumph over it. The fact is the more remarkable as unanimity was required in every act of the Tribunes, even after their number was augmented to ten. It proves the irresistible force possessed by that branch of a free government which has the people on its side. To these examples might be added that of Carthage, whose senate, according to the testimony of Polybius, instead of drawing all power into its vortex, had, at the commencement of the second Punic War, lost almost the whole of its original portion.

Besides the conclusive evidence resulting from this assemblage of facts, that the federal Senate will never be able to transform itself, by gradual usurpations, into an independent and aristocratic body, we are warranted in believing that if such a revolution should ever happen from causes which the foresight of man cannot guard against, the House of Representatives, with the people on their side, will at all times be able to bring back the Constitution to its primitive form and principles. Against the force of the immediate representatives of the people nothing will be able to maintain even the constitutional authority of the Senate, but such a display of enlightened policy and attachment to the public good, as will divide with that branch of the legislature the affections and support of the entire body of the people themselves.   PUBLIUS

Number 64

[JAY]

IT IS A just and not a new observation that enemies to particular persons, and opponents to particular measures, seldom confine their censures to such things only in either as are worthy of blame. Unless on this principle, it is difficult to explain the motives of their conduct who condemn the proposed Constitution in the aggregate, and treat with severity some of the most unexceptionable articles in it.

The second section gives power to the President, *"by and with the advice and consent of the Senate, to make treaties,* PROVIDED TWO THIRDS OF THE SENATORS PRESENT CONCUR."

The power of making treaties is an important one, especially as it relates to war, peace, and commerce; and it should not be delegated but in such a mode, and with such precautions, as will afford the highest security that it will be exercised by men the best qualified for the purpose, and in the manner most conducive to the public good. The convention appears to have been attentive to both these points: they have directed the President to be chosen by select bodies of electors, to be deputed by the people for that express purpose; and they have committed the appointment of senators to the State legislatures. This mode has, in such cases, vastly the advantage of elections by the people in their collective capacity, where the activity of party zeal, taking advantage of the supineness, the ignorance, and the hopes and fears of the unwary and uninterested, often places men in office by the votes of a small proportion of the electors.

As the select assemblies for choosing the President, as well as the State legislatures who appoint the senators, will in general be composed of the most enlightened and respectable citizens, there is reason to presume that their attention and their votes will be directed to those men only who have become the most distinguished by their abilities and virtue, and in whom the people perceive just grounds for confidence. The Constitution manifests very particular attention to this object. By excluding men under thirty-five from the first office, and those under thirty from the second, it confines the electors to men of whom the people have had time to form a judgment, and with respect to whom they will not be liable to be deceived by those brilliant appearances of genius and patriotism which, like transient meteors, sometimes mislead as well as dazzle. If the observation be well founded, that wise kings will always be served by able ministers, it is fair to argue, that as an assembly of select electors possess, in a greater degree than kings, the means of extensive and accurate information relative to men and characters, so will their appointments bear at least equal marks of discretion and discernment. The inference which naturally results from these considerations is this, that the President and senators so chosen will always be of the number of those who best understand our national interests, whether considered in relation to the several States or to foreign nations, who are best able to promote those interests, and whose reputation for integrity inspires and merits confidence. With such men the power of making treaties may be safely lodged.

Although the absolute necessity of system, in the conduct of any business, is universally known and acknowledged, yet the high importance of it in national affairs has not yet become sufficiently impressed on the public mind. They who wish to commit the power under consideration to a popular assembly, composed of members constantly coming and going in quick succession, seem not to recollect that such a body must necessarily be inadequate to the attainment of those objects which require to be steadily contemplated in all their relations and circumstances, and which can only be approached and achieved by measures which not only talents, but also exact information, and often much time, are necessary to concert and to execute. It was wise, therefore, in the convention to provide, not only that the power of making treaties should be committed to able and honest men, but also that they should continue in place a sufficient time to become perfectly acquainted with our national concerns, and to form and introduce a system for the management of them. The duration prescribed is such as will give them an opportunity of greatly extending their political information, and of rendering their accumulating experience more and more beneficial to their country. Nor has the convention discovered less prudence in providing for the frequent elections of senators in such a way as to obviate the inconvenience of periodically transferring those great affairs entirely to new men; for by leaving a considerable residue of the old ones in place, uniformity, and order, as well as a constant succession of official information, will be preserved.

There are a few who will not admit that the affairs of trade and navigation should be regulated by a system cautiously formed and steadily pursued; and that both our treaties and our laws should correspond with and be made to promote it. It is of much consequence that this correspondence and conformity be carefully maintained; and they who assent to the truth of this position will see and confess that it is well provided for by making concurrence of the Senate necessary both to treaties and to laws.

It seldom happens in the negotiation of treaties, of whatever nature, but that perfect *secrecy* and immediate *despatch* are sometimes requisite. There are cases where the most useful intelligence may be obtained if the persons possessing it can be relieved from apprehensions of discovery. Those apprehensions will operate on those persons whether they are actuated by mercenary or friendly motives; and there doubtless are many of both descriptions who would rely on the secrecy of the President, but who would not confide in that of the Senate, and still less in that of a large popular Assembly. The convention have done well, therefore, in so disposing of the power of making treaties, that although the President must, in forming them, act by the advice and consent of the Senate, yet he will be able to manage the business of intelligence in such a manner as prudence may suggest.

They who have turned their attention to the affairs of men must have perceived that there are tides in them; tides very irregular in their duration, strength, and direction, and seldom found to run twice exactly in the same manner or measure. To discern and to profit by these tides in national affairs is the business of those who preside over them; and they who have had much experience on this head inform us that there frequently are occasions when days, nay, even when hours, are precious. The loss of a battle, the death of a prince, the removal of a minister, or other circumstances intervening to change the present posture and aspect of affairs, may turn the most favourable tide into a course opposite to our wishes. As in the field, so in the cabinet, there are moments to be seized as they pass, and they who preside in either should be left in capacity to improve them. So often and so essentially have we heretofore suffered from the want of secrecy and despatch, that the Constitution would have been inexcusably defective if no attention had been paid to those objects. Those matters which in negotiations usually require the most secrecy and the most despatch are those preparatory and auxiliary measures which are not otherwise important in a national view, than as they tend to facilitate the attainment of the objects of the negotiation. For these, the President will find no difficulty to provide; and should any circumstance occur which requires the advice and consent of the Senate, he may at any time convene them. Thus we see that the Constitution provides that our negotiations for treaties shall have every advantage which can be derived from talents, information, integrity, and deliberate investigations on the one hand, and from secrecy and despatch on the other.

But to this plan, as to most others that have ever appeared, objections are contrived and urged.

Some are displeased with it, not on account of any errors or defects in it, but because, as the treaties, when made, are to have the force of laws, they should be made only by men invested with legislative authority. These gentlemen seem not to consider that the judgments of our courts, and the commissions constitutionally given by our governor, are as valid and as binding on all persons whom they concern as the laws passed by our legislature. All constitutional acts of power, whether in the executive or in the judicial department, have as much legal validity and obligation as if they proceeded from the legislature; and therefore, whatever name be given to the power of making treaties, or however obligatory they may be when made, certain it is that the people may, with much propriety, commit the power of a distinct body from the legislature, the executive, or the judicial. It surely does not follow that because they have given the power of making laws to the legislature that therefore they should likewise give them power to do every other act of sovereignty by which the citizens are to be bound and affected.

Others, though content that treaties should be made in the mode proposed, are averse to their being the *supreme* laws of the land. They insist, and profess to believe, that treaties like acts of assembly, should be repealable at pleasure. This idea seems to be new and peculiar to this country, but new errors, as well as new truths, often appear. These gentlemen would do well to reflect that a treaty is only another name for a bargain, and that it would be impossible to find a nation who would make any bargain with us which should be binding on them *absolutely*, but on us only so long and so far as we may think proper to be bound by it. They who make laws may, without doubt, amend or repeal them; and it will not be disputed that they who make treaties may alter or cancel them; but still let us not forget that treaties are made, not by only one of the contracting parties, but by both; and consequently, that as the consent of both was essential to their formation at first, so must it ever afterwards be to alter or cancel them. The proposed Constitution, therefore, has not in the least extended the obligation of treaties. They are just as binding, and just as far beyond the lawful reach of legislative acts now, as they will be at any future period, or under any form of government.

However useful jealousy may be in republics, yet when like bile in the natural, it abounds too much in the body politic, the eyes of both become very liable to be deceived by the delusive appearances which that malady casts on surrounding objects. From this cause, probably, proceed the fears and apprehensions of some that the President and Senate may make treaties without an equal eye to the interests of all the States. Others suspect that two thirds will oppress the remaining third, and ask whether those gentlemen are made sufficiently responsible for their conduct; whether, if they act corruptly, they can be punished; and if they make disadvantageous treaties, how are we to get rid of those treaties?

As all the States are equally represented in the Senate, and by men the most able and the most willing to promote the interests of their constituents, they will all have an equal degree of influence in that body, especially while they continue to be careful in appointing proper persons, and to insist on their punctual attendance. In proportion as the United States assume a national form and a national character, so will the good of the whole be more and more an object of attention, and the government must be a weak one indeed if it should forget that the good of the whole can only be promoted by advancing the good of each of the parts or members which compose the whole. It will not be in the power of the President and Senate to make any treaties by which they and their families and estates will not be equally bound and affected with the rest of the community; and, having no private interests distinct from that of the nation, they will be under no temptations to neglect the latter.

As to corruption, the case is not supposable. He must either have been very unfortunate in his intercourse with the world, or possess a heart very susceptible of such impressions, who can think it probable that the President and two thirds of the Senate will ever be capable of such unworthy conduct. The idea is too gross and too invidious to be entertained. But in such a case, if it should ever happen, the treaty so obtained from us would, like all other fraudulent contracts, be null and void by the law of nations.

With respect to their responsibility, it is difficult to conceive how it could be increased. Every consideration that can influence the human mind, such as honour, oaths, reputations, conscience, the love of country, and family affections and attachments, afford security for their fidelity. In short, as the Constitution has taken the utmost care that they shall be men of talents and integrity, we have reason to be persuaded that the treaties they make will be as advantageous as, all circumstances considered, could be made; and so far as the fear of punishment and disgrace can operate, that motive to good behaviour is amply afforded by the article on the subject of impeachments.

PUBLIUS

Number 65

[HAMILTON]

THE REMAINING powers which the plan of the convention allots to the Senate, in a distinct capacity, are comprised in their participation with the executive in the appointment to offices, and in their judicial character as a court for the trial of impeachments. As in the business of appointments the executive will be the principal agent, the provisions relating to it will most properly be discussed in the examination of that department. We will, therefore, conclude this head with a view of the judicial character of the Senate.

A well-constituted court for the trial of impeachments is an object not more to be desired than difficult to be obtained in a government wholly elective. The subjects of its jurisdiction are those offences which proceed from the misconduct of public men, or, in other words, from the abuse or violation of some public trust. They are of a nature which may with peculiar propriety be denominated POLITICAL, as they relate chiefly to injuries done immediately to the society itself. The prosecution of them, for this reason, will seldom fail to agitate the passions of the whole community, and to divide it into parties more or less friendly or inimical to the accused. In many cases it will connect itself with the pre-existing factions, and will enlist all their animosities, partialities, influence, and interest on one side or on the other; and in such cases there will always be the greatest danger that the decision will be regulated more by the comparative strength of parties, than by the real demonstrations of innocence or guilt.

The delicacy and magnitude of a trust which so deeply concerns the political reputation and existence of every man engaged in the administration of public affairs, speak for themselves. The difficulty of placing it rightly, in a government resting entirely on the basis of periodical elections, will as readily be perceived, when it is considered that the most conspicuous characters in it will, from that circumstance, be too often the leaders or the tools of the most cunning or the most numerous faction, and on this account can hardly be expected to possess the requisite neutrality towards those whose conduct may be the subject of scrutiny.

The convention, it appears, thought the Senate the most fit depositary of this important trust. Those who can best discern the intrinsic difficulty of the thing, will be least hasty in condemning that opinion, and will be most inclined to allow due weight to the arguments which may be supposed to have produced it.

What, it may be asked, is the true spirit of the institution itself? Is it not designed as a method of NATIONAL INQUEST into the conduct of public men? If this be the design of it, who can so properly be the inquisitors for the nation as the representatives of the nation themselves? It is not disputed that the power of originating the inquiry, or, in other words, of preferring the impeachment, ought to be lodged in the hands of one branch of the legislative body. Will not the reasons which indicate the propriety of this arrangement strongly plead for an admission of the other branch of that body to a share of the inquiry? The model from which the idea of this institution has been borrowed pointed out that course to the convention. In Great Britain it is the province of the House of Commons to prefer the impeachment, and of the House of Lords to decide upon it. Several of the State constitutions have followed the example. As well the latter, as the former, seem to have regarded the practice of impeachments as a bridle in the hands of the legislative body upon the executive servants of the government. Is not this the true light in which it ought to be regarded?

Where else than in the Senate could have been found a tribunal sufficiently dignified, or sufficiently independent? What other body would be likely to feel *confidence enough in its own situation* to preserve, unawed and uninfluenced, the necessary impartiality between an *individual* accused, and the *representatives of the people, his accusers?*

Could the Supreme Court have been relied upon as answering this description? It is much to be doubted whether the members of that tribunal would at all times be endowed with so eminent a portion of fortitude as would be called for in the execution of so difficult a task; and it is still more to be doubted, whether they would possess the degree of credit and authority which might, on certain occasions, be indispensable towards reconciling the people to a decision that should happen to clash with an accusation brought by their immediate representatives. A deficiency in the first would be fatal to the accused; in the last, dangerous to the public tranquillity. The hazard, in both these respects, could only be avoided, if at all, by rendering that tribunal more numerous than would consist with a reasonable attention to economy. The necessity of a numerous court for the trial of impeachments is equally dictated by the nature of the proceeding. This can never be tied down by such strict rules, either in the delineation of the offence by the prosecutors, or in the construction of it by the judges, as in common cases serve to limit the discretion of courts in favour of personal security. There will be no jury to stand between the judges who are to pronounce the sentence of the law and the party who is to receive or suffer it. The awful discretion which a court of impeachments must necessarily have, to doom to honour or to infamy the most confidential and the most distinguished characters of the community, forbids the commitment of the trust to a small number of persons.

These considerations seem alone sufficient to authorise a conclusion, that the Supreme Court would have been an improper substitute for the Senate, as a court of impeachments. There remains a further consideration, which will not a little strengthen this conclusion. It is this: The punishment which may be the consequence of conviction upon impeachment, is not to terminate the chastisement of the offender. After having been sentenced to a perpetual ostracism from the esteem and confidence, and honours and emoluments of his country, he will still be liable to prosecution and punishment in the ordinary course of law. Would it be proper that the persons who had disposed of his fame, and his most valuable rights as a citizen, in one trial, should, in another trial for the same offence, be also the disposers of his life and his fortune? Would there

not be the greatest reason to apprehend that error, in the first sentence, would be the parent of error in the second sentence? That the strong bias of one decision would be apt to overrule the influence of any new lights which might be brought to vary the complexion of another decision? Those who know anything of human nature will not hesitate to answer these questions in the affirmative; and will be at no loss to perceive that, by making the same persons judges in both cases, those who might happen to be the objects of prosecution would, in a great measure, be deprived of the double security intended them by a double trial. The loss of life and estate would often be virtually included in a sentence which, in its terms, imported nothing more than dismission from a present, and disqualification for a future, office. It may be said that the intervention of a jury, in the second instance, would obviate the danger. But juries are frequently influenced by the opinions of judges. They are sometimes induced to find special verdicts which refer the main question to the decision of the court. Who would be willing to stake his life and his estate upon the verdict of a jury acting under the auspices of judges who had predetermined his guilt?

Would it have been an improvement of the plan to have united the Supreme Court with the Senate, in the formation of the court of impeachment? This union would certainly have been attended with several advantages; but would they not have been overbalanced by the signal disadvantage, already stated, arising from the agency of the same judges in the double prosecution to which the offender would be liable? To a certain extent, the benefits of that union will be obtained from making the chief justice of the Supreme Court the president of the court of impeachments, as is proposed to be done in the plan of the convention; while the inconveniences of an entire incorporation of the former into the latter will be substantially avoided. This was perhaps the prudent mean. I forbear to remark upon the additional pretext for clamour against the judiciary, which so considerable an augmentation of its authority would have afforded.

Would it have been desirable to have composed the court for the trial of impeachments of persons wholly distinct from the other departments of the government? There are weighty arguments, as well against, as in favour of, such a plan. To some minds it will not appear a trivial objection that it could tend to increase the complexity of the political machine, and to add a new spring to the government, the utility of which would at best be questionable. But an objection which will not be thought by any unworthy of attention is this: a court formed upon such a plan would either be attended with a heavy expense, or might in practice be subject to a variety of casualties and inconveniences. It must either consist of permanent officers, stationary at the seat of government, and of course entitled to fixed and regular stipends, or of certain officers of the State governments, to be called upon whenever an impeachment was actually depending. It will not be easy to imagine any third mode materially different which could rationally be proposed. As the court, for reasons already given, ought to be numerous, the first scheme will be reprobated by every man who can compare the extent of the public wants with the means of supplying them. The second will be espoused with caution by those who will seriously consider the difficulty of collecting men dispersed over the whole Union; the injury to the innocent, from the procrastinated determination of the charges which might be brought against them; the advantage to the guilty, from the opportunities which delay would afford to intrigue and corruption; and in some cases the detriment to the State, from the prolonged inaction of men whose firm and faithful execution of their duty might have exposed them to the persecution of an intemperate or designing majority in the House of Representatives. Though this latter supposition may seem harsh, and might not be likely often to be verified, yet it ought not to be forgotten that the demon of faction will, at certain seasons, extend his sceptre over all numerous bodies of men.

But though one or the other of the substitutes which have been examined, or some other that might be devised, should be thought preferable to the plan, in this respect, reported by the convention, it will not follow that the Constitution ought for this reason to be rejected. If mankind were to resolve to agree in no institution of government, until every part of it had been adjusted to the most exact standard of perfection, society would soon become a general scene of anarchy, and the world a desert. Where is the standard of perfection to be found? Who will undertake to unite the discordant opinions of a whole community in the same judgment of it; and to prevail upon one conceited projector to renounce his *infallible* criterion for the *fallible* criterion of his

more *conceited neighbour?* To answer the purpose of the adversaries of the Constitution, they ought to prove, not merely that particular provisions in it are not the best which might have been imagined, but that the plan upon the whole is bad and pernicious.

PUBLIUS

Number 66

[HAMILTON]

A REVIEW of the principal objections that have appeared against the proposed court for the trial of impeachments will not improbably eradicate the remains of any unfavourable impressions which may still exist in regard to this matter.

The *first* of these objections is, that the provision in question confounds legislative and judiciary authorities in the same body, in violation of that important and well-established maxim which requires a separation between the different departments of power. The true meaning of this maxim has been discussed and ascertained in another place, and has been shown to be entirely compatible with a partial intermixture of those departments for special purposes, preserving them, in the main, distinct and unconnected. This partial intermixture is even, in some cases, not only proper but necessary to the mutual defence of the several members of the government against each other. An absolute or qualified negative in the executive upon the acts of the legislative body is admitted, by the ablest adepts in political science, to be an indispensable barrier against the encroachments of the latter upon the former. And it may, perhaps, with no less reason be contented that the powers relating to impeachments are, as before intimated, an essential check in the hands of that body upon the encroachments of the executive. The division of them between the two branches of the legislature, assigning to one the right of accusing, to the other the right of judging, avoids the inconvenience of making the same persons both accusers and judges; and guards against the danger of persecution, from the prevalency of a factious spirit in either of those branches. As the concurrence of two thirds of the Senate will be requisite to a condemnation, the security to innocence, from this additional circumstance, will be as complete as itself can desire.

It is curious to observe with what vehemence this part of the plan is assailed, on the principle here taken notice of, by men who profess to admire, without exception, the constitution of this State; while that constitution makes the Senate, together with the chancellor and judges of the Supreme Court, not only a court of impeachments, but the highest judicatory in the State, in all causes, civil and criminal. The proportion, in point of numbers, of the chancellor and judges to the senators is so inconsiderable that the judiciary authority of New York, in the last resort, may, with truth, be said to reside in its Senate. If the plan of the convention be, in this respect, chargeable with a departure from the celebrated maxim which has been so often mentioned, and seems to be so little understood, how much more culpable must be the constitution of New York?[1]

A *second* objection to the Senate, as a court of impeachments, is, that it contributes to an undue accumulation of power in that body, tending to give to the government a countenance too aristocratic. The Senate, it is observed, is to have concurrent authority with the Executive in the formation of treaties and in the appointment to offices: if, say the objectors, to these prerogatives is added that of deciding in all cases of impeachment, it will give a decided predominancy to senatorial influence. To an objection so little precise in itself, it is not easy to find a very precise answer. Where is the measure or criterion to which we can appeal for determining what will give the Senate too much, too little, or barely the proper degree of influence? Will it not be more safe, as well as more simple, to dismiss such vague and uncertain calculations, to examine each power by itself, and to decide, on general principles, where it may be deposited with most advantage and least inconvenience?

If we take this course, it will lead to a more intelligible, if not to a more certain result. The disposition of the power of making treaties, which has obtained in the plan of the convention, will, then, if I mistake not, appear to be fully justified by the considerations stated in a former number, and by others which will occur under the next head of our inquiries. The expediency of the junction of the Senate with the Executive, in the power of appointing to offices, will, I trust, be placed in a light not less satisfactory, in the disquisitions under the

same head. And I flatter myself the observations in my last paper must have gone no inconsiderable way towards proving that it was not easy, if practicable, to find a more fit receptacle for the power of determining impeachments, than that which has been chosen. If this be truly the case, the hypothetical dread of the too great weight of the Senate ought to be discarded from our reasonings.

But this hypothesis, such as it is, has already been refuted in the remarks applied to the duration in office prescribed for the senators. It was by them shown, as well on the credit of historical examples, as from the reason of the thing, that the most *popular* branch of every government, partaking of the republican genius, by being generally the favourite of the people, will be as generally a full match, if not an overmatch, for every other member of the Government.

But independent of this most active and operative principle, to secure the equilibrium of the national House of Representatives, the plan of the convention has provided in its favour several important counterpoises to the additional authorities to be conferred upon the Senate. The exclusive privilege of originating money bills will belong to the House of Representatives. The same house will possess the sole right of instituting impeachments: is not this a complete counterbalance to that of determining them? The same house will be the umpire in all elections of the President, which do not unite the suffrages of a majority of the whole number of electors; a case which it cannot be doubted will sometimes, if not frequently, happen. The constant possibility of the thing must be a fruitful source of influence to that body. The more it is contemplated, the more important will appear this ultimate though contingent power, of deciding the competitions of the most illustrious citizens of the Union, for the first office in it. It would not perhaps be rash to predict that as a mean of influence it will be found to outweigh all the peculiar attributes of the Senate.

A *third* objection to the Senate as a court of impeachments is drawn from the agency they are to have in the appointments to office. It is imagined that they would be too indulgent judges of the conduct of men, in whose official creation they had participated. The principle of this objection would condemn a practice which is to be seen in all the State governments, if not in all the governments with which we are acquainted: I mean that of ren-

[1] In that of New Jersey, also, the final judiciary authority is in a branch of the legislature. In New Hampshire, Massachusetts, Pennsylvania, and South Carolina, one branch of the legislature is the court for the trial of impeachments.—PUBLIUS

dering those who hold offices during pleasure dependent on the pleasure of those who appoint them. With equal plausibility might it be alleged in this case that the favouritism of the latter would always be an asylum for the misbehaviour of the former. But that practice, in contradiction to this principle, proceeds upon the presumption that the responsibility of those who appoint, for the fitness and competency of the persons on whom they bestow their choice, and the interest they will have in the respectable and prosperous administration of affairs, will inspire a sufficient disposition to dismiss from a share in it all such who, by their conduct, shall have proved themselves unworthy of the confidence reposed in them. Though facts may not always correspond with this presumption, yet if it be, in the main, just, it must destroy the supposition that the Senate, who will merely sanction the choice of the Executive, should feel a bias towards the objects of that choice, strong enough to blind them to the evidences of guilt so extraordinary, as to have induced the representatives of the nation to become its accusers.

If any further arguments were necessary to evince the improbability of such a bias, it might be found in the nature of the agency of the Senate in the business of appointments.

It will be the office of the President to *nominate,* and, with the advice and consent of the Senate, to *appoint.* There will, of course, be no exertion of *choice* on the part of the Senate. They may defeat one choice of the Executive, and oblige him to make another; but they cannot themselves *choose*—they can only ratify or reject the choice of the President. They might even entertain a preference to some other person, at the very moment they were assenting to the one proposed, because there might be no positive ground of opposition to him; and they could not be sure, if they withheld their assent, that the subsequent nomination would fall upon their own favourite, or upon any other person in their estimation more meritorious than the one rejected. Thus it could hardly happen that the majority of the Senate would feel any other complacency towards the object of an appointment than such as the appearances of merit might inspire, and the proofs of the want of it destroy.

A *fourth* objection to the Senate, in the capacity of a court of impeachments, is derived from its union with the Executive in the power of making treaties. This, it has been said, would constitute the senators their own judges, in every case of a corrupt or perfidious execution of that trust. After having combined with the Executive in betraying the interests of the nation in a ruinous treaty, what prospect, it is asked, would there be of their being made to suffer the punishment they would deserve, when they were themselves to decide upon the accusation brought against them for the treachery of which they have been guilty?

This objection has been circulated with more earnestness and with greater show of reason than any other which has appeared against this part of the plan; and yet I am deceived if it does not rest upon an erroneous foundation.

The security essentially intended by the Constitution against corruption and treachery in the formation of treaties is to be sought for in the numbers and characters of those who are to make them. The JOINT AGENCY of the Chief Magistrate of the Union, and of two thirds of the members of a body selected by the collective wisdom of the legislatures of the several States, is designed to be the pledge for the fidelity of the national councils in this particular. The convention might with propriety have meditated the punishment of the Executive, for a deviation from the instructions of the Senate, or a want of integrity in the conduct of the negotiations committed to him; they might also have had in view the punishment of a few leading individuals in the Senate, who should have prostituted their influence in that body as the mercenary instruments of foreign corruption: but they could not, with more or with equal propriety, have contemplated the impeachment and punishment of two thirds of the Senate consenting to an improper treaty, than of a majority of that or of the other branch of the national legislature consenting to a pernicious or unconstitutional law—a principle which, I believe, has never been admitted into any government. How, in fact, could a majority in the House of Representatives impeach themselves? Not better, it is evident, than two thirds of the Senate might try themselves. And yet what reason is there that a majority of the House of Representatives, sacrificing the interests of the society by an unjust and tyrannical act of legislation, should escape with impunity, more than two thirds of the Senate, sacrificing the same interests in an injurious treaty with a foreign power? The truth is, that in all such cases it is essential to the freedom and to the necessary independence of the deliberations of the body, that the members of it should be exempt from punishment for acts done in a collective capacity; and the security to the society must depend on the care which is taken to confide the trust to proper hands, to make it their interest to execute it with fidelity, and to make it as difficult as possible for them to combine in any interest opposite to that of the public good.

So far as might concern the misbehaviour of the Executive in perverting the instructions or contravening the views of the Senate, we need not be apprehensive of the want of a disposition in that body to punish the abuse of their confidence, or to vindicate their own authority. We may thus far count upon their pride, if not upon their virtue. And so far even as might concern the corruption of leading members, by whose arts and influence the majority may have been inveigled into measures odious to the community, if the proofs of that corruption should be satisfactory, the usual propensity of human nature will warrant us in concluding that there would be commonly no defect of inclination in the body to divert the public resentment from themselves by a ready sacrifice of the authors of their mismanagement and disgrace.   PUBLIUS

Number 67

[HAMILTON]

THE CONSTITUTION of the executive department of the proposed government claims next our attention.

There is hardly any part of the system which could have been attended with greater difficulty in the arrangement of it than this; and there is, perhaps, none which has been inveighed against with less candour or criticised with less judgment.

Here the writers against the Constitution seem to have taken pains to signalise their talent of misrepresentation. Calculating upon the aversion of the people to monarchy, they have endeavoured to enlist all their jealousies and apprehensions in opposition to the intended President of the United States; not merely as the embryo, but as the full-grown progeny, of that detested parent. To establish the pretended affinity, they have not scrupled to draw resources even from the regions of fiction. The authorities of a magistrate, in few instances greater, in some instances less, than those of a governor of New York, have been magnified into more than royal prerogatives.

He has been decorated with attributes superior in dignity and splendour to those of a king of Great Britain. He has been shown to us with the diadem sparkling on his brow and the imperial purple flowing in his train. He has been seated on a throne surrounded with minions and mistresses, giving audience to the envoys of foreign potentates, in all the supercilious pomp of majesty. The image of Asiatic despotism and voluptuousness have scarcely been wanting to crown the exaggerated scene. We have been taught to tremble at the terrific visages of murdering janizaries, and to blush at the unveiled mysteries of a future seraglio.

Attempts so extravagant as these to disfigure or, it might rather be said, to metamorphose the object, render it necessary to take an accurate view of its real nature and form: in order as well to ascertain its true aspect and genuine appearance, as to unmask the disingenuity and expose the fallacy of the counterfeit resemblances which have been so insidiously, as well as industriously, propagated.

In the execution of this task there is no man who would not find it an arduous effort either to behold with moderation, or to treat with seriousness, the devices, not less weak than wicked, which have been contrived to pervert the public opinion in relation to the subject. They so far exceed the usual though unjustifiable licences of party artifice, that even in a disposition the most candid and tolerant, they must force the sentiments which favour an indulgent construction of the conduct of political adversaries to give place to a voluntary and unreserved indignation. It is impossible not to bestow the imputation of deliberate imposture and deception upon the gross pretence of a similitude between a king of Great Britain and a magistrate of the character marked out for that of the President of the United States. It is still more impossible to withhold that imputation from the rash and barefaced expedients which have been employed to give success to the attempted imposition.

In one instance, which I cite as a sample of the general spirit, the temerity has proceeded so far as to ascribe to the President of the United States a power which by the instrument reported is *expressly* allotted to the Executives of the individual States. I mean the power of filling casual vacancies in the Senate.

This bold experiment upon the discernment of his countrymen has been hazarded by a writer who (whatever may be his real merit) has had no inconsiderable share in the applauses of his party[1]; and who, upon this false and unfounded suggestion, has built a series of observations equally false and unfounded. Let him now be confronted with the evidence of the fact, and let him, if he be able, justify or extenuate the shameful outrage he has offered to the dictates of truth and to the rules of fair dealing.

The second clause of the second section of the second article empowers the President of the United States "to nominate, and by and with the advice and consent of the Senate, to appoint ambassadors, other public ministers and consuls, judges of the Supreme Court, and all other *officers* of United States whose appointments are *not* in the Constitution *otherwise provided for*, and *which shall be established by law*." Immediately after this clause follows another in these words: "The President shall have power to fill up all *vacancies* that may happen *during the recess of the Senate*, by granting commissions which shall *expire at the end of their next session*." It is from this last provision that the pretended power of the President to fill vacancies in the Senate has been deduced. A slight attention to the connection of the clauses, and to the obvious meaning of the terms, will satisfy us that the deduction is not even colourable.

The first of these two clauses, it is clear, only provides a mode for appointing such officers, "whose appointments are *not otherwise provided for* in the Constitution, and which *shall be established by law*"; of course it cannot extend to the appointments of senators, whose appointments are *otherwise provided for* in the Constitution,[2] and who are *established by the Constitution*, and will not require a future establishment by law. This position will hardly be contested.

The last of these two clauses, it is equally clear, cannot be understood to comprehend the power of filling vacancies in the Senate, for the following reasons:—*First*. The relation in which that clause stands to the other, which declares the general mode of appointing officers of the United States, denotes it to be nothing more than a supplement to the other, for the purpose of establishing an auxiliary method of appointment, in cases to which the general method was inadequate. The ordinary power of appointment is confined to the President and Senate *jointly*, and can therefore only be exercised during the session

of the Senate; but as it would have been improper to oblige this body to be continually in session for the appointment of officers, and as vacancies might happen *in their recess,* which it might be necessary for the public service to fill without delay, the succeeding clause is evidently intended to authorise the President, *singly,* to make temporary appointments "during the recess of the Senate, by granting commissions which shall expire at the end of their next session." *Secondly.* If this clause is to be considered as supplementary to the one which precedes, the *vacancies* of which it speaks must be construed to relate to the "officers" described in the preceding one; and this, we have seen, excludes from its description the members of the Senate. *Thirdly.* The time within which the power is to operate, "during the recess of the Senate," and the duration of the appointments, "to the end of the next session" of that body, conspire to elucidate the sense of the provision, which, if it had been intended to comprehend senators, would naturally have referred the temporary power of filling vacancies to the recess of the State legislatures, who are to make the permanent appointments, and not to the recess of the national Senate, who are to have no concern in those appointments; and would have extended the duration in office of the temporary senators to the next session of the legislature of the State, in whose representation the vacancies had happened, instead of making it to expire at the end of the ensuing session of the national Senate. The circumstances of the body authorised to make the permanent appointments would, of course, have governed the modification of a power which related to the temporary appointments; and as the national Senate is the body whose situation is alone contemplated in the clause upon which the suggestion under examination has been founded, the vacancies to which it alludes can only be deemed to respect those officers in whose appointment that body has a concurrent agency with the President. But *lastly*, the first and second clauses of the third section of the first article, not only obviate all possibility of doubt but destroy the pretext of misconception. The former provides that "the Senate of the United States shall be composed of two Senators from each State, chosen *by the legislature thereof* for six years"; and the latter directs that, "if vacancies in that body should happen by resignation or otherwise, *during the recess of the legislature of* ANY STATE, the Executive THEREOF may make temporary appointments until the *next meeting of the legislature,* which shall then fill such vacancies." Here is an express power given, in clear and unambiguous terms, to the State Executives, to fill casual vacancies in the Senate, by temporary appointments; which not only invalidates the supposition, that the clause before considered could have been intended to confer that power upon the President of the United States, but proves that this supposition, destitute as it is even of the merit of plausibility, must have originated in an intention to deceive the people, too palpable to be obscured by sophistry, too atrocious to be palliated by hypocrisy.

I have taken the pains to select this instance of misrepresentation, and to place it in a clear and strong light, as an unequivocal proof of the unwarrantable arts which are practised to prevent a fair and impartial judgment of the real merits of the Constitution submitted to the consideration of the people. Nor have I scrupled, in so flagrant a case, to allow myself a severity of animadversion little congenial with the general spirit of these papers. I hesitate not to submit it to the decision of any candid and honest adversary of the proposed government, whether language can furnish epithets of too much asperity, for so shameless and so prostitute an attempt to impose on the citizens of America.   PUBLIUS

Number 68

[HAMILTON]

THE MODE of appointment of the Chief Magistrate of the United States is almost the only part of the system, of any consequence, which has escaped without severe censure, or which has received the slightest mark of approbation from its opponents. The most plausible of these, who has appeared in print, has even deigned to admit that the election of the President is pretty well guarded.[1] I venture somewhat further, and hesitate not to affirm, that if the manner of it be not perfect, it is at least excellent. It unites in an eminent degree all the advantages, the union of which was to be wished for.

It was desirable that the sense of the people should operate in the choice of the person to whom so important a trust was to be confided. This end will be answered by committing the right of making it, not to any pre-established body, but to men chosen by the people for the

[1] Vide *Federal Farmer.*—PUBLIUS

special purpose, and at the particular conjuncture.

It was equally desirable that the immediate election should be made by men most capable of analysing the qualities adapted to the station, and acting under circumstances favourable to deliberation, and to a judicious combination of all the reasons and inducements which were proper to govern their choice. A small number of persons, selected by their fellow-citizens from the general mass, will be most likely to possess the information and discernment requisite to such complicated investigations.

It was also peculiarly desirable to afford as little opportunity as possible to tumult and disorder. This evil was not least to be dreaded in the election of a magistrate, who was to have so important an agency in the administration of the government as the President of the United States. But the precautions which have been so happily concerted in the system under consideration, promise an effectual security against this mischief. The choice of *several,* to form an intermediate body of electors, will be much less apt to convulse the community with any extraordinary or violent movements than the choice of *one* who was himself to be the final object of the public wishes. And as the electors chosen in each State are to assemble and vote in the State in which they are chosen, this detached and divided situation will expose them much less to heats and ferments, which might be communicated from them to the people, than if they were all to be convened at one time in one place.

Nothing was more to be desired than that every practicable obstacle should be opposed to cabal, intrigue, and corruption. These most deadly aversaries of republican government might naturally have been expected to make their approaches from more than one quarter, but chiefly from the desire in foreign powers to gain an improper ascendant in our councils. How could they better gratify this than by raising a creature of their own to the chief magistracy of the Union? But the convention have guarded against all danger of this sort with the most provident and judicious attention. They have not made the appointment of the President to depend on any pre-existing bodies of men, who might be tampered with beforehand to prostitute their votes; but they have referred it in the first instance to an immediate act of the people of America, to be exerted in the choice of persons for the temporary and sole purpose of making the appointment. And they have excluded from eligibility to this trust all those who from situation might be suspected of too great devotion to the President in office. No senator, representative, or other person holding a place of trust or profit under the United States can be of the numbers of the electors. Thus without corrupting the body of the people, the immediate agents in the election will at least enter upon the task free from any sinister bias. Their transient existence, and their detached situation, already taken notice of, afford a satisfactory prospect of their continuing so to the conclusion of it. The business of corruption, when it is to embrace so considerable a number of men, requires time as well as means. Nor would it be found easy suddenly to embark them, dispersed as they would be over thirteen States, in any combinations founded upon motives which, though they could not properly be denominated corrupt, might yet be of a nature to mislead them from their duty.

Another and no less important desideratum was that the Executive should be independent for his continuance in office on all but the people themselves. He might otherwise be tempted to sacrifice his duty to his complaisance for those whose favour was necessary to the duration of his official consequence. This advantage will also be secured by making his re-election to depend on a special body of representatives, deputed by the society for the single purpose of making the important choice.

All these advantages will happily combine in the plan devised by the convention; which is, that the people of each State shall choose a number of persons as electors, equal to the number of senators and representatives of such State in the national government, who shall assemble within the State and vote for some fit person as President. Their votes, thus given, are to be transmitted to the seat of the national government, and the person who may happen to have a majority of the whole number of votes will be the President. But as a majority of the votes might not always happen to centre in one man, and as it might be unsafe to permit less than a majority to be conclusive, it is provided that, in such a contingency, the House of Representatives shall select out of the candidates who shall have the five highest number of votes, the man who in their opinion may be best qualified for the office.

The process of election affords a moral certainty that the office of President will never fall to the lot of any man who is not in an eminent degree endowed with the requisite qualifications. Talents for low intrigue and the little arts of popularity may alone suffice to elevate a man to the first honours in a single State; but it will require other talents, and a different kind of merit, to establish him in the esteem and confidence of the whole Union, or of so considerable a portion of it as would be necessary to make him a successful candidate for the distinguished office of President of the United States. It will not be too strong to say that there will be a constant probability of seeing the station filled by characters pre-eminent for ability and virtue. And this will be thought no inconsiderable recommendation of the Constitution by those who are able to estimate the share which the executive in every government must necessarily have in its good or ill administration. Though we cannot acquiesce in the political heresy of the poet who says—

For forms of government let fools contest—
That which is best administered is best,—

yet we may safely pronounce that the true test of a good government is its aptitude and tendency to produce a good administration.

The Vice-President is to be chosen in the same manner with the President; with this difference, that the Senate is to do, in respect to the former, what is to be done by the House of Representatives, in respect to the latter.

The appointment of an extraordinary person, as Vice-President, has been objected to as superfluous, if not mischievous. It has been alleged, that it would have been preferable to have authorised the Senate to elect out of their own body an officer answering that description. But two considerations seem to justify the ideas of the convention in this respect. One is, that to secure at all times the possibility of a definite resolution of the body, it is necessary that the President should have only a casting vote. And to take the senator of any State from his seat as senator, to place him in that of President of the Senate, would be to exchange, in regard to the State from which he came, a constant for a contingent vote. The other consideration is, that as the Vice-President may occasionally become a substitute for the President, in the supreme executive magistracy, all the reasons which recommend the mode of election prescribed for the one apply with great if not with equal force to the manner of appointing the other. It is remarkable that in this, as in most other instances, the objection which is made would lie against the constitution of this State. We have a Lieutenant-Governor, chosen by the people at large, who presides in the Senate, and is the constitutional substitute for the Governor in casualties similar to those which would authorise the Vice-President to exercise the authorities and discharge the duties of the President. PUBLIUS

Number 69

[HAMILTON]

I PROCEED now to trace the real characters of the proposed Executive, as they are marked out in the plan of the convention. This will serve to place in a strong light the unfairness of the representations which have been made in regard to it.

The first thing which strikes our attention is that the executive authority, with few exceptions, is to be vested in a single magistrate. This will scarcely, however, be considered as a point upon which any comparison can be grounded; for if, in this particular, there be a resemblance to the king of Great Britain, there is not less a resemblance to the Grand Seignior, to the khan of Tartary, to the Man of the Seven Mountains, or to the governor of New York.

That magistrate is to be elected for *four* years; and is to be re-eligible as often as the people of the United States shall think him worthy of their confidence. In these circumstances there is a total dissimilitude between *him* and a king of Great Britain, who is an *hereditary* monarch, possessing the crown as a patrimony descendible to his heirs for ever; but there is a close analogy between *him* and a governor of New York, who is elected for *three* years, and is re-eligible without limitation or intermission. If we consider how much less time would be requisite for establishing a dangerous influence in a single State than for establishing a like influence throughout the United States we must conclude that a duration of *four* years for the Chief Magistrate of the Union is a degree of permanency far less to be dreaded in that office than a duration of *three* years for a corresponding office in a single State.

The President of the United States would be liable to be impeached, tried, and, upon conviction of treason, bribery, or other high crimes or misdemeanours, removed from office; and would afterwards be liable to prosecution and punishment in the ordinary course of law. The person of the king of Great Britain is sacred and inviolable; there is no constitutional tribunal to which he is amenable; no punishment to which he can be subjected without involving the crisis of a national revolution. In this delicate and important circumstance of personal responsibility, the President of Confederated America would stand upon no better ground than a governor of New York, and upon worse ground than the governors of Maryland and Delaware.

The President of the United States is to have power to return a bill which shall have passed the two branches of the legislature for reconsideration; and the bill so returned is to become a law if, upon that reconsideration, it be approved by two thirds of both houses. The king of Great Britain, on his part, has an absolute negative upon the acts of the two houses of Parliament. The disuse of that power for a considerable time past does not affect the reality of its existence; and is to be ascribed wholly to the crown's having found the means of substituting influence to authority, or the art of gaining a majority in one or the other of the two houses, to the necessity of exerting a prerogative which could seldom be exerted without hazarding some degree of national agitation. The qualified negative of the President differs widely from this absolute negative of the British sovereign; and tallies exactly with the revisionary authority of the council of revision of this State, of which the governor is a constituent part. In this respect the power of the President would exceed that of the governor of New York, because the former would possess, singly, what the latter shares with the chancellor and judges; but it would be precisely the same with that of the governor of Massachusetts, whose constitution, as to this article, seems to have been the original from which the convention have copied.

The President is to be the "commander-in-chief of the army and navy of the United States, and of the militia of the several States, when called into the actual service of the United States. He is to have power to grant reprieves and pardons for offences against the United States, *except in cases of impeachment;* to recommend to the consideration of Congress such measures as he shall judge necessary and expedient; to convene, on extraordinary occasions, both houses of the legislature, or either of them, and, in case of disagreement between them *with respect to the time of adjournment,* to adjourn them to such time as he shall think proper; to take care that the laws be faithfully executed; and to commission all officers of the United States." In most of these particulars the power of the President will resemble equally that of the king of Great Britain and of the governor of New York. The most material points of difference are these:—*First.* The President will have only the occasional command of such part of the militia of the nation as by legislative provision may be called into the actual service of the Union. The king of Great Britain and the governor of New York have at all times the entire command of all the militia within their several jurisdictions. In this article, therefore, the power of the President would be inferior to that of either the monarch or the governor. *Secondly.* The President is to be commander-in-chief of the army and navy of the United States. In this respect his authority would be nominally the same with that of the king of Great Britain, but in substance much inferior to it. It would amount to nothing more than the supreme command and direction of the military and naval forces, as first general and admiral of the Confederacy; while that of the British king extends to the *declaring* of war and to the *raising* and *regulating* of fleets and armies—all which, by the Constitution under consideration, would appertain to the legislature.[1] The governor of New York, on the other hand, is by the constitution of the State vested only with the command of its militia and navy. But the constitutions of several of the States expressly declare their governors to be commanders-in-chief, as well of the army as navy; and it may well be a question whether those of New Hampshire and Massachusetts, in particular, do not, in this instance, confer larger powers upon

[1] A writer in a Pennsylvania paper, under the signature of TAMONY, has asserted that the king of Great Britain owes his prerogative as commander-in-chief to an annual mutiny bill. The truth is, on the contrary, that his prerogative, in this respect, is immemorial, and was only disputed, "contrary to all reason and precedent," as Blackstone, vol. i. page 262, expresses it, by the Long Parliament of Charles I.; but by the statute the 13th of Charles II. chap. vi., it was declared to be in the king alone, for that the sole supreme government and command of the militia within his Majesty's realms and dominions, and of all forces by sea and land, and of all forts and places of strength, EVER WAS AND IS the undoubted right of his Majesty and his royal predecessors, kings and queens of England, and that both or either house of Parliament cannot nor ought to pretend to the same.—PUBLIUS

their respective governors than could be claimed by a President of the United States. *Thirdly.* The power of the President, in respect to pardons, would extend to all cases, *except those of impeachment.* The governor of New York may pardon in all cases, even in those of impeachment, except for treason and murder. Is not the power of the governor, in this article, on a calculation of political consequences, greater than that of the President? All conspiracies and plots against the government which have not been matured into actual treason may be screened from punishment of every kind by the interposition of the prerogative of pardoning. If a governor of New York, therefore, should be at the head of any such conspiracy, until the design had been ripened into actual hostility he could insure his accomplices and adherents an entire impunity. A President of the Union, on the other hand, though he may even pardon treason when prosecuted in the ordinary course of law, could shelter no offender, in any degree, from the effects of impeachment and conviction. Would not the prospect of a total indemnity for all the preliminary steps be a greater temptation to undertake and persevere in an enterprise against the public liberty than the mere prospect of an exemption from death and confiscation if the final execution of the design, upon an actual appeal to arms, should miscarry? Would this last expectation have any influence at all when the probability was computed that the person who was to afford that exemption might himself be involved in the consequences of the measure, and might be incapacitated by his agency in it from affording the desired impunity? The better to judge of this matter, it will be necessary to recollect that, by the proposed Constitution, the offence of treason is limited "to levying war upon the United States, and adhering to their enemies, giving them aid and comfort"; and that by the laws of New York it is confined within similar bounds. *Fourthly.* The President can only adjourn the national legislature in the single case of disagreement about the time of adjournment. The British monarch may prorogue or even dissolve the Parliament. The governor of New York may also prorogue the legislature of this State for a limited time; a power which, in certain situations, may be employed to very important purposes.

The President is to have power, with the advice and consent of the Senate, to make treaties, provided two thirds of the senators present concur. The king of Great Britain is the sole and absolute representative of the nation in all foreign transactions. He can of his own accord make treaties of peace, commerce, alliance, and of every other description. It has been insinuated that his authority in this respect is not conclusive, and that his conventions with foreign powers are subject to the revision, and stand in need of the ratification, of Parliament. But I believe this doctrine was never heard of until it was broached upon the present occasion. Every jurist [1] of that kingdom, and every other man acquainted with its Constitution, knows, as an established fact, that the prerogative of making treaties exists in the crown in its utmost plenitude; and that the compacts entered into by the royal authority have the most complete legal validity and perfection, independent of any other sanction. The Parliament, it is true, is sometimes seen employing itself in altering the existing laws to conform them to the stipulations in a new treaty; and this may have possibly given birth to the imagination that its co-operation was necessary to the obligatory efficacy of the treaty. But this parliamentary interposition proceeds from a different cause: from the necessity of adjusting a most artificial and intricate system of revenue and commercial laws to the changes made in them by the operation of the treaty; and of adapting new provisions and precautions to the new state of things to keep the machine from running into disorder. In this respect, therefore, there is no comparison between the intended power of the President and the actual power of the British sovereign. The one can perform alone what the other can do only with the concurrence of a branch of the legislature. It must be admitted that, in this instance, the power of the federal Executive would exceed that of any State Executive. But this arises naturally from the sovereign power which relates to treaties. If the Confederacy were to be dissolved it would become a question whether the Executives of the several States were not solely invested with that delicate and important prerogative.

The President is also to be authorised to receive ambassadors and other public ministers. This, though it has been a rich theme of declamation, is more a matter of dignity than of authority. It is a circumstance which will be without consequence in the administration of the government; and it was far more convenient that it should be arranged in this manner than that there should be a necessity of convening the legislature, or one of its branches, upon every arrival of a foreign minister, though it were merely to take the place of a departed predecessor.

The President is to nominate and, *with the advice and consent of the Senate,* to appoint ambassadors and other public ministers, judges of the Supreme Court, and in general all officers of the United States established by law, and whose appointments are not otherwise provided for by the Constitution. The king of Great Britain is emphatically and truly styled the fountain of honour. He not only appoints to all offices, but can create offices. He can confer titles of nobility at pleasure; and has the disposal of an immense number of church preferments. There is evidently a great inferiority in the power of the President, in this particular, to that of the British king; nor is it equal to that of the governor of New York, if we are to interpret the meaning of the constitution of the State by the practice which has obtained under it. The power of appointment is with us lodged in a council composed of the governor and four members of the Senate chosen by the Assembly. The governor *claims,* and has frequently *exercised,* the right of nomination, and is *entitled* to a casting vote in the appointment. If he really has the right of nominating, his authority in this respect is equal to that of the President and exceeds it in the article of the casting vote. In the national government, if the Senate should be divided, no appointment could be made; in the government of New York, if the council should be divided, the governor can turn the scale and confirm his own nomination.[2] If we compare the publicity which must necessarily attend the mode of appointment by the President and an entire branch of the national legislature with the privacy in the mode of appointment by the governor of New York, closeted in a secret apartment with at most four, and frequently with only two persons; and if we at the same time consider how much more easy it must be to in-

[1] *Vide* Blackstone's *Commentaries,* vol. i. p. 257.
—PUBLIUS

[2] Candour, however, demands an acknowledgment that I do not think the claim of the governor to a right of nomination well founded. Yet it is always justifiable to reason from the practice of a government, till its propriety has been constitutionally questioned. And independent of this claim, when we take into view the other considerations, and pursue them through all their consequences, we shall be inclined to draw much the same conclusion.—PUBLIUS

fluence the small number of which a council of appointment consists than the considerable number of which the national Senate would consist, we cannot hesitate to pronounce that the power of the chief magistrate of this State, in the disposition of offices, must, in practice, be greatly superior to that of the Chief Magistrate of the Union.

Hence it appears that, except as to the concurrent authority of the President in the article of treaties, it would be difficult to determine whether that magistrate would, in the aggregate, possess more or less power than the Governor of New York. And it appears yet more unequivocally that there is no pretence for the parallel which has been attempted between him and the king of Great Britain. But to render the contrast in this respect still more striking, it may be of use to throw the principal circumstances of dissimilitude into a closer group.

The President of the United States would be an officer elected by the people for *four* years; the king of Great Britain is a perpetual and *hereditary* prince. The one would be amenable to personal punishment and disgrace; the person of the other is sacred and inviolable. The one would have a *qualified* negative upon the acts of the legislative body; the other has an *absolute* negative. The one would have a right to command the military and naval forces of the nation; the other, in addition to this right, possesses that of *declaring* war, and of *raising* and *regulating* fleets and armies by his own authority. The one would have a concurrent power with a branch of the legislature in the formation of treaties; the other is the *sole possessor* of the power of making treaties. The one would have a like concurrent authority in appointing to offices; the other is the sole author of all appointments. The one can confer no privileges whatever: the other can make denizens of aliens, noblemen of commoners; can erect corporations with all the rights incident to corporate bodies. The one can prescribe no rules concerning the commerce or currency of the nation; the other is in several respects the arbiter of commerce, and in this capacity can establish markets and fairs, can regulate weights and measures, can lay embargoes for a limited time, can coin money, can authorise or prohibit the circulation of foreign coin. The one has no particle of spiritual jurisdiction; the other is the supreme head and governor of the national church! What answer shall we give to those who would per-

suade us that things so unlike resemble each other? The same that ought to be given to those who tell us that a government, the whole power of which would be in the hands of the elective and periodical servants of the people, is an aristocracy, a monarchy, and a despotism.

PUBLIUS

Number 70
[HAMILTON]

THERE IS an idea, which is not without its advocates, that a vigorous Executive is inconsistent with the genius of republican government. The enlightened well-wishers to this species of government must at least hope that the supposition is destitute of foundation, since they can never admit its truth without at the same time admitting the condemnation of their own principles. Energy in the Executive is a leading character in the definition of good government. It is essential to the protection of the community against foreign attacks; it is not less essential to the steady administration of the laws; to the protection of property against those irregular and high-handed combinations which sometimes interrupt the ordinary course of justice; to the security of liberty against the enterprises and assaults of ambition, of faction, and of anarchy. Every man the least conversant in Roman story knows how often that republic was obliged to take refuge in the absolute power of a single man, under the formidable title of Dictator, as well against the intrigues of ambitious individuals who aspired to the tyranny and the seditions of whole classes of the community whose conduct threatened the existence of all government, as against the invasions of external enemies who menaced the conquest and destruction of Rome.

There can be no need, however, to multiply arguments or examples on this head. A feeble Executive implies a feeble execution of the government. A feeble execution is but another phrase for a bad execution; and a government ill executed, whatever it may be in theory, must be, in practice, a bad government.

Taking it for granted, therefore, that all men of sense will agree in the necessity of an energetic Executive, it will only remain to inquire what are the ingredients which constitute this energy? How far can they be combined with those other ingredients which constitute safety in the republican sense? And how far does this combination characterise the plan which has been reported by the convention?

The ingredients which constitute energy in the Executive are, first, unity; secondly, duration; thirdly, an adequate provision for its support; fourthly, competent powers.

The ingredients which constitute safety in the republican sense are, first, a due dependence on the people; secondly, a due responsibility.

Those politicians and statesmen who have been the most celebrated for the soundness of their principles and for the justice of their views have declared in favour of a single Executive and a numerous legislature. They have, with great propriety, considered energy as the most necessary qualification of the former, and have regarded this as most applicable to power in a single hand; while they have, with equal propriety, considered the latter as best adapted to deliberation and wisdom, and best calculated to conciliate the confidence of the people and to secure their privileges and interests.

That unity is conducive to energy will not be disputed. Decision, activity, secrecy, and despatch will generally characterise the proceedings of one man in a much more eminent degree than the proceedings of any greater number; and in proportion as the number is increased, these qualities will be diminished.

This unity may be destroyed in two ways: either by vesting the power in two or more magistrates of equal dignity and authority; or by vesting it ostensibly in one man, subject, in whole or in part, to the control and co-operation of others in the capacity of counsellors to him. Of the first, the two Consuls of Rome may serve as an example; of the last, we shall find examples in the constitutions of several of the States. New York and New Jersey, if I recollect right, are the only States which have intrusted the executive authority wholly to single men.[1] Both these methods of destroying the unity of the Executive have their partisans; but the votaries of an executive council are the most numerous. They are both liable, if not to equal, to similar objections, and may in most lights be examined in conjunction.

The experience of other nations will afford little instruction on this head. As far, however, as it teaches anything, it teaches us not to be enamoured of plurality in the Executive. We have seen that the Achæans, on an experiment

[1] New York has no council except for the single purpose of appointing to offices; New Jersey has a council whom the governor may consult. But I think, from the terms of the constitution, their resolutions do not bind him.—PUBLIUS

of two Prætors, were induced to abolish one. The Roman history records many instances of mischiefs to the republic from the dissensions between the Consuls, and between the military Tribunes, who were at times substituted for the Consuls. But it gives us no specimens of any peculiar advantages derived to the state from the circumstance of the plurality of those magistrates. That the dissensions between them were not more frequent or more fatal is matter of astonishment, until we advert to the singular position in which the republic was almost continually placed, and to the prudent policy pointed out by the circumstances of the state, and pursued by the Consuls, of making a division of the government between them. The patricians engaged in a perpetual struggle with the plebeians for the preservation of their ancient authorities and dignities; the Consuls, who were generally chosen out of the former body, were commonly united by the personal interest they had in the defence of the privileges of their order. In addition to this motive of union, after the arms of the republic had considerably expanded the bounds of its empire, it became an established custom with the Consuls to divide the administration between themselves by lot—one of them remaining at Rome to govern the city and its environs, the other taking the command in the more distant provinces. This expedient must, no doubt, have had great influence in preventing those collisions and rivalships which might otherwise have embroiled the peace of the republic.

But quitting the dim light of historical research, attaching ourselves purely to the dictates of reason and good sense, we shall discover much greater cause to reject than to approve the idea of plurality in the Executive, under any modification whatever.

Wherever two or more persons are engaged in any common enterprise or pursuit there is always danger of difference of opinion. If it be a public trust or office, in which they are clothed with equal dignity and authority, there is peculiar danger of personal emulation and even animosity. From either, and especially from all these causes, the most bitter dissensions are apt to spring. Whenever these happen, they lessen the respectability, weaken the authority, and distract the plans and operations of those whom they divide. If they should unfortunately assail the supreme executive magistracy of a country, consisting of a plurality of persons, they might impede or frustrate the most important measures of the government in the most critical emergencies of the state. And what is still worse, they might split the community into the most violent and irreconcilable factions, adhering differently to the different individuals who composed the magistracy.

Men often oppose a thing, merely because they have had no agency in planning it, or because it may have been planned by those whom they dislike. But if they have been consulted, and have happened to disapprove, opposition then becomes, in their estimation, an indispensable duty of self-love. They seem to think themselves bound in honour, and by all the motives of personal infallibility, to defeat the success of what has been resolved upon contrary to their sentiments. Men of upright, benevolent tempers have too many opportunities of remarking, with horror, to what desperate lengths this disposition is sometimes carried, and how often the great interests of society are sacrificed to the vanity, to the conceit, and to the obstinacy of individuals who have credit enough to make their passions and their caprices interesting to mankind. Perhaps the question now before the public may, in its consequences, afford melancholy proofs of the effects of this despicable frailty, or rather detestable vice, in the human character.

Upon the principles of a free government inconveniences from the source just mentioned must necessarily be submitted to in the formation of the legislature; but it is unnecessary, and therefore unwise, to introduce them into the constitution of the Executive. It is here, too, that they may be most pernicious. In the legislature, promptitude of decision is oftener an evil than a benefit. The differences of opinion, and the jarrings of parties in that department of the government, though they may sometimes obstruct salutary plans, yet often promote deliberation and circumspection, and serve to check excesses in the majority. When a resolution, too, is once taken, the opposition must be at an end. That resolution is a law, and resistance to it punishable. But no favourable circumstances palliate or atone for the disadvantages of dissension in the executive department. Here they are pure and unmixed. There is no point at which they cease to operate. They serve to embarrass and weaken the execution of the plan or measure to which they relate, from the first step to the final conclusion of it. They constantly counteract those qualities in the Executive which are the most necessary ingredients in its composition—vig-

our and expedition, and this without any counterbalancing good. In the conduct of war, in which the energy of the Executive is the bulwark of the national security, everything would be to be apprehended from its plurality.

It must be confessed that these observations apply with principal weight to the first case supposed—that is, to a plurality of magistrates of equal dignity and authority, a scheme the advocates for which are not likely to form a numerous sect; but they apply, though not with equal, yet with considerable weight to the project of a council, whose concurrence is made constitutionally necessary to the operations of the ostensible Executive. An artful cabal in that council would be able to distract and to enervate the whole system of administration. If no such cabal should exist, the mere diversity of views and opinions would alone be sufficient to tincture the exercise of the executive authority with a spirit of habitual feebleness and dilatoriness.

But one of the weightiest objections to a plurality in the Executive, and which lies as much against the last as the first plan, is that it tends to conceal faults and destroy responsibility. Responsibility is of two kinds—to censure and to punishment. The first is the more important of the two, especially in an elective office. Man, in public trust, will much oftener act in such a manner as to render him unworthy of being any longer trusted than in such a manner as to make him obnoxious to legal punishment. But the multiplication of the Executive adds to the difficulty of detection in either case. It often becomes impossible, amidst mutual accusations, to determine on whom the blame or the punishment of a pernicious measure, or series of pernicious measures, ought really to fall. It is shifted from one to another with so much dexterity, and under such plausible appearances, that the public opinion is left in suspense about the real author. The circumstances which may have led to any national miscarriage or misfortune are sometimes so complicated that, where there are a number of actors who may have had different degrees and kinds of agency, though we may clearly see upon the whole that there has been mismanagement, yet it may be impracticable to pronounce to whose account the evil which may have been incurred is truly chargeable.

"I was overruled by my council. The council were so divided in their opinions that it was impossible to obtain any better resolution on the point." These and similar pretexts are constantly at hand, whether true or false. And who is there that will either take the trouble or incur the odium of a strict scrutiny into the secret springs of the transaction? Should there be found a citizen zealous enough to undertake the unpromising task, if there happen to be collusion between the parties concerned, how easy it is to clothe the circumstances with so much ambiguity as to render it uncertain what was the precise conduct of any of those parties?

In the single instance in which the governor of this State is coupled with a council—that is, in the appointment to offices, we have seen the mischiefs of it in the view now under consideration. Scandalous appointments to important offices have been made. Some cases, indeed, have been so flagrant that ALL PARTIES have agreed in the impropriety of the thing. When inquiry has been made, the blame has been laid by the governor on the members of the council, who, on their part, have charged it upon his nomination; while the people remain altogether at a loss to determine by whose influence their interests have been committed to hands so unqualified and so manifestly improper. In tenderness to individuals, I forbear to descend to particulars.

It is evident from these considerations that the plurality of the Executive tends to deprive the people of the two greatest securities they can have for the faithful exercise of any delegated power: *first,* the restraints of public opinion, which lose their efficacy, as well on account of the division of the censure attendant on bad measures among a number as on account of the uncertainty on whom it ought to fall; and, *secondly,* the opportunity of discovering with facility and clearness the misconduct of the persons they trust, in order either to [effect] their removal from office or their actual punishment in cases which admit of it.

In England, the king is a perpetual magistrate; and it is a maxim which has obtained for the sake of the public peace, that he is unaccountable for his administration, and his person sacred. Nothing, therefore, can be wiser in that kingdom, than to annex to the king a constitutional council, who may be responsible to the nation for the advice they give. Without this, there would be no responsibility whatever in the executive department—an idea inadmissible in a free government. But even there the king is not bound by the resolutions of his council, though they are answerable for the advice they give. He is the absolute master of his own conduct in the exercise of his office, and may observe or disregard the counsel given to him at his sole discretion.

But in a republic, where every magistrate ought to be personally responsible for his behaviour in office, the reason which in the British Constitution dictates the propriety of a council, not only ceases to apply, but turns against the institution. In the monarchy of Great Britain, it furnishes a substitute for the prohibited responsibility of the chief magistrate, which serves in some degree as a hostage to the national justice for his good behaviour. In the American republic it would serve to destroy, or would greatly diminish, the intended and necessary responsibility of the Chief Magistrate himself.

The idea of a council to the Executive, which has so generally obtained in the State constitutions, has been derived from that maxim of republican jealousy which considers power as safer in the hands of a number of men than of a single man. If the maxim should be admitted to be applicable to the case, I should contend that the advantage on that side would not counterbalance the numerous disadvantages on the opposite side. But I do not think the rule at all applicable to the executive power. I clearly concur in opinion, in this particular, with a writer whom the celebrated Junius pronounces to be "deep, solid, and ingenious," that "the executive power is more easily confined when it is ONE";[1] that it is far more safe there should be a single object for the jealousy and watchfulness of the people; and, in a word, that all multiplication of the Executive is rather dangerous than friendly to liberty.

A little consideration will satisfy us that the species of security sought for in the multiplication of the EXECUTIVE is unattainable. Numbers must be so great as to render combination difficult, or they are rather a source of danger than of security. The united credit and influence of several individuals must be more formidable to liberty than the credit and influence of either of them separately. When power, therefore, is placed in the hands of so small a number of men as to admit of their interests and views being easily combined in a common enterprise, by an artful leader it becomes more liable to abuse, and more dangerous when abused, than if it be lodged in the hands of one man; who, from the very circumstance of his

[1] De Lolme.—PUBLIUS

being alone, will be more narrowly watched and more readily suspected, and who cannot unite so great a mass of influence as when he is associated with others. The Decemvirs of Rome, whose name denotes their number,[1] were more to be dreaded, in their usurpation than any ONE of them would have been. No person would think of proposing an Executive much more numerous than that body; from six to a dozen have been suggested for the number of the council. The extreme of these numbers is not too great for an easy combination; and from such a combination America would have more to fear than from the ambition of any single individual. A council to a magistrate, who is himself responsible for what he does, are generally nothing better than a clog upon his good intentions, are often the instruments and accomplices of his bad, and are almost always a cloak to his faults.

I forbear to dwell upon the subject of expense; though it be evident that if the council should be numerous enough to answer the principal end aimed at by the institution, the salaries of the members, who must be drawn from their homes to reside at the seat of government, would form an item in the catalogue of public expenditures too serious to be incurred for an object of equivocal utility. I will only add that, prior to the appearance of the Constitution, I rarely met with an intelligent man from any of the States, who did not admit, as the result of experience, that the UNITY of the executive of this State was one of the best of the distinguishing features of our constitution.   PUBLIUS

Number 71

[HAMILTON]

DURATION IN office has been mentioned as the second requisite to the energy of the Executive authority. This has relation to two objects: to the personal firmness of the executive magistrate in the employment of his constitutional powers; and to the stability of the system of administration which may have been adopted under his auspices. With regard to the first, it must be evident that the longer the duration in office, the greater will be the probability of obtaining so important an advantage. It is a general principle of human nature that a man will be interested in whatever he possesses, in proportion to the firmness or precariousness of the tenure by which he holds it;

[1] Ten.—PUBLIUS

will be less attached to what he holds by a momentary or uncertain title than to what he enjoys by a durable or certain title; and, of course, will be willing to risk more for the sake of the one than for the sake of the other. This remark is not less applicable to a political privilege, or honour, or trust, than to any article of ordinary property. The inference from it is that a man acting in the capacity of chief magistrate, under a consciousness that in a very short time he *must* lay down his office, will be apt to feel himself too little interested in it to hazard any material censure or perplexity, from the independent exertion of his powers, or from encountering the ill-humours, however transient, which may happen to prevail, either in a considerable part of the society itself, or even in a predominant faction in the legislative body. If the case should only be that he *might* lay it down, unless continued by a new choice, and if he should be desirous of being continued, his wishes, conspiring with his fears, would tend still more powerfully to corrupt his integrity, or debase his fortitude. In either case, feebleness and irresolution must be the characteristics of the station.

There are some who would be inclined to regard the servile pliancy of the Executive to a prevailing current, either in the community or in the legislature, as its best recommendation. But such men entertain very crude notions, as well of the purposes for which government was instituted as of the true means by which the public happiness may be promoted. The republican principle demands that the deliberate sense of the community should govern the conduct of those to whom they intrust the management of their affairs; but it does not require an unqualified complaisance to every sudden breeze of passion, or to every transient impulse which the people may receive from the arts of men, who flatter their prejudices to betray their interests. It is a just observation that the people commonly *intend* the PUBLIC GOOD. This often applies to their very errors. But their good sense would despise the adulator who should pretend that they always *reason right* about the *means* of promoting it. They know from experience that they sometimes err; and the wonder is that they so seldom err as they do, beset, as they continually are, by the wiles of parasites and sycophants, by the snares of the ambitious, the avaricious, the desperate, by the artifices of men who possess their confidence more than they deserve it, and of those who seek to possess rather than to deserve it. When occasions present themselves, in which the interests of the people are at variance with their inclinations, it is the duty of the persons whom they have appointed to be the guardians of those interests, to withstand the temporary delusion, in order to give them time and opportunity for more cool and sedate reflection. Instances might be cited in which a conduct of this kind has saved the people from very fatal consequences of their own mistakes, and has procured lasting monuments of their gratitude to the men who had courage and magnanimity enough to serve them at the peril of their displeasure.

But however inclined we might be to insist upon an unbounded complaisance in the Executive to the inclinations of the people, we can with no propriety contend for a like complaisance to the humour of the legislature. The latter may sometimes stand in opposition to the former, and at other times the people may be entirely neutral. In either supposition, it is certainly desirable that the Executive should be in a situation to dare to act his own opinion with vigour and decision.

The same rule which teaches the propriety of a partition between the various branches of power, teaches us likewise that this partition ought to be so contrived as to render the one independent of the other. To what purpose separate the executive or the judiciary from the legislative, if both the executive and the judiciary are so constituted as to be at the absolute devotion of the legislative? Such a separation must be merely nominal, and incapable of producing the ends for which it was established. It is one thing to be subordinate to the laws, and another to be dependent on the legislative body. The first comports with, the last violates, the fundamental principles of good government; and, whatever may be the forms of the Constitution, unites all power in the same hands. The tendency of the legislative authority to absorb every other, has been fully displayed and illustrated by examples in some preceding numbers. In governments purely republican, this tendency is almost irresistible. The representatives of the people, in a popular assembly, seem sometimes to fancy that they are the people themselves, and betray strong symptoms of impatience and disgust at the least sign of opposition from any other quarter; as if the exercise of its rights, by either the executive or judiciary, were a breach of their privilege and an outrage to their dignity.

They often appear disposed to exert an imperious control over the other departments; and as they commonly have the people on their side, they always act with such momentum as to make it very difficult for the other members of the government to maintain the balance of the Constitution.

It may perhaps be asked, how the shortness of the duration in office can affect the independence of the Executive on the legislature, unless the one were possessed of the power of appointing or displacing the other. One answer to this inquiry may be drawn from the principle already remarked—that is, from the slender interest a man is apt to take in a short-lived advantage, and the little inducement it affords him to expose himself, on account of it, to any considerable inconvenience or hazard. Another answer, perhaps more obvious, though not more conclusive, will result from the consideration of the influence of the legislative body over the people; which might be employed to prevent the re-election of a man who, by an upright resistance to any sinister project of that body, should have made himself obnoxious to its resentment.

It may be asked also, whether a duration of four years would answer the end proposed; and if it would not, whether a less period, which would at least be recommended by greater security against ambitious designs, would not, for that reason, be preferable to a longer period, which was, at the same time, too short for the purpose of inspiring the desired firmness and independence of the magistrate.

It cannot be affirmed that a duration of four years, or any other limited duration, would completely answer the end proposed; but it would contribute towards it in a degree which would have a material influence upon the spirit and character of the government. Between the commencement and termination of such a period there would always be a considerable interval in which the prospect of annihilation would be sufficiently remote not to have an improper effect upon the conduct of a man indued with a tolerable portion of fortitude; and in which he might reasonably promise himself that there would be time enough before it arrived to make the community sensible of the propriety of the measures he might incline to pursue. Though it be probable that, as he approached the moment when the public were, by a new election, to signify their sense of his conduct, his confidence, and with it his firmness, would decline; yet both the one and the other would derive support from the opportunities which his previous continuance in the station had afforded him, of establishing himself in the esteem and good-will of his constituents. He might, then, hazard with safety, in proportion to the proofs he had given to his wisdom and integrity, and to the title he had acquired to the respect and attachment of his fellow-citizens. As, on the one hand, a duration of four years will contribute to the firmness of the Executive in a sufficient degree to render it a very valuable ingredient in the composition; so, on the other, it is not enough to justify any alarm for the public liberty. If a British House of Commons, from the most feeble beginnings, *from the mere power of assenting or disagreeing to the imposition of a new tax,* have, by rapid strides, reduced the prerogatives of the crown and the privileges of the nobility within the limits they conceived to be compatible with the principles of a free government, while they raised themselves to the rank and consequence of a co-equal branch of the legislature; if they have been able, in one instance, to abolish both the royalty and the aristocracy, and to overturn all the ancient establishments, as well in the Church as State; if they have been able, on a recent occasion, to make the monarch tremble at the prospect of an innovation[1] attempted by them, what would be to be feared from an elective magistrate of four years' duration, with the confined authorities of a President of the United States? What, but that he might be unequal to the task which the Constitutions assign him? I shall only add, that if his duration be such as to leave a doubt of his firmness, that doubt is inconsistent with a jealousy of his encroachments.   PUBLIUS

Number 72

[HAMILTON]

THE ADMINISTRATION of government, in its largest sense, comprehends all the operations of the body politic, whether legislative, or judiciary; but in its most usual and perhaps in its most precise signification, it is limited to executive details, and falls peculiarly within the province of the executive department. The actual conduct of foreign negotiations, the

[1] This was the case with respect to Mr. Fox's India bill, which was carried in the House of Commons, and rejected in the House of Lords, to the entire satisfaction, as it is said, of the people. —PUBLIUS

preparatory plans of finance, the application and disbursement of the public money in conformity to the general appropriations of the legislature, the arrangement of the army and navy, the direction of the operations of war,—these, and other matters of a like nature, constitute what seems to be most properly understood by the administration of government. The persons, therefore, to whose immediate management these different matters are committed, ought to be considered as the assistants or deputies of the chief magistrate, and on this account they ought to derive their offices from his appointment, at least from his nomination, and ought to be subject to his superintendence. This view of the subject will at once suggest to us the intimate connection between the duration of the executive magistrate in office and the stability of the system of administration. To reverse and undo what has been done by a predecessor is very often considered by a successor as the best proof he can give of his own capacity and desert; and in addition to this propensity, where the alteration has been the result of public choice, the person substituted is warranted in supposing that the dismission of his predecessor has proceeded from a dislike to his measures; and that the less he resembles him the more he will recommend himself to the favour of his constituents. These considerations, and the influence of personal confidences and attachments, would be likely to induce every new President to promote a change of men to fill the subordinate stations; and these causes together could not fail to occasion a disgraceful and ruinous mutability in the administration of the government.

With a positive duration of considerable extent, I connect the circumstance of re-eligibility. The first is necessary to give to the officer himself the inclination and the resolution to act his part well, and to the community time and leisure to observe the tendency of his measures, and thence to form an experimental estimate of their merits. The last is necessary to enable the people, when they see reason to approve of his conduct, to continue him in his station, in order to prolong the utility of his talents and virtues, and to secure to the government the advantage of permanency in a wise system of administration.

Nothing appears more plausible at first sight, nor more ill-founded upon close inspection, than a scheme which in relation to the present point has had some respectable advocates,—I mean that of continuing the chief magistrate in office for a certain time, and then excluding him from it, either for a limited period or for ever after. This exclusion, whether temporary or perpetual, would have nearly the same effects, and these effects would be for the most part rather pernicious than salutary.

One ill effect of the exclusion would be a diminution of the inducements to good behaviour. There are few men who would not feel much less zeal in the discharge of a duty, when they were conscious that the advantages of the station with which it was connected must be relinquished at a determinate period, than when they were permitted to entertain a hope of *obtaining*, by *meriting*, a continuance of them. This position will not be disputed so long as it is admitted that the desire of reward is one of the strongest incentives of human conduct; or that the best security for the fidelity of mankind is to make their interest coincide with their duty. Even the love of fame, the ruling passion of the noblest minds, which would prompt a man to plan and undertake extensive and arduous enterprises for the public benefit, requiring considerable time to mature and perfect them, if he could flatter himself with the prospect of being allowed to finish what he had begun, would, on the contrary, deter him from the undertaking, when he foresaw that he must quit the scene before he could accomplish the work, and must commit that, together with his own reputation, to hands which might be unequal or unfriendly to the task. The most to be expected from the generality of men, in such a situation, is the negative merit of not doing harm, instead of the positive merit of doing good.

Another ill effect of the exclusion would be the temptation to sordid views, to peculation, and, in some instances, to usurpation. An avaricious man, who might happen to fill the office, looking forward to a time when he must at all events yield up the emoluments he enjoyed, would feel a propensity, not easy to be resisted by such a man, to make the best use of the opportunity he enjoyed while it lasted, and might not scruple to have recourse to the most corrupt expedients to make the harvest as abundant as it was transitory; though the same man, probably, with a different prospect before him, might content himself with the regular perquisites of his situation, and might even be unwilling to risk the consequences of an abuse of his opportunities. His avarice might be a guard upon his avarice. Add to this that the same man might be vain or ambitious, as well

as avaricious. And if he could expect to prolong his honours by his good conduct, he might hesitate to sacrifice his appetite for them to his appetite for gain. But with the prospect before him of approaching an inevitable annihilation, his avarice would be likely to get the victory over his caution, his vanity, or his ambition.

An ambitious man, too, when he found himself seated on the summit of his country's honours, when he looked forward to the time at which he must descend from the exalted eminence for ever, and reflected that no exertion of merit on his part could save him from the unwelcome reverse; such a man, in such a situation, would be much more violently tempted to embrace a favourable conjuncture for attempting the prolongation of his power, at every personal hazard, than if he had the probability of answering the same end by doing his duty.

Would it promote the peace of the community or the stability of the government to have half a dozen men who had had credit enough to be raised to the seat of the supreme magistracy, wandering among the people like discontented ghosts, and sighing for a place which they were destined never more to possess?

A third ill effect of the exclusion would be the depriving the community of the advantage of the experience gained by the chief magistrate in the exercise of his office. That experience is the parent of wisdom is an adage the truth of which is recognised by the wisest as well as the simplest of mankind. What more desirable or more essential than this quality in the governors of nations? Where more desirable or more essential than in the first magistrate of a nation? Can it be wise to put this desirable and essential quality under the ban of the Constitution, and to declare that the moment it is acquired its possessor shall be compelled to abandon the station in which it was acquired, and to which it is adapted? This, nevertheless, is the precise import of all those regulations which exclude men from serving their country, by the choice of their fellow-citizens, after they have by a course of service fitted themselves for doing it with a greater degree of utility.

A fourth ill effect of the exclusion would be the banishing men from stations in which, in certain emergencies of the state, their presence might be of the greatest moment to the public interest or safety. There is no nation which has not, at one period or another, experienced an absolute necessity of the services of particular men in particular situations; perhaps it would not be too strong to say, to the preservation of its political existence. How unwise, therefore, must be every such self-denying ordinance as serves to prohibit a nation from making use of its own citizens in the manner best suited to its exigencies and circumstances! Without supposing the personal essentiality of the man, it is evident that a change of the chief magistrate, at the breaking out of a war, or at any similar crisis, for another, even of equal merit, would at all times be detrimental to the community, inasmuch as it would substitute inexperience to experience, and would tend to unhinge and set afloat the already settled train of the administration.

A fifth ill effect of the exclusion would be, that it would operate as a constitutional interdiction of stability in the administration. By *necessitating* a change of men, in the first office of the nation, it would necessitate a mutability of measures. It is not generally to be expected that men will vary and measures remain uniform. The contrary is the usual course of things. And we need not be apprehensive that there will be too much stability while there is even the option of changing; nor need we desire to prohibit the people from continuing their confidence where they think it may be safely placed, and where, by constancy on their part, they may obviate the fatal inconveniences of fluctuating councils and a variable policy.

These are some of the disadvantages which would flow from the principle of exclusion. They apply most forcibly to the scheme of a perpetual exclusion; but when we consider that even a partial exclusion would always render the readmission of the person a remote and precarious object, the observations which have been made will apply nearly as fully to one case as to the other.

What are the advantages promised to counterbalance these disadvantages? They are represented to be: 1st, greater independence in the magistrate; 2nd, greater security to the people. Unless the exclusion be perpetual, there will be no pretence to infer the first advantage. But even in that case, may he have no object beyond his present station, to which he may sacrifice his independence? May he have no connections, no friends, for whom he may sacrifice it? May he not be less willing, by a firm conduct, to make personal enemies,

when he acts under the impression that a time is fast approaching on the arrival of which he not only MAY, but MUST, be exposed to their resentments, upon an equal, perhaps upon an inferior, footing? It is not an easy point to determine whether his independence would be most promoted or impaired by such an arrangement.

As to the second supposed advantage, there is still greater reason to entertain doubts concerning it. If the exclusion were to be perpetual, a man of irregular ambition, of whom alone there could be reason in any case to entertain apprehension, would, with infinite reluctance, yield to the necessity of taking his leave for ever of a post in which his passion for power and pre-eminence had acquired the force of habit. And if he had been fortunate or adroit enough to conciliate the good-will of the people, he might induce them to consider as a very odious and unjustifiable restraint upon themselves, a provision which was calculated to debar them of the right of giving a fresh proof of their attachment to a favourite. There may be conceived circumstances in which this disgust of the people, seconding the thwarted ambition of such a favourite, might occasion greater danger to liberty than could ever reasonably be dreaded from the possibility of a perpetuation in office, by the voluntary suffrages of the community, exercising a constitutional privilege.

There is an excess of refinement in the idea of disabling the people to continue in office men who had entitled themselves, in their opinion, to approbation and confidence; the advantages of which are at best speculative and equivocal, and are overbalanced by disadvantages far more certain and decisive.

PUBLIUS

Number 73

[HAMILTON]

THE THIRD ingredient towards constituting the vigour of the executive authority is an adequate provision for its support. It is evident that, without proper attention to this article, the separation of the executive from the legislative department would be merely nominal and nugatory. The legislature, with a discretionary power over the salary and emoluments of the Chief Magistrate, could render him as obsequious to their will as they might think proper to make him. They might, in most cases, either reduce him by famine, or tempt him by largesses, to surrender at discretion his judgment to their inclinations. These expressions, taken in all the latitude of the terms, would no doubt convey more than is intended. There are men who could neither be distressed nor won into a sacrifice of their duty; but this stern virtue is the growth of few soils; and in the main it will be found that a power over a man's support is a power over his will. If it were necessary to confirm so plain a truth by facts, examples would not be wanting, even in this country, of the intimidation or seduction of the Executive by the terrors or allurements of the pecuniary arrangements of the legislative body.

It is not easy, therefore, to commend too highly the judicious attention which has been paid to this subject in the proposed Constitution. It is there provided that "The President of the United States shall, at stated times, receive for his service a compensation *which shall neither be increased nor diminished during the period for which he shall have been elected;* and he *shall not receive within that period any other emolument* from the United States, or any of them." It is impossible to imagine any provision which would have been more eligible than this. The legislature, on the appointment of a President, is once for all to declare what shall be the compensation for his services during the time for which he shall have been elected. This done, they will have no power to alter it, either by increase or diminution, till a new period of service by a new election commences. They can neither weaken his fortitude by operating on his necessities, nor corrupt his integrity by appealing to his avarice. Neither the Union, nor any of its members, will be at liberty to give, nor will he be at liberty to receive, any other emolument than that which may have been determined by the first act. He can, of course, have no pecuniary inducement to renounce or desert the independence intended for him by the Constitution.

The last of the requisites to energy, which have been enumerated, are competent powers. Let us proceed to consider those which are proposed to be vested in the President of the United States.

The first thing that offers itself to our observation is the qualified negative of the President upon the acts or resolutions of the two houses of the legislature; or, in other words, his power of returning all bills with objections, to have the effect of preventing their becoming laws, unless they should afterwards be ratified by two thirds of each of the component members of the legislative body.

The propensity of the legislative department to intrude upon the rights, and to absorb the powers, of the other departments, has been already suggested and repeated; the insufficiency of a mere parchment delineation of the boundaries of each, has also been remarked upon; and the necessity of furnishing each with constitutional arms for its own defence has been inferred and proved. From these clear and indubitable principles results the propriety of a negative, either absolute or qualified, in the Executive, upon the acts of the legislative branches. Without the one or the other, the former would be absolutely unable to defend himself against the depredations of the latter. He might gradually be stripped of his authorities by successive resolutions, or annihilated by a single vote. And in the one mode or the other, the legislative and executive powers might speedily come to be blended in the same hands. If even no propensity had ever discovered itself in the legislative body to invade the rights of the Executive, the rules of just reasoning and theoretic propriety would of themselves teach us that the one ought not to be left to the mercy of the other, but ought to possess a constitutional and effectual power of self-defence.

But the power in question has a further use. It not only serves as a shield to the Executive, but it furnishes an additional security against the enaction of improper laws. It establishes a salutary check upon the legislative body, calculated to guard the community against the effects of faction, precipitancy, or of any impulse unfriendly to the public good, which may happen to influence a majority of that body.

The propriety of a negative has, upon some occasions, been combated by an observation, that it was not to be presumed a single man would possess more virtue and wisdom than a number of men; and that unless this presumption should be entertained, it would be improper to give the executive magistrate any species of control over the legislative body.

But this observation, when examined, will appear rather specious than solid. The propriety of the thing does not turn upon the supposition of superior wisdom or virtue in the Executive, but upon the supposition that the legislature will not be infallible; that the love of power may sometimes betray it into a disposition to encroach upon the rights of other members of the government; that a spirit of faction may sometimes pervert its deliberations; that impressions of the moment may sometimes hurry it into measures which itself, on maturer reflection, would condemn. The primary inducement to conferring the power in question upon the Executive is, to enable him to defend himself; the secondary one is to increase the chances in favour of the community against the passing of bad laws, through haste, inadvertence, or design. The oftener the measure is brought under examination, the greater the diversity in the situations of those who are to examine it, the less must be the danger of those errors which flow from want of due deliberation, or of those missteps which proceed from the contagion of some common passion or interest. It is far less probable that culpable views of any kind should infect all the parts of the government at the same moment and in relation to the same object, than that they should by turns govern and mislead every one of them.

It may perhaps be said that the power of preventing bad laws includes that of preventing good ones; and may be used to the one purpose as well as to the other. But this objection will have little weight with those who can properly estimate the mischiefs of that inconstancy and mutability in the laws which form the greatest blemish in the character and genius of our governments. They will consider every institution calculated to restrain the excess of law-making, and to keep things in the same state in which they happen to be at any given period, as much more likely to do good than harm; because it is favourable to greater stability in the system of legislation. The injury which may possibly be done by defeating a few good laws will be amply compensated by the advantage of preventing a number of bad ones.

Nor is this all. The superior weight and influence of the legislative body in a free government, and the hazard to the Executive in a trial of strength with that body, afford a satisfactory security that the negative would generally be employed with great caution; and there would oftener be room for a charge of timidity than of rashness in the exercise of it. A king of Great Britain, with all his train of sovereign attributes, and with all the influence he draws from a thousand sources, would, at this day, hesitate to put a negative upon the joint resolutions of the two houses of Parliament. He would not fail to exert the utmost resources of that influence to strangle a measure disagreeable to him, in its progress to the throne, to avoid being reduced to the dilemma of permitting it to take effect, or of risking the displeasure of the nation by an opposition to the sense of the legislative body. Nor is it probable that he would ultimately venture to exert his prerogatives, but in a case of manifest propriety or extreme necessity. All well-informed men in that kingdom will accede to the justness of this remark. A very considerable period has elapsed since the negative of the crown has been exercised.

If a magistrate so powerful and so well fortified as a British monarch would have scruples about the exercise of the power under consideration, how much greater caution may be reasonably expected in a President of the United States, clothed for the short period of four years with the executive authority of a government wholly and purely republican?

It is evident that there would be greater danger of his not using his power when necessary than of his using it too often, or too much. An argument, indeed, against its expediency has been drawn from this very source. It has been represented, on this account, as a power odious in appearance, useless in practice. But it will not follow that because it might be rarely exercised it would never be exercised. In the case for which it is chiefly designed, that of an immediate attack upon the constitutional rights of the Executive, or in a case in which the public good was evidently and palpably sacrificed, a man of tolerable firmness would avail himself of his constitutional means of defence, and would listen to the admonitions of duty and responsibility. In the former supposition, his fortitude would be stimulated by his immediate interest in the power of his office; in the latter, by the probability of the sanction of his constituents, who, though they would naturally incline to the legislative body in a doubtful case, would hardly suffer their partiality to delude them in a very plain case. I speak now with an eye to a magistrate possessing only a common share of firmness. There are men who, under any circumstances, will have the courage to do their duty at every hazard.

But the convention have pursued a mean in this business which will both facilitate the exercise of the power vested in this respect in the executive magistrate, and make its efficacy to depend on the sense of a considerable part of the legislative body. Instead of an absolute negative, it is proposed to give the Executive the qualified negative already described. This is a power which would be much more readily exercised than the other. A man who might be afraid to defeat a law by his single VETO, might not scruple to return it for reconsideration; subject to being finally rejected only in the event of more than one third of each house concurring in the sufficiency of his objections. He would be encouraged by the reflection that if his opposition should prevail it would embark in it a very respectable proportion of the legislative body whose influence would be united with his in supporting the propriety of his conduct in the public opinion. A direct and categorical negative has something in the appearance of it more harsh, and more apt to irritate, than the mere suggestion of argumentative objections to be approved or disapproved by those to whom they are addressed. In proportion as it would be less apt to offend, it would be more apt to be exercised; and for this very reason it may in practice be found more effectual. It is to be hoped that it will not often happen that improper views will govern so large a proportion as two thirds of both branches of the legislature at the same time; and this, too, in spite of the counterposing weight of the Executive. It is at any rate far less probable that this should be the case than that such views should taint the resolutions and conduct of a bare majority. A power of this nature in the Executive will often have a silent and unperceived, though forcible, operation. When men, engaged in unjustifiable pursuits, are aware that obstructions may come from a quarter which they cannot control, they will often be restrained by the bare apprehension of opposition from doing what they would with eagerness rush into, if no such external impediments were to be feared.

This qualified negative, as has been elsewhere remarked, is in this State vested in a council, consisting of the governor, with the chancellor and judges of the Supreme Court, or any two of them. It has been freely employed upon a variety of occasions, and frequently with success. And its utility has become so apparent that persons who, in compiling the Constitution, were violent opposers of it, have from experience become its declared admirers.[1]

[1] Mr. Abraham Yates, a warm opponent of the plan of the convention, is of this number.— PUBLIUS

I have in another place remarked that the convention, in the formation of this part of their plan, had departed from the model of the constitution of this State in favour of that of Massachusetts. Two strong reasons may be imagined for this preference. One is that the judges, who are to be the interpreters of the law, might receive an improper bias, from having given a previous opinion in their revisionary capacities; the other is, that by being often associated with the Executive, they might be induced to embark too far in the political views of that magistrate, and thus a dangerous combination might by degrees be cemented between the executive and judiciary departments. It is impossible to keep the judges too distinct from every other avocation than that of expounding the laws. It is peculiarly dangerous to place them in a situation to be either corrupted or influenced by the Executive.   PUBLIUS

Number 74

[HAMILTON]

THE PRESIDENT of the United States is to be "commander-in-chief of the army and navy of the United States, and of the militia of the several States *when called into the actual service* of the United States." The propriety of this provision is so evident in itself, and it is, at the same time, so consonant to the precedents of the State constitutions in general, that little need be said to explain or enforce it. Even those of them which have, in other respects, coupled the chief magistrate with a council, have for the most part concentrated the military authority in him alone. Of all the cares or concerns of government, the direction of war most peculiarly demands those qualities which distinguish the exercise of power by a single hand. The direction of war implies the direction of the common strength; and the power of directing and employing the common strength forms a usual and essential part in the definition of the executive authority.

"The President may require the opinion, in writing, of the principal officer in each of the executive departments, upon any subject relating to the duties of their respective officers." This I consider as a mere redundancy in the plan, as the right for which it provides would result of itself from the office.

He is also to be authorised to grant "reprieves and pardons for offences against the United States, *except in cases of impeach-*

ment." Humanity and good policy conspire to dictate that the benign prerogative of pardoning should be as little as possible fettered or embarrassed. The criminal code of every country partakes so much of necessary severity that without an easy access to exceptions in favour of unfortunate guilt, justice would wear a countenance too sanguinary and cruel. As the sense of responsibility is always strongest, in proportion as it is undivided, it may be inferred that a single man would be most ready to attend to the force of those motives which might plead for a mitigation of the rigour of the law, and least apt to yield to considerations which were calculated to shelter a fit object of its vengeance. The reflection that the fate of a fellow-creature depended on his *sole fiat* would naturally inspire scrupulousness and caution; the dread of being accused of weakness or connivance, would beget equal circumspection, though of a different kind. On the other hand, as men generally derive confidence from their numbers, they might often encourage each other in an act of obduracy, and might be less sensible to the apprehension of suspicion or censure for an injudicious or affected clemency. On these accounts, one man appears to be a more eligible dispenser of the mercy of government than a body of men.

The expediency of vesting the power of pardoning in the President has, if I mistake not, been only contested in relation to the crime of treason. This, it has been urged, ought to have depended upon the assent of one, or both, of the branches of the legislative body. I shall not deny that there are strong reasons to be assigned for requiring in this particular the concurrence of that body, or of a part of it. As treason is a crime levelled at the immediate being of the society, when the laws have once ascertained the guilt of the offender, there seems a fitness in referring the expediency of an act of mercy towards him to the judgment of the legislature. And this ought the rather to be the case, as the supposition of the connivance of the Chief Magistrate ought not to be entirely excluded. But there are also strong objections to such a plan. It is not to be doubted that a single man of prudence and good sense is better fitted, in delicate conjunctures, to balance the motives which may plead for and against the remission of the punishment, than any numerous body whatever. It deserves particular attention, that treason will often be connected with seditions which embrace a large proportion of the community; as

lately happened in Massachusetts. In every such case, we might expect to see the representation of the people tainted with the same spirit which had given birth to the offence. And when parties were pretty equally matched, the secret sympathy of the friends and favourers of the condemned person, availing itself of the good nature and weakness of others, might frequently bestow impunity where the terror of an example was necessary. On the other hand, when the sedition had proceeded from causes which had inflamed the resentments of the major party, they might often be found obstinate and inexorable when policy demanded a conduct of forbearance and clemency. But the principal argument for reposing the power of pardoning in this case to the Chief Magistrate is this: in seasons of insurrection or rebellion there are often critical moments when a well-timed offer of pardon to the insurgents or rebels may restore the tranquillity of the commonwealth; and which, if suffered to pass unimproved, it may never be possible afterwards to recall. The dilatory process of convening the legislature, or one of its branches, for the purpose of obtaining its sanction to the measure, would frequently be the occasion of letting slip the golden opportunity. The loss of a week, a day, an hour, may sometimes be fatal. If it should be observed that a discretionary power, with a view to such contingencies, might be occasionally conferred upon the President, it may be answered in the first place that it is questionable whether, in a limited Constitution, that power could be delegated by law; and in the second place, that it would generally be impolitic beforehand to take any step which might hold out the prospect of impunity. A proceeding of this kind, out of the usual course, would be likely to be construed into an argument of timidity or of weakness, and would have a tendency to embolden guilt.   PUBLIUS

Number 75

[HAMILTON]

THE PRESIDENT is to have power, "by and with the advice and consent of the Senate, to make treaties, provided two thirds of the senators present concur."

Though this provision has been assailed, on different grounds, with no small degree of vehemence, I scruple not to declare my firm persuasion that it is one of the best digested and most unexceptionable parts of the plan. One ground of objection is the trite topic of the intermixture of powers: some contending that the President ought alone to possess the power of making treaties; others, that it ought to have been exclusively deposited in the Senate. Another source of objection is derived from the small number of persons by whom a treaty may be made. Of those who espouse this objection, a part are of opinion that the House of Representatives ought to have been associated in the business, while another part seem to think that nothing more was necessary than to have substituted two thirds of *all* the members of the Senate, to two thirds of the members *present*. As I flatter myself the observations made in a preceding number upon this part of the plan must have sufficed to place it, to a discerning eye, in a very favourable light, I shall here content myself with offering only some supplementary remarks, principally with a view to the objections which have been just stated.

With regard to the intermixture of powers, I shall rely upon the explanations already given in other places, of the true sense of the rule upon which that objection is founded; and shall take it for granted, as an inference from them, that the union of the Executive with the Senate, in the article of treaties, is no infringement of that rule. I venture to add, that the particular nature of the power of making treaties indicates a peculiar propriety in that union. Though several writers on the subject of government place that power in the class of executive authorities, yet this is evidently an arbitrary disposition; for if we attend carefully to its operation, it will be found to partake more of the legislative than of the executive character, though it does not seem strictly to fall within the definition of either of them. The essence of the legislative authority is to enact laws, or, in other words, to prescribe rules for the regulation of the society; while the execution of the laws, and the employment of the common strength, either for this purpose or for the common defence, seem to comprise all the functions of the executive magistrate. The power of making treaties is, plainly, neither the one nor the other. It relates neither to the execution of the subsisting laws, nor to the enaction of new ones; and still less to an exertion of the common strength. Its objects are CONTRACTS with foreign nations, which have the force of law, but derive it from the obligations of good faith. They are not rules prescribed by the sovereign to the subject, but agreements between sovereign and sovereign. The power in question seems therefore to form a distinct department, and to belong, properly, neither to the legislative nor to the executive. The qualities elsewhere detailed as indispensable in the management of foreign negotiations, point out the Executive as the most fit agent in those transactions; while the vast importance of the trust, and the operation of treaties as laws, plead strongly for the participation of the whole or a portion of the legislative body in the office of making them.

However proper or safe it may be in governments where the executive magistrate is an hereditary monarch, to commit to him the entire power of making treaties, it would be utterly unsafe and improper to intrust that power to an elective magistrate of four years' duration. It has been remarked, upon another occasion, and the remark is unquestionably just, that an hereditary monarch, though often the oppressor of his people, has personally too much stake in the government to be in any material danger of being corrupted by foreign powers. But a man raised from the station of a private citizen to the rank of chief magistrate, possessed of a moderate or slender fortune, and looking forward to a period not very remote when he may probably be obliged to return to the station from which he was taken, might sometimes be under temptations to sacrifice his duty to his interest, which it would require superlative virtue to withstand. An avaricious man might be tempted to betray the interests of the state to the acquisition of wealth. An ambitious man might make his own aggrandisement, by the aid of a foreign power, the price of his treachery to his constituents. The history of human conduct does not warrant that exalted opinion of human virtue which could make it wise in a nation to commit interests of so delicate and momentous a kind, as those which concern its intercourse with the rest of the world, to the sole disposal of a magistrate created and circumstanced as would be a President of the United States.

To have intrusted the power of making treaties to the Senate alone, would have been to relinquish the benefits of the constitutional agency of the President in the conduct of foreign negotiations. It is true that the Senate would, in that case, have the option of employing in this capacity, but they would also have the option of letting it alone, and pique or cabal might induce the latter rather than the former. Besides this, the ministerial servant of the Senate could not be expected to enjoy the confidence and respect of foreign powers in the same degree with the constitutional representatives of the nation, and, of course, would not be able to act with an equal degree of weight or efficacy. While the Union would, from this cause, lose a considerable advantage in the management of its external concerns, the people would lose the additional security which would result from the co-operation of the Executive. Though it would be imprudent to confide in him solely so important a trust, yet it cannot be doubted that his participation would materially add to the safety of the society. It must indeed be clear to a demonstration that the joint possession of the power in question, by the President and Senate, would afford a greater prospect of security than the separate possession of it by either of them. And whoever has maturely weighed the circumstances which must concur in the appointment of a President, will be satisfied that the office will always bid fair to be filled by men of such characters as to render their concurrence in the formation of treaties peculiarly desirable, as well on the score of wisdom, as on that of integrity.

The remarks made in a former number, which have been alluded to in another part of this paper, will apply with conclusive force against the admission of the House of Representatives to a share in the formation of treaties. The fluctuating and, taking its future increase into the account, the multitudinous composition of that body, forbid us to expect in it those qualities which are essential to the proper execution of such a trust. Accurate and comprehensive knowledge of foreign politics; a steady and systematic adherence to the same views; a nice and uniform sensibility to national character; decision, *secrecy,* and despatch, are incompatible with the genius of a body so variable and so numerous. The very complication of the business, by introducing a necessity of the concurrence of so many different bodies, would of itself afford a solid objection. The greater frequency of the calls upon the House of Representatives, and the greater length of time which it would often be necessary to keep them together when convened, to obtain their sanction in the progressive stages of a treaty, would be a source of so great inconvenience and expense as alone ought to condemn the project.

The only objection which remains to be canvassed is that which would substitute the proportion of two thirds of all the members composing the senatorial body to that of two thirds of the members *present.* It has been shown, under the second head of our inquiries, that all provisions which require more than the majority of any body to its resolutions have a direct tendency to embarrass the operations of the government, and an indirect one to subject the sense of the majority to that of the minority. This consideration seems sufficient to determine our opinion that the convention have gone as far in the endeavour to secure the advantage of numbers in the formation of treaties as could have been reconciled either with the activity of the public councils or with a reasonable regard to the major sense of the community. If two thirds of the whole number of members had been required, it would, in many cases, from the non-attendance of a part, amount in practice to a necessity of unanimity. And the history of every political establishment in which this principle has prevailed is a history of impotence, perplexity, and disorder. Proofs of this position might be adduced from the examples of the Roman Tribuneship, the Polish Diet, and the States-General of the Netherlands, did not an example at home render foreign precedents unnecessary.

To require a fixed proportion of the whole body would not, in all probability, contribute to the advantages of a numerous agency better than merely to require a proportion of the attending members. The former, by making a determinate number at all times requisite to a resolution, diminishes the motives to punctual attendance. The latter, by making the capacity of the body to depend on a *proportion* which may be varied by the absence or presence of a single member, has the contrary effect. And as, by promoting punctuality, it tends to keep the body complete, there is great likelihood that its resolutions would generally be dictated by as great a number in this case as in the other; while there would be much fewer occasions of delay. It ought not to be forgotten that, under the existing Confederation, two members *may,* and usually *do,* represent a State; whence it happens that Congress, who now are solely invested with *all the powers* of the Union, rarely consist of a greater number of persons than would compose the intended Senate. If we add to this, that as the members vote by States, and that where there is only a single member present from a State, his vote is lost, it will justify a supposition that the active voices in the Senate, where the members are to vote individually, would rarely fall short in number of the active voices in the existing Congress. When, in addition to these considerations, we take into view the co-operation of the President we shall not hesitate to infer that the people of America would have greater security against an improper use of the power of making treaties under the new Constitution than they now enjoy under the Confederation. And when we proceed still one step further, and look forward to the probable augmentation of the Senate by the erection of new States, we shall not only perceive ample ground of confidence in the sufficiency of the members to whose agency that power will be intrusted, but we shall probably be led to conclude that a body more numerous than the Senate would be likely to become would be very little fit for the proper discharge of the trust.   PUBLIUS

Number 76

[HAMILTON]

THE PRESIDENT is "to *nominate,* and, by and with the advice and consent of the Senate, to appoint ambassadors, other public ministers and consuls, judges of the Supreme Court, and all other officers of the United States whose appointments are not otherwise provided for in the Constitution. But the Congress may by law vest the appointment of such inferior officers as they think proper in the President alone, or in the courts of law, or in the heads of departments. The President shall have power to fill up *all vacancies* which may happen *during the recess of the Senate,* by granting commissions which shall *expire* at the end of their next session."

It has been observed in a former paper that "the true test of a good government is its aptitude and tendency to produce a good administration." If the justness of this observation be admitted, the mode of appointing the officers of the United States contained in the foregoing clauses must, when examined, be allowed to be entitled to particular commendation. It is not easy to conceive a plan better calculated than this to promote a judicious choice of men for filling the offices of the Union; and it will not need proof that on this point must essentially depend the character of its administration.

It will be agreed on all hands that the power of appointment, in ordinary cases, ought to be modified in one of three ways. It ought either to be vested in a single man, or in a *select* assembly of a moderate number; or in a single man with the concurrence of such an assembly. The exercise of it by the people at large will be readily admitted to be impracticable; as, waiving every other consideration, it would leave them little time to do anything else. When, therefore, mention is made in the subsequent reasonings, of an assembly or body of men, what is said must be understood to relate to a select body or assembly of the description already given. The people collectively, from their number and from their dispersed situation, cannot be regulated in their movements by that systematic spirit of cabal and intrigue, which will be urged as the chief objections to reposing the power in question in a body of men.

Those who have themselves reflected upon the subject, or who have attended to the observations made in other parts of these papers in relation to the appointment of the President, will, I presume, agree to the position, that there would always be great probability of having the place supplied by a man of abilities, at least respectable. Premising this, I proceed to lay it down as a rule that one man of discernment is better fitted to analyse and estimate the peculiar qualities adapted to particular offices than a body of men of equal or perhaps even of superior discernment.

The sole and undivided responsibility of one man will naturally beget a livelier sense of duty and a more exact regard to reputation. He will, on this account, feel himself under stronger obligations, and more interested to investigate with care the qualities requisite to the stations to be filled, and to prefer with impartiality the persons who may have the fairest pretensions to them. He will have *fewer* personal attachments to gratify than a body of men who may each be supposed to have an equal number; and will be so much the less liable to be misled by the sentiments of friendship and of affection. A single well-directed man, by a single understanding, cannot be distracted and warped by that diversity of views, feelings, and interests which frequently distract and warp the resolutions of a collective body. There is nothing so apt to agitate the passions of mankind as personal considerations, whether they relate to ourselves or to others, who are to be the objects of our choice or preference. Hence, in every exercise of the power of appointing to offices by an assembly of men, we must expect to see a full display of all the private and party likings and dislikes, partialities and antipathies, attachments and animosities, which are felt by those who compose the assembly. The choice which may at any time happen to be made under such circumstances will of course be the result either of a victory gained by one party over the other or of a compromise between the parties. In either case, the intrinsic merit of the candidate will be too often out of sight. In the first, the qualifications best adapted to uniting the suffrages of the party will be more considered than those which fit the person for the station. In the last, the coalition will commonly turn upon some interested equivalent: "Give us the man we wish for this office, and you shall have the one you wish for that." This will be the usual condition of the bargain. And it will rarely happen that the advancement of the public service will be the primary object either of party victories or of party negotiations.

The truth of the principles here advanced seems to have been felt by the most intelligent of those who have found fault with the provision made, in this respect, by the convention. They contend that the President ought solely to have been authorised to make the appointments under the federal government. But it is easy to show that every advantage to be expected for such an arrangement would, in substance, be derived from the power of *nomination*, which is proposed to be conferred upon him; while several disadvantages which might attend the absolute power of appointment in the hands of that officer would be avoided. In the act of nomination, his judgment alone would be exercised; and as it would be his sole duty to point out the man who, with the approbation of the Senate, should fill an office, his responsibility would be as complete as if he were to make the final appointment. There can, in this view, be no difference between nominating and appointing. The same motives which would influence a proper discharge of his duty in one case would exist in the other. And as no man could be appointed but on his previous nomination, every man who might be appointed would be, in fact, his choice.

But might not his nomination be overruled? I grant it might, yet this could only be to make place for another nomination by himself. The person ultimately appointed must be the object of his preference, though perhaps not in the first degree. It is also not very probable that his nomination would often be overruled. The Senate could not be tempted, by the preference they might feel to another, to reject the one proposed, because they could not assure themselves that the person they might wish would be brought forward by a second or by any subsequent nomination. They could not even be certain that a future nomination would present a candidate in any degree more acceptable to them; and as their dissent might cast a kind of stigma upon the individual rejected, and might have the appearance of a reflection upon the judgment of the chief magistrate, it is not likely that their sanction would often be refused where there were not special and strong reasons for the refusal.

To what purpose then require the co-operation of the Senate? I answer, that the necessity of their concurrence would have a powerful though, in general, a silent operation. It would be an excellent check upon a spirit of favouritism in the President, and would tend greatly to prevent the appointment of unfit characters from State prejudice, from family connection, from personal attachment, or from a view to popularity. In addition to this, it would be an efficacious source of stability in the administration.

It will readily be comprehended that a man who had himself the sole disposition of offices would be governed much more by his private inclinations and interests than when he was bound to submit the propriety of his choice to the discussion and determination of a different and independent body, and that body an entire branch of the legislature. The possibility of rejection would be a strong motive to care in proposing. The danger to his own reputation and, in the case of an elective magistrate, to his political existence from betraying a spirit of favouritism, or an unbecoming pursuit of popularity, to the observation of a body whose opinion would have great weight in forming that of the public, could not fail to operate as a barrier to the one and to the other. He would be both ashamed and afraid to bring forward, for the most distinguished or lucrative stations, candidates who had no other merit than that of coming from the same State to which he particularly belonged, or of being in some way or other personally allied to him, or of possessing the necessary insignificance and pliancy to render them the obsequious instruments of his pleasure.

To this reasoning it has been objected that the President, by the influence of the power of nomination, may secure the complaisance of the Senate to his views. This supposition of universal venality in human nature is little less an error in political reasoning than the supposition of universal rectitude. The institution of delegated power implies that there is a portion of virtue and honour among mankind which may be a reasonable foundation of confidence; and experience justifies the theory. It has been found to exist in the most corrupt periods of the most corrupt governments. The venality of the British House of Commons has been long a topic of accusation against that body in the country to which they belong as well as in this; and it cannot be doubted that the charge is, to a considerable extent, well founded. But it is as little to be doubted that there is always a large proportion of the body which consists of independent and public-spirited men, who have an influential weight in the councils of the nation. Hence it is (the present reign not excepted) that the sense of that body is often seen to control the inclinations of the monarch, both with regard to men and to measures. Though it might therefore be allowable to suppose that the Executive might occasionally influence some individuals in the Senate, yet the supposition that he could in general purchase the integrity of the whole body would be forced and improbable. A man disposed to view human nature as it is, without either flattering its virtues or exaggerating its vices, will see sufficient ground of confidence in the probity of the Senate to rest satisfied, not only that it will be impracticable to the Executive to corrupt or seduce a majority of its members, but that the necessity of its co-operation, in the business of appointments, will be a considerable and salutary restraint upon the conduct of that magistrate. Nor is the integrity of the Senate the only reliance. The Constitution has provided some important guards against the danger of executive influence upon the legislative body: it declares that "No senator or representative shall, during the time *for which he was elected*, be appointed to any civil office under the United States which shall have been created, or the emoluments whereof shall have been increased, during such time; and no person, holding any office under the United States, shall be a member of either house during his continuance in office."   PUBLIUS

Number 77

[HAMILTON]

IT HAS been mentioned as one of the advantages to be expected from the co-operation of the Senate, in the business of appointments, that it would contribute to the stability of the administration. The consent of that body would be necessary to displace as well as to appoint. A change of the Chief Magistrate, therefore, would not occasion so violent or so general a revolution in the officers of the government as might be expected if he were the sole disposer of offices. Where a man in any station had given satisfactory evidence of his fitness for it, a new President would be restrained from attempting a change in favour of a person more agreeable to him by the apprehension that a discountenance of the Senate might frustrate the attempt and bring some degree of discredit upon himself. Those who can best estimate the value of a steady administration will be most disposed to prize a provision which connects the official existence of public men with the approbation or disapprobation of that body which, from the greater permanency of its own composition, will in all probability be less subject to inconstancy than any other member of the government.

To this union of the Senate with the President, in the article of appointments, it has in some cases been suggested that it would serve to give the President an undue influence over the Senate, and in others that it would have an opposite tendency—a strong proof that neither suggestion is true.

To state the first in its proper form is to refute it. It amounts to this: the President would have an improper *influence over* the Senate, because the Senate would have the power of *restraining* him. This is an absurdity in terms. It cannot admit of a doubt that the entire power of appointment would enable him much more effectually to establish a dangerous empire over that body than a mere power of nomination subject to their control.

Let us take a view of the converse of the proposition: "the Senate would influence the Executive." As I have had occasion to remark in several other instances, the indistinctness of the objection forbids a precise answer. In what manner is this influence to be exerted? In relation to what objects? The power of influencing a person, in the sense in which it is here used, must imply a power of conferring a benefit upon him. How could the Senate confer a benefit upon the President by the manner of employing their right of negative upon his nominations? If it be said they might sometimes gratify him by an acquiescence in a favourite choice when public motives might dictate a different conduct, I answer that the instances in which the President could be personally interested in the result would be too few to admit of his being materially affected by the compliances of the Senate. The POWER which can *originate* the disposition of honours and emoluments is more likely to attract than to be attracted by the POWER which can merely obstruct their course. If by influencing the President be meant *restraining* him, this is precisely what must have been intended. And it has been shown that the restraint would be salutary at the same time that it would not be such as to destroy a single advantage to be looked for from the uncontrolled agency of that Magistrate. The right of nomination would produce all the good of that of appointment, and would in a great measure avoid its evils.

Upon a comparison of the plan for the appointment of the officers of the proposed government with that which is established by the constitution of this State, a decided preference must be given to the former. In that plan the power of nomination is unequivocally vested in the Executive. And as there would be a necessity of submitting each nomination to the judgment of an entire branch of the legislature, the circumstances attending an appointment, from the mode of conducting it, would naturally become matters of notoriety; and the public would be at no loss to determine what part had been performed by the different actors. The blame of a bad nomination would fall upon the President singly and absolutely. The censure of rejecting a good one would lie entirely at the door of the Senate; aggravated by the consideration of their having counteracted the good intentions of the Executive. If an ill appointment should be made, the Executive for nominating, and the Senate for approving, would participate, though in different degrees, in the opprobrium and disgrace.

The reverse of all this characterises the manner of appointment in this State. The council of appointment consists of from three to five persons, of whom the governor is always one. This small body, shut up in a private apartment, impenetrable to the public eye, proceed to the execution of the trust committed to them. It is known that the governor claims the right of nomination, upon the strength of some ambiguous expressions in the constitution; but it is not known to what extent or in what manner he exercises it; nor upon what occasions he is contradicted or opposed. The censure of a bad appointment, on account of the uncertainty of its author, and for want of a determinate object, has neither poignancy nor duration. And while an unbounded field for cabal and intrigue lies open, all idea of responsibility is lost. The most that the public can know is that the governor claims the right of nomination; that *two* out of the inconsiderable number of *four* men can too often be managed without much difficulty; that if some of the members of a particular council should happen to be of an uncomplying character, it is frequently not impossible to get rid of their opposition by regulating the times of meeting in such a manner as to render their attendance inconvenient; and that from whatever cause it may proceed, a great number of very improper appointments are from time to time made. Whether a governor of this State avails himself of the ascendant he must necessarily have, in this delicate and important part of the administration, to prefer to offices men who are best qualified for them, or whether he prostitutes that advantage to the advancement of persons whose chief merit is their implicit devotion to his will, and to the support of a despicable and dangerous system of personal influence, are questions which, unfortunately for the community, can only be the subjects of speculation and conjecture.

Every mere council of appointment, however constituted, will be a conclave, in which cabal and intrigue will have their full scope. Their number, without an unwarrantable increase of expense, cannot be large enough to preclude a facility of combination. And as each member will have his friends and connections to provide for, the desire of mutual gratification will beget a scandalous bartering of votes and bargaining for places. The private attachments of one man might easily be satisfied; but to satisfy the private attachments of a dozen, or of twenty men, would occasion a monopoly of all the principal employments of the government in a few families, and would lead more directly to an aristocracy or an oligarchy than any measure that could be contrived. If, to avoid an accumulation of offices, there was to be a frequent change in the persons who were to compose the council, this would involve the mischiefs of a mutable administration in their full extent. Such a council would also be more liable to executive influence than the Senate, because they would be fewer in number, and would act less immediately under the public inspection. Such a council, in fine, as a substitute for the plan of the convention, would be productive of an increase of expense, a multiplication of the evils which spring from favouritism and intrigue in the distribution of public honours, a decrease of stability in the administration of the government, and a diminution of the security against an undue influence of the Executive. And yet such a council has been warmly contended for as an essential amendment in the proposed Constitution.

I could not with propriety conclude my observations on the subject of appointments without taking notice of a scheme for which there have appeared some, though but few advocates; I mean that of uniting the House of Representatives in the power of making them. I shall, however, do little more than mention it, as I cannot imagine that it is likely to gain the countenance of any considerable part of the community. A body so fluctuating, and at the same time so numerous, can never be deemed proper for the exercise of that power. Its unfitness will appear manifest to all when it is recollected that in half a century it may consist of three or four hundred persons. All the advantages of the stability, both of the Executive and of the Senate, would be defeated by this union, and infinite delays and embarrassments would be occasioned. The example of most of the States in their local constitutions encourages us to reprobate the idea.

The only remaining powers of the Executive are comprehended in giving information to Congress of the state of the Union; in recommending to their consideration such measures as he shall judge expedient; in convening them, or either branch, upon extraordinary occasions; in adjourning them when they cannot themselves agree upon the time of adjournment; in receiving ambassadors and other public ministers; in faithfully executing the laws; and in commissioning all the officers of the United States.

Except some cavils about the power of convening *either* house of the legislature, and that of receiving ambassadors, no objection has been made to this class of authorities; nor could they possibly admit of any. It required, indeed, an insatiable avidity for censure to invent exceptions to the parts which have been excepted to. In regard to the power of convening either house of the legislature, I shall barely remark that in respect to the Senate at least we can readily discover a good reason for it. As this body has a concurrent power with the Executive in the article of treaties, it might

often be necessary to call it together with a view to this object when it would be unnecessary and improper to convene the House of Representatives. As to the reception of ambassadors, what I have said in a former paper will furnish a sufficient answer.

We have now completed a survey of the structure and powers of the executive department, which, I have endeavoured to show, combines, as far as republican principles will admit, all the requisites to energy. The remaining inquiry is: Does it also combine the requisites to safety, in a republican sense—a due dependence on the people, a due responsibility? The answer to this question has been anticipated in the investigation of its other characteristics, and is satisfactorily deducible from these circumstances; from the election of the President once in four years by persons immediately chosen by the people for that purpose; and from his being at all times liable to impeachment, trial, dismission from office, incapacity to serve in any other, and to forfeiture of life and estate by subsequent prosecution in the common course of law. But these precautions, great as they are, are not the only ones which the plan of the convention has provided in favour of the public security. In the only instances in which the abuse of the executive authority was materially to be feared, the Chief Magistrate of the United States would, by that plan, be subjected to the control of a branch of the legislative body. What more could be desired by an enlightened and reasonable people? PUBLIUS

Number 78

[HAMILTON]

WE PROCEED now to an examination of the judiciary department of the proposed government.

In unfolding the defects of the existing Confederation, the utility and necessity of a federal judicature have been clearly pointed out. It is the less necessary to recapitulate the considerations there urged, as the propriety of the institution in the abstract is not disputed; the only questions which have been raised being relative to the manner of constituting it, and to its extent. To these points, therefore, our observations shall be confined.

The manner of constituting it seems to embrace these several objects: 1st. The mode of appointing the judges. 2nd. The tenure by which they are to hold their places. 3rd. The partition of the judiciary authority between different courts, and their relations to each other.

First. As to the mode of appointing the judges; this is the same with that of appointing the officers of the Union in general, and has been so fully discussed in the two last numbers that nothing can be said here which would not be useless repetition.

Second. As to the tenure by which the judges are to hold their places: this chiefly concerns their duration in office; the provisions for their support; the precautions for their responsibility.

According to the plan of the convention, all judges who may be appointed by the United States are to hold their offices *during good behaviour;* which is conformable to the most approved of the State constitutions, and among the rest, to that of this State. Its propriety having been drawn into question by the adversaries of that plan is no light symptom of the rage for objection which disorders their imaginations and judgments. The standard of good behaviour for the continuance in office of the judicial magistracy is certainly one of the most valuable of the modern improvements in the practice of government. In a monarchy it is an excellent barrier to the despotism of the prince; in a republic it is a no less excellent barrier to the encroachments and oppressions of the representative body. And it is the best expedient which can be devised in any government to secure a steady, upright, and impartial administration of the laws.

Whoever attentively considers the different departments of power must perceive that, in a government in which they are separated from each other, the judiciary, from the nature of its functions, will always be the least dangerous to the political rights of the Constitution; because it will be least in a capacity to annoy or injure them. The Executive not only dispenses the honours, but holds the sword of the community. The legislature not only commands the purse, but prescribes the rules by which the duties and rights of every citizen are to be regulated. The judiciary, on the contrary, has no influence over either the sword or the purse; no direction either of the strength or of the wealth of the society; and can take no active resolution whatever. It may truly be said to have neither FORCE nor WILL, but merely judgment; and must ultimately depend upon the aid of the executive arm even for the efficacy of its judgments.

This simple view of the matter suggests several important consequences. It proves incontestably that the judiciary is beyond comparison the weakest of the three departments of power;[1] that it can never attack with success either of the other two; and that all possible care is requisite to enable it to defend itself against their attacks. It equally proves that though individual oppression may now and then proceed from the courts of justice, the general liberty of the people can never be endangered from that quarter; I mean so long as the judiciary remains truly distinct from both the legislature and the Executive. For I agree that "there is no liberty, if the power of judging be not separated from the legislative and executive powers."[2] And it proves, in the last place, that as liberty can have nothing to fear from the judiciary alone, but would have everything to fear from its union with either of the other departments; that as all the effects of such a union must ensue from a dependence of the former on the latter, notwithstanding a nominal and apparent separation; that as, from the natural feebleness of the judiciary, it is in continual jeopardy of being overpowered, awed, or influenced by its co-ordinate branches; and that as nothing can contribute so much to its firmness and independence as permanency in office, this quality may therefore be justly regarded as an indispensable ingredient in its constitution, and, in a great measure, as the citadel of the public justice and the public security.

The complete independence of the courts of justice is peculiarly essential in a limited Constitution. By a limited Constitution I understand one which contains certain specified exceptions to the legislative authority; such, for instance, as that it shall pass no bills of attainder, no *ex post facto* laws, and the like. Limitations of this kind can be preserved in practice no other way than through the medium of courts of justice, whose duty it must be to declare all acts contrary to the manifest tenor of the Constitution void. Without this, all the reservations of particular rights or privileges would amount to nothing.

Some perplexity respecting the rights of the courts to pronounce legislative acts void, because contrary to the Constitution, has arisen

---

[1] The celebrated Montesquieu, speaking of them, says: "Of the three powers above mentioned, the judiciary is next to nothing."—*Spirit of Laws.* —PUBLIUS

[2] *Idem.*

from an imagination that the doctrine would imply a superiority of the judiciary to the legislative power. It is urged that the authority which can declare the acts of another void must necessarily be superior to the one whose acts may be declared void. As this doctrine is of great importance in all the American constitutions, a brief discussion of the ground on which it rests cannot be unacceptable.

There is no position which depends on clearer principles than that every act of a delegated authority, contrary to the tenor of the commission under which it is exercised, is void. No legislative act, therefore, contrary to the Constitution can be valid. To deny this would be to affirm that the deputy is greater than his principal; that the servant is above his master; that the representatives of the people are superior to the people themselves; that men acting by virtue of powers may do not only what their powers do not authorise, but what they forbid.

If it be said that the legislative body are themselves the constitutional judges of their own powers, and that the construction they put upon them is conclusive upon the other departments, it may be answered that this cannot be the natural presumption where it is not to be collected from any particular provisions in the Constitution. It is not otherwise to be supposed that the Constitution could intend to enable the representatives of the people to substitute their *will* to that of their constituents. It is far more rational to suppose that the courts were designed to be an intermediate body between the people and the legislature, in order, among other things, to keep the latter within the limits assigned to their authority. The interpretation of the laws is the proper and peculiar province of the courts. A constitution is, in fact, and must be regarded by the judges, as a fundamental law. It therefore belongs to them to ascertain its meaning, as well as the meaning of any particular act proceeding from the legislative body. If there should happen to be an irreconcilable variance between the two, that which has the superior obligation and validity ought, of course, to be preferred; or, in other words, the Constitution ought to be preferred to the statute, the intention of the people to the intention of their agents.

Nor does this conclusion by any means suppose a superiority of the judicial to the legislative power. It only supposes that the power of the people is superior to both; and that

where the will of the legislature, declared in its statutes, stands in opposition to that of the people, declared in the Constitution, the judges ought to be governed by the latter rather than the former. They ought to regulate their decisions by the fundamental laws, rather than by those which are not fundamental.

This exercise of judicial discretion, in determining between two contradictory laws, is exemplified in a familiar instance. It not uncommonly happens that there are two statutes existing at one time, clashing in whole or in part with each other, and neither of them containing any repealing clause or expression. In such a case it is the province of the courts to liquidate and fix their meaning and operation. So far as they can, by any fair construction, be reconciled to each other, reason and law conspire to dictate that this should be done; where this is impracticable, it becomes a matter of necessity to give effect to one in exclusion of the other. The rule which has obtained in the courts for determining their relative validity is, that the last in order of time shall be preferred to the first. But this is a mere rule of construction, not derived from any positive law, but from the nature and reason of the thing. It is a rule not enjoined upon the courts by legislative provision, but adopted by themselves, as consonant to truth and propriety, for the direction of their conduct as interpreters of the law. They thought it reasonable that between the interfering acts of an *equal* authority, that which was the last indication of its will should have the preference.

But in regard to the interfering acts of a superior and subordinate authority, of an original and derivative power, the nature and reason of the thing indicate the converse of that rule as proper to be followed. They teach us that the prior act of a superior ought to be preferred to the subsequent act of an inferior and subordinate authority; and that accordingly, whenever a particular statute contravenes the Constitution, it will be the duty of the judicial tribunals to adhere to the latter and disregard the former.

It can be of no weight to say that the courts, on the pretence of a repugnancy, may substitute their own pleasure to the constitutional intentions of the legislature. This might as well happen in the case of two contradictory statutes; or it might as well happen in every adjudication upon any single statute. The courts must declare the sense of the law; and if they should be disposed to exercise WILL instead of JUDGMENT, the consequence would equally be the substitution of their pleasure to that of the legislative body. The observation, if it prove anything, would prove that there ought to be no judges distinct from that body.

If, then, the courts of justice are to be considered as the bulwarks of a limited Constitution against legislative encroachments, this consideration will afford a strong argument for the permanent tenure of judicial offices, since nothing will contribute so much as this to that independent spirit in the judges which must be essential to the faithful performance of so arduous a duty.

This independence of the judges is equally requisite to guard the Constitution and the rights of individuals from the effects of those ill humours, which the arts of designing men, or the influence of particular conjunctures, sometimes disseminate among the people themselves, and which, though they speedily give place to better information, and more deliberate reflection, have a tendency, in the meantime, to occasion dangerous innovations in the government, and serious oppressions of the minor party in the community. Though I trust the friends of the proposed Constitution will never concur with its enemies,[1] in questioning that fundamental principle of republican government which admits the right of the people to alter or abolish the established Constitution, whenever they find it inconsistent with their happiness, yet it is not to be inferred from this principle that the representatives of the people, whenever a momentary inclination happens to lay hold of a majority of their constituents, incompatible with the provisions in the existing constitution, would, on that account, be justifiable in a violation of those provisions; or that the courts would be under a greater obligation to connive at infractions in this shape than when they had proceeded wholly from the cabals of the representative body. Until the people have, by some solemn and authoritative act, annulled or changed the established form, it is binding upon themselves collectively, as well as individually; and no presumption, or even knowledge, of their sentiments, can warrant their representatives in a departure from it, prior to such an act. But it is easy to see that it would require an uncommon portion of fortitude in the judges to do their duty as faithful guard-

[1] *Vide* "Protest of the Minority of the Convention of Pennsylvania," Martin's Speech, etc.— PUBLIUS

ians of the Constitution where legislative invasions of it had been instigated by the major voice of the community.

But it is not with a view to infractions of the Constitution only that the independence of the judges may be an essential safeguard against the effects of occasional ill humours in the society. These sometimes extend no farther than to the injury of the private rights of particular classes of citizens by unjust and partial laws. Here also the firmness of the judicial magistracy is of vast importance in mitigating the severity and confining the operation of such laws. It not only serves to moderate the immediate mischiefs of those which may have been passed, but it operates as a check upon the legislative body in passing them; who, perceiving that obstacles to the success of iniquitous intention are to be expected from the scruples of the courts, are in a manner compelled, by the very motives of the injustice they meditate to qualify their attempts. This is a circumstance calculated to have more influence upon the character of our governments than but few may be aware of. The benefits of the integrity and moderation of the judiciary have already been felt in more States than one; and though they may have displeased those whose sinister expectations they may have disappointed, they must have commanded the esteem and applause of all the virtuous and disinterested. Considerate men, of every description, ought to prize whatever will tend to beget or fortify that temper in the courts; as no man can be sure that he may not be to-morrow the victim of a spirit of injustice, by which he may be a gainer to-day. And every man must now feel that the inevitable tendency of such a spirit is to sap the foundations of public and private confidence, and to introduce in its stead universal distrust and distress.

That inflexible and uniform adherence to the rights of the Constitution, and of individuals, which we perceive to be indispensable in the courts of justice, can certainly not be expected from judges who hold their offices by a temporary commission. Periodical appointments, however regulated, or by whomsoever made, would, in some way or other, be fatal to their necessary independence. If the power of making them was committed either to the Executive or legislature, there would be danger of an improper complaisance to the branch which possessed it; if to both, there would be an unwillingness to hazard the displeasure of either; if to the people, or to persons chosen by them for the special purpose, there would be too great a disposition to consult popularity, to justify a reliance that nothing would be consulted but the Constitution and the laws.

There is yet a further and a weightier reason for the permanency of the judicial offices which is deducible from the nature of the qualifications they require. It has been frequently remarked, with great propriety, that a voluminous code of laws is one of the inconveniences necessarily connected with the advantages of a free government. To avoid an arbitrary discretion in the courts, it is indispensable that they should be bound down by strict rules and precedents, which serve to define and point out their duty in every particular case that comes before them; and it will readily be conceived from the variety of controversies which grow out of the folly and wickedness of mankind that the records of those precedents must unavoidably swell to a very considerable bulk, and must demand long and laborious study to acquire a competent knowledge of them. Hence it is, that there can be but few men in the society who will have sufficient skill in the laws to qualify them for the stations of judges. And making the proper deductions for the ordinary depravity of human nature, the number must be still smaller of those who unite the requisite integrity with the requisite knowledge. These considerations apprise us that the government can have no great option between fit character; and that a temporary duration in office, which would naturally discourage such characters from quitting a lucrative line of practice to accept a seat on the bench, would have a tendency to throw the administration of justice into hands less able, and less well qualified, to conduct it with utility and dignity. In the present circumstances of this country, and in those in which it is likely to be for a long time to come, the disadvantages on this score would be greater than they may at first sight appear; but it must be confessed that they are far inferior to those which present themselves under the other aspects of the subject.

Upon the whole, there can be no room to doubt that the convention acted wisely in copying from the models of those constitutions which have established *good behaviour* as the tenure of their judicial offices, in point of duration; and that so far from being blamable on this account, their plan would have been inexcusably defective, if it had wanted this important feature of good government. The experience of Great Britain affords an illustrious comment on the excellence of the institution.   PUBLIUS

Number 79
[HAMILTON]

NEXT TO PERMANENCY in office, nothing can contribute more to the independence of the judges than a fixed provision for their support. The remark made in relation to the President is equally applicable here. In the general course of human nature, *a power over a man's subsistence amounts to a power over his will.* And we can never hope to see realised in practice the complete separation of the judicial from the legislative power, in any system which leaves the former dependent for pecuniary resources on the occasional grants of the latter. The enlightened friends to good government in every State have seen cause to lament the want of precise and explicit precautions in the State constitutions on this head. Some of these indeed have declared that *permanent*[1] salaries should be established for the judges; but the experiment has in some instances shown that such expressions are not sufficiently definite to preclude legislative evasions. Something still more positive and unequivocal has been évinced to be requisite. The plan of the convention accordingly has provided that the judges of the United States "shall at *stated times* receive for their services a compensation which shall not be *dimished* during their continuance in office."

This, all circumstances considered, is the most eligible provision that could have been devised. It will readily be understood that the fluctuations in the value of money and in the state of society rendered a fixed rate of compensation in the Constitution inadmissible. What might be extravagant to-day might in half a century become penurious and inadequate. It was therefore necessary to leave it to the discretion of the legislature to vary its provisions in conformity to the variations in circumstances, yet under such restrictions as to put it out of the power of that body to change the condition of the individual for the worse. A man may then be sure of the ground upon which he stands, and can never be deterred from his duty by the apprehension of being placed in a less eligible situation. The clause which has been quoted combines both

[1] Vide *Constitution of Massachusetts,* chapter ii., section 1, article 13.—PUBLIUS

advantages. The salaries of judicial officers may from time to time be altered, as occasion shall require, yet so as never to lessen the allowance with which any particular judge comes into office, in respect to him. It will be observed that a difference has been made by the convention between the compensation of the President and of the judges. That of the former can neither be increased nor diminished; that of the latter can only not be diminished. This probably arose from the difference in the duration of the respective offices. As the President is to be elected for no more than four years, it can rarely happen that an adequate salary, fixed at the commencement of that period, will not continue to be such to its end. But with regard to the judges, who, if they behave properly, will be secured in their places for life, it may well happen, especially in the early stages of the government, that a stipend, which would be very sufficient at their first appointment, would become too small in the progress of their service.

This provision for the support of the judges bears every mark of prudence and efficacy; and it may be safely affirmed that, together with the permanent tenure of their offices, it affords a better prospect of their independence than is discoverable in the constitutions of any of the States in regard to their own judges.

The precautions for their responsibility are comprised in the article respecting impeachments. They are liable to be impeached for malconduct by the House of Representatives, and tried by the Senate; and, if convicted, may be dismissed from office, and disqualified for holding any other. This is the only provision on the point which is consistent with the necessary independence of the judicial character, and is the only one which we find in our own Constitution in respect to our own judges.

The want of a provision for removing the judges on account of inability has been a subject of complaint. But all considerate men will be sensible that such a provision would either not be practised upon or would be more liable to abuse than calculated to answer any good purpose. The mensuration of the faculties of the mind has, I believe, no place in the catalogue of known arts. An attempt to fix the boundary between the regions of ability and inability would much oftener give scope to personal and party attachments and enmities than advance the interests of justice or the public good. The result, except in the case of insanity, must for the most part be arbitrary; and insanity, without any formal or express provision, may be safely pronounced to be a virtual disqualification.

The constitution of New York, to avoid investigations that must for ever be vague and dangerous, has taken a particular age as the criterion of inability. No man can be a judge beyond sixty. I believe there are few at present who do not disapprove of this provision. There is no station, in relation to which it is less proper than to that of a judge. The deliberating and comparing faculties generally preserve their strength much beyond that period in men who survive it; and when, in addition to this circumstance, we consider how few there are who outlive the season of intellectual vigour, and how improbable it is that any considerable portion of the bench, whether more or less numerous, should be in such a situation at the same time, we shall be ready to conclude that limitations of this sort have little to recommend them. In a republic, where fortunes are not affluent and pensions not expedient, the dismission of men from stations in which they have served their country long and usefully, on which they depend for subsistence, and from which it will be too late to resort to any other occupation for a livelihood, ought to have some better apology to humanity than is to be found in the imaginary danger of a superannuated bench. PUBLIUS

Number 80

[HAMILTON]

To JUDGE WITH accuracy of the proper extent of the federal judicature, it will be necessary to consider, in the first place, what are its proper objects.

It seems scarcely to admit of controversy, that the judiciary authority of the Union ought to extend to these several descriptions of cases: 1st, to all those which arise out of the laws of the United States, passed in pursuance of their just and constitutional powers of legislation; 2nd, to all those which concern the execution of the provisions expressly contained in the articles of Union; 3rd, to all those in which the United States are a party; 4th, to all those which involve the PEACE of the CONFEDERACY, whether they relate to the intercourse between the United States and foreign nations, or to that between the States themselves; 5th, to all those which originate on the high seas, and are of admiralty or maritime jurisdiction; and, lastly, to all those in which the State tribunals cannot be supposed to be impartial and unbiased.

The first point depends upon this obvious consideration, that there ought always to be a constitutional method of giving efficacy to constitutional provisions. What, for instance, would avail restrictions on the authority of the State legislatures, without some constitutional mode of enforcing the observance of them? The States, by the plan of the convention, are prohibited from doing a variety of things, some of which are incompatible with the interests of the Union, and others with the principles of good government. The imposition of duties on imported articles, and the emission of paper money, are specimens of each kind. No man of sense will believe that such prohibitions would be scrupulously regarded without some effectual power in the government to restrain or correct the infractions of them. This power must either be a direct negative on the State laws, or an authority in the federal courts to overrule such as might be in manifest contravention of the articles of Union. There is no third course that I can imagine. The latter appears to have been thought by the convention preferable to the former, and, I presume, will be most agreeable to the States.

As to the second point, it is impossible, by any argument or comment, to make it clearer than it is in itself. If there are such things as political axioms, the propriety of the judicial power of a government being co-extensive with its legislative, may be ranked among the number. The mere necessity of uniformity in the interpretation of the national laws decides the question. Thirteen independent courts of final jurisdiction over the same causes, arising upon the same laws, is a hydra in government, from which nothing but contradiction and confusion can proceed.

Still less need be said in regard to the third point. Controversies between the nation and its members or citizens can only be properly referred to the national tribunals. Any other plan would be contrary to reason, to precedent, and to decorum.

The fourth point rests on this plain proposition, that the peace of the WHOLE ought not to be left at the disposal of a PART. The Union will undoubtedly be answerable to foreign powers for the conduct of its members. And the responsibility for an injury ought ever to be accompanied with the faculty of preventing it. As the denial or perversion of justice by the sentences of courts, as well as in any other manner, is with reason classed among the just causes of war, it will follow that the federal judiciary ought to have cognisance of all causes in which the citizens of other countries are concerned. This is not less essential to the preservation of the public faith than to the security of the public tranquillity. A distinction may perhaps be imagined between cases arising upon treaties and the laws of nations and those which may stand merely on the footing of the municipal law. The former kind may be supposed proper for the federal jurisdiction, the latter for that of the States. But it is at least problematical, whether an unjust sentence against a foreigner, where the subject of controversy was wholly relative to the *lex loci,* would not, if unredressed be an aggression upon his sovereign, as well as one which violated the stipulations of a treaty or the general law of nations. And a still greater objection to the distinction would result from the immense difficulty, if not impossibility, of a practical discrimination between the cases of one complexion and those of the other. So great a proportion of the cases in which foreigners are parties involve national questions, that it is by far most safe and most expedient to refer all those in which they are concerned to the national tribunals.

The power of determining causes between two States, between one State and the citizens of another, and between the citizens of different States, is perhaps not less essential to the peace of the Union than that which has been just examined. History gives us a horrid picture of the dissensions and private wars which distracted and desolated Germany prior to the institution of the Imperial Chamber by Maximilian, towards the close of the fifteenth century; and informs us, at the same time, of the vast influence of that institution in appeasing the disorders and establishing the tranquillity of the empire. This was a court invested with authority to decide finally all differences among the members of the Germanic body.

A method of terminating territorial disputes between the States, under the authority of the federal head, was not unattended to even in the imperfect system by which they have been hitherto held together. But there are many other sources, besides interfering claims of boundary, from which bickerings and animosities may spring up among the members of the Union. To some of these we have been witnesses in the course of our past experience.

It will readily be conjectured that I allude to the fraudulent laws which have been passed in too many of the States. And though the proposed Constitution establishes particular guards against the repetition of those instances which have heretofore made their appearance, yet it is warrantable to apprehend that the spirit which produced them will assume new shapes that could not be foreseen nor specifically provided against. Whatever practices may have a tendency to disturb the harmony between the States are proper objects of federal superintendence and control.

It may be esteemed the basis of the Union, that "the citizens of each State shall be entitled to all the privileges and immunities of citizens of the several States." And if it be a just principle that every government *ought to possess the means of executing its own provisions by its own authority,* it will follow that in order to [preserve] the inviolable maintenance of that equality of privileges and immunities to which the citizens of the Union will be entitled, the national judiciary ought to preside in all cases in which one State or its citizens are opposed to another State or its citizens. To secure the full effect of so fundamental a provision against all evasion and subterfuge, it is necessary that its construction should be committed to that tribunal which, having no local attachments, will be likely to be impartial between the different States and their citizens, and which, owing its official existence to the Union, will never be likely to feel any bias inauspicious to the principles on which it is founded.

The fifth point will demand little animadversion. The most bigoted idolisers of State authority have not thus far shown a disposition to deny the national judiciary the cognisances of maritime causes. These so generally depend on the laws of nations, and so commonly affect the rights of foreigners, that they fall within the considerations which are relative to the public peace. The most important part of them are, by the present Confederation, submitted to federal jurisdiction.

The reasonableness of the agency of the national courts in cases in which the State tribunals cannot be supposed to be impartial speaks for itself. No man ought certainly to be a judge in his own cause, or in any cause in respect to which he has the least interest or bias. This principle has no inconsiderable weight in designating the federal courts as the proper tribunals for the determination of controversies between different States and their

citizens. And it ought to have the same operation in regard to some cases between citizens of the same State. Claims to land under grants of different States, founded upon adverse pretensions of boundary, are of this description. The courts of neither of the granting States could be expected to be unbiased. The laws may have even prejudged the question, and tied the courts down to decisions in favour of the grants of the State to which they belonged. And even where this had not been done, it would be natural that the judges, as men, should feel a strong predilection to the claims of their own government.

Having thus laid down and discussed the principles which ought to regulate the constitution of the federal judiciary, we will proceed to test, by these principles, the particular powers of which, according to the plan of the convention, it is to be composed. It is to comprehend "all cases in law and equity arising under the Constitution, the laws of the United States, and treaties made, or which shall be made, under their authority; to all cases affecting ambassadors, other public ministers, and consuls; to all cases of admiralty and maritime jurisdiction; to controversies to which the United States shall be a party; to controversies between two or more States; between a State and citizens of another State; between citizens of different States; between citizens of the same State claiming lands and grants of different States; and between a State or the citizens thereof and foreign states, citizens, and subjects." This constitutes the entire mass of the judicial authority of the Union. Let us now review it in detail. It is, then, to extend:

First. To all cases in law and equity *arising under the Constitution* and *the laws of the United States.* This corresponds with the two first classes of causes, which have been enumerated, as proper for the judisdiction of the United States. It has been asked, what is meant by "cases arising under the Constitution," in contradistinction from those "arising under the laws of the United States"? The difference has been already explained. All the restrictions upon the authority of the State legislatures furnish examples of it. They are not, for instance, to emit paper money; but the interdiction results from the Constitution, and will have no connection with any law of the United States. Should paper money, notwithstanding, be emitted, the controversies concerning it would be cases arising under the Constitution and not the laws of the United States, in the ordinary signification of the terms. This may serve as a sample of the whole.

It has also been asked, what need of the word "equity"? What equitable causes can grow out of the Constitution and laws of the United States? There is hardly a subject of litigation between individuals, which may not involve those ingredients of *fraud, accident, trust,* or *hardship,* which would render the matter an object of equitable rather than of legal jurisdiction, as the distinction is known and established in several of the States. It is the peculiar province, for instance, of a court of equity to relieve against what are called hard bargains: these are contracts in which, though there may have been no direct fraud or deceit, sufficient to invalidate them in a court of law, yet there may have been some undue and unconscionable advantage taken of the necessities or misfortunes of one of the parties which a court of equity would not tolerate. In such cases, where foreigners were concerned on either side, it would be impossible for the federal judicatories to do justice without an equitable as well as a legal jurisdiction. Agreements to convey lands claimed under the grants of different States may afford another example of the necessity of an equitable jurisdiction in the federal courts. This reasoning may not be so palpable in those States where the formal and technical distinction between LAW and EQUITY is not maintained, as in this State, where it is exemplified by every day's practice.

The judiciary authority of the Union is to extend:

Second. To treaties made, or which shall be made, under the authority of the United States, and to all cases affecting ambassadors, other public ministers, and consuls. These belong to the fourth class of the enumerated cases, as they have an evident connection with the preservation of the national peace.

Third. To cases of admiralty and maritime jurisdiction. These form, altogether, the fifth of the enumerated classes of causes proper for the cognisance of the national courts.

Fourth. To controversies to which the United States shall be a party. These constitute the third of those classes.

Fifth. To controversies between two or more States; between a State and citizens of another State; between citizens of different States. These belong to the fourth of those classes, and partake, in some measure, of the nature of the last.

Sixth. To cases between the citizens of the same State, *claiming lands under grants of different States.* These fall within the last class, and *are the only instances in which the proposed Constitution directly contemplates the cognisance of disputes between the citizens of the same State.*

Seventh. To cases between a State and the citizens thereof, and foreign States, citizens, or subjects. These have been already explained to belong to the fourth of the enumerated classes, and have been shown to be, in a peculiar manner, the proper subjects of the national judicature.

From this review of the particular powers of the federal judiciary, as marked out in the Constitution, it appears that they are all conformable to the principles which ought to have governed the structure of that department, and which were necessary to the perfection of the system. If some partial inconveniences should appear to be connected with the incorporation of any of them into the plan, it ought to be recollected that the national legislature will have ample authority to make such *exceptions,* and to prescribe such regulations as will be calculated to obviate or remove these inconveniences. The possibility of particular mischiefs can never be viewed, by a well-informed mind, as a solid objection to a general principle, which is calculated to avoid general mischiefs and to obtain general advantages.

PUBLIUS

Number 81

[HAMILTON]

LET US NOW return to the partition of the judiciary authority between different courts, and their relations to each other.

"The judicial power of the United States is" (by the plan of the convention) "to be vested in one Supreme Court, and in such inferior courts as the Congress may, from time to time, ordain and establish."[1]

That there ought to be one court of supreme and final judisdiction is a proposition which is not likely to be contested. The reasons for it have been assigned in another place, and are too obvious to need repetition. The only question that seems to have been raised concerning it is whether it ought to be a distinct body or a branch of the legislature. The same contradiction is observable in regard to this matter which has been remarked in several other

[1] Article 3, section 1.—PUBLIUS

cases. The very men who object to the Senate as a court of impeachments, on the ground of an improper intermixture of powers, advocate, by implication at least, the propriety of vesting the ultimate decision of all causes in the whole or in a part of the legislative body.

The arguments, or rather suggestions, upon which this charge is founded, are to this effect: "The authority of the proposed Supreme Court of the United States, which is to be a separate and independent body, will be superior to that of the legislature. The power of construing the laws according to the *spirit* of the Constitution, will enable that court to mould them into whatever shape it may think proper; especially as its decisions will not be in any manner subject to the revision or correction of the legislative body. This is as unprecedented as it is dangerous. In Britain, the judicial power, in the last resort, resides in the House of Lords, which is a branch of the legislature; and this part of the British government has been imitated in the State constitutions in general. The Parliament of Great Britain, and the legislatures of the several States, can at any time rectify, by law, the exceptionable decisions of their respective courts. But the errors and usurpations of the Supreme Court of the United States will be uncontrollable and remediless." This, upon examination, will be found to be made up altogether of false reasoning upon misconceived fact.

In the first place, there is not a syllable in the plan under consideration which *directly* empowers the national courts to construe the laws according to the spirit of the Constitution, or which gives them any greater latitude in this respect than may be claimed by the courts of every State. I admit, however, that the Constitution ought to be the standard of construction for the laws, and that wherever there is an evident opposition, the laws ought to give place to the Constitution. But this doctrine is not deducible from any circumstance peculiar to the plan of the convention, but from the general theory of a limited Constitution; and as far as it is true, is equally applicable to most, if not to all the State governments. There can be no objection, therefore, on this account, to the federal judicature which will not lie against the local judicatures in general, and which will not serve to condemn every constitution that attempts to set bounds to legislative discretion.

But perhaps the force of the objection may be thought to consist in the particular organisation of the Supreme Court; in its being composed of a distinct body of magistrates, instead of being one of the branches of the legislature, as in the government of Great Britain and that of the State. To insist upon this point, the authors of the objection must renounce the meaning they have laboured to annex to the celebrated maxim, requiring a separation of the departments of power. It shall, nevertheless, be conceded to them, agreeably to the interpretation given to that maxim in the course of these papers, that it is not violated by vesting the ultimate power of judging in a *part* of the legislative body. But though this be not an absolute violation of that excellent rule, yet it verges so nearly upon it as on this account alone to be less eligible than the mode preferred by the convention. From a body which had even a partial agency in passing bad laws we could rarely expect a disposition to temper and moderate them in the application. The same spirit which had operated in making them would be too apt in interpreting them; still less could it be expected that men who had infringed the Constitution in the character of legislators would be disposed to repair the breach in the character of judges. Nor is this all. Every reason which recommends the tenure of good behaviour for judicial offices militates against placing the judiciary power, in the last resort, in a body composed of men chosen for a limited period. There is an absurdity in referring the determination of causes, in the first instance, to judges of permanent standing; in the last, to those of a temporary and mutable constitution. And there is a still greater absurdity in subjecting the decisions of men, selected for their knowledge of the laws, acquired by long and laborious study, to the revision and control of men who, for want of the same advantage, cannot but be deficient in that knowledge. The members of the legislature will rarely be chosen with a view to those qualifications which fit men for the stations of judges; and as, on this account, there will be great reason to apprehend all the ill consequences of defective information, so, on account of the natural propensity of such bodies to party divisions, there will be no less reason to fear that the pestilential breath of faction may poison the fountains of justice. The habit of being continually marshalled on opposite sides will be too apt to stifle the voice both of law and of equity.

These considerations teach us to applaud the wisdom of those States who have committed the judicial power, in the last resort, not to a part of the legislature, but to distinct and independent bodies of men. Contrary to the supposition of those who have represented the plan of the convention, in this respect, as novel and unprecedented, it is but a copy of the constitutions of New Hampshire, Massachusetts, Pennsylvania, Delaware, Maryland, Virginia, North Carolina, South Carolina, and Georgia; and the preference which has been given to those models is highly to be commended.

It is not true, in the second place, that the Parliament of Great Britain, or the legislatures of the particular States, can rectify the exceptionable decisions of their respective courts in any other sense than might be done by a future legislature of the United States. The theory, neither of the British, nor the State constitutions, authorises the revisal of a judicial sentence by a legislative act. Nor is there anything in the proposed Constitution, more than in either of them, by which it is forbidden. In the former, as well as in the latter, the impropriety of the thing, on the general principles of law and reason, is the sole obstacle. A legislature, without exceeding its province, cannot reverse a determination once made in a particular case; though it may prescribe a new rule for future cases. This is the principle, and it applies in all its consequences, exactly in the same manner and extent, to the State governments, as to the national government now under consideration. Not the least difference can be pointed out in any view of the subject.

It may in the last place be observed that the supposed danger of judiciary encroachments on the legislative authority, which has been upon many occasions reiterated, is in reality a phantom. Particular misconstructions and contraventions of the will of the legislature may now and then happen; but they can never be so extensive as to amount to an inconvenience, or in any sensible degree to affect the order of the political system. This may be inferred with certainty from the general nature of the judicial power, from the objects to which it relates, from the manner in which it is exercised, from its comparative weakness, and from its total incapacity to support its usurpations by force. And the inference is greatly fortified by the consideration of the important constitutional check which the power of instituting impeachments in one part of the legislative body, and of determining upon

them in the other, would give to that body upon the members of the judicial department. This is alone a complete security. There never can be danger that the judges, by a series of deliberate usurpations on the authority of the legislature, would hazard the united resentment of the body intrusted with it, while this body was possessed of the means of punishing their presumption by degrading them from their stations. While this ought to remove all apprehensions on the subject, it affords, at the same time, a cogent argument for constituting the Senate a court for the trial of impeachments.

Having now examined and, I trust, removed the objections to the distinct and independent organisation of the Supreme Court, I proceed to consider the propriety of the power of constituting inferior courts,[1] and the relations which will subsist between these and the former.

The power of constituting inferior courts is evidently calculated to obviate the necessity of having recourse to the Supreme Court in every case of federal cognisance. It is intended to enable the national government to institute or *authorise,* in each State or district of the United States, a tribunal competent to the determination of matters of national jurisdiction within its limits.

But why, it is asked, might not the same purpose have been accomplished by the instrumentality of the State courts? This admits of different answers. Though the fitness and competency of those courts should be allowed in the utmost latitude, yet the substance of the power in question may still be regarded as a necessary part of the plan, if it were only to empower the national legislature to commit to them the cognisance of causes arising out of the national Constitution. To confer the power of determining such causes upon the existing courts of the several States, would perhaps be as much "to constitute tribunals" as to create new courts with the like power. But ought not a more direct and explicit provision to have been made in favour of the State

[1] This power has been absurdly represented as intended to abolish all the county courts in the several States, which are commonly called inferior courts. But the expressions of the Constitution are, to constitute "tribunals INFERIOR TO THE SUPREME COURT"; and the evident design of the provision is to enable the institution of local courts, subordinate to the Supreme, either in States or larger districts. It is ridiculous to imagine that county courts were in contemplation.—PUBLIUS

courts? There are, in my opinion, substantial reasons against such a provision: the most discerning cannot foresee how far the prevalency of a local spirit may be found to disqualify the local tribunals for the jurisdiction of national causes; whilst every man may discover that courts constituted like those of some of the States would be improper channels of the judicial authority of the Union. State judges, holding their offices during pleasure, or from year to year, will be too little independent to be relied upon for an inflexible execution of the national laws. And if there was a necessity for confiding the original cognisance of causes arising under those laws to them, there would be a correspondent necessity for leaving the door of appeal as wide as possible. In proportion to the grounds of confidence in, or distrust of, the subordinate tribunals, ought to be the facility or difficulty of appeals. And well satisfied as I am of the propriety of the appellate jurisdiction, in the several classes of causes to which it is extended by the plan of the convention, I should consider everything calculated to give, in practice, an *unrestrained course* to appeals as a source of public and private inconvenience.

I am not sure but that it will be found highly expedient and useful to divide the United States into four or five or half a dozen districts; and to institute a federal court in each district in lieu of one in every State. The judges of these courts, with the aid of the State judges, may hold circuits for the trial of causes in the several parts of the respective districts. Justice through them may be administered with ease and despatch; and appeals may be safely circumscribed within a narrow compass. This plan appears to me at present the most eligible of any that could be adopted, and in order to it, it is necessary that the power of constituting inferior courts should exist in the full extent in which it is to be found in the proposed Constitution.

These reasons seem sufficient to satisfy a candid mind that the want of such a power would have been a great defect in the plan. Let us now examine in what manner the judicial authority is to be distributed between the supreme and the inferior courts of the Union.

The Supreme Court is to be invested with original jurisdiction only "in cases affecting ambassadors, other public ministers, and consuls, and those in which a STATE shall be a party." Public ministers of every class are the immediate representatives of their sovereigns.

All questions in which they are concerned are so directly connected with the public peace that, as well for the preservation of this as out of respect to the sovereignties they represent, it is both expedient and proper that such questions should be submitted in the first instance to the highest judicatory of the nation. Though consuls have not in strictness a diplomatic character, yet as they are the public agents of the nations to which they belong, the same observation is in a great measure applicable to them. In cases in which a State might happen to be a party it would ill suit its dignity to be turned over to an inferior tribunal.

Though it may rather be a digression from the immediate subject of this paper, I shall take occasion to mention here a supposition which has excited some alarm upon very mistaken grounds. It has been suggested that an assignment of the public securities of one State to the citizens of another would enable them to prosecute that State in the federal courts for the amount of those securities; a suggestion which the following considerations prove to be without foundation.

It is inherent in the nature of sovereignty not to be amenable to the suit of an individual *without its consent.* This is the general sense and the general practice of mankind; and the exemption, as one of the attributes of sovereignty, is now enjoyed by the government of every State in the Union. Unless, therefore, there is a surrender of this immunity in the plan of the convention, it will remain with the States, and the danger intimated must be merely ideal. The circumstances which are necessary to produce an alienation of State sovereignty were discussed in considering the article of taxation, and need not be repeated here. A recurrence to the principles there established will satisfy us that there is no colour to pretend that the State governments would, by the adoption of that plan, be divested of the privilege of paying their own debts in their own way, free from every constraint but that which flows from the obligations of good faith. The contracts between a nation and individuals are only binding on the conscience of the sovereign and have no pretensions to a compulsive force. They confer no right of action independent of the sovereign will. To what purpose would it be to authorise suits against States for the debts they owe? How could recoveries be enforced? It is evident it could not be done without waging war against the contracting State; and to ascribe to the federal courts, by mere implication, and in destruction of a pre-existing right of the State governments, a power which would involve such a consequence, would be altogether forced and unwarrantable.

Let us resume the train of our observations. We have seen that the original jurisdiction of the Supreme Court would be confined to two classes of causes, and those of a nature rarely to occur. In all other cases of federal cognisance, the original jurisdiction would appertain to the inferior tribunals; and the Supreme Court would have nothing more than an appellate jurisdiction, "with such *exceptions* and under such *regulations* as the Congress shall make."

The propriety of this appellate jurisdiction has been scarcely called in question in regard to matters of law; but the clamours have been loud against it as applied to matters of fact. Some well-intentioned men in this State, deriving their notions from the language and forms which obtain in our courts, have been induced to consider it as an implied supersedure of the trial by jury in favour of the civil-law mode of trial which prevails in our courts of admiralty, probate, and chancery. A technical sense has been affixed to the term "appellate," which, in our law parlance, is commonly used in reference to appeals in the course of the civil law. But if I am not misinformed, the same meaning would not be given to it in any part of New England. There an appeal from one jury to another is familiar both in language and practice, and is even a matter of course, until there have been two verdicts on one side. The word "appellate," therefore, will not be understood in the same sense in New England as in New York, which shows the impropriety of a technical interpretation derived from the jurisprudence of any particular State. The expression, taken in the abstract, denotes nothing more than the power of one tribunal to review the proceedings of another, either as to the law or fact, or both. The mode of doing it may depend on ancient custom or legislative provision (in a new government it must depend on the latter), and may be with or without the aid of a jury, as may be judged advisable. If, therefore, the re-examination of a fact once determined by a jury should in any case be admitted under the proposed Constitution, it may be so regulated as to be done by a second jury, either by remanding the cause to the court below for a second trial of the fact, or by directing an issue immediately out of the Supreme Court.

But it does not follow that the re-examination of a fact once ascertained by a jury will be permitted in the Supreme Court. Why may not it be said, with the strictest propriety, when a writ of error is brought from an inferior to a superior court of law in this State, that the latter has jurisdiction of the fact as well as the law? It is true it cannot institute a new inquiry concerning the fact, but it takes cognisance of it as it appears upon the record, and pronounces the law arising upon it.[1] This is jurisdiction of both fact and law; nor is it even possible to separate them. Though the common-law courts of this State ascertain disputed facts by a jury, yet they unquestionably have jurisdiction of both fact and law; and accordingly when the former is agreed in the pleadings, they have no recourse to a jury, but proceed at once to judgment. I contend, therefore, on this ground, that the expressions, "appellate jurisdiction, both as to law and fact," do not necessarily imply a re-examination in the Supreme Court of facts decided by juries in the inferior courts.

The following train of ideas may well be imagined to have influenced the convention in relation to this particular provision. The appellate jurisdiction of the Supreme Court (it may have been argued) will extend to causes determinable in different modes, some in the course of the COMMON LAW, others in the course of the CIVIL LAW. In the former, the revision of the law only will be, generally speaking, the proper province of the Supreme Court; in the latter, the re-examination of the fact is agreeable to usage, and in some cases, of which prize causes are an example, might be essential to the preservation of the public peace. It is therefore necessary that the appellate jurisdiction should, in certain cases, extend in the broadest sense to matters of fact. It will not answer to make an express exception of cases which shall have been originally tried by a jury, because in the courts of some of the States *all causes* are tried in this mode;[2] and such an exception would preclude the revision of matters of fact, as well where it might be proper, as where it might be improper. To avoid all inconveniences, it will be safest to

[1] This word is composed of JUS and DICTIO, *juris dictio*, or a speaking and pronouncing of the law. —PUBLIUS

[2] I hold that the States will have concurrent jurisdiction with the subordinate federal judicatories, in many cases of federal cognizance, as will be explained in my next paper.—PUBLIUS

declare generally that the Supreme Court shall possess appellate jurisdiction both as to law and *fact,* and that this jurisdiction shall be subject to such *exceptions* and regulations as the national legislature may prescribe. This will enable the government to modify it in such a manner as will best answer the ends of public justice and security.

This view of the matter, at any rate, puts it out of all doubt that the supposed *abolition* of the trial by jury, by the operation of this provision, is fallacious and untrue. The legislature of the United States would certainly have full power to provide that in appeals to the Supreme Court there should be no reexamination of facts where they had been tried in the original causes by juries. This would certainly be an authorised exception; but if, for the reason already intimated, it should be thought too extensive, it might be qualified with a limitation to such causes only as are determinable at common law in that mode of trial.

The amount of the observations hitherto made on the authority of the judicial department is this: that it has been carefully restricted to those causes which are manifestly proper for the cognisance of the national judicature; that in the partition of this authority a very small portion of original jurisdiction has been preserved to the Supreme Court, and the rest consigned to the subordinate tribunals; that the Supreme Court will possess an appellate jurisdiction, both as to law and fact, in all the cases referred to them, both subject to any *exceptions* and *regulations* which may be thought advisable; that this appellate jurisdiction does, in no case, *abolish* the trial by jury; and that an ordinary degree of prudence and integrity in the national councils will insure us solid advantages from the establishment of the proposed judiciary, without exposing us to any of the inconveniences which have been predicted from that source.

PUBLIUS

Number 82

[HAMILTON]

THE ERECTION of a new government, whatever care or wisdom may distinguish the work, cannot fail to originate questions of intricacy and nicety; and these may, in a particular manner, be expected to flow from the establishment of a constitution founded upon the total or partial incorporation of a number of distinct sovereignties. 'Tis time only that can mature and perfect so compound a system, can liquidate the meaning of all the parts, and can adjust them to each other in a harmonious and consistent WHOLE.

Such questions, accordingly, have arisen upon the plan proposed by the convention, and particularly concerning the judiciary department. The principal of these respect the situation of the State courts in regard to those causes which are to be submitted to federal jurisdiction. Is this to be exclusive, or are those courts to possess a concurrent jurisdiction? If the latter, in what relation will they stand to the national tribunals? These are inquiries which we meet with in the mouths of men of sense, and which are certainly entitled to attention.

The principles established in a former paper[1] teach us that the States will retain all *pre-existing* authorities which may not be exclusively delegated to the federal head; and that this exclusive delegation can only exist in one of three cases: where an exclusive authority is, in express terms, granted to the Union; or where a particular authority is granted to the Union, and the exercise of a like authority is prohibited to the States; or where an authority is granted to the Union, with which a similar authority in the States would be utterly incompatible. Though these principles may not apply with the same force to the judiciary as to the legislative power, yet I am inclined to think that they are, in the main, just with respect to the former as well as the latter. And under this impression, I shall lay it down as a rule that the State Courts will *retain* the jurisdiction they now have, unless it appears to be taken away in one of the enumerated modes.

The only thing in the proposed Constitution which wears the appearance of confining the causes of federal cognisance to the federal courts is contained in this passage:—"The JUDICIAL POWER of the United States *shall be vested* in one Supreme Court and in *such* inferior courts as the Congress shall from time to time ordain and establish." This might either be construed to signify that the supreme and subordinate courts of the Union should alone have the power of deciding those causes to which their authority is to extend; or simply to denote that the organs of the national judiciary should be one Supreme Court, and as many subordinate courts as Congress should think proper to appoint; or in other words,

[1] Number 31.

that the United States should exercise the judicial power with which they are to be invested through one supreme tribunal and a certain number of inferior ones to be instituted by them. The first excludes, the last admits, the concurrent jurisdiction of the State tribunals; and as the first would amount to an alienation of State power by implication, the last appears to me the most natural and the most defensible construction.

But this doctrine of concurrent jurisdiction is only clearly applicable to those descriptions of causes of which the State courts have previous cognisance. It is not equally evident in relation to cases which may grow out of, and be *peculiar* to, the Constitution to be established; for not to allow the State courts a right of jurisdiction in such cases can hardly be considered as the abridgment of a pre-existing authority. I mean not therefore to contend that the United States, in the course of legislation upon the objects intrusted to their direction, may not commit the decision of causes arising upon a particular regulation to the federal courts solely, if such a measure should be deemed expedient; but I hold that the State courts will be divested of no part of their primitive jurisdiction further than may relate to an appeal; and I am even of opinion that in every case in which they were not expressly excluded by the future acts of the national legislature they will of course take cognisance of the causes to which those acts may give birth. This I infer from the nature of judiciary power, and from the general genius of the system. The judiciary power of every government looks beyond its own local or municipal laws, and in civil cases lays hold of all subjects of litigation between parties within its jurisdiction, though the causes of dispute are relative to the laws of the most distant part of the globe. Those of Japan, not less than of New York, may furnish the objects of legal discussion to our courts. When in addition to this we consider the State governments and the national governments, as they truly are, in the light of kindred systems, and as parts of ONE WHOLE, the inference seems to be conclusive that the State courts would have a concurrent jurisdiction in all cases arising under the laws of the Union where it was not expressly prohibited.

Here another question occurs: What relation would subsist between the national and State courts in these instances of concurrent jurisdiction? I answer, that an appeal would certainly lie from the latter to the Supreme Court of the United States. The Constitution in direct terms gives an appellate jurisdiction to the Supreme Court in all the enumerated cases of federal cognisance in which it is not to have an original one, without a single expression to confine its operation to the inferior federal courts. The objects of appeal, not the tribunals from which it is to be made, are alone contemplated. From this circumstance, and from the reason of the thing, it ought to be construed to extend to the State tribunals. Either this must be the case, or the local courts must be excluded from a concurrent jurisdiction in matters of national concern, else the judiciary authority of the Union may be eluded at the pleasure of every plaintiff or prosecutor. Neither of these consequences ought, without evident necessity, to be involved; the latter would be entirely inadmissible, as it would defeat some of the most important and avowed purposes of the proposed government, and would essentially embarrass its measures. Nor do I perceive any foundation for such a supposition. Agreeably to the remark already made, the national and State systems are to be regarded as ONE WHOLE. The courts of the latter will of course be natural auxiliaries to the execution of the laws of the Union, and an appeal from them will as naturally lie to that tribunal which is destined to unite and assimilate the principles of national justice and the rules of national decisions. The evident aim of the plan of the convention is, that all the causes of the specified classes shall, for weighty public reasons, receive their original or final determination in the courts of the Union. To confine, therefore, the general expression giving appellate jurisdiction to the Supreme Court to appeals from the subordinate federal courts, instead of allowing their extension to the State courts, would be to abridge the latitude of the terms in subversion of the intent, contrary to every sound rule of interpretation.

But could an appeal be made to lie from the State courts to the subordinate federal judicatories? This is another of the questions which have been raised, and of greater difficulty than the former. The following considerations countenance the affirmative. The plan of the convention, in the first place, authorises the national legislature "to constitute tribunals inferior to the Supreme Court."[1] It declares, in the next place, that "the JUDICIAL POWER of the United States *shall be vested* in

[1] Section 8, article 1.—PUBLIUS

one Supreme Court, and in such inferior courts as Congress shall ordain and establish"; and it then proceeds to enumerate the cases to which this judicial power shall extend. It afterwards divides the jurisdiction of the Supreme Court into original and appellate, but gives no definition of that of the subordinate courts. The only outlines described for them are that they shall be "inferior to the Supreme Court," and that they shall not exceed the specified limits of the federal judiciary. Whether their authority shall be original or appellate, or both, is not declared. All this seems to be left to the discretion of the legislature. And this being the case, I perceive at present no impediment to the establishment of an appeal from the State courts to the subordinate national tribunals; and many advantages attending the power of doing it may be imagined. It would diminish the motives to the multiplication of federal courts, and would admit of arrangements calculated to contract the appellate jurisdiction of the Supreme Court. The State tribunals may then be left with a more entire charge of federal causes; and appeals, in most cases in which they may be deemed proper, instead of being carried to the Supreme Court, may be made to lie from the State courts to district courts of the Union.   PUBLIUS

Number 83

[HAMILTON]

THE OBJECTION to the plan of the convention which has met with most success in this State, and perhaps in several of the other States, is *that relative to the want of a constitutional provision* for the trial by jury in civil cases. The disingenuous form in which this objection is usually stated has been repeatedly adverted to and exposed, but continues to be pursued in all the conversations and writings of the opponents of the plan. The mere silence of the Constitution in regard to *civil causes* is represented as an abolition of the trial by jury, and the declamations to which it has afforded a pretext are artfully calculated to induce a persuasion that this pretended abolition is complete and universal, extending not only to every species of civil, but even to *criminal, causes.* To argue with respect to the latter would, however, be as vain and fruitless as to attempt the serious proof of the *existence* of *matter,* or to demonstrate any of those propositions which, by their own internal evidence, force conviction when expressed in

language adapted to convey their meaning.

With regard to civil causes, subtleties almost too contemptible for refutation have been employed to countenance the surmise that a thing which is only *not provided for* is entirely *abolished.* Every man of discernment must at once perceive the wide difference between *silence* and *abolition.* But as the inventors of this fallacy have attempted to support it by certain *legal maxims* of interpretation, which they have perverted from their true meaning, it may not be wholly useless to explore the ground they have taken.

The maxims on which they rely are of this nature: "A specification of particulars is an exclusion of generals"; or "The expression of one thing is the exclusion of another." Hence, say they, as the Constitution has established the trial by jury in criminal cases, and is silent in respect to civil, this silence is an implied prohibition of trial by jury in regard to the latter.

The rules of legal interpretation are rules of *common-sense,* adopted by the courts in the construction of the laws. The true test, therefore, of a just application of them is its conformity to the source from which they are derived. This being the case, let me ask if it is consistent with common-sense to suppose that a provision obliging the legislative power to commit the trial of criminal causes to juries is a privation of its right to authorise or permit that mode of trial in other cases? Is it natural to suppose that a command to do one thing is a prohibition to the doing of another which there was a previous power to do and which is not incompatible with the thing commanded to be done? If such a supposition would be unnatural and unreasonable, it cannot be rational to maintain that an injunction of the trial by jury in certain cases is an interdiction of it in others.

A power to constitute courts is a power to prescribe the mode of trial; and consequently, if nothing was said in the Constitution on the subject of juries, the legislature would be at liberty either to adopt that institution or to let it alone. This discretion in regard to criminal causes is abridged by the express injunction of trial by jury in all such cases; but it is, of course, left at large in relation to civil causes, there being a total silence on this head. The specification of an obligation to try all criminal causes in a particular mode excludes indeed the obligation or necessity of employing the same mode in civil causes, but does not abridge *the power* of the legislature to exercise that mode if it should be thought proper. The pretence, therefore, that the national legislature would not be at full liberty to submit all the civil causes of federal cognisance to the determination of juries is a pretence destitute of all just foundation.

From these observations this conclusion results: that the trial by jury in civil cases would not be abolished; and that the use attempted to be made of the maxims which have been quoted is contrary to reason and commonsense, and therefore not admissible. Even if these maxims had a precise technical sense, corresponding with the idea of those who employ them upon the present occasion, which, however, is not the case, they would still be inapplicable to a constitution of government. In relation to such a subject, the natural and obvious sense of its provisions, apart from any technical rules, is the true criterion of construction.

Having now seen that the maxims relied upon will not bear the use made of them, let us endeavour to ascertain their proper use and true meaning. This will be best done by examples. The plan of the convention declares that the power of Congress, or, in other words, of the *national legislature,* shall extend to certain enumerated cases. This specification of particulars evidently excludes all pretension to a general legislative authority, because an affirmative grant of special powers would be absurd, as well as useless, if a general authority was intended.

In like manner the judicial authority of the federal judicatures is declared by the Constitution to comprehend certain cases particularly specified. The expression of those cases marks the precise limits, beyond which the federal courts cannot extend their jurisdiction, because the objects of their cognisance being enumerated, the specification would be nugatory if it did not exclude all ideas of more extensive authority.

These examples are sufficient to elucidate the maxims which have been mentioned, and to designate the manner in which they should be used. But that there may be no misapprehension upon this subject, I shall add one case more, to demonstrate the proper use of these maxims, and the abuse which has been made of them.

Let us suppose that by the laws of this State a married woman was incapable of conveying her estate, and that the legislature, considering this as an evil, should enact that she might dispose of her property by deed executed in the presence of a magistrate. In such a case there can be no doubt but the specification would amount to an exclusion of any other mode of conveyance, because the woman having no previous power to alienate her property the specification determines the particular mode which she is, for that purpose, to avail herself of. But let us further suppose that in a subsequent part of the same act it should be declared that no woman should dispose of any estate of a determinate value without the consent of three of her nearest relations, signified by their signing the deed; could it be inferred from this regulation that a married woman might not procure the approbation of her relations to a deed for conveying property of inferior value? The position is too absurd to merit a refutation, and yet this is precisely the position which those must establish who contend that the trial by juries in civil cases is abolished, because it is expressly provided for in cases of a criminal nature.

From these observations it must appear unquestionably true that trial by jury is in no case abolished by the proposed Constitution, and it is equally true that in those controversies between individuals in which the great body of the people are likely to be interested, that institution will remain precisely in the same situation in which it is placed by the State constitutions, and will be in no degree altered or influenced by the adoption of the plan under consideration. The foundation of this assertion is, that the national judiciary will have no cognisance of them, and of course they will remain determinable as heretofore by the State courts only, and in the manner which the State constitutions and laws prescribe. All land causes, except where claims under the grants of different States come into question, and all other controversies between the citizens of the same State, unless where they depend upon positive violations of the articles of union by acts of the State legislatures, will belong exclusively to the jurisdiction of the State tribunals. Add to this, that admiralty causes, and almost all those which are of equity jurisdiction, are determinable under our own government without the intervention of a jury, and the inference from the whole will be that this institution, as it exists with us at present, cannot possibly be affected to any great extent by the proposed alteration in our system of government.

The friends and adversaries of the plan of

the convention, if they agree in nothing else, concur at least in the value they set upon the trial by jury; or if there is any difference between them it consists in this: the former regard it as a valuable safeguard to liberty; the latter represent it as the very palladium of free government. For my own part, the more the operation of the institution has fallen under my observation, the more reason I have discovered for holding it in high estimation; and it would be altogether superfluous to examine to what extent it deserves to be esteemed useful or essential in a representative republic, or how much more merit it may be entitled to as a defence against the oppressions of an hereditary monarch than as a barrier to the tyranny of popular magistrates in a popular government. Discussions of this kind would be more curious than beneficial, as all are satisfied of the utility of the institution and of its friendly aspect to liberty. But I must acknowledge that I cannot readily discern the inseparable connection between the existence of liberty and the trial by jury in civil cases. Arbitrary impeachments, arbitrary methods of prosecuting pretended offences, and arbitrary punishments upon arbitrary convictions, have ever appeared to me to be the great engines of judicial despotism; and these have all relation to criminal proceedings. The trial by jury in criminal cases, aided by the *habeas-corpus* act, seems therefore to be alone concerned in the question. And both of these are provided for, in the most ample manner, in the plan of the convention.

It has been observed that trial by jury is a safeguard against an oppressive exercise of the power of taxation. This observation deserves to be canvassed.

It is evident that it can have no influence upon the legislature in regard to the *amount* of taxes to be laid, to the *objects* upon which they are to be imposed, or to the *rule* by which they are to be apportioned. If it can have any influence, therefore, it must be upon the mode of collection, and the conduct of the officers intrusted with the execution of the revenue laws.

As to the mode of collection in this State, under our own Constitution, the trial by jury is in most cases out of use. The taxes are usually levied by the more summary proceeding of distress and sale, as in cases of rent. And it is acknowledged on all hands that this is essential to the efficacy of the revenue laws. The dilatory course of a trial at law to recover the taxes imposed on individuals would neither suit the exigencies of the public nor promote the convenience of the citizens. It would often occasion an accumulation of costs more burdensome than the original sum of the tax to be levied.

And as to the conduct of the officers of the revenue, the provision in favour of trial by jury in criminal cases will afford the security aimed at. Wilful abuses of a public authority, to the oppression of the subject, and every species of official extortion, are offences against the government, for which the persons who commit them may be indicted and punished according to the circumstances of the case.

The excellence of the trial by jury in civil cases appears to depend on circumstances foreign to the preservation of liberty. The strongest argument in its favour is that it is a security against corruption. As there is always more time and better opportunity to tamper with a standing body of magistrates than with a jury summoned for the occasion, there is room to suppose that a corrupt influence would more easily find its way to the former than to the latter. The force of this consideration is, however, diminished by others. The sheriff, who is the summoner of ordinary juries, and the clerks of courts, who have the nomination of special juries, are themselves standing officers, and, acting individually, may be supposed more accessible to the touch of corruption than the judges, who are a collective body. It is not difficult to see that it would be in the power of those officers to select jurors who would serve the purpose of the party as well as a corrupted bench. In the next place, it may fairly be supposed that there would be less difficulty in gaining some of the jurors promiscuously taken from the public mass than in gaining men who had been chosen by the government for their probity and good character. But making every deduction for these considerations, the trial by jury must still be a valuable check upon corruption. It greatly multiplies the impediments to its success. As matters now stand, it would be necessary to corrupt both court and jury; for where the jury have gone evidently wrong, the court will generally grant a new trial, and it would be in most cases of little use to practise upon the jury unless the court could be likewise gained. Here then is a double security; and it will readily be perceived that this complicated agency tends to preserve the purity of both institutions. By increasing the obstacles to success it discourages attempts to seduce the integrity of either. The temptations to prostitution which the judges might have to surmount must certainly be much fewer, while the cooperation of a jury is necessary, than they might be if they had themselves the exclusive determination of all causes.

Notwithstanding, therefore, the doubts I have expressed as to the essentiality of trial by jury in civil cases to liberty, I admit that it is in most cases, under proper regulations, an excellent method of determining questions of property; and that on this account alone it would be entitled to a constitutional provision in its favour if it were possible to fix the limits within which it ought to be comprehended. There is, however, in all cases, great difficulty in this; and men not blinded by enthusiasm must be sensible that in a federal government, which is a composition of societies whose ideas and institutions in relation to the matter materially vary from each other, that difficulty must be not a little augmented. For my own part, at every new view I take of the subject, I become more convinced of the reality of the obstacles which, we are authoritatively informed, prevented the insertion of a provision on this head in the plan of the convention.

The great difference between the limits of the jury trial in different States is not generally understood; and as it must have considerable influence on the sentence we ought to pass upon the omission complained of in regard to this point an explanation of it is necessary. In this State, our judicial establishments resemble, more nearly than in any other, those of Great Britain. We have courts of common law, courts of probates (analogous in certain matters to the spiritual courts in England), a court of admiralty, and a court of chancery. In the courts of common law only the trial by jury prevails, and this with some exceptions. In all the others a single judge presides, and proceeds in general either according to the course of the cannon or civil law, without the aid of a jury.[1] In New Jersey there is a court of chancery which proceeds like ours, but neither courts of admiralty nor of probates, in the sense in which these last are established with us. In that State the courts of common law

[1] It has been erroneously insinuated, with regard to the Court of Chancery, that this court generally tries disputed facts by a jury. The truth is, that references to a jury in that court rarely happen, and are in no case necessary but where the validity of a devise of land comes into question.—PUBLIUS

have the cognisance of those causes which with us are determinable in the courts of admiralty and of probates, and of course the jury trial is more extensive in New Jersey than in New York. In Pennsylvania this is perhaps still more the case, for there is no court of chancery in that State, and its common-law courts have equity jurisdiction. It has a court of admiralty, but none of probates, at least on the plan of ours. Delaware has in these respects imitated Pennsylvania. Maryland approaches more nearly to New York, as does also Virginia, except that the latter has a plurality of chancellors. North Carolina bears most affinity to Pennsylvania; South Carolina to Virginia. I believe, however, that in some of those States which have distinct courts of admiralty, the causes depending in them are triable by juries. In Georgia there are none but common-law courts, and an appeal of course lies from the verdict of one jury to another, which is called a special jury, and for which a particular mode of appointments is marked out. In Connecticut, they have no distinct courts either of chancery or of admiralty, and their courts of probates have no jurisdiction of causes. Their common-law courts have admiralty and, to a certain extent, equity jurisdiction. In cases of importance, their General Assembly is the only court of chancery. In Connecticut, therefore, the trial by jury extends in *practice* further than in any other State yet mentioned. Rhode Island is, I believe, in this particular, pretty much in the situation of Connecticut. Massachusetts and New Hampshire, in regard to the blending of law, equity, and admiralty jurisdictions, are in a similar predicament. In the four Eastern States, the trial by jury not only stands upon a broader foundation than in the other States, but it is attended with a peculiarity unknown, in its full extent, to any of them. There is an appeal *of course* from one jury to another, till there have been two verdicts out of three on one side.

From this sketch it appears that there is a material diversity, as well in the modification as in the extent of the institution of trial by jury in civil cases, in the several States; and from this fact these obvious reflections flow: first, that no general rule could have been fixed upon by the convention which would have corresponded with the circumstances of all the States; and secondly, that more or at least as much might have been hazarded by taking the system of any one State for a standard, as by omitting a provision altogether and leaving the matter, as has been done, to legislative regulation.

The propositions which have been made for supplying the omission have rather served to illustrate than to obviate the difficulty of the thing. The minority of Pennsylvania have proposed this mode of expression for the purpose —"Trial by jury shall be as heretofore"—and this I maintain would be senseless and nugatory. The United States, in their united or collective capacity, are the OBJECT to which all general provisions in the Constitution must necessarily be construed to refer. Now it is evident that though trial by jury, with various limitations, is known in each State individually, yet in the United States, *as such,* it is at this time altogether unknown, because the present federal government has no judiciary power whatever; and consequently there is no proper antecedent or previous establishment to which the term *heretofore* could relate. It would therefore be destitute of a precise meaning, and inoperative from its uncertainty.

As, on the one hand, the form of the provision would not fulfil the intent of its proposers, so, on the other, if I apprehend that intent rightly, it would be in itself inexpedient. I presume it to be, that causes in the federal courts should be tried by jury, if, in the State where the courts sat, that mode of trial would obtain in a similar case in the State courts; that is to say, admiralty causes should be tried in Connecticut by a jury, in New York without one. The capricious operation of so dissimilar a method of trial in the same cases, under the same government, is of itself sufficient to indispose every well-regulated judgment towards it. Whether the cause should be tried with or without a jury would depend, in a great number of cases, on the accidental situation of the court and parties.

But this is not, in my estimation, the greatest objection. I feel a deep and deliberate conviction that there are many cases in which the trial by jury is an ineligible one. I think it so particularly in cases which concern the public peace with foreign nations—that is, in most cases where the question turns wholly on the laws of nations. Of this nature, among others, are all prize causes. Juries cannot be supposed competent to investigations that require a thorough knowledge of the laws and usages of nations; and they will sometimes be under the influence of impressions which will not suffer them to pay sufficient regard to those consid-erations of public policy which ought to guide their inquiries. There would of course be always danger that the rights of other nations might be infringed by their decisions, so as to afford occasions of reprisal and war. Though the proper province of juries be to determine matters of fact, yet in most cases legal consequences are complicated with fact in such a manner as to render a separation impracticable.

It will add great weight to this remark, in relation to prize causes, to mention that the method of determining them has been thought worthy of particular regulation in various treaties between different powers of Europe, and that, pursuant to such treaties, they are determinable in Great Britain, in the last resort, before the king himself, in his privy council, where the fact, as well as the law, undergoes a re-examination. This alone demonstrates the impolicy of inserting a fundamental provision in the Constitution which would make the State systems a standard for the national government in the article under consideration, and the danger of encumbering the government with any constitutional provisions the propriety of which is not indisputable.

My convictions are equally strong that great advantages result from the separation of the equity from the law jurisdiction, and that the causes which belong to the former would be improperly committed to juries. The great and primary use of a court of equity is to give relief *in extraordinary cases,* which are *exceptions*[1] to general rules. To unite the jurisdiction of such cases with the ordinary jurisdiction must have a tendency to unsettle the general rules, and to subject every case that arises to a *special* determination; while a separation of the one from the other has the contrary effect of rendering one a sentinel over the other, and of keeping each within the expedient limits. Besides this, the circumstances that constitute cases proper for courts of equity are in many instances so nice and intricate that they are incompatible with the genius of trials by jury. They require often such long, deliberate, and critical investigation as would be impracticable to men called from their occupations, and obliged to decide before they were permitted to return to them. The simplicity and

---

[1] It is true that the principles by which that relief is governed are now reduced to a regular system; but it is not the less true that they are in the main applicable to SPECIAL circumstances, which form exceptions to general rules.—PUBLIUS

expedition which form the distinguishing characters of this mode of trial require that the matter to be decided should be reduced to some single and obvious point: while the litigations usual in chancery frequently comprehend a long train of minute and independent particulars.

It is true that the separation of the equity from the legal jurisdiction is peculiar to the English system of jurisprudence: which is the model that has been followed in several of the States. But it is equally true that the trial by jury has been unknown in every case in which they have been united. And the separation is essential to the preservation of that institution in its pristine purity. The nature of a court of equity will readily permit the extension of its jurisdiction to matters of law; but it is not a little to be suspected that the attempt to extend the jurisdiction of the courts of law to matters of equity will not only be unproductive of the advantages which may be derived from courts of chancery, on the plan upon which they are established in this State, but will tend gradually to change the nature of the courts of law, and to undermine the trial by jury, by introducing questions too complicated for a decision in that mode.

These appeared to be conclusive reasons against incorporating the systems of all the States, in the formation of the national judiciary, according to what may be conjectured to have been the attempt of the Pennsylvania minority. Let us now examine how far the proposition of Massachusetts is calculated to remedy the supposed defect.

It is in this form: "In civil actions between citizens of different States, every issue of fact, arising in *actions at common law,* may be tried by a jury if the parties, or either of them, request it."

This, at best, is a proposition confined to one description of causes; and the inference is fair, either that the Massachusetts convention considered that as the only class of federal causes in which the trial by jury would be proper; or that if desirous of a more extensive provision, they found it impracticable to devise one which would properly answer the end. If the first, the omission of a regulation respecting so partial an object can never be considered as a material imperfection in the system. If the last, it affords a strong corroboration of the extreme difficulty of the thing.

But this is not all: if we advert to the observations already made respecting the courts that subsist in the several States of the Union, and the different powers exercised by them, it will appear that there are no expressions more vague and indeterminate than those which have been employed to characterise *that* species of causes which it is intended shall be entitled to a trial by jury. In this State, the boundaries between actions at common law and actions of equitable jurisdiction are ascertained in conformity to the rules which prevail in England upon that subject. In many of the other States the boundaries are less precise. In some of them, every cause is to be tried in a court of common law, and upon that foundation every action may be considered as an action at common law, to be determined by a jury, if the parties, or either of them, choose it. Hence the same irregularity and confusion would be introduced by a compliance with this proposition that I have already noticed as resulting from the regulation proposed by the Pennsylvania minority. In one State a cause would receive its determination from a jury, if the parties, or either of them, requested it; but in another State, a cause exactly similar to the other must be decided without the intervention of a jury, because the State judicatories varied as to common-law jurisdiction.

It is obvious, therefore, that the Massachusetts proposition upon this subject cannot operate as a general regulation until some uniform plan, with respect to the limits of common-law and equitable jurisdictions, shall be adopted by the different States. To devise a plan of that kind is a task arduous in itself, and which it would require much time and reflection to mature. It would be extremely difficult, if not impossible, to suggest any general regulation that would be acceptable to all the States in the Union, or that would perfectly quadrate with the several State institutions.

It may be asked, Why could not a reference have been made to the constitution of this State, taking that, which is allowed by me to be a good one, as a standard for the United States? I answer that it is not very probable the other States would entertain the same opinion of our institutions as we do ourselves. It is natural to suppose that they are hitherto more attached to their own, and that each would struggle for the preference. If the plan of taking one State as a model for the whole had been thought of in the convention, it is to be presumed that the adoption of it in that body would have been rendered difficult by the predilection of each representation in favour of its own government; and it must be uncertain which of the States would have been taken as the model. It has been shown that many of them would be improper ones. And I leave it to conjecture whether, under all circumstances, it is most likely that New York, or some other State, would have been preferred. But admit that a judicious selection could have been effected in the convention, still there would have been great danger of jealousy and disgust in the other States at the partiality which had been shown to the institutions of one. The enemies of the plan would have been furnished with a fine pretext for raising a host of local prejudices against it, which perhaps might have hazarded, in no inconsiderable degree, its final establishment.

To avoid the embarrassments of a definition of the cases which the trial by jury ought to embrace, it is sometimes suggested by men of enthusiastic tempers that a provision might have been inserted for establishing it in all cases whatsoever. For this, I believe, no precedent is to be found in any member of the Union; and the considerations which have been stated in discussing the proposition of the minority of Pennsylvania must satisfy every sober mind that the establishment of the trial by jury in *all* cases would have been an unpardonable error in the plan.

In short, the more it is considered the more arduous will appear the task of fashioning a provision in such a form as not to express too little to answer the purpose, or too much to be advisable; or which might not have opened other sources of opposition to the great and essential object of introducing a firm national government.

I cannot but persuade myself, on the other hand, that the different lights in which the subject has been placed in the course of these observations will go far towards removing in candid minds the apprehensions they may have entertained on the point. They have tended to show that the security of liberty is materially concerned only in the trial by jury in criminal cases, which is provided for in the most ample manner in the plan of the convention; that even in far the greatest proportion of civil cases, and those in which the great body of the community is interested, that mode of trial will remain in its full force, as established in the State constitutions, untouched and unaffected by the plan of the convention; that it

is in no case abolished[1] by that plan; and that there are great if not insurmountable difficulties in the way of making any precise and proper provision for it in a Constitution for the United States.

The best judges of the matter will be the least anxious for a constitutional establishment of the trial by jury in civil cases, and will be the most ready to admit that the changes which are continually happening in the affairs of society may render a different mode of determining questions of property preferable in many cases in which that mode of trial now prevails. For my part, I acknowledge myself to be convinced that even in this State it might be advantageously extended to some cases to which it does not at present apply, and might as advantageously be abridged in others. It is conceded by all reasonable men that it ought not to obtain in all cases. The examples of innovations which contract its ancient limits, as well in these States as in Great Britain, afford a strong presumption that its former extent has been found inconvenient, and give room to suppose that future experience may discover the propriety and utility of other exceptions. I suspect it to be impossible in the nature of the thing to fix the salutary point at which the operation of the institution ought to stop, and this is with me a strong argument for leaving the matter to the discretion of the legislature.

This is now clearly understood to be the case in Great Britain, and it is equally so in the State of Connecticut; and yet it may be safely affirmed that more numerous encroachments have been made upon the trial by jury in this State since the Revolution, though provided for by a positive article of our constitution, than has happened in the same time either in Connecticut or Great Britain. It may be added that these encroachments have generally originated with the men who endeavour to persuade the people they are the warmest defenders of popular liberty, but who have rarely suffered constitutional obstacles to arrest them in a favourite career. The truth is that the general GENIUS of a government is all that can be substantially relied upon for permanent effects. Particular provisions, though not altogether useless, have far less virtue and efficacy than are commonly ascribed to them; and the want of them will never be, with men of

---

[1] *Vide* Number 71, in which the supposition of its being abolished by the appellate jurisdiction in matters of fact being vested in the Supreme Court, is examined and refuted.—PUBLIUS

sound discernment, a decisive objection to any plan which exhibits the leading characters of a good government.

It certainly sounds not a little harsh and extraordinary to affirm that there is no security for liberty in a Constitution which expressly establishes the trial by jury in criminal cases, because it does not do it in civil also; while it is a notorious fact that Connecticut, which has been always regarded as the most popular State in the Union, can boast of no constitutional provision for either. PUBLIUS

Number 84

[HAMILTON]

IN THE course of the foregoing review of the Constitution, I have taken notice of, and endeavoured to answer, most of the objections which have appeared against it. There, however, remain a few which either did not fall naturally under any particular head or were forgotten in their proper places. These shall now be discussed; but as the subject has been drawn into great length, I shall so far consult brevity as to comprise all my observations on these miscellaneous points in a single paper.

The most considerable of the remaining objections is that the plan of the convention contains no bill of rights. Among other answers given to this, it has been upon different occasions remarked that the constitutions of several of the States are in a similar predicament. I add that New York is of the number. And yet the opposers of the new system, in this State, who profess an unlimited admiration for its constitution, are among the most intemperate partisans of a bill of rights. To justify their zeal in this matter, they allege two things: one is, that though the constitution of New York has no bill of rights prefixed to it, yet it contains, in the body of it, various provisions in favour of particular privileges and rights, which, in substance, amount to the same thing; the other is, that the Constitution adopts, in their full extent, the common and statute law of Great Britain, by which many other rights, not expressed in it, are equally secured.

To the first I answer, that the Constitution proposed by the convention contains, as well as the constitution of this State, a number of such provisions.

Independent of those which relate to the structure of the government, we find the following: Article 1, section 3, clause 7—"Judgment in cases of impeachment shall not extend further than to removal from office, and disqualification to hold and enjoy any office of honour, trust, or profit under the United States; but the party convicted shall, nevertheless, be liable and subject to indictment, trial, judgment, and punishment according to law." Section 9 of the same article, clause 2—"The privilege of the writ of *habeas corpus* shall not be suspended, unless when in cases of rebellion or invasion the public safety may require it." Clause 3—"No bill of attainder or *ex-post-facto* law shall be passed." Clause 7—"No title of nobility shall be granted by the United States; and no person holding any office of profit or trust under them, shall, without the consent of the Congress, accept of any present, emolument, office, or title of any kind whatever, from any king, prince, or foreign state." Article 3, section 2, clause 3—"The trial of all crimes, except in cases of impeachment, shall be by jury; and such trial shall be held in the State where the said crimes shall have been committed; but when not committed within any State, the trial shall be at such place or places as the Congress may by law have directed." Section 3 of the same article—"Treason against the United States shall consist only in levying war against them, or in adhering to their enemies, giving them aid and comfort. No person shall be convicted of treason, unless on the testimony of two witnesses to the same overt act, or on confession in open court." And clause 3 of the same section—"The Congress shall have power to declare the punishment of treason; but no attainder of treason shall work corruption of blood, or forfeiture, except during the life of the person attainted."

It may well be a question whether these are not, upon the whole, of equal importance with any which are to be found in the constitution of this State. The establishment of the writ of *habeas corpus,* the prohibition of *ex-post-facto* laws, and of TITLES OF NOBILITY, *to which we have no corresponding provision in our Constitution,* are perhaps greater securities to liberty and republicanism than any it contains. The creation of crimes after the commission of the fact, or, in other words, the subjecting of men to punishment for things which, when they were done, were breaches of no law, and the practice of arbitrary imprisonments, have been, in all ages, the favourite and most formidable instruments of tyranny. The observations of the judicious Blackstone,[1] in reference

[1] *Vide* Blackstone's *Commentaries,* vol. l., p. 136. —PUBLIUS

to the latter, are well worthy of recital: "To bereave a man of life, [says he,] or by violence to confiscate his estate, without accusation or trial would be so gross and notorious an act of despotism, as must at once convey the alarm of tyranny throughout the whole nation; but confinement of the person, by secretly hurrying him to jail, where his sufferings are unknown or forgotten, is a less public, a less striking, and therefore *a more dangerous engine* of arbitrary government." And as a remedy for this fatal evil he is everywhere peculiarly emphatical in his encomiums on the *habeas-corpus* act, which in one place he calls "the BULWARK of the British Constitution."[1]

Nothing need be said to illustrate the importance of the prohibition of titles of nobility. This may truly be denominated the cornerstone of republican government; for so long as they are excluded there can never be serious danger that the government will be any other than that of the people.

To the second—that is, to the pretended establishment of the common and statute law by the Constitution, I answer, that they are expressly made subject "to such alterations and provisions as the legislature shall from time to time make concerning the same." They are therefore at any moment liable to repeal by the ordinary legislative power, and of course have no constitutional sanction. The only use of the declaration was to recognise the ancient law, and to remove doubts which might have been occasioned by the Revolution. This consequently can be considered as no part of a declaration of rights, which under our constitutions must be intended as limitations of the power of the government itself.

It has been several times truly remarked that bills of rights are, in their origin, stipulations between kings and their subjects, abridgments of prerogative in favour of privilege, reservations of rights not surrendered to the prince. Such was MAGNA CHARTA, obtained by the barons, sword in hand, from King John. Such were the subsequent confirmations of that charter by succeeding princes. Such was the *Petition of Right* assented to by Charles I., in the beginning of his reign. Such, also, was the Declaration of Right presented by the Lords and Commons to the Prince of Orange in 1688, and afterwards thrown into the form of an act of parliament called the Bill of Rights. It is evident, therefore, that, according to their

[1] *Vide* Blackstone's *Commentaries,* vol. iv., p. 438.—PUBLIUS

primitive signification they have no application to constitutions professedly founded upon the power of the people, and executed by their immediate representatives and servants. Here, in strictness, the people surrender nothing; and as they retain everything they have no need of particular reservations. "We, THE PEOPLE of the United States, to secure the blessings of liberty to ourselves and our posterity, do *ordain* and *establish* this Constitution for the United States of America." Here is a better recognition of popular rights than volumes of those aphorisms which make the principal figure in several of our State bills of rights, and which would sound much better in a treatise of ethics than in a constitution of government.

But a minute detail of particular rights is certainly far less applicable to a Constitution like that under consideration, which is merely intended to regulate the general political interests of the nation, than to a constitution which has the regulation of every species of personal and private concerns. If, therefore, the loud clamours against the plan of the convention, on this score, are well founded, no epithets of reprobation will be too strong for the constitution of this State. But the truth is, that both of them contain all which, in relation to their objects, is reasonably to be desired.

I go further and affirm that bills of rights, in the sense and to the extent in which they are contended for, are not only unnecessary in the proposed Constitution, but would even be dangerous. They would contain various exceptions to powers not granted; and, on this very account, would afford a colourable pretext to claim more than were granted. For why declare that things shall not be done which there is no power to do? Why, for instance, should it be said that the liberty of the press shall not be restrained when no power is given by which restrictions may be imposed? I will not contend that such a provision would confer a regulating power; but it is evident that it would furnish, to men disposed to usurp, a plausible pretence for claiming that power. They might urge with a semblance of reason that the Constitution ought not to be charged with the absurdity of providing against the abuse of an authority which was not given, and that the provision against restraining the liberty of the press afforded a clear implication that a power to prescribe proper regulations concerning it was intended to be vested in the national government. This may serve as a specimen of the numerous handles which would be given to the doctrine of constructive powers by the indulgence of an injudicious zeal for bills of rights.

On the subject of the liberty of the press, as much as has been said, I cannot forbear adding a remark or two: in the first place, I observe, that there is not a syllable concerning it in the constitution of this State; in the next, I contend, that whatever has been said about it in that of any other State amounts to nothing. What signifies a declaration, that "the liberty of the press shall be inviolably preserved"? What is the liberty of the press? Who can give it any definition which would not leave the utmost latitude for evasion? I hold it to be impracticable; and from this I infer that its security, whatever fine declarations may be inserted in any constitution respecting it, must altogether depend on public opinion, and on the general spirit of the people and of the government.[1] And here, after all, as is intimated upon another occasion, must we seek for the only solid basis of all our rights.

There remains but one other view of this matter to conclude the point. The truth is, after all the declamations we have heard, that the Constitution is itself, in every rational sense, and to every useful purpose, A BILL OF RIGHTS. The several bills of rights in Great Britain form its Constitution, and conversely the constitution of each State is its bill of rights. And the proposed Constitution, if adopted, will be the bill of rights of the Union. Is it one object of a bill of rights to declare and specify the political privileges of the citizens in the structure and administration of the government? This is done in the most ample and precise manner in the plan of the convention; comprehending various precautions for the public security, which are not to be found in any of the State constitutions. Is another object of a bill of rights to define certain immunities and modes of proceeding, which are relative to personal and private concerns? This we have seen has also been attended to, in a variety of cases, in the same plan. Adverting therefore to the substantial meaning of a bill of rights, it is absurd to allege that it is not to be found in the work of the convention. It may be said that it does not go far enough, though it will not be easy to make this appear; but it can with no propriety be contended that there is no such thing. It certainly must be immaterial what mode is observed as to the order of declaring the rights of the citizens, if they are to be found in any part of the instrument which establishes the government. And hence it must be apparent that much of what has been said on this subject rests merely on verbal and nominal distinctions, entirely foreign from the substance of the thing.

Another objection which has been made, and which, from the frequency of its repetition, it is to be presumed is relied on, is of this nature: "It is improper [say the objectors] to confer such large powers, as are proposed, upon the national government, because the seat of that government must of necessity be too remote from many of the States to admit of a proper knowledge on the part of the constituent of the conduct of the representative body." This argument, if it proves anything, proves that there ought to be no general government whatever. For the powers which, it seems to be agreed on all hands, ought to be vested in the Union cannot be safely intrusted to a body which is not under every requisite control. But there are satisfactory reasons to show that the objection is in reality not well founded. There is in most of the arguments which relate to distance a palpable illusion of the imagination. What are the sources of information by which the people in Montgomery County must regulate their judgment of the conduct of their representatives in the State legislature?

[1] To show that there is a power in the Constitution by which the liberty of the press may be affected, recourse has been had to the power of taxation. It is said that duties may be laid upon the publications so high as to amount to a prohibition. I know not by what logic it could be maintained, that the declarations in the State constitutions, in favour of the freedom of the press, would be a constitutional impediment to the imposition of duties upon publications by the State legislatures. It cannot certainly be pretended that any degree of duties, however low, would be an abridgment of the liberty of the press. We know that newspapers are taxed in Great Britain, and yet it is notorious that the press nowhere enjoys greater liberty than in that country. And if duties of any kind may be laid without a violation of that liberty, it is evident that the extent must depend on legislative discretion, regulated by public opinion; so that, after all, general declarations respecting the liberty of the press will give it no greater security than it will have without them. The same invasions of it may be effected under the State constitutions which contain those declarations through the means of taxation, as under the proposed Constitution, which has nothing of the kind. It would be quite as significant to declare that government ought to be free, that taxes ought not to be excessive, etc., as that the liberty of the press ought not to be restrained.—PUBLIUS

Of personal observation they can have no benefit. This is confined to the citizens on the spot. They must therefore depend on the information of intelligent men, in whom they confide; and how must these men obtain their information? Evidently from the complexion of public measures, from the public prints, from correspondences with their representatives, and with other persons who reside at the place of their deliberations. This does not apply to Montgomery County only, but to all the counties at any considerable distance from the seat of government.

It is equally evident that the same sources of information would be open to the people in relation to the conduct of their representatives in the general government, and the impediments to a prompt communication which distance may be supposed to create will be overbalanced by the effects of the vigilance of the State governments. The executive and legislative bodies of each State will be so many sentinels over the persons employed in every department of the national administration; and as it will be in their power to adopt and pursue a regular and effectual system of intelligence, they can never be at a loss to know the behaviour of those who represent their constituents in the national councils, and can readily communicate the same knowledge to the people. Their disposition to apprise the community of whatever may prejudice its interests from another quarter may be relied upon, if it were only from the rivalship of power. And we may conclude with the fullest assurance that the people, through that channel, will be better informed of the conduct of their national representatives than they can be by any means they now possess of that of their State representatives.

It ought also to be remembered that the citizens who inhabit the country at and near the seat of government will, in all questions that affect the general liberty and prosperity, have the same interest with those who are at a distance, and that they will stand ready to sound the alarm when necessary, and to point out the actors in any pernicious project. The public papers will be expeditious messengers of intelligence to the most remote inhabitants of the Union.

Among the many curious objections which have appeared against the proposed Constitution, the most extraordinary and the least colourable is derived from the want of some provision respecting the debts due *to* the United States. This has been represented as a tacit relinquishment of those debts, and as a wicked contrivance to screen public defaulters. The newspapers have teemed with the most inflammatory railings on this head; yet there is nothing clearer than that the suggestion is entirely void of foundation, the offspring of extreme ignorance or extreme dishonesty. In addition to the remarks I have made upon the subject in another place, I shall only observe that as it is a plain dictate of common-sense, so it is also an established doctrine of political law, that *"states neither lose any of their rights, nor are discharged from any of their obligations, by a change in the form of their civil government."* [1]

The last objection of any consequence, which I at present recollect, turns upon the article of expense. If it were even true that the adoption of the proposed government would occasion a considerable increase of expense, it would be an objection that ought to have no weight against the plan.

The great bulk of the citizens of America are with reason convinced that Union is the basis of their political happiness. Men of sense of all parties now, with few exceptions, agree that it cannot be preserved under the present system, nor without radical alterations; that new and extensive powers ought to be granted to the national head, and that these require a different organisation of the federal government—a single body being an unsafe depositary of such ample authorities. In conceding all this, the question of expense must be given up; for it is impossible, with any degree of safety, to narrow the foundation upon which the system is to stand. The two branches of the legislature are, in the first instance, to consist of only sixty-five persons, which is the same number of which Congress, under the existing Confederation, may be composed. It is true that this number is intended to be increased; but this is to keep pace with the progress of the population and resources of the country. It is evident that a less number would, even in the first instance, have been unsafe, and that a continuance of the present number would, in a more advanced stage of population, be a very inadequate representation of the people.

Whence is the dreaded augmentation of expense to spring? One source indicated is the multiplication of offices under the new

---

[1] *Vide* Rutherford's *Institutes*, vol. ii., book II, chap. x., sects. xiv. and xv. *Vide* also Grotius, book 11, chap. ix., sects. viii. and ix.—PUBLIUS

government. Let us examine this a little.

It is evident that the principal departments of the administration under the present government are the same which will be required under the new. There are now a Secretary of War, a Secretary of Foreign Affairs, a Secretary for Domestic Affairs, a Board of Treasury, consisting of three persons, a Treasurer, assistants, clerks, etc. These officers are indispensable under any system, and will suffice under the new as well as the old. As to ambassadors and other ministers and agents in foreign countries, the proposed Constitution can make no other difference than to render their characters, where they reside, more respectable, and their services more useful. As to persons to be employed in the collection of the revenues, it is unquestionably true that these will form a very considerable addition to the number of federal officers; but it will not follow that this will occasion an increase of public expense. It will be in most cases nothing more than an exchange of State for national officers. In the collection of all duties, for instance, the persons employed will be wholly of the latter description. The States individually will stand in no need of any for this purpose. What difference can it make in point of expense to pay officers of the customs appointed by the State or by the United States? There is no good reason to suppose that either the number or the salaries of the latter will be greater than those of the former.

Where then are we to seek for those additional articles of expense which are to swell the account to the enormous size that has been represented to us? The chief item which occurs to me respects the support of the judges of the United States. I do not add the President, because there is now a president of Congress, whose expenses may not be far, if anything, short of those which will be incurred on account of the President of the United States. The support of the judges will clearly be an extra expense, but to what extent will depend on the particular plan which may be adopted in regard to this matter. But upon no reasonable plan can it amount to a sum which will be an object of material consequence.

Let us now see what there is to counterbalance any extra expense that may attend the establishment of the proposed government. The first thing which presents itself is that a great part of the business which now keeps Congress sitting through the year will be transacted by the President. Even the management of foreign negotiations will naturally devolve upon him, according to general principles concerted with the Senate, and subject to their final concurrence. Hence it is evident that a portion of the year will suffice for the session of both the Senate and the House of Representatives; we may suppose about a fourth for the latter and a third, or perhaps half, for the former. The extra business of treaties and appointments may give this extra occupation to the Senate. From this circumstance we may infer that, until the House of Representatives shall be increased greatly beyond its present number, there will be a considerable saving of expense from the difference between the constant session of the present and the temporary session of the future Congress.

But there is another circumstance of great importance in the view of economy. The business of the United States has hitherto occupied the State legislatures, as well as Congress. The latter has made requisitions which the former have had to provide for. Hence it has happened that the sessions of the State legislatures have been protracted greatly beyond what was necessary for the execution of the mere local business of the States. More than half their time has been frequently employed in matters which related to the United States. Now the members who compose the legislatures of the several States amount to two thousand and upwards, which number has hitherto performed what under the new system will be done in the first instance by sixty-five persons, and probably at no future period by above a fourth or a fifth of that number. The Congress under the proposed government will do all the business of the United States themselves, without the intervention of the State legislatures, who thenceforth will have only to attend to the affairs of their particular States, and will not have to sit in any proportion as long as they have heretofore done. This difference in the time of the sessions of the State legislatures will be clear gain, and will alone form an article of saving which may be regarded as an equivalent for any additional objects of expense that may be occasioned by the adoption of the new system.

The result from these observations is, that the sources of additional expense from the establishment of the proposed Constitution are much fewer than may have been imagined; that they are counterbalanced by considerable objects of saving; and that while it is questionable on which side the scale will preponderate, it is certain that a government less expensive would be incompetent to the purposes of the Union.   PUBLIUS

Number 85

[HAMILTON]

ACCORDING TO the formal division of the subject of these papers, announced in my first number, there would appear still to remain for discussion two points: "the analogy of the proposed government to your own State constitution," and "the additional security which its adoption will afford to republican government, to liberty, and to property." But these heads have been so fully anticipated and exhausted in the progress of the work that it would now scarcely be possible to do anything more than repeat, in a more dilated form, what has been heretofore said, which the advanced stage of the question, and the time already spent upon it, conspire to forbid.

It is remarkable that the resemblance of the plan of the convention to the act which organises the government of this State holds, not less with regard to many of the supposed defects than to the real excellences of the former. Among the pretended defects are the re-eligibility of the Executive, the want of a council, the omission of a formal bill of rights, the omission of a provision respecting the liberty of the press. These and several others which have been noted in the course of our inquiries are as much chargeable on the existing constitution of this State as on the one proposed for the Union; and a man must have slender pretensions to consistency who can rail at the latter for imperfections which he finds no difficulty in excusing in the former. Nor indeed can there be a better proof of the insincerity and affectation of some of the zealous adversaries of the plan of the convention among us, who profess to be the devoted admirers of the government under which they live, than the fury with which they have attacked that plan, for matters in regard to which our own constitution is equally or perhaps more vulnerable.

The additional securities to republican government, to liberty, and to property, to be derived from the adoption of the plan under consideration, consist chiefly in the restraints which the preservation of the Union will impose on local factions and insurrections, and on the ambition of powerful individuals in single States who may acquire credit and influence enough, from leaders and favourites, to become the despots of the people; in the diminution of the opportunities to foreign intrigue, which the dissolution of the Confederacy would invite and facilitate; in the prevention of extensive military establishments, which could not fail to grow out of wars between the States in a disunited situation; in the express guaranty of a republican form of government to each; in the absolute and universal exclusion of titles of nobility; and in the precautions against the repetition of those practices on the part of the State governments which have undermined the foundations of property and credit, have planted mutual distrust in the breasts of all classes of citizens, and have occasioned an almost universal prostration of morals.

Thus have I, fellow-citizens, executed the task I had assigned to myself; with what success, your conduct must determine. I trust at least you will admit that I have not failed in the assurance I gave you respecting the spirit with which my endeavours should be conducted. I have addressed myself purely to your judgments, and have studiously avoided those asperities which are too apt to disgrace political disputants of all parties, and which have been not a little provoked by the language and conduct of the opponents of the Constitution. The charge of a conspiracy against the liberties of the people, which has been indiscriminately brought against the advocates of the plan, has something in it too wanton and to malignant not to excite the indignation of every man who feels in his own bosom a refutation of the calumny. The perpetual changes which have been rung upon the wealthy, the well-born, and the great, have been such as to inspire the disgust of all sensible men. And the unwarrantable concealments and misrepresentations which have been in various ways practised to keep the truth from the public eye, have been of a nature to demand the reprobation of all honest men. It is not impossible that these circumstances may have occasionally betrayed me into intemperances of expression which I did not intend; it is certain that I have frequently felt a struggle between sensibility and moderation; and if the former has in some instances prevailed, it must be my excuse that it has been neither often nor much.

Let us now pause and ask ourselves whether, in the course of these papers, the proposed Constitution has not been satisfactorily vindicated from the aspersions thrown upon it; and whether it has not been shown to be worthy of the public approbation, and necessary to the public safety and prosperity. Every man is bound to answer these questions to himself, according to the best of his conscience and understanding, and to act agreeably to the genuine and sober dictates of his judgment. This is a duty from which nothing can give him a dispensation. 'Tis one that he is called upon, nay, constrained by all the obligations that form the bands of society, to discharge sincerely and honestly. No partial motive, no particular interest, no pride of opinion, no temporary passion or prejudice, will justify to himself, to his country, or to his posterity, an improper election of the part he is to act. Let him beware of an obstinate adherence to party; let him reflect that the object upon which he is to decide is not a particular interest of the community, but the very existence of the nation; and let him remember that a majority of America has already given its sanction to the plan which he is to approve or reject.

I shall not dissemble that I feel an entire confidence in the arguments which recommend the proposed system to your adoption, and that I am unable to discern any real force in those by which it has been opposed. I am persuaded that it is the best which our political situation, habits, and opinions will admit, and superior to any the revolution has produced.

Concessions on the part of the friends of the plan, that it has not a claim to absolute perfection, have afforded matter of no small triumph to its enemies. "Why," say they, "should we adopt an imperfect thing? Why not amend it and make it perfect before it is irrevocably established?" This may be plausible enough, but it is only plausible. In the first place, I remark that the extent of these concessions has been greatly exaggerated. They have been stated as amounting to an admission that the plan is radically defective, and that without material alterations the rights and the interests of the community cannot be safely confided to it. This, as far as I have understood the meaning of those who make the concessions, is an entire perversion of their sense. No advocate of the measure can be found who will not declare as his sentiment that the system, though it may not be perfect in every part, is, upon the whole, a good one; is the best that the present views and circumstances of the country will permit; and is such an one as promises every species of security which a reasonable people can desire.

I answer, in the next place, that I should esteem it the extreme of imprudence to prolong the precarious state of our national affairs, and to expose the Union to the jeopardy of successive experiments, in the chimerical pursuit of a perfect plan. I never expect to see a perfect work from imperfect man. The result of the deliberations of all collective bodies must necessarily be a compound, as well of the errors and prejudices as of the good sense and wisdom, of the individuals of whom they are composed. The compacts which are to embrace thirteen distinct States in a common bond of amity and union, must as necessarily be a compromise of as many dissimilar interests and inclinations. How can perfection spring from such materials?

The reasons assigned in an excellent little pamphlet lately published in this city[1] are unanswerable to show the utter improbability of assembling a new convention, under circumstances in any degree so favourable to a happy issue as those in which the late convention met, deliberated, and concluded. I will not repeat the arguments there used, as I presume the production itself has had an extensive circulation. It is certainly well worthy the perusal of every friend to his country. There is, however, one point of light in which the subject of amendments still remains to be considered, and in which it has not yet been exhibited to public view. I cannot resolve to conclude without first taking a survey of it in this aspect.

It appears to me susceptible of absolute demonstration that it will be far more easy to obtain subsequent than previous amendments to the Constitution. The moment an alteration is made in the present plan, it becomes, to the purpose of adoption, a new one, and must undergo a new decision of each State. To its complete establishment throughout the Union, it will therefore require the concurrence of thirteen States. If, on the contrary, the Constitution proposed should once be ratified by all the States as it stands, alterations in it may at any time be effected by nine States. Here, then, the chances are as thirteen to nine[2] in favour of subsequent amendment, rather than of the original adoption of an entire system.

This is not all. Every Constitution for the United States must inevitably consist of a great variety of particulars, in which thirteen inde-

[1] Entitled "An Address to the People of the State of New York."—PUBLIUS
[2] It may rather be said TEN, for though two thirds may set on foot the measure, three fourths must ratify.—PUBLIUS

pendent States are to be accommodated in their interests or opinions of interest. We may of course expect to see, in any body of men charged with its original formation, very different combinations of the parts upon different points. Many of those who form a majority on one question may become the minority on a second, and an association dissimilar to either may constitute the majority on a third. Hence the necessity of moulding and arranging all the particulars which are to compose the whole in such a manner as to satisfy all the parties to the compact; and hence, also, an immense multiplication of difficulties and casualties in obtaining the collective assent to a final act. The degree of that multiplication must evidently be in a ratio to the number of particulars and the number of parties.

But every amendment to the Constitution, if once established, would be a single proposition, and might be brought forward singly. There would then be no necessity for management or compromise, in relation to any other point—no giving nor taking. The will of the requisite number would at once bring the matter to a decisive issue. And consequently, whenever nine, or rather ten States, were united in the desire of a particular amendment, that amendment must infallibly take place. There can, therefore, be no comparison between the facility of effecting an amendment, and that of establishing in the first instance a complete Constitution.

In opposition to the probability of subsequent amendments, it has been urged that the persons delegated to the administration of the national government will always be disinclined to yield up any portion of the authority of which they were once possessed. For my own part, I acknowledge a thorough conviction that any amendments which may, upon mature consideration, be thought useful, will be applicable to the organisation of the government, not to the mass of its powers; and on this account alone I think there is no weight in the observation just stated. I also think there is little weight in it on another account. The intrinsic difficulty of governing thirteen States at any rate, independent of calculations upon an ordinary degree of public spirit and integrity, will, in my opinion, constantly impose on the national rulers the necessity of a spirit of accommodation to the reasonable expectations of their constituents. But there is yet a further consideration, which proves beyond the possibility of a doubt that the observation is futile.

It is this, that the national rulers, whenever nine States concur, will have no option upon the subject. By the fifth article of the plan, the Congress will be obliged "on the application of the legislatures of two thirds of the States [which at present amount to nine], to call a convention for proposing amendments, which shall be valid, to all intents and purposes, as part of the Constitution, when ratified by the legislatures of three fourths of the States, or by conventions in three fourths thereof." The words of this article are peremptory. The Congress "shall call a convention." Nothing in this particular is left to the discretion of that body. And of consequence, all the declamation about the disinclination to a change vanishes in air. Nor however difficult it may be supposed to unite two thirds or three fourths of the State legislatures, in amendments which may affect local interests, can there be any room to apprehend any such difficulty in a union on points which are merely relative to the general liberty or security of the people. We may safely rely on the disposition of the State legislatures to erect barriers against the encroachments of the national authority.

If the foregoing argument is a fallacy, certain it is that I am myself deceived by it, for it is, in my conception, one of those rare instances in which a political truth can be brought to the test of a mathematical demonstration. Those who see the matter in the same light with me, however zealous they may be for amendments, must agree in the propriety of a previous adoption, as the most direct road to their own object.

The zeal for attempts to amend, prior to the establishment of the Constitution, must abate in every man who is ready to accede to the truth of the following observations of a writer equally solid and ingenious: "To balance a large state or society [says he], whether monarchical or republican, on general laws, is a work of so great difficulty, that no human genius, however comprehensive, is able, by the mere dint of reason and reflection, to effect it. The judgments of many must unite in the work; experience must guide their labour; time must bring it to perfection, and the feeling of inconveniences must correct the mistakes which they *inevitably* fall into in their first trials and experiments."[1] These judicious reflections contain a lesson of moderation to all the sincere lovers of the Union, and ought to put them upon their guard against hazard-

[1] Hume's *Essays*, vol. i., page 128: "The Rise of Arts and Sciences."—PUBLIUS

ing anarchy, civil war, a perpetual alienation of the States from each other, and perhaps the military despotism of a victorious demagogue, in the pursuit of what they are not likely to obtain but from time and experience. It may be in me a defect of political fortitude, but I acknowledge that I cannot entertain an equal tranquillity with those who affect to treat the dangers of a longer continuance in our present situation as imaginary. A nation without a national government is, in my view, an awful spectacle. The establishment of a Constitution, in time of profound peace, by the voluntary consent of a whole people, is a prodigy to the completion of which I look forward with trembling anxiety. I can reconcile it to no rules of prudence to let go the hold we now have, in so arduous an enterprise, upon seven out of the thirteen States, and after having passed over so considerable a part of the ground, to recommence the course. I dread the more the consequences of new attempts, because I know that powerful individuals, in this and in other States, are enemies to a general national government in every possible shape.

PUBLIUS

ON LIBERTY

REPRESENTATIVE GOVERNMENT

UTILITARIANISM

BIOGRAPHICAL NOTE
John Stuart Mill, 1806-1873

MILL, in his *Autobiography*, declared that his intellectual development was due primarily to the influence of two people: his father, James Mill, and his wife.

James Mill elaborated for his son a comprehensive educational program, modelled upon the theories of Helvétius and Bentham. It was encyclopaedic in scope and equipped Mill by the time he was thirteen with the equivalent of a thorough university education. The father acted as the boy's tutor and constant companion, allowing Mill to work in the same room with him and even to interrupt him as he was writing his *History of India* or his articles for the *Encyclopaedia Britannica*. Mill later described the result as one that "made me appear as a 'made' or manufactured man, having had a certain impress of opinion stamped upon me which I could only reproduce."

The education began with Greek and arithmetic at the age of three. By the time he was eight Mill had read through the whole of Herodotus, six dialogues of Plato, and considerable history. Before he was twelve he had studied Euclid and algebra, the Greek and Latin poets, and some English poetry. His interest in history continued, and he even attempted writing an account of Roman government. At twelve he was introduced to logic in Aristotle's *Organon* and the Latin scholastic manuals on the subject. The last year under his father's direct supervision, his thirteenth, was devoted to political economy; the son's notes later served the elder Mill in his *Elements of Political Economy*. He furthered his education by a period of studies with his father's friends, reading law with Austin and economics with Ricardo, and completed it by himself with Bentham's treatise on legislation, which he felt gave him "a creed, a doctrine, a philosophy . . . a religion" and made a "different being of him."

Although Mill never actually severed relations with his father, he experienced, at the age of twenty, a "crisis" in his mental history.

It occurred to him to pose the question: "Suppose that all your objects in life were realized; that all the changes in institutions and opinions which you are looking forward to, could be completely effected at this very instant: would this be a great joy and happiness to you?" He reported that "an irrepressible self-consciousness distinctly answered, 'No,' " and he was overcome by a depression which lasted for several years. The first break in his "gloom" came while reading Marmontel's *Mémoires:* "I . . . came to the passage which relates his father's death, the distressed position of the family, and the sudden inspiration by which he, then a mere boy, felt and made them feel that he would be everything to them—would supply the place of all that they had lost." He was moved to tears by the scene, and from this moment his "burden grew lighter."

From the time he was seventeen, Mill supported himself by working for the East India Company, where his father was an official. Although he began nominally as a clerk, he was soon promoted to assistant-examiner, and for twenty years, from his father's death in 1836, until the Company's activities were taken over by the British Government, he had charge of the relations with the Indian states, which gave him wide practical experience in the problems of government. In addition to his regular employment, he took part in many activities tending to prepare public opinion for legislative reform. He, his father, and their friends formed the group known as "philosophical radicals," which made a major contribution to the debates leading to the Reform Bill of 1832. Mill was active in exposing what he considered departures from sound principle in parliament and the courts of justice. He wrote often for the newspapers friendly to the "radical" cause, helped to found and edit the *Westminster Review* as a "radical" organ, and participated in several reading and debating societies, devoted to the discussion of the contemporary intellectual and social problems.

These activities did not prevent him from pursuing his own intellectual interests. He edited Bentham's *Rationale of Judicial Evidence*. He studied logic and science with the aim of reconciling syllogistic logic with the methods of inductive science, and published his *System of Logic* (1843). At the same time he pushed his inquiries in the field of economics. These first took the form of *Essays on Some Unsettled Questions in Political Economy* and were later given systematic treatment in the *Principles of Political Economy* (1848).

The development and productivity of these years he attributed to his relationship with Mrs. Harriet Taylor, who became his wife in 1851. Mill had known her for twenty years, since shortly after his "crisis," and he could never praise too highly her influence upon his work. Although he published less during the seven years of his married life than at any other period of his career, he thought out and partly wrote many of his important works, including the essay *On Liberty* (1859), the *Thoughts on Parliamentary Reform,* which

later led to the *Representative Government* (1861), and *Utilitarianism* (1863). He attributed to her especially his understanding of the human side of the abstract reforms he advocated. After her death he stated: "Her memory is to me a religion, and her approbation the standard by which, summing up as it does all worthiness, I endeavour to regulate my life."

Mill devoted a large part of his last years directly to political activity. In addition to his writings, he was one of the founders of the first women's suffrage society and, in 1865, consented to become a member of Parliament. Voting with the radical wing of the Liberal Party, he took an active part in the debates on Disraeli's Reform Bill and promoted the measures which he had long advocated, such as the representation of women, the reform of London government, and the alteration of land tenure in Ireland. Largely because of his support of unpopular measures, he was defeated for re-election. He retired to his cottage in Avignon, which had been built so that he might be close to the grave of his wife, and died there May 8, 1873.

CONTENTS: ON LIBERTY

ON LIBERTY

The grand, leading principle, towards which every argument unfolded in these pages directly converges, is the absolute and essential importance of human development in its richest diversity.
WILHELM VON HUMBOLDT: *Sphere and Duties of Government*

TO the beloved and deplored memory of her who was the inspirer, and in part the author, of all that is best in my writings—the friend and wife whose exalted sense of truth and right was my strongest incitement, and whose approbation was my chief reward—I dedicate this volume. Like all that I have written for many years, it belongs as much to her as to me; but the work as it stands has had, in a very insufficient degree, the inestimable advantage of her revision; some of the most important portions having been reserved for a more careful re-examination, which they are now never destined to receive. Were I but capable of interpreting to the world one half the great thoughts and noble feelings which are buried in her grave, I should be the medium of a greater benefit to it, than is ever likely to arise from anything that I can write, unprompted and unassisted by her all but unrivalled wisdom.

Chapter 1

Introductory

THE SUBJECT of this Essay is not the so-called Liberty of the Will, so unfortunately opposed to the misnamed doctrine of Philosophical Necessity; but Civil, or Social Liberty: the nature and limits of the power which can be legitimately exercised by society over the individual. A question seldom stated, and hardly ever discussed, in general terms, but which profoundly influences the practical controversies of the age by its latent presence, and is likely soon to make itself recognised as the vital question of the future. It is so far from being new, that, in a certain sense, it has divided mankind, almost from the remotest ages; but in the stage of progress into which the more civilised portions of the species have now entered, it presents itself under new conditions, and requires a different and more fundamental treatment.

The struggle between Liberty and Authority is the most conspicuous feature in the portions of history with which we are earliest familiar, particularly in that of Greece, Rome, and England. But in old times this contest was between subjects, or some classes of subjects, and the Government. By liberty, was meant protection against the tyranny of the political rulers. The rulers were conceived (except in some of the popular governments of Greece) as in a necessarily antagonistic position to the people whom they ruled. They consisted of a governing One, or a governing tribe or caste, who derived their authority from inheritance or conquest, who, at all events, did not hold it at the pleasure of the governed, and whose supremacy men did not venture, perhaps did not desire, to contest, whatever precautions might be taken against its oppressive exercise. Their power was regarded as necessary, but also as highly dangerous; as a weapon which they would attempt to use against their subjects, no less than against external enemies. To prevent the weaker members of the community from being preyed upon by innumerable vultures, it was needful that there should be an animal of prey stronger than the rest, commissioned to keep them down. But as the king of the vultures would be no less bent upon preying on the flock than any of the minor harpies, it was indispensable to be in a perpetual attitude of defence against his beak and claws. The aim, therefore, of patriots was to set limits to the power which the ruler should be suffered to exercise over the community; and this limitation was what they meant by liberty. It was attempted in two ways. First, by obtaining a recognition of certain immunities, called political liberties or rights, which it was to be regarded as a breach of duty in the ruler to infringe, and which if he did infringe, specific resistance, or general rebellion, was held to be justifiable. A second, and generally a later expedient, was the establishment of constitutional checks, by which the consent of the community, or of a body of some sort, supposed to represent its interests, was made a necessary condition to some of the more important acts of the governing power. To the first of these modes of limitation, the ruling power, in most European countries, was compelled, more or less, to submit. It was not so with the second; and, to attain this, or when already in some degree possessed, to attain it more completely, became everywhere the principal object of the lovers of liberty. And so long as mankind were content to combat one enemy by another, and to be ruled by a master, on condition of being guaranteed more or less efficaciously against his tyranny, they did not carry their aspirations beyond this point.

A time, however, came, in the progress of human affairs, when men ceased to think it a necessity of nature that their governors should be an independent power, opposed in interest to themselves. It appeared to them much better that the various magistrates of the State should be their tenants or delegates, revocable at their pleasure. In that way alone, it seemed, could they have complete security that the powers of government would never be abused to their disadvantage. By degrees this new demand for elective and temporary rulers became the prominent object of the exertions of the popular party, wherever any such party existed; and superseded, to a considerable extent, the previous efforts to limit the power of rulers. As the struggle proceeded for making

the ruling power emanate from the periodical choice of the ruled, some persons began to think that too much importance had been attached to the limitation of the power itself. *That* (it might seem) was a resource against rulers whose interests were habitually opposed to those of the people. What was now wanted was, that the rulers should be identified with the people; that their interest and will should be the interest and will of the nation. The nation did not need to be protected against its own will. There was no fear of its tyrannising over itself. Let the rulers be effectually responsible to it, promptly removable by it, and it could afford to trust them with power of which it could itself dictate the use to be made. Their power was but the nation's own power, concentrated, and in a form convenient for exercise. This mode of thought, or rather perhaps of feeling, was common among the last generation of European liberalism, in the Continental section of which it still apparently predominates. Those who admit any limit to what a government may do, except in the case of such governments as they think ought not to exist, stand out as brilliant exceptions among the political thinkers of the Continent. A similar tone of sentiment might by this time have been prevalent in our own country, if the circumstances which for a time encouraged it, had continued unaltered.

But, in political and philosophical theories, as well as in persons, success discloses faults and infirmities which failure might have concealed from observation. The notion, that the people have no need to limit their power over themselves, might seem axiomatic, when popular government was a thing only dreamed about, or read of as having existed at some distant period of the past. Neither was that notion necessarily disturbed by such temporary aberrations as those of the French Revolution, the worst of which were the work of a usurping few, and which, in any case, belonged, not to the permanent working of popular institutions, but to a sudden and convulsive outbreak against monarchical and aristocratic despotism. In time, however, a democratic republic came to occupy a large portion of the earth's surface, and made itself felt as one of the most powerful members of the community of nations; and elective and responsible government became subject to the observations and criticisms which wait upon a great existing fact. It was now perceived that such phrases as "self-government," and "the power of the people over themselves," do not express the true state of the case. The "people" who exercise the power are not always the same people with those over whom it is exercised; and the "self-government" spoken of is not the government of each by himself, but of each by all the rest. The will of the people, moreover, practically means the will of the most numerous or the most active *part* of the people; the majority, or those who succeed in making themselves accepted as the majority; the people, consequently *may* desire to oppress a part of their number; and precautions are as much needed against this as against any other abuse of power. The limitation, therefore, of the power of government over individuals loses none of its importance when the holders of power are regularly accountable to the community, that is, to the strongest party therein. This view of things, recommending itself equally to the intelligence of thinkers and to the inclination of those important classes in European society to whose real or supposed interests democracy is adverse, has had no difficulty in establishing itself; and in political speculations "the tyranny of the majority" is now generally included among the evils against which society requires to be on its guard.

Like other tyrannies, the tyranny of the majority was at first, and is still vulgarly, held in dread, chiefly as operating through the acts of the public authorities. But reflecting persons perceived that when society is itself the tyrant—society collectively over the separate individuals who compose it—its means of tyrannising are not restricted to the acts which it may do by the hands of its political functionaries. Society can and does execute its own mandates: and if it issues wrong mandates instead of right, or any mandates at all in things with which it ought not to meddle, it practises a social tyranny more formidable than many kinds of political oppression, since, though not usually upheld by such extreme penalties, it leaves fewer means of escape, penetrating much more deeply into the details of life, and enslaving the soul itself. Protection, therefore, against the tyranny of the magistrate is not enough: there needs protection also against the tyranny of the prevailing opinion and feeling; against the tendency of society to impose, by other means than civil penalties, its own ideas and practices as rules of conduct on those who dissent from them; to fetter the development, and, if possible, prevent the formation, of any individuality not in harmony with its ways, and compels all characters to fashion themselves upon the model of its own. There is a limit to the legitimate interference of collective opinion with individual independence: and to find that limit, and maintain it against encroachment, is as indispensable to a good condition of human affairs, as protection against political despotism.

But though this proposition is not likely to be contested in general terms, the practical question, where to place the limit—how to make the fitting adjustment between individual independence and social control—is a subject on which nearly everything remains to be done. All that makes existence valuable to any one, depends on the enforcement of restraints upon the actions of other people. Some rules of conduct, therefore, must be imposed, by law in the first place, and by opinion on many things which are not fit subjects for the operation of law. What these rules should be is the principal question in human affairs; but if we except a few of the most obvious cases, it is one of those which least progress has been made in resolving. No two ages, and scarcely any two countries, have decided it alike; and the decision of one age or country is a wonder to another. Yet the people of any given age and country no more suspect any difficulty in it, than if it were a subject on which mankind had always been agreed. The rules which obtain among themselves appear to them self-evident and self-justifying.

This all but universal illusion is one of the examples of the magical influence of custom, which is not only, as the proverb says, a second nature, but is continually mistaken for the first. The effect of custom, in preventing any misgiving respecting the rules of conduct which mankind impose on one another, is all the more complete because the subject is one on which it is not generally considered necessary that reasons should be given, either by one person to others or by each to himself. People are accustomed to believe, and have been encouraged in the belief by some who aspire to the character of philosophers, that their feelings, on subjects of this nature, are better than reasons, and render reasons unnecessary. The practical principle which guides them to their opinions on the regulation of human conduct, is the feeling in each person's mind that everybody should be required to act as he, and those with whom he sympathises, would like them to act. No one, indeed, acknowledges to himself that his standard of judgment is his own liking; but an opinion on a point of conduct, not supported by reasons, can only count as one person's preference; and if the reasons, when given, are a mere appeal to a similar preference felt by other people, it is still only many people's liking instead of one. To an ordinary man, however, his own preference, thus supported, is not only a perfectly satisfactory reason, but the only one he generally has for any of his notions of morality, taste, or propriety, which are not expressly written in his religious creed; and his chief guide in the interpretation even of that. Men's opinions, accordingly, on what is laudable or blamable, are affected by all the multifarious causes which influence their wishes in regard to the conduct of others, and which are as numerous as those which determine their wishes on any other subject. Sometimes their reason—at other times their prejudices or superstitions: often their social affections, not seldom their antisocial ones, their envy or jealousy, their arrogance or contemptuousness: but most commonly their desires or fears for themselves—their legitimate or illegitimate self-interest.

Wherever there is an ascendant class, a large portion of the morality of the country emanates from its class interests, and its feelings of class superiority. The morality between Spartans and Helots, between planters and negroes, between princes and subjects, between nobles and roturiers, between men and women, has been for the most part the creation of these class interests and feelings: and the sentiments thus generated react in turn upon the moral feelings of the members of the ascendant class, in their relations among themselves. Where, on the other hand, a class, formerly ascendant, has lost its ascendancy, or where its ascendancy is unpopular, the prevailing moral sentiments frequently bear the impress of an impatient dislike of superiority. Another grand determining principle of the rules of conduct, both in act and forbearance, which have been enforced by law or opinion, has been the servility of mankind towards the supposed preferences or aversions of their temporal masters or of their gods. This servility, though essentially selfish, is not hypocrisy; it gives rise to perfectly genuine sentiments of abhorrence; it made men burn magicians and heretics. Among so many baser influences, the general and obvious interests of society have of course had a share, and a large one, in the direction of the moral sentiments: less, however, as a matter of reason, and on their own account, than as a consequence of the sympathies and antipathies which grew out of them: and sympathies and antipathies which had little or nothing to do with the interests of society, have made themselves felt in the establishment of moralities with quite as great force.

The likings and dislikings of society, or of some powerful portion of it, are thus the main thing which has practically determined the rules laid down for general observance, under the penalties of law or opinion. And in general, those who have been in advance of society in thought and feeling, have left this condition of things unassailed in principle, however they may have come into conflict with it in some of its details. They have occupied themselves rather in inquiring what things society ought to like or dislike, than in questioning whether its likings or dislikings should be a law to individuals. They preferred endeavouring to alter the feelings of mankind on the particular points on which they were themselves heretical, rather than make common cause in defence of freedom, with heretics generally. The only case in which the higher ground has been taken on principle and maintained with consistency, by any but an individual here and there, is that of religious belief: a case instructive in many ways, and not least so as forming a most striking instance of the fallibility of what is called the moral sense: for the *odium theologicum*, in a sincere bigot, is one of the most unequivocal cases of moral feeling. Those who first broke the yoke of what called itself the Universal Church, were in general as little willing to permit difference of religious opinion as that church itself. But when the heat of the conflict was over, without giving a complete victory to any party, and each church or sect was reduced to limit its hopes to retaining possession of the ground it already occupied; minorities, seeing that they had no chance of becoming majorities, were under the necessity of pleading to those whom they could not convert, for permission to differ. It is accordingly on this battle field, almost solely, that the rights of the individual against society have been asserted on broad grounds of principle, and the claim of society to exercise authority over dissentients openly controverted. The great writers to whom the world owes what religious liberty it possesses, have mostly asserted freedom of conscience as an indefeasible right, and denied absolutely that a human being is accountable to others for his religious belief. Yet so natural to mankind is intolerance in whatever they really care about, that religious freedom has hardly any- where been practically realised, except where religious indifference, which dislikes to have its peace disturbed by theological quarrels, has added its weight to the scale. In the minds of almost all religious persons, even in the most tolerant countries, the duty of toleration is ad- mitted with tacit reserves. One person will bear with dissent in matters of church govern- ment, but not of dogma; another can tolerate everybody, short of a Papist or a Unitarian; another every one who believes in revealed re- ligion; a few extend their charity a little fur- ther, but stop at the belief in a God and in a future state. Wherever the sentiment of the majority is still genuine and intense, it is found to have abated little of its claim to be obeyed.

In England, from the peculiar circumstances of our political history, though the yoke of opinion is perhaps heavier, that of law is light- er, than in most other countries of Europe; and there is considerable jealousy of direct interference, by the legislative or the executive power, with private conduct; not so much from any just regard for the independence of the individual, as from the still subsisting habit of looking on the government as representing an opposite interest to the public. The ma- jority have not yet learnt to feel the power of the government their power, or its opinions their opinions. When they do so, individual liberty will probably be as much exposed to invasion from the government, as it already is from public opinion. But, as yet, there is a considerable amount of feeling ready to be called forth against any attempt of the law to control individuals in things in which they have not hitherto been accustomed to be con- trolled by it; and this with very little discrimi- nation as to whether the matter is, or is not, within the legitimate sphere of legal control; insomuch that the feeling, highly salutary on the whole, is perhaps quite as often misplaced as well grounded in the particular instances of its application. There is, in fact, no recognised principle by which the propriety or impro- priety of government interference is custom- arily tested. People decide according to their personal preferences. Some, whenever they see any good to be done, or evil to be remedied, would willingly instigate the government to undertake the business; while others prefer to bear almost any amount of social evil, rather than add one to the departments of human in- terests amenable to governmental control. And men range themselves on one or the other side

in any particular case, according to this gen- eral direction of their sentiments; or according to the degree of interest which they feel in the particular thing which it is proposed that the government should do, or according to the be- lief they entertain that the government would, or would not, do it in the manner they prefer; but very rarely on account of any opinion to which they consistently adhere, as to what things are fit to be done by a government. And it seems to me that in consequence of this absence of rule or principle, one side is at present as often wrong as the other; the inter- ference of government is, with about equal frequency, improperly invoked and improp- erly condemned.

The object of this Essay is to assert one very simple principle, as entitled to govern abso- lutely the dealings of society with the indi- vidual in the way of compulsion and control, whether the means used be physical force in the form of legal penalties, or the moral coer- cion of public opinion. That principle is, that the sole end for which mankind are warrant- ed, individually or collectively, in interfering with the liberty of action of any of their num- ber, is self-protection. That the only purpose for which power can be rightfully exercised over any member of a civilised community, against his will, is to prevent harm to others. His own good, either physical or moral, is not a sufficient warrant. He cannot rightfully be compelled to do or forbear because it will be better for him to do so, because it will make him happier, because, in the opinions of others, to do so would be wise, or even right. These are good reasons for remonstrating with him, or reasoning with him, or persuading him, or en- treating him, but not for compelling him, or visiting him with any evil in case he do other- wise. To justify that, the conduct from which it is desired to deter him must be calculated to produce evil to some one else. The only part of the conduct of any one, for which he is amenable to society, is that which concerns others. In the part which merely concerns him- self, his independence is, of right, absolute. Over himself, over his own body and mind, the individual is sovereign.

It is, perhaps, hardly necessary to say that this doctrine is meant to apply only to human beings in the maturity of their faculties. We are not speaking of children, or of young per- sons below the age which the law may fix as that of manhood or womanhood. Those who are still in a state to require being taken care of by others, must be protected against their own actions as well as against external injury. For the same reason, we may leave out of consideration those backward states of society in which the race itself may be considered as in its nonage. The early difficulties in the way of spontaneous progress are so great, that there is seldom any choice of means for overcoming them; and a ruler full of the spirit of improvement is warranted in the use of any expedients that will attain an end, perhaps otherwise unattainable. Despotism is a legitimate mode of government in dealing with barbarians, provided the end be their improvement, and the means justified by actually affecting that end. Liberty, as a principle, has no application to any state of things anterior to the time when mankind have become capable of being improved by free and equal discussion. Until then, there is nothing for them but implicit obedience to an Akbar or a Charlemagne, if they are so fortunate as to find one. But as soon as mankind have attained the capacity of being guided to their own improvement by conviction or persuasion (a period long since reached in all nations with whom we need here concern ourselves), compulsion, either in the direct form or in that of pains and penalties for non-compliance, is no longer admissible as a means to their own good, and justifiable only for the security of others.

It is proper to state that I forego any advantage which could be derived to my argument from the idea of abstract right, as a thing independent of utility. I regard utility as the ultimate appeal on all ethical questions; but it must be utility in the largest sense, grounded on the permanent interests of a man as a progressive being. Those interests, I contend, authorise the subjection of individual spontaneity to external control, only in respect to those actions of each, which concern the interest of other people. If any one does an act hurtful to others, there is a *prima facie* case for punishing him, by law, or, where legal penalties are not safely applicable, by general disapprobation. There are also many positive acts for the benefit of others, which he may rightfully be compelled to perform; such as to give evidence in a court of justice; to bear his fair share in the common defence, or in any other joint work necessary to the interest of the society of which he enjoys the protection; and to perform certain acts of individual beneficence, such as saving a fellow creature's life, or interposing to protect the defenceless against ill-usage,

things which whenever it is obviously a man's duty to do, he may rightfully be made responsible to society for not doing. A person may cause evil to others not only by his actions but by his inaction, and in either case he is justly accountable to them for the injury. The latter case, it is true, requires a much more cautious exercise of compulsion than the former. To make any one answerable for doing evil to others is the rule; to make him answerable for not preventing evil is, comparatively speaking, the exception. Yet there are many cases clear enough and grave enough to justify that exception. In all things which regard the external relations of the individual, he is *de jure* amenable to those whose interests are concerned, and, if need be, to society as their protector. There are often good reasons for not holding him to the responsibility; but these reasons must arise from the special expediencies of the case: either because it is a kind of case in which he is on the whole likely to act better, when left to his own discretion, than when controlled in any way in which society have it in their power to control him; or because the attempt to exercise control would produce other evils, greater than those which it would prevent. When such reasons as these preclude the enforcement of responsibility, the conscience of the agent himself should step into the vacant judgment seat, and protect those interests of others which have no external protection; judging himself all the more rigidly, because the case does not admit of his being made accountable to the judgment of his fellow creatures.

But there is a sphere of action in which society, as distinguished from the individual, has, if any, only an indirect interest; comprehending all that portion of a person's life and conduct which affects only himself, or if it also affects others, only with their free, voluntary, and undeceived consent and participation. When I say only himself, I mean directly, and in the first instance; for whatever affects himself, may affect others through himself; and the objection which may be grounded on this contingency, will receive consideration in the sequel. This, then, is the appropriate region of human liberty. It comprises, first, the inward domain of consciousness; demanding liberty of conscience in the most comprehensive sense; liberty of thought and feeling; absolute freedom of opinion and sentiment on all subjects, practical or speculative, scientific, moral, or theological. The liberty of expressing and publishing opinions may seem to fall under a different principle, since it belongs to that part of the conduct of an individual which concerns other people; but, being almost of as much importance as the liberty of thought itself, and resting in great part on the same reasons, is practically inseparable from it. Secondly, the principle requires liberty of tastes and pursuits; of framing the plan of our life to suit our own character; of doing as we like, subject to such consequences as may follow: without impediment from our fellow creatures, so long as what we do does not harm them, even though they should think our conduct foolish, perverse, or wrong. Thirdly, from this liberty of each individual, follows the liberty, within the same limits, of combination among individuals; freedom to unite, for any purpose not involving harm to others: the persons combining being supposed to be of full age, and not forced or deceived.

No society in which these liberties are not, on the whole, respected, is free, whatever may be its form of government; and none is completely free in which they do not exist absolute and unqualified. The only freedom which deserves the name, is that of pursuing our own good in our own way, so long as we do not attempt to deprive others of theirs, or impede their efforts to obtain it. Each is the proper guardian of his own health, whether bodily, *or* mental and spiritual. Mankind are greater gainers by suffering each other to live as seems good to themselves, than by compelling each to live as seems good to the rest.

Though this doctrine is anything but new, and, to some persons, may have the air of a truism, there is no doctrine which stands more directly opposed to the general tendency of existing opinion and practice. Society has expended fully as much effort in the attempt (according to its lights) to compel people to conform to its notions of personal as of social excellence. The ancient commonwealths thought themselves entitled to practise, and the ancient philosophers countenanced, the regulation of every part of private conduct by public authority, on the ground that the State had a deep interest in the whole bodily and mental discipline of every one of its citizens; a mode of thinking which may have been admissible in small republics surrounded by powerful enemies, in constant peril of being subverted by foreign attack or internal commotion, and to which even a short interval of relaxed energy and self-command might so

easily be fatal that they could not afford to wait for the salutary permanent effects of freedom. In the modern world, the greater size of political communities, and, above all, the separation between spiritual and temporal authority (which placed the direction of men's consciences in other hands than those which controlled their worldly affairs), prevented so great an interference by law in the details of private life; but the engines of moral repression have been wielded more strenuously against divergence from the reigning opinion in self-regarding, than even in social matters; religion, the most powerful of the elements which have entered into the formation of moral feeling, having almost always been governed either by the ambition of a hierarchy, seeking control over every department of human conduct, or by the spirit of Puritanism. And some of those modern reformers who have placed themselves in strongest opposition to the religions of the past, have been noway behind either churches or sects in their assertion of the right of spiritual domination: M. Comte, in particular, whose social system, as unfolded in his *Système de Politique Positive,* aims at establishing (though by moral more than by legal appliances) a despotism of society over the individual, surpassing anything contemplated in the political ideal of the most rigid disciplinarian among the ancient philosophers.

Apart from the peculiar tenets of individual thinkers, there is also in the world at large an increasing inclination to stretch unduly the powers of society over the individual, both by the force of opinion and even by that of legislation; and as the tendency of all the changes taking place in the world is to strengthen society, and diminish the power of the individual, this encroachment is not one of the evils which tend spontaneously to disappear, but, on the contrary, to grow more and more formidable. The disposition of mankind, whether as rulers or as fellow-citizens, to impose their own opinions and inclinations as a rule of conduct on others, is so energetically supported by some of the best and by some of the worst feelings incident to human nature, that it is hardly ever kept under restraint by anything but want of power; and as the power is not declining, but growing, unless a strong barrier of moral conviction can be raised against the mischief, we must expect, in the present circumstances of the world, to see it increase.

It will be convenient for the argument, if, instead of at once entering upon the general thesis, we confine ourselves in the first instance to a single branch of it, on which the principle here stated is, if not fully, yet to a certain point, recognised by the current opinions. This one branch is the Liberty of Thought: from which it is impossible to separate the cognate liberty of speaking and of writing. Although these liberties, to some considerable amount, form part of the political morality of all countries which profess religious toleration and free institutions, the grounds, both philosophical and practical, on which they rest, are perhaps not so familiar to the general mind, nor so thoroughly appreciated by many even of the leaders of opinion, as might have been expected. Those grounds, when rightly understood, are of much wider application than to only one division of the subject, and a thorough consideration of this part of the question will be found the best introduction to the remainder. Those to whom nothing which I am about to say will be new, may therefore, I hope, excuse me, if on a subject which for now three centuries has been so often discussed, I venture on one discussion more.

Chapter 2
Of the Liberty of Thought and Discussion

THE TIME, it is to be hoped, is gone by, when any defence would be necessary of the "liberty of the press" as one of the securities against corrupt or tyrannical government. No argument, we may suppose, can now be needed, against permitting a legislature or an executive, not identified in interest with the people, to prescribe opinions to them, and determine what doctrines or what arguments they shall be allowed to hear. This aspect of the question, besides, has been so often and so triumphantly enforced by preceding writers, that it needs not be specially insisted on in this place. Though the law of England, on the subject of the press, is as servile to this day as it was in the time of the Tudors, there is little danger of its being actually put in force against political discussion, except during some temporary panic, when fear of insurrection drives ministers and judges from their propriety;[1] and, speaking generally, it is not, in

constitutional countries, to be apprehended, that the government, whether completely responsible to the people or not, will often attempt to control the expression of opinion, except when in doing so it makes itself the organ of the general intolerance of the public. Let us suppose, therefore, that the government is entirely at one with the people, and never thinks of exerting any power of coercion unless in agreement with what it conceives to be their voice. But I deny the right of the people to exercise such coercion, either by themselves or by their government. The power itself is illegitimate. The best government has no more title to it than the worst. It is as noxious, or more noxious, when exerted in accordance with public opinion, than when in opposition to it. If all mankind minus one were of one opinion, and only one person were of the contrary opinion, mankind would be no more justified in silencing that one person, than he, if he had the power, would be justified in silencing mankind. Were an opinion a personal possession of no value except to the owner; if to be obstructed in the enjoyment of it were

---

[1] These words had scarcely been written, when, as if to give them an emphatic contradiction, occurred the Government Press Prosecutions of 1858. That ill-judged interference with the liberty of public discussion has not, however, induced me to alter a single word in the text, nor has it at all weakened my conviction that, moments of panic excepted, the era of pains and penalties for political discussion has, in our own country, passed away. For, in the first place, the prosecutions were not persisted in; and, in the second, they were never, properly speaking, political prosecutions. The offence charged was not that of criticising institutions, or the acts or persons of rulers, but of circulating what was deemed an immoral doctrine, the lawfulness of Tyrannicide.

If the arguments of the present chapter are of any validity, there ought to exist the fullest liberty of professing and discussing, as a matter of ethical conviction, any doctrine, however immoral it may be considered. It would, therefore, be irrelevant and out of place to examine here, whether the doctrine of Tyrannicide deserves that title. I shall content myself with saying that the subject has been at all times one of the open questions of morals; that the act of a private citizen in striking down a criminal, who, by raising himself above the law, has placed himself beyond the reach of legal punishment or control, has been accounted by whole nations, and by some of the best and wisest of men, not a crime, but an act of exalted virtue; and that, right or wrong, it is not of the nature of assassination, but of civil war. As such, I hold that the instigation to it, in a specific case, may be a proper subject of punishment, but only if an overt act has followed, and at least a probable connection can be established between the act and the instigation. Even then, it is not a foreign government, but the very government assailed, which alone, in the exercise of self-defence, can legitimately punish attacks directed against its own existence.

simply a private injury, it would make some difference whether the injury was inflicted only on a few persons or on many. But the peculiar evil of silencing the expression of an opinion is, that it is robbing the human race; posterity as well as the existing generation; those who dissent from the opinion, still more than those who hold it. If the opinion is right, they are deprived of the opportunity of exchanging error for truth: if wrong, they lose, what is almost as great a benefit, the clearer perception and livelier impression of truth, produced by its collision with error.

It is necessary to consider separately these two hypotheses, each of which has a distinct branch of the argument corresponding to it. We can never be sure that the opinion we are endeavouring to stifle is a false opinion; and if we were sure, stifling it would be an evil still.

First: the opinion which it is attempted to suppress by authority may possibly be true. Those who desire to suppress it, of course deny its truth; but they are not infallible. They have no authority to decide the question for all mankind, and exclude every other person from the means of judging. To refuse a hearing to an opinion, because they are sure that it is false, is to assume that *their* certainty is the same thing as *absolute* certainty. All silencing of discussion is an assumption of infallibility. Its condemnation may be allowed to rest on this common argument, not the worse for being common.

Unfortunately for the good sense of mankind, the fact of their fallibility is far from carrying the weight in their practical judgment which is always allowed to it in theory; for while every one well knows himself to be fallible, few think it necessary to take any precautions against their own fallibility, or admit the supposition that any opinion, of which they feel very certain, may be one of the examples of the error to which they acknowledge themselves to be liable. Absolute princes, or others who are accustomed to unlimited deference, usually feel this complete confidence in their own opinions on nearly all subjects. People more happily situated, who sometimes hear their opinions disputed, and are not wholly unused to be set right when they are wrong, place the same unbounded reliance only on such of their opinions as are shared by all who surround them, or to whom they habitually defer; for in proportion to a man's want of confidence in his own solitary judgment, does he usually repose, with implicit trust, on the infallibility of "the world" in general. And the world, to each individual, means the part of it with which he comes in contact; his party, his sect, his church, his class of society; the man may be called, by comparison, almost liberal and large-minded to whom it means anything so comprehensive as his own country or his own age. Nor is his faith in this collective authority at all shaken by his being aware that other ages, countries, sects, churches, classes, and parties have thought, and even now think, the exact reverse. He devolves upon his own world the responsibility of being in the right against the dissentient worlds of other people; and it never troubles him that mere accident has decided which of these numerous worlds is the object of his reliance, and that the same causes which make him a Churchman in London, would have made him a Buddhist or a Confucian in Pekin. Yet it is as evident in itself, as any amount of argument can make it, that ages are no more infallible than individuals; every age having held many opinions which subsequent ages have deemed not only false but absurd; and it is as certain that many opinions now general will be rejected by future ages, as it is that many, once general, are rejected by the present.

The objection likely to be made to this argument would probably take some such form as the following. There is no greater assumption of infallibility in forbidding the propagation of error, than in any other thing which is done by public authority on its own judgment and responsibility. Judgment is given to men that they may use it. Because it may be used erroneously, are men to be told that they ought not to use it at all? To prohibit what they think pernicious, is not claiming exemption from error, but fulfilling the duty incumbent on them, although fallible, of acting on their conscientious conviction. If we were never to act on our opinions, because those opinions may be wrong, we should leave all our interests uncared for, and all our duties unperformed. An objection which applies to all conduct can be no valid objection to any conduct in particular. It is the duty of governments, and of individuals, to form the truest opinions they can; to form them carefully, and never impose them upon others unless they are quite sure of being right. But when they are sure (such reasoners may say), it is not conscientiousness but cowardice to shrink from acting on their opinions, and allow doctrines which they honestly think dangerous to the welfare of mankind, either in this life or in another, to be scattered abroad without restraint, because other people, in less enlightened times, have persecuted opinions now believed to be true. Let us take care, it may be said, not to make the same mistake: but governments and nations have made mistakes in other things, which are not denied to be fit subjects for the exercise of authority: they have laid on bad taxes, made unjust wars. Ought we therefore to lay on no taxes, and, under whatever provocation, make no wars? Men, and governments, must act to the best of their ability. There is no such thing as absolute certainty, but there is assurance sufficient for the purposes of human life. We may, and must, assume our opinion to be true for the guidance of our own conduct: and it is assuming no more when we forbid bad men to pervert society by the propagation of opinions which we regard as false and pernicious.

I answer, that it is assuming very much more. There is the greatest difference between presuming an opinion to be true, because, with every opportunity for contesting it, it has not been refuted, and assuming its truth for the purpose of not permitting its refutation. Complete liberty of contradicting and disproving our opinion is the very condition which justifies us in assuming its truth for purposes of action; and on no other terms can a being with human faculties have any rational assurance of being right.

When we consider either the history of opinion, or the ordinary conduct of human life, to what is it to be ascribed that the one and the other are no worse than they are? Not certainly to the inherent force of the human understanding; for, on any matter not self-evident, there are ninety-nine persons totally incapable of judging of it for one who is capable; and the capacity of the hundredth person is only comparative; for the majority of the eminent men of every past generation held many opinions now known to be erroneous, and did or approved numerous things which no one will now justify. Why is it, then, that there is on the whole a preponderance among mankind of rational opinions and rational conduct? If there really is this preponderance—which there must be unless human affairs are, and have always been, in an almost desperate state—it is owing to a quality of the human mind, the source of everything respectable in man either as an intellectual or as a moral

being, namely, that his errors are corrigible. He is capable of rectifying his mistakes, by discussion and experience. Not by experience alone. There must be discussion, to show how experience is to be interpreted. Wrong opinions and practices gradually yield to fact and argument; but facts and arguments, to produce any effect on the mind, must be brought before it. Very few facts are able to tell their own story, without comments to bring out their meaning. The whole strength and value, then, of human judgment, depending on the one property, that it can be set right when it is wrong, reliance can be placed on it only when the means of setting it right are kept constantly at hand. In the case of any person whose judgment is really deserving of confidence, how has it become so? Because he has kept his mind open to criticism of his opinions and conduct. Because it has been his practice to listen to all that could be said against him; to profit by as much of it as was just, and expound to himself, and upon occasion to others, the fallacy of what was fallacious. Because he has felt, that the only way in which a human being can make some approach to knowing the whole of a subject, is by hearing what can be said about it by persons of every variety of opinion, and studying all modes in which it can be looked at by every character of mind. No wise man ever acquired his wisdom in any mode but this; nor is it in the nature of human intellect to become wise in any other manner. The steady habit of correcting and completing his own opinion by collating it with those of others, so far from causing doubt and hesitation in carrying it into practice, is the only stable foundation for a just reliance on it: for, being cognisant of all that can, at least obviously, be said against him, and having taken up his position against all gainsayers—knowing that he has sought for objections and difficulties, instead of avoiding them, and has shut out no light which can be thrown upon the subject from any quarter—he has a right to think his judgment better than that of any person, or any multitude, who have not gone through a similar process.

It is not too much to require that what the wisest of mankind, those who are best entitled to trust their own judgment, find necessary to warrant their relying on it, should be submitted to by that miscellaneous collection of a few wise and many foolish individuals, called the public. The most intolerant of churches, the Roman Catholic Church, even at the canonisation of a saint, admits, and listens patiently to, a "devil's advocate." The holiest of men, it appears, cannot be admitted to posthumous honours, until all that the devil could say against him is known and weighed. If even the Newtonian philosophy were not permitted to be questioned, mankind could not feel as complete assurance of its truth as they now do. The beliefs which we have most warrant for have no safeguard to rest on, but a standing invitation to the whole world to prove them unfounded. If the challenge is not accepted, or is accepted and the attempt fails, we are far enough from certainty still; but we have done the best that the existing state of human reason admits of; we have neglected nothing that could give the truth a chance of reaching us: if the lists are kept open, we may hope that if there be a better truth, it will be found when the human mind is capable of receiving it; and in the meantime we may rely on having attained such approach to truth as is possible in our own day. This is the amount of certainty attainable by a fallible being, and this the sole way of attaining it.

Strange it is, that men should admit the validity of the arguments for free discussion, but object to their being "pushed to an extreme"; not seeing that unless the reasons are good for an extreme case, they are not good for any case. Strange that they should imagine that they are not assuming infallibility, when they acknowledge that there should be free discussion on all subjects which can possibly be *doubtful*, but think that some particular principle or doctrine should be forbidden to be questioned because it is so *certain*, that is, because *they are certain* that it is certain. To call any proposition certain, while there is any one who would deny its certainty if permitted, but who is not permitted, is to assume that we ourselves, and those who agree with us, are the judges of certainty, and judges without hearing the other side.

In the present age—which has been described as "destitute of faith, but terrified at scepticism"—in which people feel sure, not so much that their opinions are true, as that they should not know what to do without them—the claims of an opinion to be protected from public attack are rested not so much on its truth, as on its importance to society. There are, it is alleged, certain beliefs so useful, not to say indispensable, to well-being that it is as much the duty of governments to uphold those beliefs, as to protect any other of the interests of society.

In a case of such necessity, and so directly in the line of their duty, something less than infallibility may, it is maintained, warrant, and even bind, governments to act on their own opinion, confirmed by the general opinion of mankind. It is also often argued, and still oftener thought, that none but bad men would desire to weaken these salutary beliefs; and there can be nothing wrong, it is thought, in restraining bad men, and prohibiting what only such men would wish to practise. This mode of thinking makes the justification of restraints on discussion not a question of the truth of doctrines, but of their usefulness; and flatters itself by that means to escape the responsibility of claiming to be an infallible judge of opinions.

But those who thus satisfy themselves, do not perceive that the assumption of infallibility is merely shifted from one point to another. The usefulness of an opinion is itself matter of opinion: as disputable, as open to discussion, and requiring discussion as much as the opinion itself. There is the same need of an infallible judge of opinions to decide an opinion to be noxious, as to decide it to be false, unless the opinion condemned has full opportunity of defending itself. And it will not do to say that the heretic may be allowed to maintain the utility or harmlessness of his opinion, though forbidden to maintain its truth. The truth of an opinion is part of its utility. If we would know whether or not it is desirable that a proposition should be believed, is it possible to exclude the consideration of whether or not it is true? In the opinion, not of bad men, but of the best men, no belief which is contrary to truth can be really useful: and can you prevent such men from urging that plea, when they are charged with culpability for denying some doctrine which they are told is useful, but which they believe to be false? Those who are on the side of received opinions never fail to take all possible advantage of this plea; you do not find *them* handling the question of utility as if it could be completely abstracted from that of truth: on the contrary, it is, above all, because their doctrine is "the truth," that the knowledge or the belief of it is held to be so indispensable. There can be no fair discussion of the question of usefulness when an argument so vital may be employed on one side, but not on the other. And in point of fact, when law or public feeling do not permit the truth of an opinion to be disputed, they are just as little tolerant of a denial of its usefulness. The utmost they allow is an extenuation of its absolute necessity, or of the positive guilt of rejecting it.

In order more fully to illustrate the mischief of denying a hearing to opinions because we, in our own judgment, have condemned them, it will be desirable to fix down the discussion to a concrete case; and I choose, by preference, the cases which are least favourable to me—in which the argument against freedom of opinion, both on the score of truth and on that of utility, is considered the strongest. Let the opinions impugned be the belief in a God and in a future state, or any of the commonly received doctrines of morality. To fight the battle on such ground gives a great advantage to an unfair antagonist; since he will be sure to say (and many who have no desire to be unfair will say it internally), Are these the doctrines which you do not deem sufficiently certain to be taken under the protection of law? Is the belief in a God one of the opinions to feel sure of which you hold to be assuming infallibility? But I must be permitted to observe, that it is not the feeling sure of a doctrine (be it what it may) which I call an assumption of infallibility. It is the undertaking to decide that question *for others,* without allowing them to hear what can be said on the contrary side. And I denounce and reprobate this pretension not the less, if put forth on the side of my most solemn convictions. However positive any one's persuasion may be, not only of the falsity but of the pernicious consequences—not only of the pernicious consequences, but (to adopt expressions which I altogether condemn) the immorality and impiety of an opinion; yet if, in pursuance of that private judgment, though backed by the public judgment of his country or his contemporaries, he prevents the opinion from being heard in its defence, he assumes infallibility. And so far from the assumption being less objectionable or less dangerous because the opinion is called immoral or impious, this is the case of all others in which it is most fatal. These are exactly the occasions on which the men of one generation commit those dreadful mistakes which excite the astonishment and horror of posterity. It is among such that we find the instances memorable in history, when the arm of the law has been employed to root out the best men and the noblest doctrines; with deplorable success as to the men, though some of the doctrines have survived to be (as if in mockery) invoked in defence of similar conduct towards those who dissent from *them,* or from their received interpretation.

Mankind can hardly be too often reminded, that there was once a man named Socrates, between whom and the legal authorities and public opinion of his time there took place a memorable collision. Born in an age and country abounding in individual greatness, this man has been handed down to us by those who best knew both him and the age, as the most virtuous man in it; while *we* know him as the head and prototype of all subsequent teachers of virtue, the source equally of the lofty inspiration of Plato and the judicious utilitarianism of Aristotle, "*i mastri di color che sanno,*" the two headsprings of ethical as of all other philosophy. This acknowledged master of all the eminent thinkers who have since lived—whose fame, still growing after more than two thousand years, all but outweighs the whole remainder of the names which make his native city illustrious—was put to death by his countrymen, after a judicial conviction, for impiety and immorality. Impiety, in denying the gods recognised by the State; indeed his accuser asserted (see the *Apologia*) that he believed in no gods at all. Immorality, in being, by his doctrines and instructions, a "corruptor of youth." Of these charges the tribunal, there is every ground for believing, honestly found him guilty, and condemned the man who probably of all then born had deserved best of mankind to be put to death as a criminal.

To pass from this to the only other instance of judicial iniquity, the mention of which, after the condemnation of Socrates, would not be an anti-climax: the event which took place on Calvary rather more than eighteen hundred years ago. The man who left on the memory of those who witnessed his life and conversation such an impression of his moral grandeur that eighteen subsequent centuries have done homage to him as the Almighty in person, was ignominiously put to death, as what? As a blasphemer. Men did not merely mistake their benefactor; they mistook him for the exact contrary of what he was, and treated him as that prodigy of impiety which they themselves are now held to be for their treatment of him. The feelings with which mankind now regard these lamentable transactions, especially the later of the two, render them extremely unjust in their judgment of the unhappy actors. These were, to all appearance, not bad men—not worse than men commonly are, but rather the contrary; men who possessed in a full, or somewhat more than a full measure, the religious, moral, and patriotic feelings of their time and people: the very kind of men who, in all times, our own included, have every chance of passing through life blameless and respected. The high-priest who rent his garments when the words were pronounced, which, according to all the ideas of his country, constituted the blackest guilt, was in all probability quite as sincere in his horror and indignation as the generality of respectable and pious men now are in the religious and moral sentiments they profess; and most of those who now shudder at his conduct, if they had lived in his time, and been born Jews, would have acted precisely as he did. Orthodox Christians who are tempted to think that those who stoned to death the first martyrs must have been worse men than they themselves are, ought to remember that one of those persecutors was Saint Paul.

Let us add one more example, the most striking of all, if the impressiveness of an error is measured by the wisdom and virtue of him who falls into it. If ever any one, possessed of power, had grounds for thinking himself the best and most enlightened among his contemporaries, it was the Emperor Marcus Aurelius. Absolute monarch of the whole civilised world, he preserved through life not only the most unblemished justice, but what was less to be expected from his Stoical breeding, the tenderest heart. The few failings which are attributed to him were all on the side of indulgence: while his writings, the highest ethical product of the ancient mind, differ scarcely perceptibly, if they differ at all, from the most characteristic teachings of Christ. This man, a better Christian in all but the dogmatic sense of the word than almost any of the ostensibly Christian sovereigns who have since reigned, persecuted Christianity. Placed at the summit of all the previous attainments of humanity, with an open, unfettered intellect, and a character which led him of himself to embody in his moral writings the Christian ideal, he yet failed to see that Christianity was to be a good and not an evil to the world, with his duties to which he was so deeply penetrated. Existing society he knew to be in a deplorable state. But such as it was, he saw, or thought he saw, that it was held together, and prevented from being worse, by belief and reverence of the received divinities. As a ruler of mankind, he deemed it his duty not to suffer society to fall in pieces; and saw not how, if its existing ties were removed, any

others could be formed which could again knit it together. The new religion openly aimed at dissolving these ties: unless, therefore, it was his duty to adopt that religion, it seemed to be his duty to put it down. Inasmuch then as the theology of Christianity did not appear to him true or of divine origin; inasmuch as this strange history of a crucified God was not credible to him, and a system which purported to rest entirely upon a foundation to him so wholly unbelievable, could not be foreseen by him to be that renovating agency which, after all abatements, it has in fact proved to be; the gentlest and most amiable of philosophers and rulers, under a solemn sense of duty, authorised the persecution of Christianity.

To my mind this is one of the most tragical facts in all history. It is a bitter thought, how different a thing the Christianity of the world might have been, if the Christian faith had been adopted as the religion of the empire under the auspices of Marcus Aurelius instead of those of Constantine. But it would be equally unjust to him and false to truth to deny, that no one plea which can be urged for punishing anti-Christian teaching was wanting to Marcus Aurelius for punishing, as he did, the propagation of Christianity. No Christian more firmly believes that Atheism is false, and tends to the dissolution of society, than Marcus Aurelius believed the same things of Christianity; he who, of all men then living, might have been thought the most capable of appreciating it. Unless any one who approves of punishment for the promulgation of opinions, flatters himself that he is a wiser and better man than Marcus Aurelius—more deeply versed in the wisdom of his time, more elevated in his intellect above it—more earnest in his search for truth, or more single-minded in his devotion to it when found; let him abstain from that assumption of the joint infallibility of himself and the multitude, which the great Antoninus made with so unfortunate a result.

Aware of the impossibility of defending the use of punishment for restraining irreligious opinions by any argument which will not justify Marcus Antoninus, the enemies of religious freedom, when hard pressed, occasionally accept this consequence, and say, with Dr. Johnson, that the persecutors of Christianity were in the right; that persecution is an ordeal through which truth ought to pass, and always passes successfully, legal penalties being, in the end, powerless against truth, though sometimes beneficially effective against mischievous errors. This is a form of the argument for religious intolerance sufficiently remarkable not to be passed without notice.

A theory which maintains that truth may justifiably be persecuted because persecution cannot possibly do it any harm, cannot be charged with being intentionally hostile to the reception of new truths; but we cannot commend the generosity of its dealing with the persons to whom mankind are indebted for them. To discover to the world something which deeply concerns it, and of which it was previously ignorant; to prove to it that it had been mistaken on some vital point of temporal or spiritual interest, is as important a service as a human being can render to his fellow creatures, and in certain cases, as in those of the early Christians and of the Reformers, those who think with Dr. Johnson believe it to have been the most precious gift which could be bestowed on mankind. That the authors of such splendid benefits should be requited by martyrdom; that their reward should be to be dealt with as the vilest of criminals, is not, upon this theory, a deplorable error and misfortune, for which humanity should mourn in sackcloth and ashes, but the normal and justifiable state of things. The propounder of a new truth, according to this doctrine, should stand, as stood, in the legislation of the Locrians, the proposer of a new law, with a halter round his neck, to be instantly tightened if the public assembly did not, on hearing his reasons, then and there adopt his proposition. People who defend this mode of treating benefactors cannot be supposed to set much value on the benefit; and I believe this view of the subject is mostly confined to the sort of persons who think that new truths may have been desirable once, but that we have had enough of them now.

But, indeed, the dictum that truth always triumphs over persecution is one of those pleasant falsehoods which men repeat after one another till they pass into commonplaces, but which all experience refutes. History teems with instances of truth put down by persecution. If not suppressed for ever, it may be thrown back for centuries. To speak only of religious opinions: the Reformation broke out at least twenty times before Luther, and was put down. Arnold of Brescia was put down. Fra Dolcino was put down. Savonarola was put down. The Albigeois were put down. The Vaudois were put down. The Lollards were put down. The Hussites were put down. Even

after the era of Luther, wherever persecution was persisted in, it was successful. In Spain, Italy, Flanders, the Austrian empire, Protestantism was rooted out; and, most likely, would have been so in England, had Queen Mary lived, or Queen Elizabeth died. Persecution has always succeeded, save where the heretics were too strong a party to be effectually persecuted. No reasonable person can doubt that Christianity might have been extirpated in the Roman Empire. It spread, and became predominant, because the persecutions were only occasional, lasting but a short time, and separated by long intervals of almost undisturbed propagandism. It is a piece of idle sentimentality that truth, merely as truth, has any inherent power denied to error of prevailing against the dungeon and the stake. Men are not more zealous for truth than they often are for error, and a sufficient application of legal or even of social penalties will generally succeed in stopping the propagation of either. The real advantage which truth has consists in this, that when an opinion is true, it may be extinguished once, twice, or many times, but in the course of ages there will generally be found persons to rediscover it, until some one of its reappearances falls on a time when from favourable circumstances it escapes persecution until it has made such head as to withstand all subsequent attempts to suppress it.

It will be said, that we do not now put to death the introducers of new opinions: we are not like our fathers who slew the prophets, we even build sepulchres to them. It is true we no longer put heretics to death; and the amount of penal infliction which modern feeling would probably tolerate, even against the most obnoxious opinions, is not sufficient to extirpate them. But let us not flatter ourselves that we are yet free from the stain even of legal persecution. Penalties for opinion, or at least for its expression, still exist by law; and their enforcement is not, even in these times, so unexampled as to make it at all incredible that they may some day be revived in full force. In the year 1857, at the summer assizes of the county of Cornwall, an unfortunate man,[1] said to be of unexceptionable conduct in all relations of life, was sentenced to twenty-one months' imprisonment, for uttering, and writing on a gate, some offensive words concerning Christianity. Within a month of the same time, at

[1] Thomas Pooley, Bodmin Assizes, July 31, 1857. In December following, he received a free pardon from the Crown.

the Old Bailey, two persons, on two separate occasions,[1] were rejected as jurymen, and one of them grossly insulted by the judge and by one of the counsel, because they honestly declared that they had no theological belief; and a third, a foreigner,[2] for the same reason, was denied justice against a thief.

This refusal of redress took place in virtue of the legal doctrine, that no person can be allowed to give evidence in a court of justice who does not profess belief in a God (any god is sufficient) and in a future state; which is equivalent to declaring such persons to be outlaws, excluded from the protection of the tribunals; who may not only be robbed or assaulted with impunity, if no one but themselves, or persons of similar opinions, be present, but any one else may be robbed or assaulted with impunity, if the proof of the fact depends on their evidence. The assumption on which this is grounded is that the oath is worthless of a person who does not believe in a future state; a proposition which betokens much ignorance of history in those who assent to it (since it is historically true that a large proportion of infidels in all ages have been persons of distinguished integrity and honour); and would be maintained by no one who had the smallest conception how many of the persons in greatest repute with the world, both for virtues and attainments, are well known, at least to their intimates, to be unbelievers. The rule, besides, is suicidal, and cuts away its own foundation. Under pretence that atheists must be liars, it admits the testimony of all atheists who are willing to lie, and rejects only those who brave the obloquy of publicly confessing a detested creed rather than affirm a falsehood. A rule thus self-convicted of absurdity so far as regards its professed purpose, can be kept in force only as a badge of hatred, a relic of persecution; a persecution, too, having the peculiarity that the qualification for undergoing it is the being clearly proved not to deserve it. The rule, and the theory it implies, are hardly less insulting to believers than to infidels. For if he who does not believe in a future state necessarily lies, it follows that they who do believe are only prevented from lying, if prevented they are, by the fear of hell. We will not do the authors and abettors of the rule the injury of supposing that the conception which

[1] George Jacob Holyoake, August 17, 1857; Edward Trueelove, July, 1857.
[2] Baron de Gleichen, Marlborough Street Police Court, August 4, 1857.

they have formed of Christian virtue is drawn from their own consciousness.

These, indeed, are but rags and remnants of persecution, and may be thought to be not so much an indication of the wish to persecute, as an example of that very frequent infirmity of English minds, which makes them take a preposterous pleasure in the assertion of a bad principle, when they are no longer bad enough to desire to carry it really into practice. But unhappily there is no security in the state of the public mind that the suspension of worse forms of legal persecution, which has lasted for about the space of a generation, will continue. In this age the quiet surface of routine is as often ruffled by attempts to resuscitate past evils, as to introduce new benefits. What is boasted of at the present time as the revival of religion, is always, in narrow and uncultivated minds, at least as much the revival of bigotry; and where there is the strong permanent leaven of intolerance in the feelings of a people, which at all times abides in the middle classes of this country, it needs but little to provoke them into actively persecuting those whom they have never ceased to think proper objects of persecution.[3] For it is this—it is the

[3] Ample warning may be drawn from the large infusion of the passions of a persecutor, which mingled with the general display of the worst parts of our national character on the occasion of the Sepoy insurrection. The ravings of fanatics or charlatans from the pulpit may be unworthy of notice; but the heads of the Evangelical party have announced as their principle for the government of Hindoos and Mahometans, that no schools be supported by public money in which the Bible is not taught, and by necessary consequence that no public employment be given to any but real or pretended Christians. An Under-Secretary of State, in a speech delivered to his constituents on the 12th of November, 1857, is reported to have said: "Toleration of their faith" (the faith of a hundred millions of British subjects), "the superstition which they called religion, by the British Government, had had the effect of retarding the ascendancy of the British name, and preventing the salutary growth of Christianity.... Toleration was the great corner-stone of the religious liberties of this country; but do not let them abuse that precious word toleration. As he understood it, it meant the complete liberty to all, freedom of worship, *among Christians, who worshipped upon the same foundation.* It meant toleration of all sects and denominations of *Christians who believed in the one mediation.*" I desire to call attention to the fact, that a man who has been deemed fit to fill a high office in the government of this country under a liberal ministry, maintains the doctrine that all who do not believe in the divinity of Christ are beyond the pale of toleration. Who, after this imbecile display, can in-

opinions men entertain, and the feelings they cherish, respecting those who disown the beliefs they deem important, which makes this country not a place of mental freedom.

For a long time past, the chief mischief of the legal penalties is that they strengthen the social stigma. It is that stigma which is really effective, and so effective is it, that the profession of opinions which are under the ban of society is much less common in England than is, in many other countries, the avowal of those which incur risk of judicial punishment. In respect to all persons but those whose pecuniary circumstances make them independent of the good will of other people, opinion, on this subject, is as efficacious as law; men might as well be imprisoned, as excluded from the means of earning their bread. Those whose bread is already secured, and who desire no favours from men in power, or from bodies of men, or from the public, have nothing to fear from the open avowal of any opinions, but to be ill-thought of and ill-spoken of, and this it ought not to require a very heroic mould to enable them to bear. There is no room for any appeal *ad misericordiam* in behalf of such persons. But though we do not now inflict so much evil on those who think differently from us as it was formerly our custom to do, it may be that we do ourselves as much evil as ever by our treatment of them. Socrates was put to death, but the Socratic philosophy rose like the sun in heaven, and spread its illumination over the whole intellectual firmament. Christians were cast to the lions, but the Christian church grew up a stately and spreading tree, overtopping the older and less vigorous growths, and stifling them by its shade. Our merely social intolerance kills no one, roots out no opinions, but induces men to disguise them, or to abstain from any active effort for their diffusion. With us, heretical opinions do not perceptibly gain, or even lose, ground in each decade or generation; they never blaze out far and wide, but continue to smoulder in the narrow circles of thinking and studious persons among whom they originate, without ever lighting up the general affairs of mankind with either a true or a deceptive light.

And thus is kept up a state of things very satisfactory to some minds, because, without the unpleasant process of fining or imprisoning anybody, it maintains all prevailing opinions outwardly undisturbed, while it does not absolutely interdict the exercise of reason by dissentients afflicted with the malady of thought. A convenient plan for having peace in the intellectual world, and keeping all things going on therein very much as they do already. But the price paid for this sort of intellectual pacification is the sacrifice of the entire moral courage of the human mind. A state of things in which a large portion of the most active and inquiring intellects find it advisable to keep the general principles and grounds of their convictions within their own breasts, and attempt, in what they address to the public, to fit as much as they can of their own conclusions to premises which they have internally renounced, cannot send forth the open, fearless characters, and logical, consistent intellects who once adorned the thinking world. The sort of men who can be looked for under it, are either mere conformers to commonplace, or time-servers for truth, whose arguments on all great subjects are meant for their hearers, and are not those which have convinced themselves. Those who avoid this alternative, do so by narrowing their thoughts and interests to things which can be spoken of without venturing within the region of principles, that is, to small practical matters, which would come right of themselves, if but the minds of mankind were strengthened and enlarged, and which will never be made effectually right until then: while that which would strengthen and enlarge men's minds, free and daring speculation on the highest subjects, is abandoned.

Those in whose eyes this reticence on the part of heretics is no evil should consider, in the first place, that in consequence of it there is never any fair and thorough discussion of heretical opinions; and that such of them as could not stand such a discussion, though they may be prevented from spreading, do not disappear. But it is not the minds of heretics that are deteriorated most by the ban placed on all inquiry which does not end in the orthodox conclusions. The greatest harm done is to those who are not heretics, and whose whole mental development is cramped, and their reason cowed, by the fear of heresy. Who can compute what the world loses in the multitude of promising intellects combined with timid characters, who dare not follow out any bold, vigorous, independent train of thought, lest it should land them in something which would admit of being considered irreligious or immoral?

---

dulge the illusion that religious persecution has passed away, never to return?

Among them we may occasionally see some man of deep conscientiousness, and subtle and refined understanding, who spends a life in sophisticating with an intellect which he cannot silence, and exhausts the resources of ingenuity in attempting to reconcile the promptings of his conscience and reason with orthodoxy, which yet he does not, perhaps, to the end succeed in doing.

No one can be a great thinker who does not recognise, that as a thinker it is his first duty to follow his intellect to whatever conclusions it may lead. Truth gains more even by the errors of one who, with due study and preparation, thinks for himself, than by the true opinions of those who only hold them because they do not suffer themselves to think. Not that it is solely, or chiefly, to form great thinkers, that freedom of thinking is required. On the contrary, it is as much and even more indispensable to enable average human beings to attain the mental stature which they are capable of. There have been, and may again be, great individual thinkers in a general atmosphere of mental slavery. But there never has been, nor ever will be, in that atmosphere an intellectually active people. Where any people has made a temporary approach to such a character, it has been because the dread of heterodox speculation was for a time suspended. Where there is a tacit convention that principles are not to be disputed; where the discussion of the greatest questions which can occupy humanity is considered to be closed, we cannot hope to find that generally high scale of mental activity which has made some periods of history so remarkable. Never when controversy avoided the subjects which are large and important enough to kindle enthusiasm, was the mind of a people stirred up from its foundations, and the impulse given which raised even persons of the most ordinary intellect to something of the dignity of thinking beings. Of such we have had an example in the condition of Europe during the times immediately following the Reformation; another, though limited to the Continent and to a more cultivated class, in the speculative movement of the latter half of the eighteenth century; and a third, of still briefer duration, in the intellectual fermentation of Germany during the Goethian and Fichtean period. These periods differed widely in the particular opinions which they developed; but were alike in this, that during all three the yoke of authority was broken. In each, an old mental despotism had been thrown off, and no new one had

yet taken its place. The impulse given at these three periods has made Europe what it now is. Every single improvement which has taken place either in the human mind or in institutions, may be traced distinctly to one or other of them. Appearances have for some time indicated that all three impulses are well nigh spent; and we can expect no fresh start until we again assert our mental freedom.

Let us now pass to the second division of the argument, and dismissing the supposition that any of the received opinions may be false, let us assume them to be true, and examine into the worth of the manner in which they are likely to be held, when their truth is not freely and openly canvassed. However unwillingly a person who has a strong opinion may admit the possibility that his opinion may be false, he ought to be moved by the consideration that, however true it may be, if it is not fully, frequently, and fearlessly discussed, it will be held as a dead dogma, not a living truth.

There is a class of persons (happily not quite so numerous as formerly) who think it enough if a person assents undoubtingly to what they think true, though he has no knowledge whatever of the grounds of the opinion, and could not make a tenable defence of it against the most superficial objections. Such persons, if they can once get their creed taught from authority, naturally think that no good, and some harm, comes of its being allowed to be questioned. Where their influence prevails, they make it nearly impossible for the received opinion to be rejected wisely and considerately, though it may still be rejected rashly and ignorantly; for to shut out discussion entirely is seldom possible, and when it once gets in, beliefs not grounded on conviction are apt to give way before the slightest semblance of an argument. Waiving, however, this possibility—assuming that the true opinion abides in the mind, but abides as a prejudice, a belief independent of, and proof against, argument—this is not the way in which truth ought to be held by a rational being. This is not knowing the truth. Truth, thus held, is but one superstition the more, accidentally clinging to the words which enunciate a truth.

If the intellect and judgment of mankind ought to be cultivated, a thing which Protestants at least do not deny, on what can these faculties be more appropriately exercised by any one, than on the things which concern him so much that it is considered necessary for him to hold opinions on them? If the cultivation of the understanding consists in one thing more than in another, it is surely in learning the grounds of one's own opinions. Whatever people believe, on subjects on which it is of the first importance to believe rightly, they ought to be able to defend against at least the common objections. But, some one may say, "Let them be *taught* the grounds of their opinions. It does not follow that opinions must be merely parroted because they are never heard controverted. Persons who learn geometry do not simply commit the theorems to memory, but understand and learn likewise the demonstrations; and it would be absurd to say that they remain ignorant of the grounds of geometrical truths, because they never hear any one deny, and attempt to disprove them." Undoubtedly: and such teaching suffices on a subject like mathematics, where there is nothing at all to be said on the wrong side of the question. The peculiarity of the evidence of mathematical truths is that all the argument is on one side. There are no objections, and no answers to objections. But on every subject on which difference of opinion is possible, the truth depends on a balance to be struck between two sets of conflicting reasons. Even in natural philosophy, there is always some other explanation possible of the same facts; some geocentric theory instead of heliocentric, some phlogiston instead of oxygen; and it has to be shown why that other theory cannot be the true one: and until this is shown, and until we know how it is shown, we do not understand the grounds of our opinion.

But when we turn to subjects infinitely more complicated, to morals, religion, politics, social relations, and the business of life, three-fourths of the arguments for every disputed opinion consist in dispelling the appearances which favour some opinion different from it. The greatest orator, save one, of antiquity, has left it on record that he always studied his adversary's case with as great, if not still greater, intensity than even his own. What Cicero practised as the means of forensic success requires to be imitated by all who study any subject in order to arrive at the truth. He who knows only his own side of the case, knows little of that. His reasons may be good, and no one may have been able to refute them. But if he is equally unable to refute the reasons on the opposite side; if he does not so much as know what they are, he has no ground for preferring either opinion. The rational position for him would be suspension of judgment, and unless he con-

tents himself with that, he is either led by authority, or adopts, like the generality of the world, the side to which he feels most inclination. Nor is it enough that he should hear the arguments of adversaries from his own teachers, presented as they state them, and accompanied by what they offer as refutations. That is not the way to do justice to the arguments, or bring them into real contact with his own mind. He must be able to hear them from persons who actually believe them; who defend them in earnest, and do their very utmost for them. He must know them in their most plausible and persuasive form; he must feel the whole force of the difficulty which the true view of the subject has to encounter and dispose of; else he will never really possess himself of the portion of truth which meets and removes that difficulty.

Ninety-nine in a hundred of what are called educated men are in this condition; even of those who can argue fluently for their opinions. Their conclusion may be true, but it might be false for anything they know: they have never thrown themselves into the mental position of those who think differently from them, and considered what such persons may have to say; and consequently they do not, in any proper sense of the word, know the doctrine which they themselves profess. They do not know those parts of it which explain and justify the remainder; the considerations which show that a fact which seemingly conflicts with another is reconcilable with it, or that, of two apparently strong reasons, one and not the other ought to be preferred. All that part of the truth which turns the scale, and decides the judgment of a completely informed mind, they are strangers to; nor is it ever really known, but to those who have attended equally and impartially to both sides, and endeavoured to see the reasons of both in the strongest light. So essential is this discipline to a real understanding of moral and human subjects, that if opponents of all important truths do not exist, it is indispensable to imagine them, and supply them with the strongest arguments which the most skilful devil's advocate can conjure up.

To abate the force of these considerations, an enemy of free discussion may be supposed to say, that there is no necessity for mankind in general to know and understand all that can be said against or for their opinions by philosophers and theologians. That it is not needful for common men to be able to expose all the misstatements or fallacies of an ingenious opponent. That it is enough if there is always some-body capable of answering them, so that nothing likely to mislead uninstructed persons remains unrefuted. That simple minds, having been taught the obvious grounds of the truths inculcated on them, may trust to authority for the rest, and being aware that they have neither knowledge nor talent to resolve every difficulty which can be raised, may repose in the assurance that all those which have been raised have been or can be answered, by those who are specially trained to the task.

Conceding to this view of the subject the utmost that can be claimed for it by those most easily satisfied with the amount of understanding of truth which ought to accompany the belief of it; even so, the argument for free discussion is no way weakened. For even this doctrine acknowledges that mankind ought to have a rational assurance that all objections have been satisfactorily answered; and how are they to be answered if that which requires to be answered is not spoken? or how can the answer be known to be satisfactory, if the objectors have no opportunity of showing that it is unsatisfactory? If not the public, at least the philosophers and theologians who are to resolve the difficulties, must make themselves familiar with those difficulties in their most puzzling form; and this cannot be accomplished unless they are freely stated, and placed in the most advantageous light which they admit of. The Catholic Church has its own way of dealing with this embarrassing problem. It makes a broad separation between those who can be permitted to receive its doctrines on conviction, and those who must accept them on trust. Neither, indeed, are allowed any choice as to what they will accept; but the clergy, such at least as can be fully confided in, may admissibly and meritoriously make themselves acquainted with the arguments of opponents, in order to answer them, and may, therefore, read heretical books; the laity, not unless by special permission, hard to be obtained. This discipline recognises a knowledge of the enemy's case as beneficial to the teachers, but finds means, consistent with this, of denying it to the rest of the world: thus giving to the *élite* more mental culture, though not more mental freedom, than it allows to the mass. By this device it succeeds in obtaining the kind of mental superiority which its purposes require; for though culture without freedom never made a large and liberal mind, it can make a clever *nisi prius* advocate of a cause. But in countries professing Protestantism, this resource is denied; since Protestants hold, at least in theory, that the responsibility for the choice of a religion must be borne by each for himself, and cannot be thrown off upon teachers. Besides, in the present state of the world, it is practically impossible that writings which are read by the instructed can be kept from the uninstructed. If the teachers of mankind are to be cognisant of all that they ought to know, everything must be free to be written and published without restraint.

If, however, the mischievous operation of the absence of free discussion, when the received opinions are true, were confined to leaving men ignorant of the grounds of those opinions, it might be thought that this, if an intellectual, is no moral evil, and does not affect the worth of the opinions, regarded in their influence on the character. The fact, however, is, that not only the grounds of the opinion are forgotten in the absence of discussion, but too often the meaning of the opinion itself. The words which convey it cease to suggest ideas, or suggest only a small portion of those they were originally employed to communicate. Instead of a vivid conception and a living belief, there remain only a few phrases retained by rote; or, if any part, the shell and husk only of the meaning is retained, the finer essence being lost. The great chapter in human history which this fact occupies and fills, cannot be too earnestly studied and meditated on.

It is illustrated in the experience of almost all ethical doctrines and religious creeds. They are all full of meaning and vitality to those who originate them, and to the direct disciples of the originators. Their meaning continues to be felt in undiminished strength, and is perhaps brought out into even fuller consciousness, so long as the struggle lasts to give the doctrine or creed an ascendancy over other creeds. At last it either prevails, and becomes the general opinion, or its progress stops; it keeps possession of the ground it has gained, but ceases to spread further. When either of these results has become apparent, controversy on the subject flags, and gradually dies away. The doctrine has taken its place, if not as a received opinion, as one of the admitted sects or divisions of opinion: those who hold it have generally inherited, not adopted it; and conversion from one of these doctrines to another, being now an exceptional fact, occupies little place in the thoughts of their professors. Instead of being, as at first, constantly on the alert either to defend themselves against the world, or to bring the world over to them, they have subsided into acquiescence, and neither listen, when they can help it, to arguments against their creed, nor trouble dissentients (if there be such) with arguments in its favour. From this time may usually be dated the decline in the living power of the doctrine.

We often hear the teachers of all creeds lamenting the difficulty of keeping up in the minds of believers a lively apprehension of the truth which they nominally recognise, so that it may penetrate the feelings, and acquire a real mastery over the conduct. No such difficulty is complained of while the creed is still fighting for its existence: even the weaker combatants then know and feel what they are fighting for, and the difference between it and other doctrines; and in that period of every creed's existence, not a few persons may be found, who have realised its fundamental principles in all the forms of thought, have weighed and considered them in all their important bearings, and have experienced the full effect on the character which belief in that creed ought to produce in a mind thoroughly imbued with it. But when it has come to be an hereditary creed, and to be received passively, not actively—when the mind is no longer compelled, in the same degree as at first, to exercise its vital powers on the questions which its belief presents to it, there is a progressive tendency to forget all of the belief except the formularies, or to give it a dull and torpid assent, as if accepting it on trust dispensed with the necessity of realising it in consciousness, or testing it by personal experience, until it almost ceases to connect itself at all with the inner life of the human being. Then are seen the cases, so frequent in this age of the world as almost to form the majority, in which the creed remains as it were outside the mind, incrusting and petrifying it against all other influences addressed to the higher parts of our nature; manifesting its power by not suffering any fresh and living conviction to get in, but itself doing nothing for the mind or heart, except standing sentinel over them to keep them vacant.

To what an extent doctrines intrinsically fitted to make the deepest impression upon the mind may remain in it as dead beliefs, without being ever realised in the imagination, the feelings, or the understanding, is exemplified by the manner in which the majority of believers hold the doctrines of Christianity. By Christianity I here mean what is accounted such by all churches and sects—the maxims and precepts contained in the New Testament. These are considered sacred, and accepted as laws, by all professing Christians. Yet it is scarcely too much to say that not one Christian in a thousand guides or tests his individual conduct by reference to those laws. The standard to which he does refer it, is the custom of his nation, his class, or his religious profession. He has thus, on the one hand, a collection of ethical maxims, which he believes to have been vouchsafed to him by infallible wisdom as rules for his government; and on the other a set of every-day judgments and practices, which go a certain length with some of those maxims, not so great a length with others, stand in direct opposition to some, and are, on the whole, a compromise between the Christian creed and the interests and suggestions of worldly life. To the first of these standards he gives his homage; to the other his real allegiance.

All Christians believe that the blessed are the poor and humble, and those who are ill-used by the world; that it is easier for a camel to pass through the eye of a needle than for a rich man to enter the kingdom of heaven; that they should judge not, lest they be judged; that they should swear not at all; that they should love their neighbour as themselves; that if one take their cloak, they should give him their coat also; that they should take no thought for the morrow; that if they would be perfect they should sell all that they have and give it to the poor. They are not insincere when they say that they believe these things. They do believe them, as people believe what they have always heard lauded and never discussed. But in the sense of that living belief which regulates conduct, they believe these doctrines just up to the point to which it is usual to act upon them. The doctrines in their integrity are serviceable to pelt adversaries with; and it is understood that they are to be put forward (when possible) as the reasons for whatever people do that they think laudable. But any one who reminded them that the maxims require an infinity of things which they never even think of doing, would gain nothing but to be classed among those very unpopular characters who affect to be better than other people. The doctrines have no hold on ordinary believers—are not a power in their minds. They have an habitual respect for the sound of them, but no feeling which spreads from the words to the things signified, and forces the mind to take *them* in, and make them conform to the formula. Whenever conduct is concerned, they look round for Mr. A and B to direct them how far to go in obeying Christ.

Now we may be well assured that the case was not thus, but far otherwise, with the early Christians. Had it been thus, Christianity never would have expanded from an obscure sect of the despised Hebrews into the religion of the Roman empire. When their enemies said, "See how these Christians love one another" (a remark not likely to be made by anybody now), they assuredly had a much livelier feeling of the meaning of their creed than they have ever had since. And to this cause, probably, it is chiefly owing that Christianity now makes so little progress in extending its domain, and after eighteen centuries is still nearly confined to Europeans and the descendants of Europeans. Even with the strictly religious, who are much in earnest about their doctrines, and attach a greater amount of meaning to many of them than people in general, it commonly happens that the part which is thus comparatively active in their minds is that which was made by Calvin, or Knox, or some such person much nearer in character to themselves. The sayings of Christ coexist passively in their minds, producing hardly any effect beyond what is caused by mere listening to words so amiable and bland. There are many reasons, doubtless, why doctrines which are the badge of a sect retain more of their vitality than those common to all recognised sects, and why more pains are taken by teachers to keep their meaning alive; but one reason certainly is, that the peculiar doctrines are more questioned, and have to be oftener defended against open gainsayers. Both teachers and learners go to sleep at their post, as soon as there is no enemy in the field.

The same thing holds true, generally speaking, of all traditional doctrines—those of prudence and knowledge of life, as well as of morals or religion. All languages and literatures are full of general observations on life, both as to what it is, and how to conduct oneself in it; observations which everybody knows, which everybody repeats, or hears with acquiescence, which are received as truisms, yet of which most people first truly learn the meaning when experience, generally of a painful kind, has made it a reality to them. How often, when smarting under some unforeseen misfortune or disappointment, does a person call to mind some proverb or common saying, familiar to him all his life, the meaning of which, if he had ever before felt it as he does now, would have saved him from the calamity. There are indeed reasons for this, other than the absence of discussion; there are many truths of which the full meaning *cannot* be realised until personal experience has brought it home. But much more of the meaning even of these would have been understood, and what was understood would have been far more deeply impressed on the mind, if the man had been accustomed to hear it argued *pro* and *con* by people who did understand it. The fatal tendency of mankind to leave off thinking about a thing when it is no longer doubtful, is the cause of half their errors. A contemporary author has well spoken of "the deep slumber of a decided opinion."

But what! (it may be asked) Is the absence of unanimity an indispensable condition of true knowledge? Is it necessary that some part of mankind should persist in error to enable any to realise the truth? Does a belief cease to be real and vital as soon as it is generally received—and is a proposition never thoroughly understood and felt unless some doubt of it remains? As soon as mankind have unanimously accepted a truth, does the truth perish within them? The highest aim and best result of improved intelligence, it has hitherto been thought, is to unite mankind more and more in the acknowledgment of all important truths; and does the intelligence only last as long as it has not achieved its object? Do the fruits of conquest perish by the very completeness of the victory?

I affirm no such thing. As mankind improve, the number of doctrines which are no longer disputed or doubted will be constantly on the increase: and the well-being of mankind may almost be measured by the number and gravity of the truths which have reached the point of being uncontested. The cessation, on one question after another, of serious controversy, is one of the necessary incidents of the consolidation of opinion; a consolidation as salutary in the case of true opinions, as it is dangerous and noxious when the opinions are erroneous. But though this gradual narrowing of the bounds of diversity of opinion is necessary in both senses of the term, being at once inevitable and indispensable, we are not therefore obliged to conclude that all its consequences must be beneficial. The loss of so important an aid to the intelligent and living apprehension of a truth, as is afforded by the necessity of explaining it to, or defending it against, opponents, though not sufficient to outweigh, is no trifling drawback from, the benefit of its universal recognition. Where this advantage can no longer be had, I confess I should like to see the teachers of mankind endeavouring to provide a substitute for it; some contrivance for making the difficulties of the question as present to the learner's consciousness, as if they were pressed upon him by a dissentient champion, eager for his conversion.

But instead of seeking contrivances for this purpose, they have lost those they formerly had. The Socratic dialectics, so magnificently exemplified in the dialogues of Plato, were a contrivance of this description. They were essentially a negative discussion of the great question of philosophy and life, directed with consummate skill to the purpose of convincing any one who had merely adopted the commonplaces of received opinion that he did not understand the subject—that he as yet attached no definite meaning to the doctrines he professed; in order that, becoming aware of his ignorance, he might be put in the way to obtain a stable belief, resting on a clear apprehension both of the meaning of doctrines and of their evidence. The school disputations of the Middle Ages had a somewhat similar object. They were intended to make sure that the pupil understood his own opinion, and (by necessary correlation) the opinion opposed to it, and could enforce the grounds of the one and confute those of the other. These last-mentioned contests had indeed the incurable defect, that the premises appealed to were taken from authority, not from reason; and, as a discipline to the mind, they were in every respect inferior to the powerful dialectics which formed the intellects of the "Socratici viri"; but the modern mind owes far more to both than it is generally willing to admit, and the present modes of education contain nothing which in the smallest degree supplies the place either of the one or of the other. A person who derives all his instruction from teachers or books, even if he escape the besetting temptation of contenting himself with cram, is under no compulsion to hear both sides; accordingly it is far from a frequent accomplishment, even among thinkers, to know both sides; and the weakest part of what everybody says in defence of his opinion is what he intends as a reply to antagonists.

It is the fashion of the present time to disparage negative logic—that which points out weaknesses in theory or errors in practice, without establishing positive truths. Such negative criticism would indeed be poor enough as an ultimate result; but as a means to attaining any positive knowledge or conviction worthy the name, it cannot be valued too highly; and until people are again systematically trained to it, there will be few great thinkers, and a low general average of intellect, in any but the mathematical and physical departments of speculation. On any other subject no one's opinions deserve the name of knowledge, except so far as he has either had forced upon him by others, or gone through of himself, the same mental process which would have been required of him in carrying on an active controversy with opponents. That, therefore, which when absent, it is so indispensable, but so difficult, to create, how worse than absurd it is to forego, when spontaneously offering itself! If there are any persons who contest a received opinion, or who will do so if law or opinion will let them, let us thank them for it, open our minds to listen to them, and rejoice that there is some one to do for us what we otherwise ought, if we have any regard for either the certainty or the vitality of our convictions, to do with much greater labour for ourselves.

It still remains to speak of one of the principal causes which make diversity of opinion advantageous, and will continue to do so until mankind shall have entered a stage of intellectual advancement which at present seems at an incalculable distance. We have hitherto considered only two possibilities: that the received opinion may be false, and some other opinion, consequently, true; or that, the received opinion being true, a conflict with the opposite error is essential to a clear apprehension and deep feeling of its truth. But there is a commoner case than either of these; when the conflicting doctrines, instead of being one true and the other false, share the truth between them; and the nonconforming opinion is needed to supply the remainder of the truth, of which the received doctrine embodies only a part. Popular opinions, on subjects not palpable to sense, are often true, but seldom or never the whole truth. They are a part of the truth; sometimes a greater, sometimes a smaller part, but exaggerated, distorted, and disjointed from the truths by which they ought to be accompanied and limited. Heretical opinions, on the other hand, are generally some of these suppressed and neglected truths, bursting the bonds which kept them down, and either seeking reconciliation with the truth contained in the common opinion, or fronting it as enemies, and setting themselves up, with similar exclusiveness, as the whole truth. The latter case is hitherto the most frequent, as, in the human mind, one-sidedness has always been the rule, and many-sidedness the exception. Hence, even in revolutions of opinion, one part of the truth usually sets while another rises. Even progress, which ought to superadd, for the most part only substitutes, one partial and incomplete truth for another; improvement consisting chiefly in this, that the new fragment of truth is more wanted, more adapted to the needs of the time, than that which it displaces. Such being the partial character of prevailing opinions, even when resting on a true foundation, every opinion which embodies somewhat of the portion of truth which the common opinion omits, ought to be considered precious, with whatever amount of error and confusion that truth may be blended. No sober judge of human affairs will feel bound to be indignant because those who force on our notice truths which we should otherwise have overlooked, overlook some of those which we see. Rather, he will think that so long as popular truth is one-sided, it is more desirable than otherwise that unpopular truth should have one-sided assertors too; such being usually the most energetic, and the most likely to compel reluctant attention to the fragment of wisdom which they proclaim as if it were the whole.

Thus, in the eighteenth century, when nearly all the instructed, and all those of the uninstructed who were led by them, were lost in admiration of what is called civilisation, and of the marvels of modern science, literature, and philosophy, and while greatly overrating the amount of unlikeness between the men of modern and those of ancient times, indulged the belief that the whole of the difference was in their own favour; with what a salutary shock did the paradoxes of Rousseau explode like bombshells in the midst, dislocating the compact mass of one-sided opinion, and forcing its elements to recombine in a better form and with additional ingredients. Not that the current opinions were on the whole farther from the truth than Rousseau's were; on the contrary, they were nearer to it; they contained more of positive truth, and very much less of error. Nevertheless there lay in Rousseau's doctrine, and has floated down the stream of opinion along with it, a considerable amount of exactly those truths which the popular opinion wanted; and these are the deposit which was left behind when the flood subsided. The superior worth of simplicity of life, the enervating and demoralising effect of the trammels and hypocrisies of artificial society, are ideas which have never been entirely absent from cultivated minds since Rousseau wrote; and they will in time produce their due effect, though at present needing to be asserted as much as ever, and to be asserted by deeds, for words, on this subject, have nearly exhausted their power.

In politics, again, it is almost a commonplace, that a party of order or stability, and a party of progress or reform, are both necessary elements of a healthy state of political life; until the one or the other shall have so enlarged its mental grasp as to be a party equally of order and of progress, knowing and distinguishing what is fit to be preserved from what ought to be swept away. Each of these modes of thinking derives its utility from the deficiencies of the other; but it is in a great measure the opposition of the other that keeps each within the limits of reason and sanity. Unless opinions favourable to democracy and to aristocracy, to property and to equality, to co-operation and to competition, to luxury and to abstinence, to sociality and individuality, to liberty and discipline, and all the other standing antagonisms of practical life, are expressed with equal freedom, and enforced and defended with equal talent and energy, there is no chance of both elements obtaining their due; one scale is sure to go up, and the other down. Truth, in the great practical concerns of life, is so much a question of the reconciling and combining of opposites, that very few have minds sufficiently capacious and impartial to make the adjustment with an approach to correctness, and it has to be made by the rough process of a struggle between combatants fighting under hostile banners. On any of the great open questions just enumerated, if either of the two opinions has a better claim than the other, not merely to be tolerated, but to be encouraged and countenanced, it is the one which happens at the particular time and place to be in a minority. That is the opinion which, for the time being, represents the neglected interests, the side of human well-being which is in danger of obtaining less than its share. I am aware that there is not, in this country, any intolerance of differences of opinion on most of these topics. They are adduced to show, by admitted and multiplied examples, the universality of the fact, that only through diversity of opinion is there, in the existing state of human intellect, a chance of fair play to all sides of the truth. When there are persons to be found who form an exception to the apparent unanimity of the world on any subject, even if the world is in the right, it is always probable that dissentients have something worth hearing to say for themselves, and that truth would lose something by their silence.

It may be objected, "But *some* received principles, especially on the highest and most vital subjects, are more than half-truths. The Christian morality, for instance, is the whole truth on that subject, and if any one teaches a morality which varies from it, he is wholly in error." As this is of all cases the most important in practice, none can be fitter to test the general maxim. But before pronouncing what Christian morality is or is not, it would be desirable to decide what is meant by Christian morality. If it means the morality of the New Testament, I wonder that any one who derives his knowledge of this from the book itself, can suppose that it was announced, or intended, as a complete doctrine of morals. The Gospel always refers to a pre-existing morality, and confines its precepts to the particulars in which that morality was to be corrected, or superseded by a wider and higher; expressing itself, moreover, in terms most general, often impossible to be interpreted literally, and possessing rather the impressiveness of poetry or eloquence than the precision of legislation. To extract from it a body of ethical doctrine, has never been possible without eking it out from the Old Testament, that is, from a system elaborate indeed, but in many respects barbarous, and intended only for a barbarous people. St. Paul, a declared enemy to this Judaical mode of interpreting the doctrine and filling up the scheme of his Master, equally assumes a pre-existing morality, namely that of the Greeks and Romans; and his advice to Christians is in a great measure a system of accommodation to that; even to the extent of giving an apparent sanction to slavery. What is called Christian, but should rather be termed theological, morality, was not the work of Christ or the Apostles, but is of much later origin, having been gradually built up by the Catholic church of the first five centuries, and though not im-

plicitly adopted by moderns and Protestants, has been much less modified by them than might have been expected. For the most part, indeed, they have contented themselves with cutting off the additions which had been made to it in the Middle Ages, each sect supplying the place by fresh additions, adapted to its own character and tendencies.

That mankind owe a great debt to this morality, and to its early teachers, I should be the last person to deny; but I do not scruple to say of it that it is, in many important points, incomplete and one-sided, and that unless ideas and feelings, not sanctioned by it, had contributed to the formation of European life and character, human affairs would have been in a worse condition than they now are. Christian morality (so called) has all the characters of a reaction; it is, in great part, a protest against Paganism. Its ideal is negative rather than positive; passive rather than active; Innocence rather than Nobleness; Abstinence from Evil, rather than energetic Pursuit of Good; in its precepts (as has been well said) "thou shalt not" predominates unduly over "thou shalt." In its horror of sensuality, it made an idol of asceticism, which has been gradually compromised away into one of legality. It holds out the hope of heaven and the threat of hell, as the appointed and appropriate motives to a virtuous life: in this falling far below the best of the ancients, and doing what lies in it to give to human morality an essentially selfish character, by disconnecting each man's feelings of duty from the interests of his fellow creatures, except so far as a self-interested inducement is offered to him for consulting them. It is essentially a doctrine of passive obedience; it inculcates submission to all authorities found established; who indeed are not to be actively obeyed when they command what religion forbids, but who are not to be resisted, far less rebelled against, for any amount of wrong to ourselves. And while, in the morality of the best Pagan nations, duty to the State holds even a disproportionate place, infringing on the just liberty of the individual; in purely Christian ethics, that grand department of duty is scarcely noticed or acknowledged. It is in the Koran, not the New Testament, that we read the maxim—"A ruler who appoints any man to an office, when there is in his dominions another man better qualified for it, sins against God and against the State." What little recognition the idea of obligation to the public obtains in modern morality is derived from Greek and Roman sources, not from Christian; as, even in the morality of private life, whatever exists of magnanimity, highmindedness, personal dignity, even the sense of honour, is derived from the purely human, not the religious part of our education, and never could have grown out of a standard of ethics in which the only worth, professedly recognised, is that of obedience.

I am as far as any one from pretending that these defects are necessarily inherent in the Christian ethics in every manner in which it can be conceived, or that the many requisites of a complete moral doctrine which it does not contain do not admit of being reconciled with it. Far less would I insinuate this of the doctrines and precepts of Christ himself. I believe that the sayings of Christ are all that I can see any evidence of their having been intended to be; that they are irreconcilable with nothing which a comprehensive morality requires; that everything which is excellent in ethics may be brought within them, with no greater violence to their language than has been done to it by all who have attempted to deduce from them any practical system of conduct whatever. But it is quite consistent with this to believe that they contain, and were meant to contain, only a part of the truth; that many essential elements of the highest morality are among the things which are not provided for, nor intended to be provided for, in the recorded deliverances of the Founder of Christianity, and which have been entirely thrown aside in the system of ethics erected on the basis of those deliverances by the Christian Church. And this being so, I think it a great error to persist in attempting to find in the Christian doctrine that complete rule for our guidance which its author intended it to sanction and enforce, but only partially to provide. I believe, too, that this narrow theory is becoming a grave practical evil, detracting greatly from the moral training and instruction which so many well-meaning persons are now at length exerting themselves to promote. I much fear that by attempting to form the mind and feelings on an exclusively religious type, and discarding those secular standards (as for want of a better name they may be called) which heretofore coexisted with and supplemented the Christian ethics, receiving some of its spirit, and infusing into it some of theirs, there will result, and is even now resulting, a low, abject, servile type of character, which, submit itself as it may to what it deems the Supreme Will, is incapable of rising to or sympathising in the conception of Supreme Goodness. I believe that other ethics than any which can be evolved from exclusively Christian sources, must exist side by side with Christian ethics to produce the moral regeneration of mankind; and that the Christian system is no exception to the rule, that in an imperfect state of the human mind the interests of truth require a diversity of opinions.

It is not necessary that in ceasing to ignore the moral truths not contained in Christianity men should ignore any of those which it does contain. Such prejudice, or oversight, when it occurs, is altogether an evil; but it is one from which we cannot hope to be always exempt, and must be regarded as the price paid for an inestimable good. The exclusive pretension made by a part of the truth to be the whole, must and ought to be protested against; and if a reactionary impulse should make the protestors unjust in their turn, this one-sidedness, like the other, may be lamented, but must be tolerated. If Christians would teach infidels to be just to Christianity, they should themselves be just to infidelity. It can do truth no service to blink the fact, known to all who have the most ordinary acquaintance with literary history, that a large portion of the noblest and most valuable moral teaching has been the work, not only of men who did not know, but of men who knew and rejected, the Christian faith.

I do not pretend that the most unlimited use of the freedom of enunciating all possible opinions would put an end to the evils of religious or philosophical sectarianism. Every truth which men of narrow capacity are in earnest about, is sure to be asserted, inculcated, and in many ways even acted on, as if no other truth existed in the world, or at all events none that could limit or qualify the first. I acknowledge that the tendency of all opinions to become sectarian is not cured by the freest discussion, but is often heightened and exacerbated thereby; the truth which ought to have been, but was not, seen, being rejected all the more violently because proclaimed by persons regarded as opponents. But it is not on the impassioned partisan, it is on the calmer and more disinterested bystander, that this collision of opinions works its salutary effect. Not the violent conflict between parts of the truth, but the quiet suppression of half of it, is the formidable evil; there is always hope when people are forced to listen to both sides; it is when they attend only to one that errors harden into prejudices, and truth itself ceases to have the effect of truth, by being exaggerated into falsehood. And since there are few mental attributes more rare than that judicial faculty which can sit in intelligent judgment between two sides of a question, of which only one is represented by an advocate before it, truth has no chance but in proportion as every side of it, every opinion which embodies any fraction of the truth, not only finds advocates, but is so advocated as to be listened to.

We have now recognised the necessity to the mental well-being of mankind (on which all their other well-being depends) of freedom of opinion, and freedom of the expression of opinion, on four distinct grounds; which we will now briefly recapitulate.

First, if any opinion is compelled to silence, that opinion may, for aught we can certainly know, be true. To deny this is to assume our own infallibility.

Secondly, though the silenced opinion be an error, it may, and very commonly does, contain a portion of truth; and since the general or prevailing opinion on any subject is rarely or never the whole truth, it is only by the collision of adverse opinions that the remainder of the truth has any chance of being supplied.

Thirdly, even if the received opinion be not only true, but the whole truth; unless it is suffered to be, and actually is, vigorously and earnestly contested, it will, by most of those who receive it, be held in the manner of a prejudice, with little comprehension or feeling of its rational grounds. And not only this, but, fourthly, the meaning of the doctrine itself will be in danger of being lost, or enfeebled, and deprived of its vital effect on the character and conduct: the dogma becoming a mere formal profession, inefficacious for good, but cumbering the ground, and preventing the growth of any real and heartfelt conviction, from reason or personal experience.

Before quitting the subject of freedom of opinion, it is fit to take some notice of those who say that the free expression of all opinions should be permitted, on condition that the manner be temperate, and do not pass the bounds of fair discussion. Much might be said on the impossibility of fixing where these supposed bounds are to be placed; for if the test be offence to those whose opinions are attacked,

I think experience testifies that this offence is given whenever the attack is telling and powerful, and that every opponent who pushes them hard, and whom they find it difficult to answer, appears to them, if he shows any strong feeling on the subject, an intemperate opponent.

But this, though an important consideration in a practical point of view, merges in a more fundamental objection. Undoubtedly the manner of asserting an opinion, even though it be a true one, may be very objectionable, and may justly incur severe censure. But the principal offences of the kind are such as it is mostly impossible, unless by accidental self-betrayal, to bring home to conviction. The gravest of them is, to argue sophistically, to suppress facts or arguments, to misstate the elements of the case, or misrepresent the opposite opinion. But all this, even to the most aggravated degree, is so continually done in perfect good faith, by persons who are not considered, and in many other respects may not deserve to be considered, ignorant or incompetent, that it is rarely possible, on adequate grounds, conscientiously to stamp the misrepresentation as morally culpable; and still less could law presume to interfere with this kind of controversial misconduct. With regard to what is commonly meant by intemperate discussion, namely invective, sarcasm, personality, and the like, the denunciation of these weapons would deserve more sympathy if it were ever proposed to interdict them equally to both sides; but it is only desired to restrain the employment of them against the prevailing opinion: against the unprevailing they may not only be used without general disapproval, but will be likely to obtain for him who uses them the praise of honest zeal and righteous indignation. Yet whatever mischief arises from their use is greatest when they are employed against the comparatively defenceless; and whatever unfair advantage can be derived by any opinion from this mode of asserting it, accrues almost exclusively to received opinions. The worst offence of this kind which can be committed by a polemic is to stigmatise those who hold the contrary opinion as bad and immoral men. To calumny of this sort, those who hold any unpopular opinion are peculiarly exposed, because they are in general few and uninfluential, and nobody but themselves feels much interested in seeing justice done them; but this weapon is, from the nature of the case, denied to those who attack a prevailing opinion:

they can neither use it with safety to themselves, nor, if they could, would it do anything but recoil on their own cause. In general, opinions contrary to those commonly received can only obtain a hearing by studied moderation of language, and the most cautious avoidance of unnecessary offence, from which they hardly ever deviate even in a slight degree without losing ground: while unmeasured vituperation employed on the side of the prevailing opinion really does deter people from professing contrary opinions, and from listening to those who profess them.

For the interest, therefore, of truth and justice, it is far more important to restrain this employment of vituperative language than the other; and, for example, if it were necessary to choose, there would be much more need to discourage offensive attacks on infidelity than on religion. It is, however, obvious that law and authority have no business with restraining either, while opinion ought, in every instance, to determine its verdict by the circumstances of the individual case; condemning every one, on whichever side of the argument he places himself, in whose mode of advocacy either want of candour, or malignity, bigotry, or intolerance of feeling manifest themselves; but not inferring these vices from the side which a person takes, though it be the contrary side of the question to our own; and giving merited honour to every one, whatever opinion he may hold, who has calmness to see and honesty to state what his opponents and their opinions really are, exaggerating nothing to their discredit, keeping nothing back which tells, or can be supposed to tell, in their favour. This is the real morality of public discussion: and if often violated, I am happy to think that there are many controversialists who to a great extent observe it, and a still greater number who conscientiously strive towards it.

Chapter 3
Of Individuality, as one of the Elements of Well-being

SUCH BEING the reasons which make it imperative that human beings should be free to form opinions, and to express their opinions without reserve; and such the baneful consequences to the intellectual, and through that to the moral nature of man, unless this liberty is either conceded, or asserted in spite of prohibition; let us next examine whether the same reasons do not require that men should be free to act upon their opinions—to carry these out in their lives, without hindrance, either physical or moral, from their fellow-men, so long as it is at their own risk and peril.

This last proviso is of course indispensable. No one pretends that actions should be as free as opinions. On the contrary, even opinions lose their immunity when the circumstances in which they are expressed are such as to constitute their expression a positive instigation to some mischievous act. An opinion that corn-dealers are starvers of the poor, or that private property is robbery, ought to be unmolested when simply circulated through the press, but may justly incur punishment when delivered orally to an excited mob assembled before the house of a corn-dealer, or when handed about among the same mob in the form of a placard. Acts, of whatever kind, which, without justifiable cause, do harm to others, may be, and in the more important cases absolutely require to be, controlled by the unfavourable sentiments, and, when needful, by the active interference of mankind. The liberty of the individual must be thus far limited; he must not make himself a nuisance to other people. But if he refrains from molesting others in what concerns them, and merely acts according to his own inclination and judgment in things which concern himself, the same reasons which show that opinion should be free, prove also that he should be allowed, without molestation, to carry his opinions into practice at his own cost. That mankind are not infallible; that their truths, for the most part, are only half-truths; that unity of opinion, unless resulting from the fullest and freest comparison of opposite opinions, is not desirable, and diversity not an evil, but a good, until mankind are much more capable than at present of recognising all sides of the truth, are principles applicable to men's modes of action, not less than to their opinions. As it is useful that while mankind are imperfect there should be different opinions, so it is that there should be different experiments of living; that free scope should be given to varieties of character, short of injury to others; and that the worth of different modes of life should be proved practically, when any one thinks fit to try them. It is desirable, in short, that in things which do not primarily concern others, individuality should assert itself. Where, not the person's own character, but the traditions or customs of other people are the rule of conduct, there is wanting one of the principal ingredients of human happiness, and quite the chief ingredient of individual and social progress.

In maintaining this principle, the greatest difficulty to be encountered does not lie in the appreciation of means towards an acknowledged end, but in the indifference of persons in general to the end itself. If it were felt that the free development of individuality is one of the leading essentials of well-being; that it is not only a co-ordinate element with all that is designated by the terms civilisation, instruction, education, culture, but is itself a necessary part and condition of all those things; there would be no danger that liberty should be undervalued, and the adjustment of the boundaries between it and social control would present no extraordinary difficulty. But the evil is, that individual spontaneity is hardly recognised by the common modes of thinking as having any intrinsic worth, or deserving any regard on its own account. The majority, being satisfied with the ways of mankind as they now are (for it is they who make them what they are), cannot comprehend why those ways should not be good enough for everybody; and what is more, spontaneity forms no part of the ideal of the majority of moral and social reformers, but is rather looked on with jealousy, as a troublesome and perhaps rebellious obstruction to the general acceptance of what these reformers, in their own judgment, think would be best for mankind. Few persons, out of Germany, even comprehend the meaning of the doctrine which Wilhelm von Humboldt, so eminent both as a *savant* and as a politician, made the text of a treatise—that "the end of man, or that which is prescribed by the eternal or immutable dictates of reason, and not suggested by vague and transient desires, is the highest and most harmonious development of his powers to a complete and consistent whole"; that, therefore, the object "towards which every human being must ceaselessly direct his efforts, and on which especially those who design to influence their fellow-men must ever keep their eyes, is the individuality of power and development"; that for this there are two requisites, "freedom, and variety of situations"; and that from the union of these arise "individual vigour and manifold diversity," which combine themselves in "originality."[1]

Little, however, as people are accustomed to a doctrine like that of Von Humboldt, and

surprising as it may be to them to find so high a value attached to individuality, the question, one must nevertheless think, can only be one of degree. No one's idea of excellence in conduct is that people should do absolutely nothing but copy one another. No one would assert that people ought not to put into their mode of life, and into the conduct of their concerns, any impress whatever of their own judgment, or of their own individual character. On the other hand, it would be absurd to pretend that people ought to live as if nothing whatever had been known in the world before they came into it; as if experience had as yet done nothing towards showing that one mode of existence, or of conduct, is preferable to another. Nobody denies that people should be so taught and trained in youth as to know and benefit by the ascertained results of human experience. But it is the privilege and proper condition of a human being, arrived at the maturity of his faculties, to use and interpret experience in his own way. It is for him to find out what part of recorded experience is properly applicable to his own circumstances and character. The traditions and customs of other people are, to a certain extent, evidence of what their experience has taught *them;* presumptive evidence, and as such, have a claim to his deference: but, in the first place, their experience may be too narrow; or they may not have interpreted it rightly. Secondly, their interpretation of experience may be correct, but unsuitable to him. Customs are made for customary circumstances and customary characters; and his circumstances or his character may be uncustomary. Thirdly, though the customs be both good as customs, and suitable to him, yet to conform to custom, merely *as* custom, does not educate or develop in him any of the qualities which are the distinctive endowment of a human being. The human faculties of perception, judgment, discriminative feeling, mental activity, and even moral preference, are exercised only in making a choice. He who does anything because it is the custom makes no choice. He gains no practice either in discerning or in desiring what is best. The mental and moral, like the muscular powers, are improved only by being used. The faculties are called into no exercise by doing a thing merely because others do it, no more than by believing a thing only because others believe it. If the grounds of an opinion are not conclusive to the person's own reason, his reason cannot be strengthened, but is likely to be weakened, by his adopting

---

[1] *The Sphere and Duties of Government,* from the German of Baron Wilhelm von Humboldt, pp. 11-13.

it: and if the inducements to an act are not such as are consentaneous to his own feelings and character (where affection, or the rights of others, are not concerned) it is so much done towards rendering his feelings and character inert and torpid, instead of active and energetic.

He who lets the world, or his own portion of it, choose his plan of life for him, has no need of any other faculty than the ape-like one of imitation. He who chooses his plan for himself, employs all his faculties. He must use observation to see, reasoning and judgment to foresee, activity to gather materials for decision, discrimination to decide, and when he has decided, firmness and self-control to hold to his deliberate decision. And these qualities he requires and exercises exactly in proportion as the part of his conduct which he determines according to his own judgment and feelings is a large one. It is possible that he might be guided in some good path, and kept out of harm's way, without any of these things. But what will be his comparative worth as a human being? It really is of importance, not only what men do, but also what manner of men they are that do it. Among the works of man, which human life is rightly employed in perfecting and beautifying, the first in importance surely is man himself. Supposing it were possible to get houses built, corn grown, battles fought, causes tried, and even churches erected and prayers said, by machinery—by automatons in human form—it would be a considerable loss to exchange for these automatons even the men and women who at present inhabit the more civilised parts of the world, and who assuredly are but starved specimens of what nature can and will produce. Human nature is not a machine to be built after a model, and set to do exactly the work prescribed for it, but a tree, which requires to grow and develop itself on all sides, according to the tendency of the inward forces which make it a living thing.

It will probably be conceded that it is desirable people should exercise their understandings, and that an intelligent following of custom, or even occasionally an intelligent deviation from custom, is better than a blind and simply mechanical adhesion to it. To a certain extent it is admitted that our understanding should be our own: but there is not the same willingness to admit that our desires and impulses should be our own likewise; or that to possess impulses of our own, and of any strength, is anything but a peril and a snare. Yet desires and impulses are as much a part

of a perfect human being as beliefs and restraints: and strong impulses are only perilous when not properly balanced; when one set of aims and inclinations is developed into strength, while others, which ought to co-exist with them, remain weak and inactive. It is not because men's desires are strong that they act ill; it is because their consciences are weak. There is no natural connection between strong impulses and a weak conscience. The natural connection is the other way. To say that one person's desires and feelings are stronger and more various than those of another, is merely to say that he has more of the raw material of human nature, and is therefore capable, perhaps of more evil, but certainly of more good. Strong impulses are but another name for energy. Energy may be turned to bad uses; but more good may always be made of an energetic nature, than of an indolent and impassive one. Those who have most natural feeling are always those whose cultivated feelings may be made the strongest. The same strong susceptibilities which make the personal impulses vivid and powerful, are also the source from whence are generated the most passionate love of virtue, and the sternest self-control. It is through the cultivation of these that society both does its duty and protects its interests: not by rejecting the stuff of which heroes are made, because it knows not how to make them. A person whose desires and impulses are his own—are the expression of his own nature, as it has been developed and modified by his own culture—is said to have a character. One whose desires and impulses are not his own, has no character, no more than a steam-engine has a character. If, in addition to being his own, his impulses are strong, and are under the government of a strong will, he has an energetic character. Whoever thinks that individuality of desires and impulses should not be encouraged to unfold itself, must maintain that society has no need of strong natures—is not the better for containing many persons who have much character—and that a high general average of energy is not desirable.

In some early states of society, these forces might be, and were, too much ahead of the power which society then possessed of disciplining and controlling them. There has been a time when the element of spontaneity and individuality was in excess, and the social principle had a hard struggle with it. The difficulty then was to induce men of strong bodies or minds to pay obedience to any rules which required them to control their impulses. To overcome this difficulty, law and discipline, like the Popes struggling against the Emperors, asserted a power over the whole man, claiming to control all his life in order to control his character—which society had not found any other sufficient means of binding. But society has now fairly got the better of individuality; and the danger which threatens human nature is not the excess, but the deficiency, of personal impulses and preferences. Things are vastly changed since the passions of those who were strong by station or by personal endowment were in a state of habitual rebellion against laws and ordinances, and required to be rigorously chained up to enable the persons within their reach to enjoy any particle of security. In our times, from the highest class of society down to the lowest, every one lives as under the eye of a hostile and dreaded censorship. Not only in what concerns others, but in what concerns only themselves, the individual or the family do not ask themselves—what do I prefer? or, what would suit my character and disposition? or, what would allow the best and highest in me to have fair play, and enable it to grow and thrive? They ask themselves, what is suitable to my position? what is usually done by persons of my station and pecuniary circumstances? or (worse still) what is usually done by persons of a station and circumstances superior to mine? I do not mean that they choose what is customary in preference to what suits their own inclination. It does not occur to them to have any inclination, except for what is customary. Thus the mind itself is bowed to the yoke: even in what people do for pleasure, conformity is the first thing thought of; they like in crowds; they exercise choice only among things commonly done: peculiarity of taste, eccentricity of conduct, are shunned equally with crimes: until by dint of not following their own nature they have no nature to follow: their human capacities are withered and starved: they become incapable of any strong wishes or native pleasures, and are generally without either opinions or feelings of home growth, or properly their own. Now is this, or is it not, the desirable condition of human nature?

It is so, on the Calvinistic theory. According to that, the one great offence of man is self-will. All the good of which humanity is capable is comprised in obedience. You have no choice; thus you must do, and no otherwise: "whatever is not a duty, is a sin." Human nature being radically corrupt, there is no redemption for any one until human nature is killed within him. To one holding this theory of life, crushing out any of the human faculties, capacities, and susceptibilities, is no evil: man needs no capacity, but that of surrendering himself to the will of God: and if he uses any of his faculties for any other purpose but to do that supposed will more effectually, he is better without them. This is the theory of Calvinism; and it is held, in a mitigated form, by many who do not consider themselves Calvinists; the mitigation consisting in giving a less ascetic interpretation to the alleged will of God; asserting it to be his will that mankind should gratify some of their inclinations; of course not in the manner they themselves prefer, but in the way of obedience, that is, in a way prescribed to them by authority; and, therefore, by the necessary condition of the case, the same for all.

In some such insidious form there is at present a strong tendency to this narrow theory of life, and to the pinched and hidebound type of human character which it patronises. Many persons, no doubt, sincerely think that human beings thus cramped and dwarfed are as their Maker designed them to be; just as many have thought that trees are a much finer thing when clipped into pollards, or cut out into figures of animals, than as nature made them. But if it be any part of religion to believe that man was made by a good Being, it is more consistent with that faith to believe that this Being gave all human faculties that they might be cultivated and unfolded, not rooted out and consumed, and that he takes delight in every nearer approach made by his creatures to the ideal conception embodied in them, every increase in any of their capabilities of comprehension, of action, or of enjoyment. There is a different type of human excellence from the Calvinistic: a conception of humanity as having its nature bestowed on it for other purposes than merely to be abnegated. "Pagan self-assertion" is one of the elements of human worth, as well as "Christian self-denial."[1] There is a Greek ideal of self-development, which the Platonic and Christian ideal of self-government blends with, but does not supersede. It may be better to be a John Knox than an Alcibiades, but it is better to be a Pericles than either; nor would a Pericles, if we had one in these days, be without anything good which belonged to John Knox.

[1] Sterling's *Essays*.

It is not by wearing down into uniformity all that is individual in themselves, but by cultivating it, and calling it forth, within the limits imposed by the rights and interests of others, that human beings become a noble and beautiful object of contemplation; and as the works partake the character of those who do them, by the same process human life also becomes rich, diversified, and animating, furnishing more abundant aliment to high thoughts and elevating feelings, and strengthening the tie which binds every individual to the race, by making the race infinitely better worth belonging to. In proportion to the development of his individuality, each person becomes more valuable to himself, and is therefore capable of being more valuable to others. There is a greater fulness of life about his own existence, and when there is more life in the units there is more in the mass which is composed of them. As much compression as is necessary to prevent the stronger specimens of human nature from encroaching on the rights of others cannot be dispensed with; but for this there is ample compensation even in the point of view of human development. The means of development which the individual loses by being prevented from gratifying his inclinations to the injury of others, are chiefly obtained at the expense of the development of other people. And even to himself there is a full equivalent in the better development of the social part of his nature, rendered possible by the restraint put upon the selfish part. To be held to rigid rules of justice for the sake of others, develops the feelings and capacities which have the good of others for their object. But to be restrained in things not affecting their good, by their mere displeasure, develops nothing valuable, except such force of character as may unfold itself in resisting the restraint. If acquiesced in, it dulls and blunts the whole nature. To give any fair play to the nature of each, it is essential that different persons should be allowed to lead different lives. In proportion as this latitude has been exercised in any age, has that age been noteworthy to posterity. Even despotism does not produce its worst effects, so long as individuality exists under it; and whatever crushes individuality is despotism, by whatever name it may be called, and whether it professes to be enforcing the will of God or the injunctions of men.

Having said that the individuality is the same thing with development, and that it is only the cultivation of individuality which produces, or can produce, well-developed human beings, I might here close the argument: for what more or better can be said of any condition of human affairs than that it brings human beings themselves nearer to the best thing they can be? or what worse can be said of any obstruction to good than that it prevents this? Doubtless, however, these considerations will not suffice to convince those who most need convincing; and it is necessary further to show, that these developed human beings are of some use to the undeveloped—to point out to those who do not desire liberty, and would not avail themselves of it, that they may be in some intelligible manner rewarded for allowing other people to make use of it without hindrance.

In the first place, then, I would suggest that they might possibly learn something from them. It will not be denied by anybody, that originality is a valuable element in human affairs. There is always need of persons not only to discover new truths, and point out when what were once truths are true no longer, but also to commence new practices, and set the example of more enlightened conduct, and better taste and sense in human life. This cannot well be gainsaid by anybody who does not believe that the world has already attained perfection in all its ways and practices. It is true that this benefit is not capable of being rendered by everybody alike: there are but few persons, in comparison with the whole of mankind, whose experiments, if adopted by others, would be likely to be any improvement on established practice. But these few are the salt of the earth; without them, human life would become a stagnant pool. Not only is it they who introduce good things which did not before exist; it is they who keep the life in those which already exist. If there were nothing new to be done, would human intellect cease to be necessary? Would it be a reason why those who do the old things should forget why they are done, and do them like cattle, not like human beings? There is only too great a tendency in the best beliefs and practices to degenerate into the mechanical; and unless there were a succession of persons whose ever-recurring originality prevents the grounds of those beliefs and practices from becoming merely traditional, such dead matter would not resist the smallest shock from anything really alive, and there would be no reason why civilisation should not die out, as in the Byzantine Empire. Persons of genius, it is true, are, and are always likely to be, a small minority; but in order to have them, it is necessary to preserve the soil in which they grow. Genius can only breathe freely in an *atmosphere* of freedom. Persons of genius are, *ex vi termini,* more individual than any other people—less capable, consequently, of fitting themselves, without hurtful compression, into any of the small number of moulds which society provides in order to save its members the trouble of forming their own character. If from timidity they consent to be forced into one of these moulds, and to let all that part of themselves which cannot expand under the pressure remain unexpanded, society will be little the better for their genius. If they are of a strong character, and break their fetters, they become a mark for the society which has not succeeded in reducing them to commonplace, to point out with solemn warning as "wild," "erratic," and the like; much as if one should complain of the Niagara river for not flowing smoothly between its banks like a Dutch canal.

I insist thus emphatically on the importance of genius, and the necessity of allowing it to unfold itself freely both in thought and in practice, being well aware that no one will deny the position in theory, but knowing also that almost every one, in reality, is totally indifferent to it. People think genius a fine thing if it enables a man to write an exciting poem, or paint a picture. But in its true sense, that of originality in thought and action, though no one says that it is not a thing to be admired, nearly all, at heart, think that they can do very well without it. Unhappily this is too natural to be wondered at. Originality is the one thing which unoriginal minds cannot feel the use of. They cannot see what it is to do for them: how should they? If they could see what it would do for them, it would not be originality. The first service which originality has to render them, is that of opening their eyes: which being once fully done, they would have a chance of being themselves original. Meanwhile, recollecting that nothing was ever yet done which some one was not the first to do, and that all good things which exist are the fruits of originality, let them be modest enough to believe that there is something still left for it to accomplish, and assure themselves that they are more in need of originality, the less they are conscious of the want.

In sober truth, whatever homage may be professed, or even paid, to real or supposed mental superiority, the general tendency of things throughout the world is to render medi-ocrity the ascendant power among mankind. In ancient history, in the Middle Ages, and in a diminishing degree through the long transition from feudality to the present time, the individual was a power in himself; and if he had either great talents or a high social position, he was a considerable power. At present individuals are lost in the crowd. In politics it is almost a triviality to say that public opinion now rules the world. The only power deserving the name is that of masses, and of governments while they make themselves the organ of the tendencies and instincts of masses. This is as true in the moral and social relations of private life as in public transactions. Those whose opinions go by the name of public opinion are not always the same sort of public: in America they are the whole white population; in England, chiefly the middle class. But they are always a mass, that is to say, collective mediocrity. And what is a still greater novelty, the mass do not now take their opinions from dignitaries in Church or State, from ostensible leaders, or from books. Their thinking is done for them by men much like themselves, addressing them or speaking in their name, on the spur of the moment, through the newspapers.

I am not complaining of all this. I do not assert that anything better is compatible, as a general rule, with the present low state of the human mind. But that does not hinder the government of mediocrity from being mediocre government. No government by a democracy or a numerous aristocracy, either in its political acts or in the opinions, qualities, and tone of mind which it fosters, ever did or could rise above mediocrity, except in so far as the sovereign Many have let themselves be guided (which in their best times they always have done) by the counsels and influence of a more highly gifted and instructed One or Few. The initiation of all wise or noble things comes and must come from individuals; generally at first from some one individual. The honour and glory of the average man is that he is capable of following that initiative; that he can respond internally to wise and noble things, and be led to them with his eyes open. I am not countenancing the sort of "hero-worship" which applauds the strong man of genius for forcibly seizing on the government of the world and making it do his bidding in spite of itself. All he can claim is, freedom to point out the way. The power of compelling others into it is not only inconsistent with the freedom and development of all the rest, but corrupting to the strong man himself. It does seem, however, that when the opinions of masses of merely average men are everywhere become or becoming the dominant power, the counterpoise and corrective to that tendency would be the more and more pronounced individuality of those who stand on the higher eminences of thought. It is in these circumstances most especially, that exceptional individuals, instead of being deterred, should be encouraged in acting differently from the mass. In other times there was no advantage in their doing so, unless they acted not only differently but better. In this age, the mere example of non-conformity, the mere refusal to bend the knee to custom, is itself a service. Precisely because the tyranny of opinion is such as to make eccentricity a reproach, it is desirable, in order to break through that tyranny, that people should be eccentric. Eccentricity has always abounded when and where strength of character has abounded; and the amount of eccentricity in a society has generally been proportional to the amount of genius, mental vigour, and moral courage it contained. That so few now dare to be eccentric marks the chief danger of the time.

I have said that it is important to give the freest scope possible to uncustomary things, in order that it may in time appear which of these are fit to be converted into customs. But independence of action, and disregard of custom, are not solely deserving of encouragement for the chance they afford that better modes action, and customs more worthy of general adoption, may be struck out; nor is it only persons of decided mental superiority who have a just claim to carry on their lives in their own way. There is no reason that all human existence should be constructed on some one or some small number of patterns. If a person possesses any tolerable amount of common sense and experience, his own mode of laying out his existence is the best, not because it is the best in itself, but because it is his own mode. Human beings are not like sheep; and even sheep are not undistinguishably alike. A man cannot get a coat or a pair of boots to fit him unless they are either made to his measure, or he has a whole warehouseful to choose from: and is it easier to fit him with a life than with a coat, or are human beings more like one another in their whole physical and spiritual conformation than in the shape of their feet? If it were only that people have diversities of taste, that is reason enough for not attempting to shape them all after one model.

But different persons also require different conditions for their spiritual development; and can no more exist healthily in the same moral, than all the variety of plants can in the same physical, atmosphere and climate. The same things which are helps to one person towards the cultivation of his higher nature are hindrances to another. The same mode of life is a healthy excitement to one, keeping all his faculties of action and enjoyment in their best order, while to another it is a distracting burthen, which suspends or crushes all internal life. Such are the differences among human beings in their sources of pleasure, their susceptibilities of pain, and the operation on them of different physical and moral agencies, that unless there is a corresponding diversity in their modes of life, they neither obtain their fair share of happiness, nor grow up to the mental, moral, and æsthetic stature of which their nature is capable. Why then should tolerance, as far as the public sentiment is concerned, extend only to tastes and modes of life which extort acquiescence by the multitude of their adherents? Nowhere (except in some monastic institutions) is diversity of taste entirely unrecognised; a person may, without blame, either like or dislike rowing, or smoking, or music, or athletic exercises, or chess, or cards, or study, because both those who like each of these things, and those who dislike them, are too numerous to be put down. But the man, and still more the woman, who can be accused either of doing "what nobody does," or of not doing "what everybody does," is the subject of as much depreciatory remark as if he or she had committed some grave moral delinquency. Persons require to possess a title, or some other badge of rank, or of the consideration of people of rank, to be able to indulge somewhat in the luxury of doing as they like without detriment to their estimation. To indulge somewhat, I repeat: for whoever allow themselves much of that indulgence, incur the risk of something worse than disparaging speeches—they are in peril of a commission *de lunatico,* and of having their property taken from them and given to their relations.[1]

[1] There is something both contemptible and frightful in the sort of evidence on which, of late years, any person can be judicially declared unfit for the management of his affairs; and after his death, his disposal of his property can be set aside, if there is enough of it to pay the expenses of litigation—which are charged on the property itself.

There is one characteristic of the present direction of public opinion peculiarly calculated to make it intolerant of any marked demonstration of individuality. The general average of mankind are not only moderate in intellect, but also moderate in inclinations: they have no tastes or wishes strong enough to incline them to do anything unusual, and they consequently do not understand those who have, and class all such with the wild and intemperate whom they are accustomed to look down upon. Now, in addition to this fact which is general, we have only to suppose that a strong movement has set in towards the improvement of morals, and it is evident what we have to expect. In these days such a movement has set in; much has actually been effected in the way of increased regularity of conduct and discouragement of excesses; and there is a philanthropic spirit abroad, for the exercise of which there is no more inviting field than the moral and prudential improvement of our fellow creatures. These tendencies of the times cause the public to be more disposed than at most former periods to prescribe general rules of conduct, and endeavour to make every one conform to the approved standard. And that standard, express or tacit, is to desire nothing strongly. Its ideal of character is to be without any marked character; to maim by compression, like a Chinese lady's foot, every part of human nature which stands out prominently, and

---

All the minute details of his daily life are pried into, and whatever is found which, seen through the medium of the perceiving and describing faculties of the lowest of the low, bears an appearance unlike absolute commonplace, is laid before the jury as evidence of insanity, and often with success; the jurors being little, if at all, less vulgar and ignorant than the witnesses; while the judges, with that extraordinary want of knowledge of human nature and life which continually astonishes us in English lawyers, often help to mislead them. These trials speak volumes as to the state of feeling and opinion among the vulgar with regard to human liberty. So far from setting any value on individuality—so far from respecting the right of each individual to act, in things indifferent, as seems good to his own judgment and inclinations, judges and juries cannot even conceive that a person in a state of sanity can desire such freedom. In former days, when it was proposed to burn atheists, charitable people used to suggest putting them in a madhouse instead: it would be nothing surprising now-a-days were we to see this done, and the doers applauding themselves, because, instead of persecuting for religion, they had adopted so humane and Christian a mode of treating these unfortunates, not without a silent satisfaction at their having thereby obtained their deserts.

tends to make the person markedly dissimilar in outline to commonplace humanity.

As is usually the case with ideals which exclude one-half of what is desirable, the present standard of approbation produces only an inferior imitation of the other half. Instead of great energies guided by vigorous reason, and strong feelings strongly controlled by a conscientious will, its result is weak feelings and weak energies, which therefore can be kept in outward conformity to rule without any strength either of will or of reason. Already energetic characters on any large scale are becoming merely traditional. There is now scarcely any outlet for energy in this country except business. The energy expended in this may still be regarded as considerable. What little is left from that employment is expended on some hobby; which may be a useful, even a philanthropic hobby, but is always some one thing, and generally a thing of small dimensions. The greatness of England is now all collective; individually small, we only appear capable of anything great by our habit of combining; and with this our moral and religious philanthropists are perfectly contented. But it was men of another stamp than this that made England what it has been; and men of another stamp will be needed to prevent its decline.

The despotism of custom is everywhere the standing hindrance to human advancement, being in unceasing antagonism to that disposition to aim at something better than customary, which is called, according to circumstances, the spirit of liberty, or that of progress or improvement. The spirit of improvement is not always a spirit of liberty, for it may aim at forcing improvements on an unwilling people; and the spirit of liberty, in so far as it resists such attempts, may ally itself locally and temporarily with the opponents of improvement; but the only unfailing and permanent source of improvement is liberty, since by it there are as many possible independent centres of improvement as there are individuals. The progressive principle, however, in either shape, whether as the love of liberty or of improvement, is antagonistic to the sway of Custom, involving at least emancipation from that yoke; and the contest between the two constitutes the chief interest of the history of mankind. The greater part of the world has, properly speaking, no history, because the despotism of Custom is complete. This is the case over the whole East. Custom is there, in all things, the final appeal; justice and right mean conformity to custom; the argument of custom no one, unless some tyrant intoxicated with power, thinks of resisting. And we see the result. Those nations must once have had originality; they did not start out of the ground populous, lettered, and versed in many of the arts of life; they made themselves all this, and were then the greatest and most powerful nations of the world. What are they now? The subjects or dependents of tribes whose forefathers wandered in the forests when theirs had magnificent palaces and gorgeous temples, but over whom custom exercised only a divided rule with liberty and progress.

A people, it appears, may be progressive for a certain length of time, and then stop: when does it stop? When it ceases to possess individuality. If a similar change should befall the nations of Europe, it will not be in exactly the same shape: the despotism of custom with which these nations are threatened is not precisely stationariness. It proscribes singularity, but it does not preclude change, provided all change together. We have discarded the fixed costumes of our forefathers; every one must still dress like other people, but the fashion may change once or twice a year. We thus take care that when there is a change, it shall be for change's sake, and not from any idea of beauty or convenience; for the same idea of beauty or convenience would not strike all the world at the same moment, and be simultaneously thrown aside by all at another moment. But we are progressive as well as changeable: we continually make new inventions in mechanical things, and keep them until they are again superseded by better; we are eager for improvement in politics, in education, even in morals, though in this last our idea of improvement chiefly consists in persuading or forcing other people to be as good as ourselves. It is not progress that we object to; on the contrary, we flatter ourselves that we are the most progressive people who ever lived. It is individuality that we war against: we should think we had done wonders if we had made ourselves all alike; forgetting that the unlikeness of one person to another is generally the first thing which draws the attention of either to the imperfection of his own type, and the superiority of another, or the possibility, by combining the advantages of both, of producing something better than either. We have a warning example in China—a nation of much talent, and, in some respects, even wisdom, owing to the rare good fortune of having been provided at an early period with a particularly good set of customs, the work, in some measure, of men to whom even the most enlightened European must accord, under certain limitations, the title of sages and philosophers. They are remarkable, too, in the excellence of their apparatus for impressing, as far as possible, the best wisdom they possess upon every mind in the community, and securing that those who have appropriated most of it shall occupy the posts of honour and power. Surely the people who did this have discovered the secret of human progressiveness, and must have kept themselves steadily at the head of the movement of the world. On the contrary, they have become stationary—have remained so for thousands of years; and if they are ever to be farther improved, it must be by foreigners. They have succeeded beyond all hope in what English philanthropists are so industriously working at—in making a people all alike, all governing their thoughts and conduct by the same maxims and rules; and these are the fruits. The modern *régime* of public opinion is, in an unorganised form, what the Chinese educational and political systems are in an organised; and unless individuality shall be able successfully to assert itself against this yoke, Europe, notwithstanding its noble antecedents and its professed Christianity, will tend to become another China.

What is it that has hitherto preserved Europe from this lot? What has made the European family of nations an improving, instead of a stationary portion of mankind? Not any superior excellence in them, which, when it exists, exists as the effect not as the cause; but their remarkable diversity of character and culture. Individuals, classes, nations, have been extremely unlike one another: they have struck out a great variety of paths, each leading to something valuable; and although at every period those who travelled in different paths have been intolerant of one another, and each would have thought it an excellent thing if all the rest could have been compelled to travel his road, their attempts to thwart each other's development have rarely had any permanent success, and each has in time endured to receive the good which the others have offered. Europe is, in my judgment, wholly indebted to this plurality of paths for its progressive and many-sided development. But it already begins to possess this benefit in a considerably less degree. It is decidedly advancing towards the Chinese ideal of making all people alike.

M. de Tocqueville, in his last important work, remarks how much more the Frenchmen of the present day resemble one another than did those even of the last generation. The same remark might be made of Englishmen in a far greater degree.

In a passage already quoted from Wilhelm von Humboldt, he points out two things as necessary conditions of human development, because necessary to render people unlike one another; namely, freedom, and variety of situations. The second of these two conditions is in this country every day diminishing. The circumstances which surround different classes and individuals, and shape their characters, are daily becoming more assimilated. Formerly, different ranks, different neighbourhoods, different trades and professions, lived in what might be called different worlds; at present to a great degree in the same. Comparatively speaking, they now read the same things, listen to the same things, see the same things, go to the same places, have their hopes and fears directed to the same objects, have the same rights and liberties, and the same means of asserting them. Great as are the differences of position which remain, they are nothing to those which have ceased. And the assimilation is still proceeding. All the political changes of the age promote it, since they all tend to raise the low and to lower the high. Every extension of education promotes it, because education brings people under common influences, and gives them access to the general stock of facts and sentiments. Improvement in the means of communication promotes it, by bringing the inhabitants of distant places into personal contact, and keeping up a rapid flow of changes of residence between one place and another. The increase of commerce and manufactures promotes it, by diffusing more widely the advantages of easy circumstances, and opening all objects of ambition, even the highest, to general competition, whereby the desire of rising becomes no longer the character of a particular class, but of all classes. A more powerful agency than even all these, in bringing about a general similarity among mankind, is the complete establishment, in this and other free countries, of the ascendancy of public opinion in the State. As the various social eminences which enabled persons entrenched on them to disregard the opinion of the multitude gradually become levelled; as the very idea of resisting the will of the public, when it is positively known that they have a

will, disappears more and more from the minds of practical politicians; there ceases to be any social support for nonconformity—any substantive power in society which, itself opposed to the ascendancy of numbers, is interested in taking under its protection opinions and tendencies at variance with those of the public.

The combination of all these causes forms so great a mass of influences hostile to Individuality, that it is not easy to see how it can stand its ground. It will do so with increasing difficulty, unless the intelligent part of the public can be made to feel its value—to see that it is good there should be differences, even though not for the better, even though, as it may appear to them, some should be for the worse. If the claims of Individuality are ever to be asserted, the time is now, while much is still wanting to complete the enforced assimilation. It is only in the earlier stages that any stand can be successfully made against the encroachment. The demand that all other people shall resemble ourselves grows by what it feeds on. If resistance waits till life is reduced *nearly* to one uniform type, all deviations from that type will come to be considered impious, immoral, even monstrous and contrary to nature. Mankind speedily become unable to conceive diversity, when they have been for some time unaccustomed to see it.

Chapter 4
Of the Limits to the Authority of Society over the Individual

WHAT, THEN, is the rightful limit to the sovereignty of the individual over himself? Where does the authority of society begin? How much of human life should be assigned to individuality, and how much to society?

Each will receive its proper share, if each has that which more particularly concerns it. To individuality should belong the part of life in which it is chiefly the individual that is interested; to society, the part which chiefly interests society.

Though society is not founded on a contract, and though no good purpose is answered by inventing a contract in order to deduce social obligations from it, every one who receives the protection of society owes a return for the benefit, and the fact of living in society renders it indispensable that each should be bound to observe a certain line of conduct towards the rest. This conduct consists, first, in not injuring the interests of one another; or rather certain interests, which, either by express legal provision or by tacit understanding, ought to be considered as rights; and secondly, in each person's bearing his share (to be fixed on some equitable principle) of the labours and sacrifices incurred for defending the society or its members from injury and molestation. These conditions society is justified in enforcing, at all costs to those who endeavour to withhold fulfilment. Nor is this all that society may do. The acts of an individual may be hurtful to others, or wanting in due consideration for their welfare, without going to the length of violating any of their constituted rights. The offender may then be justly punished by opinion, though not by law. As soon as any part of a person's conduct affects prejudicially the interests of others, society has jurisdiction over it, and the question whether the general welfare will or will not be promoted by interfering with it, becomes open to discussion. But there is no room for entertaining any such question when a person's conduct affects the interests of no persons besides himself, or needs not affect them unless they like (all the persons concerned being of full age, and the ordinary amount of understanding). In all such cases, there should be perfect freedom, legal and social, to do the action and stand the consequences.

It would be a great misunderstanding of this doctrine to suppose that it is one of selfish indifference, which pretends that human beings have no business with each other's conduct in life, and that they should not concern themselves about the well-doing or well-being of one another, unless their own interest is involved. Instead of any diminution, there is need of a great increase of disinterested exertion to promote the good of others. But disinterested benevolence can find other instruments to persuade people to their good than whips and scourges, either of the literal or the metaphorical sort. I am the last person to undervalue the self-regarding virtues; they are only second in importance, if even second, to the social. It is equally the business of education to cultivate both. But even education works by conviction and persuasion as well as by compulsion, and it is by the former only that, when the period of education is passed, the self-regarding virtues should be inculcated. Human beings owe to each other help to distinguish the better from the worse, and encouragement to choose the former and avoid the latter. They should be for ever stimulating each other to increased exercise of their higher faculties, and increased direction of their feelings and aims towards wise instead of foolish, elevating instead of degrading, objects and contemplations. But neither one person, nor any number of persons, is warranted in saying to another human creature of ripe years, that he shall not do with his life for his own benefit what he chooses to do with it. He is the person most interested in his own well-being: the interest which any other person, except in cases of strong personal attachment, can have in it, is trifling, compared with that which he himself has; the interest which society has in him individually (except as to his conduct to others) is fractional, and altogether indirect; while with respect to his own feelings and circumstances, the most ordinary man or woman has means of knowledge immeasurably surpassing those that can be possessed by any one else. The interference of society to overrule his judgment and purposes in what only regards himself must be grounded on general presumptions; which may be altogether wrong, and even if right, are as likely as not to be misapplied to individual cases, by persons no better acquainted with the circumstances of such cases than those are who look at them merely from without. In this department, therefore, of human affairs, Individuality has its proper field of action. In the conduct of human beings towards one another it is necessary that general rules should for the most part be observed, in order that people may know what they have to expect: but in each person's own concerns his individual spontaneity is entitled to free exercise. Considerations to aid his judgment, exhortations to strengthen his will, may be offered to him, even obtruded on him, by others: but he himself is the final judge. All errors which he is likely to commit against advice and warning are far outweighed by the evil of allowing others to constrain him to what they deem his good.

I do not mean that the feelings with which a person is regarded by others ought not to be in any way affected by his self-regarding qualities or deficiencies. This is neither possible nor desirable. If he is eminent in any of the qualities which conduce to his own good, he is, so far, a proper object of admiration. He is so much the nearer to the ideal perfection of human nature. If he is grossly deficient in those qualities, a sentiment the opposite of admiration will follow. There is a degree of folly, and a degree of what may be called (though the phrase is not unobjectionable) lowness or depravation of taste, which, though it cannot justify doing harm to the person who manifests it, renders him necessarily and properly a subject of distaste, or, in extreme cases, even of contempt: a person could not have the opposite qualities in due strength without entertaining these feelings. Though doing no wrong to any one, a person may so act as to compel us to judge him, and feel to him, as a fool, or as a being of an inferior order: and since this judgment and feeling are a fact which he would prefer to avoid, it is doing him a service to warn him of it beforehand, as of any other disagreeable consequence to which he exposes himself. It would be well, indeed, if this good office were much more freely rendered than the common notions of politeness at present permit, and if one person could honestly point out to another that he thinks him in fault, without being considered unmannerly or presuming. We have a right, also, in various ways, to act upon our unfavourable opinion of any one, not to the oppression of his individuality, but in the exercise of ours. We are not bound, for example, to seek his society; we have a right to avoid it (though not to parade the avoidance), for we have a right to choose the society most acceptable to us. We have a right, and it may be our duty, to caution others against him, if we think his example or conversation likely to have a pernicious effect on those with whom he associates. We may give others a preference over him in optional good offices, except those which tend to his improvement. In these various modes a person may suffer very severe penalties at the hands of others for faults which directly concern only himself; but he suffers these penalties only in so far as they are the natural and, as it were, the spontaneous consequences of the faults themselves, not because they are purposely inflicted on him for the sake of punishment. A person who shows rashness, obstinacy, self-conceit—who cannot live within moderate means—who cannot restrain himself from hurtful indulgences—who pursues animal pleasures at the expense of those of feeling and intellect —must expect to be lowered in the opinion of others, and to have a less share of their favourable sentiments; but of this he has no right to complain, unless he has merited their favour by special excellence in his social relations, and has thus established a title to their good offices, which is not affected by his demerits towards himself.

What I contend for is, that the inconveniences which are strictly inseparable from the unfavourable judgment of others, are the only ones to which a person should ever be subjected for that portion of his conduct and character which concerns his own good, but which does not affect the interest of others in their relations with him. Acts injurious to others require a totally different treatment. Encroachment on their rights; infliction on them of any loss or damage not justified by his own rights; falsehood or duplicity in dealing with them; unfair or ungenerous use of advantages over them; even selfish abstinence from defending them against injury—these are fit objects of moral reprobation, and, in grave cases, of moral retribution and punishment. And not only these acts, but the dispositions which lead to them, are properly immoral, and fit subjects of disapprobation which may rise to abhorrence. Cruelty of disposition; malice and ill-nature; that most anti-social and odious of all passions, envy; dissimulation and insincerity, irascibility on insufficient cause, and resentment disproportioned to the provocation; the love of domineering over others; the desire to engross more than one's share of advantages (the πλεονεξία of the Greeks); the pride which derives gratification from the abasement of others; the egotism which thinks self and its concerns more important than everything else, and decides all doubtful questions in its own favour;—these are moral vices, and constitute a bad and odious moral character: unlike the self-regarding faults previously mentioned, which are not properly immoralities, and to whatever pitch they may be carried, do not constitute wickedness. They may be proofs of any amount of folly, or want of personal dignity and self-respect; but they are only a subject of moral reprobation when they involve a breach of duty to others, for whose sake the individual is bound to have care for himself. What are called duties to ourselves are not socially obligatory, unless circumstances render them at the same time duties to others. The term duty to oneself, when it means anything more than prudence, means self-respect or self-development, and for none of these is any one accountable to his fellow creatures, because for none of them is it for the good of mankind that he be held accountable to them.

The distinction between the loss of consideration which a person may rightly incur by defect of prudence or of personal dignity, and the reprobation which is due to him for an offence against the rights of others, is not a merely nominal distinction. It makes a vast difference both in our feelings and in our conduct towards him whether he displeases us in things in which we think we have a right to control him, or in things in which we know that we have not. If he displeases us, we may express our distaste, and we may stand aloof from a person as well as from a thing that displeases us; but we shall not therefore feel called on to make his life uncomfortable. We shall reflect that he already bears, or will bear, the whole penalty of his error; if he spoils his life by mismanagement, we shall not, for that reason, desire to spoil it still further: instead of wishing to punish him, we shall rather endeavour to alleviate his punishment, by showing him how he may avoid or cure the evils his conduct tends to bring upon him. He may be to us an object of pity, perhaps of dislike, but not of anger or resentment; we shall not treat him like an enemy of society: the worst we shall think ourselves justified in doing is leaving him to himself, if we do not interfere benevolently by showing interest or concern for him. It is far otherwise if he has infringed the rules necessary for the protection of his fellow creatures, individually or collectively. The evil consequences of his acts do not then fall on himself, but on others; and society, as the protector of all its members, must retaliate on him; must inflict pain on him for the express purpose of punishment, and must take care that it be sufficiently severe. In the one case, he is an offender at our bar, and we are called on not only to sit in judgment on him, but, in one shape or another, to execute our own sentence: in the other case, it is not our part to inflict any suffering on him, except what may incidentally follow from our using the same liberty in the regulation of our own affairs, which we allow to him in his.

The distinction here pointed out between the part of a person's life which concerns only himself, and that which concerns others, many persons will refuse to admit. How (it may be asked) can any part of the conduct of a member of society be a matter of indifference to the other members? No person is an entirely isolated being; it is impossible for a person to do anything seriously or permanently hurtful to himself, without mischief reaching at least to his near connections, and often far beyond them. If he injures his property, he does harm to those who directly or indirectly derived support from it, and usually diminishes, by a greater or less amount, the general resources of the community. If he deteriorates his bodily or mental faculties, he not only brings evil upon all who depended on him for any portion of their happiness, but disqualifies himself for rendering the services which he owes to his fellow creatures generally; perhaps becomes a burthen on their affection or benevolence; and if such conduct were very frequent, hardly any offence that is committed would detract more from the general sum of good. Finally, if by his vices or follies a person does no direct harm to others, he is nevertheless (it may be said) injurious by his example; and ought to be compelled to control himself, for the sake of those whom the sight or knowledge of his conduct might corrupt or mislead.

And even (it will be added) if the consequences of misconduct could be confined to the vicious or thoughtless individual, ought society to abandon to their own guidance those who are manifestly unfit for it? If protection against themselves is confessedly due to children and persons under age, is not society equally bound to afford it to persons of mature years who are equally incapable of self-government? If gambling, or drunkenness, or incontinence, or idleness, or uncleanliness, are as injurious to happiness, and as great a hindrance to improvement, as many or most of the acts prohibited by law, why (it may be asked) should not law, so far as is consistent with practicability and social convenience, endeavour to repress these also? And as a supplement to the unavoidable imperfections of law, ought not opinion at least to organise a powerful police against these vices, and visit rigidly with social penalties those who are known to practise them? There is no question here (it may be said) about restricting individuality, or impeding the trial of new and original experiments in living. The only things it is sought to prevent are things which have been tried and condemned from the beginning of the world until now; things which experience has shown not to be useful or suitable to any person's individuality. There must be some length of time and amount of experience after which a moral or prudential truth may be regarded as established: and it is merely desired to prevent generation after generation from falling over the same precipice which has been fatal to their predecessors.

I fully admit that the mischief which a person does to himself may seriously affect, both through their sympathies and their interests, those nearly connected with him and, in a minor degree, society at large. When, by conduct of this sort, a person is led to violate a distinct and assignable obligation to any other person or persons, the case is taken out of the self-regarding class, and becomes amenable to moral disapprobation in the proper sense of the term. If, for example, a man, through intemperance or extravagance, becomes unable to pay his debts, or, having undertaken the moral responsibility of a family, becomes from the same cause incapable of supporting or educating them, he is deservedly reprobated, and might be justly punished; but it is for the breach of duty to his family or creditors, not for the extravagance. If the resources which ought to have been devoted to them, had been diverted from them for the most prudent investment, the moral culpability would have been the same. George Barnwell murdered his uncle to get money for his mistress, but if he had done it to set himself up in business, he would equally have been hanged. Again, in the frequent case of a man who causes grief to his family by addiction to bad habits, he deserves reproach for his unkindness or ingratitude; but so he may for cultivating habits not in themselves vicious, if they are painful to those with whom he passes his life, or who from personal ties are dependent on him for their comfort. Whoever fails in the consideration generally due to the interests and feelings of others, not being compelled by some more imperative duty, or justified by allowable self-preference, is a subject of moral disapprobation for that failure, but not for the cause of it, nor for the errors, merely personal to himself, which may have remotely led to it. In like manner, when a person disables himself, by conduct purely self-regarding, from the performance of some definite duty incumbent on him to the public, he is guilty of a social offence. No person ought to be punished simply for being drunk; but a soldier or a policeman should be punished for being drunk on duty. Whenever, in short, there is a definite damage, or a definite risk of damage, either to an individual or to the public, the case is taken out of the province of liberty, and placed in that of morality or law.

But with regard to the merely contingent, or, as it may be called, constructive injury which a person causes to society, by conduct which neither violates any specific duty to the public, nor occasions perceptible hurt to any assignable individual except himself; the inconvenience is one which society can afford to bear, for the sake of the greater good of human freedom. If grown persons are to be punished for not taking proper care of themselves, I would rather it were for their own sake, than under pretence of preventing them from impairing their capacity or rendering to society benefits which society does not pretend it has a right to exact. But I cannot consent to argue the point as if society had no means of bringing its weaker members up to its ordinary standard of rational conduct, except waiting till they do something irrational, and then punishing them, legally or morally, for it. Society has had absolute power over them during all the early portion of their existence: it has had the whole period of childhood and nonage in which to try whether it could make them capable of rational conduct in life. The existing generation is master both of the training and the entire circumstances of the generation to come; it cannot indeed make them perfectly wise and good, because it is itself so lamentably deficient in goodness and wisdom; and its best efforts are not always, in individual cases, its most successful ones; but it is perfectly well able to make the rising generation, as a whole, as good as, and a little better than, itself. If society lets any considerable number of its members grow up mere children, incapable of being acted on by rational consideration of distant motives, society has itself to blame for the consequences. Armed not only with all the powers of education, but with the ascendency which the authority of a received opinion always exercises over the minds who are least fitted to judge for themselves; and aided by the *natural* penalties which cannot be prevented from falling on those who incur the distaste or the contempt of those who know them; let not society pretend that it needs, besides all this, the power to issue commands and enforce obedience in the personal concerns of individuals, in which, on all principles of justice and policy, the decision ought to rest with those who are to abide the consequences.

Nor is there anything which tends more to discredit and frustrate the better means of influencing conduct than a resort to the worse. If there be among those whom it is attempted to coerce into prudence or temperance any of the material of which vigorous and independent characters are made, they will infallibly rebel against the yoke. No such person will ever feel that others have a right to control him in his concerns, such as they have to prevent him from injuring them in theirs; and it easily comes to be considered a mark of spirit and courage to fly in the face of such usurped authority, and do with ostentation the exact opposite of what it enjoins; as in the fashion of grossness which succeeded, in the time of Charles II., to the fanatical moral intolerance of the Puritans. With respect to what is said of the necessity of protecting society from the bad example set to others by the vicious or the self-indulgent; it is true that bad example may have a pernicious effect, especially the example of doing wrong to others with impunity to the wrong-doer. But we are now speaking of conduct which, while it does no wrong to others, is supposed to do great harm to the agent himself: and I do not see how those who believe this can think otherwise than that the example, on the whole, must be more salutary than hurtful, since, if it displays the misconduct, it displays also the painful or degrading consequences which, if the conduct is justly censured, must be supposed to be in all or most cases attendant on it.

But the strongest of all the arguments against the interference of the public with purely personal conduct is that, when it does interfere, the odds are that it interferes wrongly, and in the wrong place. On questions of social morality, of duty to others, the opinion of the public, that is, of an overruling majority, though often wrong, is likely to be still oftener right; because on such questions they are only required to judge of their own interests; of the manner in which some mode of conduct, if allowed to be practised, would effect themselves. But the opinion of a similar majority, imposed as a law on the minority, on questions of self-regarding conduct, is quite as likely to be wrong as right; for in these cases public opinion means, at the best, some people's opinion of what is good or bad for other people; while very often it does not even mean that; the public, with the most perfect indifference, passing over the pleasure or convenience of those whose conduct they censure, and considering only their own preference. There are many who consider as an injury to themselves any conduct which they have a distaste for, and resent it as an outrage to their feelings; as a religious bigot, when charged with disregarding the religious feelings of others, has been known to retort that they disregard his feelings, by persisting in their abominable worship or creed. But there is no parity between the feeling of a person for his own opinion, and the feeling of another who is offended at his holding it; no more than between the desire of a thief to take a purse, and the desire of the right owner to keep it. And a person's taste is as much his own peculiar concern as his opinion or his purse. It is easy for any one to imagine an ideal public which leaves the freedom and choice of individuals in all uncertain matters undisturbed, and only requires them to abstain from modes of conduct which universal experience has condemned. But where has there been seen a public which set any such limit to its censorship? or when does the public trouble itself about universal experience? In its interferences with personal conduct it is seldom thinking of anything but the enormity of acting or feeling differently from itself; and this standard of judgment, thinly disguised, is held up to mankind as the dictate of religion and philosophy, by nine-tenths of all moralists and speculative writers. These teach that things are right because they are right; because we feel them to be so. They tell us to search in our own minds and hearts for laws of conduct binding on ourselves and on all others. What can the poor public do but apply these instructions, and make their own personal feelings of good and evil, if they are tolerably unanimous in them, obligatory on all the world?

The evil here pointed out is not one which exists only in theory; and it may perhaps be expected that I should specify the instances in which the public of this age and country improperly invests its own preferences with the character of moral laws. I am not writing an essay on the aberrations of existing moral feeling. That is too weighty a subject to be discussed parenthetically, and by way of illustration. Yet examples are necessary to show that the principle I maintain is of serious and practical moment, and that I am not endeavouring to erect a barrier against imaginary evils. And it is not difficult to show, by abundant instances, that to extend the bounds of what may be called moral police, until it encroaches on the most unquestionably legitimate liberty of the individual, is one of the most universal of all human propensities.

As a first instance, consider the antipathies which men cherish on no better grounds than that persons whose religious opinions are different from theirs do not practise their religious observances, especially their religious abstinences. To cite a rather trivial example, nothing in the creed or practice of Christians does more to envenom the hatred of Mahomedans against them than the fact of their eating pork. There are few acts which Christians and Europeans regard with more unaffected disgust than Mussulmans regard this particular mode of satisfying hunger. It is, in the first place, an offence against their religion; but this circumstance by no means explains either the degree or the kind of their repugnance; for wine also is forbidden by their religion, and to partake of it is by all Mussulmans accounted wrong, but not disgusting. Their aversion to the flesh of the "unclean beast" is, on the contrary, of that peculiar character, resembling an instinctive antipathy, which the idea of uncleanness, when once it thoroughly sinks into the feelings, seems always to excite even in those whose personal habits are anything but scrupulously cleanly, and of which the sentiment of religious impurity, so intense in the Hindoos, is a remarkable example. Suppose now that in a people, of whom the majority were Mussulmans, that majority should insist upon not permitting pork to be eaten within the limits of the country. This would be nothing new in Mahomedan countries.[1] Would it be a legitimate exercise of the moral authority of public opinion? and if not, why not? The practice is really revolting to such a public. They also sincerely think that it is forbidden and abhorred by the Deity. Neither could the prohibition be censured as religious persecution. It might be religious in its origin, but it would not be persecution for religion, since nobody's religion makes it a duty to eat pork. The only tenable ground of condemnation would be that with the personal tastes and self-regarding concerns of individuals the public has no business to interfere.

To come somewhat nearer home: the major-

ity of Spaniards consider it a gross impiety, offensive in the highest degree to the Supreme Being, to worship him in any other manner than the Roman Catholic; and no other public worship is lawful on Spanish soil. The people of all Southern Europe look upon a married clergy as not only irreligious, but unchaste, indecent, gross, disgusting. What do Protestants think of these perfectly sincere feelings, and of the attempt to enforce them against non-Catholics? Yet, if mankind are justified in interfering with each other's liberty in things which do not concern the interests of others, on what principle is it possible consistently to exclude these cases? or who can blame people for desiring to suppress what they regard as a scandal in the sight of God and man? No stronger case can be shown for prohibiting anything which is regarded as a personal immorality, than is made out for suppressing these practices in the eyes of those who regard them as impieties; and unless we are willing to adopt the logic of persecutors, and to say that we may persecute others because we are right, and that they must not persecute us because they are wrong, we must beware of admitting a principle of which we should resent as a gross injustice the application to ourselves.

The preceding instances may be objected to, although unreasonably, as drawn from contingencies impossible among us: opinion, in this country, not being likely to enforce abstinence from meats, or to interfere with people for worshipping, and for either marrying or not marrying, according to their creed or inclination. The next example, however, shall be taken from an interference with liberty which we have by no means passed all danger of. Wherever the Puritans have been sufficiently powerful, as in New England, and in Great Britain at the time of the Commonwealth, they have endeavoured, with considerable success, to put down all public, and nearly all private, amusements: especially music, dancing, public games, or other assemblages for purposes of diversion, and the theatre. There are still in this country large bodies of persons by whose notions of morality and religion these recreations are condemned; and those persons belonging chiefly to the middle class, who are the ascendant power in the present social and political condition of the kingdom, it is by no means impossible that persons of these sentiments may at some time or other command a majority in Parliament. How will the remaining portion of the community like

[1] The case of the Bombay Parsees is a curious instance in point. When this industrious and enterprising tribe, the descendants of the Persian fire-worshippers, flying from their native country before the Caliphs, arrived in Western India, they were admitted to toleration by the Hindoo sovereigns, on condition of not eating beef. When those regions afterwards fell under the dominion of Mahomedan conquerors, the Parsees obtained from them a continuance of indulgence, on condition of refraining from pork. What was at first obedience to authority became a second nature, and the Parsees to this day abstain both from beef and pork. Though not required by their religion, the double abstinence has had time to grow into a custom of their tribe; and custom, in the East, is a religion.

to have the amusements that shall be permitted to them regulated by the religious and moral sentiments of the stricter Calvinists and Methodists? Would they not, with considerable peremptoriness, desire these intrusively pious members of society to mind their own business? This is precisely what should be said to every government and every public, who have the pretension that no person shall enjoy any pleasure which they think wrong. But if the principle of the pretension be admitted, no one can reasonably object to its being acted on in the sense of the majority, or other preponderating power in the country; and all persons must be ready to conform to the idea of a Christian commonwealth, as understood by the early settlers in New England, if a religious profession similar to theirs should ever succeed in regaining its lost ground, as religions supposed to be declining have so often been known to do.

To imagine another contingency, perhaps more likely to be realised than the one last mentioned. There is confessedly a strong tendency in the modern world towards a democratic constitution of society, accompanied or not by popular political institutions. It is affirmed that in the country where this tendency is most completely realised—where both society and the government are most democratic —the United States—the feeling of the majority, to whom any appearance of a more showy or costly style of living than they can hope to rival is disagreeable, operates as a tolerably effectual sumptuary law, and that in many parts of the Union it is really difficult for a person possessing a very large income to find any mode of spending it which will not incur popular disapprobation. Though such statements as these are doubtless much exaggerated as a representation of existing facts, the state of things they describe is not only a conceivable and possible, but a probable result of democratic feeling, combined with the notion that the public has a right to a veto on the manner in which individuals shall spend their incomes. We have only further to suppose a considerable diffusion of Socialist opinions, and it may become infamous in the eyes of the majority to possess more property than some very small amount, or any income not earned by manual labour. Opinions similar in principle to these already prevail widely among the artisan class, and weigh oppressively on those who are amenable to the opinion chiefly of that class, namely, its own members. It is

known that the bad workmen who form the majority of the operatives in many branches of industry, are decidedly of opinion that bad workmen ought to receive the same wages as good, and that no one ought to be allowed, through piecework or otherwise, to earn by superior skill or industry more than others can without it. And they employ a moral police, which occasionally becomes a physical one, to deter skilful workmen from receiving, and employers from giving, a larger remuneration for a more useful service. If the public have any jurisdiction over private concerns, I cannot see that these people are in fault, or that any individual's particular public can be blamed for asserting the same authority over his individual conduct which the general public asserts over people in general.

But, without dwelling upon supposititious cases, there are, in our own day, gross usurpations upon the liberty of private life actually practised, and still greater ones threatened with some expectation of success, and opinions propounded which assert an unlimited right in the public not only to prohibit by law everything which it thinks wrong, but, in order to get at what it thinks wrong, to prohibit a number of things which it admits to be innocent.

Under the name of preventing intemperance, the people of one English colony, and of nearly half the United States, have been interdicted by law from making any use whatever of fermented drinks, except for medical purposes: for prohibition of their sale is in fact, as it is intended to be, prohibition of their use. And though the impracticability of executing the law has caused its repeal in several of the States which had adopted it, including the one from which it derives its name, an attempt has notwithstanding been commenced, and is prosecuted with considerable zeal by many of the professed philanthropists, to agitate for a similar law in this country. The association, or "Alliance" as it terms itself, which has been formed for this purpose, has acquired some notoriety through the publicity given to a correspondence between its secretary and one of the very few English public men who hold that a politician's opinions ought to be founded on principles. Lord Stanley's share in this correspondence is calculated to strengthen the hopes already built on him, by those who know how rare such qualities as are manifested in some of his public appearances unhappily are among those who figure in political life. The organ of the Alliance, who would "deeply deplore the recognition of any principle which could be wrested to justify bigotry and persecution," undertakes to point out the "broad and impassable barrier" which divides such principles from those of the association. "All matters relating to thought, opinion, conscience, appear to me," he says, "to be without the sphere of legislation; all pertaining to social act, habit, relation, subject only to a discretionary power vested in the State itself, and not in the individual, to be within it."

No mention is made of a third class, different from either of these, viz., acts and habits which are not social, but individual; although it is to this class, surely, that the act of drinking fermented liquors belongs. Selling fermented liquors, however, is trading, and trading is a social act. But the infringement complained of is not on the liberty of the seller, but on that of the buyer and consumer; since the State might just as well forbid him to drink wine as purposely make it impossible for him to obtain it. The secretary, however, says, "I claim, as a citizen, a right to legislate whenever my social rights are invaded by the social act of another." And now for the definition of these "social rights." "If anything invades my social rights, certainly the traffic in strong drink does. It destroys my primary right of security, by constantly creating and stimulating social disorder. It invades my right of equality, by deriving a profit from the creation of a misery I am taxed to support. It impedes my right to free moral and intellectual development, by surrounding my path with dangers, and by weakening and demoralising society, from which I have a right to claim mutual aid and intercourse." A theory of "social rights" the like of which probably never before found its way into distinct language: being nothing short of this—that it is the absolute social right of every individual, that every other individual shall act in every respect exactly as he ought; that whosoever fails thereof in the smallest particular violates my social right, and entitles me to demand from the legislature the removal of the grievance. So monstrous a principle is far more dangerous than any single interference with liberty; there is no violation of liberty which it would not justify; it acknowledges no right to any freedom whatever, except perhaps to that of holding opinions in secret, without ever disclosing them: for, the moment an opinion which I consider noxious passes any one's lips, it invades all the "social rights" attributed to me by the Alliance. The doctrine ascribes to all mankind a vested interest in each other's moral, intellectual, and even physical perfection, to be defined by each claimant according to his own standard.

Another important example of illegitimate interference with the rightful liberty of the individual, not simply threatened, but long since carried into triumphant effect, is Sabbatarian legislation. Without doubt, abstinence on one day in the week, so far as the exigencies of life permit, from the usual daily occupation, though in no respect religiously binding on any except Jews, is a highly beneficial custom. And inasmuch as this custom cannot be observed without a general consent to that effect among the industrious classes, therefore, in so far as some persons by working may impose the same necessity on others, it may be allowable and right that the law should guarantee to each the observance by others of the custom, by suspending the greater operations of industry on a particular day. But this justification, grounded on the direct interest which others have in each individual's observance of the practice, does not apply to the self-chosen occupations in which a person may think fit to employ his leisure; nor does it hold good, in the smallest degree, for legal restrictions on amusements. It is true that the amusement of some is the day's work of others; but the pleasure, not to say the useful recreation, of many, is worth the labour of a few, provided the occupation is freely chosen, and can be freely resigned. The operatives are perfectly right in thinking that if all worked on Sunday, seven days' work would have to be given for six days' wages; but so long as the great mass of employments are suspended, the small number who for the enjoyment of others must still work, obtain a proportional increase of earnings; and they are not obliged to follow those occupations if they prefer leisure to emolument. If a further remedy is sought, it might be found in the establishment by custom of a holiday on some other day of the week for those particular classes of persons. The only ground, therefore, on which restrictions on Sunday amusements can be defended, must be that they are religiously wrong; a motive of legislation which can never be too earnestly protested against. *Deorum injuriæ Diis curæ.* It remains to be proved that society or any of its officers holds a commission from on high to avenge any supposed offence to Omnipotence, which is not also a wrong to our fellow creatures. The notion that it is one man's duty that another should be religious, was the foundation of all the religious persecutions ever perpetrated, and, if admitted, would fully justify them. Though the feeling which breaks out in the repeated attempts to stop railway travelling on Sunday, in the resistance to the opening of Museums, and the like, has not the cruelty of the old persecutors, the state of mind indicated by it is fundamentally the same. It is a determination not to tolerate others in doing what is permitted by their religion, because it is not permitted by the persecutor's religion. It is a belief that God not only abominates the act of the misbeliever, but will not hold us guiltless if we leave him unmolested.

I cannot refrain from adding to these examples of the little account commonly made of human liberty, the language of downright persecution which breaks out from the press of this country whenever it feels called on to notice the remarkable phenomenon of Mormonism. Much might be said on the unexpected and instructive fact that an alleged new revelation, and a religion founded on it, the product of palpable imposture, not even supported by the *prestige* of extraordinary qualities in its founder, is believed by hundreds of thousands, and has been made the foundation of a society, in the age of newspapers, railways, and the electric telegraph. What here concerns us is, that this religion, like other and better religions, has its martyrs: that its prophet and founder was, for his teaching, put to death by a mob; that others of its adherents lost their lives by the same lawless violence; that they were forcibly expelled, in a body, from the country in which they first grew up; while, now that they have been chased into a solitary recess in the midst of a desert, many in this country openly declare that it would be right (only that it is not convenient) to send an expedition against them, and compel them by force to conform to the opinions of other people. The article of the Mormonite doctrine which is the chief provocative to the antipathy which thus breaks through the ordinary restraints of religious tolerance, is its sanction of polygamy; which, though permitted to Mahomedans, and Hindoos, and Chinese, seems to excite unquenchable animosity when practised by persons who speak English and profess to be a kind of Christians. No one has a deeper disapprobation than I have of this Mormon institution; both for other reasons, and because, far from being in any way countenanced by the principle of liberty, it is a direct infraction of that principle, being a mere riveting of the chains of one half of the community, and an emancipation of the other from reciprocity of obligation towards them. Still, it must be remembered that this relation is as much voluntary on the part of the women concerned in it, and who may be deemed the sufferers by it, as is the case with any other form of the marriage institution; and however surprising this fact may appear, it has its explanation in the common ideas and customs of the world, which teaching women to think marriage the one thing needful, make it intelligible that many a woman should prefer being one of several wives, to not being a wife at all. Other countries are not asked to recognise such unions, or release any portion of their inhabitants from their own laws on the score of Mormonite opinions. But when the dissentients have conceded to the hostile sentiments of others far more than could justly be demanded; when they have left the countries to which their doctrines were unacceptable, and established themselves in a remote corner of the earth, which they have been the first to render habitable to human beings; it is difficult to see on what principles but those of tyranny they can be prevented from living there under what laws they please, provided they commit no aggression on other nations, and allow perfect freedom of departure to those who are dissatisfied with their ways.

A recent writer, in some respects of considerable merit, proposes (to use his own words) not a crusade, but a *civilisade,* against this polygamous community, to put an end to what seems to him a retrograde step in civilisation. It also appears so to me, but I am not aware that any community has a right to force another to be civilised. So long as the sufferers by the bad law do not invoke assistance from other communities, I cannot admit that persons entirely unconnected with them ought to step in and require that a condition of things with which all who are directly interested appear to be satisfied, should be put an end to because it is a scandal to persons some thousands of miles distant, who have no part or concern in it. Let them send missionaries, if they please, to preach against it; and let them, by any fair means (of which silencing the teachers is not one), oppose the progress of similar doctrines among their own people. If civilisation has got the better of barbarism when barbarism had the world to itself, it is too much to profess to be afraid lest barbarism, after having been fairly got under, should revive and conquer civilisation. A civilisation that can thus succumb to its vanquished enemy, must first have become so degenerate, that neither its appointed priests and teachers, nor anybody else, has the capacity, or will take the trouble, to stand up for it. If this be so, the sooner such a civilisation receives notice to quit the better. It can only go on from bad to worse, until destroyed and regenerated (like the Western Empire) by energetic barbarians.

Chapter 5
Applications

THE PRINCIPLES asserted in these pages must be more generally admitted as the basis for discussion of details, before a consistent application of them to all the various departments of government and morals can be attempted with any prospect of advantage. The few observations I propose to make on questions of detail are designed to illustrate the principles, rather than to follow them out to their consequences. I offer, not so much applications, as specimens of application; which may serve to bring into greater clearness the meaning and limits of the two maxims which together form the entire doctrine of this Essay, and to assist the judgment in holding the balance between them, in the cases where it appears doubtful which of them is applicable to the case.

The maxims are, first, that the individual is not accountable to society for his actions, in so far as these concern the interests of no person but himself. Advice, instruction, persuasion, and avoidance by other people if thought necessary by them for their own good, are the only measures by which society can justifiably express its dislike or disapprobation of his conduct. Secondly, that for such actions as are prejudicial to the interests of others, the individual is accountable, and may be subjected either to social or to legal punishment, if society is of opinion that the one or the other is requisite for its protection.

In the first place, it must by no means be supposed, because damage, or probability of damage, to the interests of others, can alone justify the interference of society, that therefore it always does justify such interference. In many cases, an individual, in pursuing a legitimate object, necessarily and therefore legitimately causes pain or loss to others, or intercepts a good which they had a reasonable hope

of obtaining. Such oppositions of interest between individuals often arise from bad social institutions, but are unavoidable while those institutions last; and some would be unavoidable under any institutions. Whoever succeeds in an overcrowded profession, or in a competitive examination; whoever is preferred to another in any contest for an object which both desire, reaps benefit from the loss of others, from their wasted exertion and their disappointment. But it is, by common admission, better for the general interest of mankind, that persons should pursue their objects undeterred by this sort of consequences. In other words, society admits no right, either legal or moral, in the disappointed competitors to immunity from this kind of suffering; and feels called on to interfere, only when means of success have been employed which it is contrary to the general interest to permit—namely, fraud or treachery, and force.

Again, trade is a social act. Whoever undertakes to sell any description of goods to the public, does what affects the interest of other persons, and of society in general; and thus his conduct, in principle, comes within the jurisdiction of society: accordingly, it was once held to be the duty of governments, in all cases which were considered of importance, to fix prices, and regulate the processes of manufacture. But it is now recognised, though not till after a long struggle, that both the cheapness and the good quality of commodities are most effectually provided for by leaving the producers and sellers perfectly free, under the sole check of equal freedom to the buyers for supplying themselves elsewhere. This is the so-called doctrine of Free Trade, which rests on grounds different from, though equally solid with, the principle of individual liberty asserted in this Essay. Restrictions on trade, or on production for purposes of trade, are indeed restraints; and all restraint, *quâ* restraint, is an evil: but the restraints in question affect only that part of conduct which society is competent to restrain, and are wrong solely because they do not really produce the results which it is desired to produce by them. As the principle of individual liberty is not involved in the doctrine of Free Trade, so neither is it in most of the questions which arise respecting the limits of that doctrine; as, for example, what amount of public control is admissible for the prevention of fraud by adulteration; how far sanitary precautions, or arrangements to protect workpeople employed in dangerous occupations, should be enforced on employers. Such questions involve considerations of liberty, only in so far as leaving people to themselves is always better, *cæteris paribus,* than controlling them: but that they may be legitimately controlled for these ends is in principle undeniable. On the other hand, there are questions relating to interference with trade which are essentially questions of liberty; such as the Maine Law, already touched upon; the prohibition of the importation of opium into China; the restriction of the sale of poisons; all cases, in short, where the object of the interference is to make it impossible or difficult to obtain a particular commodity. These interferences are objectionable, not as infringements on the liberty of the producer or seller, but on that of the buyer.

One of these examples, that of the sale of poisons, opens a new question; the proper limits of what may be called the functions of police; how far liberty may legitimately be invaded for the prevention of crime, or of accident. It is one of the undisputed functions of government to take precautions against crime before it has been committed, as well as to detect and punish it afterwards. The preventive function of government, however, is far more liable to be abused, to the prejudice of liberty, than the punitory function; for there is hardly any part of the legitimate freedom of action of a human being which would not admit of being represented, and fairly too, as increasing the facilities for some form or other of delinquency. Nevertheless, if a public authority, or even a private person, sees any one evidently preparing to commit a crime, they are not bound to look on inactive until the crime is committed, but may interfere to prevent it. If poisons were never bought or used for any purpose except the commission of murder it would be right to prohibit their manufacture and sale. They may, however, be wanted not only for innocent but for useful purposes, and restrictions cannot be imposed in the one case without operating in the other. Again, it is a proper office of public authority to guard against accidents. If either a public officer or any one else saw a person attempting to cross a bridge which had been ascertained to be unsafe, and there were no time to warn him of his danger, they might seize him and turn him back, without any real infringement of his liberty; for liberty consists in doing what one desires, and he does not desire to fall into the river. Nevertheless, when there is not a

certainty, but only a danger of mischief, no one but the person himself can judge of the sufficiency of the motive which may prompt him to incur the risk: in this case, therefore (unless he is a child, or delirious, or in some state of excitement or absorption incompatible with the full use of the reflecting faculty), he ought, I conceive, to be only warned of the danger; not forcibly prevented from exposing himself to it. Similar considerations, applied to such a question as the sale of poisons, may enable us to decide which among the possible modes of regulation are or are not contrary to principle. Such a precaution, for example, as that of labelling the drug with some word expressive of its dangerous character, may be enforced without violation of liberty: the buyer cannot wish not to know that the thing he possesses has poisonous qualities. But to require in all cases the certificate of a medical practitioner would make it sometimes impossible, always expensive, to obtain the article for legitimate uses.

The only mode apparent to me, in which difficulties may be thrown in the way of crime committed through this means, without any infringement worth taking into account upon the liberty of those who desire the poisonous substance for other purposes, consists in providing what, in the apt language of Bentham, is called "preappointed evidence." This provision is familiar to every one in the case of contracts. It is usual and right that the law, when a contract is entered into, should require as the condition of its enforcing performance, that certain formalities should be observed, such as signatures, attestation of witnesses, and the like, in order that in case of subsequent dispute there may be evidence to prove that the contract was really entered into, and that there was nothing in the circumstances to render it legally invalid: the effect being to throw great obstacles in the way of fictitious contracts, or contracts made in circumstances which, if known, would destroy their validity. Precautions of a similar nature might be enforced in the sale of articles adapted to be instruments of crime. The seller, for example, might be required to enter in a register the exact time of the transaction, the name and address of the buyer, the precise quality and quantity sold; to ask the purpose for which it was wanted, and record the answer he received. When there was no medical prescription, the presence of some third person might be required, to bring home the fact to the purchaser, in case there should afterwards be reason to believe that the article had been applied to criminal purposes. Such regulations would in general be no material impediment to obtaining the article, but a very considerable one to making an improper use of it without detection.

The right inherent in society, to ward off crimes against itself by antecedent precautions, suggests the obvious limitations to the maxim, that purely self-regarding misconduct cannot properly be meddled with in the way of prevention or punishment. Drunkenness, for example, in ordinary cases, is not a fit subject for legislative interference; but I should deem it perfectly legitimate that a person, who had once been convicted of any act of violence to others under the influence of drink, should be placed under a special legal restriction, personal to himself; that if he were afterwards found drunk, he should be liable to a penalty, and that if when in that state he committed another offence, the punishment to which he would be liable for that other offence should be increased in severity. The making himself drunk, in a person whom drunkenness excites to do harm to others, is a crime against others. So, again, idleness, except in a person receiving support from the public, or except when it constitutes a breach of contract, cannot without tyranny be made a subject of legal punishment; but if, either from idleness or from any other avoidable cause, a man fails to perform his legal duties to others, as for instance to support his children, it is no tyranny to force him to fulfil that obligation, by compulsory labour, if no other means are available.

Again, there are many acts which, being directly injurious only to the agents themselves, ought not to be legally interdicted, but which, if done publicly, are a violation of good manners, and coming thus within the category of offences against others, may rightly be prohibited. Of this kind are offences against decency; on which it is unnecessary to dwell, the rather as they are only connected indirectly with our subject, the objection to publicity being equally strong in the case of many actions not in themselves condemnable, nor supposed to be so.

There is another question to which an answer must be found, consistent with the principles which have been laid down. In cases of personal conduct supposed to be blamable, but which respect for liberty precludes society from preventing or punishing, because the evil directly resulting falls wholly on the agent; what the agent is free to do, ought other persons to be equally free to counsel or instigate? This question is not free from difficulty. The case of a person who solicits another to do an act is not strictly a case of self-regarding conduct. To give advice or offer inducements to any one is a social act, and may, therefore, like actions in general which affect others, be supposed amenable to social control. But a little reflection corrects the first impression, by showing that if the case is not strictly within the definition of individual liberty, yet the reasons on which the principle of individual liberty is grounded are applicable to it. If people must be allowed, in whatever concerns only themselves, to act as seems best to themselves, at their own peril, they must equally be free to consult with one another about what is fit to be so done; to exchange opinions, and give and receive suggestions. Whatever it is permitted to do, it must be permitted to advise to do. The question is doubtful only when the instigator derives a personal benefit from his advice; when he makes it his occupation, for subsistence or pecuniary gain, to promote what society and the State consider to be an evil. Then, indeed, a new element of complication is introduced; namely, the existence of classes of persons with an interest opposed to what is considered as the public weal, and whose mode of living is grounded on the counteraction of it. Ought this to be interfered with, or not? Fornication, for example, must be tolerated, and so must gambling; but should a person be free to be a pimp, or to keep a gambling-house? The case is one of those which lie on the exact boundary line between two principles, and it is not at once apparent to which of the two it properly belongs.

There are arguments on both sides. On the side of toleration it may be said that the fact of following anything as an occupation, and living or profiting by the practice of it, cannot make that criminal which would otherwise be admissible; that the act should either be consistently permitted or consistently prohibited; that if the principles which we have hitherto defended are true, society has no business, *as* society, to decide anything to be wrong which concerns only the individual; that it cannot go beyond dissuasion, and that one person should be as free to persuade as another to dissuade. In opposition to this it may be contended, that although the public, or the State, are not warranted in authoritatively deciding, for purposes of repression or punishment, that such or such conduct affecting only the interests of the individual is good or bad, they are fully justified in assuming, if they regard it as bad, that its being so or not is at least a disputable question: That, this being supposed, they cannot be acting wrongly in endeavouring to exclude the influence of solicitations which are not disinterested, of instigators who cannot possibly be impartial—who have a direct personal interest on one side, and that side the one which the State believes to be wrong, and who confessedly promote it for personal objects only. There can surely, it may be urged, be nothing lost, no sacrifice of good, by so ordering matters that persons shall make their election, either wisely or foolishly, on their own prompting, as free as possible from the arts of persons who stimulate their inclinations for interested purposes of their own. Thus (it may be said) though the statutes respecting unlawful games are utterly indefensible—though all persons should be free to gamble in their own or each other's houses, or in any place of meeting established by their own subscriptions, and open only to the members and their visitors—yet public gambling-houses should not be permitted. It is true that the prohibition is never effectual, and that, whatever amount of tyrannical power may be given to the police, gambling-houses can always be maintained under other pretences; but they may be compelled to conduct their operations with a certain degree of secrecy and mystery, so that nobody knows anything about them but those who seek them; and more than this society ought not to aim at.

There is considerable force in these arguments. I will not venture to decide whether they are sufficient to justify the moral anomaly of punishing the accessary, when the principal is (and must be) allowed to go free; of fining or imprisoning the procurer, but not the fornicator—the gambling-house keeper, but not the gambler. Still less ought the common operations of buying and selling to be interfered with on analogous grounds. Almost every article which is bought and sold may be used in excess, and the sellers have a pecuniary interest in encouraging that excess; but no argument can be founded on this, in favour, for instance, of the Maine Law; because the class of dealers in strong drinks, though interested in their abuse, are indispensably required for the sake of their legitimate use. The interest, however, of these dealers in promoting intemperance is a real evil, and justifies the State in imposing restrictions and requiring guarantees which, but for that justification, would be infringements of legitimate liberty.

A further question is, whether the State, while it permits, should nevertheless indirectly discourage conduct which it deems contrary to the best interests of the agent; whether, for example, it should take measures to render the means of drunkenness more costly, or add to the difficulty of procuring them by limiting the number of the places of sale. On this as on most other practical questions, many distinctions require to be made. To tax stimulants for the sole purpose of making them more difficult to be obtained, is a measure differing only in degree from their entire prohibition; and would be justifiable only if that were justifiable. Every increase of cost is a prohibition, to those whose means do not come up to the augmented price; and to those who do, it is a penalty laid on them for gratifying a particular taste. Their choice of pleasures, and their mode of expending their income, after satisfying their legal and moral obligations to the State and to individuals, are their own concern, and must rest with their own judgment. These considerations may seem at first sight to condemn the selection of stimulants as special subjects of taxation for purposes of revenue. But it must be remembered that taxation for fiscal purposes is absolutely inevitable; that in most countries it is necessary that a considerable part of that taxation should be indirect; that the State, therefore, cannot help imposing penalties, which to some persons may be prohibitory, on the use of some articles of consumption. It is hence the duty of the State to consider, in the imposition of taxes, what commodities the consumers can best spare; and *à fortiori,* to select in preference those of which it deems the use, beyond a very moderate quantity, to be positively injurious. Taxation, therefore, of stimulants, up to the point which produces the largest amount of revenue (supposing that the State needs all the revenue which it yields) is not only admissible, but to be approved of.

The question of making the sale of these commodities a more or less exclusive privilege, must be answered differently, according to the purposes to which the restriction is intended to be subservient. All places of public resort require the restraint of a police, and places of this kind peculiarly, because offences against society are especially apt to originate there. It is, therefore, fit to confine the power of selling these commodities (at least for consumption on the spot) to persons of known or vouched-for respectability of conduct; to make such regulations respecting hours of opening and closing as may be requisite for public surveillance, and to withdraw the licence if breaches of the peace repeatedly take place through the connivance or incapacity of the keeper of the house, or if it becomes a rendezvous for concocting and preparing offences against the law. Any further restriction I do not conceive to be, in principle, justifiable. The limitation in number, for instance, of beer and spirit houses, for the express purpose of rendering them more difficult of access, and dimishing the occasions of temptation, not only exposes all to an inconvenience because there are some by whom the facility would be abused, but is suited only to a state of society in which the labouring classes are avowedly treated as children or savages, and placed under an education of restraint, to fit them for future admission to the privileges of freedom. This is not the principle on which the labouring classes are professedly governed in any free country; and no person who sets due value on freedom will give his adhesion to their being so governed, unless after all efforts have been exhausted to educate them for freedom and govern them as freemen, and it has been definitively proved that they can only be governed as children. The bare statement of the alternative shows the absurdity of supposing that such efforts have been made in any case which needs be considered here. It is only because the institutions of this country are a mass of inconsistencies, that things find admittance into our practice which belong to the system of despotic, or what is called paternal, government, while the general freedom of our institutions precludes the exercise of the amount of control necessary to render the restraint of any real efficacy as a moral education.

It was pointed out in an early part of this Essay, that the liberty of the individual, in things wherein the individual is alone concerned, implies a corresponding liberty in any number of individuals to regulate by mutual agreement such things as regard them jointly, and regard no persons but themselves. This question presents no difficulty, so long as the will of all the persons implicated remains unaltered; but since that will may change, it is often necessary, even in things in which they alone are concerned, that they should enter into engagements with one another; and when

they do, it is fit, as a general rule, that those engagements should be kept. Yet, in the laws, probably, of every country, this general rule has some exceptions. Not only persons are not held to engagements which violate the rights of third parties, but it is sometimes considered a sufficient reason for releasing them from an engagement, that it is injurious to themselves. In this and most other civilised countries, for example, an engagement by which a person should sell himself, or allow himself to be sold, as a slave, would be null and void; neither enforced by law nor by opinion. The ground for thus limiting his power of voluntarily disposing of his own lot in life, is apparent, and is very clearly seen in this extreme case. The reason for not interfering, unless for the sake of others, with a person's voluntary acts, is consideration for his liberty. His voluntary choice is evidence that what he so chooses is desirable, or at least endurable, to him, and his good is on the whole best provided for by allowing him to take his own means of pursuing it. But by selling himself for a slave, be abdicates his liberty; he foregoes any future use of it beyond that single act. He therefore defeats, in his own case, the very purpose which is the justification of allowing him to dispose of himself. He is no longer free; but is thenceforth in a position which has no longer the presumption in its favour, that would be afforded by his voluntarily remaining in it. The principle of freedom cannot require that he should be free not to be free. It is not freedom to be allowed to alienate his freedom. These reasons, the force of which is so conspicuous in this peculiar case, are evidently of far wider application; yet a limit is everywhere set to them by the necessities of life, which continually require, not indeed that we should resign our freedom, but that we should consent to this and the other limitation of it. The principle, however, which demands uncontrolled freedom of action in all that concerns only the agents themselves, requires that those who have become bound to one another, in things which concern no third party, should be able to release one another from the engagement: and even without such voluntary release there are perhaps no contracts or engagements, except those that relate to money or money's worth, of which one can venture to say that there ought to be no liberty whatever of retractation.

Baron Wilhelm von Humboldt, in the excellent essay from which I have already quoted, states it as his conviction, that engagements which involve personal relations or services should never be legally binding beyond a limited duration of time; and that the most important of these engagements, marriage, having the peculiarity that its objects are frustrated unless the feelings of both the parties are in harmony with it, should require nothing more than the declared will of either party to dissolve it. This subject is too important, and too complicated, to be discussed in a parenthesis, and I touch on it only so far as is necessary for purposes of illustration. If the conciseness and generality of Baron Humboldt's dissertation had not obliged him in this instance to content himself with enunciating his conclusion without discussing the premises, he would doubtless have recognised that the question cannot be decided on grounds so simple as those to which he confines himself. When a person, either by express promise or by conduct, has encouraged another to rely upon his continuing to act in a certain way—to build expectations and calculations, and stake any part of his plan of life upon that supposition—a new series of moral obligations arises on his part towards that person, which may possibly be overruled, but cannot be ignored. And again, if the relation between two contracting parties has been followed by consequences to others; if it has placed third parties in any peculiar position, or, as in the case of marriage, has even called third parties into existence, obligations arise on the part of both the contracting parties towards those third persons, the fulfilment of which, or at all events the mode of fulfilment, must be greatly affected by the continuance or disruption of the relation between the original parties to the contract. It does not follow, nor can I admit, that these obligations extend to requiring the fulfilment of the contract at all costs to the happiness of the reluctant party; but they are a necessary element in the question; and even if, as Von Humboldt maintains, they ought to make no difference in the *legal* freedom of the parties to release themselves from the engagement (and I also hold that they ought not to make *much* difference), they necessarily make a great difference in the *moral* freedom. A person is bound to take all these circumstances into account before resolving on a step which may affect such important interests of others; and if he does not allow proper weight to those interests, he is morally responsible for the wrong. I have made these obvious remarks for the better illustration of the general principle of liberty, and not because they are at all needed on the particular question, which, on the contrary, is usually discussed as if the interest of children was everything, and that of grown persons nothing.

I have already observed that, owing to the absence of any recognised general principles, liberty is often granted where it should be withheld, as well as withheld where it should be granted; and one of the cases in which, in the modern European world, the sentiment of liberty is the strongest, is a case where, in my view, it is altogether misplaced. A person should be free to do as he likes in his own concerns; but he ought not to be free to do as he likes in acting for another, under the pretext that the affairs of the other are his own affairs. The State, while it respects the liberty of each in what specially regards himself, is bound to maintain a vigilant control over his exercise of any power which it allows him to possess over others. This obligation is almost entirely disregarded in the case of the family relations, a case, in its direct influence on human happiness, more important than all others taken together. The almost despotic power of husbands over wives needs not be enlarged upon here, because nothing more is needed for the complete removal of the evil than that wives should have the same rights, and should receive the protection of law in the same manner, as all other persons; and because, on this subject, the defenders of established injustice do not avail themselves of the plea of liberty, but stand forth openly as the champions of power. It is in the case of children that misapplied notions of liberty are a real obstacle to the fulfilment by the State of its duties. One would almost think that a man's children were supposed to be literally, and not metaphorically, a part of himself, so jealous is opinion of the smallest interference of law with his absolute and exclusive control over them; more jealous than of almost any interference with his own freedom of action: so much less do the generality of mankind value liberty than power. Consider, for example, the case of education. Is it not almost a self-evident axiom, that the State should require and compel the education, up to a certain standard, of every human being who is born its citizen? Yet who is there that is not afraid to recognise and assert this truth? Hardly any one indeed will deny that it is one of the most sacred duties of the parents (or, as law and usage now stand, the father), after summoning a human being into the world, to give to that being an education fitting him to perform his part well in life towards others and towards himself. But while this is unanimously declared to be the father's duty, scarcely anybody, in this country, will bear to hear of obliging him to perform it. Instead of his being required to make any exertion or sacrifice for securing education to his child, it is left to his choice to accept it or not when it is provided gratis! It still remains unrecognised, that to bring a child into existence without a fair prospect of being able, not only to provide food for its body, but instruction and training for its mind, is a moral crime, both against the unfortunate offspring and against society; and that if the parent does not fulfil this obligation, the State ought to see it fulfilled, at the charge, as far as possible, of the parent.

Were the duty of enforcing universal education once admitted there would be an end to the difficulties about what the State should teach, and how it should teach, which now convert the subject into a mere battlefield for sects and parties, causing the time and labour which should have been spent in educating to be wasted in quarreling about education. If the government would make up its mind to require for every child a good education, it might save itself the trouble of providing one. It might leave to parents to obtain the education where and how they pleased, and content itself with helping to pay the school fees of the poorer classes of children, and defraying the entire school expenses of those who have no one else to pay for them. The objections which are urged with reason against State education do not apply to the enforcement of education by the State, but to the State's taking upon itself to direct that education; which is a totally different thing. That the whole or any large part of the education of the people should be in State hands, I go as far as any one in deprecating. All that has been said of the importance of individuality of character, and diversity in opinions and modes of conduct, involves, as of the same unspeakable importance, diversity of education. A general State education is a mere contrivance for moulding people to be exactly like one another: and as the mould in which it casts them is that which pleases the predominant power in the government, whether this be a monarch, a priesthood, an aristocracy, or the majority of the existing generation; in proportion as it is efficient and successful, it establishes a despotism

over the mind, leading by natural tendency to one over the body. An education established and controlled by the State should only exist, if it exist at all, as one among many competing experiments, carried on for the purpose of example and stimulus, to keep the others up to a certain standard of excellence. Unless, indeed, when society in general is in so backward a state that it could not or would not provide for itself any proper institutions of education unless the government undertook the task: then, indeed, the government may, as the less of two great evils, take upon itself the business of schools and universities, as it may that of joint stock companies, when private enterprise, in a shape fitted for undertaking great works of industry, does not exist in the country. But in general, if the country contains a sufficient number of persons qualified to provide education under government auspices, the same persons would be able and willing to give an equally good education on the voluntary principle, under the assurance of remuneration afforded by a law rendering education compulsory, combined with State aid to those unable to defray the expense.

The instrument for enforcing the law could be no other than public examinations, extending to all children, and beginning at an early age. An age might be fixed at which every child must be examined, to ascertain if he (or she) is able to read. If a child proves unable, the father, unless he has some sufficient ground of excuse, might be subjected to a moderate fine, to be worked out, if necessary, by his labour, and the child might be put to school at his expense. Once in every year the examination should be renewed, with a gradually extending range of subjects, so as to make the universal acquisition, and what is more, retention, of a certain minimum of general knowledge virtually compulsory. Beyond that minimum there should be voluntary examinations on all subjects, at which all who come up to a certain standard of proficiency might claim a certificate. To prevent the State from exercising, through these arrangements, an improper influence over opinion, the knowledge required for passing an examination (beyond the merely instrumental parts of knowledge, such as languages and their use) should, even in the higher classes of examinations, be confined to facts and positive science exclusively. The examinations on religion, politics, or other disputed topics, should not turn on the truth or falsehood of opinions, but on the matter of fact that such and such an opinion is held, on such grounds, by such authors, or schools, or churches.

Under this system, the rising generation would be no worse off in regard to all disputed truths than they are at present; they would be brought up either churchmen or dissenters as they now are, the State merely taking care that they should be instructed churchmen, or instructed dissenters. There would be nothing to hinder them from being taught religion, if their parents chose, at the same schools where they were taught other things. All attempts by the State to bias the conclusions of its citizens on disputed subjects are evil; but it may very properly offer to ascertain and certify that a person possesses the knowledge requisite to make his conclusions, on any given subject, worth attending to. A student of philosophy would be the better for being able to stand an examination both in Locke and in Kant, whichever of the two he takes up with, or even if with neither: and there is no reasonable objection to examining an atheist in the evidences of Christianity, provided he is not required to profess a belief in them. The examinations, however, in the higher branches of knowledge should, I conceive, be entirely voluntary. It would be giving too dangerous a power to governments were they allowed to exclude any one from professions, even from the profession of teacher, for alleged deficiency of qualifications: and I think, with Wilhelm von Humboldt, that degrees, or other public certificates of scientific or professional acquirements, should be given to all who present themselves for examination, and stand the test; but that such certificates should confer no advantage over competitors other than the weight which may be attached to their testimony by public opinion.

It is not in the matter of education only that misplaced notions of liberty prevent moral obligations on the part of parents from being recognised, and legal obligations from being imposed, where there are the strongest grounds for the former always, and in many cases for the latter also. The fact itself, of causing the existence of a human being, is one of the most responsible actions in the range of human life. To undertake this responsibility—to bestow a life which may be either a curse or a blessing —unless the being on whom it is to be bestowed will have at least the ordinary chances of a desirable existence, is a crime against that being. And in a country either over-peopled, or threatened with being so, to produce children, beyond a very small number, with the effect of reducing the reward of labour by their competition, is a serious offence against all who live by the remuneration of their labour. The laws which, in many countries on the Continent, forbid marriage unless the parties can show that they have the means of supporting a family, do not exceed the legitimate powers of the State: and whether such laws be expedient or not (a question mainly dependent on local circumstances and feelings), they are not objectionable as violations of liberty. Such laws are interferences of the State to prohibit a mischievous act—an act injurious to others, which ought to be a subject of reprobation, and social stigma, even when it is not deemed expedient to superadd legal punishment. Yet the current ideas of liberty, which bend so easily to real infringements of the freedom of the individual in things which concern only himself, would repel the attempt to put any restraint upon his inclinations when the consequence of their indulgence is a life or lives of wretchedness and depravity to the offspring, with manifold evils to those sufficiently within reach to be in any way affected by their actions. When we compare the strange respect of mankind for liberty, with their strange want of respect for it, we might imagine that a man had an indispensable right to do harm to others, and no right at all to please himself without giving pain to any one.

I have reserved for the last place a large class of questions respecting the limits of government interference, which, though closely connected with the subject of this Essay, do not, in strictness, belong to it. These are cases in which the reasons against interference do not turn upon the principle of liberty: the question is not about restraining the actions of individuals, but about helping them; it is asked whether the government should do, or cause to be done, something for their benefit, instead of leaving it to be done by themselves, individually or in voluntary combination.

The objections to government interference, when it is not such as to involve infringement of liberty, may be of three kinds.

The first is, when the thing to be done is likely to be better done by individuals than by the government. Speaking generally, there is no one so fit to conduct any business, or to determine how or by whom it shall be conducted, as those who are personally interested in it. This principle condemns the interferences, once so common, of the legislature, or the officers of government, with the ordinary processes of industry. But this part of the subject has been sufficiently enlarged upon by political economists, and is not particularly related to the principles of this Essay.

The second objection is more nearly allied to our subject. In many cases, though individuals may not do the particular thing so well, on the average, as the officers of government, it is nevertheless desirable that it should be done by them, rather than by the government, as a means to their own mental education—a mode of strengthening their active faculties, exercising their judgment, and giving them a familiar knowledge of the subjects with which they are thus left to deal. This is a principal, though not the sole, recommendation of jury trial (in cases not political); of free and popular local and municipal institutions; of the conduct of industrial and philanthropic enterprises by voluntary associations. These are not questions of liberty, and are connected with that subject only by remote tendencies; but they are questions of development. It belongs to a different occasion from the present to dwell on these things as parts of national education; as being, in truth, the peculiar training of a citizen, the practical part of the political education of a free people, taking them out of the narrow circle of personal and family selfishness, and accustoming them to the comprehension of joint interests, the management of joint concerns—habituating them to act from public or semi-public motives, and guide their conduct by aims which unite instead of isolating them from one another. Without these habits and powers, a free constitution can neither be worked nor preserved; as is exemplified by the too-often transitory nature of political freedom in countries where it does not rest upon a sufficient basis of local liberties. The management of purely local business by the localities, and of the great enterprises of industry by the union of those who voluntarily supply the pecuniary means, is further recommended by all the advantages which have been set forth in this Essay as belonging to individuality of development, and diversity of modes of action. Government operations tend to be everywhere alike. With individuals and voluntary associations, on the contrary, there are varied experiments, and endless diversity of experience. What the State can usefully do is to make itself a central depository, and active circulator and diffuser, of the experience resulting from many trials. Its business is to enable each experimentalist to benefit by the experiments of others; instead of tolerating no experiments but its own.

The third and most cogent reason for restricting the interference of government is the great evil of adding unnecessarily to its power. Every function superadded to those already exercised by the government causes its influence over hopes and fears to be more widely diffused, and converts, more and more, the active and ambitious part of the public into hangers-on of the government, or of some party which aims at becoming the government. If the roads, the railways, the banks, the insurance offices, the great joint-stock companies, the universities, and the public charities, were all of them branches of the government; if, in addition, the municipal corporations and local boards, with all that now devolves on them, became departments of the central administration; if the employés of all these different enterprises were appointed and paid by the government, and looked to the government for every rise in life; not all the freedom of the press and popular constitution of the legislature would make this or any other country free otherwise than in name. And the evil would be greater, the more efficiently and scientifically the administrative machinery was constructed—the more skilful the arrangements for obtaining the best qualified hands and heads with which to work it. In England it has of late been proposed that all the members of the civil service of government should be selected by competitive examination, to obtain for these employments the most intelligent and instructed persons procurable; and much has been said and written for and against this proposal. One of the arguments most insisted on by its opponents is that the occupation of a permanent official servant of the State does not hold out sufficient prospects of emolument and importance to attract the highest talents, which will always be able to find a more inviting career in the professions, or in the service of companies and other public bodies. One would not have been surprised if this argument had been used by the friends of the proposition, as an answer to its principal difficulty. Coming from the opponents it is strange enough. What is urged as an objection is the safety-valve of the proposed system. If indeed all the high talent of the country *could* be drawn into the service of the government, a proposal tending to bring about that result might well inspire uneasiness. If every part of the business of society which required organised concert, or large and comprehensive views, were in the hands of the government, and if government offices were universally filled by the ablest men, all the enlarged culture and practised intelligence in the country, except the purely speculative, would be concentrated in a numerous bureaucracy, to whom alone the rest of the community would look for all things: the multitude for direction and dictation in all they had to do; the able and aspiring for personal advancement. To be admitted into the ranks of this bureaucracy, and when admitted, to rise therein, would be the sole objects of ambition. Under this *régime,* not only is the outside public ill-qualified, for want of practical experience, to criticise or check the mode of operation of the bureaucracy, but even if the accidents of despotic or the natural working of popular institutions occasionally raise to the summit a ruler or rulers of reforming inclinations, no reform can be effected which is contrary to the interest of the bureaucracy.

Such is the melancholy condition of the Russian empire, as shown in the accounts of those who have had sufficient opportunity of observation. The Czar himself is powerless against the bureaucratic body; he can send any one of them to Siberia, but he cannot govern without them, or against their will. On every decree of his they have a tacit veto, by merely refraining from carrying it into effect. In countries of more advanced civilisation and of a more insurrectionary spirit, the public, accustomed to expect everything to be done for them by the State, or at least to do nothing for themselves without asking from the State not only leave to do it, but even how it is to be done, naturally hold the State responsible for all evil which befalls them, and when the evil exceeds their amount of patience, they rise against the government, and make what is called a revolution; whereupon somebody else, with or without legitimate authority from the nation, vaults into the seat, issues his orders to the bureaucracy, and everything goes on much as it did before; the bureaucracy being unchanged, and nobody else being capable of taking their place.

A very different spectacle is exhibited among a people accustomed to transact their own business. In France, a large part of the people, having been engaged in military service, many of whom have held at least the rank of non commissioned officers, there are in every popular insurrection several persons competent to take the lead, and improvise some tolerable plan of action. What the French are in military affairs, the Americans are in every kind of civil business; let them be left without a government, every body of Americans is able to improvise one, and to carry on that or any other public business with a sufficient amount of intelligence, order, and decision. This is what every free people ought to be: and a people capable of this is certain to be free; it will never let itself be enslaved by any man or body of men because these are able to seize and pull the reins of the central administration. No bureaucracy can hope to make such a people as this do or undergo anything that they do not like. But where everything is done through the bureaucracy, nothing to which the bureaucracy is really adverse can be done at all. The constitution of such countries is an organisation of the experience and practical ability of the nation into a disciplined body for the purpose of governing the rest; and the more perfect that organisation is in itself, the more successful in drawing to itself and educating for itself the persons of greatest capacity from all ranks of the community, the more complete is the bondage of all, the members of the bureaucracy included. For the governors are as much the slaves of their organisation and discipline as the governed are of the governors. A Chinese mandarin is as much the tool and creature of a despotism as the humblest cultivator. An individual Jesuit is to the utmost degree of abasement the slave of his order, though the order itself exists for the collective power and importance of its members.

It is not, also, to be forgotten, that the absorption of all the principal ability of the country into the governing body is fatal, sooner or later, to the mental activity and progressiveness of the body itself. Banded together as they are—working a system which, like all systems, necessarily proceeds in a great measure by fixed rules—the official body are under the constant temptation of sinking into indolent routine, or, if they now and then desert that mill-horse round, of rushing into some half-examined crudity which has struck the fancy of some leading member of the corps; and the sole check to these closely allied, though seemingly opposite, tendencies, the only stimulus which can keep the ability of the body itself up to a high standard, is liability to the watchful criticism of equal ability outside the body. It is indispensable, therefore, that the means should exist, independently of the government, of forming such ability, and furnishing it with the opportunities and experience necessary for a correct judgment of great practical affairs. If we would possess permanently a skilful and efficient body of functionaries—above all, a body able to originate and willing to adopt improvements; if we would not have our bureaucracy degenerate into a pedantocracy, this body must not engross all the occupations which form and cultivate the faculties required for the government of mankind.

To determine the point at which evils, so formidable to human freedom and advancement, begin, or rather at which they begin to predominate over the benefits attending the collective application of the force of society, under its recognised chiefs, for the removal of the obstacles which stand in the way of its wellbeing; to secure as much of the advantages of centralised power and intelligence as can be had without turning into governmental channels too great a proportion of the general activity—is one of the most difficult and complicated questions in the art of government. It is, in a great measure, a question of detail, in which many and various considerations must be kept in view, and no absolute rule can be laid down. But I believe that the practical principle in which safety resides, the ideal to be kept in view, the standard by which to test all arrangements intended for overcoming the difficulty, may be conveyed in these words: the greatest dissemination of power consistent with efficiency; but the greatest possible centralisation of information, and diffusion of it from the centre. Thus, in municipal administration, there would be, as in the New England States, a very minute division among separate officers, chosen by the localities, of all business which is not better left to the persons directly interested; but besides this, there would be, in each department of local affairs, a central superintendence, forming a branch of the general government. The organ of this superintendence would concentrate, as in a focus, the variety of information and experience derived from the conduct of that branch of public business in all the localities, from everything analogous which is done in foreign countries, and from the general principles of political science. This central organ should have a right to know all that is done, and its special duty should be that of making the knowledge acquired in one place available for others. Emancipated from the petty prejudices and narrow views of a locality by its elevated position and comprehensive sphere of observation, its advice would naturally carry much authority; but its actual power, as a permanent institution, should, I conceive, be limited to compelling the local officers to obey the laws laid down for their guidance. In all things not provided for by general rules, those officers should be left to their own judgment, under responsibility to their constituents. For the violation of rules, they should be responsible to law, and the rules themselves should be laid down by the legislature; the central administrative authority only watching over their execution, and if they were not properly carried into effect, appealing, according to the nature of the case, to the tribunals to enforce the law, or to the constituencies to dismiss the functionaries who had not executed it according to its spirit.

Such, in its general conception, is the central superintendence which the Poor Law Board is intended to exercise over the administrators of the Poor Rate throughout the country. Whatever powers the Board exercises beyond this limit were right and necessary in that peculiar case, for the cure of rooted habits of maladministration in matters deeply affecting not the localities merely, but the whole community; since no locality has a moral right to make itself by mismanagement a nest of pauperism, necessarily overflowing into other localities, and impairing the moral and physical condition of the whole labouring community. The powers of administrative coercion and subordinate legislation possessed by the Poor Law Board (but which, owing to the state of opinion on the subject, are very scantily exercised by them), though perfectly justifiable in a case of first-rate national interest, would be wholly out of place in the superintendence of interests purely local. But a central organ of information and instruction for all the localities would be equally valuable in all departments of administration. A government cannot have too much of the kind of activity which does not impede, but aids and stimulates, individual exertion and development. The mischief begins when, instead of calling forth the activity and powers of individuals and bodies, it substitutes its own activity for theirs; when, instead of informing, advising, and, upon occasion, denouncing, it makes them work in fetters, or bids them stand aside and does their work instead of them. The worth of a State, in the long run, is the worth of the individuals composing it; and a State which postpones the interests of *their* mental expansion and elevation to a little more of administrative skill, or of that semblance of it which practice gives, in the details of business; a State which dwarfs its men, in order that they may be more docile instruments in its hands even for beneficial purposes—will find that with small men no great thing can really be accomplished; and that the perfection of machinery to which it has sacrificed everything will in the end avail it nothing, for want of the vital power which, in order that the machine might work more smoothly, it has preferred to banish.

CONTENTS: REPRESENTATIVE
GOVERNMENT

REPRESENTATIVE GOVERNMENT

THOSE who have done me the honour of reading my previous writings will probably receive no strong impression of novelty from the present volume; for the principles are those to which I have been working up during the greater part of my life, and most of the practical suggestions have been anticipated by others or by myself. There is novelty, however, in the fact of bringing them together, and exhibiting them in their connection; and also, I believe, in much that is brought forward in their support. Several of the opinions at all events, if not new, are for the present as little likely to meet with general acceptance as if they were.

It seems to me, however, from various indications, and from none more than the recent debates on Reform of Parliament, that both Conservatives and Liberals (if I may continue to call them what they still call themselves) have lost confidence in the political creeds which they nominally profess, while neither side appears to have made any progress in providing itself with a better. Yet such a better doctrine must be possible; not a mere compromise, by splitting the difference between the two, but something wider than either, which, in virtue of its superior comprehensiveness, might be adopted by either Liberal or Conservative without renouncing anything which he really feels to be valuable in his own creed. When so many feel obscurely the want of such a doctrine, and so few even flatter themselves that they have attained it, any one may without presumption offer what his own thoughts, and the best that he knows of those of others, are able to contribute towards its formation.

Chapter 1

To what extent Forms of Government are a Matter of Choice

ALL SPECULATIONS concerning forms of government bear the impress, more or less exclusive, of two conflicting theories respecting political institutions; or, to speak more properly, conflicting conceptions of what political institutions are.

By some minds, government is conceived as strictly a practical art, giving rise to no questions but those of means and an end. Forms of government are assimilated to any other expedients for the attainment of human objects. They are regarded as wholly an affair of invention and contrivance. Being made by man, it is assumed that man has the choice either to make them or not, and how or on what pattern they shall be made. Government, according to this conception, is a problem, to be worked like any other question of business. The first step is to define the purposes which governments are required to promote. The next, is to inquire what form of government is best fitted to fulfil those purposes. Having satisfied ourselves on these two points, and ascertained the form of government which combines the greatest amount of good with the least of evil, what further remains is to obtain the concurrence of our countrymen, or those for whom the institutions are intended, in the opinion which we have privately arrived at. To find the best form of government; to persuade others that it is the best; and having done so, to stir them up to insist on having it, is the order of ideas in the minds of those who adopt this view of political philosophy. They look upon a constitution in the same light (difference of scale being allowed for) as they would upon a steam plough, or a threshing machine.

To these stand opposed another kind of political reasoners, who are so far from assimilating a form of government to a machine, that they regard it as a sort of spontaneous product, and the science of government as a branch (so to speak) of natural history. According to them, forms of government are not a matter of choice. We must take them, in the main, as we find them. Governments cannot be constructed by premeditated design. They "are not made, but grow." Our business with them, as with the other facts of the universe, is to acquaint ourselves with their natural properties, and adapt ourselves to them. The fundamental political institutions of a people are considered by this school as a sort of organic growth from the nature and life of that people: a product of their habits, instincts, and unconscious wants and desires, scarcely at all of their deliberate purposes. Their will has had no part in the matter but that of meeting the necessities of the moment by the contrivances of the moment, which contrivances, if in sufficient conformity to the national feelings and character, commonly last, and by successive aggregation constitute a polity, suited to the people who possess it, but which it would be vain to attempt to superduce upon any people whose nature and circumstances had not spontaneously evolved it.

It is difficult to decide which of these doctrines would be the most absurd, if we could suppose either of them held as an exclusive theory. But the principles which men profess, on any controverted subject, are usually a very incomplete exponent of the opinions they really hold. No one believes that every people is capable of working every sort of institutions. Carry the analogy of mechanical contrivances as far as we will, a man does not choose even an instrument of timber and iron on the sole ground that it is in itself the best.

He considers whether he possesses the other requisites which must be combined with it to render its employment advantageous, and in particular whether those by whom it will have to be worked possess the knowledge and skill necessary for its management. On the other hand, neither are those who speak of institutions as if they were a kind of living organisms really the political fatalists they give themselves out to be. They do not pretend that mankind have absolutely no range of choice as to the government they will live under, or that a consideration of the consequences which flow from different forms of polity is no element at all in deciding which of them should be preferred. But though each side greatly exaggerates its own theory, out of opposition to the other, and no one holds without modification to either, the two doctrines correspond to a deep-seated difference between two modes of thought; and though it is evident that neither of these is entirely in the right, yet it being equally evident that neither is wholly in the wrong, we must endeavour to get down to what is at the root of each, and avail ourselves of the amount of truth which exists in either.

Let us remember, then, in the first place, that political institutions (however the proposition may be at times ignored) are the work of men; owe their origin and their whole existence to human will. Men did not wake on a summer morning and find them sprung up. Neither do they resemble trees, which, once planted, "are aye growing" while men "are sleeping." In every stage of their existence they are made what they are by human voluntary agency. Like all things, therefore, which are made by men, they may be either well or ill made; judgment and skill may have been exercised in their production, or the reverse of these. And again, if a people have omitted, or from outward pressure have not had it in their power, to give themselves a constitution by the tentative process of applying a corrective to each evil as it arose, or as the sufferers gained strength to resist it, this retardation of political progress is no doubt a great disadvantage to them, but it does not prove that what has been found good for others would not have been good also for them, and will not be so still when they think fit to adopt it.

On the other hand, it is also to be borne in mind that political machinery does not act of itself. As it is first made, so it has to be worked, by men, and even by ordinary men. It needs, not their simple acquiescence, but their active participation; and must be adjusted to the capacities and qualities of such men as are available. This implies three conditions. The people for whom the form of government is intended must be willing to accept it; or at least not so unwilling as to oppose an insurmountable obstacle to its establishment. They must be willing and able to do what is necessary to keep it standing. And they must be willing and able to do what it requires of them to enable it to fulfil its purposes. The word "do" is to be understood as including forbearances as well as acts. They must be capable of fulfilling the conditions of action, and the conditions of self-restraint, which are necessary either for keeping the established polity in existence, or for enabling it to achieve the ends, its conduciveness to which forms its recommendation.

The failure of any of these conditions renders a form of government, whatever favourable promise it may otherwise hold out, unsuitable to the particular case.

The first obstacle, the repugnance of the people to the particular form of government, needs little illustration, because it never can in theory have been overlooked. The case is of perpetual occurrence. Nothing but foreign force would induce a tribe of North American Indians to submit to the restraints of a regular and civilised government. The same might have been said, though somewhat less absolutely, of the barbarians who overran the Roman Empire. It required centuries of time, and an entire change of circumstances, to discipline them into regular obedience even to their own leaders, when not actually serving under their banner. There are nations who will not voluntarily submit to any government but that of certain families, which have from time immemorial had the privilege of supplying them with chiefs. Some nations could not, except by foreign conquest, be made to endure a monarchy; others are equally averse to a republic. The hindrance often amounts, for the time being, to impracticability.

But there are also cases in which, though not averse to a form of government—possibly even desiring it—a people may be unwilling or unable to fulfil its conditions. They may be incapable of fulfilling such of them as are necessary to keep the government even in nominal existence. Thus a people may prefer a free government, but if, from indolence, or carelessness, or cowardice, or want of public spirit, they are unequal to the exertions necessary for preserving it; if they will not fight for it when it is directly attacked; if they can be deluded by the artifices used to cheat them out of it; if by momentary discouragement, or temporary panic, or a fit of enthusiasm for an individual, they can be induced to lay their liberties at the feet even of a great man, or trust him with powers which enable him to subvert their institutions; in all these cases they are more or less unfit for liberty: and though it may be for their good to have had it even for a short time, they are unlikely long to enjoy it. Again, a people may be unwilling or unable to fulfil the duties which a particular form of government requires of them. A rude people, though in some degree alive to the benefits of civilised society, may be unable to practise the forbearance which it demands: their passions may be too violent, or their personal pride too exacting, to forego private conflict, and leave to the laws the avenging of their real or supposed wrongs. In such a case, a civilised government, to be really advantageous to them, will require to be in a considerable degree despotic: to be one over which they do not themselves exercise control, and which imposes a great amount of forcible restraint upon their actions.

Again, a people must be considered unfit for more than a limited and qualified freedom, who will not co-operate actively with the law and the public authorities in the repression of evil-doers. A people who are more disposed to shelter a criminal than to apprehend him; who, like the Hindoos, will perjure themselves to screen the man who has robbed them, rather than take trouble or expose themselves to vindictiveness by giving evidence against him; who, like some nations of Europe down to a recent date, if a man poniards another in the public street, pass by on the other side, because it is the business of the police to look to the matter, and it is safer not to interfere in what does not concern them; a people who are revolted by an execution, but not shocked at an assassination—require that the public authorities should be armed with much sterner powers of repression than elsewhere, since the first indispensable requisites of civilised life have nothing else to rest on. These deplorable states of feeling, in any people who have emerged from savage life, are, no doubt, usually the consequence of previous bad government, which has taught them to regard the law as made for other ends than their good, and its administrators as worse enemies than those who openly violate it. But however little blame may be due to those in whom these mental habits have grown up, and however the habits may be ultimately conquerable by better government, yet while they exist a people so disposed cannot be governed with as little power exercised over them as a people whose sympathies are on the side of the law, and who are willing to give active assistance in its enforcement. Again, representative institutions are of little value, and may be a mere instrument of tyranny or intrigue, when the generality of electors are not sufficiently interested in their own government to give their vote, or, if they vote at all, do not bestow their suffrages on public grounds, but sell them for money, or vote at the beck of some one who has control over them, or whom for private reasons they desire to propitiate. Popular election thus practised, instead of a security against misgovernment, is but an additional wheel in its machinery.

Besides these moral hindrances, mechanical difficulties are often an insuperable impediment to forms of government. In the ancient world, though there might be, and often was, great individual or local independence, there could be nothing like a regulated popular government beyond the bounds of a single city-community; because there did not exist the physical conditions for the formation and propagation of a public opinion, except among those who could be brought together to discuss public matters in the same agora. This obstacle is generally thought to have ceased by the adoption of the representative system. But to surmount it completely, required the press, and even the newspaper press, the real equivalent, though not in all respects an adequate one, of the Pnyx and the Forum. There have been states of society in which even a monarchy of any great territorial extent could not subsist, but unavoidably broke up into petty principalities, either mutually independent, or held together by a loose tie like the feudal: because the machinery of authority was not perfect enough to carry orders into effect at a great distance from the person of the ruler. He depended mainly upon voluntary fidelity for the obedience even of his army, nor did there exist the means of making the people pay an amount of taxes sufficient for keeping up the force necessary to compel obedience throughout a large territory. In these and all similar cases, it must be understood that the amount of the hindrance may be either greater or less. It may be so great as to make the form of government

work very ill, without absolutely precluding its existence, or hindering it from being practically preferable to any other which can be had. This last question mainly depends upon a consideration which we have not yet arrived at—the tendencies of different forms of government to promote Progress.

We have now examined the three fundamental conditions of the adaptation of forms of government to the people who are to be governed by them. If the supporters of what may be termed the naturalistic theory of politics, mean but to insist on the necessity of these three conditions; if they only mean that no government can permanently exist which does not fulfil the first and second conditions, and, in some considerable measure, the third; their doctrine, thus limited, is incontestable. Whatever they mean more than this appears to me untenable. All that we are told about the necessity of an historical basis for institutions, of their being in harmony with the national usages and character, and the like, means either this, or nothing to the purpose. There is a great quantity of mere sentimentality connected with these and similar phrases, over and above the amount of rational meaning contained in them. But, considered practically, these alleged requisites of political institutions are merely so many facilities for realising the three conditions. When an institution, or a set of institutions, has the way prepared for it by the opinions, tastes, and habits of the people, they are not only more easily induced to accept it, but will more easily learn, and will be, from the beginning, better disposed, to do what is required of them both for the preservation of the institutions, and for bringing them into such action as enables them to produce their best results. It would be a great mistake in any legislator not to shape his measures so as to take advantage of such pre-existing habits and feelings when available. On the other hand, it is an exaggeration to elevate these mere aids and facilities into necessary conditions. People are more easily induced to do, and do more easily, what they are already used to; but people also learn to do things new to them. Familiarity is a great help; but much dwelling on an idea will make it familiar, even when strange at first. There are abundant instances in which a whole people have been eager for untried things. The amount of capacity which a people possess for doing new things, and adapting themselves to new circumstances; is itself one of the elements of the question. It is a quality in which different nations, and different stages of civilisation, differ much from one another. The capability of any given people for fulfilling the conditions of a given form of government cannot be pronounced on by any sweeping rule. Knowledge of the particular people, and general practical judgment and sagacity, must be the guides.

There is also another consideration not to be lost sight of. A people may be unprepared for good institutions; but to kindle a desire for them is a necessary part of the preparation. To recommend and advocate a particular institution or form of government, and set its advantages in the strongest light, is one of the modes, often the only mode within reach, of educating the mind of the nation not only for accepting or claiming, but also for working, the institution. What means had Italian patriots, during the last and present generation, of preparing the Italian people for freedom in unity, but by inciting them to demand it? Those, however, who undertake such a task, need to be duly impressed, not solely with the benefits of the institution or polity which they recommend, but also with the capacities, moral, intellectual, and active, required for working it; that they may avoid, if possible, stirring up a desire too much in advance of the capacity.

The result of what has been said is, that, within the limits set by the three conditions so often adverted to, institutions and forms of government are a matter of choice. To inquire into the best form of government in the abstract (as it is called) is not a chimerical, but a highly practical employment of scientific intellect; and to introduce into any country the best institutions which, in the existing state of that country, are capable of, in any tolerable degree, fulfilling the conditions, is one of the most rational objects to which practical effort can address itself. Everything which can be said by way of disparaging the efficacy of human will and purpose in matters of government might be said of it in every other of its applications. In all things there are very strict limits to human power. It can only act by wielding some one or more of the forces of nature. Forces, therefore, that can be applied to the desired use must exist; and will only act according to their own laws. We cannot make the river run backwards; but we do not therefore say that watermills "are not made, but grow." In politics, as in mechanics, the power which is to keep the engine going must be sought for outside the machinery; and if it is not forthcoming, or is insufficient to surmount the obstacles which may reasonably be expected, the contrivance will fail. This is no peculiarity of the political art; and amounts only to saying that it is subject to the same limitations and conditions as all other arts.

At this point we are met by another objection, or the same objection in a different form. The forces, it is contended, on which the greater political phenomena depend, are not amenable to the direction of politicians or philosophers. The government of a country, it is affirmed, is, in all substantial respects, fixed and determined beforehand by the state of the country in regard to the distribution of the elements of social power. Whatever is the strongest power in society will obtain the governing authority; and a change in the political constitution cannot be durable unless preceded or accompanied by an altered distribution of power in society itself. A nation, therefore, cannot choose its form of government. The mere details, and practical organisation, it may choose; but the essence of the whole, the seat of the supreme power, is determined for it by social circumstances.

That there is a portion of truth in this doctrine I at once admit; but to make it of any use, it must be reduced to a distinct expression and proper limits. When it is said that the strongest power in society will make itself strongest in the government, what is meant by power? Not thews and sinews; otherwise pure democracy would be the only form of polity that could exist. To mere muscular strength, add two other elements, property and intelligence, and we are nearer the truth, but far from having yet reached it. Not only is a greater number often kept down by a less, but the greater number may have a preponderance in property, and individually in intelligence, and may yet be held in subjection, forcibly or otherwise, by a minority in both respects inferior to it. To make these various elements of power politically influential they must be organised; and the advantage in organisation is necessarily with those who are in possession of the government. A much weaker party in all other elements of power may greatly preponderate when the powers of government are thrown into the scale; and may long retain its predominance through this alone: though, no doubt, a government so situated is in the condition called in mechanics unstable equilibrium, like a thing balanced on its smaller end, which, if once disturbed, tends more and more to depart from, instead of reverting to, its previous state.

But there are still stronger objections to this theory of government in the terms in which it is usually stated. The power in society which has any tendency to convert itself into political power is not power quiescent, power merely passive, but active power; in other words, power actually exerted; that is to say, a very small portion of all the power in existence. Politically speaking, a great part of all power consists in will. How is it possible, then, to compute the elements of political power, while we omit from the computation anything which acts on the will? To think that because those who wield the power in society wield in the end that of government, therefore it is of no use to attempt to influence the constitution of the government by acting on opinion, is to forget that opinion is itself one of the greatest active social forces. One person with a belief is a social power equal to ninety-nine who have only interests. They who can succeed in creating a general persuasion that a certain form of government, or social fact of any kind, deserves to be preferred, have made nearly the most important step which can possibly be taken towards ranging the powers of society on its side. On the day when the proto-martyr was stoned to death at Jerusalem, while he who was to be the Apostle of the Gentiles stood by "consenting unto his death," would any one have supposed that the party of that stoned man were then and there the strongest power in society? And has not the event proved that they were so? Because theirs was the most powerful of then existing beliefs. The same element made a monk of Wittenberg, at the meeting of the Diet of Worms, a more powerful social force than the Emperor Charles the Fifth, and all the princes there assembled. But these, it may be said, are cases in which religion was concerned, and religious convictions are something peculiar in their strength. Then let us take a case purely political, where religion, so far as concerned at all, was chiefly on the losing side. If any one requires to be convinced that speculative thought is one of the chief elements of social power, let him bethink himself of the age in which there was scarcely a throne in Europe which was not filled by a liberal and reforming king, a liberal and reforming emperor, or, strangest of all, a liberal and reforming pope; the age of Frederic the Great, of Catherine the Second, of Joseph the Second, of Peter Leopold, of Benedict XIV., of Ganganelli, of Pombal, of Aranda; when the very Bourbons of Naples were liberals and reformers, and all the active minds among the noblesse of France were filled with the ideas which were soon after to cost them so dear. Surely a conclusive example how far mere physical and economic power is from being the whole of social power.

It was not by any change in the distribution of material interests, but by the spread of moral convictions, that negro slavery has been put an end to in the British Empire and elsewhere. The serfs in Russia owe their emancipation, if not to a sentiment of duty, at least to the growth of a more enlightened opinion respecting the true interest of the State. It is what men think that determines how they act; and though the persuasions and convictions of average men are in a much greater degree determined by their personal position than by reason, no little power is exercised over them by the persuasions and convictions of those whose personal position is different, and by the united authority of the instructed. When, therefore, the instructed in general can be brought to recognise one social arrangement, or political or other institution, as good, and another as bad, one as desirable, another as condemnable, very much has been done towards giving to the one, or withdrawing from the other, that preponderance of social force which enables it to subsist. And the maxim, that the government of a country is what the social forces in existence compel it to be, is true only in the sense in which it favours, instead of discouraging, the attempt to exercise, among all forms of government practicable in the existing condition of society, a rational choice.

Chapter 2

The Criterion of a Good Form of Government

THE FORM of government for any given country being (within certain definite conditions) amenable to choice, it is now to be considered by what test the choice should be directed; what are the distinctive characteristics of the form of government best fitted to promote the interests of any given society.

Before entering into this inquiry, it may seem necessary to decide what are the proper functions of government; for, government altogether being only a means, the eligibility of the means must depend on their adaptation to the end. But this mode of stating the problem gives less aid to its investigation than might be supposed, and does not even bring the whole of the question into view. For, in the first place, the proper functions of a government are not a fixed thing, but different in different states of society; much more extensive in a backward than in an advanced state. And, secondly, the character of a government or set of political institutions cannot be sufficiently estimated while we confine our attention to the legitimate sphere of governmental functions. For though the goodness of a government is necessarily circumscribed within that sphere, its badness unhappily is not. Every kind and degree of evil of which mankind are susceptible may be inflicted on them by their government; and none of the good which social existence is capable of can be any further realised than as the constitution of the government is compatible with, and allows scope for, its attainment. Not to speak of indirect effects, the direct meddling of the public authorities has no necessary limits but those of human existence; and the influence of government on the well-being of society can be considered or estimated in reference to nothing less than the whole of the interests of humanity.

Being thus obliged to place before ourselves, as the test of good and bad government, so complex an object as the aggregate interests of society, we would willingly attempt some kind of classification of those interests, which, bringing them before the mind in definite groups, might give indication of the qualities by which a form of government is fitted to promote those various interests respectively. It would be a great facility if we could say the good of society consists of such and such elements; one of these elements requires such conditions, another such others; the government, then, which unites in the greatest degree all these conditions, must be the best. The theory of government would thus be built up from the separate theorems of the elements which compose a good state of society.

Unfortunately, to enumerate and classify the constituents of social well-being, so as to admit of the formation of such theorems, is no easy task. Most of those who, in the last or present generation, have applied themselves to the philosophy of politics in any comprehensive spirit, have felt the importance of such a classification; but the attempts which have been made towards it are as yet limited, so far as I am aware, to a single step. The classification begins and ends with a partition of the exigencies of society between the two heads of Order and Progress (in the phraseology of French thinkers); Permanence and Progression in the words of Coleridge. This division is plausible and seductive, from the apparently clean-cut opposition between its two members, and the remarkable difference between the sentiments to which they appeal. But I apprehend that (however admissible for purposes of popular discourse) the distinction between Order, or Permanence, and Progress, employed to define the qualities necessary in a government, is unscientific and incorrect.

For, first, what are Order and Progress? Concerning Progress there is no difficulty, or none which is apparent at first sight. When Progress is spoken of as one of the wants of human society, it may be supposed to mean Improvement. That is a tolerably distinct idea. But what is Order? Sometimes it means more, sometimes less, but hardly ever the whole of what human society needs except improvement.

In its narrowest acceptation Order means Obedience. A government is said to preserve order if it succeeds in getting itself obeyed. But there are different degrees of obedience, and it is not every degree that is commendable. Only an unmitigated despotism demands that the individual citizen shall obey unconditionally every mandate of persons in authority. We must at least limit the definition to such mandates as are general and issued in the deliberate form of laws. Order, thus understood, expresses, doubtless, an indispensable attribute of government. Those who are unable to make their ordinances obeyed, cannot be said to govern. But though a necessary condition, this is not the object of government. That it should make itself obeyed is requisite, in order that it may accomplish some other purpose. We are still to seek what is this other purpose, which government ought to fulfil, abstractedly from the idea of improvement, and which has to be fulfilled in every society, whether stationary or progressive.

In a sense somewhat more enlarged, Order means the preservation of peace by the cessation of private violence. Order is said to exist where the people of the country have, as a general rule, ceased to prosecute their quarrels by private force, and acquired the habit of referring the decision of their disputes and the redress of their injuries to the public authorities. But in this larger use of the term, as well as in the former narrow one, Order expresses rather one of the conditions of government, than either its purpose or the criterion of its excellence. For the habit may be well established of submitting to the government, and referring all disputed matters to its authority, and yet the manner in which the government deals with those disputed matters, and with the other things about which it concerns itself, may differ by the whole interval which divides the best from the worst possible.

If we intend to comprise in the idea of Order all that society requires from its government which is not included in the idea of Progress, we must define Order as the preservation of all kinds and amounts of good which already exist, and Progress as consisting in the increase of them. This distinction does comprehend in one or the other section everything which a government can be required to promote. But, thus understood, it affords no basis for a philosophy of government. We cannot say that, in constituting a polity, certain provisions ought to be made for Order and certain others for Progress; since the conditions of Order, in the sense now indicated, and those of Progress, are not opposite, but the same. The agencies which tend to preserve the social good which already exists are the very same which promote the increase of it, and *vice versa:* the sole difference being, that a greater degree of those agencies is required for the latter purpose than for the former.

What, for example, are the qualities in the citizens individually which conduce most to keep up the amount of good conduct, of good management, of success and prosperity, which already exist in society? Everybody will agree that those qualities are industry, integrity, justice, and prudence. But are not these, of all qualities, the most conducive to improvement? and is not any growth of these virtues in the community in itself the greatest of improvements? If so, whatever qualities in the government are promotive of industry, integrity, justice, and prudence, conduce alike to permanence and to progression; only there is needed more of those qualities to make the society decidedly progressive than merely to keep it permanent.

What, again, are the particular attributes in human beings which seem to have a more especial reference to Progress, and do not so directly suggest the ideas of Order and Preservation? They are chiefly the qualities of mental activity, enterprise, and courage. But are not all these qualities fully as much required for preserving the good we have, as for adding to it? If there is anything certain in human affairs, it is that valuable acquisitions are only to be retained by the continuation of the same energies which gained them. Things left to take care of themselves inevitably decay. Those whom success induces to relax their habits of care and thoughtfulness, and their willingness to encounter disagreeables, seldom long retain their good fortune at its height. The mental attribute which seems exclusively dedicated to Progress, and is the culmination of the tendencies to it, is Originality, or Invention. Yet this is no less necessary for Permanence; since, in the inevitable changes of human affairs, new inconveniences and dangers continually grow up, which must be encountered by new resources and contrivances, in order to keep things going on even only as well as they did before. Whatever qualities, therefore, in a government, tend to encourage activity, energy, courage, originality, are requisites of Permanence as well as of Progress; only a somewhat less degree of them will on the average suffice for the former purpose than for the latter.

To pass now from the mental to the outward and objective requisites of society; it is impossible to point out any contrivance in politics, or arrangement of social affairs, which conduces to Order only, or to Progress only; whatever tends to either promotes both. Take, for instance, the common institution of a police. Order is the object which seems most immediately interested in the efficiency of this part of the social organisation. Yet if it is effectual to promote Order, that is, if it represses crime, and enables every one to feel his person and property secure, can any state of things be more conducive to Progress? The greater security of property is one of the main conditions and causes of greater production, which is Progress in its most familiar and vulgarest aspect. The better repression of crime represses the dispositions which tend to crime, and this is Progress in a somewhat higher sense. The release of the individual from the cares and anxieties of a state of imperfect protection, sets his faculties free to be employed in any new effort for improving his own state and that of others: while the same cause, by attaching him to social existence, and making him no longer see present or prospective enemies in his fellow creatures, fosters all those feelings of kindness and fellowship towards others, and interest in the general well-being of the community, which are such important parts of social improvement.

Take, again, such a familiar case as that of a good system of taxation and finance. This would generally be classed as belonging to the province of Order. Yet what can be more conducive to Progress? A financial system which promotes the one, conduces, by the very same excellences, to the other. Economy, for example, equally preserves the existing stock of national wealth, and favours the creation of more. A just distribution of burthens, by holding up to every citizen an example of morality and good conscience applied to difficult adjustments, and an evidence of the value which the highest authorities attach to them, tends in an eminent degree to educate the moral sentiments of the community, both in respect of strength and of discrimination. Such a mode of levying the taxes as does not impede the industry, or unnecessarily interfere with the liberty, of the citizen, promotes, not the preservation only, but the increase of the national wealth, and encourages a more active use of the individual faculties. And *vice versa,* all errors in finance and taxation which obstruct the improvement of the people in wealth and morals tend also, if of sufficiently serious amount, positively to impoverish and demoralise them. It holds, in short, universally, that when Order and Permanence are taken in their widest sense, for the stability of existing advantages, the requisites of Progress are but the requisites of Order in a greater degree; those of Permanence merely those of Progress in a somewhat smaller measure.

In support of the position that Order is intrinsically different from Progress, and that preservation of existing and acquisition of additional good are sufficiently distinct to afford the basis of a fundamental classification, we shall perhaps be reminded that Progress may be at the expense of Order; that while we are acquiring, or striving to acquire, good of one kind, we may be losing ground in respect to others: thus there may be progress in wealth, while there is deterioration in virtue. Granting this, what it proves is not that Progress is generically a different thing from Permanence, but that wealth is a different thing from virtue. Progress is permanence and something more; and it is no answer to this to say that Progress in one thing does not imply Permanence in everything. No more does Progress in one thing imply Progress in everything. Progress of any kind includes Permanence in that same

kind; whenever Permanence is sacrificed to some particular kind of Progress, other Progress is still more sacrificed to it; and if it be not worth the sacrifice, not the interest of Permanence alone has been disregarded, but the general interest of Progress has been mistaken.

If these improperly contrasted ideas are to be used at all in the attempt to give a first commencement of scientific precision to the notion of good government, it would be more philosophically correct to leave out of the definition the word Order, and to say that the best government is that which is most conducive to Progress. For Progress includes Order, but Order does not include Progress. Progress is a greater degree of that of which Order is a less. Order, in any other sense, stands only for a part of the pre-requisites of good government, not for its idea and essence. Order would find a more suitable place among the conditions of Progress; since, if we would increase our sum of good, nothing is more indispensable than to take due care of what we already have. If we are endeavouring after more riches, our very first rule should be not to squander uselessly our existing means. Order, thus considered, is not an additional end to be reconciled with Progress, but a part and means of Progress itself. If a gain in one respect is purchased by a more than equivalent loss in the same or in any other, there is not Progress. Conduciveness to Progress, thus understood, includes the whole excellence of a government.

But, though metaphysically defensible, this definition of the criterion of good government is not appropriate, because, though it contains the whole of the truth, it recalls only a part. What is suggested by the term Progress is the idea of moving onward, whereas the meaning of it here is quite as much the prevention of falling back. The very same social causes—the same beliefs, feelings, institutions, and practices—are as much required to prevent society from retrograding, as to produce a further advance. Were there no improvement to be hoped for, life would not be the less an unceasing struggle against causes of deterioration; as it even now is. Politics, as conceived by the ancients, consisted wholly in this. The natural tendency of men and their works was to degenerate, which tendency, however, by good institutions virtuously administered, it might be possible for an indefinite length of time to counteract. Though we no longer hold this opinion; though most men in the present age profess the contrary creed, believing that the tendency of things, on the whole, is towards improvement; we ought not to forget that there is an incessant and ever-flowing current of human affairs towards the worse, consisting of all the follies, all the vices, all the negligences, indolences, and supinenesses of mankind; which is only controlled, and kept from sweeping all before it, by the exertions which some persons constantly, and others by fits, put forth in the direction of good and worthy objects. It gives a very insufficient idea of the importance of the strivings which take place to improve and elevate human nature and life, to suppose that their chief value consists in the amount of actual improvement realised by their means, and that the consequence of their cessation would merely be that we should remain as we are. A very small diminution of those exertions would not only put a stop to improvement, but would turn the general tendency of things towards deterioration; which, once begun, would proceed with increasingly rapidity, and become more and more difficult to check, until it reached a state often seen in history, and in which many large portions of mankind even now grovel; when hardly anything short of superhuman power seems sufficient to turn the tide, and give a fresh commencement to the upward movement.

These reasons make the word Progress as unapt as the terms Order and Permanence to become the basis for a classification of the requisites of a form of government. The fundamental antithesis which these words express does not lie in the things themselves, so much as in the types of human character which answer to them. There are, we know, some minds in which caution, and others in which boldness, predominates: in some, the desire to avoid imperilling what is already possessed is a stronger sentiment than that which prompts to improve the old and acquire new advantages; while there are others who lean the contrary way, and are more eager for future than careful of present good. The road to the ends of both is the same; but they are liable to wander from it in opposite directions. This consideration is of importance in composing the *personnel* of any political body: persons of both types ought to be included in it, that the tendencies of each may be tempered, in so far as they are excessive, by a due proportion of the other. There needs no express provision to ensure this object, provided care is taken to admit nothing inconsistent with it. The natural and spontaneous admixture of the old and

the young, of those whose position and reputation are made and those who have them still to make, will in general sufficiently answer the purpose, if only this natural balance is not disturbed by artificial regulation.

Since the distinction most commonly adopted for the classification of social exigencies does not possess the properties needful for that use, we have to seek for some other leading distinction better adapted to the purpose. Such a distinction would seem to be indicated by the considerations to which I now proceed.

If we ask ourselves on what causes and conditions good government in all its senses, from the humblest to the most exalted, depends, we find that the principal of them, the one which transcends all others, is the qualities of the human beings composing the society over which the government is exercised.

We may take, as a first instance, the administration of justice; with the more propriety, since there is no part of public business in which the mere machinery, the rules and contrivances for conducting the details of the operation, are of such vital consequence. Yet even these yield in importance to the qualities of the human agents employed. Of what efficacy are rules of procedure in securing the ends of justice, if the moral condition of the people is such that the witnesses generally lie, and the judges and their subordinates take bribes? Again, how can institutions provide a good municipal administration if there exists such indifference to the subject that those who would administer honestly and capably cannot be induced to serve, and the duties are left to those who undertake them because they have some private interest to be promoted? Of what avail is the most broadly popular representative system if the electors do not care to choose the best member of parliament, but choose him who will spend most money to be elected? How can a representative assembly work for good if its members can be bought, or if their excitability of temperament, uncorrected by public discipline or private self-control, makes them incapable of calm deliberation, and they resort to manual violence on the floor of the House, or shoot at one another with rifles? How, again, can government, or any joint concern, be carried on in a tolerable manner by people so envious that, if one among them seems likely to succeed in anything, those who ought to cooperate with him form a tacit combination to make him fail? Whenever the general disposition of the people is such that each individual regards those only of his interests which are selfish, and does not dwell on, or concern himself for, his share of the general interest, in such a state of things good government is impossible. The influence of defects of intelligence in obstructing all the elements of good government requires no illustration. Government consists of acts done by human beings; and if the agents, or those who choose the agents, or those to whom the agents are responsible, or the lookers-on whose opinion ought to influence and check all these, are mere masses of ignorance, stupidity, and baleful prejudice, every operation of government will go wrong; while, in proportion as the men rise above this standard, so will the government improve in quality; up to the point of excellence, attainable but nowhere attained, where the officers of government, themselves persons of superior virtue and intellect, are surrounded by the atmosphere of a virtuous and enlightened public opinion.

The first element of good government, therefore, being the virtue and intelligence of the human beings composing the community, the most important point of excellence which any form of government can possess is to promote the virtue and intelligence of the people themselves. The first question in respect to any political institutions is, how far they tend to foster in the members of the community the various desirable qualities, moral and intellectual; or rather (following Bentham's more complete classification) moral, intellectual, and active. The government which does this the best has every likelihood of being the best in all other respects, since it is on these qualities, so far as they exist in the people, that all possibility of goodness in the practical operations of the government depends.

We may consider, then, as one criterion of the goodness of a government, the degree in which it tends to increase the sum of good qualities in the governed, collectively and individually; since, besides that their well-being is the sole object of government, their good qualities supply the moving force which works the machinery. This leaves, as the other constituent element of the merit of a government, the quality of the machinery itself; that is, the degree in which it is adapted to take advantage of the amount of good qualities which may at any time exist, and make them instrumental to the right purposes. Let us again take the subject of judicature as an example

and illustration. The judicial system being given, the goodness of the administration of justice is in the compound ratio of the worth of the men composing the tribunals, and the worth of the public opinion which influences or controls them. But all the difference between a good and a bad system of judicature lies in the contrivances adopted for bringing whatever moral and intellectual worth exists in the community to bear upon the administration of justice, and making it duly operative on the result. The arrangements for rendering the choice of the judges such as to obtain the highest average of virtue and intelligence; the salutary forms of procedure; the publicity which allows observation and criticism of whatever is amiss; the liberty of discussion and censure through the press; the mode of taking evidence, according as it is well or ill adapted to elicit truth; the facilities, whatever be their amount, for obtaining access to the tribunals; the arrangements for detecting crimes and apprehending offenders; —all these things are not the power, but the machinery for bringing the power into contact with the obstacle: and the machinery has no action of itself, but without it the power, let it be ever so ample, would be wasted and of no effect.

A similar distinction exists in regard to the constitution of the executive departments of administration. Their machinery is good, when the proper tests are prescribed for the qualifications of officers, the proper rules for their promotion; when the business is conveniently distributed among those who are to transact it, a convenient and methodical order established for its transaction, a correct and intelligible record kept of it after being transacted; when each individual knows for what he is responsible, and is known to others as responsible for it; when the best-contrived checks are provided against negligence, favouritism, or jobbery, in any of the acts of the department. But political checks will no more act of themselves than a bridle will direct a horse without a rider. If the checking functionaries are as corrupt or as negligent as those whom they ought to check, and if the public, the mainspring of the whole checking machinery, are too ignorant, too passive, or too careless and inattentive, to do their part, little benefit will be derived from the best administrative apparatus. Yet a good apparatus is always preferable to a bad. It enables such insufficient moving or checking power as exists to act at the greatest advantage;

and without it, no amount of moving or checking power would be sufficient. Publicity, for instance, is no impediment to evil nor stimulus to good if the public will not look at what is done; but without publicity, how could they either check or encourage what they were not permitted to see? The ideally perfect constitution of a public office is that in which the interest of the functionary is entirely coincident with his duty. No mere system will make it so, but still less can it be made so without a system, aptly devised for the purpose.

What we have said of the arrangements for the detailed administration of the government is still more evidently true of its general constitution. All government which aims at being good is an organisation of some part of the good qualities existing in the individual members of the community for the conduct of its collective affairs. A representative constitution is a means of bringing the general standard of intelligence and honesty existing in the community, and the individual intellect and virtue of its wisest members, more directly to bear upon the government, and investing them with greater influence in it, than they would in general have under any other mode of organisation; though, under any, such influence as they do have is the source of all good that there is in the government, and the hindrance of every evil that there is not. The greater the amount of these good qualities which the institutions of a country succeed in organising, and the better the mode of organisation, the better will be the government.

We have now, therefore, obtained a foundation for a twofold division of the merit which any set of political institutions can possess. It consists partly of the degree in which they promote the general mental advancement of the community, including under that phrase advancement in intellect, in virtue, and in practical activity and efficiency; and partly of the degree of perfection with which they organise the moral, intellectual, and active worth already existing, so as to operate with the greatest effect on public affairs. A government is to be judged by its action upon men, and by its action upon things; by what it makes of the citizens, and what it does with them; its tendency to improve or deteriorate the people themselves, and the goodness or badness of the work it performs for them, and by means of them. Government is at once a great influence acting on the human mind, and a set of organised arrangements for public business: in the first ca-

pacity its beneficial action is chiefly indirect, but not therefore less vital, while its mischievous action may be direct.

The difference between these two functions of a government is not, like that between Order and Progress, a difference merely in degree, but in kind. We must not, however, suppose that they have no intimate connection with one another. The institutions which ensure the best management of public affairs practicable in the existing state of cultivation tend by this alone to the further improvement of that state. A people which had the most just laws, the purest and most efficient judicature, the most enlightened administration, the most equitable and least onerous system of finance, compatible with the stage it had attained in moral and intellectual advancement, would be in a fair way to pass rapidly into a higher stage. Nor is there any mode in which political institutions can contribute more effectually to the improvement of the people than by doing their more direct work well. And, reversely, if their machinery is so badly constructed that they do their own particular business ill, the effect is felt in a thousand ways in lowering the morality and deadening the intelligence and activity of the people. But the distinction is nevertheless real, because this is only one of the means by which political institutions improve or deteriorate the human mind, and the causes and modes of that beneficial or injurious influence remain a distinct and much wider subject of study.

Of the two modes of operation by which a form of government or set of political institutions affects the welfare of the community—its operation as an agency of national education, and its arrangements for conducting the collective affairs of the community in the state of education in which they already are; the last evidently varies much less, from difference of country and state of civilisation, than the first. It has also much less to do with the fundamental constitution of the government. The mode of conducting the practical business of government, which is best under a free constitution, would generally be best also in an absolute monarchy: only an absolute monarchy is not so likely to practise it. The laws of property, for example; the principles of evidence and judicial procedure; the system of taxation and of financial administration, need not necessarily be different in different forms of government. Each of these matters has principles and rules of its own, which are a subject of separate study. General jurisprudence, civil and penal legislation, financial and commercial policy, are sciences in themselves, or rather, separate members of the comprehensive science or art of government: and the most enlightened doctrines on all these subjects, though not equally likely to be understood, or acted on under all forms of government, yet, if understood and acted on, would in general be equally beneficial under them all. It is true that these doctrines could not be applied without some modifications to all states of society and of the human mind: nevertheless, by far the greater number of them would require modifications solely of details, to adapt them to any state of society sufficiently advanced to possess rulers capable of understanding them. A government to which they would be wholly unsuitable must be one so bad in itself, or so opposed to public feeling, as to be unable to maintain itself in existence by honest means.

It is otherwise with that portion of the interests of the community which relate to the better or worse training of the people themselves. Considered as instrumental to this, institutions need to be radically different, according to the stage of advancement already reached. The recognition of this truth, though for the most part empirically rather than philosophically, may be regarded as the main point of superiority in the political theories of the present above those of the last age; in which it was customary to claim representative democracy for England or France by arguments which would equally have proved it the only fit form of government for Bedouins or Malays. The state of different communities, in point of culture and development, ranges downwards to a condition very little above the highest of the beasts. The upward range, too, is considerable, and the future possible extension vastly greater. A community can only be developed out of one of these states into a higher by a concourse of influences, among the principal of which is the government to which they are subject. In all states of human improvement ever yet attained, the nature and degree of authority exercised over individuals, the distribution of power, and the conditions of command and obedience, are the most powerful of the influences, except their religious belief, which make them what they are, and enable them to become what they can be. They may be stopped short at any point in their progress by defective adaptation of their government to that particular stage of advance-

ment. And the one indispensable merit of a government, in favour of which it may be forgiven almost any amount of other demerit compatible with progress, is that its operation on the people is favourable, or not unfavourable, to the next step which it is necessary for them to take, in order to raise themselves to a higher level.

Thus (to repeat a former example), a people in a state of savage independence, in which every one lives for himself, exempt, unless by fits, from any external control, is practically incapable of making any progress in civilisation until it has learnt to obey. The indispensable virtue, therefore, in a government which establishes itself over a people of this sort is, that it make itself obeyed. To enable it to do this, the constitution of the government must be nearly, or quite, despotic. A constitution in any degree popular, dependent on the voluntary surrender by the different members of the community of their individual freedom of action, would fail to enforce the first lesson which the pupils, in this stage of their progress, require. Accordingly, the civilisation of such tribes, when not the result of juxtaposition with others already civilised, is almost always the work of an absolute ruler, deriving his power either from religion or military prowess; very often from foreign arms.

Again, uncivilised races, and the bravest and most energetic still more than the rest, are averse to continuous labour of an unexciting kind. Yet all real civilisation is at this price; without such labour, neither can the mind be disciplined into the habits required by civilised society, nor the material world prepared to receive it. There needs a rare concurrence of circumstances, and for that reason often a vast length of time, to reconcile such a people to industry, unless they are for a while compelled to it. Hence even personal slavery, by giving a commencement to industrial life, and enforcing it as the exclusive occupation of the most numerous portion of the community, may accelerate the transition to a better freedom than that of fighting and rapine. It is almost needless to say that this excuse for slavery is only available in a very early state of society. A civilised people have far other means of imparting civilisation to those under their influence; and slavery is, in all its details, so repugnant to that government of law, which is the foundation of all modern life, and so corrupting to the master-class when they have once come under civilised influences, that its adoption under any circumstances whatever in modern society is a relapse into worse than barbarism.

At some period, however, of their history, almost every people, now civilised, have consisted, in majority, of slaves. A people in that condition require to raise them out of it a very different polity from a nation of savages. If they are energetic by nature, and especially if there be associated with them in the same community an industrious class who are neither slaves nor slave-owners (as was the case in Greece), they need, probably, no more to ensure their improvement than to make them free: when freed, they may often be fit, like Roman freedmen, to be admitted at once to the full rights of citizenship. This, however, is not the normal condition of slavery, and is generally a sign that it is becoming obsolete. A slave, properly so called, is a being who has not learnt to help himself. He is, no doubt, one step in advance of a savage. He has not the first lesson of political society still to acquire. He has learnt to obey. But what he obeys is only a direct command. It is the characteristic of *born* slaves to be incapable of conforming their conduct to a rule, or law. They can only do what they are ordered, and only when they are ordered to do it. If a man whom they fear is standing over them and threatening them with punishment, they obey; but when his back is turned, the work remains undone. The motive determining them must appeal not to their interests, but to their instincts; immediate hope or immediate terror. A despotism, which may tame the savage, will, in so far as it is a despotism, only confirm the slaves in their incapacities. Yet a government under their own control would be entirely unmanageable by them. Their improvement cannot come from themselves, but must be superinduced from without. The step which they have to take, and their only path to improvement, is to be raised from a government of will to one of law. They have to be taught self-government, and this, in its initial stage, means the capacity to act on general instructions. What they require is not a government of force, but one of guidance. Being, however, in too low a state to yield to the guidance of any but those to whom they look up as the possessors of force, the sort of government fittest for them is one which possesses force, but seldom uses it: a parental despotism or aristocracy, resembling the St. Simonian form of Socialism; maintaining a general superintendence over all the operations of society, so as to keep before each the sense of a present force sufficient to compel his obedience to the rule laid down, but which, owing to the impossibility of descending to regulate all the minutiæ of industry and life, necessarily leaves and induces individuals to do much of themselves. This, which may be termed the government of leading-strings, seems to be the one required to carry such a people the most rapidly through the next necessary step in social progress. Such appears to have been the idea of the government of the Incas of Peru; and such was that of the Jesuits of Paraguay. I need scarcely remark that leading-strings are only admissible as a means of gradually training the people to walk alone.

It would be out of place to carry the illustration further. To attempt to investigate what kind of government is suited to every known state of society would be to compose a treatise, not on representative government, but on political science at large. For our more limited purpose we borrow from political philosophy only its general principles. To determine the form of government most suited to any particular people, we must be able, among the defects and shortcomings which belong to that people, to distinguish those that are the immediate impediment to progress; to discover what it is which (as it were) stops the way. The best government for them is the one which tends most to give them that for want of which they cannot advance, or advance only in a lame and lopsided manner. We must not, however, forget the reservation necessary in all things which have for their object improvement, or Progress; namely, that in seeking the good which is needed, no damage, or as little as possible, be done to that already possessed. A people of savages should be taught obedience, but not in such a manner as to convert them into a people of slaves. And (to give the observation a higher generality) the form of government which is most effectual for carrying a people through the next stage of progress will still be very improper for them if it does this in such a manner as to obstruct, or positively unfit them for, the step next beyond. Such cases are frequent, and are among the most melancholy facts in history. The Egyptian hierarchy, the paternal despotism of China, were very fit instruments for carrying those nations up to the point of civilisation which they attained. But having reached that point, they were brought to a permanent halt for want of mental liberty and individuality; requisites of improvement which the institutions that had carried them thus far entirely incapacitated them from acquiring; and as the institutions did not break down and give place to others, further improvement stopped.

In contrast with these nations, let us consider the example of an opposite character afforded by another and a comparatively insignificant Oriental people—the Jews. They, too, had an absolute monarchy and a hierarchy, and their organised institutions were as obviously of sacerdotal origin as those of the Hindoos. These did for them what was done for other Oriental races by their institutions—subdued them to industry and order, and gave them a national life. But neither their kings nor their priests ever obtained, as in those other countries, the exclusive moulding of their character. Their religion, which enabled persons of genius and a high religious tone to be regarded and to regard themselves as inspired from heaven, gave existence to an inestimably precious unorganised institution—the Order (if it may be so termed) of Prophets. Under the protection, generally though not always effectual, of their sacred character, the Prophets were a power in the nation, often more than a match for kings and priests, and kept up, in that little corner of the earth, the antagonism of influences which is the only real security for continued progress. Religion consequently was not there what it has been in so many other places—a consecration of all that was once established, and a barrier against further improvement. The remark of a distinguished Hebrew, M. Salvador, that the Prophets were, in Church and State, the equivalent of the modern liberty of the press, gives a just but not an adequate conception of the part fulfilled in national and universal history by this great element of Jewish life; by means of which, the canon of inspiration never being complete, the persons most eminent in genius and moral feeling could not only denounce and reprobate, with the direct authority of the Almighty, whatever appeared to them deserving of such treatment, but could give forth better and higher interpretations of the national religion, which thenceforth became part of the religion. Accordingly, whoever can divest himself of the habit of reading the Bible as if it was one book, which until lately was equally inveterate in Christians and in unbelievers, sees with admiration the vast interval between the morality and religion of the Pentateuch, or even of the historical books (the unmistak-

able work of Hebrew Conservatives of the sacerdotal order), and the morality and religion of the Prophecies: a distance as wide as between these last and the Gospels. Conditions more favourable to Progress could not easily exist: accordingly, the Jews, instead of being stationary like other Asiatics, were, next to the Greeks, the most progressive people of antiquity, and, jointly with them, have been the starting-point and main propelling agency of modern cultivation.

It is, then, impossible to understand the question of the adaptation of forms of government to states of society without taking into account not only the next step, but all the steps which society has yet to make; both those which can be foreseen, and the far wider indefinite range which is at present out of sight. It follows, that to judge of the merits of forms of government, an ideal must be constructed of the form of government most eligible in itself, that is, which, if the necessary conditions existed for giving effect to its beneficial tendencies, would, more than all others, favour and promote not some one improvement, but all forms and degrees of it. This having been done, we must consider what are the mental conditions of all sorts, necessary to enable this government to realise its tendencies, and what, therefore, are the various defects by which a people is made incapable of reaping its benefits. It would then be possible to construct a theorem of the circumstances in which that form of government may wisely be introduced; and also to judge, in cases in which it had better not be introduced, what inferior forms of polity will best carry those communities through the intermediate stages which they must traverse before they can become fit for the best form of government.

Of these inquiries, the last does not concern us here; but the first is an essential part of our subject: for we may, without rashness, at once enunciate a proposition, the proofs and illustrations of which will present themselves in the ensuing pages; that this ideally best form of government will be found in some one or other variety of the Representative System.

Chapter 3

That the ideally best Form of Government is Representative Government

IT HAS long (perhaps throughout the entire duration of British freedom) been a common saying, that if a good despot could be ensured, despotic monarchy would be the best form of government. I look upon this as a radical and most pernicious misconception of what good government is; which, until it can be got rid of, will fatally vitiate all our speculations on government.

The supposition is, that absolute power, in the hands of an eminent individual, would ensure a virtuous and intelligent performance of all the duties of government. Good laws would be established and enforced, bad laws would be reformed; the best men would be placed in all situations of trust; justice would be as well administered, the public burthens would be as light and as judiciously imposed, every branch of administration would be as purely and as intelligently conducted, as the circumstances of the country and its degree of intellectual and moral cultivation would admit. I am willing, for the sake of the argument, to concede all this; but I must point out how great the concession is; how much more is needed to produce even an approximation to these results than is conveyed in the simple expression, a good despot. Their realisation would in fact imply, not merely a good monarch, but an all-seeing one. He must be at all times informed correctly, in considerable detail, of the conduct and working of every branch of administration, in every district of the country, and must be able, in the twenty-four hours per day which are all that is granted to a king as to the humblest labourer, to give an effective share of attention and superintendence to all parts of this vast field; or he must at least be capable of discerning and choosing out, from among the mass of his subjects, not only a large abundance of honest and able men, fit to conduct every branch of public administration under supervision and control, but also the small number of men of eminent virtues and talents who can be trusted not only to do without that supervision, but to exercise it themselves over others. So extraordinary are the faculties and energies required for performing this task in any supportable manner, that the good despot whom we are supposing can hardly be imagined as consenting to undertake it, unless as a refuge from intolerable evils, and a transitional preparation for something beyond. But the argument can do without even this immense item in the account. Suppose the difficulty vanquished. What should we then have? One man of superhuman mental activity managing the entire affairs of a mentally passive people. Their passivity is implied in the very idea of absolute power. The nation as a whole, and every individual composing it, are without any potential voice in their own destiny. They exercise no will in respect to their collective interests. All is decided for them by a will not their own, which it is legally a crime for them to disobey.

What sort of human beings can be formed under such a regimen? What development can either their thinking or their active faculties attain under it? On matters of pure theory they might perhaps be allowed to speculate, so long as their speculations either did not approach politics, or had not the remotest connection with its practice. On practical affairs they could at most be only suffered to suggest; and even under the most moderate of despots, none but persons of already admitted or reputed superiority could hope that their suggestions would be known to, much less regarded by, those who had the management of affairs. A person must have a very unusual taste for intellectual exercise in and for itself, who will put himself to the trouble of thought when it is to have no outward effect, or qualify himself for functions which he has no chance of being allowed to exercise. The only sufficient incitement to mental exertion, in any but a few minds in a generation, is the prospect of some practical use to be made of its results. It does not follow that the nation will be wholly destitute of intellectual power. The common business of life, which must necessarily be performed by each individual or family for themselves, will call forth some amount of intelligence and practical ability, within a certain narrow range of ideas. There may be a select class of *savants,* who cultivate science with a view to its physical uses, or for the pleasure of the pursuit. There will be a bureaucracy, and persons in training for the bureaucracy, who will be taught at least some empirical maxims of government and public administration. There may be, and often has been, a systematic organisation of the best mental power in the country in some special direction (commonly military) to promote the grandeur of the despot. But the public at large remain without information and without interest on all greater matters of practice; or, if they have any knowledge of them, it is but a *dilettante* knowledge, like that which people have of the mechanical arts who have never handled a tool.

Nor is it only in their intelligence that they

suffer. Their moral capacities are equally stunted. Wherever the sphere of action of human beings is artificially circumscribed, their sentiments are narrowed and dwarfed in the same proportion. The food of feeling is action: even domestic affection lives upon voluntary good offices. Let a person have nothing to do for his country, and he will not care for it. It has been said of old, that in a despotism there is at most but one patriot, the despot himself; and the saying rests on a just appreciation of the effects of absolute subjection, even to a good and wise master. Religion remains: and here at least, it may be thought, is an agency that may be relied on for lifting men's eyes and minds above the dust at their feet. But religion, even supposing it to escape perversion for the purposes of despotism, ceases in these circumstances to be a social concern, and narrows into a personal affair between an individual and his Maker, in which the issue at stake is but his private salvation. Religion in this shape is quite consistent with the most selfish and contracted egoism, and identifies the votary as little in feeling with the rest of his kind as sensuality itself.

A good despotism means a government in which, so far as depends on the despot, there is no positive oppression by officers of state, but in which all the collective interests of the people are managed for them, all the thinking that has relation to collective interests done for them, and in which their minds are formed by, and consenting to, this abdication of their own energies. Leaving things to the Government, like leaving them to Providence, is synonymous with caring nothing about them, and accepting their results, when disagreeable, as visitations of Nature. With the exception, therefore, of a few studious men who take an intellectual interest in speculation for its own sake, the intelligence and sentiments of the whole people are given up to the material interests, and, when these are provided for, to the amusement and ornamentation, of private life. But to say this is to say, if the whole testimony of history is worth anything, that the era of national decline has arrived: that is, if the nation had ever attained anything to decline from. If it has never risen above the condition of an Oriental people, in that condition it continues to stagnate. But if, like Greece or Rome, it had realised anything higher, through the energy, patriotism, and enlargement of mind, which as national qualities are the fruits solely of freedom, it relapses in a few genera-

tions into the Oriental state. And that state does not mean stupid tranquillity, with security against change for the worse; it often means being overrun, conquered, and reduced to domestic slavery, either by a stronger despot, or by the nearest barbarous people who retain along with their savage rudeness the energies of freedom.

Such are not merely the natural tendencies, but the inherent necessities of despotic government; from which there is no outlet, unless in so far as the despotism consents not to be despotism; in so far as the supposed good despot abstains from exercising his power, and, though holding it in reserve, allows the general business of government to go on as if the people really governed themselves. However little probable it may be, we may imagine a despot observing many of the rules and restraints of constitutional government. He might allow such freedom of the press and of discussion as would enable a public opinion to form and express itself on national affairs. He might suffer local interests to be managed, without the interference of authority, by the people themselves. He might even surround himself with a council or councils of government, freely chosen by the whole or some portion of the nation; retaining in his own hands the power of taxation, and the supreme legislative as well as executive authority. Were he to act thus, and so far abdicate as a despot, he would do away with a considerable part of the evils characteristic of despotism. Political activity and capacity for public affairs would no longer be prevented from growing up in the body of the nation; and a public opinion would form itself not the mere echo of the government. But such improvement would be the beginning of new difficulties. This public opinion, independent of the monarch's dictation, must be either with him or against him; if not the one, it will be the other. All governments must displease many persons, and these having now regular organs, and being able to express their sentiments, opinions adverse to the measures of government would often be expressed. What is the monarch to do when these unfavourable opinions happen to be in the majority? Is he to alter his course? Is he to defer to the nation? If so, he is no longer a despot, but a constitutional king; an organ or first minister of the people, distinguished only by being irremovable. If not, he must either put down opposition by his despotic power, or there will arise a permanent antagonism between the people and one man, which can have but one possible ending. Not even a religious principle of passive obedience and "right divine" would long ward off the natural consequences of such a position. The monarch would have to succumb, and conform to the conditions of constitutional royalty, or give place to some one who would. The despotism, being thus chiefly nominal, would possess few of the advantages supposed to belong to absolute monarchy; while it would realise in a very imperfect degree those of a free government; since however great an amount of liberty the citizens might practically enjoy, they could never forget that they held it on sufferance, and by a concession which under the existing constitution of the state might at any moment be resumed; that they were legally slaves, though of a prudent, or indulgent, master.

It is not much to be wondered at if impatient or disappointed reformers, groaning under the impediments opposed to the most salutary public improvements by the ignorance, the indifference, the intractableness, the perverse obstinacy of a people, and the corrupt combinations of selfish private interests armed with the powerful weapons afforded by free institutions, should at times sigh for a strong hand to bear down all these obstacles, and compel a recalcitrant people to be better governed. But (setting aside the fact, that for one despot who now and then reforms an abuse, there are ninety-nine who do nothing but create them) those who look in any such direction for the realisation of their hopes leave out of the idea of good government its principal element, the improvement of the people themselves. One of the benefits of freedom is that under it the ruler cannot pass by the people's minds, and amend their affairs for them without amending them. If it were possible for the people to be well governed in spite of themselves, their good government would last no longer than the freedom of a people usually lasts who have been liberated by foreign arms without their own co-operation. It is true, a despot may educate the people; and to do so really, would be the best apology for his despotism. But any education which aims at making human beings other than machines, in the long run makes them claim to have the control of their own actions. The leaders of French philosophy in the eighteenth century had been educated by the Jesuits. Even Jesuit education, it seems, was sufficiently real to call forth the appetite for freedom. Whatever invigorates the faculties, in however small a measure, creates an increased desire for their more unimpeded exercise; and a popular education is a failure, if it educates the people for any state but that which it will certainly induce them to desire, and most probably to demand.

I am far from condemning, in cases of extreme exigency, the assumption of absolute power in the form of a temporary dictatorship. Free nations have, in times of old, conferred such power by their own choice, as a necessary medicine for diseases of the body politic which could not be got rid of by less violent means. But its acceptance, even for a time strictly limited, can only be excused, if, like Solon or Pittacus, the dictator employs the whole power he assumes in removing the obstacles which debar the nation from the enjoyment of freedom. A good despotism is an altogether false ideal, which practically (except as a means to some temporary purpose) becomes the most senseless and dangerous of chimeras. Evil for evil, a good despotism, in a country at all advanced in civilisation, is more noxious than a bad one; for it is far more relaxing and enervating to the thoughts, feelings, and energies of the people. The despotism of Augustus prepared the Romans for Tiberius. If the whole tone of their character had not first been prostrated by nearly two generations of that mild slavery, they would probably have had spirit enough left to rebel against the more odious one.

There is no difficulty in showing that the ideally best form of government is that in which the sovereignty, or supreme controlling power in the last resort, is vested in the entire aggregate of the community; every citizen not only having a voice in the exercise of that ultimate sovereignty, but being, at least occasionally, called on to take an actual part in the government, by the personal discharge of some public function, local or general.

To test this proposition, it has to be examined in reference to the two branches into which, as pointed out in the last chapter, the inquiry into the goodness of a government conveniently divides itself, namely, how far it promotes the good management of the affairs of society by means of the existing faculties, moral, intellectual, and active, of its various members, and what is its effect in improving or deteriorating those faculties.

The ideally best form of government, it is

scarcely necessary to say, does not mean one which is practicable or eligible in all states of civilisation, but the one which, in the circumstances in which it is practicable and eligible, is attended with the greatest amount of beneficial consequences, immediate and prospective. A completely popular government is the only polity which can make out any claim to this character. It is pre-eminent in both the departments between which the excellence of a political constitution is divided. It is both more favourable to present good government, and promotes a better and higher form of national character, than any other polity whatsoever.

Its superiority in reference to present wellbeing rests upon two principles, of as universal truth and applicability as any general propositions which can be laid down respecting human affairs. The first is, that the rights and interests of every or any person are only secure from being disregarded when the person interested is himself able, and habitually disposed, to stand up for them. The second is, that the general prosperity attains a greater height, and is more widely diffused, in proportion to the amount and variety of the personal energies enlisted in promoting it.

Putting these two propositions into a shape more special to their present application; human beings are only secure from evil at the hands of others in proportion as they have the power of being, and are, self-*protecting;* and they only achieve a high degree of success in their struggle with Nature in proportion as they are self-*dependent,* relying on what they themselves can do, either separately or in concert, rather than on what others do for them.

The former proposition—that each is the only safe guardian of his own rights and interests—is one of those elementary maxims of prudence, which every person, capable of conducting his own affairs, implicitly acts upon, wherever he himself is interested. Many, indeed, have a great dislike to it as a political doctrine, and are fond of holding it up to obloquy, as a doctrine of universal selfishness. To which we may answer, that whenever it ceases to be true that mankind, as a rule, prefer themselves to others, and those nearest to them to those more remote, from that moment Communism is not only practicable, but the only defensible form of society; and will, when that time arrives, be assuredly carried into effect. For my own part, not believing in universal selfishness, I have no difficulty in admitting that Communism would even now be practicable among the *élite* of mankind, and may become so among the rest. But as this opinion is anything but popular with those defenders of existing institutions who find fault with the doctrine of the general predominance of self-interest, I am inclined to think they do in reality believe that most men consider themselves before other people. It is not, however, necessary to affirm even thus much in order to support the claim of all to participate in the sovereign power. We need not suppose that when power resides in an exclusive class, that class will knowingly and deliberately sacrifice the other classes to themselves: it suffices that, in the absence of its natural defenders, the interest of the excluded is always in danger of being overlooked; and, when looked at, is seen with very different eyes from those of the persons whom it directly concerns.

In this country, for example, what are called the working classes may be considered as excluded from all direct participation in the government. I do not believe that the classes who do participate in it have in general any intention of sacrificing the working classes to themselves. They once had that intention; witness the persevering attempts so long made to keep down wages by law. But in the present day their ordinary disposition is the very opposite: they willingly make considerable sacrifices, especially of their pecuniary interest, for the benefit of the working classes, and err rather by too lavish and indiscriminating beneficence; nor do I believe that any rulers in history have been actuated by a more sincere desire to do their duty towards the poorer portion of their countrymen. Yet does Parliament, or almost any of the members composing it, ever for an instant look at any question with the eyes of a working man? When a subject arises in which the labourers as such have an interest, is it regarded from any point of view but that of the employers of labour? I do not say that the working men's view of these questions is in general nearer to the truth than the other: but it is sometimes quite as near; and in any case it ought to be respectfully listened to, instead of being, as it is, not merely turned away from, but ignored. On the question of strikes, for instance, it is doubtful if there is so much as one among the leading members of either House who is not firmly convinced that the reason of the matter is unqualifiedly on the side of the masters, and that the men's view of it is simply absurd. Those who have studied the question know well how far this is from being the case; and in how different, and how infinitely less superficial a manner the point would have to be argued, if the classes who strike were able to make themselves heard in Parliament.

It is an adherent condition of human affairs that no intention, however sincere, of protecting the interests of others can make it safe or salutary to tie up their own hands. Still more obviously true is it, that by their own hands only can any positive and durable improvement of their circumstances in life be worked out. Through the joint influence of these two principles, all free communities have both been more exempt from social injustice and crime, and have attained more brilliant prosperity, than any others, or than they themselves after they lost their freedom. Contrast the free states of the world, while their freedom lasted, with the cotemporary subjects of monarchical or oligarchical despotism: the Greek cities with the Persian satrapies; the Italian republics and the free towns of Flanders and Germany, with the feudal monarchies of Europe; Switzerland, Holland, and England, with Austria or anterevolutionary France. Their superior prosperity was too obvious ever to have been gainsaid: while their superiority in good government and social relations is proved by the prosperity, and is manifest besides in every page of history. If we compare, not one age with another, but the different governments which co-existed in the same age, no amount of disorder which exaggeration itself can pretend to have existed amidst the publicity of the free states can be compared for a moment with the contemptuous trampling upon the mass of the people which pervaded the whole life of the monarchical countries, or the disgusting individual tyranny which was of more than daily occurrence under the systems of plunder which they called fiscal arrangements, and in the secrecy of their frightful courts of justice.

It must be acknowledged that the benefits of freedom, so far as they have hitherto been enjoyed, were obtained by the extension of its privileges to a part only of the community; and that a government in which they are extended impartially to all is a desideratum still unrealised. But though every approach to this has an independent value, and in many cases more than an approach could not, in the existing state of general improvement, be made, the participation of all in these benefits is the ideally perfect conception of free government.

In proportion as any, no matter who, are excluded from it, the interests of the excluded are left without the guarantee accorded to the rest, and they themselves have less scope and encouragement than they might otherwise have to that exertion of their energies for the good of themselves and of the community, to which the general prosperity is always proportioned.

Thus stands the case as regards present well-being; the good management of the affairs of the existing generation. If we now pass to the influence of the form of government upon character, we shall find the superiority of popular government over every other to be, if possible, still more decided and indisputable.

This question really depends upon a still more fundamental one, viz., which of two common types of character, for the general good of humanity, it is most desirable should predominate—the active, or the passive type; that which struggles against evils, or that which endures them; that which bends to circumstances, or that which endeavours to make circumstances bend to itself.

The commonplaces of moralists, and the general sympathies of mankind, are in favour of the passive type. Energetic characters may be admired, but the acquiescent and submissive are those which most men personally prefer. The passiveness of our neighbours increases our sense of security, and plays into the hands of our wilfulness. Passive characters, if we do not happen to need their activity, seem an obstruction the less in our own path. A contented character is not a dangerous rival. Yet nothing is more certain than that improvement in human affairs is wholly the work of the uncontented characters; and, moreover, that it is much easier for an active mind to acquire the virtues of patience than for a passive one to assume those of energy.

Of the three varieties of mental excellence, intellectual, practical, and moral, there never could be any doubt in regard to the first two which side had the advantage. All intellectual superiority is the fruit of active effort. Enterprise, the desire to keep moving, to be trying and accomplishing new things for our own benefit or that of others, is the parent even of speculative, and much more of practical, talent. The intellectual culture compatible with the other type is of that feeble and vague description which belongs to a mind that stops at amusement, or at simple contemplation. The test of real and vigourous thinking, the thinking which ascertains truths instead of dreaming dreams, is successful application to practice. Where that purpose does not exist, to give definiteness, precision, and an intelligible meaning to thought, it generates nothing better than the mystical metaphysics of the Pythagoreans or the Vedas. With respect to practical improvement, the case is still more evident. The character which improves human life is that which struggles with natural powers and tendencies, not that which gives way to them. The self-benefiting qualities are all on the side of the active and energetic character: and the habits and conduct which promote the advantage of each individual member of the community must be at least a part of those which conduce most in the end to the advancement of the community as a whole.

But on the point of moral preferability, there seems at first sight to be room for doubt. I am not referring to the religious feeling which has so generally existed in favour of the inactive character, as being more in harmony with the submission due to the divine will. Christianity as well as other religions has fostered this sentiment; but it is the prerogative of Christianity, as regards this and many other perversions, that it is able to throw them off. Abstractedly from religious considerations, a passive character, which yields to obstacles instead of striving to overcome them, may not indeed be very useful to others, no more than to itself, but it might be expected to be at least inoffensive. Contentment is always counted among the moral virtues. But it is a complete error to suppose that contentment is necessarily or naturally attendant on passivity of character; and useless it is, the moral consequences are mischievous. Where there exists a desire for advantages not possessed, the mind which does not potentially possess them by means of its own energies is apt to look with hatred and malice on those who do. The person bestirring himself with hopeful prospects to improve his circumstances is the one who feels good-will towards others engaged in, or who have succeeded in, the same pursuit. And where the majority are so engaged, those who do not attain the object have had the tone given to their feelings by the general habit of the country, and ascribe their failure to want of effort or opportunity, or to their personal ill luck. But those who, while desiring what others possess, put no energy into striving for it, are either incessantly grumbling that fortune does not do for them what they do not attempt to do for themselves, or overflowing with envy and ill-will towards those who possess what they would like to have.

In proportion as success in life is seen or believed to be the fruit of fatality or accident, and not of exertion, in that same ratio does envy develop itself as a point of national character. The most envious of all mankind are the Orientals. In Oriental moralists, in Oriental tales, the envious man is remarkably prominent. In real life, he is the terror of all who possess anything desirable, be it a palace, a handsome child, or even good health and spirits: the supposed effect of his mere look constitutes the all-pervading superstition of the evil eye. Next to Orientals in envy, as in activity, are some of the Southern Europeans. The Spaniards pursued all their great men with it, embittered their lives, and generally succeeded in putting an early stop to their successes.[1] With the French, who are essentially a southern people, the double education of despotism and Catholicism has, in spite of their impulsive temperament, made submission and endurance the common character of the people, and their most received notion of wisdom and excellence: and if envy of one another, and of all superiority, is not more rife among them than it is, the circumstance must be ascribed to the many valuable counteracting elements in the French character, and most of all to the great individual energy which, though less persistent and more intermittent than in the self-helping and struggling Anglo-Saxons, has nevertheless manifested itself among the French in nearly every direction in which the operation of their institutions has been favourable to it.

There are, no doubt, in all countries, really contented characters, who not merely do not seek, but do not desire, what they do not already possess, and these naturally bear no ill-will towards such as have apparently a more favoured lot. But the great mass of seeming contentment is real discontent, combined with indolence or self-indulgence, which, while taking no legitimate means of raising itself, delights in bringing others down to its own level. And if we look narrowly even at the cases of

[1] I limit the expression to past time, because I would say nothing derogatory of a great, and now at last a free, people, who are entering into the general movement of European progress with a vigour which bids fair to make up rapidly the ground they have lost. No one can doubt what Spanish intellect and energy are capable of; and their faults as a people are chiefly those for which freedom and industrial ardour are a real specific.

innocent contentment, we perceive that they only win our admiration when the indifference is solely to improvement in outward circumstances, and there is a striving for perpetual advancement in spiritual worth, or at least a disinterested zeal to benefit others. The contented man, or the contented family, who have no ambition to make any one else happier, to promote the good of their country or their neighbourhood, or to improve themselves in moral excellence, excite in us neither admiration nor approval. We rightly ascribe this sort of contentment to mere unmanliness and want of spirit. The content which we approve is an ability to do cheerfully without what cannot be had, a just appreciation of the comparative value of different objects of desire, and a willing renunciation of the less when incompatible with the greater. These, however, are excellences more natural to the character, in proportion as it is actively engaged in the attempt to improve its own or some other lot. He who is continually measuring his energy against difficulties learns what are the difficulties insuperable to him, and what are those which, though he might overcome, the success is not worth the cost. He whose thoughts and activities are all needed for, and habitually employed in, practicable and useful enterprises, is the person of all others least likely to let his mind dwell with brooding discontent upon things either not worth attaining, or which are not so to him. Thus the active, self-helping character is not only intrinsically the best, but is the likeliest to acquire all that is really excellent or desirable in the opposite type

The striving, go-ahead character of England and the United States is only a fit subject of disapproving criticism on account of the very secondary objects on which it commonly expends its strength. In itself it is the foundation of the best hopes for the general improvement of mankind. It has been acutely remarked that whenever anything goes amiss the habitual impulse of French people is to say, "Il faut de la patience"; and of English people, "What a shame." The people who think it a shame when anything goes wrong—who rush to the conclusion that the evil could and ought to have been prevented, are those who, in the long run, do most to make the world better. If the desires are low placed, if they extend to little beyond physical comfort, and the show of riches, the immediate results of the energy will not be much more than the continual extension of man's power over material objects;

but even this makes room, and prepares the mechanical appliances, for the greatest intellectual and social achievements; and while the energy is there, some persons will apply it, and it will be applied more and more, to the perfecting not of outward circumstances alone, but of man's inward nature. Inactivity, unaspiringness, absence of desire, are a more fatal hindrance to improvement than any misdirection of energy; and are that through which alone, when existing in the mass, any very formidable misdirection by an energetic few becomes possible. It is this, mainly, which retains in a savage or semi-savage state the great majority of the human race.

Now there can be no kind of doubt that the passive type of character is favoured by the government of one or a few, and the active self-helping type by that of the Many. Irresponsible rulers need the quiescence of the ruled more than they need any activity but that which they can compel. Submissiveness to the prescriptions of men as necessities of nature is the lesson inculcated by all governments upon those who are wholly without participation in them. The will of superiors, and the law as the will of superiors, must be passively yielded to. But no men are mere instruments or materials in the hands of their rulers who have will or spirit or a spring of internal activity in the rest of their proceedings: and any manifestation of these qualities, instead of receiving encouragement from despots, has to get itself forgiven by them. Even when irresponsible rulers are not sufficiently conscious of danger from the mental activity of their subjects to be desirous of repressing it, the position itself is a repression. Endeavour is even more effectually restrained by the certainty of its impotence than by any positive discouragement. Between subjection to the will of others, and the virtues of self-help and self-government, there is a natural incompatibility. This is more or less complete, according as the bondage is strained or relaxed. Rulers differ very much in the length to which they carry the control of the free agency of their subjects, or the supersession of it by managing their business for them. But the difference is in degree, not in principle; and the best despots often go the greatest lengths in chaining up the free agency of their subjects. A bad despot, when his own personal indulgences have been provided for, may sometimes be willing to let the people alone; but a good despot insists on doing them good, by making them do their own business in a better way than they themselves know of. The regulations which restricted to fixed processes all the leading branches of French manufactures were the work of the great Colbert.

Very different is the state of the human faculties where a human being feels himself under no other external restraint than the necessities of nature, or mandates of society which he has his share in imposing, and which it is open to him, if he thinks them wrong, publicly to dissent from, and exert himself actively to get altered. No doubt, under a government partially popular, this freedom may be exercised even by those who are not partakers in the full privileges of citizenship. But it is a great additional stimulus to any one's self-help and self-reliance when he starts from even ground, and has not to feel that his success depends on the impression he can make upon the sentiments and dispositions of a body of whom he is not one. It is a great discouragement to an individual, and a still greater one to a class, to be left out of the constitution; to be reduced to plead from outside the door to the arbiters of their destiny, not taken into consultation within. The maximum of the invigorating effect of freedom upon the character is only obtained when the person acted on either is, or is looking forward to becoming, a citizen as fully privileged as any other.

What is still more important than even this matter of feeling is the practical discipline which the character obtains from the occasional demand made upon the citizens to exercise, for a time and in their turn, some social function. It is not sufficiently considered how little there is in most men's ordinary life to give any largeness either to their conceptions or to their sentiments. Their work is a routine; not a labour of love, but of self-interest in the most elementary form, the satisfaction of daily wants; neither the thing done, nor the process of doing it, introduces the mind to thoughts or feelings extending beyond individuals; if instructive books are within their reach, there is no stimulus to read them; and in most cases the individual has no access to any person of cultivation much superior to his own. Giving him something to do for the public, supplies, in a measure, all these deficiencies. If circumstances allow the amount of public duty assigned him to be considerable, it makes him an educated man. Notwithstanding the defects of the social system and moral ideas of antiquity, the practice of the dicastery and the ecclesia raised the intellectual standard of an average Athenian citizen far beyond anything of which there is yet an example in any other mass of men, ancient or modern. The proofs of this are apparent in every page of our great historian of Greece; but we need scarcely look further than to the high quality of the addresses which their great orators deemed best calculated to act with effect on their understanding and will. A benefit of the same kind, though far less in degree, is produced on Englishmen of the lower middle class by their liability to be placed on juries and to serve parish offices; which, though it does not occur to so many, nor is so continuous, nor introduces them to so great a variety of elevated considerations, as to admit of comparison with the public education which every citizen of Athens obtained from her democratic institutions, must make them nevertheless very different beings, in range of ideas and development of faculties, from those who have done nothing in their lives but drive a quill, or sell goods over a counter.

Still more salutary is the moral part of the instruction afforded by the participation of the private citizen, if even rarely, in public functions. He is called upon, while so engaged, to weigh interests not his own; to be guided, in case of conflicting claims, by another rule than his private partialities; to apply, at every turn, principles and maxims which have for their reason of existence the common good: and he usually finds associated with him in the same work minds more familiarised than his own with these ideas and operations, whose study it will be to supply reasons to his understanding, and stimulation to his feeling for the general interest. He is made to feel himself one of the public, and whatever is for their benefit to be for his benefit. Where this school of public spirit does not exist, scarcely any sense is entertained that private persons, in no eminent social situation, owe any duties to society, except to obey the laws and submit to the government. There is no unselfish sentiment of identification with the public. Every thought or feeling, either of interest or of duty, is absorbed in the individual and in the family. The man never thinks of any collective interest, of any objects to be pursued jointly with others, but only in competition with them, and in some measure at their expense. A neighbour, not being an ally or an associate, since he is never engaged in any common undertaking for joint benefit, is therefore only a rival. Thus even private morality suffers, while public is actually extinct. Were this the universal and only possible state of things, the utmost aspirations of the lawgiver or the moralist could only stretch to make the bulk of the community a flock of sheep innocently nibbling the grass side by side.

From these accumulated considerations it is evident that the only government which can fully satisfy all the exigencies of the social state is one in which the whole people participate; that any participation, even in the smallest public function, is useful; that the participation should everywhere be as great as the general degree of improvement of the community will allow; and that nothing less can be ultimately desirable than the admission of all to a share in the sovereign power of the state. But since all cannot, in a community exceeding a single small town, participate personally in any but some very minor portions of the public business, it follows that the ideal type of a perfect government must be representative.

Chapter 4
Under what Social Conditions Representative Government is Inapplicable

WE HAVE recognised in representative government the ideal type of the most perfect polity, for which, in consequence, any portion of mankind are better adapted in proportion to their degree of general improvement. As they range lower and lower in development, that form of government will be, generally speaking, less suitable to them; though this is not true universally: for the adaptation of a people to representative government does not depend so much upon the place they occupy in the general scale of humanity as upon the degree in which they possess certain special requisites; requisites, however, so closely connected with their degree of general advancement, that any variation between the two is rather the exception than the rule. Let us examine at what point in the descending series representative government ceases altogether to be admissible, either through its own unfitness, or the superior fitness of some other regimen.

First, then, representative, like any other government, must be unsuitable in any case in which it cannot permanently subsist—*i.e.* in which it does not fulfil the three fundamental conditions enumerated in the first chapter. These were—1. That the people should be willing to receive it. 2. That they should be willing

and able to do what is necessary for its preservation. 3. That they should be willing and able to fulfil the duties and discharge the functions which it imposes on them.

The willingness of the people to accept representative government only becomes a practical question when an enlightened ruler, or a foreign nation or nations who have gained power over the country, are disposed to offer it the boon. To individual reformers the question is almost irrelevant, since, if no other objection can be made to their enterprise than that the opinion of the nation is not yet on their side, they have the ready and proper answer, that to bring it over to their side is the very end they aim at. When opinion is really adverse, its hostility is usually to the fact of change, rather than to representative government in itself. The contrary case is not indeed unexampled; there has sometimes been a religious repugnance to any limitation of the power of a particular line of rulers; but, in general, the doctrine of passive obedience meant only submission to the will of the powers that be, whether monarchical or popular. In any case in which the attempt to introduce representative government is at all likely to be made, indifference to it, and inability to understand its processes and requirements, rather than positive opposition, are the obstacles to be expected. These, however, are as fatal, and may be as hard to be got rid of, as actual aversion; it being easier, in most cases, to change the direction of an active feeling, than to create one in a state previously passive. When a people have no sufficient value for, and attachment to, a representative constitution, they have next to no chance of retaining it. In every country, the executive is the branch of the government which wields the immediate power, and is in direct contact with the public; to it, principally, the hopes and fears of individuals are directed, and by it both the benefits, and the terrors and *prestige*, of government are mainly represented to the public eye. Unless, therefore, the authorities whose office it is to check the executive are backed by an effective opinion and feeling in the country, the executive has always the means of setting them aside, or compelling them to subservience, and is sure to be well supported in doing so. Representative institutions necessarily depend for permanence upon the readiness of the people to fight for them in case of their being endangered. If too little valued for this, they seldom obtain a footing at all, and if they do, are almost sure to be overthrown, as soon as the head of the government, or any party leader who can muster force for a *coup de main,* is willing to run some small risk for absolute power.

These considerations relate to the first two causes of failure in a representative government. The third is, when the people want either the will or the capacity to fulfil the part which belongs to them in a representative constitution. When nobody, or only some small fraction, feels the degree of interest in the general affairs of the State necessary to the formation of a public opinion, the electors will seldom make any use of the right of suffrage but to serve their private interest, or the interest of their locality, or of some one with whom they are connected as adherents or dependents. The small class who, in this state of public feeling, gain the command of the representative body, for the most part use it solely as a means of seeking their fortune. If the executive is weak, the country is distracted by mere struggles for place; if strong, it makes itself despotic, at the cheap price of appeasing the representatives, or such of them as are capable of giving trouble, by a share of the spoil; and the only fruit produced by national representation is, that in addition to those who really govern, there is an assembly quartered on the public, and no abuse in which a portion of the assembly are interested is at all likely to be removed. When, however, the evil stops here, the price may be worth paying, for the publicity and discussion which, though not an invariable, are a natural accompaniment of any, even nominal, representation. In the modern Kingdom of Greece, for example,[1] it can hardly be doubted, that the placehunters who chiefly compose the representative assembly, though they contribute little or nothing directly to good government, nor even much temper the arbitrary power of the executive, yet keep up the idea of popular rights, and conduce greatly to the real liberty of the press which exists in that country. This benefit, however, is entirely dependent on the co-existence with the popular body of an hereditary king. If, instead of struggling for the favours of the chief ruler, these selfish and sordid factions struggled for the chief place itself, they would

[1] Written before the salutary revolution of 1862, which, provoked by popular disgust at the system of governing by corruption, and the general demoralisation of political men, has opened to that rapidly improving people a new and hopeful chance of real constitutional government.

certainly, as in Spanish America, keep the country in a state of chronic revolution and civil war. A despotism, not even legal, but of illegal violence, would be alternately exercised by a succession of political adventurers, and the name and forms of representation would have no effect but to prevent despotism from attaining the stability and security by which alone its evils can be mitigated, or its few advantages realised.

The preceding are the cases in which representative government cannot permanently exist. There are others in which it possibly might exist, but in which some other form of government would be preferable. These are principally when the people, in order to advance in civilisation, have some lesson to learn, some habit not yet acquired, to the acquisition of which representative government is likely to be an impediment.

The most obvious of these cases is the one already considered, in which the people have still to learn the first lesson of civilisation, that of obedience. A race who have been trained in energy and courage by struggles with Nature and their neighbours, but who have not yet settled down into permanent obedience to any common superior, would be little likely to acquire this habit under the collective government of their own body. A representative assembly drawn from among themselves would simply reflect their own turbulent insubordination. It would refuse its authority to all proceedings which would impose, on their savage independence, any improving restraint. The mode in which such tribes are usually brought to submit to the primary conditions of civilised society is through the necessities of warfare, and the despotic authority indispensable to military command. A military leader is the only superior to whom they will submit, except occasionally some prophet supposed to be inspired from above, or conjurer regarded as possessing miraculous power. These may exercise a temporary ascendancy, but as it is merely personal, it rarely effects any change in the general habits of the people, unless the prophet, like Mahomet, is also a military chief, and goes forth the armed apostle of a new religion; or unless the military chiefs ally themselves with his influence, and turn it into a prop for their own government.

A people are no less unfitted for representative government by the contrary fault to that last specified; by extreme passiveness, and ready submission to tyranny. If a people thus prostrated by character and circumstances could obtain representative institutions, they would inevitably choose their tyrants as their representatives, and the yoke would be made heavier on them by the contrivance which *prima facie* might be expected to lighten it. On the contrary, many a people has gradually emerged from this condition by the aid of a central authority, whose position has made it the rival, and has ended by making it the master, of the local despots, and which, above all, has been single. French history, from Hugh Capet to Richelieu and Louis XIV., is a continued example of this course of things. Even when the King was scarcely so powerful as many of his chief feudatories, the great advantage which he derived from being but one has been recognised by French historians. To him the eyes of *all* the locally oppressed were turned; he was the object of hope and reliance throughout the kingdom; while each local potentate was only powerful within a more or less confined space. At his hands, refuge and protection were sought from every part of the country, against first one, then another, of the immediate oppressors. His progress to ascendancy was slow; but it resulted from successively taking advantage of opportunities which offered themselves only to him. It was, therefore, sure; and, in proportion as it was accomplished, it abated, in the oppressed portion of the community, the habit of submitting to oppression. The king's interest lay in encouraging all partial attempts on the part of the serfs to emancipate themselves from their masters, and place themselves in immediate subordination to himself. Under his protection numerous communities were formed which knew no one above them but the King. Obedience to a distant monarch is liberty itself compared with the dominion of the lord of the neighbouring castle: and the monarch was long compelled by necessities of position to exert his authority as the ally, rather than the master, of the classes whom he had aided in affecting their liberation. In this manner a central power, despotic in principle though generally much restricted in practice, was mainly instrumental in carrying the people through a necessary stage of improvement, which representative government, if real, would most likely have prevented them from entering upon. Nothing short of despotic rule, or a general massacre, could have effected the emancipation of the serfs in the Russian Empire.

The same passages of history forcibly illustrate another mode in which unlimited monarchy overcomes obstacles to the progress of civilisation which representative government would have had a decided tendency to aggravate. One of the strongest hindrances to improvement, up to a rather advanced stage, is an inveterate spirit of locality. Portions of mankind, in many other respects capable of, and prepared for, freedom, may be unqualified for amalgamating into even the smallest nation. Not only may jealousies and antipathies repel them from one another, and bar all possibility of voluntary union, but they may not yet have acquired any of the feelings or habits which would make the union real, supposing it to be nominally accomplished. They may, like the citizens of an ancient community, or those of an Asiatic village, have had considerable practice in exercising their faculties on village or town interests, and have even realised a tolerably effective popular government on that restricted scale, and may yet have but slender sympathies with anything beyond, and no habit or capacity of dealing with interests common to many such communities.

I am not aware that history furnishes any example in which a number of these political atoms or corpuscles have coalesced into a body, and learnt to feel themselves one people, except through previous subjection to a central authority common to all.[1] It is through the habit of deferring to that authority, entering into its plans and subserving its purposes, that a people such as we have supposed receive into their minds the conception of large interests, common to a considerable geographical extent. Such interests, on the contrary, are necessarily the predominant consideration in the mind of the central ruler; and through the relations, more or less intimate, which he progressively establishes with the localities, they become familiar to the general mind. The most favourable concurrence of circumstances under which this step in improvement could be made, would be one which should raise up representative institutions without representative government; a representative body, or bodies, drawn from the localities, making itself the auxiliary and instrument of the central power, but seldom attempting to thwart or

[1] Italy, which alone can be quoted as an exception, is only so in regard to the final stage of its transformation. The more difficult previous advance from the city isolation of Florence, Pisa, or Milan, to the provincial unity of Tuscany or Lombardy, took place in the usual manner.

control it. The people being thus taken, as it were, into council, though not sharing the supreme power, the political education given by the central authority is carried home, much more effectually than it could otherwise be, to the local chiefs and to the population generally; while, at the same time, a tradition is kept up of government by general consent, or at least, the sanction of tradition is not given to government without it, which, when consecrated by custom, has so often put a bad end to a good beginning, and is one of the most frequent causes of the sad fatality which in most countries has stopped improvement in so early a stage, because the work of some one period has been so done as to bar the needful work of the ages following. Meanwhile, it may be laid down as a political truth, that by irresponsible monarchy rather than by representative government can a multitude of insignificant political units be welded into a people, with common feelings of cohesion, power enough to protect itself against conquest or foreign aggression, and affairs sufficiently various and considerable of its own to occupy worthily and expand to fit proportions the social and political intelligence of the population.

For these several reasons, kingly government, free from the control (though perhaps strengthened by the support) of representative institutions, is the most suitable form of polity for the earliest stages of any community, not excepting a city-community like those of ancient Greece: where, accordingly, the government of kings, under some real but no ostensible or constitutional control by public opinion, did historically precede by an unknown and probably great duration all free institutions, and gave place at last, during a considerable lapse of time, to oligarchies of a few families.

A hundred other infirmities or short-comings in a people might be pointed out, which *pro tanto* disqualify them from making the best use of representative government; but in regard to these it is not equally obvious that the government of One or a Few would have any tendency to cure or alleviate the evil. Strong prejudices of any kind; obstinate adherence to old habits; positive defects of national character, or mere ignorance, and deficiency of mental cultivation, if prevalent in a people, will be in general faithfully reflected in their representative assemblies: and should it happen that the executive administration, the direct management of public affairs, is in the hands of persons comparatively free from

these defects, more good would frequently be done by them when not hampered by the necessity of carrying with them the voluntary assent of such bodies. But the mere position of the rulers does not in these, as it does in the other cases which we have examined, of itself invest them with interests and tendencies operating in the beneficial direction. From the general weaknesses of the people or of the state of civilisation, the One and his counsellors, or the Few, are not likely to be habitually exempt; except in the case of their being foreigners, belonging to a superior people or a more advanced state of society. Then, indeed, the rulers may be, to almost any extent, superior in civilisation to those over whom they rule; and subjection to a foreign government of this description, notwithstanding its inevitable evils, is often of the greatest advantage to a people, carrying them rapidly through several stages of progress, and clearing away obstacles to improvement which might have lasted indefinitely if the subject population had been left unassisted to its native tendencies and chances. In a country not under the dominion of foreigners, the only cause adequate to producing similar benefits is the rare accident of a monarch of extraordinary genius. There have been in history a few of these, who, happily for humanity, have reigned long enough to render some of their improvements permanent, by leaving them under the guardianship of a generation which had grown up under their influence. Charlemagne may be cited as one instance; Peter the Great is another. Such examples however are so unfrequent that they can only be classed with the happy accidents which have so often decided at a critical moment whether some leading portion of humanity should make a sudden start, or sink back towards barbarism: chances like the existence of Themistocles at the time of the Persian invasion, or of the first or third William of Orange.

It would be absurd to construct institutions for the mere purpose of taking advantage of such possibilities; especially as men of this calibre, in any distinguished position, do not require despotic power to enable them to exert great influence, as is evidenced by the three last mentioned. The case most requiring consideration in reference to institutions is the not very uncommon one in which a small but leading portion of the population, from difference of race, more civilised origin, or other peculiarities of circumstance, are markedly superior in civilisation and general character to the remainder. Under those conditions, government by the representatives of the mass would stand a chance of depriving them of much of the benefit they might derive from the greater civilisation of the superior ranks; while government by the representatives of those ranks would probably rivet the degradation of the multitude, and leave them no hope of decent treatment except by ridding themselves of one of the most valuable elements of future advancement. The best prospect of improvement for a people thus composed lies in the existence of a constitutionally unlimited, or at least a practically preponderant, authority in the chief ruler of the dominant class. He alone has by his position an interest in raising and improving the mass of whom he is not jealous, as a counterpoise to his associates of whom he is. And if fortunate circumstances place beside him, not as controllers but as subordinates, a body representative of the superior caste, which by its objections and questionings, and by its occasional outbreaks of spirit, keeps alive habits of collective resistance, and may admit of being, in time and by degrees, expanded into a really national representation (which is in substance the history of the English Parliament), the nation has then the most favourable prospects of improvement which can well occur to a community thus circumstanced and constituted.

Among the tendencies which, without absolutely rendering a people unfit for representative government, seriously incapacitate them from reaping the full benefit of it, one deserves particular notice. There are two states of the inclinations, intrinsically very different, but which have something in common, by virtue of which they often coincide in the direction they give to the efforts of individuals and of nations: one is, the desire to exercise power over others; the other is disinclination to have power exercised over themselves.

The difference between different portions of mankind in the relative strength of these two dispositions is one of the most important elements in their history. There are nations in whom the passion for governing others is so much stronger than the desire of personal independence, that for the mere shadow of the one they are found ready to sacrifice the whole of the other. Each one of their number is willing, like the private soldier in an army, to abdicate his personal freedom of action into the hands of his general, provided the army is triumphant and victorious, and he is able to flatter himself that he is one of a conquering host, though the notion that he has himself any share in the domination exercised over the conquered is an illusion. A government strictly limited in its powers and attributions, required to hold its hands from over-meddling, and to let most things go on without its assuming the part of guardian or director, is not to the taste of such a people. In their eyes the possessors of authority can hardly take too much upon themselves, provided the authority itself is open to general competition. An average individual among them prefers the chance, however distant or improbable, of wielding some share of power over his fellow-citizens, above the certainty, to himself and others, of having no unnecessary power exercised over them. These are the elements of a people of place-hunters; in whom the course of politics is mainly determined by place-hunting; where equality alone is cared for, but not liberty; where the contests of political parties are but struggles to decide whether the power of meddling in everything shall belong to one class or another, perhaps merely to one knot of public men or another; where the idea entertained of democracy is merely that of opening offices to the competition of all instead of a few; where, the more popular the institutions, the more innumerable are the places created, and the more monstrous the over-government exercised by all over each, and by the executive over all. It would be as unjust as it would be ungenerous to offer this, or anything approaching to it, as an unexaggerated picture of the French people; yet the degree in which they do participate in this type of character has caused representative government by a limited class to break down by excess of corruption, and the attempt at representative government by the whole male population to end in giving one man the power of consigning any number of the rest, without trial, to Lambessa or Cayenne, provided he allows all of them to think themselves not excluded from the possibility of sharing his favours.

The point of character which, beyond any other, fits the people of this country for representative government is that they have almost universally the contrary characteristic. They are very jealous of any attempt to exercise power over them not sanctioned by long usage and by their own opinion of right; but they in general care very little for the exercise of power over others. Not having the smallest sympathy with the passion for governing, while they are but too well acquainted with the motives of private interest from which that office is sought, they prefer that it should be performed by those to whom it comes without seeking, as a consequence of social position. If foreigners understood this, it would account to them for some of the apparent contradictions in the political feelings of Englishmen; their unhesitating readiness to let themselves be governed by the higher classes, coupled with so little personal subservience to them, that no people are so fond of resisting authority when it oversteps certain prescribed limits, or so determined to make their rulers always remember that they will only be governed in the way they themselves like best. Place-hunting, accordingly, is a form of ambition to which the English, considered nationally, are almost strangers. If we except the few families or connections of whom official employment lies directly in the way, Englishmen's views of advancement in life take an altogether different direction—that of success in business, or in a profession. They have the strongest distaste for any mere struggle for office by political parties or individuals: and there are few things to which they have a greater aversion than to the multiplication of public employments: a thing, on the contrary, always popular with the bureaucracy-ridden nations of the Continent, who would rather pay higher taxes than diminish by the smallest fraction their individual chances of a place for themselves or their relatives, and among whom a cry for retrenchment never means abolition of offices, but the reduction of the salaries of those which are too considerable for the ordinary citizen to have any chance of being appointed to them.

Chapter 5
Of the Proper Functions of Representative Bodies

IN TREATING of representative government, it is above all necessary to keep in view the distinction between its idea or essence, and the particular forms in which the idea has been clothed by accidental historical developments, or by the notions current at some particular period.

The meaning of representative government is, that the whole people, or some numerous portion of them, exercise through deputies periodically elected by themselves the ultimate controlling power, which, in every constitution, must reside somewhere. This ultimate power they must possess in all its completeness. They must be masters, whenever they please, of all the operations of government. There is no need that the constitutional law should itself give them this mastery. It does not in the British Constitution. But what it does give practically amounts to this. The power of final control is as essentially single, in a mixed and balanced government, as in a pure monarchy or democracy. This is the portion of truth in the opinion of the ancients, revived by great authorities in our own time, that a balanced constitution is impossible. There is almost always a balance, but the scales never hang exactly even. Which of them preponderates is not always apparent on the face of the political institutions. In the British Constitution, each of the three co-ordinate members of the sovereignty is invested with powers which, if fully exercised, would enable it to stop all the machinery of government. Nominally, therefore, each is invested with equal power of thwarting and obstructing the others: and if, by exerting that power, any of the three could hope to better its position, the ordinary course of human affairs forbids us to doubt that the power would be exercised. There can be no question that the full powers of each would be employed defensively if it found itself assailed by one or both of the others. What then prevents the same powers from being exerted aggressively? The unwritten maxims of the Constitution—in other words, the positive political morality of the country: and this positive political morality is what we must look to, if we would know in whom the really supreme power in the Constitution resides.

By constitutional law, the Crown can refuse its assent to any Act of Parliament, and can appoint to office and maintain in it any Minister, in opposition to the remonstrances of Parliament. But the constitutional morality of the country nullifies these powers, preventing them from being ever used; and, by requiring that the head of the Administration should always be virtually appointed by the House of Commons, makes that body the real sovereign of the State. These unwritten rules, which limit the use of lawful powers, are, however, only effectual, and maintain themselves in existence, on condition of harmonising with the actual distribution of real political strength. There is in every constitution a strongest power—one which would gain the victory if the compromises by which the Constitution habitually works were suspended and there came a trial of strength. Constitutional maxims are adhered to, and are practically operative, so long as they give the predominance in the Constitution to that one of the powers which has the preponderance of active power out of doors. This, in England, is the popular power. If, therefore, the legal provisions of the British Constitution, together with the unwritten maxims by which the conduct of the different political authorities is in fact regulated, did not give to the popular element in the Constitution that substantial supremacy over every department of the government which corresponds to its real power in the country, the Constitution would not possess the stability which characterises it; either the laws or the unwritten maxims would soon have to be changed. The British government is thus a representative government in the correct sense of the term: and the powers which it leaves in hands not directly accountable to the people can only be considered as precautions which the ruling power is willing should be taken against its own errors. Such precautions have existed in all well-constructed democracies. The Athenian Constitution had many such provisions; and so has that of the United States.

But while it is essential to representative government that the practical supremacy in the state should reside in the representatives of the people, it is an open question what actual functions, what precise part in the machinery of government, shall be directly and personally discharged by the representative body. Great varieties in this respect are compatible with the essence of representative government, provided the functions are such as secure to the representative body the control of everything in the last resort.

There is a radical distinction between controlling the business of government and actually doing it. The same person or body may be able to control everything, but cannot possibly do everything; and in many cases its control over everything will be more perfect the less it personally attempts to do. The commander of an army could not direct its movements effectually if he himself fought in the ranks, or led an assault. It is the same with bodies of men. Some things cannot be done except by bodies; other things cannot be well done by them. It is one question, therefore, what a popular assembly should control, another what it should itself do. It should, as we have already seen, control all the operations of government. But in order to determine through what channel this general control may most expediently be exercised, and what portion of the business of government the representative assembly should hold in its own hands, it is necessary to consider what kinds of business a numerous body is competent to perform properly. That alone which it can do well it ought to take personally upon itself. With regard to the rest, its proper province is not to do it, but to take means for having it well done by others.

For example, the duty which is considered as belonging more peculiarly than any other to an assembly representative of the people, is that of voting the taxes. Nevertheless, in no country does the representative body undertake, by itself or its delegated officers, to prepare the estimates. Though the supplies can only be voted by the House of Commons, and though the sanction of the House is also required for the appropriation of the revenues to the different items of the public expenditure, it is the maxim and the uniform practice of the Constitution that money can be granted only on the proposition of the Crown. It has, no doubt, been felt, that moderation as to the amount, and care and judgment in the detail of its application, can only be expected when the executive government, through whose hands it is to pass, is made responsible for the plans and calculations on which the disbursements are grounded. Parliament, accordingly, is not expected, nor even permitted, to originate directly either taxation or expenditure. All it is asked for is its consent, and the sole power it possesses is that of refusal.

The principles which are involved and recognised in this constitutional doctrine, if followed as far as they will go, are a guide to the limitation and definition of the general functions of representative assemblies. In the first place, it is admitted in all countries in which the representative system is practically understood, that numerous representative bodies ought not to administer. The maxim is grounded not only on the most essential principles of good government, but on those of the successful conduct of business of any description. No body of men, unless organised and under command, is fit for action, in the proper sense. Even a select board, composed of few members, and these specially conversant with the business to be done, is always an inferior instrument to some one individual who could be found among them, and would be improved in character if that one person were made the chief, and all the others reduced to subordinates. What can be done better by a body than by any individual is deliberation. When it is necessary or important to secure hearing and consideration to many conflicting opinions, a deliberative body is indispensable. Those bodies, therefore, are frequently useful, even for administrative business, but in general only as advisers; such business being, as a rule, better conducted under the responsibility of one. Even a joint-stock company has always in practice, if not in theory, a managing director; its good or bad management depends essentially on some one person's qualifications, and the remaining directors, when of any use, are so by their suggestions to him, or by the power they possess of watching him, and restraining or removing him in case of misconduct. That they are ostensibly equal shares with him in the management is no advantage, but a considerable set-off against any good which they are capable of doing: it weakens greatly the sense in his own mind, and in those of other people, of that individual responsibility in which he should stand forth personally and undividedly.

But a popular assembly is still less fitted to administer, or to dictate in detail to those who have the charge of administration. Even when honestly meant, the interference is almost always injurious. Every branch of public administration is a skilled business, which has its own peculiar principles and traditional rules, many of them not even known, in any effectual way, except to those who have at some time had a hand in carrying on the business, and none of them likely to be duly appreciated by persons not practically acquainted with the department. I do not mean that the transaction of public business has esoteric mysteries, only to be understood by the initiated. Its principles are all intelligible to any person of good sense, who has in his mind a true picture of the circumstances and conditions to be dealt with: but to have this he must know those circumstances and conditions; and the knowledge does not come by intuition. There are many rules of the greatest importance in every branch of public business (as there are in every private occupation), of which a person fresh to the subject neither knows the reason or even suspects the existence, because they are intended to meet dangers or provide against inconveniences which never entered into his thoughts. I have known public men, ministers, of more than ordinary natural capacity, who on their first introduction to a department of business new to them, have excited the mirth of their inferiors by the air with which they announced as a truth hitherto set at nought, and brought to light by themselves, something which was probably the first thought of everybody who ever looked at the subject, given up as soon as he had got on to a second. It is true that a great statesman is he who knows when to depart from traditions, as well as when to adhere to them. But it is a great mistake to suppose that he will do this better for being ignorant of the traditions. No one who does not thoroughly know the modes of action which common experience has sanctioned is capable of judging of the circumstances which require a departure from those ordinary modes of action. The interests dependent on the acts done by a public department, the consequences liable to follow from any particular mode of conducting it, require for weighing and estimating them a kind of knowledge, and of specially exercised judgment, almost as rarely found in those not bred to it, as the capacity to reform the law in those who have not professionally studied it.

All these difficulties are sure to be ignored by a representative assembly which attempts to decide on special acts of administration. At its best, it is inexperience sitting in judgment on experience, ignorance on knowledge: ignorance which never suspecting the existence of what it does not know, is equally careless and supercilious, making light of, if not resenting, all pretensions to have a judgment better worth attending to than its own. Thus it is when no interested motives intervene: but when they do, the result is jobbery more unblushing and audacious than the worst corruption which can well take place in a public office under a government of publicity. It is not necessary that the interested bias should extend to the majority of the assembly. In any particular case it is often enough that it affects two or three of their number. Those two or three will have a greater interest in misleading the body, than any other of its members are likely to have in putting it right. The bulk of the assembly may keep their hands clean, but they cannot keep their minds vigilant or their judgments discerning in matters they know nothing about; and an indolent majority, like an indolent individual, belongs to the person who takes most pains with it. The bad measures or bad appointments of a minister may be checked by Parliament; and the interest of ministers in defending, and of rival partisans in attacking, secures a tolerably equal discussion: but *quis custodiet custodes?* who shall check the Parliament? A minister, a head of an office, feels himself under some responsibility. An assembly in such cases feels under no responsibility at all: for when did any member of Parliament lose his seat for the vote he gave on any detail of administration? To a minister, or the head of an office, it is of more importance what will be thought of his proceedings some time hence than what is thought of them at the instant: but an assembly, if the cry of the moment goes with it, however hastily raised or artificially stirred up, thinks itself and is thought by everybody to be completely exculpated however disastrous may be the consequences. Besides, an assembly never personally experiences the inconveniences of its bad measures until they have reached the dimensions of national evils. Ministers and administrators see them approaching, and have to bear all the annoyance and trouble of attempting to ward them off.

The proper duty of a representative assembly in regard to matters of administration is not to decide them by its own vote, but to take care that the persons who have to decide them shall be the proper persons. Even this they cannot advantageously do by nominating the individuals. There is no act which more imperatively requires to be performed under a strong sense of individual responsibility than the nomination to employments. The experience of every person conversant with public affairs bears out the assertion, that there is scarcely any act respecting which the conscience of an average man is less sensitive; scarcely any case in which less consideration is paid to qualifications, partly because men do not know, and partly because they do not care for, the difference in qualifications between one person and another. When a minister makes what is meant to be an honest appointment, that is when he does not actually job it for his personal connections or his party, an ignorant person might suppose that he would try to give it to the person best qualified. No such thing. An ordinary minister thinks himself a miracle of virtue if he gives it to a person of merit, or who has a claim on the public on any account, though the claim or the merit may be of the most opposite description to that required. *Il fallait un calculateur, ce fut un danseur qui l'obtint,* is hardly more of a caricature than in the days of Figaro; and the min-

ister doubtless thinks himself not only blameless but meritorious if the man dances well. Besides, the qualifications which fit special individuals for special duties can only be recognised by those who know the individuals, or who make it their business to examine and judge of persons from what they have done, or from the evidence of those who are in a position to judge. When these conscientious obligations are so little regarded by great public officers who can be made responsible for their appointments, how must it be with assemblies who cannot? Even now, the worst appointments are those which are made for the sake of gaining support or disarming opposition in the representative body: what might we expect if they were made by the body itself? Numerous bodies never regard special qualifications at all. Unless a man is fit for the gallows, he is thought to be about as fit as other people for almost anything for which he can offer himself as a candidate. When appointments made by a public body are not decided, as they almost always are, by party connection or private jobbing, a man is appointed either because he has a reputation, often quite undeserved, for *general* ability, or frequently for no better reason than that he is personally popular.

It has never been thought desirable that Parliament should itself nominate even the members of a Cabinet. It is enough that it virtually decides who shall be prime minister, or who shall be the two or three individuals from whom the prime minister shall be chosen. In doing this it merely recognises the fact that a certain person is the candidate of the party whose general policy commands its support. In reality, the only thing which Parliament decides is, which of two, or at most three, parties or bodies of men, shall furnish the executive government: the opinion of the party itself decides which of its members is fittest to be placed at the head. According to the existing practice of the British Constitution, these things seem to be on as good a footing as they can be. Parliament does not nominate any minister, but the Crown appoints the head of the administration in conformity to the general wishes and inclinations manifested by Parliament, and the other ministers on the recommendation of the chief; while every minister has the undivided moral responsibility of appointing fit persons to the other offices of administration which are not permanent. In a republic, some other arrangement would be necessary: but the nearer it approached in practice to that which has long existed in England, the more likely it would be to work well. Either, as in the American republic, the head of the Executive must be elected by some agency entirely independent of the representative body; or the body must content itself with naming the prime minister, and making him responsible for the choice of his associates and subordinates. To all these considerations, at least theoretically, I fully anticipate a general assent: though, practically, the tendency is strong in representative bodies to interfere more and more in the details of administration, by virtue of the general law, that whoever has the strongest power is more and more tempted to make an excessive use of it; and this is one of the practical dangers to which the futurity of representative governments will be exposed.

But it is equally true, though only of late and slowly beginning to be acknowledged, that a numerous assembly is as little fitted for the direct business of legislation as for that of administration. There is hardly any kind of intellectual work which so much needs to be done, not only by experienced and exercised minds, but by minds trained to the task through long and laborious study, as the business of making laws. This is a sufficient reason, were there no other, why they can never be well made but by a committee of very few persons. A reason no less conclusive is, that every provision of a law requires to be framed with the most accurate and long-sighted perception of its effect on all the other provisions; and the law when made should be capable of fitting into a consistent whole with the previously existing laws. It is impossible that these conditions should be in any degree fulfilled when laws are voted clause by clause in a miscellaneous assembly. The incongruity of such a mode of legislating would strike all minds, were it not that our laws are already, as to form and construction, such a chaos, that the confusion and contradiction seem incapable of being made greater by any addition to the mass.

Yet even now, the utter unfitness of our legislative machinery for its purpose is making itself practically felt every year more and more. The mere time necessarily occupied in getting through Bills renders Parliament more and more incapable of passing any, except on detached and narrow points. If a Bill is prepared which even attempts to deal with the whole of any subject (and it is impossible to legislate properly on any part without having the whole present to the mind), it hangs over from session to session through sheer impossibility of finding time to dispose of it. It matters not though the Bill may have been deliberately drawn up by the authority deemed the best qualified, with all appliances and means to boot; or by a select commission, chosen for their conversancy with the subject, and having employed years in considering and digesting the particular measure; it cannot be passed, because the House of Commons will not forego the precious privilege of tinkering it with their clumsy hands. The custom has of late been to some extent introduced, when the principle of a Bill has been affirmed on the second reading, of referring it for consideration in detail to a Select Committee: but it has not been found that this practice causes much less time to be lost afterwards in carrying it through the Committee of the whole House: the opinions or private crotchets which have been overruled by knowledge always insist on giving themselves a second chance before the tribunal of ignorance. Indeed, the practice itself has been adopted principally by the House of Lords, the members of which are less busy and fond of meddling, and less jealous of the importance of their individual voices, than those of the elective House. And when a Bill of many clauses does succeed in getting itself discussed in detail, what can depict the state in which it comes out of Committee! Clauses omitted which are essential to the working of the rest; incongruous ones inserted to conciliate some private interest, or some crotchety member who threatens to delay the Bill; articles foisted in on the motion of some sciolist with a mere smattering of the subject, leading to consequences which the member who introduced or those who supported the Bill did not at the moment foresee, and which need an amending Act in the next session to correct their mischiefs.

It is one of the evils of the present mode of managing these things that the explaining and defending of a Bill, and of its various provisions, is scarcely ever performed by the person from whose mind they emanated, who probably has not a seat in the House. Their defence rests upon some minister or member of Parliament who did not frame them, who is dependent on cramming for all his arguments but those which are perfectly obvious, who does not know the full strength of his case, nor the best reasons by which to support it, and is wholly incapable of meeting unforeseen objections. This evil, as far as Government bills are concerned, admits of remedy, and has been remedied in some representative constitutions, by allowing the Government to be represented in either House by persons in its confidence, having a right to speak, though not to vote.

If that, as yet considerable, majority of the House of Commons who never desire to move an amendment or make a speech would no longer leave the whole regulation of business to those who do; if they would bethink themselves that better qualifications for legislation exist, and may be found if sought for, than a fluent tongue and the faculty of getting elected by a constituency; it would soon be recognised that, in legislation as well as administration, the only task to which a representative assembly can possibly be competent is not that of doing the work, but of causing it to be done; of determining to whom or to what sort of people it shall be confided, and giving or withholding the national sanction to it when performed. Any government fit for a high state of civilisation would have as one of its fundamental elements a small body, not exceeding in number the members of a Cabinet, who should act as a Commission of legislation, having for its appointed office to make the laws. If the laws of this country were, as surely they will soon be, revised and put into a connected form, the Commission of Codification by which this is effected should remain as a permanent institution, to watch over the work, protect it from deterioration, and make further improvements as often as required. No one would wish that this body should of itself have any power of *enacting* laws: the Commission would only embody the element of intelligence in their construction; Parliament would represent that of will. No measure would become a law until expressly sanctioned by Parliament: and Parliament, or either House, would have the power not only of rejecting but of sending back a Bill to the Commission for reconsideration or improvement. Either House might also exercise its initiative, by referring any subject to the Commission, with directions to prepare a law. The Commission, of course, would have no power of refusing its instrumentality to any legislation which the country desired. Instructions, concurred in by both Houses, to draw up a Bill which should effect a particular purpose, would be imperative on the Commissioners, unless they preferred to resign their office. Once framed, however, Parliament should have no power to alter the measure, but solely to pass or reject it; or, if partially disapproved of, re-

mit it to the Commission for reconsideration. The Commissioners should be appointed by the Crown, but should hold their offices for a time certain, say five years, unless removed on an address from the two Houses of Parliament, grounded either on personal misconduct (as in the case of judges), or on refusal to draw up a Bill in obedience to the demands of Parliament. At the expiration of the five years a member should cease to hold office unless reappointed, in order to provide a convenient mode of getting rid of those who had not been found equal to their duties, and of infusing new and younger blood into the body.

The necessity of some provision corresponding to this was felt even in the Athenian Democracy, where, in the time of its most complete ascendancy, the popular Ecclesia could pass Psephisms (mostly decrees on single matters of policy), but laws, so called, could only be made or altered by a different and less numerous body, renewed annually, called the Nomothetæ, whose duty it also was to revise the whole of the laws, and keep them consistent with one another. In the English Constitution there is great difficulty in introducing any arrangement which is new both in form and in substance, but comparatively little repugnance is felt to the attainment of new purposes by an adaptation of existing forms and traditions.

It appears to me that the means might be devised of enriching the Constitution with this great improvement through the machinery of the House of Lords. A Commission for preparing Bills would in itself be no more an innovation on the Constitution than the Board for the administration of the Poor Laws, or the Inclosure Commission. If, in consideration of the great importance and dignity of the trust, it were made a rule that every person appointed a member of the Legislative Commission, unless removed from office on an address from Parliament, should be a Peer for life, it is probable that the same good sense and taste which leave the judicial functions of the Peerage practically to the exclusive care of the law lords, would leave the business of legislation, except on questions involving political principles and interests, to the professional legislators; that Bills originating in the Upper House would always be drawn up by them; that the Government would devolve on them the framing of all its Bills; and that private members of the House of Commons would gradually find it convenient, and likely to facilitate the passing of their measures through the two Houses, if instead of bringing in a Bill and submitting it directly to the House, they obtained leave to introduce it and have it referred to the Legislative Commission. For it would, of course, be open to the House to refer for the consideration of that body not a subject merely, but any specific proposal, or a Draft of a Bill *in extenso*, when any member thought himself capable of preparing one such as ought to pass; and the House would doubtless refer every such draft to the Commission, if only as materials, and for the benefit of the suggestions it might contain: as they would, in like manner, refer every amendment or objection which might be proposed in writing by any member of the House after a measure had left the Commissioners' hands. The alteration of Bills by a Committee of the whole House would cease, not by formal abolition, but by desuetude; the right not being abandoned, but laid up in the same armoury with the royal veto, the right of withholding the supplies, and other ancient instruments of political warfare, which no one desires to see used, but no one likes to part with, lest they should at any time be found to be still needed in an extraordinary emergency. By such arrangements as these, legislation would assume its proper place as a work of skilled labour and special study and experience; while the most important liberty of the nation, that of being governed only by laws assented to by its elected representatives, would be fully preserved, and made more valuable by being detached from the serious, but by no means unavoidable, drawbacks which now accompany it in the form of ignorant and ill-considered legislation.

Instead of the function of governing, for which it is radically unfit, the proper office of a representative assembly is to watch and control the government: to throw the light of publicity on its acts: to compel a full exposition and justification of all of them which any one considers questionable; to censure them if found condemnable, and, if the men who compose the government abuse their trust, or fulfil it in a manner which conflicts with the deliberate sense of the nation, to expel them from office, and either expressly or virtually appoint their successors. This is surely ample power, and security enough for the liberty of the nation. In addition to this, the Parliament has an office, not inferior even to this in importance; to be at once the nation's Committee of Grievances, and its Congress of Opinions; an arena in which not only the general opinion of the nation, but that of every section of it, and as far as possible of every eminent individual whom it contains, can produce itself in full light and challenge discussion; where every person in the country may count upon finding somebody who speaks his mind, as well or better than he could speak it himself—not to friends and partisans exclusively, but in the face of opponents, to be tested by adverse controversy; where those whose opinion is overruled, feel satisfied that it is heard, and set aside not by a mere act of will, but for what are thought superior reasons, and commend themselves as such to the representatives of the majority of the nation; where every party or opinion in the country can muster its strength, and be cured of any illusion concerning the number or power of its adherents; where the opinion which prevails in the nation makes itself manifest as prevailing, and marshals its hosts in the presence of the government, which is thus enabled and compelled to give way to it on the mere manifestation, without the actual employment, of its strength; where statesmen can assure themselves, far more certainly than by any other signs, what elements of opinion and power are growing, and what declining, and are enabled to shape their measures with some regard not solely to present exigencies, but to tendencies in progress.

Representative assemblies are often taunted by their enemies with being places of mere talk and *bavardage*. There has seldom been more misplaced derision. I know not how a representative assembly can more usefully employ itself than in talk, when the subject of talk is the great public interests of the country, and every sentence of it represents the opinion either of some important body of persons in the nation, or of an individual in whom some such body have reposed their confidence. A place where every interest and shade of opinion in the country can have its cause even passionately pleaded, in the face of the government and of all other interests and opinions, can compel them to listen, and either comply, or state clearly why they do not, is in itself, if it answered no other purpose, one of the most important political institutions that can exist anywhere, and one of the foremost benefits of free government. Such "talking" would never be looked upon with disparagement if it were not allowed to stop "doing"; which it never would, if assemblies knew and acknowledged that talking and discussion are their proper business, while *doing*, as the result of discussion, is the task not of a miscellaneous body, but of individuals specially trained to it; that the fit office of an assembly is to see that those individuals are honestly and intelligently chosen, and to interfere no further with them, except by unlimited latitude of suggestion and criticism, and by applying or withholding the final seal of national assent. It is for want of this judicious reserve that popular assemblies attempt to do what they cannot do well—to govern and legislate—and provide no machinery but their own for much of it, when of course every hour spent in talk is an hour withdrawn from actual business.

But the very fact which most unfits such bodies for a Council of Legislation qualifies them the more for their other office—namely, that they are not a selection of the greatest political minds in the country, from whose opinions little could with certainty be inferred concerning those of the nation, but are, when properly constituted, a fair sample of every grade of intellect among the people which is at all entitled to a voice in public affairs. Their part is to indicate wants, to be an organ for popular demands, and a place of adverse discussion for all opinions relating to public matters, both great and small; and, along with this, to check by criticism, and eventually by withdrawing their support, those high public officers who really conduct the public business, or who appoint those by whom it is conducted. Nothing but the restriction of the function of representative bodies within these rational limits will enable the benefits of popular control to be enjoyed in conjunction with the no less important requisites (growing ever more important as human affairs increase in scale and in complexity) of skilled legislation and administration. There are no means of combining these benefits except by separating the functions which guarantee the one from those which essentially require the other; by disjoining the office of control and criticism from the actual conduct of affairs, and devolving the former on the representatives of the Many, while securing for the latter, under strict responsibility to the nation, the acquired knowledge and practised intelligence of a specially trained and experienced Few.

The preceding discussion of the functions which ought to devolve on the sovereign representative assembly of the nation would require to be followed by an inquiry into those properly vested in the minor representative bodies, which ought to exist for purposes that regard only localities. And such an inquiry forms an essential part of the present treatise; but many reasons require its postponement, until we have considered the most proper composition of the great representative body, destined to control as sovereign the enactment of laws and the administration of the general affairs of the nation.

Chapter 6
Of the Infirmities and Dangers to which Representative Government is Liable

THE DEFECTS of any form of government may be either negative or positive. It is negatively defective if it does not concentrate in the hands of the authorities power sufficient to fulfil the necessary offices of a government; or if it does not sufficiently develop by exercise the active capacities and social feelings of the individual citizens. On neither of these points is it necessary that much should be said at this stage of our inquiry.

The want of an amount of power in the government, adequate to preserve order and allow of progress in the people, is incident rather to a wild and rude state of society generally, than to any particular form of political union. When the people are too much attached to savage independence to be tolerant of the amount of power to which it is for their good that they should be subject, the state of society (as already observed) is not yet ripe for representative government. When the time for that government has arrived, sufficient power for all needful purposes is sure to reside in the sovereign assembly; and if enough of it is not entrusted to the executive, this can only arise from a jealous feeling on the part of the assembly towards the administration, never likely to exist but where the constitutional power of the assembly to turn them out of office has not yet sufficiently established itself. Wherever that constitutional right is admitted in principle, and fully operative in practice, there is no fear that the assembly will not be willing to trust its own ministers with any amount of power really desirable; the danger is, on the contrary, lest they should grant it too ungrudgingly, and too indefinite in extent, since the power of the minister is the power of the body who make and who keep him so. It is, however, very likely, and is one of the dangers of a controlling assembly, that it may be lavish of powers, but afterwards interfere with their exercise; may give power by wholesale, and take it back in detail, by multiplied single acts of interference in the business of administration. The evils arising from this assumption of the actual function of governing, in lieu of that of criticising and checking those who govern, have been sufficiently dwelt upon in the preceding chapter. No safeguard can in the nature of things be provided against this improper meddling, except a strong and general conviction of its injurious character.

The other negative defect which may reside in a government, that of not bringing into sufficient exercise the individual faculties, moral, intellectual, and active, of the people, has been exhibited generally in setting forth the distinctive mischiefs of despotism. As between one form of popular government and another, the advantage in this respect lies with that which most widely diffuses the exercise of public functions; on the one hand, by excluding fewest from the suffrage; on the other, by opening to all classes of private citizens, so far as is consistent with other equally important objects, the widest participation in the details of judicial and administrative business; as by jury trial, admission to municipal offices, and above all by the utmost possible publicity and liberty of discussion, whereby not merely a few individuals in succession, but the whole public, are made, to a certain extent, participants in the government, and sharers in the instruction and mental exercise derivable from it. The further illustration of these benefits, as well as of the limitations under which they must be aimed at, will be better deferred until we come to speak of the details of administration.

The *positive* evils and dangers of the representative, as of every other form of government, may be reduced to two heads: first, general ignorance and incapacity, or, to speak more moderately, insufficient mental qualifications, in the controlling body; secondly, the danger of its being under the influence of interests not identical with the general welfare of the community.

The former of these evils, deficiency in high mental qualifications, is one to which it is generally supposed that popular government is liable in a greater degree than any other. The energy of a monarch, the steadiness and prudence of an aristocracy, are thought to contrast most favourably with the vacillation and shortsightedness of even a qualified democracy.

These propositions, however, are not by any means so well founded as they at first sight appear.

Compared with simple monarchy, representative government is in these respects at no disadvantage. Except in a rude age, hereditary monarchy, when it is really such, and not aristocracy in disguise, far surpasses democracy in all the forms of incapacity supposed to be characteristic of the last. I say, except in a rude age, because in a really rude state of society there is a considerable guarantee for the intellectual and active capacities of the sovereign. His personal will is constantly encountering obstacles from the wilfulness of his subjects, and of powerful individuals among their number. The circumstances of society do not afford him much temptation to mere luxurious self-indulgence; mental and bodily activity, especially political and military, are his principal excitements; and among turbulent chiefs and lawless followers he has little authority, and is seldom long secure even of his throne, unless he possesses a considerable amount of personal daring, dexterity, and energy. The reason why the average of talent is so high among the Henries and Edwards of our history may be read in the tragical fate of the second Edward and the second Richard, and the civil wars and disturbances of the reigns of John and his incapable successor. The troubled period of the Reformation also produced several eminent hereditary monarchs, Elizabeth, Henri Quatre, Gustavus Adolphus; but they were mostly bred up in adversity, succeeded to the throne by the unexpected failure of nearer heirs, or had to contend with great difficulties in the commencement of their reign. Since European life assumed a settled aspect, anything above mediocrity in an hereditary king has become extremely rare, while the general average has been even below mediocrity, both in talent and in vigour of character. A monarchy constitutionally absolute now only maintains itself in existence (except temporarily in the hands of some active-minded usurper) through the mental qualifications of a permanent bureaucracy. The Russian and Austrian Governments, and even the French Government in its normal condition, are oligarchies of officials, of whom the head of the State does little more than select the chiefs. I am speaking of the regular course of their administration; for the will of the master of course determines many of their particular acts.

The governments which have been remarkable in history for sustained mental ability and vigour in the conduct of affairs have generally been aristocracies. But they have been, without any exception, aristocracies of public functionaries. The ruling bodies have been so narrow, that each member, or at least each influential member, of the body, was able to make, and did make, public business an active profession, and the principal occupation of his life. The only aristocracies which have manifested high governing capacities, and acted on steady maxims of policy, through many generations, are those of Rome and Venice. But, at Venice, though the privileged order was numerous, the actual management of affairs was rigidly concentrated in a small oligarchy within the oligarchy, whose whole lives were devoted to the study and conduct of the affairs of the state. The Roman government partook more of the character of an open aristocracy like our own. But the really governing body, the Senate, was in general exclusively composed of persons who had exercised public functions, and had either already filled or were looking forward to fill the higher offices of the state, at the peril of a severe responsibility in case of incapacity and failure. When once members of the Senate, their lives were pledged to the conduct of public affairs; they were not permitted even to leave Italy except in the discharge of some public trust; and unless turned out of the Senate by the censors for character or conduct deemed disgraceful, they retained their powers and responsibilities to the end of life. In an aristocracy thus constituted, every member felt his personal importance entirely bound up with the dignity and estimation of the commonwealth which he administered, and with the part he was able to play in its councils. This dignity and estimation were quite different things from the prosperity or happiness of the general body of the citizens, and were often wholly incompatible with it. But they were closely linked with the external success and aggrandisement of the State: and it was, consequently, in the pursuit of that object almost exclusively that either the Roman or the Venetian aristocracies manifested the systematically wise collective policy, and the great individual capacities for government, for which history has deservedly given them credit.

It thus appears that the only governments, not representative, in which high political skill and ability have been other than exceptional, whether under monarchical or aristocratic forms, have been essentially bureaucracies. The work of government has been in the hands of governors by profession; which is the essence and meaning of bureaucracy. Whether the work is done by them because they have been trained to it, or they are trained to it because it is to be done by them, makes a great difference in many respects, but none at all as to the essential character of the rule. Aristocracies, on the other hand, like that of England, in which the class who possessed the power derived it merely from their social position, without being specially trained or devoting themselves exclusively to it (and in which, therefore, the power was not exercised directly, but through representative institutions oligarchically constituted) have been, in respect to intellectual endowments, much on a par with democracies; that is, they have manifested such qualities in any considerable degree only during the temporary ascendancy which great and popular talents, united with a distinguished position, have given to some one man. Themistocles and Pericles, Washington and Jefferson, were not more completely exceptions in their several democracies, and were assuredly much more splendid exceptions, than the Chathams and Peels of the representative aristocracy of Great Britain, or even the Sullys and Colberts of the aristocratic monarchy of France. A great minister, in the aristocratic governments of modern Europe, is almost as rare a phenomenon as a great king.

The comparison, therefore, as to the intellectual attributes of a government, has to be made between a representative democracy and a bureaucracy; all other governments may be left out of the account. And here it must be acknowledged that a bureaucratic government has, in some important respects, greatly the advantage. It accumulates experience, acquires well-tried and well-considered traditional maxims, and makes provision for appropriate practical knowledge in those who have the actual conduct of affairs. But it is not equally favourable to individual energy of mind. The disease which afflicts bureaucratic governments, and which they usually die of, is routine. They perish by the immutability of their maxims; and, still more, by the universal law that whatever becomes a routine loses its vital principle, and having no longer a mind acting within it, goes on revolving mechanically though the work it is intended to do remains undone. A bureaucracy always tends to become a pedantocracy. When the bureaucracy is the real government, the spirit of the corps (as with the Jesuits) bears down the individuality of its more distinguished members. In the profession of government, as in other professions, the sole idea of the majority is to do what they have been taught; and it requires a popular government to enable the conceptions of the man of original genius among them to prevail over the obstructive spirit of trained mediocrity. Only in a popular government (setting apart the accident of a highly intelligent despot) could Sir Rowland Hill have been victorious over the Post Office. A popular government installed him *in* the Post Office, and made the body, in spite of itself, obey the impulse given by the man who united special knowledge with individual vigour and originality. That the Roman aristocracy escaped this characteristic disease of a bureaucracy was evidently owing to its popular element. All special offices, both those which gave a seat in the Senate and those which were sought by senators, were conferred by popular election. The Russian government is a characteristic exemplification of both the good and bad side of bureaucracy; its fixed maxims, directed with Roman perseverance to the same unflinchingly-pursued ends from age to age; the remarkable skill with which those ends are generally pursued; the frightful internal corruption, and the permanent organised hostility to improvements from without, which even the autocratic power of a vigorous-minded Emperor is seldom or never sufficient to overcome; the patient obstructiveness of the body being in the long run more than a match for the fitful energy of one man. The Chinese Government, a bureaucracy of Mandarins, is, as far as known to us, another apparent example of the same qualities and defects.

In all human affairs conflicting influences are required to keep one another alive and efficient even for their own proper uses; and the exclusive pursuit of one good object, apart from some other which should accompany it, ends not in excess of one and defect of the other, but in the decay and loss even of that which has been exclusively cared for. Government by trained officials cannot do, for a country, the things which can be done by a free government; but it might be supposed capable of doing some things which free government, of itself, cannot do. We find, however, that an outside element of freedom is necessary to enable it to do effectually or permanently even its own business. And so, also, freedom cannot produce its best effects, and often breaks down altogether, unless means

can be found of combining it with trained and skilled administration. There could not be a moment's hesitation between representative government, among a people in any degree ripe for it, and the most perfect imaginable bureaucracy. But it is, at the same time, one of the most important ends of political institutions, to attain as many of the qualities of the one as are consistent with the other; to secure, as far as they can be made compatible, the great advantage of the conduct of affairs by skilled persons, bred to it as an intellectual profession, along with that of a general control vested in, and seriously exercised by, bodies representative of the entire people. Much would be done towards this end by recognising the line of separation, discussed in the preceding chapter, between the work of government properly so called, which can only be well performed after special cultivation, and that of selecting, watching, and, when needful, controlling the governors, which in this case, as in others, properly devolves, not on those who do the work, but on those for whose benefit it ought to be done. No progress at all can be made towards obtaining a skilled democracy unless the democracy are willing that the work which requires skill should be done by those who possess it. A democracy has enough to do in providing itself with an amount of mental competency sufficient for its own proper work, that of superintendence and check.

How to obtain and secure this amount is one of the questions to be taken into consideration in judging of the proper constitution of a representative body. In proportion as its composition fails to secure this amount, the assembly will encroach, by special acts, on the province of the executive; it will expel a good, or elevate and uphold a bad, ministry; it will connive at, or overlook in them, abuses of trust, will be deluded by their false pretences, or will withhold support from those who endeavour to fulfil their trust conscientiously; it will countenance, or impose, a selfish, a capricious and impulsive, a short-sighted, ignorant, and prejudiced general policy, foreign and domestic; it will abrogate good laws, or enact bad ones, let in new evils, or cling with perverse obstinacy to old; it will even, perhaps, under misleading impulses, momentary or permanent, emanating from itself or from its constituents, tolerate or connive at proceedings which set law aside altogether, in cases where equal justice would not be agreeable to popular feeling. Such are among the dangers of representative government, arising from a constitution of the representation which does not secure an adequate amount of intelligence and knowledge in the representative assembly.

We next proceed to the evils arising from the prevalence of modes of action in the representative body, dictated by sinister interests (to employ the useful phrase introduced by Bentham), that is, interests conflicting more or less with the general good of the community.

It is universally admitted that, of the evils incident to monarchical and aristocratic governments, a large proportion arise from this cause. The interest of the monarch, or the interest of the aristocracy, either collective or that of its individual members, is promoted, or they themselves think that it will be promoted, by conduct opposed to that which the general interest of the community requires. The interest, for example, of the government is to tax heavily: that of the community is to be as little taxed as the necessary expenses of good government permit. The interest of the king, and of the governing aristocracy, is to possess, and exercise, unlimited power over the people; to enforce, on their part, complete conformity to the will and preferences of the rulers. The interest of the people is to have as little control exercised over them in any respect as is consistent with attaining the legitimate ends of government. The interest, or apparent and supposed interest, of the king or aristocracy is to permit no censure of themselves, at least in any form which they may consider either to threaten their power, or seriously to interfere with their free agency. The interest of the people is that there should be full liberty of censure on every public officer, and on every public act or measure. The interest of a ruling class, whether in an aristocracy or an aristocratic monarchy, is to assume to themselves an endless variety of unjust privileges, sometimes benefiting their pockets at the expense of the people, sometimes merely tending to exalt them above others, or, what is the same thing in different words, to degrade others below themselves. If the people are disaffected, which under such a government they are very likely to be, it is the interest of the king or aristocracy to keep them at a low level of intelligence and education, foment dissensions among them, and even prevent them from being too well off, lest they should "wax fat, and kick"; agreeably to the maxim of Cardinal Richelieu in his celebrated *Testament Politi-*

que. All these things are for the interest of a king or aristocracy, in a purely selfish point of view, unless a sufficiently strong counter-interest is created by the fear of provoking resistance. All these evils have been, and many of them still are, produced by the sinister interests of kings and aristocracies, where their power is sufficient to raise them above the opinion of the rest of the community; nor is it rational to expect, as a consequence of such a position, any other conduct.

These things are superabundantly evident in the case of a monarchy or an aristocracy; but it is sometimes rather gratuitously assumed that the same kind of injurious influences do not operate in a democracy. Looking at democracy in the way in which it is commonly conceived, as the rule of the numerical majority, it is surely possible that the ruling power may be under the dominion of sectional or class interests, pointing to conduct different from that which would be dictated by impartial regard for the interest of all. Suppose the majority to be whites, the minority negroes, or *vice versa:* is it likely that the majority would allow equal justice to the minority? Suppose the majority Catholics, the minority Protestants, or the reverse; will there not be the same danger? Or let the majority be English, the minority Irish, or the contrary: is there not a great probability of similar evil? In all countries there is a majority of poor, a minority who, in contradistinction, may be called rich. Between these two classes, on many questions, there is complete opposition of apparent interest. We will suppose the majority sufficiently intelligent to be aware that it is not for their advantage to weaken the security of property, and that it would be weakened by any act of arbitrary spoliation. But is there not a considerable danger lest they should throw upon the possessors of what is called realised property, and upon the larger incomes, an unfair share, or even the whole, of the burden of taxation; and having done so, add to the amount without scruple, expending the proceeds in modes supposed to conduce to the profit and advantage of the labouring class? Suppose, again, a minority of skilled labourers, a majority of unskilled: the experience of many trade unions, unless they are greatly calumniated, justifies the apprehension that equality of earnings might be imposed as an obligation, and that piecework, payment by the hour, and all practices which enable superior industry or abilities to gain a superior reward might be put down. Legislative attempts to raise wages, limitation of competition in the labour market, taxes or restrictions on machinery, and on improvements of all kinds tending to dispense with any of the existing labour—even, perhaps, protection of the home producer against foreign industry—are very natural (I do not venture to say whether probable) results of a feeling of class interest in a governing majority of manual labourers.

It will be said that none of these things are for the *real* interest of the most numerous class: to which I answer, that if the conduct of human beings was determined by no other interested considerations than those which constitute their "real" interest, neither monarchy nor oligarchy would be such bad governments as they are; for assuredly very strong arguments may be, and often have been, adduced to show that either a king or a governing senate are in much the most enviable position, when ruling justly and vigilantly over an active, wealthy, enlightened, and high-minded people. But a king only now and then, and an oligarchy in no known instance, have taken this exalted view of their self-interest: and why should we expect a loftier mode of thinking from the labouring classes? It is not what their interest is, but what they suppose it to be, that is the important consideration with respect to their conduct: and it is quite conclusive against any theory of government that it assumes the numerical majority to do habitually what is never done, nor expected to be done, save in very exceptional cases, by any other depositaries of power—namely, to direct their conduct by their real ultimate interest, in opposition to their immediate and apparent interest. No one, surely, can doubt that many of the pernicious measures above enumerated, and many others as bad, would be for the immediate interest of the general body of unskilled labourers. It is quite possible that they would be for the selfish interest of the whole existing generation of the class. The relaxation of industry and activity, and diminished encouragement to saving which would be their ultimate consequence, might perhaps be little felt by the class of unskilled labourers in the space of a single lifetime.

Some of the most fatal changes in human affairs have been, as to their more manifest immediate effects, beneficial. The establishment of the despotism of the Cæsars was a great benefit to the entire generation in which it

took place. It put a stop to civil war, abated a vast amount of malversation and tyranny by prætors and proconsuls; it fostered many of the graces of life, and intellectual cultivation in all departments not political; it produced monuments of literary genius dazzling to the imaginations of shallow readers of history, who do not reflect that the men to whom the despotism of Augustus (as well as of Lorenzo de' Medici and of Louis XIV.) owes its brilliancy, were all formed in the generation preceding. The accumulated riches, and the mental energy and activity, produced by centuries of freedom, remained for the benefit of the first generation of slaves. Yet this was the commencement of a *régime* by whose gradual operation all the civilisation which had been gained insensibly faded away, until the Empire, which had conquered and embraced the world in its grasp, so completely lost even its military efficiency, that invaders whom three or four legions had always sufficed to coerce were able to overrun and occupy nearly the whole of its vast territory. The fresh impulse given by Christianity came but just in time to save arts and letters from perishing, and the human race from sinking back into perhaps endless night.

When we talk of the interest of a body of men, or even of an individual man, as a principle determining their actions, the question what would be considered their interest by an unprejudiced observer is one of the least important parts of the whole matter. As Coleridge observes, the man makes the motive, not the motive the man. What it is the man's interest to do or refrain from depends less on any outward circumstances than upon what sort of man he is. If you wish to know what is practically a man's interest, you must know the cast of his habitual feelings and thoughts. Everybody has two kinds of interests, interests which he cares for, and interests which he does not care for. Everybody has selfish and unselfish interests, and a selfish man has cultivated the habit of caring for the former, and not caring for the latter. Every one has present and distant interests, and the improvident man is he who cares for the present interests and does not care for the distant. It matters little that on any correct calculation the latter may be the more considerable, if the habits of his mind lead him to fix his thoughts and wishes solely on the former. It would be vain to attempt to persuade a man who beats his wife and illtreats his children that he would be happier if he lived in love and kindness with them. He would be happier if he were the kind of person who *could* so live; but he is not, and it is probably too late for him to become, that kind of person. Being what he is, the gratification of his love of domineering, and the indulgence of his ferocious temper, are to his perceptions a greater good to himself than he would be capable of deriving from the pleasure and affection of those dependent on him. He has no pleasure in their pleasure, and does not care for their affection. His neighbour, who does, is probably a happier man than he; but could he be persuaded of this, the persuasion would, most likely, only still further exasperate his malignity or his irritability. On the average, a person who cares for other people, for his country, or for mankind, is a happier man than one who does not; but of what use is it to preach this doctrine to a man who cares for nothing but his own ease, or his own pocket? He cannot care for other people if he would. It is like preaching to the worm who crawls on the ground how much better it would be for him if he were an eagle.

Now it is a universally observed fact that the two evil dispositions in question, the disposition to prefer a man's selfish interests to those which he shares with other people, and his immediate and direct interests to those which are indirect and remote, are characteristics most especially called forth and fostered by the possession of power. The moment a man, or a class of men, find themselves with power in their hands, the man's individual interest, or the class's separate interest, acquires an entirely new degree of importance in their eyes. Finding themselves worshipped by others, they become worshippers of themselves, and think themselves entitled to be counted at a hundred times the value of other people; while the facility they acquire of doing as they like without regard to consequences insensibly weakens the habits which make men look forward even to such consequences as affect themselves. This is the meaning of the universal tradition, grounded on universal experience, of men's being corrupted by power. Every one knows how absurd it would be to infer from what a man is or does when in a private station, that he will be and do exactly the like when a despot on a throne; where the bad parts of his human nature, instead of being restrained and kept in subordination by every circumstance of his life and by every person surrounding him, are courted by all persons, and ministered to by all circumstances. It would be quite as absurd to entertain a similar expectation in regard to a class of men; the Demos, or any other. Let them be ever so modest and amenable to reason while there is a power over them stronger than they, we ought to expect a total change in this respect when they themselves become the strongest power.

Governments must be made for human beings as they are, or as they are capable of speedily becoming: and in any state of cultivation which mankind, or any class among them, have yet attained, or are likely soon to attain, the interests by which they will be led, when they are thinking only of self-interest, will be almost exclusively those which are obvious at first sight, and which operate on their present condition. It is only a disinterested regard for others, and especially for what comes after them, for the idea of posterity, of their country, or of mankind, whether grounded on sympathy or on a conscientious feeling, which ever directs the minds and purposes of classes or bodies of men towards distant or unobvious interests. And it cannot be maintained that any form of government would be rational which required as a condition that these exalted principles of action should be the guiding and master motives in the conduct of average human beings. A certain amount of conscience, and of disinterested public spirit, may fairly be calculated on in the citizens of any community ripe for representative government. But it would be ridiculous to expect such a degree of it, combined with such intellectual discernment, as would be proof against any plausible fallacy tending to make that which was for their class interest appear the dictate of justice and of the general good.

We all know what specious fallacies may be urged in defence of every act of injustice yet proposed for the imaginary benefit of the mass. We know how many, not otherwise fools or bad men, have thought it justifiable to repudiate the national debt. We know how many, not destitute of ability, and of considerable popular influence, think it fair to throw the whole burthen of taxation upon savings, under the name of realised property, allowing those whose progenitors and themselves have always spent all they received to remain, as a reward for such exemplary conduct, wholly untaxed. We know what powerful arguments, the more dangerous because there is a portion of truth in them, may be brought against all inheritance, against the power of bequest, against every advantage which one person seems to have over another. We know how easily the uselessness of almost every branch of knowledge may be proved, to the complete satisfaction of those who do not possess it. How many, not altogether stupid men, think the scientific study of languages useless, think ancient literature useless, all erudition useless, logic and metaphysics useless, poetry and the fine arts idle and frivolous, political economy purely mischievous? Even history has been pronounced useless and mischievous by able men. Nothing but that acquaintance with external nature, empirically acquired, which serves directly for the production of objects necessary to existence or agreeable to the senses, would get its utility recognised if people had the least encouragement to disbelieve it. Is it reasonable to think that even much more cultivated minds than those of the numerical majority can be expected to be will have so delicate a conscience, and so just an appreciation of what is against their own apparent interest, that they will reject these and the innumerable other fallacies which will press in upon them from all quarters as soon as they come into power, to induce them to follow their own selfish inclinations and short-sighted notions of their own good, in opposition to justice, at the expense of all other classes and of posterity?

One of the greatest dangers, therefore, of democracy, as of all other forms of government, lies in the sinister interest of the holders of power: it is the danger of class legislation; of government intended for (whether really effecting it or not) the immediate benefit of the dominant class, to the lasting detriment of the whole. And one of the most important questions demanding consideration, in determining the best constitution of a representative government, is how to provide efficacious securities against this evil.

If we consider as a class, politically speaking, any number of persons who have the same sinister interest—that is, whose direct and apparent interest points towards the same description of bad measures; the desirable object would be that no class, and no combination of classes likely to combine, should be able to exercise a preponderant influence in the government. A modern community, not divided within itself by strong antipathies of race, language, or nationality, may be considered as in the main divisible into two sections, which, inspite of partial variations, corre-

spond on the whole with two divergent directions of apparent interest. Let us call them (in brief general terms) labourers on the one hand, employers of labour on the other: including however along with employers of labour, not only retired capitalists, and the possessors of inherited wealth, but all that highly paid description of labourers (such as the professions) whose education and way of life assimilate them with the rich, and whose prospect and ambition it is to raise themselves into that class. With the labourers, on the other hand, may be ranked those smaller employers of labour, who by interests, habits, and educational impressions are assimilated in wishes, tastes, and objects to the labouring classes; comprehending a large proportion of petty tradesmen. In a state of society thus composed, if the representative system could be made ideally perfect, and if it were possible to maintain it in that state, its organisation must be such that these two classes, manual labourers and their affinities on one side, employers of labour and their affinities on the other, should be, in the arrangement of the representative system, equally balanced, each influencing about an equal number of votes in Parliament: since, assuming that the majority of each class, in any difference between them, would be mainly governed by their class interests, there would be a minority of each in whom that consideration would be subordinate to reason, justice, and the good of the whole; and this minority of either, joining with the whole of the other, would turn the scale against any demands of their own majority which were not such as ought to prevail.

The reason why, in any tolerable constituted society, justice and the general interest mostly in the end carry their point, is that the separate and selfish interests of mankind are almost always divided; some are interested in what is wrong, but some, also, have their private interest on the side of what is right: and those who are governed by higher considerations, though too few and weak to prevail against the whole of the others, usually after sufficient discussion and agitation become strong enough to turn the balance in favour of the body of private interests which is on the same side with them. The representative system ought to be so constituted as to maintain this state of things: it ought not to allow any of the various sectional interests to be so powerful as to be capable of prevailing against truth and justice and the other sectional interests combined.

There ought always to be such a balance preserved among personal interests as may render any one of them dependent for its successes on carrying with it at least a large proportion of those who act on higher motives and more comprehensive and distant views.

Chapter 7
Of True and False Democracy; Representation of All, and Representation of the Majority only

IT HAS been seen that the dangers incident to a representative democracy are of two kinds: danger of a low grade of intelligence in the representative body, and in the popular opinion which controls it; and danger of class legislation on the part of the numerical majority, these being all composed of the same class. We have next to consider how far it is possible so to organise the democracy as, without interfering materially with the characteristic benefits of democratic government, to do away with these two great evils, or at least to abate them, in the utmost degree attainable by human contrivance.

The common mode of attempting this is by limiting the democratic character of the representation, through a more or less restricted suffrage. But there is a previous consideration which, duly kept in view, considerably modifies the circumstances which are supposed to render such a restriction necessary. A completely equal democracy, in a nation in which a single class composes the numerical majority, cannot be divested of certain evils; but those evils are greatly aggravated by the fact that the democracies which at present exist are not equal, but systematically unequal in favour of the predominant class. Two very different ideas are usually confounded under the name democracy. The pure idea of democracy, according to its definition, is the government of the whole people by the whole people, equally represented. Democracy as commonly conceived and hitherto practised is the government of the whole people by a mere majority of the people, exclusively represented. The former is synonymous with the equality of all citizens; the latter, strangely confounded with it, is a government of privilege, in favour of the numerical majority, who alone possess practically any voice in the State. This is the inevitable consequence of the manner in which the votes are now taken, to the complete disfranchisement of minorities.

The confusion of ideas here is great, but it is so easily cleared up that one would suppose the slightest indication would be sufficient to place the matter in its true light before any mind of average intelligence. It would be so, but for the power of habit; owing to which the simplest idea, if unfamiliar, has as great difficulty in making its way to the mind as a far more complicated one. That the minority must yield to the majority, the smaller number to the greater, is a familiar idea; and accordingly men think there is no necessity for using their minds any further, and it does not occur to them that there is any medium between allowing the smaller number to be equally powerful with the greater, and blotting out the smaller number altogether. In a representative body actually deliberating, the minority must of course be overruled; and in an equal democracy (since the opinions of the constituents, when they insist on them, determine those of the representative body) the majority of the people, through their representatives, will outvote and prevail over the minority and their representatives. But does it follow that the minority should have no representatives at all? Because the majority ought to prevail over the minority, must the majority have all the votes, the minority none? Is it necessary that the minority should not even be heard? Nothing but habit and old association can reconcile any reasonable being to the needless injustice. In a really equal democracy, every or any section would be represented, not disproportionately, but proportionately. A majority of the electors would always have a majority of the representatives; but a minority of the electors would always have a minority of the representatives. Man for man they would be as fully represented as the majority. Unless they are, there is not equal government, but a government of inequality and privilege: one part of the people rule over the rest: there is a part whose fair and equal share of influence in the representation is withheld from them; contrary to all just government, but, above all, contrary to the principle of democracy, which professes equality as its very root and foundation.

The injustice and violation of principle are not less flagrant because those who suffer by them are a minority; for there is not equal suffrage where every single individual does not count for as much as any other single individual in the community. But it is not only a minority who suffer. Democracy, thus constituted, does not even attain its ostensible object, that of giving the powers of government in all cases to the numerical majority. It does something very different: it gives them to a majority of the majority; who may be, and often are, but a minority of the whole. All principles are most effectually tested by extreme cases. Suppose then, that, in a country governed by equal and universal suffrage, there is a contested election in every constituency, and every election is carried by a small majority. The Parliament thus brought together represents little more than a bare majority of the people. This Parliament proceeds to legislate, and adopts important measures by a bare majority of itself. What guarantee is there that these measures accord with the wishes of a majority of the people? Nearly half the electors, having been outvoted at the hustings, have had no influence at all in the decision; and the whole of these may be, a majority of them probably are, hostile to the measures, having voted against those by whom they have been carried. Of the remaining electors, nearly half have chosen representatives who, by supposition, have voted against the measures. It is possible, therefore, and not at all improbable, that the opinion which has prevailed was agreeable only to a minority of the nation, though a majority of that portion of it whom the institutions of the country have erected into a ruling class. If democracy means the certain ascendancy of the majority, there are no means of insuring that but by allowing every individual figure to tell equally in the summing up. Any minority left out, either purposely or by the play of the machinery, gives the power not to the majority, but to a minority in some other part of the scale.

The only answer which can possibly be made to this reasoning is, that as different opinions predominate in different localities, the opinion which is in a minority in some places has a majority in others, and on the whole every opinion which exists in the constituencies obtains its fair share of voices in the representation. And this is roughly true in the present state of the constituency; if it were not, the discordance of the House with the general sentiment of the country would soon become evident. But it would be no longer true if the present constituency were much enlarged; still less, if made co-extensive with the whole population; for in that case the majority in every locality would consist of manual labourers; and when there was any question pending, on which these classes were at issue with the rest

of the community, no other class could succeed in getting represented anywhere. Even now, is it not a great grievance that in every Parliament a very numerous portion of the electors, willing and anxious to be represented, have no member in the House for whom they have voted? Is it just that every elector of Marylebone is obliged to be represented by two nominees of the vestries, every elector of Finsbury or Lambeth by those (as is generally believed) of the publicans? The constituencies to which most of the highly educated and public spirited persons in the country belong, those of the large towns, are now, in great part, either unrepresented or misrepresented. The electors who are on a different side in party politics from the local majority are unrepresented. Of those who are on the same side, a large proportion are misrepresented; having been obliged to accept the man who had the greatest number of supporters in their political party, though his opinions may differ from theirs on every other point. The state of things is, in some respects, even worse than if the minority were not allowed to vote at all; for then, at least, the majority might have a member who would represent their own best mind: while now, the necessity of not dividing the party, for fear of letting in its opponents, induces all to vote either for the first person who presents himself wearing their colours, or for the one brought forward by their local leaders; and these, if we pay them the compliment, which they very seldom deserve, of supposing their choice to be unbiassed by their personal interests, are compelled, that they may be sure of mustering their whole strength, to bring forward a candidate whom none of the party will strongly object to—that is, a man without any distinctive peculiarity, any known opinions except the shibboleth of the party.

This is strikingly exemplified in the United States; where, at the election of President, the strongest party never dares put forward any of its strongest men, because every one of these, from the mere fact that he has been long in the public eye, has made himself objectionable to some portion or other of the party, and is therefore not so sure a card for rallying all their votes as a person who has never been heard of by the public at all until he is produced as the candidate. Thus, the man who is chosen, even by the strongest party, represents perhaps the real wishes only of the narrow margin by which that party outnumbers the other. Any section whose support is necessary to success possesses a veto on the candidate. Any section which holds out more obstinately than the rest can compel all the others to adopt its nominee; and this superior pertinacity is unhappily more likely to be found among those who are holding out for their own interest than for that of the public. The choice of the majority is therefore very likely to be determined by that portion of the body who are the most timid, the most narrow-minded and prejudiced, or who cling most tenaciously to the exclusive class-interest; in which case the electoral rights of the minority, while useless for the purposes for which votes are given, serve only for compelling the majority to accept the candidate of the weakest or worst portion of themselves.

That, while recognising these evils, many should consider them as the necessary price paid for a free government is in no way surprising: it was the opinion of all the friends of freedom up to a recent period. But the habit of passing them over as irremediable has become so inveterate that many persons seem to have lost the capacity of looking at them as things which they would be glad to remedy if they could. From despairing of a cure, there is too often but one step to denying the disease; and from this follows dislike to having a remedy proposed, as if the proposer were creating a mischief instead of offering relief from one. People are so inured to the evils that they feel as if it were unreasonable, if not wrong, to complain of them. Yet, avoidable or not, he must be a purblind lover of liberty on whose mind they do not weigh; who would not rejoice at the discovery that they could be dispensed with. Now, nothing is more certain than that the virtual blotting-out of the minority is no necessary or natural consequence of freedom; that, far from having any connection with democracy, it is diametrically opposed to the first principle of democracy, representation in proportion to numbers. It is an essential part of democracy that minorities should be adequately represented. No real democracy, nothing but a false show of democracy, is possible without it.

Those who have seen and felt, in some degree, the force of these considerations, have proposed various expedients by which the evil may be, in a greater or less degree, mitigated. Lord John Russell, in one of his Reform Bills, introduced a provision, that certain constituencies should return three members, and that in these each elector should be allowed to vote

only for two; and Mr. Disraeli, in the recent debates, revived the memory of the fact by reproaching him for it; being of opinion, apparently, that it befits a Conservative statesman to regard only means, and to disown scornfully all fellow-feeling with any one who is betrayed, even once, into thinking of ends.[1] Others have proposed that each elector should be allowed to vote only for one. By either of these plans, a minority equalling or exceeding a third of the local constituency, would be able, if it attempted no more, to return one out of three members. The same result might be attained in a still better way if, as proposed in an able pamphlet by Mr. James Garth Marshall, the elector retained his three votes, but was at liberty to bestow them all upon the same candidate. These schemes, though infinitely better than none at all, are yet but makeshifts, and attain the end in a very imperfect manner; since all local minorities of less than a third, and all minorities, however numerous, which are made up from several constituencies, would remain unrepresented. It is much to be lamented, however, that none of these plans have been carried into effect, as any of them would have recognised the right principle, and prepared the way for its more complete application. But real equality of representation is not obtained unless any set of electors amounting to the average number of a constituency, wherever in the country they happen to reside, have the power of combining with one another to return a representa-

[1] This blunder of Mr. Disraeli (from which, greatly to his credit, Sir John Pakington took an opportunity, soon after, of separating himself) is a speaking instance among many, how little the Conservative leaders understand Conservative principles. Without presuming to require from political parties such an amount of virtue and discernment as that they should comprehend, and know when to apply, the principles of their opponents, we may yet say that it would be a great improvement if each party understood and acted upon its own. Well would it be for England if Conservatives voted consistently for everything conservative, and Liberals for everything liberal. We should not then have to wait long for things which, like the present and many other great measures, are eminently both the one and the other. The Conservatives, as being by the law of their existence the stupidest party, have much the greatest sins of this description to answer for: and it is a melancholy truth, that if any measure were proposed, on any subject, truly, largely, and far-sightedly conservative, even if Liberals were willing to vote for it, the great bulk of the Conservative party would rush blindly in and prevent it from being carried.

tive. This degree of perfection in representation appeared impracticable until a man of great capacity, fitted alike for large general views and for the contrivance of practical details—Mr. Thomas Hare—had proved its possibility by drawing up a scheme for its accomplishment, embodied in a Draft of an Act of Parliament: a scheme which has the almost unparalleled merit of carrying out a great principle of government in a manner approaching to ideal perfection as regards the special object in view, while it attains incidentally several other ends of scarcely inferior importance.

According to this plan, the unit of representation, the quota of electors who would be entitled to have a member to themselves, would be ascertained by the ordinary process of taking averages, the number of voters being divided by the number of seats in the House: and every candidate who obtained that quota would be returned, from however great a number of local constituencies it might be gathered. The votes would, as at present, be given locally; but any elector would be at liberty to vote for any candidate in whatever part of the country he might offer himself. Those electors, therefore, who did not wish to be represented by any of the local candidates, might aid by their vote in the return of the person they liked best among all those throughout the country who had expressed a willingness to be chosen. This would, so far, give reality to the electoral rights of the otherwise virtually disfranchised minority. But it is important that not those alone who refuse to vote for any of the local candidates, but those also who vote for one of them and are defeated, should be enabled to find elsewhere the representation which they have not succeeded in obtaining in their own district. It is therefore provided that an elector may deliver a voting paper, containing other names in addition to the one which stands foremost in his preference. His vote would only be counted for one candidate; but if the object of his first choice failed to be returned, from not having obtained the quota, his second perhaps might be more fortunate. He may extend his list to a greater number, in the order of his preference, so that if the names which stand near the top of the list either cannot make up the quota, or are able to make it up without his vote, the vote may still be used for some one whom it may assist in returning. To obtain the full number of members required to complete the House, as well as to prevent very popular candidates from engrossing nearly all

the suffrages, it is necessary, however many votes a candidate may obtain, that no more of them than the quota should be counted for his return: the remainder of those who voted for him would have their votes counted for the next person on their respective lists who needed them, and could by their aid complete the quota. To determine which of a candidate's votes should be used for his return, and which set free for others, several methods are proposed, into which we shall not here enter. He would of course retain the votes of all those who would not otherwise be represented; and for the remainder, drawing lots, in default of better, would be an unobjectionable expedient. The voting papers would be conveyed to a central office, where the votes would be counted, the number of first, second, third, and other votes given for each candidate ascertained, and the quota would be allotted to every one who could make it up, until the number of the House was complete: first votes being preferred to second, second to third, and so forth. The voting papers, and all the elements of the calculation, would be placed in public repositories, accessible to all whom they concerned; and if any one who had obtained the quota was not duly returned it would be in his power easily to prove it.

These are the main provisions of the scheme. For a more minute knowledge of its very simple machinery, I must refer to Mr. Hare's *Treatise on the Election of Representatives* (a small volume published in 1859),[1] and to a pamphlet by Mr. Henry Fawcett (now Professor of Political Economy in the University of Cambridge), published in 1860, and entitled *Mr. Hare's Reform Bill simplified and explained*. This last is a very clear and concise exposition of the plan, reduced to its simplest elements, by the omission of some of Mr. Hare's original provisions, which, though in themselves beneficial, were thought to take more from the simplicity of the scheme than they added to its practical usefulness. The more these works are studied the stronger, I venture to predict, will be the impression of the perfect feasibility of the scheme, and its transcendant advantages. Such and so numerous are these, that, in my conviction, they place Mr. Hare's plan among the very greatest improvements yet made in the theory and practice of government.

[1] In a second edition, published recently, Mr. Hare has made important improvements in some of the detailed provisions.

In the first place, it secures a representation, in proportion to numbers, of every division of the electoral body: not two great parties alone, with perhaps a few large sectional minorities in particular places, but every minority in the whole nation, consisting of a sufficiently large number to be, on principles of equal justice, entitled to a representative. Secondly, no elector would, as at present, be nominally represented by some one whom he had not chosen. Every member of the House would be the representative of a unanimous constituency. He would represent a thousand electors, or two thousand, or five thousand, or ten thousand, as the quota might be, every one of whom would have not only voted for him, but selected him from the whole country; not merely from the assortment of two or three perhaps rotten oranges, which may be the only choice offered to him in his local market. Under this relation the tie between the elector and the representative would be of a strength, and a value, of which at present we have no experience. Every one of the electors would be personally identified with his representative, and the representative with his constituents. Every elector who voted for him would have done so either because, among all the candidates for Parliament who are favourably known to a certain number of electors, he is the one who best expresses the voter's own opinions, or because he is one of those whose abilities and character the voter most respects, and whom he most willingly trusts to think for him. The member would represent persons, not the mere bricks and mortar of the town—the voters themselves, not a few vestrymen or parish notabilities merely. All, however, that is worth preserving in the representation of places would be preserved. Though the Parliament of the nation ought to have as little as possible to do with purely local affairs, yet, while it has to do with them, there ought to be members specially commissioned to look after the interests of every important locality: and these there would still be. In every locality which could make up the quota within itself, the majority would generally prefer to be represented by one of themselves; by a person of local knowledge, and residing in the locality, if there is any such person to be found among the candidates, who is otherwise well qualified to be their representative. It would be the minorities chiefly, who being unable to return the local member, would look out elsewhere for a candidate likely to obtain other votes in addition to their own.

Of all modes in which a national representation can possibly be constituted, this one affords the best security for the intellectual qualifications desirable in the representatives. At present, by universal admission, it is becoming more and more difficult for any one who has only talents and character to gain admission into the House of Commons. The only persons who can get elected are those who possess local influence, or make their way by lavish expenditure, or who, on the invitation of three or four tradesmen or attorneys, are sent down by one of the two great parties from their London clubs, as men whose votes the party can depend on under all circumstances. On Mr. Hare's system, those who did not like the local candidates, or who could not succeed in carrying the local candidate they preferred, would have the power to fill up their voting papers by a selection from all the persons of national reputation, on the list of candidates, with whose general political principles they were in sympathy. Almost every person, therefore, who had made himself in any way honourably distinguished, though devoid of local influence, and having sworn allegiance to no political party, would have a fair chance of making up the quota; and with this encouragement such persons might be expected to offer themselves, in numbers hitherto undreamt of. Hundreds of able men of independent thought, who would have no chance whatever of being chosen by the majority of any existing constituency, have by their writings, or their exertions in some field of public usefulness, made themselves known and approved by a few persons in almost every district of the kingdom; and if every vote that would be given for them in every place could be counted for their election, they might be able to complete the number of the quota. In no other way which it seems possible to suggest would Parliament be so certain of containing the very *élite* of the country.

And it is not solely through the votes of minorities that this system of election would raise the intellectual standard of the House of Commons. Majorities would be compelled to look out for members of a much higher calibre. When the individuals composing the majority would no longer be reduced to Hobson's choice, of either voting for the person brought forward by their local leaders or not voting at all; when the nominee of the leaders would have to encounter the competition not solely of the candidate of the minority, but of all the men of established reputation in the country who were willing to serve; it would be impossible any longer to foist upon the electors the first person who presents himself with the catchwords of the party in his mouth and three or four thousand pounds in his pocket. The majority would insist on having a candidate worthy of their choice, or they would carry their votes somewhere else, and the minority would prevail. The slavery of the majority to the least estimable portion of their number would be at an end: the very best and most capable of the local notabilities would be put forward by preference; if possible, such as were known in some advantageous way beyond the locality, that their local strength might have a chance of being fortified by stray votes from elsewhere. Constituencies would become competitors for the best candidates, and would vie with one another in selecting from among the men of local knowledge and connections those who were most distinguished in every other respect.

The natural tendency of representative government, as of modern civilisation, is towards collective mediocrity: and this tendency is increased by all reductions and extensions of the franchise, their effect being to place the principal power in the hands of classes more and more below the highest level of instruction in the community. But though the superior intellects and characters will necessarily be outnumbered, it makes a great difference whether or not they are heard. In the false democracy which, instead of giving representation to all gives it only to the local majorities, the voice of the instructed minority may have no organs at all in the representative body. It is an admitted fact that in the American democracy, which is constructed on this faulty model, the highly-cultivated members of the community, except such of them as are willing to sacrifice their own opinions and modes of judgment, and become the servile mouthpieces of their inferiors in knowledge, seldom even offer themselves for Congress or the State Legislatures, so little likelihood have they of being returned.

Had a plan like Mr. Hare's by good fortune suggested itself to the enlightened and patriotic founders of the American Republic, the Federal and State Assemblies would have contained many of these distinguished men, and democracy would have been spared its greatest reproach and one of its most formidable evils. Against this evil the system of personal

representation, proposed by Mr. Hare, is almost a specific. The minority of instructed minds scattered through the local constituencies would unite to return a number, proportioned to their own numbers, of the very ablest men the country contains. They would be under the strongest inducement to choose such men, since in no other mode could they make their small numerical strength tell for anything considerable. The representatives of the majority, besides that they would themselves be improved in quality by the operation of the system, would no longer have the whole field to themselves. They would indeed outnumber the others, as much as the one class of electors outnumbers the other in the country: they could always outvote them, but they would speak and vote in their presence, and subject to their criticism. When any difference arose, they would have to meet the arguments of the instructed few by reasons, at least apparently, as cogent; and since they could not, as those do who are speaking to persons already unanimous, simply assume that they are in the right, it would occasionally happen to them to become convinced that they were in the wrong. As they would in general be well-meaning (for thus much may reasonably be expected from a fairly-chosen national representation), their own minds would be insensibly raised by the influence of the minds with which they were in contact, or even in conflict. The champions of unpopular doctrines would not put forth their arguments merely in books and periodicals, read only by their own side; the opposing ranks would meet face to face and hand to hand, and there would be a fair comparison of their intellectual strength in the presence of the country. It would then be found out whether the opinion which prevailed by counting votes would also prevail if the votes were weighed as well as counted.

The multitude have often a true instinct for distinguishing an able man, when he has the means of displaying his ability in a fair field before them. If such a man fails to obtain at least some portion of his just weight, it is through institutions or usages which keep him out of sight. In the old democracies there were no means of keeping out of sight any able man: the bema was open to him; he needed nobody's consent to become a public adviser. It is not so in a representative government; and the best friends of representative democracy can hardly be without misgivings that the Themistocles or Demosthenes, whose counsels would have saved the nation, might be unable during his whole life ever to obtain a seat. But if the presence in the representative assembly can be insured of even a few of the first minds in the country, though the remainder consist only of average minds, the influence of these leading spirits is sure to make itself sensibly felt in the general deliberations, even though they be known to be, in many respects, opposed to the tone of popular opinion and feeling. I am unable to conceive any mode by which the presence of such minds can be so positively insured as by that proposed by Mr. Hare.

This portion of the Assembly would also be the appropriate organ of a great social function, for which there is no provision in any existing democracy, but which in no government can remain permanently unfulfilled without condemning that government to infallible degeneracy and decay. This may be called the function of Antagonism. In every government there is some power stronger than all the rest; and the power which is strongest tends perpetually to become the sole power. Partly by intention, and partly unconsciously, it is ever striving to make all other things bend to itself; and is not content while there is anything which makes permanent head against it, any influence not in agreement with its spirit. Yet if it succeeds in suppressing all rival influences, and moulding everything after its own model, improvement, in that country, is at an end, and decline commences. Human improvement is a product of many factors, and no power ever yet constituted among mankind includes them all: even the most beneficent power only contains in itself some of the requisites of good, and the remainder, if progress is to continue, must be derived from some other source. No community has ever long continued progressive, but while a conflict was going on between the strongest power in the community and some rival power; between the spiritual and temporal authorities; the military or territorial and the industrious classes; the king and the people; the orthodox and religious reformers. When the victory on either side was so complete as to put an end to the strife, and no other conflict took its place, first stagnation followed, and then decay. The ascendancy of the numerical majority is less unjust, and on the whole less mischievous, than many others, but it is attended with the very same kind of dangers, and even more certainly; for when the government is in the hands of One or a Few, the Many are always existent as a rival power, which may not be strong enough ever to control the other, but whose opinion and sentiment are a moral, and even a social, support to all who, either from conviction or contrariety of interest, are opposed to any of the tendencies of the ruling authority. But when the Democracy is supreme, there is no One or Few strong enough for dissentient opinions and injured or menaced interests to lean upon. The great difficulty of democratic government has hitherto seemed to be, how to provide, in a democratic society, what circumstances have provided hitherto in all the societies which have maintained themselves ahead of others—a social support, a *point d'appui,* for individual resistance to the tendencies of the ruling power; a protection, a rallying point, for opinions and interests which the ascendant public opinion views with disfavour. For want of such a *point d'appui,* the older societies, and all but a few modern ones, either fell into dissolution or became stationary (which means slow deterioration) through the exclusive predominance of a part only of the conditions of social and mental well-being.

Now, this great want the system of Personal Representation is fitted to supply in the most perfect manner which the circumstances of modern society admit of. The only quarter in which to look for a supplement, or completing corrective, to the instincts of a democratic majority, is the instructed minority: but, in the ordinary mode of constituting democracy, this minority has no organ: Mr. Hare's system provides one. The representatives who would be returned to Parliament by the aggregate of minorities would afford that organ in its greatest perfection. A separate organisation of the instructed classes, even if practicable, would be invidious, and could only escape from being offensive by being totally without influence. But if the *élite* of these classes formed part of the Parliament, by the same title as any other of its members—by representing the same number of citizens, the same numerical fraction of the national will—their presence could give umbrage to nobody, while they would be in the position of highest vantage, both for making their opinions and counsels heard on all important subjects, and for taking an active part in public business. Their abilities would probably draw to them more than their numerical share of the actual administration of government; as the Athenians did not confide responsible public functions to Cleon or Hyperbolus (the employment of

Cleon at Pylos and Amphipolis was purely exceptional), but Nicias, and Theramenes, and Alcibiades, were in constant employment both at home and abroad, though known to sympathise more with oligarchy than with democracy. The instructed minority would, in the actual voting, count only for their numbers, but as a moral power they would count for much more, in virtue of their knowledge, and of the influence it would give them over the rest. An arrangement better adapted to keep popular opinion within reason and justice, and to guard it from the various deteriorating influences which assail the weak side of democracy, could scarcely by human ingenuity be devised. A democratic people would in this way be provided with what in any other way it would almost certainly miss—leaders of a higher grade of intellect and character than itself. Modern democracy would have its occasional Pericles, and its habitual group of superior and guiding minds.

With all this array of reasons, of the most fundamental character, on the affirmative side of the question, what is there on the negative? Nothing that will sustain examination, when people can once be induced to bestow any real examination upon a new thing. Those indeed, if any such there be, who, under pretence of equal justice, aim only at substituting the class ascendancy of the poor for that of the rich, will of course be unfavourable to a scheme which places both on a level. But I do not believe that any such wish exists at present among the working classes of this country, though I would not answer for the effect which opportunity and demagogic artifices may hereafter have in exciting it. In the United States, where the numerical majority have long been in full possession of collective despotism, they would probably be as unwilling to part with it as a single despot or an aristocracy. But I believe that the English democracy would as yet be content with protection against the class legislation of others, without claiming the power to exercise it in their turn.

Among the ostensible objectors to Mr. Hare's scheme, some profess to think the plan unworkable; but these, it will be found, are generally people who have barely heard of it, or have given it a very slight and cursory examination. Others are unable to reconcile themselves to the loss of what they term the local character of the representation. A nation does not seem to them to consist of persons, but of artificial units, the creation of geography and statistics. Parliament must represent towns and counties, not human beings. But no one seeks to annihilate towns and counties. Towns and counties, it may be presumed, are represented, when the human beings who inhabit them are represented. Local feelings cannot exist without somebody who feels them; nor local interests without somebody interested in them. If the human beings whose feelings and interests these are have their proper share of representation, these feelings and interests are represented in common with all other feelings and interests of those persons. But I cannot see why the feelings and interests which arrange mankind according to localities should be the only one thought worthy of being represented; or why people who have other feelings and interests, which they value more than they do their geographical ones, should be restricted to these as the sole principle of their political classification. The notion that Yorkshire and Middlesex have rights apart from those of their inhabitants, or that Liverpool and Exeter are the proper objects of the legislator's care, in contradistinction to the population of those places, is a curious specimen of delusion produced by words.

In general, however, objectors cut the matter short by affirming that the people of England will never consent to such a system. What the people of England are likely to think of those who pass such a summary sentence on their capacity of understanding and judgment, deeming it superfluous to consider whether a thing is right or wrong before affirming that they are certain to reject it, I will not undertake to say. For my own part, I do not think that the people of England have deserved to be, without trial, stigmatised as insurmountably prejudiced against anything which can be proved to be good either for themselves or for others. It also appears to me that when prejudices persist obstinately, it is the fault of nobody so much as of those who make a point of proclaiming them insuperable, as an excuse to themselves for never joining in an attempt to remove them. Any prejudice whatever will be insurmountable if those who do not share it themselves truckle to it, and flatter it, and accept it as a law of nature. I believe, however, that in this case there is in general, among those who have yet heard of the proposition, no other hostility to it than the natural and healthy distrust attaching to all novelties which have not been sufficiently canvassed to make generally manifest all the pros and cons of the question. The only serious obstacle is the unfamiliarity: this indeed is a formidable one, for the imagination much more easily reconciles itself to a great alteration in substance, than to a very small one in names and forms. But unfamiliarity is a disadvantage which, when there is any real value in an idea, it only requires time to remove. And in these days of discussion, and generally awakened interest in improvement, what formerly was the work of centuries, often requires only years.

Since the first publication of this Treatise, several adverse criticisms have been made on Mr. Hare's plan, which indicate at least a careful examination of it, and a more intelligent consideration than had previously been given to its pretensions. This is the natural progress of the discussion of great improvements. They are at first met by a blind prejudice, and by arguments to which only blind prejudice could attach any value. As the prejudice weakens, the arguments it employs for some time increase in strength; since, the plan being better understood, its inevitable inconveniences, and the circumstances which militate against its at once producing all the benefits it is intrinsically capable of, come to light along with its merits. But, of all the objections, having any semblance of reason, which have come under my notice, there is not one which had not been foreseen, considered, and canvassed by the supporters of the plan, and found either unreal or easily surmountable.

The most serious, in appearance, of the objections may be the most briefly answered; the assumed impossibility of guarding against fraud, or suspicion of fraud, in the operations of the Central Office. Publicity, and complete liberty of inspecting the voting papers after the election, were the securities provided; but these, it is maintained, would be unavailing; because, to check the returns, a voter would have to go over all the work that had been done by the staff of clerks. This would be a very weighty objection, if there were any necessity that the returns should be verified individually by every voter. All that a simple voter could be expected to do in the way of verification would be to check the use made of his own voting paper; for which purpose every paper would be returned, after a proper interval, to the place from whence it came. But what he could not do would be done for him by the unsuccessful candidates and their agents. Those among the defeated who thought that

they ought to have been returned would, singly or a number together, employ an agency for verifying the entire process of the election; and if they detected material error, the documents would be referred to a Committee of the House of Commons, by whom the entire electoral operations of the nation would be examined and verified, at a tenth part the expense of time and money necessary for the scrutiny of a single return before an Election Committee under the system now in force.

Assuming the plan to be workable, two modes have been alleged in which its benefits might be frustrated, and injurious consequences produced in lieu of them. First, it is said that undue power would be given to knots or cliques; sectarian combinations; associations for special objects, such as the Maine Law League, the Ballot or Liberation Society; or bodies united by class interests or community of religious persuasion. It is in the second place objected that the system would admit of being worked for party purposes. A central organ of each political party would send its list of 658 candidates all through the country, to be voted for by the whole of its supporters in every constituency. Their votes would far outnumber those which could ever be obtained by any independent candidate. The "ticket" system, it is contended, would, as it does in America, operate solely in favour of the great organised parties, whose tickets would be accepted blindly, and voted for in their integrity; and would hardly ever be outvoted, except occasionally, by the sectarian groups, or knots of men bound together by a common crotchet, who have been already spoken of.

The answer to this appears to be conclusive. No one pretends that under Mr. Hare's or any other plan organisation would cease to be an advantage. Scattered elements are always at a disadvantage compared with organised bodies. As Mr. Hare's plan cannot alter the nature of things, we must expect that all parties or sections, great or small, which possess organisation, would avail themselves of it to the utmost to strengthen their influence. But under the existing system those influences are everything. The scattered elements are absolutely nothing. The voters who are neither bound to the great political nor to any of the little sectarian divisions have no means of making their votes available. Mr. Hare's plan gives them the means. They might be more, or less, dexterous in using it. They might obtain their share of influence, or much less than their share. But whatever they did acquire would be clear gain. And when it is assumed that every petty interest, or combination for a petty object, would give itself an organisation, why should we suppose that the great interest of national intellect and character would alone remain unorganised? If there would be Temperance tickets, and Ragged School tickets, and the like, would not one public-spirited person in a constituency be sufficient to put forth a "personal merit" ticket, and circulate it through a whole neighbourhood? And might not a few such persons, meeting in London, select from the list of candidates the most distinguished names, without regard to technical divisions of opinion, and publish them at a trifling expense through all the constituencies? It must be remembered that the influence of the two great parties, under the present mode of election, is unlimited: in Mr. Hare's scheme it would be great, but confined within bounds. Neither they, nor any of the smaller knots, would be able to elect more members than in proportion to the relative number of their adherents. The ticket system in America operates under conditions the reverse of this. In America electors vote for the party ticket, because the election goes by a mere majority, and a vote for any one who is certain not to obtain the majority is thrown away. But, on Mr. Hare's system, a vote given to a person of known worth has almost as much chance of obtaining its object as one given to a party candidate. It might be hoped, therefore, that every Liberal or Conservative, who was anything besides a Liberal or a Conservative—who had any preferences of his own in addition to those of his party—would scratch through the names of the more obscure and insignificant party candidates, and inscribe in their stead some of the men who are an honour to the nation. And the probability of this fact would operate as a strong inducement with those who drew up the party lists not to confine themselves to pledged party men, but to include along with these, in their respective tickets, such of the national notabilities as were more in sympathy with their side than with the opposite.

The real difficulty, for it is not to be dissembled that there is a difficulty, is that the independent voters, those who are desirous of voting for unpatronised persons of merit, would be apt to put down the names of a few such persons, and to fill up the remainder of their list with mere party candidates, thus helping to swell the numbers against those by whom they would prefer to be represented. There would be an easy remedy for this, should it be necessary to resort to it, namely, to impose a limit to the number of secondary or contingent votes. No voter is likely to have an independent preference, grounded on knowledge, for 658, or even for 100 candidates. There would be little objection to his being limited to twenty, fifty, or whatever might be the number in the selection of whom there was some probability that his own choice would be exercised—that he would vote as an individual, and not as one of the mere rank and file of a party. But even without this restriction, the evil would be likely to cure itself as soon as the system came to be well understood. To counteract it would become a paramount object with all the knots and cliques whose influence is so much deprecated. From these, each in itself a small minority, the word would go forth, "Vote for your *special* candidates only; or at least put their names foremost, so as to give them the full chance which your numerical strength warrants, of obtaining the quota by means of first votes, or without descending low in the scale." And those voters who did not belong to any clique would profit by the lesson.

The minor groups would have precisely the amount of power which they ought to have. The influence they could exercise would be exactly that which their number of voters entitled them to; not a particle more; while, to ensure even that, they would have a motive to put up, as representatives of their special objects, candidates whose other recommendations would enable them to obtain the suffrages of voters not of the sect or clique. It is curious to observe how the popular line of argument in defence of existing systems veers round, according to the nature of the attack made upon them. Not many years ago it was the favourite argument in support of the then existing system of representation, that under it all "interests" or "classes" were represented. And certainly, all interests or classes of any importance ought to be represented, that is, ought to have spokesmen, or advocates, in Parliament. But from thence it was argued that a system ought to be supported which gave to the partial interests not advocates merely, but the tribunal itself. Now behold the change. Mr. Hare's system makes it impossible for partial interests to have the command of the tribunal, but it ensures them advocates, and for doing even this it is reproached. Because it unites the good points of class representation and the good points of numerical representation, it is attacked from both sides at once.

But it is not such objections as these that are the real difficulty in getting the system accepted; it is the exaggerated notion entertained of its complexity, and the consequent doubt whether it is capable of being carried into effect. The only complete answer to this objection would be actual trial. When the merits of the plan shall have become more generally known, and shall have gained for it a wider support among impartial thinkers, an effort should be made to obtain its introduction experimentally in some limited field, such as the municipal election of some great town. An opportunity was lost when the decision was taken to divide the West Riding of Yorkshire for the purpose of giving it four members; instead of trying the new principle, by leaving the constituency undivided, and allowing a candidate to be returned on obtaining either in first or secondary votes a fourth part of the whole number of votes given. Such experiments would be a very imperfect test of the worth of the plan: but they would be an exemplification of its mode of working; they would enable people to convince themselves that it is not impracticable; would familiarise them with its machinery, and afford some materials for judging whether the difficulties which are thought to be so formidable are real or only imaginary. The day when such a partial trial shall be sanctioned by Parliament will, I believe, inaugurate a new era of Parliamentary Reform; destined to give to Representative Government a shape fitted to its mature and triumphant period, when it shall have passed through the militant stage in which alone the world has yet seen it.[1]

[1] In the interval between the last and present editions of this treatise, it has become known that the experiment here suggested has actually been made on a larger than any municipal or provincial scale, and has been in course of trial for several years. In the Danish Constitution (not that of Denmark proper, but the Constitution framed for the entire Danish kingdom) the equal representation of minorities was provided for on a plan so nearly identical with Mr. Hare's, as to add another to the many examples how the ideas which resolve difficulties arising out of a general situation of the human mind or of society, present themselves, without communication, to several superior minds at once. This feature of the Danish electoral law has been brought fully and clearly before the British public in an able paper by Mr. Robert Lytton, forming one of the valuable reports by Secretaries of Legation, printed by order of the House of Commons in 1864. Mr. Hare's plan, which may now be also called M. Andræ's, has thus advanced from the position of a simple project to that of a realised political fact.

Chapter 8
Of the Extension of the Suffrage

SUCH A representative democracy as has now been sketched, representative of all, and not solely of the majority—in which the interests, the opinions, the grades of intellect which are outnumbered would nevertheless be heard, and would have a chance of obtaining by weight of character and strength of argument an influence which would not belong to their numerical force—this democracy, which is alone equal, alone impartial, alone the government of all by all, the only true type of democracy—would be free from the greatest evils of the falsely-called democracies which now prevail, and from which the current idea of democracy is exclusively derived. But even in this democracy, absolute power, if they chose to

Though Denmark is as yet the only country in which Personal Representation has become an institution, the progress of the idea among thinking minds has been very rapid. In almost all the countries in which universal suffrage is now regarded as a necessity, the scheme is rapidly making its way: with the friends of democracy, as a logical consequence of their principle; with those who rather accept than prefer democratic government, as an indispensable corrective of its inconveniences. The political thinkers of Switzerland led the way. Those of France followed. To mention no others, within a very recent period two of the most influential and authoritative political writers in France, one belonging to the moderate liberal and the other to the extreme democratic school, have given in a public adhesion to the plan. Among its German supporters is numbered one of the most eminent political thinkers in Germany, who is also a distinguished member of the liberal Cabinet of the Grand Duke of Baden. This subject, among others, has its share in the important awakening of thought in the American republic, which is already one of the fruits of the great pending contest for human freedom. In the two principal of our Australian colonies Mr. Hare's plan has been brought under the consideration of their respective legislatures, and though not yet adopted, has already a strong party in its favour; while the clear and complete understanding of its principles, shown by the majority of the speakers both on the Conservative and on the Radical side of general politics, shows how unfounded is the notion of its being too complicated to be capable of being generally comprehended and acted on. Nothing is required to make both the plan and its advantages perfectly intelligible to all, except that the time should have come when they will think it worth their while to take the trouble of really attending to it.

exercise it, would rest with the numerical majority; and these would be composed exclusively of a single class, alike in biasses, prepossessions, and general modes of thinking, and a class, to say no more, not the most highly cultivated. The constitution would therefore still be liable to the characteristic evils of class government: in a far less degree, assuredly, than that exclusive government by a class, which new usurps the name of democracy; but still, under no effective restraint, except what might be found in the good sense, moderation, and forbearance of the class itself. If checks of this description are sufficient, the philosophy of constitutional government is but solemn trifling. All trust in constitutions is grounded on the assurance they may afford, not that the depositaries of power will not, but that they cannot, misemploy it. Democracy is not the ideally best form of government unless this weak side of it can be strengthened; unless it can be so organised that no class, not even the most numerous, shall be able to reduce all but itself to political insignificance, and direct the course of legislation and administration by its exclusive class interest. The problem is, to find the means of preventing this abuse, without sacrificing the characteristic advantages of popular government.

These twofold requisites are not fulfilled by the expedient of a limitation of the suffrage, involving the compulsory exclusion of any portion of the citizens from a voice in the representation. Among the foremost benefits of free government is that education of the intelligence and of the sentiments which is carried down to the very lowest ranks of the people when they are called to take a part in acts which directly affect the great interests of their country. On this topic I have already dwelt so emphatically that I only return to it because there are few who seem to attach to this effect of popular institutions all the importance to which it is entitled. People think it fanciful to expect so much from what seems so slight a cause—to recognise a potent instrument of mental improvement in the exercise of political franchises by manual labourers. Yet unless substantial mental cultivation in the mass of mankind is to be a mere vision, this is the road by which it must come. If any one supposes that this road will not bring it, I call to witness the entire contents of M. de Tocqueville's great work; and especially his estimate of the Americans. Almost all travellers are struck by the fact that every American is in some sense both

a patriot, and a person of cultivated intelligence; and M. de Tocqueville has shown how close the connection is between these qualities and their democratic institutions. No such wide diffusion of the ideas, tastes, and sentiments of educated minds has ever been seen elsewhere, or even conceived as attainable.[1]

Yet this is nothing to what we might look for in a government equally democratic in its unexclusiveness, but better organised in other important points. For political life is indeed in America a most valuable school, but it is a school from which the ablest teachers are excluded; the first minds in the country being as effectually shut out from the national representation, and from public functions generally, as if they were under a formal disqualification. The Demos, too, being in America the one source of power, all the selfish ambition of the country gravitates towards it, as it does in despotic countries towards the monarch: the people, like the despot, is pursued with adulation and sycophancy, and the corrupting effects of power fully keep pace with its improving and ennobling influences. If, even with this alloy, democratic institutions produce so marked a superiority of mental development in the lowest class of Americans, compared with the corresponding classes in England and elsewhere, what would it be if the good portion of the influence could be retained without the bad? And this, to a certain extent, may be done; but not by excluding that portion of the people who have fewest intellectual stimuli of other kinds from so inestimable an in-

[1] The following "extract from the Report of the English Commissioner to the New York Exhibition," which I quote from Mr. Carey's *Principles of Social Science* bears striking testimony to one part, at least, of the assertion in the text:—

"We have a few great engineers and mechanics, and a large body of clever workmen; but the Americans seem likely to become a whole nation of such people. Already, their rivers swarm with steamboats; their valleys are becoming crowded with factories; their towns, surpassing those of every state of Europe, except Belgium, Holland, and England, are the abodes of all the skill which now distinguishes a town population; and there is scarcely an art in Europe not carried on in America with equal or greater skill than in Europe, though it has been here cultivated and improved through ages. A whole nation of Franklins, Stephensons, and Watts in prospect, is something wonderful for other nations to contemplate. In contrast with the comparative inertness and ignorance of the bulk of the people of Europe, whatever may be the superiority of a few well-instructed and gifted persons, the great intelligence of the whole people of America is the circumstance most worthy of public attention."

troduction to large, distant, and complicated interests as is afforded by the attention they may be induced to bestow on political affairs. It is by political discussion that the manual labourer, whose employment is a routine, and whose way of life brings him in contact with no variety of impressions, circumstances, or ideas, is taught that remote causes, and events which take place far off, have a most sensible effect even on his personal interests; and it is from political discussion, and collective political action, that one whose daily occupations concentrate his interests in a small circle round himself, learns to feel for and with his fellow-citizens, and becomes consciously a member of a great community. But political discussions fly over the heads of those who have no votes, and are not endeavouring to acquire them. Their position, in comparison with the electors, is that of the audience in a court of justice, compared with the twelve men in the jury-box. It is not *their* suffrages that are asked, it is not their opinion that is sought to be influenced; the appeals are made, the arguments addressed, to others than them; nothing depends on the decision they may arrive at, and there is no necessity and very little inducement to them to come to any. Whoever, in an otherwise popular government, has no vote, and no prospect of obtaining it, will either be a permanent malcontent, or will feel as one whom the general affairs of society do not concern; for whom they are to be managed by others; who "has no business with the laws except to obey them," nor with public interests and concerns except as a looker-on. What he will know or care about them from this position may partly be measured by what an average woman of the middle class knows and cares about politics, compared with her husband or brothers.

Independently of all these considerations, it is a personal injustice to withhold from any one, unless for the prevention of greater evils, the ordinary privilege of having his voice reckoned in the disposal of affairs in which he has the same interest as other people. If he is compelled to pay, if he may be compelled to fight, if he is required implicitly to obey, he should be legally entitled to be told what for; to have his consent asked, and his opinion counted at its worth, though not at more than its worth. There ought to be no pariahs in a full-grown and civilised nation; no persons disqualified, except through their own default. Every one is degraded, whether aware of it or not, when

other people, without consulting him, take upon themselves unlimited power to regulate his destiny. And even in a much more improved state than the human mind has ever yet reached, it is not in nature that they who are thus disposed of should meet with as fair play as those who have a voice. Rulers and ruling classes are under a necessity of considering the interests and wishes of those who have the suffrage; but of those who are excluded, it is in their option whether they will do so or not, and, however honestly disposed, they are in general too fully occupied with things which they *must* attend to, to have much room in their thoughts for anything which they can with impunity disregard. No arrangement of the suffrage, therefore, can be permanently satisfactory in which any person or class is peremptorily excluded; in which the electoral privilege is not open to all persons of full age who desire to obtain it.

There are, however, certain exclusions, required by positive reasons, which do not conflict with this principle, and which, though an evil in themselves, are only to be got rid of by the cessation of the state of things which requires them. I regard it as wholly inadmissible that any person should participate in the suffrage without being able to read, write, and, I will add, perform the common operations of arithmetic. Justice demands, even when the suffrage does not depend on it, that the means of attaining these elementary acquirements should be within the reach of every person, either gratuitously, or at an expense not exceeding what the poorest who earn their own living can afford. If this were really the case, people would no more think of giving the suffrage to a man who could not read, than of giving it to a child who could not speak; and it would not be society that would exclude him, but his own laziness. When society has not performed its duty, by rendering this amount of instruction accessible to all, there is some hardship in the case, but it is a hardship that ought to be borne. If society has neglected to discharge two solemn obligations, the more important and more fundamental of the two must be fulfilled first: universal teaching must precede universal enfranchisement. No one but those in whom an *à priori* theory has silenced common sense will maintain that power over others, over the whole community, should be imparted to people who have not acquired the commonest and most essential requisites for taking care of themselves; for pursuing intelligently their own interests, and those of the persons most nearly allied to them. This argument, doubtless, might be pressed further, and made to prove much more. It would be eminently desirable that other things besides reading, writing, and arithmetic could be made necessary to the suffrage; that some knowledge of the conformation of the earth, its natural and political divisions, the elements of general history, and of the history and institutions of their own country, could be required from all electors. But these kinds of knowledge, however indispensable to an intelligent use of the suffrage, are not, in this country, nor probably anywhere save in the Northern United States, accessible to the whole people; nor does there exist any trustworthy machinery for ascertaining whether they have been acquired or not. The attempt, at present, would lead to partiality, chicanery, and every kind of fraud. It is better that the suffrage should be conferred indiscriminately, or even withheld indiscriminately, than that it should be given to one and withheld from another at the discretion of a public officer. In regard, however, to reading, writing, and calculating, there need be no difficulty. It would be easy to require from every one who presented himself for registry that he should, in the presence of the registrar, copy a sentence from an English book, and perform a sum in the rule of three; and to secure, by fixed rules and complete publicity, the honest application of so very simple a test. This condition, therefore, should in all cases accompany universal suffrage; and it would, after a few years, exclude none but those who cared so little for the privilege, that their vote, if given, would not in general be an indication of any real political opinion.

It is also important, that the assembly which votes the taxes, either general or local, should be elected exclusively by those who pay something towards the taxes imposed. Those who pay no taxes, disposing by their votes of other people's money, have every motive to be lavish and none to economise. As for as money matters are concerned, any power of voting possessed by them is a violation of the fundamental principle of free government; a severance of the power of control from the interest in its beneficial exercise. It amounts to allowing them to put their hands into other people's pockets for any purpose which they think fit to call a public one; which in some of the great towns of the United States is known to have produced a scale of local taxation onerous beyond example, and wholly borne by the wealthier classes. That representation should be co-extensive with taxation, not stopping short of it, but also not going beyond it, is in accordance with the theory of British institutions. But to reconcile this, as a condition annexed to the representation, with universality, it is essential, as it is on many other accounts desirable, that taxation, in a visible shape, should descend to the poorest class. In this country, and in most others, there is probably no labouring family which does not contribute to the indirect taxes, by the purchase of tea, coffee, sugar, not to mention narcotics or stimulants. But this mode of defraying a share of the public expenses is hardly felt: the payer, unless a person of education and reflection, does not identify his interest with a low scale of public expenditure as closely as when money for its support is demanded directly from himself; and even supposing him to do so, he would doubtless take care that, however lavish an expenditure he might, by his vote, assist in imposing upon the government, it should not be defrayed by any additional taxes on the articles which he himself consumes. It would be better that a direct tax, in the simple form of a capitation, should be levied on every grown person in the community; or that every such person should be admitted an elector on allowing himself to be rated *extra ordinem* to the assessed taxes; or that a small annual payment, rising and falling with the gross expenditure of the country, should be required from every registered elector; that so everyone might feel that the money which he assisted in voting was partly his own, and that he was interested in keeping down its amount.

However this may be, I regard it as required by first principles, that the receipt of parish relief should be a peremptory disqualification for the franchise. He who cannot by his labour suffice for his own support has no claim to the privilege of helping himself to the money of others. By becoming dependent on the remaining members of the community for actual subsistence, he abdicates his claim to equal rights with them in other respects. Those to whom he is indebted for the continuance of his very existence may justly claim the exclusive management of those common concerns, to which he now brings nothing, or less than he takes away. As a condition of the franchise, a term should be fixed, say five years previous to the registry, during which the applicant's name has not been on the parish books as a recipient of relief. To be an uncertified bankrupt, or to have taken the benefit of the Insolvent Act, should disqualify for the franchise until the person has paid his debts, or at least proved that he is not now, and has not for some long period been, dependent on eleemosynary support. Non-payment of taxes, when so long persisted in that it cannot have arisen from inadvertence, should disqualify while it lasts. These exclusions are not in their nature permanent. They exact such conditions only as all are able, or ought to be able, to fulfil if they choose. They leave the suffrage accessible to all who are in the normal condition of a human being: and if any one has to forego it, he either does not care sufficiently for it to do for its sake what he is already bound to do, or he is in a general condition of depression and degradation in which this slight addition, necessary for the security of others, would be unfelt, and on emerging from which, this mark of inferiority would disappear with the rest.

In the long run, therefore (supposing no restrictions to exist but those of which we have now treated), we might expect that all, except that (it is to be hoped) progressively diminishing class, the recipients of parish relief, would be in possession of votes, so that the suffrage would be, with that slight abatement, universal. That it should be thus widely expanded is, as we have seen, absolutely necessary to an enlarged and elevated conception of good government. Yet in this state of things, the great majority of voters, in most countries, and emphatically in this, would be manual labourers; and the twofold danger, that of too low a standard of political intelligence, and that of class legislation, would still exist in a very perilous degree. It remains to be seen whether any means exist by which these evils can be obviated.

They are capable of being obviated, if men sincerely wish it; not by any artificial contrivance, but by carrying out the natural order of human life, which recommends itself to every one in things in which he has no interest or traditional opinion running counter to it. In all human affairs, every person directly interested, and not under positive tutelage, has an admitted claim to a voice, and when his exercise of it is not inconsistent with the safety of the whole, cannot justly be excluded from it. But though every one ought to have a voice —that every one should have an equal voice is a totally different proposition. When two persons who have a joint interest in any business differ in opinion, does justice require that both opinions should be held of exactly equal value? If, with equal virtue, one is superior to the other in knowledge and intelligence—or if, with equal intelligence, one excels the other in virtue—the opinion, the judgment, of the higher moral or intellectual being is worth more than that of the inferior: and if the institutions of the country virtually assert that they are of the same value, they assert a thing which is not. One of the two, as the wiser or better man, has a claim to superior weight: the difficulty is in ascertaining which of the two it is; a thing impossible as between individuals, but, taking men in bodies and in numbers, it can be done with a certain approach to accuracy. There would be no pretence for applying this doctrine to any case which could with reason be considered as one of individual and private right. In an affair which concerns only one of two persons, that one is entitled to follow his own opinion, however much wiser the other may be than himself. But we are speaking of things which equally concern them both; where, if the more ignorant does not yield his share of the matter to the guidance of the wiser man, the wiser man must resign his to that of the more ignorant. Which of these modes of getting over the difficulty is most for the interest of both, and most conformable to the general fitness of things? If it be deemed unjust that either should have to give way, which injustice is greatest? that the better judgment should give way to the worse, or the worse to the better?

Now, national affairs are exactly such a joint concern, with the difference, that no one needs ever be called upon for a complete sacrifice of his own opinion. It can always be taken into the calculation, and counted at a certain figure, a higher figure being assigned to the suffrages of those whose opinion is entitled to greater weight. There is not, in this arrangement, anything necessarily invidious to those to whom it assigns the lower degrees of influence. Entire exclusion from a voice in the common concerns is one thing: the concession to others of a more potential voice, on the ground of greater capacity for the management of the joint interests, is another. The two things are not merely different, they are incommensurable. Every one has a right to feel insulted by being made a nobody, and stamped as of no account at all. No one but a fool, and only a fool of a peculiar description, feels offended by the acknowledgment that there are others whose opinion, and even whose wish, is entitled to a greater amount of consideration than his. To have no voice in what are partly his own concerns is a thing which nobody willingly submits to; but when what is partly his concern is also partly another's, and he feels the other to understand the subject better than himself, that the other's opinion should be counted for more than his own accords with his expectations, and with the course of things which in all other affairs of life he is accustomed to acquiese in. It is only necessary that this superior influence should be assigned on grounds which he can comprehend, and of which he is able to perceive the justice.

I hasten to say that I consider it entirely inadmissible, unless as a temporary makeshift, that the superiority of influence should be conferred in consideration of property. I do not deny that property is a kind of test; education in most countries, though anything but proportional to riches, is on the average better in the richer half of society than in the poorer. But the criterion is so imperfect; accident has so much more to do than merit with enabling men to rise in the world; and it is so impossible for any one, by acquiring any amount of instruction, to make sure of the corresponding rise in station, that this foundation of electoral privilege is always, and will continue to be, supremely odious. To connect plurality of votes with any pecuniary qualification would be not only objectionable in itself, but a sure mode of discrediting the principle, and making its permanent maintenance impracticable. The Democracy, at least of this country, are not at present jealous of personal superiority, but they are naturally and must justly so of that which is grounded on mere pecuniary circumstances. The only thing which can justify reckoning one person's opinion as equivalent to more than one is individual mental superiority; and what is wanted is some approximate means of ascertaining that. If there existed such a thing as a really national education or a trustworthy system of general examination, education might be tested directly. In the absence of these, the nature of a person's occupation is some test. An employer of labour is on the average more intelligent than a labourer; for he must labour with his head, and not solely with his hands. A foreman is generally more intelligent than an ordinary labourer, and a labourer in the skilled trades than in the unskilled. A banker, merchant, or manufacturer is likely to be more intelligent than a

tradesman, because he has larger and more complicated interests to manage.

In all these cases it is not the having merely undertaken the superior function, but the successful performance of it, that tests the qualifications; for which reason, as well as to prevent persons from engaging nominally in an occupation for the sake of the vote, it would be proper to require that the occupation should have been persevered in for some length of time (say three years). Subject to some such condition, two or more votes might be allowed to every person who exercises any of these superior functions. The liberal professions, when really and not nominally practised, imply, of course, a still higher degree of instruction; and wherever a sufficient examination, or any serious conditions of education, are required before entering on a profession, its members could be admitted at once to a plurality of votes. The same rule might be applied to graduates of universities; and even to those who bring satisfactory certificates of having passed through the course of study required by any school at which the higher branches of knowledge are taught, under proper securities that the teaching is real, and not a mere pretence. The "local" or "middle class" examination for the degree of Associate, so laudably and public-spiritedly established by the Universities of Oxford and Cambridge, and any similar ones which may be instituted by other competent bodies (provided they are fairly open to all comers), afford a ground on which plurality of votes might with great advantage be accorded to those who have passed the test. All these suggestions are open to much discussion in the detail, and to objections which it is of no use to anticipate. The time is not come for giving to such plans a practical shape, nor should I wish to be bound by the particular proposals which I have made. But it is to me evident, that in this direction lies the true ideal of representative government; and that to work towards it, by the best practical contrivances which can be found, is the path of real political improvement.

If it be asked to what length the principle admits of being carried, or how many votes might be accorded to an individual on the ground of superior qualifications, I answer, that this is not in itself very material, provided the distinctions and gradations are not made arbitrarily, but are such as can be understood and accepted by the general conscience and understanding. But it is an absolute condition not to overpass the limit prescribed by the fundamental principle laid down in a former chapter as the condition of excellence in the constitution of a representative system. The plurality of votes must on no account be carried so far that those who are privileged by it, or the class (if any) to which they mainly belong, shall outweigh by means of it all the rest of the community. The distinction in favour of education, right in itself, is further and strongly recommended by its preserving the educated from the class legislation of the uneducated; but it must stop short of enabling them to practise class legislation on their own account. Let me add, that I consider it an absolutely necessary part of the plurality scheme that it be open to the poorest individual in the community to claim its privileges, if he can prove that, in spite of all difficulties and obstacles, he is, in point of intelligence, entitled to them. There ought to be voluntary examinations at which any person whatever might present himself, might prove that he came up to the standard of knowledge and ability laid down as sufficient, and be admitted, in consequence, to the plurality of votes. A privilege which is not refused to any one who can show that he has realised the conditions on which in theory and principle it is dependent would not necessarily be repugnant to any one's sentiment of justice: but it would certainly be so, if, while conferred on general presumptions not always infallible, it were denied to direct proof.

Plural voting, though practised in vestry elections and those of poor-law guardians, is so unfamiliar in elections to Parliament that it is not likely to be soon or willingly adopted: but as the time will certainly arrive when the only choice will be between this and equal universal suffrage, whoever does not desire the last, cannot too soon begin to reconcile himself to the former. In the meantime, though the suggestion, for the present, may not be a practical one, it will serve to mark what is best in principle, and enable us to judge of the eligibility of any indirect means, either existing or capable of being adopted, which may promote in a less perfect manner the same end. A person may have a double vote by other means than that of tendering two votes at the same hustings; he may have a vote in each of two different constituencies: and though this exceptional privilege at present belongs rather to superiority of means than of intelligence, I would not abolish it where it exists, since until

a truer test of education is adopted it would be unwise to dispense with even so imperfect a one as is afforded by pecuniary circumstances. Means might be found of giving a further extension to the privilege, which would connect it in a more direct manner with superior education. In any future Reform Bill which lowers greatly the pecuniary conditions of the suffrage, it might be a wise provision to allow all graduates of universities, all persons who have passed creditably through the higher schools, all members of the liberal professions, and perhaps some others, to be registered specifically in those characters, and to give their votes as such in any constituency in which they choose to register; retaining, in addition, their votes as simple citizens in the localities in which they reside.

Until there shall have been devised, and until opinion is willing to accept, some mode of plural voting which may assign to education, as such, the degree of superior influence due to it, and sufficient as a counterpoise to the numerical weight of the least educated class; for so long the benefits of completely universal suffrage cannot be obtained without bringing with them, as it appears to me, a chance of more than equivalent evils. It is possible, indeed (and this is perhaps one of the transitions through which we may have to pass in our progress to a really good representative system), that the barriers which restrict the suffrage might be entirely levelled in some particular constituencies, whose members, consequently, would be returned principally by manual labourers; the existing electoral qualification being maintained elsewhere, or any alteration in it being accompanied by such a grouping of the constituencies as to prevent the labouring class from becoming preponderant in Parliament. By such a compromise, the anomalies in the representation would not only be retained, but augmented: this however is not a conclusive objection; for if the country does not choose to pursue the right ends by a regular system directly leading to them, it must be content with an irregular makeshift, as being greatly preferable to a system free from irregularities, but regularly adapted to wrong ends, or in which some ends equally necessary with the others have been left out. It is a far graver objection, that this adjustment is incompatible with the intercommunity of local constituencies which Mr. Hare's plan requires; that under it every voter would remain imprisoned within the one or more constituencies in which his name is registered, and unless willing to be represented by one of the candidates for those localities, would not be represented at all.

So much importance do I attach to the emancipation of those who already have votes, but whose votes are useless, because always outnumbered; so much should I hope from the natural influence of truth and reason, if only secured a hearing and a competent advocacy—that I should not despair of the operation even of equal and universal suffrage, if made real by the proportional representation of all minorities, on Mr. Hare's principle. But if the best hopes which can be formed on this subject were certainties, I should still contend for the principle of plural voting. I do not propose the plurality as a thing in itself undesirable, which, like the exclusion of part of the community from the suffrage, may be temporarily tolerated while necessary to prevent greater evils. I do not look upon equal voting as among the things which are good in themselves, provided they can be guarded against inconveniences. I look upon it as only relatively good; less objectionable than inequality of privilege grounded on irrelevant or adventitious circumstances, but in principle wrong, because recognising a wrong standard, and exercising a bad influence on the voter's mind. It is not useful, but hurtful, that the constitution of the country should declare ignorance to be entitled to as much political power as knowledge. The national institutions should place all things that they are concerned with before the mind of the citizen in the light in which it is for his good that he should regard them: and as it is for his good that he should think that every one is entitled to some influence, but the better and wiser to more than others, it is important that this conviction should be professed by the State, and embodied in the national institutions. Such things constitute the *spirit* of the institutions of a country: that portion of their influence which is least regarded by common, and especially by English, thinkers; though the institutions of every country, not under great positive oppression, produce more effect by their spirit than by any of their direct provisions, since by it they shape the national character. The American institutions have imprinted strongly on the American mind that any one man (with a white skin) is as good as any other; and it is felt that this false creed is nearly connected with some of the more unfavourable points in American character. It is not a small mischief that the constitution of any country should sanction this creed; for the belief in it, whether express or tacit, is almost as detrimental to moral and intellectual excellence as any effect which most forms of government can produce.

It may, perhaps, be said, that a constitution which gives equal influence, man for man, to the most and to the least instructed, is nevertheless conducive to progress, because the appeals constantly made to the less instructed classes, the exercise given to their mental powers, and the exertions which the more instructed are obliged to make for enlightening their judgment and ridding them of errors and prejudices, are powerful stimulants to their advance in intelligence. That this most desirable effect really attends the admission of the less educated classes to some, and even to a large share of power, I admit, and have already strenuously maintained. But theory and experience alike prove that a counter current sets in when they are made the possessors of all power. Those who are supreme over everything, whether they be One, or Few, or Many, have no longer need of the arms of reason: they can make their mere will prevail; and those who cannot be resisted are usually far too well satisfied with their own opinions to be willing to change them, or listen without impatience to any one who tells them that they are in the wrong. The position which gives the strongest stimulus to the growth of intelligence is that of rising into power, not that of having achieved it; and of all resting-points, temporary or permanent, in the way to ascendancy, the one which develops the best and highest qualities is the position of those who are strong enough to make reason prevail, but not strong enough to prevail against reason. This is the position in which, according to the principles we have laid down, the rich and the poor, the much and the little educated, and all the other classes and denominations which divide society between them, ought as far as practicable to be placed. And by combining this principle with the otherwise just one of allowing superiority of weight to superiority of mental qualities, a political constitution would realise that kind of relative perfection which is alone compatible with the complicated nature of human affairs.

In the preceding argument for universal, but graduated suffrage, I have taken no account of difference of sex. I consider it to be as entirely irrelevant to political rights as difference in height or in the colour of the hair. All human beings have the same interest in good government; the welfare of all is alike affected by it, and they have equal need of a voice in it to secure their share of its benefits. If there be any difference, women require it more than men, since, being physically weaker, they are more dependent on law and society for protection. Mankind have long since abandoned the only premises which will support the conclusion that women ought not to have votes. No one now holds that women should be in personal servitude; that they should have no thought, wish, or occupation, but to be the domestic drudges of husbands, fathers, or brothers. It is allowed to unmarried, and wants but little of being conceded to married women, to hold property, and have pecuniary and business interests, in the same manner as men. It is considered suitable and proper that women should think, and write, and be teachers. As soon as these things are admitted, the political disqualification has no principle to rest on. The whole mode of thought of the modern world is with increasing emphasis pronouncing against the claim of society to decide for individuals what they are and are not fit for, and what they shall and shall not be allowed to attempt. If the principles of modern politics and political economy are good for anything, it is for proving that these points can only be rightly judged of by the individuals themselves: and that, under complete freedom of choice, wherever there are real diversities of aptitude, the great number will apply themselves to the things for which they are on the average fittest, and the exceptional course will only be taken by the exceptions. Either the whole tendency of modern social improvements has been wrong, or it ought to be carried out to the total abolition of all exclusions and disabilities which close any honest employment to a human being.

But it is not even necessary to maintain so much in order to prove that women should have the suffrage. Were it as right, as it is wrong, that they should be a subordinate class, confined to domestic occupations and subject to domestic authority, they would not the less require the protection of the suffrage to secure them from the abuse of that authority. Men, as well as women, do not need political rights in order that they may govern, but in order that they may not be misgoverned. The majority of the male sex are, and will be all their lives, nothing else than labourers in cornfields or manufactories; but this does not render the suffrage less desirable for them, nor their claim to it less irresistible, when not likely to make a bad use of it. Nobody pretends to think that woman would make a bad use of the suffrage. The worst that is said is that they would vote as mere dependents, at the bidding of their male relations. If it be so, so let it be. If they think for themselves, great good will be done, and if they do not, no harm. It is a benefit to human beings to take off their fetters, even if they do not desire to walk. It would already be a great improvement in the moral position of women to be no longer declared by law incapable of an opinion, and not entitled to a preference, respecting the most important concerns of humanity. There would be some benefit to them individually in having something to bestow which their male relatives cannot exact, and are yet desirous to have. It would also be no small benefit that the husband would necessarily discuss the matter with his wife, and that the vote would not be his exclusive affair, but a joint concern. People do not sufficiently consider how markedly the fact that she is able to have some action on the outward world independently of him raises her dignity and value in a vulgar man's eyes, and makes her the object of a respect which no personal qualities would ever obtain for one whose social existence he can entirely appropriate.

The vote itself, too, would be improved in quality. The man would often be obliged to find honest reasons for his vote, such as might induce a more upright and impartial character to serve with him under the same banner. The wife's influence would often keep him true to his own sincere opinion. Often, indeed, it would be used, not on the side of public principle, but of the personal interest or worldly vanity of the family. But wherever this would be the tendency of the wife's influence, it is exerted to the full already in that bad direction; and with the more certainty, since under the present law and custom she is generally too utter a stranger to politics in any sense in which they involve principle to be able to realise to herself that there is a point of honour in them, and most people have as little sympathy in the point of honour of others, when their own is not placed in the same thing, as they have in the religious feelings of those whose religion differs from theirs. Give the woman a vote, and she comes under the operation of the political point of honour. She learns to look on politics as a thing on which she is allowed to have an opinion, and in which if one has an opinion it ought to be acted upon; she acquires a sense of personal accountability in the matter, and will no longer feel, as she does at present, that whatever amount of bad influence she may exercise, if the man can but be persuaded, all is right, and his responsibility covers all. It is only by being herself encouraged to form an opinion, and obtain an intelligent comprehension of the reasons which ought to prevail with the conscience against the temptations of personal or family interest, that she can ever cease to act as a disturbing force on the political conscience of the man. Her indirect agency can only be prevented from being politically mischievous by being exchanged for direct.

I have supposed the right of suffrage to depend, as in a good state of things it would, on personal conditions. Where it depends, as in this and most other countries, on conditions of property, the contradiction is even more flagrant. There is something more than ordinarily irrational in the fact that when a woman can give all the guarantees required from a male elector, independent circumstances, the position of a householder and head of a family, payment of taxes, or whatever may be the conditions imposed, the very principle and system of a representation based on property is set aside, and an exceptionally personal disqualification is created for the mere purpose of excluding her. When it is added that in the country where this is done a woman now reigns, and that the most glorious ruler whom that country ever had was a woman, the picture of unreason, and scarcely disguised injustice, is complete. Let us hope that as the work proceeds of pulling down, one after another, the remains of the mouldering fabric of monopoly and tyranny, this one will not be the last to disappear; that the opinion of Bentham, of Mr. Samuel Bailey, of Mr. Hare, and many other of the most powerful political thinkers of this age and country (not to speak of others), will make its way to all minds not rendered obdurate by selfishness or inveterate prejudice; and that, before the lapse of another generation, the accident of sex, no more than the accident of skin, will be deemed a sufficient justification for depriving its possessor of the equal protection and just privileges of a citizen.

Chapter 9
Should there be Two Stages of Election?

IN SOME representative constitutions the plan has been adopted of choosing the members of the representative body by a double process, the primary electors only choosing other electors, and these electing the member of parliament. This contrivance was probably intended as a slight impediment to the full sweep of popular feeling; giving the suffrage, and with it the complete ultimate power, to the Many, but compelling them to exercise it through the agency of a comparatively few, who, it was supposed, would be less moved than the Demos by the gusts of popular passion; and as the electors, being already a select body, might be expected to exceed in intellect and character the common level of their constituents, the choice made by them was thought likely to be more careful and enlightened, and would in any case be made under a greater feeling of responsibility, than election by the masses themselves. This plan of filtering, as it were, the popular suffrage through an intermediate body admits of a very plausible defence; since it may be said, with great appearance of reason, that less intellect and instruction are required for judging who among our neighbours can be most safely trusted to choose a member of parliament, than who is himself fittest to be one.

In the first place, however, if the dangers incident to popular power may be thought to be in some degree lessened by this indirect arrangement, so also are its benefits; and the latter effect is much more certain than the former. To enable the system to work as desired, it must be carried into effect in the spirit in which it is planned; the electors must use the suffrage in the manner supposed by the theory, that is, each of them must not ask himself who the member of parliament should be, but only whom he would best like to choose one for him. It is evident that the advantages which indirect is supposed to have over direct election require this disposition of mind in the voter, and will only be realised by his taking the doctrine *au sérieux*, that his sole business is to choose the choosers, not the member himself. The supposition must be, that he will not occupy his thoughts with political opinions and measures, or political men, but will be guided by his personal respect for some private individual, to whom he will give a general power of attorney to act for him. Now if the primary electors adopt this view of their position, one of the principal uses of giving them a vote at all is defeated: the political function to which they are called fails of developing public spirit and political intelligence; of making public affairs an object of interest to their feelings and of exercise to their faculties. The supposition, moreover, involves inconsistent conditions; for if the voter feels no interest in the final result, how or why can he be expected to feel any in the process which leads to it? To wish to have a particular individual for his representative in parliament is possible to a person of a very moderate degree of virtue and intelligence; and to wish to choose an elector who will elect that individual is a natural consequence: but for a person who does not care who is elected, or feels bound to put that consideration in abeyance, to take any interest whatever in merely naming the worthiest person to elect another according to his own judgment, implies a zeal for what is right in the abstract, an habitual principle of duty for the sake of duty, which is possible only to persons of a rather high grade of cultivation, who, by the very possession of it, show that they may be, and deserve to be, trusted with political power in a more direct shape. Of all public functions which it is possible to confer on the poorer members of the community this surely is the least calculated to kindle their feelings, and holds out least natural inducement to care for it, other than a virtuous determination to discharge conscientiously whatever duty one has to perform: and if the mass of electors cared enough about political affairs to set any value on so limited a participation in them, they would not be likely to be satisfied without one much more extensive.

In the next place, admitting that a person who, from his narrow range of cultivation, cannot judge well of the qualifications of a candidate for parliament may be a sufficient judge of the honesty and general capacity of somebody whom he may depute to choose a member of Parliament for him; I may remark, that if the voter acquiesces in this estimate of his capabilities, and really wishes to have the choice made for him by a person in whom he places reliance, there is no need of any constitutional provision for the purpose; he has only to ask this confidential person privately what candidate he had better vote for. In that case the two modes of election coincide in their result, and every advantage of indirect election is obtained under direct. The systems only diverge in their operation, if we suppose that the voter would prefer to use his own judgment in the choice of a representative, and only lets another choose for him because the law does not allow him a more direct mode of action. But if this be his state of mind; if his will does not go along with the limitation which the law imposes, and he desires to make a direct choice, he can do so notwithstanding the law. He has only to choose as elector a known partisan of the candidate he prefers, or some one who will pledge himself to vote for that candidate. And this is so much the natural working of election by two stages that, except in a condition of complete political indifference, it can scarcely be expected to act otherwise. It is in this way that the election of the President of the United States practically takes place. Nominally, the election is indirect: the population at large does not vote for the President; it votes for electors who choose the President. But the electors are always chosen under an express engagement to vote for a particular candidate: nor does a citizen ever vote for an elector because of any preference for the man; he votes for the Lincoln ticket, or the Breckenridge ticket. It must be remembered that the electors are not chosen in order that they may search the country and find the fittest person in it to be President, or to be a member of Parliament. There would be something to be said for the practice if this were so: but it is not so; nor ever will be until mankind in general are of opinion, with Plato, that the proper person to be entrusted with power is the person most unwilling to accept it. The electors are to make choice of one of those who have offered themselves as candidates: and those who choose the electors already know who these are. If there is any political activity in the country, all electors, who care to vote at all, have made up their minds which of these candidates they would like to have; and will make that the sole consideration in giving their vote. The partisans of each candidate will have their list of electors ready, all pledged to vote for that individual; and the only question practically asked of the primary elector will be which of these lists he will support.

The case in which election by two stages answers well in practice is when the electors are not chosen solely as electors, but have other important functions to discharge, which precludes their being selected solely as delegates to give a particular vote. This combination of circumstances exemplifies itself in another American institution, the Senate of the United States. That assembly, the Upper House, as it were, of Congress, is considered to represent not the people directly, but the States as such, and to be the guardian of that portion of their sovereign rights which they have not alienated. As the internal sovereignty of each State is, by the nature of an equal federation, equally sacred whatever be the size or importance of the State, each returns to the Senate the same number of members (two), whether it be little Delaware or the "Empire State" of New York. These members are not chosen by the population, but by the State Legislatures, themselves elected by the people of each State; but as the whole ordinary business of a legislative assembly, internal legislation and the control of the executive, devolves upon these bodies, they are elected with a view to those objects more than to the other; and in naming two persons to represent the State in the Federal Senate they for the most part exercise their own judgment, with only that general reference to public opinion necessary in all acts of the government of a democracy. The elections, thus made, have proved eminently successful, and are conspicuously the best of all the elections in the United States, the Senate invariably consisting of the most distinguished men among those who have made themselves sufficiently known in public life.

After such an example, it cannot be said that indirect popular election is never advantageous. Under certain conditions it is the very best system that can be adopted. But those conditions are hardly to be obtained in practice, except in a federal government like that of the United States, where the election can be entrusted to local bodies whose other functions extend to the most important concerns of the nation. The only bodies in any analogous position which exist, or are likely to exist, in this country are the municipalities, or any other boards which have been or may be created for similar local purposes. Few persons, however, would think it any improvement in our parliamentary constitution if the members for the City of London were chosen by the Aldermen and Common Council, and those for the borough of Marylebone avowedly, as they already are virtually, by the vestries of the component parishes. Even if those bodies, considered merely as local boards, were far less

objectionable than they are, the qualities that would fit them for the limited and peculiar duties of municipal or parochial ædileship are no guarantee of any special fitness to judge of the comparative qualifications of candidates for a seat in Parliament. They probably would not fulfil this duty any better than it is fulfilled by the inhabitants voting directly; while, on the other hand, if fitness for electing members of Parliament had to be taken into consideration in selecting persons for the office of vestrymen or town councillors, many of those who are fittest for that more limited duty would inevitably be excluded from it, if only by the necessity there would be of choosing persons whose sentiments in general politics agreed with those of the voters who elected them. The mere indirect political influence of town-councils has already led to a considerable perversion of municipal elections from their intended purpose, by making them a matter of party politics. If it were part of the duty of a man's book-keeper or steward to choose his physician, he would not be likely to have a better medical attendant than if he chose one for himself, while he would be restricted in his choice of a steward or book-keeper to such as might without too great danger to his health be entrusted with the other office.

It appears, therefore, that every benefit of indirect election which is attainable at all is attainable under direct; that such of the benefits expected from it, as would not be obtained under direct election, will just as much fail to be obtained under indirect; while the latter has considerable disadvantages peculiar to itself. The mere fact that it is an additional and superfluous wheel in the machinery is no trifling objection. Its decided inferiority as a means of cultivating public spirit and political intelligence has already been dwelt upon: and if it had any effective operation at all—that is, if the primary electors did to any extent leave to their nominees the selection of their parliamentary representative—the voter would be prevented from identifying himself with his member of Parliament, and the member would feel a much less active sense of responsibility to his constituents. In addition to all this, the comparatively small number of persons in whose hands, at last, the election of a member of Parliament would reside, could not but afford great additional facilities to intrigue, and to every form of corruption compatible with the station in life of the electors. The constituencies would universally be reduced, in point of conveniences for bribery, to the condition of the small boroughs at present. It would be sufficient to gain over a small number of persons to be certain of being returned. If it be said that the electors would be responsible to those who elected them, the answer is obvious, that, holding no permanent office, or position in the public eye, they would risk nothing by a corrupt vote except what they would care little for, not to be appointed electors again: and the main reliance must still be on the penalties for bribery, the insufficiency of which reliance, in small constituencies, experience has made notorious to all the world. The evil would be exactly proportional to the amount of discretion left to the chosen electors. The only case in which they would probably be afraid to employ their vote for the promotion of their personal interest would be when they were elected under an express pledge, as mere delegates, to carry, as it were, the votes of their constituents to the hustings. The moment the double stage of election began to have any effect, it would begin to have a bad effect. And this we shall find true of the principle of indirect election however applied, except in circumstances similar to those of the election of Senators in the United States.

The best which could be said for this political contrivance is that in some states of opinion it might be a more practicable expedient than that of plural voting for giving to every member of the community a vote of some sort, without rendering the mere numerical majority predominant in Parliament: as, for instance, if the present constituency of this country were increased by the addition of a numerous and select portion of the labouring classes, elected by the remainder. Circumstances might render such a scheme a convenient mode of temporary compromise, but it does not carry out any principle sufficiently thoroughly to be likely to recommend itself to any class of thinkers as a permanent arrangement.

Chapter 10
Of the Mode of Voting

THE QUESTION of greatest moment in regard to modes of voting is that of secrecy or publicity; and to this we will at once address ourselves.

It would be a great mistake to make the discussion turn on sentimentalities about skulking or cowardice. Secrecy is justifiable in many cases, imperative in some, and it is not cowardice to seek protection against evils which are honestly avoidable. Nor can it be reasonably maintained that no cases are conceivable in which secret voting is preferable to public. But I must contend that these cases, in affairs of a political character, are the exception, not the rule.

The present is one of the many instances in which, as I have already had occasion to remark, the *spirit* of an institution, the impression it makes on the mind of the citizen, is one of the most important parts of its operation. The spirit of vote by ballot—the interpretation likely to be put on it in the mind of an elector—is that the suffrage is given to him for himself; for his particular use and benefit, and not as a trust for the public. For if it is indeed a trust, if the public are entitled to his vote, are not they entitled to know his vote? This false and pernicious impression may well be made on the generality, since it has been made on most of those who of late years have been conspicuous advocates of the ballot. The doctrine was not so understood by its earlier promoters; but the effect of a doctrine on the mind is best shown, not in those who form it, but in those who are formed by it. Mr. Bright and his school of democrats think themselves greatly concerned in maintaining that the franchise is what they term a right, not a trust. Now this one idea, taking root in the general mind, does a moral mischief outweighing all the good that the ballot could do, at the highest possible estimate of it. In whatever way we define or understand the idea of a right, no person can have a right (except in the purely legal sense) to power over others: every such power, which he is allowed to possess, is morally, in the fullest force of the term, a trust. But the exercise of any political function, either as an elector or as a representative, is power over others.

Those who say that the suffrage is not a trust but a right will scarcely accept the conclusions to which their doctrine leads. If it is a right, if it belongs to the voter for his own sake, on what ground can we blame him for selling it, or using it to recommend himself to any one whom it is his interest to please? A person is not expected to consult exclusively the public benefit in the use he makes of his house, or his three per cent. stock, or anything else to which he really has a right. The suffrage is indeed due to him, among other reasons, as a means to his own protection, but only against treatment from which he is equally bound, so far as depends on his vote, to protect every one of his fellow-citizens. His vote is not a thing in which he has an option; it has no more to do with his personal wishes than the verdict of a juryman. It is strictly a matter of duty; he is bound to give it according to his best and most conscientious opinion of the public good. Whoever has any other idea of it is unfit to have the suffrage; its effect on him is to pervert, not to elevate his mind. Instead of opening his heart to an exalted patriotism and the obligation of public duty, it awakens and nourishes in him the disposition to use a public function for his own interest, pleasure, or caprice; the same feelings and purposes, on a humbler scale, which actuate a despot and oppressor. Now an ordinary citizen in any public position, or on whom there devolves any social function, is certain to think and feel, respecting the obligations it imposes on him, exactly what society appears to think and feel in conferring it. What seems to be expected from him by society forms a standard which he may fall below, but which he will seldom rise above. And the interpretation which he is almost sure to put upon secret voting is that he is not bound to give his vote with any reference to those who are not allowed to know how he gives it; but may bestow it simply as he feels inclined.

This is the decisive reason why the argument does not hold, from the use of the ballot in clubs and private societies, to its adoption in parliamentary elections. A member of a club is really, what the elector falsely believes himself to be, under no obligation to consider the wishes or interests of any one else. He declares nothing by his vote but that he is or is not willing to associate, in a manner more or less close, with a particular person. This is a matter on which, by universal admission, his own pleasure or inclination is entitled to decide: and that he should be able so to decide it without risking a quarrel is best for everybody, the rejected person included. An additional reason rendering the ballot unobjectionable in these cases is that it does not necessarily or naturally lead to lying. The persons concerned are of the same class or rank, and it would be considered improper in one of them to press another with questions as to how he had voted. It is far otherwise in parliamentary elections, and is likely to remain so, as long as the social relations exist which produce the demand for the ballot; as long as one person is sufficiently the superior of another to think himself entitled to dictate his vote. And while this is the case, silence or an evasive answer is certain to be construed as proof that the vote given has not been that which was desired.

In any political election, even by universal suffrage (and still more obviously in the case of a restricted suffrage), the voter is under an absolute moral obligation to consider the interest of the public, not his private advantage, and give his vote, to the best of his judgment, exactly as he would be bound to do if he were the sole voter, and the election depended upon him alone. This being admitted, it is at least a *prima facie* consequence that the duty of voting, like any other public duty, should be performed under the eye and criticism of the public; every one of whom has not only an interest in its performance, but a good title to consider himself wronged if it is performed otherwise than honestly and carefully. Undoubtedly neither this nor any other maxim of political morality is absolutely inviolable; it may be overruled by still more cogent considerations. But its weight is such that the cases which admit of a departure from it must be of a strikingly exceptional character.

It may, unquestionably, be the fact that if we attempt, by publicity, to make the voter responsible to the public for his vote, he will practically be made responsible for it to some powerful individual, whose interest is more opposed to the general interest of the community than that of the voter himself would be if, by the shield of secrecy, he were released from responsibility altogether. When this is the condition, in a high degree, of a large proportion of the voters, the ballot may be the smaller evil. When the voters are slaves, anything may be tolerated which enables them to throw off the yoke. The strongest case for the ballot is when the mischievous power of the Few over the Many is increasing. In the decline of the Roman republic the reasons for the ballot were irresistible. The oligarchy was yearly becoming richer and more tyrannical, the people poorer and more dependent, and it was necessary to erect stronger and stronger barriers against such abuse of the franchise as rendered it but an instrument the more in the hands of unprincipled persons of consequence. As little can it be doubted that the ballot, so far as it existed, had a beneficial operation in the Athenian constitution. Even in the least unstable of the Grecian commonwealths freedom might be for the time destroyed by a single unfairly obtained popular vote; and though the Athenian voter was not sufficiently dependent to be habitually coerced, he might have been bribed, or intimidated by the lawless outrages of some knot of individuals, such as were not uncommon even at Athens among the youth of rank and fortune. The ballot was in these cases a valuable instrument of order, and conduced to the Eunomia by which Athens was distinguished among the ancient commonwealths.

But in the more advanced states of modern Europe, and especially in this country, the power of coercing voters has declined and is declining; and bad voting is now less to be apprehended from the influences to which the voter is subject at the hands of others than from the sinister interests and discreditable feelings which belong to himself, either individually or as a member of a class. To secure him against the first, at the cost of removing all restraint from the last, would be to exchange a smaller and a diminishing evil for a greater and increasing one. On this topic, and on the question generally, as applicable to England at the present date, I have, in a pamphlet on Parliamentary Reform, expressed myself in terms which, as I do not feel that I can improve upon, I will venture here to transcribe.

"Thirty years ago it was still true that in the election of members of Parliament the main evil to be guarded against was that which the ballot would exclude—coercion by landlords, employers, and customers. At present, I conceive, a much greater source of evil is the selfishness, or the selfish partialities, of the voter himself. A base and mischievous vote is now, I am convinced, much oftener given from the voter's personal interest, or class interest, or some mean feeling in his own mind, than from any fear of consequences at the hands of others: and to these influences the ballot would enable him to yield himself up, free from all sense of shame or responsibility.

"In times not long gone by, the higher and richer classes were in complete possession of the government. Their power was the master grievance of the country. The habit of voting at the bidding of an employer, or of a landlord, was so firmly established, that hardly anything was capable of shaking it but a strong popular enthusiasm, seldom known to exist but in a good cause. A vote given in opposition to those influences was therefore, in general, an honest, a public-spirited vote; but in any case, and by whatever motive dictated, it was almost sure to be a good vote, for it was a vote against the monster evil, the over-ruling influence of oligarchy. Could the voter at that time have been enabled, with safety to himself, to exercise his privilege freely, even though neither honestly nor intelligently, it would have been a great gain to reform; for it would have broken the yoke of the then ruling power in the country—the power which had created and which maintained all that was bad in the institutions and the administration of the State—the power of landlords and boroughmongers.

"The ballot was not adopted; but the progress of circumstances has done and is doing more and more, in this respect, the work of the ballot. Both the political and the social state of the country, as they affect this question, have greatly changed, and are changing every day. The higher classes are not now masters of the country. A person must be blind to all the signs of the times who could think that the middle classes are as subservient to the higher, or the working classes as dependent on the higher and middle, as they were a quarter of a century ago. The events of that quarter of a century have not only taught each class to know its own collective strength, but have put the individuals of a lower class in a condition to show a much bolder front to those of a higher. In a majority of cases, the vote of the electors, whether in opposition to or in accordance with the wishes of their superiors, is not now the effect of coercion, which there are no longer the same means of applying, but the expression of their own personal or political partialities. The very vices of the present electoral system are a proof of this. The growth of bribery, so loudly complained of, and the spread of the contagion to places formerly free from it, are evidence that the local influences are no longer paramount; that the electors now vote to please themselves, and not other people. There is, no doubt, in counties, and in the smaller boroughs, a large amount of servile dependence still remaining; but the temper of the times is adverse to it, and the force of events is constantly tending to diminish it. A good tenant can now feel that he is as valuable to his landlord as his landord is to him; a prosperous tradesman can afford to feel independent of any particular customer. At every election the votes are more and more the voter's own. It is their minds, far more than their personal circumstances, that now require to be emancipated. They are no longer passive instruments of other men's will—mere organs for putting power into the hands of a controlling oligarchy. The electors themselves are becoming the oligarchy.

"Exactly in proportion as the vote of the elector is determined by his own will, and not by that of somebody who is his master, his position is similar to that of a member of Parliament, and publicity is indispensable. So long as any portion of the community are unrepresented, the argument of the Chartists against ballot in conjunction with a restricted suffrage is unassailable. The present electors, and the bulk of those whom any probable Reform Bill would add to the number, are the middle class; and have as much a class interest, distinct from the working classes, as landlords or great manufacturers. Were the suffrage extended to all skilled labourers, even these would, or might, still have a class interest distinct from the unskilled. Suppose it extended to all men—suppose that what was formerly called by the misapplied name of universal suffrage, and now by the silly title of manhood suffrage, became the law; the voters would still have a class interest, as distinguished from women. Suppose that there were a question before the Legislature specially affecting women; as whether women should be allowed to graduate at Universities; whether the mild penalties inflicted on ruffians who beat their wives daily almost to death's door should be exchanged for something more effectual; or suppose that any one should propose in the British Parliament, what one State after another in America is enacting, not by a mere law, but by a provision of their revised Constitutions—that married women should have a right to their own property. Are not a man's wife and daughters entitled to know whether he votes for or against a candidate who will support these propositions?

"It will of course be objected that these arguments derive all their weight from the supposition of an unjust state of the suffrage: That if the opinion of the non-electors is likely to make the elector vote more honestly, or more beneficially, than he would vote if left to himself, they are more fit to be electors than he is, and ought to have the franchise: That whoever is fit to influence electors is fit to be an elector: That those to whom voters ought to be responsible should be themselves voters; and being such, should have the safeguard of the ballot to shield them from the undue influence of powerful individuals or classes to whom they ought not to be responsible.

"This argument is specious, and I once thought it conclusive. It now appears to me fallacious. All who are fit to influence electors are not, for that reason, fit to be themselves electors. This last is a much greater power than the former, and those may be ripe for the minor political function who could not as yet be safely trusted with the superior. The opinions and wishes of the poorest and rudest class of labourers may be very useful as one influence among others on the minds of the voters, as well as on those of the Legislature; and yet it might be highly mischievous to give them the preponderant influence by admitting them, in their present state of morals and intelligence, to the full exercise of the suffrage. It is precisely this indirect influence of those who have not the suffrage over those who have which, by its progressive growth, softens the transition to every fresh extension of the franchise, and is the means by which, when the time is ripe, the extension is peacefully brought about. But there is another and a still deeper consideration, which should never be left out of the account in political speculations. The notion is itself unfounded, that publicity, and the sense of being answerable to the public, are of no use unless the public are qualified to form a sound judgment. It is a very superficial view of the utility of public opinion to suppose that it does good only when it succeeds in enforcing a servile conformity to itself. To be under the eyes of others—to have to defend oneself to others—is never more important than to those who act in opposition to the opinion of others, for it obliges them to have sure ground of their own. Nothing has so steadying an influence as working against pressure. Unless when under the temporary sway of passionate excitement, no one will do that which he expects to be greatly blamed for, unless from a preconceived and fixed purpose of his own; which is always evidence of a thoughtful and deliberate character, and, except in radically bad men, generally proceeds from sincere and strong personal convictions. Even the bare fact of having to give an account of their conduct is a powerful inducement to adhere to conduct of which at least some decent account can be given. If any one thinks that the mere obligation of preserving decency is not a very considerable check on the abuse of power, he has never had his attention called to the conduct of those who do not feel under the necessity of observing that restraint. Publicity is inappreciable, even when it does no more than prevent that which can by no possibility be plausibly defended—than compel deliberation, and force every one to determine, before he acts, what he shall say if called to account for his actions.

"But, if not now (it may be said), at least hereafter, when all are fit to have votes, and when all men and women are admitted to vote in virtue of their fitness; *then* there can no longer be danger of class legislation; then the electors, being the nation, can have no interest apart from the general interest: even if individuals still vote according to private or class inducements, the majority will have no such inducement; and as there will then be no non-electors to whom they ought to be responsible, the effect of the ballot, excluding none but the sinister influences, will be wholly beneficial.

"Even in this I do not agree. I cannot think that even if the people were fit for, and had obtained, universal suffrage, the ballot would be desirable. First, because it could not, in such circumstances, be supposed to be needful. Let us only conceive the state of things which the hypothesis implies; a people universally educated, and every grown-up human being possessed of a vote. If, even when only a small proportion are electors, and the majority of the population almost uneducated, public opinion is already, as every one now sees that it is, the ruling power in the last resort; it is a chimera to suppose that over a community who all read, and who all have votes, any power could be exercised by landlords and rich people against their own inclination which it would be at all difficult for them to throw off. But though the protection of secrecy would then be needless, the control of publicity would be as needful as ever. The universal observation of mankind has been very fallacious if the mere fact of being one of the community, and not being in a position of pronounced contrariety of interest to the public at large, is enough to ensure the performance of a public duty, without either the stimulus or the restraint derived from the opinion of our fellow creatures. A man's own particular share of the public interest, even though he may have no private interest drawing him in the opposite direction, is not, as a general rule, found sufficient to make him do his duty to the public without other external inducements. Neither can it be admitted that even if all had votes they would give their votes as honestly in secret as in public.

"The proposition that the electors when they compose the whole of the community cannot have an interest in voting against the interest of the community will be found on examination to have more sound than meaning in it. Though the community as a whole can have (as the terms imply) no other interest than its collective interest, any or every individual in it may. A man's interest consists of whatever he takes an interest *in*. Everybody has as many different interests as he has feelings; likings or dislikings, either of a selfish or of a better kind. It cannot be said that any of these, taken by itself, constitutes 'his interest'; he is a good man or a bad according as he prefers one class of his interests or another. A man who is a tyrant at home will be apt to sympathise with tyranny (when not exercised over himself): he will be almost certain not to sympathise with resistance to tyranny. An envious man will vote against Aristides because he is called the Just. A selfish man will prefer even a trifling individual benefit to his share of the advantage which his country would derive from a good law; because interests peculiar to himself are those which the habits of his mind both dispose him to dwell on, and make him best able to estimate. A great number of the electors will have two sets of preferences—those on private and those on public grounds. The last are the only ones which the elector would like to avow. The best side of their character is that which people are anxious to show, even to those who are no better than themselves. People will give dishonest or mean votes from lucre, from malice, from pique, from personal rivalry, even from the interests or prejudices of class or sect, more readily in secret than in public. And cases exist—they may come to be more frequent—in which almost the only restraint upon a majority of knaves consists in their involuntary respect for the opinion of an honest minority. In such a case as that of the repudiating States of North America, is there not some check to the unprincipled voter in the shame of looking an honest man in the face? Since all this good would be sacrificed by the ballot, even in the circumstances most favourable to it, a much stronger case is requisite than can now be made out for its necessity (and the case is continually becoming still weaker) to make its adoption desirable." [1]

On the other debateable points connected with the mode of voting it is not necessary to expend so many words. The system of personal representation, as organised by Mr. Hare, renders necessary the employment of voting papers. But it appears to me indispensable

[1] *Thoughts on Parliamentary Reform*, 2nd ed. pp. 32-36.

that the signature of the elector should be affixed to the paper at a public polling place, or if there be no such place conveniently accessible, at some office open to all the world, and in the presence of a responsible public officer. The proposal which has been thrown out of allowing the voting papers to be filled up at the voter's own residence, and sent by the post, or called for by a public officer, I should regard as fatal. The act would be done in the absence of the salutary and the presence of all the pernicious influences. The briber might, in the shelter of privacy, behold with his own eyes his bargain fulfilled, and the intimidator could see the extorted obedience rendered irrevocably on the spot; while the beneficent counter-influence of the presence of those who knew the voter's real sentiments, and the inspiring effect of the sympathy of those of his own party or opinion, would be shut out.[1]

[1] "This expedient has been recommended, both on the score of saving expense, and on that of obtaining the votes of many electors who otherwise would not vote, and who are regarded by the advocates of the plan as a particularly desirable class of voters. The scheme has been carried into practice in the election of poor-law guardians, and its success in that instance is appealed to in favour of adopting it in the more important case of voting for a member of the Legislature. But the two cases appear to me to differ in the point on which the benefits of the expedient depend. In a local election for a special kind of administrative business, which consists mainly in the dispensation of a public fund, it is an object to prevent the choice from being exclusively in the hands of those who actively concern themselves about it; for the public interest which attaches to the election being of a limited kind, and in most cases not very great in degree, the disposition to make themselves busy in the matter is apt to be in a great measure confined to persons who hope to turn their activity to their own private advantage; and it may be very desirable to render the intervention of other people as little onerous to them as possible, if only for the purpose of swamping these private interests. But when the matter in hand is the great business of national government, in which every one must take an interest who cares for anything out of himself, or who cares even for himself intelligently, it is much rather an object to prevent those from voting who are indifferent to the subject, than to induce them to vote by any other means than that of awakening their dormant minds. The voter who does not care enough about the election to go to the poll, is the very man who, if he can vote without that small trouble, will give his vote to the first person who asks for it, or on the most trifling or frivolous inducement. A man who does not care whether he votes, is not likely to care much which way he votes; and he who is in that state of mind has no moral right to vote at all; since, if he does so, a vote which is not the ex-

The polling places should be so numerous as to be within easy reach of every voter; and no expenses of conveyance, at the cost of the candidate, should be tolerated under any pretext. The infirm, and they only on medical certificate, should have the right of claiming suitable carriage conveyance, at the cost of the State, or of the locality. Hustings, poll clerks, and all the necessary machinery of elections, should be at the public charge. Not only the candidate should not be required, he should not be permitted, to incur any but a limited and trifling expense for his election. Mr. Hare thinks it desirable that a sum of £50 should be required from every one who places his name on the list of candidates, to prevent persons who have no chance of success, and no real intention of attempting it, from becoming candidates in wantonness or from mere love of notoriety, and perhaps carrying off a few votes which are needed for the return of more serious aspirants. There is one expense which a candidate or his supporters cannot help incurring, and which it can hardly be expected that the public should defray for every one who may choose to demand it; that of making his claims known to the electors, by advertisements, placards, and circulars. For all necessary expenses of this kind the £50 proposed by Mr. Hare, if allowed to be drawn upon for these purposes (it might be made £100 if requisite), ought to be sufficient. If the friends of the candidate choose to go to expense for committees and canvassing there are no means of preventing them; but such expenses out of the candidates's own pocket, or any expenses whatever beyond the deposit of £50 (or £100), should be illegal and punishable. If there appeared any likelihood that opinion would refuse to connive at falsehood, a declaration on oath or honour should be required from every member on taking his seat that he had not expended, nor would expend, money or money's worth beyond the £50, directly or indirectly, for the purposes of his election; and if the assertion were proved to be false or the pledge to have been broken, he should be liable to the penalties of perjury.

It is probable that those penalties, by showing that the Legislature was in earnest, would turn the course of opinion in the same direction, and would hinder it from regarding, as

pression of a conviction, counts for as much, and goes as far in determining the result, as one which represents the thoughts and purposes of a life."—*Thoughts, etc.*, p. 39.

it has hitherto done, this most serious crime against society as a venial peccadillo. When once this effect has been produced, there need be no doubt that the declaration on oath or honour would be considered binding.[1] "Opinion tolerates a false disclaimer, only when it already tolerates the thing disclaimed." This is notoriously the case with regard to electoral corruption. There has never yet been, among political men, any real and serious attempt to

[1] Several of the witnesses before the Committee of the House of Commons in 1860, on the operation of the Corrupt Practices Prevention Act, some of them of great practical experience in election matters, were favourable (either absolutely or as a last resort) to the principle of requiring a declaration from members of Parliament; and were of opinion that, if supported by penalties, it would be, to a great degree, effectual. (*Evidence*, pp. 46, 54-7, 67, 123, 198-202, 208.) The Chief Commissioner of the Wakefield Inquiry said (in reference certainly to a different proposal), "If they see that the Legislature is earnest upon the subject, the machinery will work. . . . I am quite sure that if some personal stigma were applied upon conviction of bribery, it would change the current of public opinion" (pp. 26 and 32). A distinguished member of the Committee (and of the present Cabinet) seemed to think it very objectionable to attach the penalties of perjury to a merely promissory as distinguished from an assertory oath; but he was reminded, that the oath taken by a witness in a court of justice is a promissory oath: and the rejoinder (that the witness's promise relates to an act to be done at once, while the member's would be a promise for all future time) would only be to the purpose, if it could be supposed that the swearer might forget the obligation he had entered into, or could possibly violate it unawares: contingencies which, in a case like the present, are out of the question.

A more substantial difficulty is that one of the forms most frequently assumed by election expenditure is that of subscriptions to local charities, or other local objects; and it would be a strong measure to enact that money should not be given in charity, within a place, by the member for it. When such subscriptions are *bona fide*, the popularity which may be derived from them is an advantage which it seems hardly possible to deny to superior riches. But the greatest part of the mischief consists in the fact that money so contributed is employed in bribery, under the euphemistic name of keeping up the member's interest. To guard against this, it should be part of the member's promissory declaration, that all sums expended by him in the place, or for any purpose connected with it or with any of its inhabitants (with the exception perhaps of his own hotel expenses), should pass through the hands of the election auditor, and be by him (and not by the member himself or his friends) applied to its declared purpose.

The principle of making all lawful expenses of elections a charge not upon the candidate, but upon the locality, was upheld by two of the best witnesses (pp. 20, 65-70, 277).

prevent bribery, because there has been no real desire that elections should not be costly. Their costliness is an advantage to those who can afford the expense, by excluding a multitude of competitors; and anything, however noxious, is cherished as having a conservative tendency if it limits the access to Parliament to rich men. This is a rooted feeling among our legislators of both political parties, and is almost the only point on which I believe them to be really ill-intentioned. They care comparatively little who votes, as long as they feel assured that none but persons of their own class can be voted for. They know that they can rely on the fellow-feeling of one of their class with another, while the subservience of *nouveaux enrichis,* who are knocking at the door of the class, is a still surer reliance; and that nothing very hostile to the class interests or feelings of the rich need be apprehended under the most democratic suffrage as long as democratic persons can be prevented from being elected to Parliament. But, even from their own point of view, this balancing of evil by evil, instead of combining good with good, is a wretched policy. The object should be to bring together the best members of both classes, under such a tenure as shall induce them to lay aside their class preferences, and pursue jointly the path traced by the common interest; instead of allowing the class feelings of the Many to have full swing in the constituencies, subject to the impediment of having to act through persons imbued with the class feelings of the Few.

There is scarcely any mode in which political institutions are more morally mischievous —work greater evil through their spirit—than by representing political functions as a favour to be conferred, a thing which the depositary is to ask for as desiring it for himself, and even pay for as if it were designed for his pecuniary benefit. Men are not fond of paying large sums for leave to perform a laborious duty. Plato had a much juster view of the conditions of good government when he asserted that the persons who should be sought out to be invested with political power are those who are personally most averse to it, and that the only motive which can be relied on for inducing the fittest men to take upon themselves the toils of government is the fear of being governed by worse men. What must an elector think, when he sees three or four gentlemen, none of them previously observed to be lavish of their money on projects of disinterested beneficence, vying with one another in the sums they expend to be enabled to write M.P. after their names? Is it likely he will suppose that it is for *his* interest they incur all this cost? And if he forms an uncomplimentary opinion of their part in the affair, what moral obligation is he likely to feel as to his own? Politicians are fond of treating it as the dream of enthusiasts that the electoral body will ever be uncorrupt: truly enough, until they are willing to become so themselves: for the electors, assuredly, will take their moral tone from the candidates. So long as the elected member, in any shape or manner, pays for his seat, all endeavours will fail to make the business of election anything but a selfish bargain on all sides. "So long as the candidate himself, and the customs of the world, seem to regard the function of a member of Parliament less as a duty to be discharged than a personal favour to be solicited, no effort will avail to implant in an ordinary voter the feeling that the election of a member of Parliament is also a matter of duty, and that he is not at liberty to bestow his vote on any other consideration than that of personal fitness."

The same principle which demands that no payment of money for election purposes should be either required or tolerated on the part of the person elected dictates another conclusion, apparently of contrary tendency, but really directed to the same object. It negatives what has often been proposed as a means of rendering Parliament accessible to persons of all ranks and circumstances; the payment of members of Parliament. If, as in some of our colonies, there are scarcely any fit persons who can afford to attend to an unpaid occupation, the payment should be an indemnity for loss of time or money, not a salary. The greater latitude of choice which a salary would give is an illusory advantage. No remuneration which any one would think of attaching to the post would attract to it those who were seriously engaged in other lucrative professions with a prospect of succeeding in them. The business of a member of Parliament would therefore become an occupation in itself; carried on, like other professions, with a view chiefly to its pecuniary returns, and under the demoralising influences of an occupation essentially precarious. It would become an object of desire to adventurers of a low class; and 658 persons in possession, with ten or twenty times as many in expectancy, would be incessantly bidding

to attract or retain the suffrages of the electors, by promising all things, honest or dishonest, possible or impossible, and rivalling each other in pandering to the meanest feelings and most ignorant prejudices of the vulgarest part of the crowd. The auction between Cleon and the sausage-seller in Aristophanes is a fair caricature of what would be always going on. Such an institution would be a perpetual blister applied to the most peccant parts of human nature. It amounts to offering 658 prizes for the most successful flatterer, the most adroit misleader, of a body of his fellow-countrymen. Under no despotism has there been such an organised system of tillage for raising a rich crop of vicious courtiership.[1] When, by reason of pre-eminent qualifications (as may at any time happen to be the case), it is desirable that a person entirely without independent means, either derived from property or from a trade or profession, should be brought into Parliament to render services which no other person accessible can render as well, there is the resource of a public subscription; he may be supported while in Parliament, like Andrew Marvell, by the contributions of his constituents. This mode is unobjectionable for such an honour will never be paid to mere subserviency: bodies of men do not care so much for the difference between one sycophant and another as to go to the expense of his maintenance in order to be flattered by that particular individual. Such a support will only be given in consideration of striking and impressive personal qualities, which, though no absolute proof of fitness to be a national representative, are some presumption of it, and, at all events, some guarantee for the possession of an independent opinion and will.

[1] "As Mr. Lorimer remarks, by creating a pecuniary inducement to persons of the lowest class to devote themselves to public affairs, the calling of the demagogue would be formally inaugurated. Nothing is more to be deprecated than making it the private interest of a number of active persons to urge the form of government in the direction of its natural perversion. The indications which either a multitude or an individual can give, when merely left to their own weaknesses, afford but a faint idea of what those weaknesses would become when played upon by a thousand flatterers. If there were 658 places of certain, however moderate, emolument, to be gained by persuading the multitude that ignorance is as good as knowledge, and better, it is terrible odds that they would believe and act upon the lesson."—(Article in *Fraser's Magazine* for April 1859, headed "Recent Writers on Reform.")

Chapter 11
Of the Duration of Parliaments

AFTER HOW long a term should members of Parliament be subject to re-election? The principles involved are here very obvious; the difficulty lies in their application. On the one hand, the member ought not to have so long a tenure of his seat as to make him forget his responsibility, take his duties easily, conduct them with a view to his own personal advantage, or neglect those free and public conferences with his constituents which, whether he agrees or differs with them, are one of the benefits of representative government. On the other hand, he should have such a term of office to look forward to as will enable him to be judged, not by a single act, but by his course of action. It is important that he should have the greatest latitude of individual opinion and discretion compatible with the popular control essential to free government; and for this purpose it is necessary that the control should be exercised, as in any case it is best exercised, after sufficient time has been given him to show all the qualities he possesses, and to prove that there is some other way than that of a mere obedient voter and advocate of their opinions, by which he can render himself in the eyes of his constituents a desirable and creditable representative.

It is impossible to fix, by any universal rule, the boundary between these principles. Where the democratic power in the constitution is weak or over-passive, and requires stimulation; where the representative, on leaving his constituents, enters at once into a courtly or aristocratic atmosphere, whose influences all tend to deflect his course into a different direction from the popular one, to tone down any democratic feelings which he may have brought with him, and make him forget the wishes and grow cool to the interests of those who chose him—the obligation of a frequent return to them for a renewal of his commission is indispensable to keeping his temper and character up to the right mark. Even three years, in such circumstances, are almost too long a period; and any longer term is absolutely inadmissible. Where, on the contrary, democracy is the ascendant power, and still tends to increase, requiring rather to be moderated in its exercise than encouraged to any abnormal activity; where unbounded publicity, and an ever-present newspaper press, give the representative assurance that his every act will be immediately known, discussed, and judged by his constituents, and that he is always either gaining or losing ground in their estimation; while by the same means the influence of their sentiments, and all other democratic influences, are kept constantly alive and active in his own mind—less than five years would hardly be a sufficient period to prevent timid subserviency. The change which has taken place in English politics as to all these features explains why annual Parliaments, which forty years ago stood prominently in front of the creed of the more advanced reformers, are so little cared for and so seldom heard of at present. It deserves consideration that, whether the term is short or long, during the last year of it the members are in position in which they would always be if Parliaments were annual: so that if the term were very brief, there would virtually be annual Parliaments during a great proportion of all time. As things now are, the period of seven years, though of unnecessary length, is hardly worth altering for any benefit likely to be produced; especially since the possibility, always impending, of an earlier dissolution keeps the motives for standing well with constituents always before the member's eyes.

Whatever may be the term most eligible for the duration of the mandate, it might seem natural that the individual member should vacate his seat at the expiration of that term from the day of his election, and that there should be no general renewal of the whole House. A great deal might be said for this system if there were any practical object in recommending it. But it is condemned by much stronger reasons than can be alleged in its support. One is, that there would be no means of promptly getting rid of a majority which had pursued a course offensive to the nation. The certainty of a general election after a limited, which would often be a nearly expired, period, and the possibility of it at any time when the minister either desires it for his own sake, or thinks that it would make him popular with the country, tend to prevent that wide divergence between the feelings of the assembly and those of the constituency, which might subsist indefinitely if the majority of the House had always several years of their term still to run—if it received new infusions drop by drop, which would be more likely to assume than to modify the qualities of the mass they were joined to. It is as essential that the general sense of the House should accord in the main with that of the nation as it is that distinguished individuals should be able, without forfeiting their seats, to give free utterance to the most unpopular sentiments. There is another reason, of much weight, against the gradual and partial renewal of a representative assembly. It is useful that there should be a periodical general muster of opposing forces, to gauge the state of the national mind, and ascertain, beyond dispute, the relative strength of different parties and opinions. This is not done conclusively by any partial renewal, even where, as in some of the French constitutions, a large fraction, a fifth or a third, go out at once.

The reasons for allowing to the executive the power of dissolution will be considered in a subsequent chapter, relating to the constitution and functions of the Executive in a representative government.

Chapter 12
Ought Pledges to be Required from Members of Parliament?

SHOULD A member of the legislature be bound by the instructions of his constituents? Should he be the organ of their sentiments, or of his own? their ambassador to a congress, or their professional agent, empowered not only to act for them, but to judge for them what ought to be done? These two theories of the duty of a legislator in a representative government have each its supporters, and each is the recognised doctrine of some representative governments. In the Dutch United Provinces, the members of the States General were mere delegates; and to such a length was the doctrine carried, that when any important question arose which had not been provided for in their instructions, they had to refer back to their constituents, exactly as an ambassador does to the government from which he is accredited. In this and most other countries which possess representative constitutions, law and custom warrant a member of Parliament in voting according to his opinion of right, however different from that of his constituents: but there is a floating notion of the opposite kind, which has considerable practical operation on many minds, even of members of Parliament, and often makes them, independently of desire for popularity, or concern for their re-election, feel bound in conscience to let their conduct, on questions on which their constituents have a decided opinion, be the expression of that opinion rather than of their own. Abstractedly

from positive law, and from the historical traditions of any particular people, which of these notions of the duty of a representative is the true one?

Unlike the questions which we have hitherto treated, this is not a question of constitutional legislation, but of what may more properly be called constitutional morality—the ethics of representative government. It does not so much concern institutions, as the temper of mind which the electors ought to bring to the discharge of their functions; the ideas which should prevail as to the moral duties of an elector. For, let the system of representation be what it may, it will be converted into one of mere delegation if the electors so choose. As long as they are free not to vote, and free to vote as they like, they cannot be prevented from making their vote depend on any condition they think fit to annex to it. By refusing to elect any one who will not pledge himself to all their opinions, and even, if they please, to consult with them before voting on any important subject not foreseen, they can reduce their representative to their mere mouthpiece, or compel him in honour, when no longer willing to act in that capacity, to resign his seat. And since they have the power of doing this, the theory of the Constitution ought to suppose that they will wish to do it; since the very principle of constitutional government requires it to be assumed that political power will be abused to promote the particular purposes of the holder; not because it always is so, but because such is the natural tendency of things, to guard against which is the especial use of free institutions. However wrong, therefore, or however foolish, we may think it in the electors to convert their representative into a delegate, that stretch of the electoral privilege being a natural and not improbable one, the same precautions ought to be taken as if it were certain. We may hope that the electors will not act on this notion of the use of the suffrage; but a representative government needs to be so framed that, even if they do, they shall not be able to effect what ought not to be in the power of any body of persons —class legislation for their own benefit.

When it is said that the question is only one of political morality, this does not extenuate its importance. Questions of constitutional morality are of no less practical moment than those relating to the constitution itself. The very existence of some governments, and all that renders others endurable, rests on the practical observance of doctrines of constitutional morality; traditional notions in the minds of the several constituted authorities, which modify the use that might otherwise be made of their powers. In unbalanced governments—pure monarchy, pure aristocracy, pure democracy—such maxims are the only barrier which restrains the government from the utmost excesses in the direction of its characteristic tendency. In imperfectly balanced governments, where some attempt is made to set constitutional limits to the impulses of the strongest power, but where that power is strong enough to overstep them with at least temporary impunity, it is only by doctrines of constitutional morality, recognised and sustained by opinion, that any regard at all is preserved for the checks and limitations of the constitution. In well-balanced governments, in which the supreme power is divided, and each sharer is protected against the usurpations of the others in the only manner possible—namely, by being armed for defence with weapons as strong as the others can wield for attack—the government can only be carried on by forbearance on all sides to exercise those extreme powers, unless provoked by conduct equally extreme on the part of some other sharer of power: and in this case we may truly say that only by the regard paid to maxims of constitutional morality is the constitution kept in existence. The question of pledges is not one of those which vitally concern the existence of representative governments; but it is very material to their beneficial operation. The laws cannot prescribe to the electors the principles by which they shall direct their choice; but it makes a great practical difference by what principles they think they ought to direct it. And the whole of that great question is involved in the inquiry whether they should make it a condition that the representative shall adhere to certain opinions laid down for him by his constituents.

No reader of this treatise can doubt what conclusion, as to this matter, results from the general principles which it professes. We have from the first affirmed, and unveryingly kept in view, the co-equal importance of two great resquisites of government: responsibility to those for whose benefit political power ought to be, and always professes to be, employed; and jointly therewith to obtain, in the greatest measure possible, for the function of government the benefits of superior intellect, trained by long meditation and practical discipline to that special task. If this second purpose is worth attaining, it is worth the necessary price. Superior powers of mind and profound study are of no use if they do not sometimes lead a person to different conclusions from those which are formed by ordinary powers of mind without study: and if it be an object to possess representatives in any intellectual respect superior to average electors, it must be counted upon that the representative will sometimes differ in opinion from the majority of his constituents, and that when he does, his opinion will be the oftenest right of the two. It follows that the electors will not do wisely if they insist on absolute conformity to their opinions as the condition of his retaining his seat.

The principle is, thus far, obvious; but there are real difficulties in its application: and we will begin by stating them in their greatest force. It it is important that the electors should choose a representative more highly instructed than themselves, it is no less necessary that this wiser man should be responsible to them; in other words, they are the judges of the manner in which he fulfils his trust: and how are they to judge, except by the standard of their own opinions? How are they even to select him in the first instance but by the same standard? It will not do to choose by mere brilliancy—by superiority of showy talent. The tests by which an ordinary man can judge beforehand of mere ability are very imperfect: such as they are, they have almost exclusive reference to the arts of expression, and little or none to the worth of what is expressed. The latter cannot be inferred from the former; and if the electors are to put their own opinions in abeyance, what criterion remains to them of the ability to govern well? Neither, if they could ascertain, even infallibly, the ablest man, ought they to allow him altogether to judge for them, without any reference to their own opinions. The ablest candidate may be a Tory and the electors Liberals; or a Liberal and they may be Tories. The political questions of the day may be Church questions, and he may be a High Churchman or a Rationalist, while they may be Dissenters or Evangelicals; and *vice versa*. His abilities, in these cases, might only enable him to go greater lengths, and act with greater effect, in what they may conscientiously believe to be a wrong course; and they may be bound, by their sincere convictions, to think it more important that their representative should be kept, on these points, to what they deem the dictate of duty, than that they should be represented by a person of more than average abilities. They may also have to consider, not solely how they can be most ably represented, but how their particular moral position and mental point of view shall be represented at all.

The influence of every mode of thinking which is shared by numbers ought to be felt in the legislature: and the constitution being supposed to have made due provision that other and conflicting modes of thinking shall be represented likewise, to secure the proper representation for their own mode may be the most important matter which the electors on the particular occasion have to attend to. In some cases, too, it may be necessary that the representative should have his hands tied, to keep him true to their interest, or rather to the public interest as they conceive it. This would not be needful under a political system which assured them an indefinite choice of honest and unprejudiced candidates; but under the existing system, in which the electors are almost always obliged, by the expenses of election and the general circumstances of society, to select their representative from persons of a station in life widely different from theirs, and having a different class-interest, who will affirm that they ought to abandon themselves to his discretion? Can we blame an elector of the poorer classes, who has only the choice among two or three rich men, for requiring from the one he votes for a pledge to those measures which he considers as a test of emancipation from the class-interests of the rich? It moreover always happens to some members of the electoral body to be obliged to accept the representative selected by a majority of their own side. But though a candidate of their own choosing would have no chance, their votes may be necessary to the success of the one chosen for them; and their only means of exerting their share of influence on his subsequent conduct, may be to make their support of him dependent on his pledging himself to certain conditions.

These considerations and counter-considerations are so intimately interwoven with one another; it is so important that the electors should choose as their representatives wiser men than themselves, and should consent to be governed according to that superior wisdom, while it is impossible that conformity to their own opinions, when they have opinions, should not enter largely into their judgment as to who possesses the wisdom, and how far its presumed possessor has verified the presumption by his conduct; that it seems quite impracticable to lay down for the elector any

positive rule of duty: and the result will depend, less on any exact prescription, or authoritative doctrine of political morality, than on the general tone of mind of the electoral body, in respect to the important requisite of deference to mental superiority. Individuals, and peoples, who are acutely sensible of the value of superior wisdom, are likely to recognise it, where it exists, by other signs than thinking exactly as they do, and even in spite of considerable differences of opinion: and when they have recognised it they will be far too desirous to secure it, at any admissible cost, to be prone to impose their own opinion as a law upon persons whom they look up to as wiser than themselves. On the other hand, there is a character of mind which does not look up to any one; which thinks no other person's opinion much better than its own, or nearly so good as that of a hundred or a thousand persons like itself. Where this is the turn of mind of the electors, they will elect no one who is not, or at least who does not profess to be, the image of their own sentiments, and will continue him no longer than while he reflects those sentiments in his conduct: and all aspirants to political honours will endeavour, as Plato says in the "Gorgias," to fashion themselves after the model of the Demos, and make themselves as like to it as possible. It cannot be denied that a complete democracy has a strong tendency to cast the sentiments of the electors in this mould. Democracy is not favourable to the reverential spirit. That it destroys reverence for mere social position must be counted among the good, not the bad part of its influences; though by doing this it closes the principal *school* of reverence (as to merely human relations) which exists in society. But also democracy, in its very essence, insists so much more forcibly on the things in which all are entitled to be considered equally, than on those in which one person is entitled to more consideration than another, that respect for even personal superiority is likely to be below the mark. It is for this, among other reasons, I hold it of so much importance that the institutions of the country should stamp the opinions of persons of a more educated class as entitled to greater weight than those of the less educated: and I should still contend for assigning plurality of votes to authenticated superiority of education, were it only to give the tone to public feeling, irrespective of any direct political consequences.

When there does exist in the electoral body

an adequate sense of the extraordinary difference in value between one person and another, they will not lack signs by which to distinguish the persons whose worth for their purposes is the greatest. Actual public services will naturally be the foremost indication: to have filled posts of magnitude, and done important things in them, of which the wisdom has been justified by the results; to have been the author of measures which appear from their effects to have been wisely planned; to have made predictions which appear from their effects to have been often verified by the event, seldom or never falsified by it; to have given advice, which when taken has been followed by good consequences, when neglected, by bad. There is doubtless a large portion of uncertainty in these signs of wisdom; but we are seeking for such as can be applied by persons of ordinary discernment. They will do well not to rely much on any one indication, unless corroborated by the rest; and, in their estimation of the success or merit of any practical effort, to lay great stress on the general opinion of disinterested persons conversant with the subject matter. The tests which I have spoken of are only applicable to tried men; among whom must be reckoned those who, though untried practically, have been tried speculatively; who, in public speech or in print, have discussed public affairs in a manner which proves that they have given serious study to them. Such persons may, in the mere character of political thinkers, have exhibited a considerable amount of the same titles to confidence as those who have been proved in the position of practical statesmen. When it is necessary to choose persons wholly untried, the best criteria are, reputation for ability among those who personally know them, and the confidence placed and recommendations given by persons already looked up to. By tests like these, constituencies who sufficiently value mental ability, and eagerly seek for it, will generally succeed in obtaining men beyond mediocrity, and often men whom they can trust to carry on public affairs according to their unfettered judgment; to whom it would be an affront to require that they should give up that judgment at the behest of their inferiors in knowledge.

If such persons, honestly sought, are not to be found, then indeed the electors are justified in taking other precautions; for they cannot be expected to postpone their particular opinions, unless in order that they may be served by a person of superior knowledge to

their own. They would do well, indeed, even then, to remember, that when once chosen, the representative, if he devotes himself to his duty, has greater opportunities of correcting an original false judgment than fall to the lot of most of his constituents; a consideration which generally ought to prevent them (unless compelled by necessity to choose some one whose impartiality they do not fully trust) from exacting a pledge not to change his opinion, or, if he does, to resign his seat. But when an unknown person, not certified in unmistakable terms by some high authority, is elected for the first time, the elector cannot be expected not to make conformity to his own sentiments the primary requisite. It is enough if he does not regard a subsequent change of those sentiments, honestly avowed, with its grounds undisguisedly stated, as a peremptory reason for withdrawing his confidence.

Even supposing the most tried ability and acknowledged eminence of character in the representative, the private opinions of the electors are not to be placed entirely in abeyance. Deference to mental superiority is not to go the length of self-annihilation—abnegation of any personal opinion. But when the difference does not relate to the fundamentals of politics, however decided the elector may be in his own sentiments, he ought to consider that when an able man differs from him there is at least a considerable chance of his being in the wrong, and that even if otherwise, it is worth while to give up his opinion in things not absolutely essential, for the sake of the inestimable advantage of having an able man to act for him in the many matters in which he himself is not qualified to form a judgment. In such cases he often endeavours to reconcile both wishes, by inducing the able man to sacrifice his own opinion on the points of difference: but, for the able man to lend himself to this compromise, is treason against his especial office; abdication of the peculiar duties of mental superiority, of which it is one of the most sacred not to desert the cause which has the clamour against it, nor to deprive of his services those of his opinions which need them the most. A man of conscience and known ability should insist on full freedom to act as he in his own judgment deems best; and should not consent to serve on any other terms. But the electors are entitled to know how he means to act; what opinions, on all things which concern his public duty, he intends should guide his conduct. If some of these are unacceptable to them, it is for him to satisfy them that he nevertheless deserves to be their representative; and if they are wise, they will overlook, in favour of his general value, many and great differences between his opinions and their own.

There are some differences, however, which they cannot be expected to overlook. Whoever feels the amount of interest in the government of his country which befits a freeman, has some convictions on national affairs which are like his life-blood; which the strength of his belief in their truth, together with the importance he attaches to them, forbid him to make a subject of compromise, or postpone to the judgment of any person, however greatly his superior. Such convictions, when they exist in a people, or in any appreciable portion of one, are entitled to influence in virtue of their mere existence, and not solely in that of the probability of their being grounded in truth. A people cannot be well governed in opposition to their primary notions of right, even though these may be in some points erroneous. A correct estimate of the relation which should subsist between governors and governed, does not require the electors to consent to be represented by one who intends to govern them in opposition to their fundamental convictions. If they avail themselves of his capacities of useful service in other respects, at a time when the points on which he is vitally at issue with them are not likely to be mooted, they are justified in dismissing him at the first moment when a question arises involving these, and on which there is not so assured a majority for what they deem right as to make the dissenting voice of that particular individual unimportant. Thus (I mention names to illustrate my meaning, not for any personal application) the opinions supposed to be entertained by Mr. Cobden and Mr. Bright on resistance to foreign aggression might be overlooked during the Crimean war, when there was an overwhelming national feeling on the contrary side, and might yet very properly lead to their rejection by the electors at the time of the Chinese quarrel (though in itself a more doubtful question), because it was then for some time a moot point whether their view of the case might not prevail.

As the general result of what precedes, we may affirm that actual pledges should not be required, unless, from unfavourable social circumstances or faulty institutions, the electors are so narrowed in their choice as to be compelled to fix it on a person presumptively under the influence of partialities hostile to their interest: That they are entitled to a full knowledge of the political opinions and sentiments of the candidate; and not only entitled, but often bound, to reject one who differs from themselves on the few articles which are the foundation of their political belief: That in proportion to the opinion they entertain of the mental superiority of a candidate, they ought to put up with his expressing and acting on opinions different from theirs on any number of things not included in their fundamental articles of belief: That they ought to be unremitting in their search for a representative of such calibre as to be entrusted with full power of obeying the dictates of his own judgment: That they should consider it a duty which they owe to their fellow-countrymen, to do their utmost towards placing men of this quality in the legislature: and that it is of much greater importance to themselves to be represented by such a man than by one who professes agreement in a greater number of their opinions: for the benefits of his ability are certain, while the hypothesis of his being wrong and their being right on the points of difference is a very doubtful one.

I have discussed this question on the assumption that the electoral system, in all that depends on positive institution, conforms to the principles laid down in the preceding chapters. Even on this hypothesis, the delegation theory of representation seems to me false, and its practical operation hurtful, though the mischief would in that case be confined within certain bounds. But if the securities by which I have endeavoured to guard the representative principle are not recognised by the Constitution; if provision is not made for the representation of minorities, nor any difference admitted in the numerical value of votes, according to some criterion of the amount of education possessed by the voters; in that case no words can exaggerate the importance in principle of leaving an unfettered discretion to the representative; for it would then be the only chance, under universal suffrage, for any other opinions than those of the majority to be heard in Parliament. In that falsely called democracy which is really the exclusive rule of the operative classes, all others being unrepresented and unheard, the only escape from class legislation in its narrowest, and political ignorance in its most dangerous, form, would lie in such disposition as the uneducated might have to choose educated representatives, and to defer to their opinions. Some willingness to do this might reasonably be expected, and everything would depend upon cultivating it to the highest point. But, once invested with political omnipotence, if the operative classes voluntarily concurred in imposing in this or any other manner any considerable limitation upon their self-opinion and self-will, they would prove themselves wiser than any class, possessed of absolute power, has shown itself, or, we may venture to say, is ever likely to show itself, under that corrupting influence.

Chapter 13
Of a Second Chamber

OF ALL topics relating to the theory of representative government, none has been the subject of more discussion, especially on the Continent, than what is known as the question of the Two Chambers. It has occupied a greater amount of the attention of thinkers than many questions of ten times its importance, and has been regarded as a sort of touchstone which distinguishes the partisans of limited from those of uncontrolled democracy. For my own part, I set little value on any check which a Second Chamber can apply to a democracy otherwise unchecked; and I am inclined to think that if all other constitutional questions are rightly decided, it is but of secondary importance whether the Parliament consists of two Chambers, or only of one.

If there are two Chambers, they may either be of similar, or of dissimilar composition. If of similar, both will obey the same influences, and whatever has a majority in one of the Houses will be likely to have it in the other. It is true that the necessity of obtaining the consent of both to the passing of any measure may at times be a material obstacle to improvement, since, assuming both the Houses to be representative, and equal in their numbers, a number slightly exceeding a fourth of the entire representation may prevent the passing of a Bill; while, if there is but one House, a Bill is secure of passing if it has a bare majority. But the case supposed is rather abstractedly possible than likely to occur in practice. It will not often happen that of two Houses similarly composed, one will be almost unanimous, and the other nearly equally divided: if a majority in one rejects a measure, there will generally have been a large minority unfavourable to it in the other; any improvement, therefore,

which could be thus impeded, would in almost all cases be one which had not much more than a simple majority in the entire body, and the worst consequence that could ensue would be to delay for a short time the passing of the measure, or give rise to a fresh appeal to the electors to ascertain if the small majority in Parliament corresponded to an effective one in the country. The inconvenience of delay, and the advantages of the appeal to the nation, might be regarded in this case as about equally balanced.

I attach little weight to the argument oftenest urged for having two Chambers—to prevent precipitancy, and compel a second deliberation; for it must be a very ill-constituted representative assembly in which the established forms of business do not require many more than two deliberations. The consideration which tells most, in my judgment, in favour of two Chambers (and this I do regard as of some moment) is the evil effect produced upon the mind of any holder of power, whether an individual or an assembly, by the consciousness of having only themselves to consult. It is important that no set of persons should, in great affairs, be able, even temporarily, to make their *sic volo* prevail without asking any one else for his consent. A majority in a single assembly, when it has assumed a permanent character—when composed of the same persons habitually acting together, and always assured of victory in their own House—easily becomes despotic and overweening, if released from the necessity of considering whether its acts will be concurred in by another constituted authority. The same reason which induced the Romans to have two consuls makes it desirable there should be two Chambers: that neither of them may be exposed to the corrupting influence of undivided power, even for the space of a single year. One of the most indispensable requisites in the practical conduct of politics, especially in the management of free institutions, is conciliation: a readiness to compromise; a willingness to concede something to opponents, and to shape good measures so as to be as little offensive as possible to persons of opposite views; and of this salutary habit, the mutual give and take (as it has been called) between two Houses is a perpetual school; useful as such even now, and its utility would probably be even more felt in a more democratic constitution of the Legislature.

But the Houses need not both be of the same composition; they may be intended as a check on one another. One being supposed democratic, the other will naturally be constituted with a view to its being some restraint upon the democracy. But its efficacy in this respect wholly depends on the social support which it can command outside the House. An assembly which does not rest on the basis of some great power in the country is ineffectual against one which does. An aristocratic House is only powerful in an aristocratic state of society. The House of Lords was once the strongest power in our Constitution, and the Commons only a checking body: but this was when the Barons were almost the only power out of doors. I cannot believe that, in a really democratic state of society, the House of Lords would be of any practical value as a moderator of democracy. When the force on one side is feeble in comparison with that on the other, the way to give it effect is not to draw both out in line, and muster their strength in open field over against one another. Such tactics would ensure the utter defeat of the less powerful. It can only act to advantage by not holding itself apart, and compelling every one to declare himself either with or against it, but taking a position among, rather than in opposition to, the crowd, and drawing to itself the elements most capable of allying themselves with it on any given point; not appearing at all as an antagonist body, to provoke a general rally against it, but working as one of the elements in a mixed mass, infusing its leaven, and often making what would be the weaker part the stronger, by the addition of its influence. The really moderating power in a democratic constitution must act in and through the democratic House.

That there should be, in every polity, a centre of resistance to the predominant power in the Constitution—and in a democratic constitution, therefore, a nucleus of resistance to the democracy—I have already maintained; and I regard it as a fundamental maxim of government. If any people, who possess a democratic representation, are, from their historical antecedents, more willing to tolerate such a centre of resistance in the form of a Second Chamber or House of Lords than in any other shape, this constitutes a strong reason for having it in that shape. But it does not appear to me the best shape in itself, nor by any means the most efficacious for its object. If there are two Houses, one considered to represent the people, the other to represent only a class, or not to be representative at all, I cannot think that where democracy is the ruling power in society the Second House would have any real ability to resist even the aberrations of the first. It might be suffered to exist in deference to habit and association, but not as an effective check. If it exercised an independent will, it would be required to do so in the same general spirit as the other House; to be equally democratic with it, and to content itself with correcting the accidental oversights of the more popular branch of the legislature, or competing with it in popular measures.

The practicability of any real check to the ascendancy of the majority depends henceforth on the distribution of strength in the most popular branch of the governing body; and I have indicated the mode in which, to the best of my judgment, a balance of forces might most advantageously be established there. I have also pointed out, that even if the numerical majority were allowed to exercise complete predominance by means of a corresponding majority in Parliament, yet if minorities also are permitted to enjoy the equal right due to them on strictly democratic principles, of being represented proportionally to their numbers, this provision will ensure the perpetual presence in the House, by the same popular title as its other members, of so many of the first intellects in the country, that without being in any way banded apart, or invested with any invidious prerogative, this portion of the national representation will have a personal weight much more than in proportion to its numerical strength, and will afford, in a most effective form, the moral centre of resistance which is needed. A Second Chamber, therefore, is not required for this purpose, and would not contribute to it, but might even, in some conceivable modes, impede its attainment. If, however, for the other reasons already mentioned, the decision were taken that there should be such a Chamber, it is desirable that it should be composed of elements which, without being open to the imputation of class interests adverse to the majority, would incline it to oppose itself to the class interests of the majority, and qualify it to raise its voice with authority against their errors and weaknesses. These conditions evidently are not found in a body constituted in the manner of our House of Lords. So soon as conventional rank and individual riches no longer overawe the democracy, a House of Lords becomes insignificant.

Of all principles on which a wisely conservative body, destined to moderate and regulate democratic ascendancy, could possibly be constructed, the best seems to be that exemplified in the Roman Senate, itself the most consistently prudent and sagacious body that ever administered public affairs. The deficiencies of a democratic assembly, which represents the general public, are the deficiencies of the public itself, want of special training and knowledge. The appropriate corrective is to associate with it a body of which special training and knowledge should be the characteristics. If one House represents popular feeling, the other should represent personal merit, tested and guaranteed by actual public service, and fortified by practical experience. If one is the People's Chamber, the other should be the Chamber of Statesmen; a council composed of all living public men who have passed through important political offices or employments. Such a Chamber would be fitted for much more than to be a merely moderating body. It would not be exclusively a check, but also an impelling force. In its hands the power of holding the people back would be vested in those most competent, and who would generally be most inclined, to lead them forward in any right course. The council to whom the task would be entrusted of rectifying the people's mistakes would not represent a class believed to be opposed to their interest, but would consist of their own natural leaders in the path of progress. No mode of composition could approach to this in giving weight and efficacy to their function of moderators. It would be impossible to cry down a body always foremost in promoting improvements as a mere obstructive body, whatever amount of mischief it might obstruct.

Were the place vacant in England for such a Senate (I need scarcely say that this is a mere hypothesis), it might be composed of some such elements as the following. All who were or had been members of the Legislative Commission described in a former chapter, and which I regard as an indispensable ingredient in a well-constituted popular government. All who were or had been Chief Justices, or heads of any of the superior courts of law or equity. All who had for five years filled the office of puisne judge. All who had held for two years any Cabinet office: but these should also be eligible to the House of Commons, and if elected members of it, their peerage or senatorial office should be held in suspense. The condition of time is needed to prevent persons from being named Cabinet Ministers merely to give them a seat in the Senate; and the period of two years is suggested, that the same term which qualifies them for a pension might entitle them to a senatorship. All who had filled the office of Commander-in-Chief; and all who, having commanded an army or a fleet, had been thanked by Parliament for military or naval successes. All who had held, during ten years, first-class diplomatic appointments. All who had been Governors-General of India or British America, and all who had held for ten years any Colonial Governorships. The permanent civil service should also be represented; all should be senators who had filled, during ten years, the important offices of Under-Secretary to the Treasury, permanent Under-Secretary of State, or any others equally high and responsible. If, along with the persons thus qualified by practical experience in the administration of public affairs, any representation of the speculative class were to be included—a thing in itself desirable—it would be worth consideration whether certain professorships, in certain national institutions, after a tenure of a few years, might confer a seat in the Senate. Mere scientific and literary eminence are too indefinite and disputable: they imply a power of selection, whereas the other qualifications speak for themselves; if the writings by which reputation has been gained are unconnected with politics, they are no evidence of the special qualities required, while if political, they would enable successive Ministries to deluge the House with party tools.

The historical antecedents of England render it all but certain that, unless in the improbable case of a violent subversion of the existing Constitution, any Second Chamber which could possibly exist would have to be built on the foundation of the House of Lords. It is out of the question to think practically of abolishing that assembly, to replace it by such a Senate as I have sketched, or by any other; but there might not be the same insuperable difficulty in aggregating the classes or categories just spoken of to the existing body, in the character of Peers for life. An ulterior, and perhaps, on this supposition, a necessary step, might be, that the hereditary Peerage should be present in the House by their representatives instead of personally: a practice already established in the case of the Scotch and Irish Peers, and which the mere multiplication of the order will probably at some time or other render inevitable. An easy adaptation of Mr. Hare's plan would prevent the representative

Peers from representing exclusively the party which has the majority in the Peerage. If, for example, one representative were allowed for every ten Peers, any ten might be admitted to choose a representative, and the Peers might be free to group themselves for that purpose as they pleased. The election might be thus conducted: All Peers who were candidates for the representation of their order should be required to declare themselves such, and enter their names in a list. A day and place should be appointed at which Peers desirous of voting should be present, either in person, or, in the usual parliamentary manner, by their proxies. The votes should be taken, each Peer voting for only one. Every candidate who had as many as ten votes should be declared elected. If any one had more, all but ten should be allowed to withdraw their votes, or ten of the number should be selected by lot. These ten would form his constituency, and the remainder of his voters would be set free to give their votes over again for some one else. This process should be repeated until (so far as possible) every Peer present either personally or by proxy was represented. When a number less than ten remained over, if amounting to five they might still be allowed to agree on a representative; if fewer than five, their votes must be lost, or they might be permitted to record them in favour of somebody already elected. With this inconsiderable exception, every representative Peer would represent ten members of the Peerage, all of whom had not only voted for him, but selected him as the one, among all open to their choice, by whom they were most desirous to be represented. As a compensation to the Peers who were not chosen representatives of their order, they should be eligible to the House of Commons; a justice now refused to Scotch Peers, and to Irish Peers in their own part of the kingdom, while the representation in the House of Lords of any but the most numerous party in the Peerage is denied equally to both.

The mode of composing a Senate, which has been here advocated, not only seems the best in itself, but is that for which historical precedent, and actual brilliant success, can to the greatest extent be pleaded. It is not, however, the only feasible plan that might be proposed. Another possible mode of forming a Second Chamber would be to have it elected by the First; subject to the restriction that they should not nominate any of their own members. Such an assembly, emanating like the American Senate from popular choice, only once removed, would not be considered to clash with democratic institutions, and would probably acquire considerable popular influence. From the mode of its nomination it would be peculiarly unlikely to excite the jealousy of, or to come into any hostile collision with, the popular House. It would, moreover (due provision being made for the representation of the minority), be almost sure to be well composed, and to comprise many of that class of highly capable men, who, either from accident or for want of showy qualities, had been unwilling to seek, or unable to obtain, the suffrages of a popular constituency.

The best constitution of a Second Chamber is that which embodies the greatest number of elements exempt from the class interests and prejudices of the majority, but having in themselves nothing offensive to democratic feeling. I repeat, however, that the main reliance for tempering the ascendancy of the majority cannot be placed in a Second Chamber of any kind. The character of a representative government is fixed by the constitution of the popular House. Compared with this, all other questions relating to the form of government are insignificant.

Chapter 14
Of the Executive in a Representative Government

IT WOULD be out of place, in this treatise, to discuss the question into what departments or branches the executive business of government may most conveniently be divided. In this respect the exigencies of different governments are different; and there is little probability that any great mistake will be made in the classification of the duties when men are willing to begin at the beginning, and do not hold themselves bound by the series of accidents which, in an old government like ours, has produced the existing division of the public business. It may be sufficient to say that the classification of functionaries should correspond to that of subjects, and that there should not be several departments independent of one another to superintend different parts of the same natural whole; as in our own military administration down to a recent period, and in a less degree even at present. Where the object to be attained is single (such as that of having an efficient army), the authority commissioned to attend to it should be single likewise. The entire aggregate of means provided for one end should be under one and the same control and responsibility. If they are divided among independent authorities, the means, with each of those authorities, become ends, and it is the business of nobody except the head of the Government, who is probably without the appropriate departmental experience, to take care of the real end. The different classes of means are not combined and adapted to one another under the guidance of any leading idea; and while every department pushes forward its own requirements, regardless of those of the rest, the purpose of the work is perpetually sacrificed to the work itself.

As a general rule, every executive function, whether superior or subordinate, should be the appointed duty of some given individual. It should be apparent to all the world who did everything, and through whose default anything was left undone. Responsibility is null when nobody knows who is responsible. Nor, even when real, can it be divided without being weakened. To maintain it at its highest there must be one person who receives the whole praise of what is well done, the whole blame of what is ill. There are, however, two modes of sharing responsibility: by one it is only enfeebled, by the other, absolutely destroyed. It is enfeebled when the concurrence of more than one functionary is required to the same act. Each one among them has still a real responsibility; if a wrong has been done, none of them can say he did not do it; he is as much a participant as an accomplice is in an offence: if there has been legal criminality they may all be punished legally, and their punishment needs not be less severe than if there had been only one person concerned. But it is not so with the penalties, any more than with the rewards, of opinion: these are always diminished by being shared. Where there has been no definite legal offence, no corruption or malversation, only an error or an imprudence, or what may pass for such, every participator has an excuse to himself and to the world, in the fact that other persons are jointly involved with him. There is hardly anything, even to pecuniary dishonesty, for which men will not feel themselves almost absolved, if those whose duty it was to resist and remonstrate have failed to do it, still more if they have given a formal assent.

In this case, however, though responsibility is weakened, there still is responsibility: every one of those implicated has in his individual capacity assented to, and joined in, the act. Things are much worse when the act itself is only that of a majority—a Board, deliberating with closed doors, nobody knowing, or, except in some extreme case, being ever likely to know, whether an individual member voted for the act or against it. Responsibility in this case is a mere name. "Boards," it is happily said by Bentham, "are screens." What "the Board" does is the act of nobody; and nobody can be made to answer for it. The Board suffers, even in reputation, only in its collective character; and no individual member feels this further than his disposition leads him to identify his own estimation with that of the body— a feeling often very strong when the body is a permanent one, and he is wedded to it for better for worse; but the fluctuations of a modern official career give no time for the formation of such an *esprit de corps;* which, if it exists at all, exists only in the obscure ranks of the permanent subordinates. Boards, therefore, are not a fit instrument for executive business; and are only admissible in it when, for other reasons, to give full discretionary power to a single minister would be worse.

On the other hand, it is also a maxim of experience that in the multitude of counsellors there is wisdom; and that a man seldom judges right, even in his own concerns, still less in those of the public, when he makes habitual use of no knowledge but his own, or that of some single adviser. There is no necessary incompatibility between this principle and the other. It is easy to give the effective power, and the full responsibility, to one, providing him when necessary with advisers, each of whom is responsible only for the opinion he gives.

In general, the head of a department of the executive government is a mere politician. He may be a good politician, and a man of merit; and unless this is usually the case, the government is bad. But his general capacity, and the knowledge he ought to possess of the general interests of the country, will not, unless by occasional accident, be accompanied by adequate, and what may be called professional, knowledge of the department over which he is called to preside. Professional advisers must therefore be provided for him. Wherever mere experience and attainments are sufficient— wherever the qualities required in a professional adviser may possibly be united in a single well-selected individual (as in the case, for example, of a law officer), one such person for general purposes, and a staff of clerks to supply knowledge of details, meet the demands of the case. But, more frequently, it is not sufficient that the minister should consult some one competent person, and, when himself not conversant with the subject, act implicitly on that person's advice. It is often necessary that he should, not only occasionally but habitually, listen to a variety of opinions, and inform his judgment by the discussions among a body of advisers. This, for example, is emphatically necessary in military and naval affairs. The military and naval ministers, therefore, and probably several others, should be provided with a Council, composed, at least in those two departments, of able and experienced professional men. As a means of obtaining the best men for the purpose under every change of administration, they ought to be permanent: by which I mean, that they ought not, like the Lords of the Admiralty, to be expected to resign with the ministry by whom they were appointed: but it is a good rule that all who hold high appointments to which they have risen by selection, and not by the ordinary course of promotion, should retain their office only for a fixed term, unless reappointed; as is now the rule with Staff appointments in the British army. This rule renders appointments somewhat less likely to be jobbed, not being a provision for life, and at the same time affords a means, without affront to any one, of getting rid of those who are least worth keeping, and bringing in highly qualified persons of younger standing, for whom there might never be room if death vacancies, or voluntary resignations, were waited for.

The Councils should be consultative merely, in this sense, that the ultimate decision should rest undividedly with the minister himself: but neither ought they to be looked upon, or to look upon themselves, as ciphers, or as capable of being reduced to such at his pleasure. The advisers attached to a powerful and perhaps self-willed man ought to be placed under conditions which make it impossible for them, without discredit, not to express an opinion, and impossible for him not to listen to and consider their recommendations, whether he adopts them or not. The relation which ought to exist between a chief and this description of advisers is very accurately hit by the constitution of the Council of the Governor-General and those of the different Presidencies in India. These Councils are composed of persons who have professional knowledge of Indian affairs, which the Governor-General and

Governors usually lack, and which it would not be desirable to require of them. As a rule, every member of Council is expected to give an opinion, which is of course very often a simple acquiescence: but if there is a difference of sentiment, it is at the option of every member, and is the invariable practice, to record the reasons of his opinion: the Governor-General, or Governor, doing the same. In ordinary cases the decision is according to the sense of the majority; the Council, therefore, has a substantial part in the government: but if the Governor-General, or Governor, thinks fit, he may set aside even their unanimous opinion, recording his reasons. The result is, that the chief is individually and effectively responsible for every act of the Government. The members of Council have only the responsibility of advisers; but it is always known, from documents capable of being produced, and which if called for by Parliament or public opinion always are produced, what each has advised, and what reasons he gave for his advice: while, from their dignified position, and ostensible participation in all acts of government, they have nearly as strong motives to apply themselves to the public business, and to form and express a well-considered opinion on every part of it, as if the whole responsibility rested with themselves.

This mode of conducting the highest class of administrative business is one of the most successful instances of the adaptation of means to ends which political history, not hitherto very prolific in works of skill and contrivance, has yet to show. It is one of the acquisitions with which the art of politics has been enriched by the experience of the East India Company's rule; and, like most of the other wise contrivances by which India has been preserved to this country, and an amount of good government produced which is truly wonderful considering the circumstances and the materials, it is probably destined to perish in the general holocaust which the traditions of Indian government seem fated to undergo, since they have been placed at the mercy of public ignorance, and the presumptuous vanity of political men. Already an outcry is raised for abolishing the Councils, as a superfluous and expensive clog on the wheels of government: while the clamour has long been urgent, and is daily obtaining more countenance in the highest quarters, for the abrogation of the professional civil service which breeds the men that compose the Councils, and the existence of which is the sole guarantee for their being of any value.

A most important principle of good government in a popular constitution is that no executive functionaries should be appointed by popular election: neither by the votes of the people themselves, nor by those of their representatives. The entire business of government is skilled employment; the qualifications for the discharge of it are of that special and professional kind which cannot be properly judged of except by persons who have themselves some share of those qualifications, or some practical experience of them. The business of finding the fittest persons to fill public employments—not merely selecting the best who offer, but looking out for the absolutely best, and taking note of all fit persons who are met with, that they may be found when wanted—is very laborious, and requires a delicate as well as highly conscientious discernment; and as there is no public duty which is in general so badly performed, so there is none for which it is of greater importance to enforce the utmost practicable amount of personal responsibility, by imposing it as a special obligation on high functionaries in the several departments. All subordinate public officers who are not appointed by some mode of public competition should be selected on the direct responsibility of the minister under whom they serve. The ministers, all but the chief, will naturally be selected by the chief; and the chief himself, though really designated by Parliament, should be, in a regal government, officially appointed by the Crown. The functionary who appoints should be the sole person empowered to remove any subordinate officer who is liable to removal; which the far greater number ought not to be, except for personal misconduct; since it would be vain to expect that the body of persons by whom the whole detail of the public business is transacted, and whose qualifications are generally of much more importance to the public than those of the minister himself, will devote themselves to their profession, and acquire the knowledge and skill on which the minister must often place entire dependence, if they are liable at any moment to be turned adrift for no fault, that the minister may gratify himself, or promote his political interest, by appointing somebody else.

To the principle which condemns the appointment of executive officers by popular suffrage, ought the chief of the executive, in a republican government, to be an exception? Is it a good rule, which, in the American Constitution, provides for the election of the President once in every four years by the entire people? The question is not free from difficulty. There is unquestionably some advantage, in a country like America, where no apprehension needs be entertained of a *coup d'état*, in making the chief minister constitutionally independent of the legislative body, and rendering the two great branches of the government, while equally popular both in their origin and in their responsibility, an effective check on one another. The plan is in accordance with that sedulous avoidance of the concentration of great masses of power in the same hands, which is a marked characteristic of the American Federal Constitution. But the advantage, in this instance, is purchased at a price above all reasonable estimates of its value. It seems far better that the chief magistrate in a republic should be appointed avowedly, as the chief minister in a constitutional monarchy is virtually, by the representative body. In the first place, he is certain, when thus appointed, to be a more eminent man. The party which has the majority in Parliament would then, as a rule, appoint its own leader; who is always one of the foremost, and often the very foremost person in political life: while the President of the United States, since the last survivor of the founders of the republic disappeared from the scene, is almost always either an obscure man, or one who has gained any reputation he may possess in some other field than politics. And this, as I have before observed, is no accident, but the natural effect of the situation. The eminent men of a party, in an election extending to the whole country, are never its most available candidates. All eminent men have made personal enemies, or have done something, or at the lowest professed some opinion, obnoxious to some local or other considerable division of the community, and likely to tell with fatal effect upon the number of votes; whereas a man without antecedents, of whom nothing is known but that he professes the creed of the party, is readily voted for by its entire strength. Another important consideration is the great mischief of unintermitted electioneering. When the highest dignity in the State is to be conferred by popular election once in every few years, the whole intervening time is spent in what is virtually a canvass. President, ministers, chiefs of parties, and their followers, are all electioneerers: the whole community is kept intent on the mere personalities of politics, and every public question is discussed and decided with less reference to its merits than to its expected bearing on the presidential election. If a system had been devised to make party spirit the ruling principle of action in all public affairs, and create an inducement not only to make every question a party question, but to raise questions for the purpose of founding parties upon them, it would have been difficult to contrive any means better adapted to the purpose.

I will not affirm that it would at all times and places be desirable that the head of the executive should be so completely dependent upon the votes of a representative assembly as the Prime Minister is in England, and is without inconvenience. If it were thought best to avoid this, he might, though appointed by Parliament, hold his office for a fixed period, independent of a parliamentary vote: which would be the American system, minus the popular election and its evils. There is another mode of giving the head of the administration as much independence of the legislature as is at all compatible with the essentials of free government. He never could be unduly dependent on a vote of Parliament, if he had, as the British Prime Minister practically has, the power to dissolve the House and appeal to the people: if instead of being turned out of office by a hostile vote, he could only be reduced by it to the alternative of resignation or dissolution. The power of dissolving Parliament is one which I think it desirable he should possess, even under the system by which his own tenure of office is secured to him for a fixed period. There ought not to be any possibility of that deadlock in politics which would ensue on a quarrel breaking out between a President and an Assembly, neither of whom, during an interval which might amount to years, would have any legal means of ridding itself of the other. To get through such a period without a *coup d'état* being attempted, on either side or on both, requires such a combination of the love of liberty and the habit of self-restraint as very few nations have yet shown themselves capable of: and though this extremity were avoided, to expect that the two authorities would not paralyse each other's operations is to suppose that the political life of the country will always be pervaded by a spirit of mutual forbearance and compromise, imperturbable by the pas-

sions and excitements of the keenest party struggles. Such a spirit may exist, but even where it does there is imprudence in trying it too far.

Other reasons make it desirable that some power in the state (which can only be the executive) should have the liberty of at any time, and at discretion, calling a new Parliament. When there is a real doubt which of two contending parties has the strongest following, it is important that there should exist a constitutional means of immediately testing the point, and setting it at rest. No other political topic has a chance of being properly attended to while this is undecided: and such an interval is mostly an interregnum for purposes of legislative or administrative improvement; neither party having sufficient confidence in its strength to attempt things likely to promote opposition in any quarter that has either direct or indirect influence in the pending struggle.

I have not taken account of the case in which the vast power centralised in the chief magistrate, and the insufficient attachment of the mass of the people to free institutions, give him a chance of success in an attempt to subvert the Constitution, and usurp sovereign power. Where such peril exists, no first magistrate is admissible whom the Parliament cannot, by a single vote, reduce to a private station. In a state of things holding out any encouragement to that most audacious and profligate of all breaches of trust, even this entireness of constitutional dependence is but a weak protection.

Of all officers of government, those in whose appointment any participation of popular suffrage is the most objectionable are judicial officers. While there are no functionaries whose special and professional qualifications the popular judgment is less fitted to estimate, there are none in whose case absolute impartiality, and freedom from connection with politicians or sections of politicians, are of anything like equal importance. Some thinkers, among others Mr. Bentham, have been of opinion that, although it is better that judges should not be appointed by popular election, the people of their district ought to have the power, after sufficient experience, of removing them from their trust. It cannot be denied that the irremovability of any public officer, to whom great interests are entrusted, is in itself an evil. It is far from desirable that there should be no means of getting rid of a bad or incompetent judge, unless for such misconduct as he can be made to answer for in a criminal court; and that a functionary on whom so much depends should have the feeling of being free from responsibility except to opinion and his own conscience. The question however is, whether in the peculiar position of a judge, and supposing that all practicable securities have been taken for an honest appointment, irresponsibility, except to his own and the public conscience, has not on the whole less tendency to pervert his conduct than responsibility to the government, or to a popular vote. Experience has long decided this point in the affirmative as regards responsibility to the executive; and the case is quite equally strong when the responsibility sought to be enforced is to the suffrages of electors. Among the good qualities of a popular constituency, those peculiarly incumbent upon a judge, calmness and impartiality, are not numbered. Happily, in that intervention of popular suffrage which is essential to freedom they are not the qualities required. Even the quality of justice, though necessary to all human beings, and therefore to all electors, is not the inducement which decides any popular election. Justice and impartiality are as little wanted for electing a member of Parliament as they can be in any transaction of men. The electors have not to award something which either candidate has a right to, nor to pass judgment on the general merits of the competitors, but to declare which of them has most of their personal confidence, or best represents their political convictions. A judge is bound to treat his political friend, or the person best known to him, exactly as he treats other people; but it would be a breach of duty as well as an absurdity if an elector did so. No argument can be grounded on the beneficial effect produced on judges, as on all other functionaries, by the moral jurisdiction of opinion; for even in this respect, that which really exercises a useful control over the proceedings of a judge, when fit for the judicial office, is not (except sometimes in political cases) the opinion of the community generally, but that of the only public by whom his conduct or qualifications can be duly estimated, the bar of his own court.

I must not be understood to say that the participation of the general public in the administration of justice is of no importance; it is of the greatest: but in what manner? By the actual discharge of a part of the judicial office,

in the capacity of jurymen. This is one of the few cases in politics in which it is better that the people should act directly and personally than through their representatives; being almost the only case in which the errors that a person exercising authority may commit can be better borne than the consequences of making him responsible for them. If a judge could be removed from office by a popular vote, whoever was desirous of supplanting him would make capital for that purpose out of all his judicial decisions; would carry all of them, as far as he found practicable, by irregular appeal before a public opinion wholly incompetent, for want of having heard the case, or from having heard it without either the precautions or the impartiality belonging to a judicial hearing; would play upon popular passion and prejudice where they existed, and take pains to arouse them where they did not. And in this, if the case were interesting, and he took sufficient trouble, he would infallibly be successful, unless the judge or his friends descended into the arena, and made equally powerful appeals on the other side. Judges would end by feeling that they risked their office upon every decision they gave in a case susceptible of general interest, and that it was less essential for them to consider what decision was just than what would be most applauded by the public, or would least admit of insidious misrepresentation. The practice introduced by some of the new or revised State Constitutions in America, of submitting judicial officers to periodical popular re-election, will be found, I apprehend, to be one of the most dangerous errors ever yet committed by democracy: and, were it not that the practical good sense which never totally deserts the people of the United States is said to be producing a reaction, likely in no long time to lead to the retraction of the error, it might with reason be regarded as the first great downward step in the degeneration of modern democratic government. [1]

[1] I have been informed, however, that in the States which have made their judges elective, the choice is not really made by the people, but by the leaders of parties; no elector ever thinking of voting for any one but the party candidate: and that, in consequence, the person elected is usually in effect the same who would have been appointed to the office by the President or by the Governor of the State. Thus one bad practice limits and corrects another; and the habit of voting *en masse* under a party banner, which is so full of evil in all cases in which the function of electing is rightly vested in the people, tends to alleviate a still great-

With regard to that large and important body which constitutes the permanent strength of the public service, those who do not change with changes of politics, but remain to aid every minister by their experience and traditions, inform him by their knowledge of business, and conduct official details under his general control; those, in short, who form the class of professional public servants, entering their profession as others do while young, in the hope of rising progressively to its higher grades as they advance in life; it is evidently inadmissible that these should be liable to be turned out, and deprived of the whole benefit of their previous service, except for positive, proved, and serious misconduct. Not, of course, such delinquency only as makes them amenable to the law; but voluntary neglect of duty, or conduct implying untrustworthiness for the purposes for which their trust is given them. Since, therefore, unless in case of personal culpability, there is no way of getting rid of them except by quartering them on the public as pensioners, it is of the greatest importance that the appointments should be well made in the first instance; and it remains to be considered by what mode of appointment this purpose can best be attained.

In making first appointments, little danger is to be apprehended from want of special skill and knowledge in the choosers, but much from partiality, and private or political interest. Being, as a rule, appointed at the commencement of manhood, not as having learnt, but in order that they may learn, their profession, the only thing by which the best candidates can be discriminated is proficiency in the ordinary branches of liberal education: and this can be ascertained without difficulty, provided there be the requisite pains and the requisite impartiality in those who are appointed to inquire into it. Neither the one nor the other can reasonably be expected from a minister; who must rely wholly on recommendations, and however disinterested as to his personal wishes, never will be proof against the solicitations of persons who have the power of influencing his own election, or whose political adherence is important to the ministry to which he belongs. These considerations have introduced the practice of submitting all candidates for first appointments to a public examina-

tion, conducted by persons not engaged in politics, and of the same class and quality with the examiners for honours at the Universities. This would probably be the best plan under any system; and under our parliamentary government it is the only one which affords a chance, I do not say of honest appointment, but even of abstinence from such as are manifestly and flagrantly profligate.

It is also absolutely necessary that the examinations should be competitive, and the appointments given to those who are most successful. A mere pass examination never, in the long run, does more than exclude absolute dunces. When the question, in the mind of an examiner, lies between blighting the prospects of an individual, and neglecting a duty to the public which, in the particular instance, seldom appears of first-rate importance; and when he is sure to be bitterly reproached for doing the first, while in general no one will either know or care whether he has done the latter; the balance, unless he is a man of very unusual stamp, inclines to the side of good nature. A relaxation in one instance establishes a claim to it in others, which every repetition of indulgence makes it more difficult to resist; each of these in succession becomes a precedent for more, until the standard of proficiency sinks gradually to something almost contemptible. Examinations for degrees at the two great Universities have generally been as slender in their requirements as those for honours are trying and serious. Where there is no inducement to exceed a certain minimum, the minimum comes to be the maximum: it becomes the general practice not to aim at more, and as in everything there are some who do not attain all they aim at, however low the standard may be pitched, there are always several who fall short of it. When, on the contrary, the appointments are given to those, among a great number of candidates, who most distinguish themselves, and where the successful competitors are classed in order of merit, not only each is stimulated to do his very utmost, but the influence is felt in every place of liberal education throughout the country. It becomes with every schoolmaster an object of ambition, and an avenue to success, to have furnished pupils who have gained a high place in these competitions; and there is hardly any other mode in which the State can do so much to raise the quality of educational institutions throughout the country.

Though the principle of competitive exam-

---

er mischief in a case where the officer to be elected is one who *ought* to be chosen not by the people but for them.

inations for public employment is of such recent introduction in this country, and is still so imperfectly carried out, the Indian service being as yet nearly the only case in which it exists in its completeness, a sensible effect has already begun to be produced on the places of middle-class education; notwithstanding the difficulties which the principle has encountered from the disgracefully low existing state of education in the country, which these very examinations have brought into strong light. So contemptible has the standard of acquirement been found to be among the youths who obtain the nomination from the minister which entitles them to offer themselves as candidates, that the competition of such candidates produces almost a poorer result than would be obtained from a mere pass examination; for no one would think of fixing the conditions of a pass examination so low as is actually found sufficient to enable a young man to surpass his fellow-candidates. Accordingly, it is said that successive years show on the whole a decline of attainments, less effort being made because the results of former examinations have proved that the exertions then used were greater than would have been sufficient to attain the object. Partly from this decrease of effort, and partly because, even at the examinations which do not require a previous nomination, conscious ignorance reduces the number of competitors to a mere handful, it has so happened that though there have always been a few instances of great proficiency, the lower part of the list of successful candidates represents but a very moderate amount of acquirement; and we have it on the word of the Commissioners that nearly all who have been unsuccessful have owed their failure to ignorance not of the higher branches of instruction, but of its very humblest elements—spelling and arithmetic.

The outcries which continue to be made against these examinations by some of the organs of opinion, are often, I regret to say, as little creditable to the good faith as to the good sense of the assailants. They proceed partly by misrepresentation of the kind of ignorance which, as a matter of fact, actually leads to failure in the examinations. They quote with emphasis the most recondite questions[1] which

can be shown to have been ever asked, and make it appear as if unexceptionable answers to all these were made the *sine qua non* of success. Yet it has been repeated to satiety that such questions are not put because it is expected of every one that he should answer them, but in order that whoever is able to do so may have the means of proving and availing himself of that portion of his knowledge. It is not as a ground of rejection, but as an additional means of success, that this opportunity is given. We are then asked whether the kind of knowledge supposed in this, that, or the other question is calculated to be of any use to the candidate after he has attained his object. People differ greatly in opinion as to what knowledge is useful. There are persons in existence, and a late Foreign Secretary of State is one of them, who think English spelling a useless accomplishment in a diplomatic attaché, or a clerk in a government office. About one thing the objectors seem to be unanimous, that general mental cultivation is not useful in these employments, whatever else may be so. If, however (as I presume to think), it is useful, or if any education at all is useful, it must be tested by the tests most likely to show whether the candidate possesses it or not. To ascertain whether he has been well educated, he must be interrogated in the things which he is likely to know if he has been well educated, even though not directly pertinent to the work to which he is to be appointed. Will those who object to his being questioned in classics and mathematics, in a country where the only things regularly taught are classics and mathematics, tell us what they would have him questioned in? There seems, however, to be equal objection to examining him in these, and to examining him in anything *but* these. If the Commissioners—anxious to open a door of admission to those who have not gone through the routine of a grammar school, or who make up for the smallness of their knowledge of what is there taught by greater knowledge of something else—allow marks to be gained by proficiency in any other subject of real utility, they are reproached for that too. Nothing will satisfy the objectors but free admission of total ignorance.

We are triumphantly told that neither Clive nor Wellington could have passed the test which is prescribed for an aspirant to an engineer cadetship. As if, because Clive and Wellington did not do what was not required of them, they could not have done it if it had

[1] Not always, however, the most recondite; for a late denouncer of competitive examination in the House of Commons had the *naïveté* to produce a set of almost elementary questions in algebra, history, and geography, as a proof of the exorbitant amount of high scientific attainment which the Commissioners were so wild as to exact.

been required. If it be only meant to inform us that it is possible to be a great general without these things, so it is without many other things which are very useful to great generals. Alexander the Great had never heard of Vauban's rules, nor could Julius Cæsar speak French. We are next informed that bookworms, a term which seems to be held applicable to whoever has the smallest tincture of book-knowledge, may not be good at bodily exercises, or have the habits of gentlemen. This is a very common line of remark with dunces of condition; but whatever the dunces may think, they have no monopoly of either gentlemanly habits or bodily activity. Wherever these are needed, let them be inquired into and separately provided for, not to the exclusion of mental qualifications, but in addition. Meanwhile, I am credibly informed, that in the Military Academy at Woolwich the competition cadets are as superior to those admitted on the old system of nomination in these respects as in all others; that they learn even their drill more quickly; as indeed might be expected, for an intelligent person learns all things sooner than a stupid one: and that in general demeanour they contrast so favourably with their predecessors, that the authorities of the institutions are impatient for the day to arrive when the last remains of the old leaven shall have disappeared from the place. If this be so, and it is easy to ascertain whether it is so, it is to be hoped we shall soon have heard for the last time that ignorance is a better qualification than knowledge for the military, and *à fortiori* for every other, profession; or that any one good quality, however little apparently connected with liberal education, is at all likely to be promoted by going without it.

Though the first admission to government employment be decided by competitive examination, it would in most cases be impossible that subsequent promotion should be so decided: and it seems proper that this should take place, as it usually does at present, on a mixed system of seniority and selection. Those whose duties are of a routine character should rise by seniority to the highest point to which duties merely of that description can carry them; while those to whom functions of particular trust, and requiring special capacity, are confided, should be selected from the body on the discretion of the chief of the office. And this selection will generally be made honestly by him if the original appointments take place by open competition: for under that system his establishment will generally consist of individuals to whom, but for the official connection, he would have been a stranger. If among them there be any in whom he, or his political friends and supporters, take an interest, it will be but occasionally, and only when, to this advantage of connection, is added, as far as the initiatory examination could test it, at least equality of real merit. And, except when there is a very strong motive to job these appointments, there is always a strong one to appoint the fittest person; being the one who gives to his chief the most useful assistance, saves him most trouble, and helps most to build up that reputation for good management of public business which necessarily and properly redounds to the credit of the minister, however much the qualities to which it is immediately owing may be those of his subordinates.

Chapter 15
Of Local Representative Bodies

IT IS BUT a small portion of the public business of a country which can be well done, or safely attempted, by the central authorities; and even in our own government, the least centralised in Europe, the legislative portion at least of the governing body busies itself far too much with local affairs, employing the supreme power of the State in cutting small knots which there ought to be other and better means of untying. The enormous amount of private business which takes up the time of Parliament, and the thoughts of its individual members, distracting them from the proper occupations of the great council of the nation, is felt by all thinkers and observers as a serious evil, and what is worse, an increasing one.

It would not be appropriate to the limited design of this treatise to discuss at large the great question, in no way peculiar to representative government, of the proper limits of governmental action. I have said elsewhere[1] what seemed to me most essential respecting the principles by which the extent of that action ought to be determined. But after subtracting from the functions performed by most European governments those which ought not to be undertaken by public authorities at all, there still remains so great and various an ag-

[1] *On Liberty*, concluding chapter; and, at greater length, in the final chapter of *Principles of Political Economy*.

gregate of duties that, if only on the principle of division of labour, it is indispensable to share them between central and local authorities. Not only are separate executive officers required for purely local duties (an amount of separation which exists under all governments), but the popular control over those officers can only be advantageously exerted through a separate organ. Their original appointment, the function of watching and checking them, the duty of providing, or the discretion of withholding, the supplies necessary for their operations, should rest, not with the national Parliament or the national executive, but with the people of the locality. In some of the New England States these functions are still exercised directly by the assembled people; it is said with better results than might be expected; and those highly educated communities are so well satisfied with this primitive mode of local government, that they have no desire to exchange it for the only representative system they are acquainted with, by which all minorities are disfranchised. Such very peculiar circumstances, however, are required to make this arrangement work tolerably in practice, that recourse must generally be had to the plan of representative sub-Parliaments for local affairs. These exist in England, but very incompletely, and with great irregularity and want of system: in some other countries much less popularly governed their constitution is far more rational. In England there has always been more liberty, but worse organisation, while in other countries there is better organisation, but less liberty. It is necessary, then, that in addition to the national representation there should be municipal and provincial representations: and the two questions which remain to be resolved are, how the local representative bodies should be constituted, and what should be the extent of their functions.

In considering these questions two points require an equal degree of our attention: how the local business itself can be best done; and how its transaction can be made most instrumental to the nourishment of public spirit and the development of intelligence. In an earlier part of this inquiry I have dwelt in strong language—hardly any language is strong enough to express the strength of my conviction—on the importance of that portion of the operation of free institutions which may be called the public education of the citizens. Now, of this operation the local administra-

tive institutions are the chief instrument. Except by the part they may take as jurymen in the administration of justice, the mass of the population have very little opportunity of sharing personally in the conduct of the general affairs of the community. Reading newspapers, and perhaps writing to them, public meetings, and solicitations of different sorts addressed to the political authorities, are the extent of the participation of private citizens in general politics during the interval between one parliamentary election and another. Though it is impossible to exaggerate the importance of these various liberties, both as securities for freedom and as means of general cultivation, the practice which they give is more in thinking than in action, and in thinking without the responsibilities of action; which with most people amounts to little more than passively receiving the thoughts of some one else. But in the case of local bodies, besides the function of electing, many citizens in turn have the chance of being elected, and many, either by selection or by rotation, fill one or other of the numerous local executive offices. In these positions they have to act for public interests, as well as to think and to speak, and the thinking cannot all be done by proxy. It may be added, that these local functions, not being in general sought by the higher ranks, carry down the important political education which they are the means of conferring to a much lower grade in society. The mental discipline being thus a more important feature in local concerns than in the general affairs of the State, while there are not such vital interests dependent on the quality of the administration, a greater weight may be given to the former consideration, and the latter admits much more frequently of being postponed to it than in matters of general legislation and the conduct of imperial affairs.

The proper constitution of local representative bodies does not present much difficulty. The principles which apply to it do not differ in any respect from those applicable to the national representation. The same obligation exists, as in the case of the more important function, for making the bodies elective; and the same reasons operate as in that case, but with still greater force, for giving them a widely democratic basis: the dangers being less, and the advantages, in point of popular education and cultivation, in some respects even greater. As the principal duty of the local bodies consists of the imposition and expenditure of local taxation, the electoral franchise should vest in all who contribute to the local rates, to the exclusion of all who do not. I assume that there is no indirect taxation, no *octroi* duties, or that if there are, they are supplementary only; those on whom their burden falls being also rated to a direct assessment. The representation of minorities should be provided for in the same manner as in the national Parliament, and there are the same strong reasons for plurality of votes. Only, there is not so decisive an objection, in the inferior as in the higher body, to making the plural voting depend (as in some of the local elections of our own country) on a mere money qualification: for the honest and frugal dispensation of money forms so much larger a part of the business of the local than of the national body, that there is more justice as well as policy in allowing a greater proportional influence to those who have a larger money interest at stake.

In the most recently established of our local representative institutions, the Boards of Guardians, the justices of peace of the district sit *ex officio* along with the elected members, in number limited by law to a third of the whole. In the peculiar constitution of English society I have no doubt of the beneficial effect of this provision. It secures the presence, in these bodies, of a more educated class than it would perhaps be practicable to attract thither on any other terms; and while the limitation in number of the *ex officio* members precludes them from acquiring predominance by mere numerical strength, they, as a virtual representation of another class, having sometimes a different interest from the rest, are a check upon the class interests of the farmers or petty shopkeepers who form the bulk of the elected Guardians. A similar commendation cannot be given to the constitution of the only provincial boards we possess, the Quarter Sessions, consisting of the justices of peace alone; on whom, over and above their judicial duties, some of the most important parts of the administrative business of the country depend for their performance. The mode of formation of these bodies is most anomalous, they being neither elected, nor, in any proper sense of the term, nominated, but holding their important functions, like the feudal lords to whom they succeeded, virtually by right of their acres: the appointment vested in the Crown (or, speaking practically, in one of themselves, the Lord Lieutenant) being made use of only as a means of excluding any one who it is thought would do discredit to the body, or, now and then, one who is on the wrong side in politics. The institution is the most aristocratic in principle which now remains in England; far more so than the House of Lords, for it grants public money and disposes of important public interests, not in conjunction with a popular assembly, but alone. It is clung to with proportionate tenacity by our aristocratic classes; but is obviously at variance with all the principles which are the foundation of representative government. In a County Board there is not the same justification as in Boards of Guardians, for even an admixture of *ex officio* with elected members: since the business of a county being on a sufficiently large scale to be an object of interest and attraction to country gentlemen, they would have no more difficulty in getting themselves elected to the Board than they have in being returned to Parliament as county members.

In regard to the proper circumscription of the constituencies which elect the local representative bodies; the principle which, when applied as an exclusive and unbending rule to parliamentary representation, is inappropriate, namely community of local interests, is here the only just and applicable one. The very object of having a local representation is in order that those who have any interest in common, which they do not share with the general body of their countrymen, may manage that joint interest by themselves: and the purpose is contradicted if the distribution of the local representation follows any other rule than the grouping of those joint interests. There are local interests peculiar to every town, whether great or small, and common to all its inhabitants: every town, therefore, without distinction of size, ought to have its municipal council. It is equally obvious that every town ought to have but one. The different quarters of the same town have seldom or never any material diversities of local interest; they all require to have the same things done, the same expenses incurred; and, except as to their churches, which it is probably desirable to leave under simply parochial management, the same arrangements may be made to serve for all. Paving, lighting, water supply, drainage, port and market regulations, cannot without great waste and inconvenience be different for different quarters of the same town. The subdivision of London into six or seven independent districts, each with its separate arrangements for local business (several of them without unity of administration even within themselves), prevents the possibility of consecutive or well-regulated cooperation for common objects, precludes any uniform principle for the discharge of local duties, compels the general government to take things upon itself which would be best left to local authorities if there were any whose authority extended to the entire metropolis, and answers no purpose but to keep up the fantastical trappings of that union of modern jobbing and antiquated foppery, the Corporation of the City of London.

Another equally important principle is, that in each local circumscription there should be but one elected body for all local business, not different bodies for different parts of it. Division of labour does not mean cutting up every business into minute fractions; it means the union of such operations as are fit to be performed by the same persons, and the separation of such as can be better performed by different persons. The executive duties of the locality do indeed require to be divided into departments, for the same reason as those of the State; because they are of diverse kinds, each requiring knowledge peculiar to itself, and needing, for its due performance, the undivided attention of a specially qualified functionary. But the reasons for subdivision which apply to the execution do not apply to the control. The business of the elective body is not to do the work, but to see that it is properly done, and that nothing necessary is left undone. This function can be fulfilled for all departments by the same superintending body; and by a collective and comprehensive far better than by a minute and microscopic view. It is as absurd in public affairs as it would be in private that every workman should be looked after by a superintendent to himself. The Government of the Crown consists of many departments, and there are many ministers to conduct them, but those ministers have not a Parliament apiece to keep them to their duty. The local, like the national Parliament, has for its proper business to consider the interest of the locality as a whole, composed of parts all of which must be adapted to one another, and attended to in the order and ratio of their importance.

There is another very weighty reason for uniting the control of all the business of a locality under one body. The greatest imperfection of popular local institutions, and the chief cause of the failure which so often attends them, is the low calibre of the men by whom they are almost always carried on. That these should be of a very miscellaneous character is, indeed, part of the usefulness of the institution; it is that circumstance chiefly which renders it a school of political capacity and general intelligence. But a school supposes teachers as well as scholars; the utility of the instruction greatly depends on its bringing inferior minds into contact with superior, a contact which in the ordinary course of life is altogether exceptional, and the want of which contributes more than anything else to keep the generality of mankind on one level of contented ignorance. The school, moreover, is worthless, and a school of evil instead of good, if through the want of due surveillance, and of the presence within itself of a higher order of characters, the action of the body is allowed, as it so often is, to degenerate into an equally unscrupulous and stupid pursuit of the self-interest of its members. Now it is quite hopeless to induce persons of a high class, either socially or intellectually, to take a share of local administration in a corner by piece-meal, as members of a Paving Board or a Drainage Commission. The entire local business of their town is not more than a sufficient object to induce men whose tastes incline them and whose knowledge qualifies them for national affairs to become members of a mere local body, and devote to it the time and study which are necessary to render their presence anything more than a screen for the jobbing of inferior persons under the shelter of their responsibility. A mere Board of Works, though it comprehend the entire metropolis, is sure to be composed of the same class of persons as the vestries of the London parishes; nor is it practicable, or even desirable, that such should not form the majority; but it is important for every purpose which local bodies are designed to serve, whether it be the enlightened and honest performance of their special duties, or the cultivation of the political intelligence of the nation, that every such body should contain a portion of the very best minds of the locality: who are thus brought into perpetual contact, of the most useful kind, with minds of a lower grade, receiving from them what local or professional knowledge they have to give, and in return inspiring them with a portion of their own more enlarged ideas, and higher and more enlightened purposes.

A mere village has no claim to a municipal representation. By a village I mean a place whose inhabitants are not markedly distinguished by occupation or social relations from those of the rural districts adjoining, and for whose local wants the arrangements made for the surrounding territory will suffice. Such small places have rarely a sufficient public to furnish a tolerable municipal council: if they contain any talent or knowledge applicable to public business, it is apt to be all concentrated in some one man, who thereby becomes the dominator of the place. It is better that such places should be merged in a larger circumscription. The local representation of rural districts will naturally be determined by geographical considerations; with due regard to those sympathies of feeling by which human beings are so much aided to act in concert, and which partly follow historical boundaries, such as those of counties or provinces, and partly community of interest and occupation, as in agricultural, maritime, manufacturing, or mining districts. Different kinds of local business may require different areas of representation. The Unions of parishes have been fixed on as the most appropriate basis for the representative bodies which superintend the relief of indigence; while, for the proper regulation of highways, or prisons, or police, a large extent, like that of an average county, is not more than sufficient. In these large districts, therefore, the maxim, that an elective body constituted in any locality should have authority over all the local concerns common to the locality, requires modification from another principle—as well as from the competing consideration of the importance of obtaining for the discharge of the local duties the highest qualifications possible. For example, if it be necessary (as I believe it to be) for the proper administration of the Poor Laws that the area of rating should not be more extensive than most of the present Unions, a principle which requires a Board of Guardians for each Union—yet, as a much more highly qualified class of persons is likely to be obtainable for a County Board than those who compose an average Board of Guardians, it may on that ground be expedient to reserve for the County Boards some higher descriptions of local business, which might otherwise have been conveniently managed within itself by each separate Union.

Besides the controlling Council, or local sub-Parliament, local business has its executive department. With respect to this, the same questions arise as with respect to the executive authorities in the State; and they may, for the most part, be answered in the same manner. The principles applicable to all public trusts are in substance the same. In the first place,

each executive officer should be single, and singly responsible for the whole of the duty committed to his charge. In the next place, he should be nominated, not elected. It is ridiculous that a surveyor, or a health officer, or even a collector of rates, should be appointed by popular suffrage. The popular choice usually depends on interest with a few local leaders, who, as they are not supposed to make the appointment, are not responsible for it; or on an appeal to sympathy, founded on having twelve children, and having been a rate-payer in the parish for thirty years. If in cases of this description election by the population is a farce, appointment by the local representative body is little less objectionable. Such bodies have a perpetual tendency to become joint-stock associations for carrying into effect the private jobs of their various members. Appointments should be made on the individual responsibility of the Chairman of the body, let him be called Mayor, Chairman of Quarter Sessions, or by whatever other title. He occupies in the locality a position analogous to that of the prime minister in the State, and under a well-organised system the appointment and watching of the local officers would be the most important part of his duty: he himself being appointed by the Council from its own number, subject either to annual re-election, or to removal by a vote of the body.

From the constitution of the local bodies I now pass to the equally important and more difficult subject of their proper attributions. This question divides itself into two parts: what should be their duties, and whether they should have full authority within the sphere of those duties, or should be liable to any, and what, interference on the part of the central government.

It is obvious, to begin with, that all business purely local—all which concerns only a single locality—should devolve upon the local authorities. The paving, lighting, and cleansing of the streets of a town, and in ordinary circumstances the draining of its houses, are of little consequence to any but its inhabitants. The nation at large is interested in them in no other way than that in which it is interested in the private well-being of all its individual citizens. But among the duties classed as local, or performed by local functionaries, there are many which might with equal propriety be termed national, being the share, belonging to the locality, of some branch of the public administration in the efficiency of which the whole nation is alike interested: the gaols, for instance, most of which in this country are under county management; the local police; the local administration of justice, much of which, especially in corporate towns, is performed by officers elected by the locality, and paid from local funds. None of these can be said to be matters of local, as distinguished from national, importance. It would not be a matter personally indifferent to the rest of the country if any part of it became a nest of robbers or a focus of demoralisation, owing to the maladministration of its police; or if, through the bad regulations of its gaol, the punishment which the courts of justice intended to inflict on the criminals confined therein (who might have come from, or committed their offences in, any other district) might be doubled in intensity, or lowered to practical impunity. The points, moreover, which constitute good management of these things are the same everywhere; there is no good reason why police, or gaols, or the administration of justice, should be differently managed in one part of the kingdom and in another; while there is great peril that in things so important, and to which the most instructed minds available to the State are not more than adequate, the lower average of capacities which alone can be counted on for the service of the localities might commit errors of such magnitude as to be a serious blot upon the general administration of the country.

Security of person and property, and equal justice between individuals, are the first needs of society, and the primary ends of government: if these things can be left to any responsibility below the highest, there is nothing, except war and treaties, which requires a general government at all. Whatever are the best arrangements for securing these primary objects should be made universally obligatory, and, to secure their enforcement, should be placed under central superintendence. It is often useful, and with the institutions of our own country even necessary, from the scarcity, in the localities, of officers representing the general government, that the execution of duties imposed by the central authority should be entrusted to functionaries appointed for local purposes by the locality. But experience is daily forcing upon the public a conviction of the necessity of having at least inspectors appointed by the general government to see that the local officers do their duty. If prisons are under local management, the central government appoints inspectors of prisons to take

care that the rules laid down by Parliament are observed, and to suggest others if the state of the gaols shows them to be requisite: as there are inspectors of factories, and inspectors of schools, to watch over the observance of the Acts of Parliament relating to the first, and the fulfilment of the conditions on which State assistance is granted to the latter.

But, if the administration of justice, police and gaols included, is both so universal a concern, and so much a matter of general science independent of local peculiarities, that it may be, and ought to be, uniformly regulated throughout the country, and its regulation enforced by more trained and skilful hands than those of purely local authorities—there is also business, such as the administration of the poor laws, sanitary regulation, and others, which, while really interesting to the whole country, cannot consistently with the very purposes of local administration, be managed otherwise than by the localities. In regard to such duties the question arises, how far the local authorities ought to be trusted with discretionary power, free from any superintendence or control of the State.

To decide this question it is essential to consider what is the comparative position of the central and the local authorities as to capacity for the work, and security against negligence or abuse. In the first place, the local representative bodies and their officers are almost certain to be of a much lower grade of intelligence and knowledge than Parliament and the national executive. Secondly, besides being themselves of inferior qualifications, they are watched by, and accountable to, an inferior public opinion. The public under whose eyes they act, and by whom they are criticised, is both more limited in extent, and generally far less enlightened, than that which surrounds and admonishes the highest authorities at the capital; while the comparative smallness of the interests involved causes even that inferior public to direct its thoughts to the subject less intently, and with less solicitude. Far less interference is exercised by the press and by public discussion, and that which is exercised may with much more impunity be disregarded in the proceedings of local than in those of national authorities.

Thus far the advantage seems wholly on the side of management by the central government. But, when we look more closely, these motives of preference are found to be balanced by others fully as substantial. If the local authorities and public are inferior to the central ones in knowledge of the principles of administration, they have the compensating advantage of a far more direct interest in the result. A man's neighbours or his landlord may be much cleverer than himself, and not without an indirect interest in his prosperity, but for all that his interests will be better attended to in his own keeping than in theirs. It is further to be remembered, that even supposing the central government to administer through its own officers, its officers do not act at the centre, but in the locality: and however inferior the local public may be to the central, it is the local public alone which has any opportunity of watching them, and it is the local opinion alone which either acts directly upon their own conduct, or calls the attention of the government to the points in which they may require correction. It is but in extreme cases that the general opinion of the country is brought to bear at all upon details of local administration, and still more rarely has it the means of deciding upon them with any just appreciation of the case. Now, the local opinion necessarily acts far more forcibly upon purely local administrators. They, in the natural course of things, are permanent residents, not expecting to be withdrawn from the place when they cease to exercise authority in it; and their authority itself depends, by supposition, on the will of the local public. I need not dwell on the deficiencies of the central authority in detailed knowledge of local persons and things, and the too great engrossment of its time and thoughts by other concerns, to admit of its acquiring the quantity and quality of local knowledge necessary even for deciding on complaints, and enforcing responsibility from so great a number of local agents. In the details of management, therefore, the local bodies will generally have the advantage; but in comprehension of the principles even of purely local management, the superiority of the central government, when rightly constituted, ought to be prodigious: not only by reason of the probably great personal superiority of the individuals composing it, and the multitude of thinkers and writers who are at all times engaged in pressing useful ideas upon their notice, but also because the knowledge and experience of any local authority is but local knowledge and experience, confined to their own part of the country and its modes of management, whereas the central government has the means of knowing all that is to be learnt from the united experience of the whole kingdom, with the addition of easy access to that of foreign countries.

The practical conclusion from these premises is not difficult to draw. The authority which is most conversant with principles should be supreme over principles, while that which is most competent in details should have the details left to it. The principal business of the central authority should be to give instruction, of the local authority to apply it. Power may be localised, but knowledge, to be most useful, must be centralised; there must be somewhere a focus at which all its scattered rays are collected, that the broken and coloured lights which exist elsewhere may find there what is necessary to complete and purify them. To every branch of local administration which affects the general interest there should be a corresponding central organ, either a minister, or some specially appointed functionary under him; even if that functionary does no more than collect information from all quarters, and bring the experience acquired in one locality to the knowledge of another where it is wanted. But there is also something more than this for the central authority to do. It ought to keep open a perpetual communication with the localities: informing itself by their experience, and them by its own; giving advice freely when asked, volunteering it when seen to be required; compelling publicity and recordation of proceedings, and enforcing obedience to every general law which the legislature has laid down on the subject of local management.

That some such laws ought to be laid down few are likely to deny. The localities may be allowed to mismanage their own interests, but not to prejudice those of others, nor violate those principles of justice between one person and another of which it is the duty of the State to maintain the rigid observance. If the local majority attempts to oppress the minority, or one class another, the State is bound to interpose. For example, all local rates ought to be voted exclusively by the local representative body; but that body, though elected solely by rate-payers, may raise its revenues by imposts of such a kind, or assess them in such a manner, as to throw an unjust share of the burden on the poor, the rich, or some particular class of the population: it is the duty, therefore, of the legislature, while leaving the mere amount of the local taxes to the discretion of the local body, to lay down authoritatively the modes of taxation, and rules of assessment, which alone the localities shall be permitted to use.

Again, in the administration of public charity the industry and morality of the whole labouring population depend, to a most serious extent, upon adherence to certain fixed principles in awarding relief. Though it belongs essentially to the local functionaries to determine who, according to those principles, is entitled to be relieved, the national Parliament is the proper authority to prescribe the principles themselves; and it would neglect a most important part of its duty if it did not, in a matter of such grave national concern, lay down imperative rules, and make effectual provision that those rules should not be departed from. What power of actual interference with the local administrators it may be necessary to retain, for the due enforcement of the laws, is a question of detail into which it would be useless to enter. The laws themselves will naturally define the penalties, and fix the mode of their enforcement. It may be requisite, to meet extreme cases, that the power of the central authority should extend to dissolving the local representative council, or dismissing the local executive: but not to making new appointments, or suspending the local institutions. Where Parliament has not interfered, neither ought any branch of the executive to interfere with authority; but as an adviser and critic, an enforcer of the laws, and a denouncer to Parliament or the local constituencies of conduct which it deems condemnable, the functions of the executive are of the greatest possible value.

Some may think that however much the central authority surpasses the local in knowledge of the principles of administration, the great object which has been so much insisted on, the social and political education of the citizens, requires that they should be left to manage these matters by their own, however imperfect, lights. To this it might be answered, that the education of the citizens is not the only thing to be considered; government and administration do not exist for that alone, great as its importance is. But the objection shows a very imperfect understanding of the function of popular institutions as a means of political instruction. It is but a poor education that associates ignorance with ignorance, and leaves them, if they care for knowledge, to grope their way to it without help, and to do without it if they do not. What is wanted is, the means of making ignorance aware of itself, and able to profit by knowledge; accustoming minds which know only routine to act upon, and feel the

value of, principles: teaching them to compare different modes of action, and learn, by the use of their reason, to distinguish the best. When we desire to have a good school, we do not eliminate the teacher. The old remark, "as the schoolmaster is, so will be the school," is as true of the indirect schooling of grown people by public business as of the schooling of youth in academies and colleges. A government which attempts to do everything is aptly compared by M. Charles de Rémusat to a schoolmaster who does all the pupils' tasks for them; he may be very popular with the pupils, but he will teach them little. A government, on the other hand, which neither does anything itself that can possibly be done by any one else, nor shows any one else how to do anything, is like a school in which there is no schoolmaster, but only pupil teachers who have never themselves been taught.

Chapter 16
Of Nationality, as connected with Representative Government

A PORTION of mankind may be said to constitute a Nationality if they are united among themselves by common sympathies which do not exist between them and any others—which make them co-operate with each other more willingly than with other people, desire to be under the same government, and desire that it should be government by themselves or a portion of themselves exclusively. This feeling of nationality may have been generated by various causes. Sometimes it is the effect of identity of race and descent. Community of language, and community of religion, greatly contribute to it. Geographical limits are one of its causes. But the strongest of all is identity of political antecedents; the possession of a national history, and consequent community of recollections; collective pride and humiliation, pleasure and regret, connected with the same incidents in the past. None of these circumstances, however, are either indispensable, or necessarily sufficient by themselves. Switzerland has a strong sentiment of nationality, though the cantons are of different races, different languages, and different religions. Sicily has, throughout history, felt itself quite distinct in nationality from Naples, notwithstanding identity of religion, almost identity of language, and a considerable amount of common historical antecedents. The Flemish and the Walloon provinces of Belgium, notwithstanding diversity of race and language, have a much greater feeling of common nationality than the former have with Holland, or the latter with France. Yet in general the national feeling is proportionally weakened by the failure of any of the causes which contribute to it. Identity of language, literature, and, to some extent, of race and recollections, have maintained the feeling of nationality in considerable strength among the different portions of the German name, though they have at no time been really united under the same government; but the feeling has never reached to making the separate states desire to get rid of their autonomy. Among Italians an identity far from complete, of language and literature, combined with a geographical position which separates them by a distinct line from other countries, and, perhaps more than everything else, the possession of a common name, which makes them all glory in the past achievements in arts, arms, politics, religious primacy, science, and literature, of any who share the same designation, give rise to an amount of national feeling in the population which, though still imperfect, has been sufficient to produce the great events now passing before us, notwithstanding a great mixture of races, and although they have never, in either ancient or modern history, been under the same government, except while that government extended or was extending itself over the greater part of the known world.

Where the sentiment of nationality exists in any force, there is a *prima facie* case for uniting all the members of the nationality under the same government, and a government to themselves apart. This is merely saying that the question of government ought to be decided by the governed. One hardly knows what any division of the human race should be free to do if not to determine with which of the various collective bodies of human beings they choose to associate themselves.

But, when a people are ripe for free institutions, there is a still more vital consideration. Free institutions are next to impossible in a country made up of different nationalities. Among a people without fellow-feeling, especially if they read and speak different languages, the united public opinion, necessary to the working of representative government, cannot exist. The influences which form opinions and decide political acts are different in the different sections of the country. An altogether different set of leaders have the confidence of one part of the country and of another. The same books, newspapers, pamphlets, speeches, do not reach them. One section does not know what opinions, or what instigations, are circulating in another. The same incidents, the same acts, the same system of government, affect them in different ways; and each fears more injury to itself from the other nationalities than from the common arbiter, the state. Their mutual antipathies are generally much stronger than jealousy of the government. That any one of them feels aggrieved by the policy of the common ruler is sufficient to determine another to support that policy. Even if all are aggrieved, none feel that they can rely on the others for fidelity in a joint resistance; the strength of none is sufficient to resist alone, and each may reasonably think that it consults its own advantage most by bidding for the favour of the government against the rest. Above all, the grand and only effectual security in the last resort against the despotism of the government is in that case wanting: the sympathy of the army with the people. The military are the part of every community in whom, from the nature of the case, the distinction between their fellow-countrymen and foreigners is the deepest and strongest. To the rest of the people foreigners are merely strangers; to the soldier, they are men against whom he may be called, at a week's notice, to fight for life or death. The difference to him is that between friends and foes—we may almost say between fellow-men and another kind of animals: for as respects the enemy, the only law is that of force, and the only mitigation the same as in the case of other animals—that of simple humanity. Soldiers to whose feelings half or three-fourths of the subjects of the same government are foreigners will have no more scruple in mowing them down, and no more desire to ask the reason why, than they would have in doing the same thing against declared enemies. An army composed of various nationalities has no other patriotism than devotion to the flag. Such armies have been the executioners of liberty through the whole duration of modern history. The sole bond which holds them together is their officers and the government which they serve; and their only idea, if they have any, of public duty is obedience to orders. A government thus supported, by keeping its Hungarian regiments in Italy and its Italian in Hungary, can long continue to rule in both places with the iron rod of foreign conquerors.

If it be said that so broadly marked a distinction between what is due to a fellow-countryman and what is due merely to a human creature is more worthy of savages than of civilised beings, and ought, with the utmost energy, to be contended against, no one holds that opinion more strongly than myself. But this object, one of the worthiest to which human endeavour can be directed, can never, in the present state of civilisation, be promoted by keeping different nationalities of anything like equivalent strength under the same government. In a barbarous state of society the case is sometimes different. The government may then be interested in softening the antipathies of the races that peace may be preserved and the country more easily governed. But when there are either free institutions or a desire for them, in any of the peoples artificially tied together, the interest of the government lies in an exactly opposite direction. It is then interested in keeping up and envenoming their antipathies that they may be prevented from coalescing, and it may be enabled to use some of them as tools for the enslavement of others. The Austrian Court has now for a whole generation made these tactics its principal means of government; with what fatal success, at the time of the Vienna insurrection and the Hungarian contest, the world knows too well. Happily there are now signs that improvement is too far advanced to permit this policy to be any longer successful.

For the preceding reasons, it is in general a necessary condition of free institutions that the boundaries of governments should coincide in the main with those of nationalities. But several considerations are liable to conflict in practice with this general principle. In the first place, its application is often precluded by geographical hindrances. There are parts even of Europe in which different nationalities are so locally intermingled that it is not practicable for them to be under separate governments. The population of Hungary is composed of Magyars, Slovaks, Croats, Serbs, Roumans, and in some districts Germans, so mixed up as to be incapable of local separation; and there is no course open to them but to make a virtue of necessity, and reconcile themselves to living together under equal rights and laws. Their community of servitude, which dates only from the destruction of Hungarian independence in 1849, seems to be ripening and disposing them for such an equal union. The German colony of East Prussia is cut off from Germany by part of the ancient Poland, and being too weak to maintain separate independence, must, if geographical continuity is to be maintained, be either under a non-German government, or the intervening Polish territory must be under a German one. Another considerable region in which the dominant element of the population is German, the provinces of Courland, Esthonia, and Livonia, is condemned by its local situation to form part of a Slavonian state. In Eastern Germany itself there is a large Slavonic population: Bohemia is principally Slavonic, Silesia and other districts partially so. The most united country in Europe, France, is far from being homogeneous: independently of the fragments of foreign nationalities at its remote extremities, it consists, as language and history prove, of two portions, one occupied almost exclusively by a Gallo-Roman population, while in the other the Frankish, Burgundian, and other Teutonic races form a considerable ingredient.

When proper allowance has been made for geographical exigencies, another more purely moral and social consideration offers itself. Experience proves that it is possible for one nationality to merge and be absorbed in another: and when it was originally an inferior and more backward portion of the human race the absorption is greatly to its advantage. Nobody can suppose that it is not more beneficial to a Breton, or a Basque of French Navarre, to be brought into the current of the ideas and feelings of a highly civilised and cultivated people—to be a member of the French nationality, admitted on equal terms to all the privileges of French citizenship, sharing the advantages of French protection, and the dignity and prestige of French power—than to sulk on his own rocks, the half-savage relic of past times, revolving in his own little mental orbit, without participation or interest in the general movement of the world. The same remark applies to the Welshman or the Scottish Highlander as members of the British nation.

Whatever really tends to the admixture of nationalities, and the blending of their attributes and peculiarities in a common union, is a benefit to the human race. Not by extinguishing types, of which, in these cases, sufficient examples are sure to remain, but by softening their extreme forms, and filling up the intervals between them. The united people, like a crossed breed of animals (but in a still greater degree, because the influences in operation are moral as well as physical), inherits the special aptitudes and excellences of all its progenitors, protected by the admixture from being exaggerated into the neighbouring vices. But to render this admixture possible, there must be peculiar conditions. The combinations of circumstances which occur, and which effect the result, are various.

The nationalities brought together under the same government may be about equal in numbers and strength, or they may be very unequal. If unequal, the least numerous of the two may either be the superior in civilisation, or the inferior. Supposing it to be superior, it may either, through that superiority, be able to acquire ascendancy over the other, or it may be overcome by brute strength and reduced to subjection. This last is a sheer mischief to the human race, and one which civilised humanity with one accord should rise in arms to prevent. The absorption of Greece by Macedonia was one of the greatest misfortunes which ever happened to the world: that of any of the principal countries of Europe by Russia would be a similar one.

If the smaller nationality, supposed to be the more advanced in improvement, is able to overcome the greater, as the Macedonians, reinforced by the Greeks, did Asia, and the English India, there is often a gain to civilisation: but the conquerors and the conquered cannot in this case live together under the same free institutions. The absorption of the conquerors in the less advanced people would be an evil: these must be governed as subjects, and the state of things is either a benefit or a misfortune, according as the subjugated people have or have not reached the state in which it is an injury not to be under a free government, and according as the conquerors do or do not use their superiority in a manner calculated to fit the conquered for a higher stage of improvement. This topic will be particularly treated of in a subsequent chapter.

When the nationality which succeeds in overpowering the other is both the most numerous and the most improved; and especially if the subdued nationality is small, and has no hope of reasserting its independence; then, if it is governed with any tolerable justice, and if the members of the more powerful nationality are not made odious by being invested with exclusive privileges, the smaller nationality is gradually reconciled to its position, and becomes amalgamated with the larger. No Bas-Breton, nor even any Alsatian, has the smallest wish at the present day to be separated from France. If all Irishmen have not yet arrived at the same disposition towards England, it is partly because they are sufficiently numerous to be capable of constituting a respectable nationality by themselves; but principally because, until of late years, they had been so atrociously governed, that all their best feelings combined with their bad ones in rousing bitter resentment against the Saxon rule. This disgrace to England, and calamity to the whole empire, has, it may be truly said, completely ceased for nearly a generation. No Irishman is now less free than an Anglo-Saxon, nor has a less share of every benefit either to his country or to his individual fortunes than if he were sprung from any other portion of the British dominions. The only remaining real grievance of Ireland, that of the State Church, is one which half, or nearly half, the people of the larger island have in common with them. There is now next to nothing, except the memory of the past, and the difference in the predominant religion, to keep apart two races, perhaps the most fitted of any two in the world to be the completing counterpart of one another. The consciousness of being at last treated not only with equal justice but with equal consideration is making such rapid way in the Irish nation as to be wearing off all feelings that could make them insensible to the benefits which the less numerous and less wealthy people must necessarily derive from being fellow-citizens instead of foreigners to those who are not only their nearest neighbours, but the wealthiest, and one of the freest, as well as most civilised and powerful, nations of the earth.

The cases in which the greatest practical obstacles exist to the blending of nationalities are when the nationalities which have been bound together are nearly equal in numbers and in the other elements of power. In such cases, each, confiding in its strength, and feeling itself capable of maintaining an equal struggle with any of the others, is unwilling to be merged in it: each cultivates with party obstinacy its distinctive peculiarities; obsolete customs, and even declining languages, are revived to deepen the separation; each deems itself tyrannised over if any authority is exercised within itself by functionaries of a rival race; and whatever is given to one of the conflicting nationalities is considered to be taken from all the rest. When nations, thus divided, are under a despotic government which is a stranger to all of them, or which, though sprung from one, yet feeling greater interest in its own power than in any sympathies of nationality, assigns no privilege to either nation, and chooses its instruments indifferently from all; in the course of a few generations, identity of situation often produces harmony of feeling, and the different races come to feel towards each other as fellow-countrymen; particularly if they are dispersed over the same tract of country. But if the era of aspiration to free government arrives before this fusion has been effected, the opportunity has gone by for effecting it. From that time, if the unreconciled nationalities are geographically separate, and especially if their local position is such that there is no natural fitness or convenience in their being under the same government (as in the case of an Italian province under a French or German yoke), there is not only an obvious propriety, but, if either freedom or concord is cared for, a necessity, for breaking the connection altogether. There may be cases in which the provinces, after separation, might usefully remain united by a federal tie: but it generally happens that if they are willing to forego complete independence, and become members of a federation, each of them has other neighbours with whom it would prefer to connect itself, having more sympathies in common, if not also greater community of interest.

Chapter 17
Of Federal Representative Governments

PORTIONS OF mankind who are not fitted, or not disposed, to live under the same internal government, may often with advantage be federally united as to their relations with foreigners: both to prevent wars among themselves, and for the sake of more effectual protection against the aggression of powerful States.

To render a federation advisable, several conditions are necessary. The first is, that there should be a sufficient amount of mutual sympathy among the populations. The federation binds them always to fight on the same side; and if they have such feelings towards one another, or such diversity of feeling towards their neighbours, that they would generally prefer to fight on opposite sides, the federal tie is neither likely to be of long duration, not to be well observed while it subsists. The sympathies available for the purpose are those of race, language, religion, and, above all, of political institutions, as conducing most to a feeling of

identity of political interest. When a few free states, separately insufficient for their own defence, are hemmed in on all sides by military or feudal monarchs, who hate and despise freedom even in a neighbour, those states have no chance for preserving liberty and its blessings but by a federal union. The common interest arising from this cause has in Switzerland, for several centuries, been found adequate to maintain efficiently the federal bond, in spite not only of difference of religion when religion was the grand source of irreconcilable political enmity throughout Europe, but also in spite of great weakness in the constitution of the federation itself. In America, where all the conditions for the maintenance of union existed at the highest point, with the sole drawback of difference of institutions in the single but most important article of Slavery, this one difference has gone so far in alienating from each other's sympathies the two divisions of the Union, that the maintenance or disruption of a tie of so much value to them both depends on the issue of an obstinate civil war.

A second condition of the stability of a federal government is that the separate states be not so powerful as to be able to rely, for protection against foreign encroachment, on their individual strength. If they are, they will be apt to think that they do not gain, by union with others, the equivalent of what they sacrifice in their own liberty of action; and consequently, whenever the policy of the Confederation, in things reserved to its cognisance, is different from that which any one of its members would separately pursue, the internal and sectional breach will, through absence of sufficient anxiety to preserve the union, be in danger of going so far as to dissolve it.

A third condition, not less important than the two others, is that there be not a very marked inequality of strength among the several contracting states. They cannot, indeed, be exactly equal in resources: in all federations there will be a gradation of power among the members; some will be more populous, rich, and civilised than others. There is a wide difference in wealth and population between New York and Rhode Island; between Bern and Zug or Glaris. The essential is, that there should not be any one State so much more powerful than the rest as to be capable of vying in strength with many of them combined. If there be such a one, and only one, it will insist on being master of the joint deliberations: if there be two, they will be irresistible when they agree; and whenever they differ everything will be decided by a struggle for ascendancy between the rivals. This cause is alone enough to reduce the German Bund to almost a nullity, independently of its wretched internal constitution. It effects none of the real purposes of a confederation. It has never bestowed on Germany a uniform system of customs, nor so much as a uniform coinage; and has served only to give Austria and Prussia a legal right of pouring in their troops to assist the local sovereigns in keeping their subjects obedient to despotism: while in regard to external concerns, the Bund would make all Germany a dependency of Prussia if there were no Austria, and of Austria if there were no Prussia: and in the meantime each petty prince has little choice but to be a partisan of one or the other, or to intrigue with foreign governments against both.

There are two different modes of organising a Federal Union. The federal authorities may represent the Governments solely, and their acts may be obligatory only on the Governments as such; or they may have the power of enacting laws and issuing orders which are binding directly on individual citizens. The former is the plan of the German so-called Confederation, and of the Swiss Constitution previous to 1847. It was tried in America for a few years immediately following the War of Independence. The other principle is that of the existing Constitution of the United States, and has been adopted within the last dozen years by the Swiss Confederacy. The Federal Congress of the American Union is a substantive part of the government of every individual State. Within the limits of its attributions, it makes laws which are obeyed by every citizen individually, executes them through its own officers, and enforces them by its own tribunals. This is the only principle which has been found, or which is ever likely, to produce an effective federal government. A union between the governments only is a mere alliance, and subject to all the contingencies which render alliances precarious. If the acts of the President and of Congress were binding solely on the Governments of New York, Virginia, or Pennsylvania, and could only be carried into effect through orders issued by those Governments to officers appointed by them, under responsibility to their own courts of justice, no mandates of the Federal Government which were disagreeable to a local majority would ever be executed. Requisitions issued to a gov-

ernment have no other sanction, or means of enforcement, than war: and a federal army would have to be always in readiness to enforce the decrees of the Federation against any recalcitrant State; subject to the probability that other States, sympathising with the recusant, and perhaps sharing its sentiments on the particular point in dispute, would withhold their contingents, if not send them to fight in the ranks of the disobedient State.

Such a federation is more likely to be a cause than a preventive of internal wars: and if such was not its effect in Switzerland until the events of the years immediately preceding 1847, it was only because the Federal Government felt its weakness so strongly that it hardly ever attempted to exercise any real authority. In America, the experiment of a Federation on this principle broke down in the first few years of its existence; happily while the men of enlarged knowledge and acquired ascendancy, who founded the independence of the Republic, were still alive to guide it through the difficult transition. The *Federalist,* a collection of papers by three of these eminent men, written in explanation and defence of the new Federal Constitution while still awaiting the national acceptance, is even now the most instructive treatise we possess on federal government.[1]

In Germany, the more imperfect kind of federation, as all know, has not even answered the purpose of maintaining an alliance. It has never, in any European war, prevented single members of the Confederation from allying themselves with foreign powers against the rest. Yet this is the only federation which seems possible among monarchical states. A king, who holds his power by inheritance, not by delegation, and who cannot be deprived of it, nor made responsible to any one for its use, is not likely to renounce having a separate army, or to brook the exercise of sovereign authority over his own subjects, not through him but directly, by another power. To enable two or more countries under kingly government to be joined together in an effectual confederation it seems necessary that they should all be under the same king. England and Scotland were a federation of this description during the interval of about a century between the

---

[1] Mr. Freeman's *History of Federal Governments,* of which only the first volume has yet appeared, is already an accession to the literature of the subject, equally valuable by its enlightened principles and its mastery of historical details.

union of the Crowns and that of the Parliaments. Even this was effective, not through federal institutions, for none existed, but because the regal power in both Constitutions was during the greater part of that time so nearly absolute as to enable the foreign policy of both to be shaped according to a single will.

Under the more perfect mode of federation, where every citizen of each particular State owes obedience to two Governments, that of his own state and that of the federation, it is evidently necessary not only that the constitutional limits of the authority of each should be precisely and clearly defined, but that the power to decide between them in any case of dispute should not reside in either of the Governments, or in any functionary subject to it, but in an umpire independent of both. There must be a Supreme Court of Justice, and a system of subordinate Courts in every State of the Union, before whom such questions shall be carried, and whose judgment on them, in the last stage of appeal, shall be final. Every State of the Union, and the Federal Government itself, as well as every functionary of each, must be liable to be sued in those Courts for exceeding their powers, or for non-performance of their federal duties, and must in general be obliged to employ those Courts as the instrument for enforcing their federal rights. This involves the remarkable consequence, actually realised in the United States, that a Court of Justice, the highest federal tribunal, is supreme over the various Governments, both State and Federal; having the right to declare that any law made, or act done by them, exceeds the powers assigned to them by the Federal Constitution, and, in consequence, has no legal validity. It was natural to feel strong doubts, before trial had been made, how such a provision would work; whether the tribunal would have the courage to exercise its constitutional power; if it did, whether it would exercise it wisely and whether the Governments would consent to submit peaceably to its decision. The discussions on the American Constitution, before its final adoption, give evidence that these natural apprehensions were strongly felt; but they are now entirely quieted, since, during the two generations and more which have subsequently elapsed, nothing has occurred to verify them, though there have at times been disputes of considerable acrimony, and which became the badges of parties, respecting the limits of the authority of the Federal and State Governments.

The eminently beneficial working of so singular a provision is probably, as M. de Tocqueville remarks, in a great measure attributable to the peculiarity inherent in a Court of Justice acting as such—namely, that it does not declare the law *eo nomine* and in the abstract, but waits until a case between man and man is brought before it judicially involving the point in dispute: from which arises the happy effect that its declarations are not made in a very early stage of the controversy; that much popular discussion usually precedes them; that the Court decides after hearing the point fully argued on both sides by lawyers of reputation; decides only as much of the question at a time as is required by the case before it, and its decision, instead of being volunteered for political purposes, is drawn from it by the duty which it cannot refuse to fulfil, of dispensing justice impartially between adverse litigants. Even these grounds of confidence would not have sufficed to produce the respectful submission with which all authorities have yielded to the decisions of the Supreme Court on the interpretation of the Constitution, were it not that complete reliance has been felt, not only on the intellectual pre-eminence of the judges composing that exalted tribunal, but on their entire superiority over either private or sectional partialities. This reliance has been in the main justified; but there is nothing which more vitally imports the American people than to guard with the most watchful solicitude against everything which has the remotest tendency to produce deterioration in the quality of this great national institution. The confidence on which depends the stability of federal institutions was for the first time impaired by the judgment declaring slavery to be of common right, and consequently lawful in the Territories while not yet constituted as States, even against the will of a majority of their inhabitants. This memorable decision has probably done more than anything else to bring the sectional division to the crisis which has issued in civil war. The main pillar of the American Constitution is scarcely strong enough to bear many more such shocks.

The tribunals which act as umpires between the Federal and the State Governments naturally also decide all disputes between two States, or between a citizen of one State and the government of another. The usual remedies between nations, war and diplomacy, being precluded by the federal union, it is necessary that a judicial remedy should supply their place. The Supreme Court of the Federation dispenses international law, and is the first great example of what is now one of the most prominent wants of civilised society, a real International Tribunal.

The powers of a Federal Government naturally extend not only to peace and war, and all questions which arise between the country and foreign governments, but to making any other arrangements which are, in the opinion of the States, necessary to their enjoyment of the full benefits of union. For example, it is a great advantage to them that their mutual commerce should be free, without the impediment of frontier duties and custom-houses. But this internal freedom cannot exist if each State has the power of fixing the duties on interchange of commodities between itself and foreign countries; since every foreign product let in by one State would be let into all the rest. And hence all custom duties and trade regulations, in the United States, are made or repealed by the Federal Government exclusively. Again, it is a great convenience to the States to have but one coinage, and but one system of weights and measures; which can only be ensured if the regulation of these matters is entrusted to the Federal Government. The certainty and celerity of Post Office communication is impeded, and its expense increased, if a letter has to pass through half a dozen sets of public offices, subject to different supreme authorities: it is convenient, therefore, that all Post Offices should be under the Federal Government. But on such questions the feelings of different communities are liable to be different. One of the American States, under the guidance of a man who has displayed powers as a speculative political thinker superior to any who has appeared in American politics since the authors of the *Federalist*,[1] claimed a veto for each State on the custom laws of the Federal Congress: and that statesman, in a posthumous work of great ability, which has been printed and widely circulated by the legislature of South Carolina, vindicated this pretension on the general principle of limiting the tyranny of the majority, and protecting minorities by admitting them to a substantial participation in political power. One of the most disputed topics in American politics, during the early part of this century, was whether the power of the Federal Government ought to extend, and whether by the Constitution it did extend, to making roads

[1] Mr. Calhoun.

and canals at the cost of the Union. It is only in transactions with foreign powers that the authority of the Federal Government is of necessity complete. On every other subject, the question depends on how closely the people in general wish to draw the federal tie; what portion of their local freedom of action they are willing to surrender, in order to enjoy more fully the benefit of being one nation.

Respecting the fitting constitution of a federal government within itself much need not be said. It of course consists of a legislative branch and an executive, and the constitution of each is amenable to the same principles as that of representative governments generally. As regards the mode of adapting these general principles to a federal government, the provision of the American Constitution seems exceedingly judicious, that Congress should consist of two Houses, and that while one of them is constituted according to population, each State being entitled to representatives in the ratio of the number of its inhabitants, the other should represent not the citizens, but the State Governments, and every State, whether large or small, should be represented in it by the same number of members. This provision precludes any undue power from being exercised by the more powerful States over the rest, and guarantees the reserved rights of the State Governments, by making it impossible, as far as the mode of representation can prevent, that any measure should pass Congress unless approved not only by a majority of the citizens, but by a majority of the States. I have before adverted to the further incidental advantage obtained of raising the standard of qualifications in one of the Houses. Being nominated by select bodies, the Legislatures of the various States, whose choice, for reasons already indicated, is more likely to fall on eminent men than any popular election—who have not only the power of electing such, but a strong motive to do so, because the influence of their State in the general deliberations must be materially affected by the personal weight and abilities of its representatives; the Senate of the United States, thus chosen, has always contained nearly all the political men of established and high reputation in the Union: while the Lower House of Congress has, in the opinion of competent observers, been generally as remarkable for the absence of conspicuous personal merit as the Upper House for its presence.

When the conditions exist for the formation of efficient and durable Federal Unions, the multiplication of them is always a benefit to the world. It has the same salutary effect as any other extension of the practice of co-operation, through which the weak, by uniting, can meet on equal terms with the strong. By diminishing the number of those petty states which are not equal to their own defence, it weakens the temptations to an aggressive policy, whether working directly by arms, or through the prestige of superior power. It of course puts an end to war and diplomatic quarrels, and usually also to restrictions on commerce, between the States composing the Union; while, in reference to neighbouring nations, the increased military strength conferred by it is of a kind to be almost exclusively available for defensive, scarcely at all for aggressive, purposes. A federal government has not a sufficiently concentrated authority to conduct with much efficiency any war but one of self-defence, in which it can rely on the voluntary co-operation of every citizen: nor is there anything very flattering to national vanity or ambition in acquiring, by a successful war, not subjects, nor even fellow-citizens, but only new, and perhaps troublesome, independent members of the confederation. The warlike proceedings of the Americans in Mexico were purely exceptional, having been carried on principally by volunteers, under the influence of the migratory propensity which prompts individual Americans to possess themselves of unoccupied land; and stimulated, if by any public motive, not by that of national aggrandisement, but by the purely sectional purpose of extending slavery. There are few signs in the proceedings of Americans, nationally or individually, that the desire of territorial acquisition for their country as such has any considerable power over them. Their hankering after Cuba is, in the same manner, merely sectional, and the northern States, those opposed to slavery, have never in any way favoured it.

The question may present itself (as in Italy at its present uprising) whether a country, which is determined to be united, should form a complete or a merely federal union. The point is sometimes necessarily decided by the mere territorial magnitude of the united whole. There is a limit to the extent of country which can advantageously be governed, or even whose government can be conveniently superintended, from a single centre. There are vast countries so governed; but they, or at least their distant provinces, are in general deplorably ill administered, and it is only when the inhabi-

tants are almost savages that they could not manage their affairs better separately. This obstacle does not exist in the case of Italy, the size of which does not come up to that of several very efficiently governed single states in past and present times. The question then is, whether the different parts of the nation require to be governed in a way so essentially different that it is not probable the same Legislature, and the same ministry or administrative body, will give satisfaction to them all. Unless this be the case, which is a question of fact, it is better for them to be completely united. That a totally different system of laws, and very different administrative institutions, may exist in two portions of a country without being any obstacle to legislative unity is proved by the case of England and Scotland. Perhaps, however, this undisturbed co-existence of two legal systems, under one united legislature, making different laws for the two sections of the country in adaptation to the previous differences, might not be so well preserved, or the same confidence might not be felt in its preservation, in a country whose legislators were more possessed (as is apt to be the case on the Continent) with the mania for uniformity. A people having that unbounded toleration which is characteristic of this country for every description of anomaly, so long as those whose interests it concerns do not feel aggrieved by it, afforded an exceptionally advantageous field for trying this difficult experiment. In most countries, if it was an object to retain different systems of law, it might probably be necessary to retain distinct legislatures as guardians of them; which is perfectly compatible with a national Parliament and King, or a national Parliament without a King, supreme over the external relations of all the members of the body.

Whenever it is not deemed necessary to maintain permanently, in the different provinces, different systems of jurisprudence, and fundamental institutions grounded on different principles, it is always practicable to reconcile minor diversities with the maintenance of unity of government. All that is needful is to give a sufficiently large sphere of action to the local authorities. Under one and the same central government there may be local governors, and provincial assemblies for local purposes. It may happen, for instance, that the people of different provinces may have preferences in favour of different modes of taxation. If the general legislature could not be depended on for being guided by the members for each province in modifying the general system of taxation to suit that province, the Constitution might provide that as many of the expenses of the government as could by any possibility be made local should be defrayed by local rates imposed by the provincial assemblies, and that those which must of necessity be general, such as the support of an army and navy, should, in the estimates for the year, be apportioned among the different provinces according to some general estimate of their resources, the amount assigned to each being levied by the local assembly on the principles most acceptable to the locality, and paid *en bloc* into the national treasury. A practice approaching to this existed even in the old French monarchy, so far as regarded the *pays d'états;* each of which, having consented or been required to furnish a fixed sum, was left to assess it upon the inhabitants by its own officers, thus escaping the grinding despotism of the royal *intendants* and *subdélégués;* and this privilege is always mentioned as one of the advantages which mainly contributed to render them, as some of them were, the most flourishing provinces of France.

Identity of central government is compatible with many different degrees of centralisation, not only administrative, but even legislative. A people may have the desire, and the capacity, for a closer union than one merely federal, while yet their local peculiarities and antecedents render considerable diversities desirable in the details of their government. But if there is a real desire on all hands to make the experiment successful, there needs seldom be any difficulty in not only preserving these diversities, but giving them the guarantee of a constitutional provision against any attempt at assimilation, except by the voluntary act of those who would be affected by the change.

Chapter 18
Of the Government of Dependencies by a Free State

FREE STATES, like all others, may possess dependencies, acquired either by conquest or by colonisation; and our own is the greatest instance of the kind in modern history. It is a most important question how such dependencies ought to be governed.

It is unnecessary to discuss the case of small posts, like Gibraltar, Aden, or Heligoland, which are held only as naval or military positions. The military or naval object is in this case paramount, and the inhabitants cannot, consistently with it, be admitted to the government of the place; though they ought to be allowed all liberties and privileges compatible with that restriction, including the free management of municipal affairs; and as a compensation for being locally sacrificed to the convenience of the governing State, should be admitted to equal rights with its native subjects in all other parts of the empire.

Outlying territories of some size and population, which are held as dependencies, that is, which are subject, more or less, to acts of sovereign power on the part of the paramount country, without being equally represented (if represented at all) in its legislature, may be divided into two classes. Some are composed of people of similar civilisation to the ruling country, capable of, and ripe for, representative government: such as the British possessions in America and Australia. Others, like India, are still at a great distance from that state.

In the case of dependencies of the former class, this country has at length realised, in rare completeness, the true principle of government. England has always felt under a certain degree of obligation to bestow on such of her outlying populations as were of her own blood and language, and on some who were not, representative institutions formed in imitation of her own: but until the present generation, she has been on the same bad level with other countries as to the amount of self-government which she allowed them to exercise through the representative institutions that she conceded to them. She claimed to be the supreme arbiter even of their purely internal concerns, according to her own, not their, ideas of how those concerns could be best regulated. This practice was a natural corollary from the vicious theory of colonial policy—once common to all Europe, and not yet completely relinquished by any other people —which regarded colonies as valuable by affording markets for our commodities, that could be kept entirely to ourselves: a privilege we valued so highly that we thought it worth purchasing by allowing to the colonies the same monopoly of our market for their own productions which we claimed for our commodities in theirs. This notable plan for enriching them and ourselves, by making each pay enormous sums to the other, dropping the greatest part by the way, has been for some time abandoned. But the bad habit of meddling in the internal government of the colonies did not at once terminate when we relinquished the idea of making any profit by it. We continued to torment them, not for any benefit to ourselves, but for that of a section or faction among the colonists: and this persistence in domineering cost us a Canadian rebellion before we had the happy thought of giving it up. England was like an ill-brought-up elder brother, who persists in tyrannising over the younger ones from mere habit, till one of them, by a spirited resistance, though with unequal strength, gives him notice to desist. We were wise enough not to require a second warning. A new era in the colonial policy of nations began with Lord Durham's Report; the imperishable memorial of that nobleman's courage, patriotism, and enlightened liberality, and of the intellect and practical sagacity of its joint authors, Mr. Wakefield and the lamented Charles Buller.[1]

It is now a fixed principle of the policy of Great Britain, professed in theory and faithfully adhered to in practice, that her colonies of European race, equally with the parent country, possess the fullest measure of internal self-government. They have been allowed to make their own free representative constitutions by altering in any manner they thought fit the already very popular constitutions which we had given them. Each is governed by its own legislature and executive, constituted on highly democratic principles. The veto of the Crown and of Parliament, though nominally reserved, is only exercised (and that very rarely) on questions which concern the empire, and not solely the particular colony. How liberal a construction has been given to the distinction between imperial and colonial questions is shown by the fact that the whole of the unappropriated lands in the regions behind our American and Australian colonies have been given up to the uncontrolled disposal of the colonial communities; though they might, without injustice, have been kept in the hands of the Imperial Government, to be administered for the greatest advantage of future emigrants from all parts of the empire. Every colony has thus as full power over its own affairs as it could have if it were a member of even the loosest federation; and much fuller than would belong to it under the Constitution of the United

States, being free even to tax at its pleasure the commodities imported from the mother country. Their union with Great Britain is the slightest kind of federal union; but not a strictly equal federation, the mother country retaining to itself the powers of a Federal Government, though reduced in practice to their very narrowest limits. This inequality is, of course, as far as it goes, a disadvantage to the dependencies, which have no voice in foreign policy, but are bound by the decisions of the superior country. They are compelled to join England in war, without being in any way consulted previous to engaging in it.

Those (now happily not a few) who think that justice is as binding on communities as it is on individuals, and that men are not warranted in doing to other countries, for the supposed benefit of their own country, what they would not be justified in doing to other men for their own benefit—feel even this limited amount of constitutional subordination on the part of the colonies to be a violation of principle, and have often occupied themselves in looking out for means by which it may be avoided. With this view it has been proposed by some that the colonies should return representatives to the British legislature; and by others, that the powers of our own, as well as of their Parliaments, should be confined to internal policy, and that there should be another representative body for foreign and imperial concerns, in which last the dependencies of Great Britain should be represented in the same manner, and with the same completeness, as Great Britain itself. On this system there would be a perfectly equal federation between the mother country and her colonies, then no longer dependencies.

The feelings of equity, and conceptions of public morality, from which these suggestions emanate, are worthy of all praise; but the suggestions themselves are so inconsistent with rational principles of government that it is doubtful if they have been seriously accepted as a possibility by any reasonable thinker. Countries separated by half the globe do not present the natural conditions for being under one government, or even members of one federation. If they had sufficiently the same interests, they have not, and never can have, a sufficient habit of taking counsel together. They are not part of the same public; they do not discuss and deliberate in the same arena, but apart, and have only a most imperfect knowledge of what passes in the minds of one an-

---

[1] I am speaking here of the *adoption* of this improved policy, not, of course, of its original suggestion. The honour of having been its earliest champion belongs unquestionably to Mr. Roebuck.

other. They neither know each other's objects, nor have confidence in each other's principles of conduct. Let any Englishman ask himself how he should like his destinies to depend on an assembly of which one-third was British American, and another third South African and Australian. Yet to this it must come if there were anything like fair or equal representation; and would not every one feel that the representatives of Canada and Australia, even in matters of an imperial character, could not know, or feel any sufficient concern for, the interests, opinions, or wishes of English, Irish, and Scotch? Even for strictly federative purposes the conditions do not exist which we have seen to be essential to a federation. England is sufficient for her own protection without the colonies; and would be in a much stronger, as well as more dignified position, if separated from them, than when reduced to be a single member of an American, African, and Australian confederation. Over and above the commerce which she might equally enjoy after separation, England derives little advantage, except in prestige, from her dependencies; and the little she does derive is quite outweighed by the expense they cost her, and the dissemination they necessitate of her naval and military force, which in case of war, or any real apprehension of it, requires to be double or treble what would be needed for the defence of this country alone.

But though Great Britain could do perfectly well without her colonies, and though on every principle of morality and justice she ought to consent to their separation, should the time come when, after full trial of the best form of union, they deliberately desire to be dissevered—there are strong reasons for maintaining the present slight bond of connection, so long as not disagreeable to the feelings of either party. It is a step, as far as it goes, towards universal peace, and general friendly co-operation among nations. It renders war impossible among a large number of otherwise independent communities; and moreover hinders any of them from being absorbed into a foreign state, and becoming a source of additional aggressive strength to some rival power, either more despotic or closer at hand, which might not always be so unambitious or so pacific as Great Britain. It at least keeps the markets of the different countries open to one another, and prevents that mutual exclusion by hostile tariffs, which none of the great communities of mankind, except England, have yet completely

outgrown. And in the case of the British possessions it has the advantage, especially valuable at the present time, of adding to the moral influence, and weight in the councils of the world, of the Power which, of all in existence, best understands liberty—and whatever may have been its errors in the past, has attained to more of conscience and moral principle in its dealings with foreigners than any other great nation seems either to conceive as possible or recognise as desirable. Since, then, the union can only continue, while it does continue, on the footing of an unequal federation, it is important to consider by what means this small amount of inequality can be prevented from being either onerous or humiliating to the communities occupying the less exalted position.

The only inferiority necessarily inherent in the case is that the mother country decides, both for the colonies and for herself, on questions of peace and war. They gain, in return, the obligation on the mother country to repel aggressions directed against them; but, except when the minor community is so weak that the protection of a stronger power is indispensable to it, reciprocity of obligation is not a full equivalent for non-admission to a voice in the deliberations. It is essential, therefore, that in all wars, save those which, like the Caffre or New Zealand wars, are incurred for the sake of the particular colony, the colonists should not (without their own voluntary request) be called on to contribute anything to the expense, except what may be required for the specific local defence of their own ports, shores, and frontiers against invasion. Moreover, as the mother country claims the privilege, at her sole discretion, of taking measures or pursuing a policy which may expose them to attack, it is just that she should undertake a considerable portion of the cost of their military defence even in time of peace; the whole of it, so far as it depends upon a standing army.

But there is a means, still more effectual than these, by which, and in general by which alone, a full equivalent can be given to a smaller community for sinking its individuality, as a substantive power among nations, in the greater individuality of a wide and powerful empire. This one indispensable and, at the same time, sufficient expedient, which meets at once the demands of justice and the growing exigencies of policy, is to open the service of Government in all its departments, and in every part of the empire, on perfectly equal terms, to the inhabitants of the Colonies. Why does no one ever hear a breath of disloyalty from the Islands in the British Channel? By race, religion, and geographical position they belong less to England than to France. But, while they enjoy, like Canada and New South Wales, complete control over their internal affairs and their taxation, every office or dignity in the gift of the Crown is freely open to the native of Guernsey or Jersey. Generals, admirals, peers of the United Kingdom, are made, and there is nothing which hinders prime ministers to be made, from those insignificant islands. The same system was commenced in reference to the Colonies generally by an enlightened Colonial Secretary, too early lost, Sir William Molesworth, when he appointed Mr. Hinckes, a leading Canadian politician, to a West Indian government. It is a very shallow view of the springs of political action in a community which thinks such things unimportant because the number of those in a position actually to profit by the concession might not be very considerable. That limited number would be composed precisely of those who have most moral power over the rest: and men are not so destitute of the sense of collective degradation as not to feel the withholding of an advantage from even one person, because of a circumstance which they all have in common with him, an affront to all. If we prevent the leading men of a community from standing forth to the world as its chiefs and representatives in the general councils of mankind, we owe it both to their legitimate ambition, and to the just pride of the community, to give them in return an equal chance of occupying the same prominent position in a nation of greater power and importance.

Thus far of the dependencies whose population is in a sufficiently advanced state to be fitted for representative government. But there are others which have not attained that state, and which, if held at all, must be governed by the dominant country, or by persons delegated for that purpose by it. This mode of government is as legitimate as any other if it is the one which in the existing state of civilisation of the subject people most facilitates their transition to a higher stage of improvement. There are, as we have already seen, conditions of society in which a vigorous despotism is in itself the best mode of government for training the people in what is specifically wanting to render them capable of a higher civilisation. There are others, in which the mere fact of despotism has

indeed no beneficial effect, the lessons which it teaches having already been only too completely learnt; but in which, there being no spring of spontaneous improvement in the people themselves, their almost only hope of making any steps in advance depends on the chances of a good despot. Under a native despotism, a good despot is a rare and transitory accident: but when the dominion they are under is that of a more civilised people, that people ought to be able to supply it constantly. The ruling country ought to be able to do for its subjects all that could be done by a succession of absolute monarchs, guaranteed by irresistible force against the precariousness of tenure attendant on barbarous despotisms, and qualified by their genius to anticipate all that experience has taught to the more advanced nation. Such is the ideal rule of a free people over a barbarous or semi-barbarous one. We need not expect to see that ideal realised; but unless some approach to it is, the rulers are guilty of a dereliction of the highest moral trust which can devolve upon a nation: and if they do not even aim at it, they are selfish usurpers, on a par in criminality with any of those whose ambition and rapacity have sported from age to age with the destiny of masses of mankind.

As it is already a common, and is rapidly tending to become the universal, condition of the more backward populations, to be either held in direct subjection by the more advanced, or to be under their complete political ascendancy; there are in this age of the world few more important problems than how to organise this rule, so as to make it a good instead of an evil to the subject people; providing them with the best attainable present government, and with the conditions most favourable to future permanent improvement. But the mode of fitting the government for this purpose is by no means so well understood as the conditions of good government in a people capable of governing themselves. We may even say that it is not understood at all.

The thing appears perfectly easy to superficial observers. If India (for example) is not fit to govern itself, all that seems to them required is that there should be a minister to govern it: and that this minister, like all other British ministers, should be responsible to the British Parliament. Unfortunately this, though the simplest mode of attempting to govern a dependency, is about the worst; and betrays in its advocates a total want of comprehension of the conditions of good government. To govern a country under responsibility to the people of that country, and to govern one country under responsibility to the people of another, are two very different things. What makes the excellence of the first is that freedom is preferable to despotism: but the last *is* despotism. The only choice the case admits is a choice of despotisms: and it is not certain that the despotism of twenty millions is necessarily better than that of a few, or of one. But it is quite certain that the despotism of those who neither hear, nor see, nor know anything about their subjects, has many chances of being worse than that of those who do. It is not usually thought that the immediate agents of authority govern better because they govern in the name of an absent master, and of one who has a thousand more pressing interests to attend to. The master may hold them to a strict responsibility, enforced by heavy penalties; but it is very questionable if those penalties will often fall in the right place.

It is always under great difficulties, and very imperfectly, that a country can be governed by foreigners; even when there is no extreme disparity, in habits and ideas, between the rulers and the ruled. Foreigners do not feel with the people. They cannot judge, by the light in which a thing appears to their own minds, or the manner in which it affects their feelings, how it will affect the feelings or appear to the minds of the subject population. What a native of the country, of average practical ability, knows as it were by instinct, they have to learn slowly, and after all imperfectly, by study and experience. The laws, the customs, the social relations, for which they have to legislate, instead of being familiar to them from childhood, are all strange to them. For most of their detailed knowledge they must depend on the information of natives; and it is difficult for them to know whom to trust. They are feared, suspected, probably disliked by the population; seldom sought by them except for interested purposes; and they are prone to think that the servilely submissive are the trustworthy. Their danger is of despising the natives; that of the natives is of disbelieving that anything the strangers do can be intended for their good. These are but a part of the difficulties that any rulers have to struggle with who honestly attempt to govern well a country in which they are foreigners. To overcome these difficulties in any degree will always be a work of much labour, requiring a very superior degree of capacity in the chief administrators, and a high average among the subordinates: and the best organisation of such a government is that which will best ensure the labour, develop the capacity, and place the highest specimens of it in the situations of greatest trust. Responsibility to an authority which has gone through none of the labour, acquired none of the capacity, and for the most part is not even aware that either, in any peculiar degree, is required, cannot be regarded as a very effectual expedient for accomplishing these ends.

The government of a people by itself has a meaning and a reality; but such a thing as government of one people by another does not and cannot exist. One people may keep another as a warren or preserve for its own use, a place to make money in, a human cattle farm to be worked for the profit of its own inhabitants. But if the good of the governed is the proper business of a government, it is utterly impossible that a people should directly attend to it. The utmost they can do is to give some of their best men a commission to look after it; to whom the opinion of their own country can neither be much of a guide in the performance of their duty, nor a competent judge of the mode in which it has been performed. Let any one consider how the English themselves would be governed if they knew and cared no more about their own affairs than they know and care about the affairs of the Hindoos. Even this comparison gives no adequate idea of the state of the case: for a people thus indifferent to politics altogether would probably be simply acquiescent and let the government alone: whereas in the case of India, a politically active people like the English, amidst habitual acquiescence, are every now and then interfering, and almost always in the wrong place. The real causes which determine the prosperity or wretchedness, the improvement or deterioration, of the Hindoos are too far off to be within their ken. They have not the knowledge necessary for suspecting the existence of those causes, much less for judging of their operation. The most essential interests of the country may be well administered without obtaining any of their approbation, or mismanaged to almost any excess without attracting their notice.

The purposes for which they are principally tempted to interfere and control the proceedings of their delegates are of two kinds. One is to force English ideas down the throats of the natives; for instance, by measures of prose-lytism, or acts intentionally or unintentionally offensive to the religious feelings of the people. This misdirection of opinion in the ruling country is instructively exemplified (the more so, because nothing is meant but justice and fairness, and as much impartiality as can be expected from persons really convinced) by the demand now so general in England for having the Bible taught, at the option of pupils or of their parents, in the Government schools. From the European point of view nothing can wear a fairer aspect, or seem less open to objec-tion on the score of religious freedom. To Asiatic eyes it is quite another thing. No Asiatic people ever believes that a government puts its paid officers and official machinery into mo-tion unless it is bent upon an object; and when bent on an object, no Asiatic believes that any government, except a feeble and contemptible one, pursues it by halves. If Government schools and schoolmasters taught Christianity, whatever pledges might be given of teaching it only to those who spontaneously sought it, no amount of evidence would ever persuade the parents that improper means were not used to make their children Christians, or at all events, outcasts from Hindooism. If they could, in the end, be convinced of the contrary, it would only be by the entire failure of the schools, so conducted, to make any converts. If the teaching had the smallest effect in pro-moting its object it would compromise not only the utility and even existence of the govern-ment education, but perhaps the safety of the government itself. An English Protestant would not be easily induced, by disclaimers of proselytism, to place his children in a Roman Catholic seminary: Irish Catholics will not send their children to schools in which they can be made Protestants: and we expect that Hindoos, who believe that the privileges of Hindooism can be forfeited by a merely phys-ical act, will expose theirs to the danger of being made Christians!

Such is one of the modes in which the opin-ion of the dominant country tends to act more injuriously than beneficially on the conduct of its deputed governors. In other respects, its interference is likely to be oftenest exercised where it will be most pertinaciously demand-ed, and that is on behalf of some interest of the English settlers. English settlers have friends at home, have organs, have access to the public; they have a common language and common ideas with their countrymen: any complaint by an Englishman is more sympathetically heard, even if no unjust preference is intentionally accorded to it. Now, if there be a fact to which all experience testifies, it is that when a country holds another in subjection, the individuals of the ruling people who resort to the foreign country to make their fortunes are of all others those who most need to be held under power-ful restraint. They are always one of the chief difficulties of the government. Armed with the prestige and filled with the scornful overbear-ingness of the conquering nation, they have the feelings inspired by absolute power without its sense of responsibility.

Among a people like that of India the utmost efforts of the public authorities are not enough for the effectual protection of the weak against the strong; and of all the strong, the European settlers are the strongest. Wherever the demor-alising effect of the situation is not in a most remarkable degree corrected by the personal character of the individual, they think the peo-ple of the country mere dirt under their feet: it seems to them monstrous that any rights of the natives should stand in the way of their smallest pretensions: the simplest act of pro-tection to the inhabitants against any act of power on their part which they may consider useful to their commercial objects, they de-nounce, and sincerely regard, as an injury. So natural is this state of feeling in a situation like theirs that even under the discouragement which it has hitherto met with from the ruling authorities it is impossible that more or less of the spirit should not perpetually break out. The Government, itself free from this spirit, is never able sufficiently to keep it down in the young and raw even of its own civil and mili-tary officers, over whom it has so much more control than over the independent residents.

As it is with the English in India, so, accord-ing to trustworthy testimony, it is with the French in Algiers; so with the Americans in the countries conquered from Mexico; so it seems to be with the Europeans in China, and already even in Japan: there is no necessity to recall how it was with the Spaniards in South America. In all these cases, the government to which these private adventurers are subject is better than they, and does the most it can to protect the natives against them. Even the Spanish Government did this, sincerely and earnestly, though ineffectually, as is known to every reader of Mr. Helps' instructive history. Had the Spanish Government been directly ac-countable to Spanish opinion we may question if it would have made the attempt: for the Spaniards, doubtless, would have taken part with their Christian friends and relations rather than with Pagans. The settlers, not the natives, have the ear of the public at home; it is they whose representations are likely to pass for truth, because they alone have both the means and the motive to press them perseveringly upon the inattentive and uninterested public mind. The distrustful criticism with which Englishmen, more than any other people, are in the habit of scanning the conduct of their country towards foreigners, they usually reserve for the proceedings of the public authorities. In all questions between a government and an individual the presumption in every Englishman's mind is that the government is in the wrong. And when the resident English bring the batteries of English political action to bear upon any of the bulwarks erected to protect the natives against their encroachments, the executive, with their real but faint velleities of something better, generally find it safer to their parliamentary interest, and at any rate less troublesome, to give up the disputed position than to defend it.

What makes matters worse is that when the public mind is invoked (as, to its credit, the English mind is extremely open to be) in the name of justice and philanthropy, in behalf of the subject community or race, there is the same probability of its missing the mark. For in the subject community also there are oppressors and oppressed; powerful individuals or classes, and slaves prostrate before them; and it is the former, not the latter, who have the means of access to the English public. A tyrant or sensualist who has been deprived of the power he had abused, and, instead of punishment, is supported in as great wealth and splendour as he ever enjoyed; a knot of privileged landholders, who demand that the State should relinquish to them its reserved right to a rent from their lands, or who resent as a wrong any attempt to protect the masses from their extortion; these have no difficulty in procuring interested or sentimental advocacy in the British Parliament and press. The silent myriads obtain none.

The preceding observations exemplify the operation of a principle—which might be called an obvious one, were it not that scarcely anybody seems to be aware of it—that, while responsibility to the governed is the greatest of all securities for good government, responsibility to somebody else not only has no such tendency, but is as likely to produce evil as good. The responsibility of the British rulers of India to the British nation is chiefly useful because, when any acts of the government are called in question, it ensures publicity and discussion; the utility of which does not require that the public at large should comprehend the point at issue, provided there are any individuals among them who do; for, a merely moral responsibility not being responsibility to the collective people, but to every separate person among them who forms a judgment, opinions may be weighed as well as counted, and the approbation or disapprobation of one person well versed in the subject may outweigh that of thousands who know nothing about it at all. It is doubtless a useful restraint upon the immediate rulers that they can be put upon their defence, and that one or two of the jury will form an opinion worth having about their conduct, though that of the remainder will probably be several degrees worse than none. Such as it is, this is the amount of benefit to India, from the control exercised over the Indian government by the British Parliament and people.

It is not by attempting to rule directly a country like India, but by giving it good rulers, that the English people can do their duty to that country; and they can scarcely give it a worse one than an English Cabinet Minister, who is thinking of English, not Indian politics; who seldom remains long enough in office to acquire an intelligent interest in so complicated a subject; upon whom the factitious public opinion got up in Parliament, consisting of two or three fluent speakers, acts with as much force as if it were genuine; while he is under none of the influences of training and position which would lead or qualify him to form an honest opinion of his own. A free country which attempts to govern a distant dependency, inhabited by a dissimilar people, by means of a branch of its own executive, will almost inevitably fail. The only mode which has any chance of tolerable success is to govern through a delegated body of a comparatively permanent character; allowing only a right of inspection, and a negative voice, to the changeable Administration of the State. Such a body did exist in the case of India; and I fear that both India and England will pay a severe penalty for the shortsighted policy by which this intermediate instrument of government was done away with.

It is of no avail to say that such a delegated

body cannot have all the requisites of good government; above all, cannot have that complete and ever-operative identity of interest with the governed which it is so difficult to obtain even where the people to be ruled are in some degree qualified to look after their own affairs. Real good government is not compatible with the conditions of the case. There is but a choice of imperfections. The problem is, so to construct the governing body that, under the difficulties of the position, it shall have as much interest as possible in good government, and as little in bad. Now these conditions are best found in an intermediate body. A delegated administration has always this advantage over a direct one, that it has, at all events, no duty to perform except to the governed. It has no interests to consider except theirs. Its own power of deriving profit from misgovernment may be reduced—in the latest constitution of the East India Company it was reduced—to a singularly small amount: and it can be kept entirely clear of bias from the individual or class interests of any one else.

When the home government and Parliament are swayed by those partial influences in the exercise of the power reserved to them in the last resort, the intermediate body is the certain advocate and champion of the dependency before the imperial tribunal. The intermediate body, moreover, is, in the natural course of things, chiefly composed of persons who have acquired professional knowledge of this part of their country's concerns; who have been trained to it in the place itself, and have made its administration the main occupation of their lives. Furnished with these qualifications, and not being liable to lose their office from the accidents of home politics, they identify their character and consideration with their special trust, and have a much more permanent interest in the success of their administration, and in the prosperity of the country which they administer, than a member of a Cabinet under a representative constitution can possibly have in the good government of any country except the one which he serves. So far as the choice of those who carry on the management on the spot devolves upon this body, the appointments are kept out of the vortex of party and parliamentary jobbing, and freed from the influence of those motives to the abuse of patronage, for the reward of adherents, or to buy off those who would otherwise be opponents, which are always stronger, with statesmen of average honesty, than a con-

scientious sense of the duty of appointing the fittest man. To put this one class of appointments as far as possible out of harm's way is of more consequence than the worst which can happen to all other offices in the state; for, in every other department, if the officer is unqualified, the general opinion of the community directs him in a certain degree what to do: but in the position of the administrators of a dependency where the people are not fit to have the control in their own hands, the character of the government entirely depends on the qualifications, moral and intellectual, of the individual functionaries.

It cannot be too often repeated, that in a country like India everything depends on the personal qualities and capacities of the agents of government. This truth is the cardinal principle of Indian administration. The day when it comes to be thought that the appointment of persons to situations of trust from motives of convenience, already so criminal in England, can be practised with impunity in India, will be the beginning of the decline and fall of our empire there. Even with a sincere intention of preferring the best candidate, it will not do to rely on chance for supplying fit persons. The system must be calculated to form them. It has done this hitherto; and because it has done so, our rule in India has lasted, and been one of constant, if not very rapid, improvement in prosperity and good administration. As much bitterness is now manifested against this system, and as much eagerness displayed to overthrow it, as if educating and training the officers of government for their work were a thing utterly unreasonable and indefensible, an unjustifiable interference with the rights of ignorance and inexperience. There is a tacit conspiracy between those who would like to job in first-rate Indian offices for their connections here, and those who, being already in India, claim to be promoted from the indigo factory or the attorney's office, to administer justice or fix the payments due to government from millions of people. The "monopoly" of the Civil Service, so much inveighed against, is like the monopoly of judicial offices by the bar; and its abolition would be like opening the bench in Westminster Hall to the first comer whose friends certify that he has now and then looked into Blackstone. Were the course ever adopted of sending men from this country, or encouraging them in going out, to get themselves put into high appointments without having learnt their business by passing through the lower ones, the most important offices would be thrown to Scotch cousins and adventurers, connected by no professional feeling with the country or the work, held to no previous knowledge, and eager only to make money rapidly and return home.

The safety of the country is, that those by whom it is administered be sent out in youth, as candidates only, to begin at the bottom of the ladder, and ascend higher or not, as, after a proper interval, they are proved qualified. The defect of the East India Company's system was, that though the best men were carefully sought out for the most important posts, yet if an officer remained in the service, promotion, though it might be delayed, came at last in some shape or other, to the least as well as to the most competent. Even the inferior in qualifications, among such a corps of functionaries, consisted, it must be remembered, of men who had been brought up to their duties, and had fulfilled them for many years, at lowest without disgrace, under the eye and authority of a superior. But though this diminished the evil, it was nevertheless considerable. A man who never becomes fit for more than an assistant's duty should remain an assistant all his life, and his juniors should be promoted over him. With this exception, I am not aware of any real defect in the old system of Indian appointments. It had already received the greatest other improvement it was susceptible of, the choice of the original candidates by competitive examination: which, besides the advantage of recruiting from a higher grade of industry and capacity, has the recommendation, that under it, unless by accident, there are no personal ties between the candidates for offices and those who have a voice in conferring them.

It is in no way unjust that public officers thus selected and trained should be exclusively eligible to offices which require specially Indian knowledge and experience. If any door to the higher appointments, without passing through the lower, be opened even for occasional use, there will be such incessant knocking at it by persons of influence that it will be impossible ever to keep it closed. The only excepted appointment should be the highest one of all. The Viceroy of British India should be a person selected from all Englishmen for his great general capacity for government. If he have this, he will be able to distinguish in others, and turn to his own use, that special knowledge and judgment in local affairs which he has not himself had the opportunity of acquiring. There are good reasons why (saving exceptional cases) the Viceroy should not be a member of the regular service. All services have, more or less, their class prejudices, from which the supreme ruler ought to be exempt. Neither are men, however able and experienced, who have passed their lives in Asia, so likely to possess the most advanced European ideas in general statesmanship; which the chief ruler should carry out with him, and blend with the results of Indian experience. Again, being of a different class, and especially if chosen by a different authority, he will seldom have any personal partialities to warp his appointments to office. This great security for honest bestowal of patronage existed in rare perfection under the mixed government of the Crown and the East India Company. The supreme dispensers of office, the Governor-General and Governors, were appointed, in fact though not formally, by the Crown, that is, by the general Government, not by the intermediate body; and a great officer of the Crown probably had not a single personal or political connection in the local service: while the delegated body, most of whom had themselves served in the country, had and were likely to have such connections.

This guarantee for impartiality would be much impaired if the civil servants of Government, even though sent out in boyhood as mere candidates for employment, should come to be furnished, in any considerable proportion, by the class of society which supplies Viceroys and Governors. Even the initiatory competitive examination would then be an insufficient security. It would exclude mere ignorance and incapacity; it would compel youths of family to start in the race with the same amount of instruction and ability as other people; the stupidest son could not be put into the Indian service as he can be into the Church; but there would be nothing to prevent undue preference afterwards. No longer all equally unknown and unheard of by the arbiter of their lot, a portion of the service would be personally, and a still greater number politically, in close relation with him. Members of certain families, and of the higher classes and influential connections generally, would rise more rapidly than their competitors, and be often kept in situations for which they were unfit, or placed in those for which others were fitter. The same influences would be brought into play which affect promotions in the army: and those alone, if such miracles of simplicity there be, who believe that these are impartial, would expect impartiality in those of India. This evil is, I fear, irremediable by any general measures which can be taken under the present system. No such will afford a degree of security comparable to that which once flowed spontaneously from the so-called double government.

What is accounted so great an advantage in the case of the English system of government at home has been its misfortune in India—that it grew up of itself, not from preconceived design, but by successive expedients, and by the adaptation of machinery originally created for a different purpose. As the country on which its maintenance depended was not the one out of whose necessities it grew, its practical benefits did not come home to the mind of that country, and it would have required theoretic recommendations to render it acceptable. Unfortunately, these were exactly what it seemed to be destitute of: and undoubtedly the common theories of government did not furnish it with such, framed as those theories have been for states of circumstances differing in all the most important features from the case concerned. But in government, as in other departments of human agency, almost all principles which have been durable were first suggested by observation of some particular case in which the general laws of nature acted in some new or previously unnoticed combination of circumstances. The institutions of Great Britain, and those of the United States, have had the distinction of suggesting most of the theories of government which, through good and evil fortune, are now, in the course of generations, reawakening political life in the nations of Europe. It has been the destiny of the government of the East India Company to suggest the true theory of the government of a semi-barbarous dependency by a civilised country, and after having done this, to perish. It would be a singular fortune if, at the end of two or three more generations, this speculative result should be the only remaining fruit of our ascendancy in India; if posterity should say of us, that having stumbled accidentally upon better arrangements than our wisdom would ever have devised, the first use we made of our awakened reason was to destroy them, and allow the good which had been in course of being realised to fall through and be lost, from ignorance of the principles on which it depended. *Di meliora:* but if a fate so disgraceful to England and to civilisation can be averted, it must be through far wider political conceptions than merely English or European practice can supply, and through a much more profound study of Indian experience, and of the conditions of Indian government, than either English politicians, or those who supply the English public with opinions, have hitherto shown any willingness to undertake.

CONTENTS: UTILITARIANISM

UTILITARIANISM

Chapter 1

General Remarks

THERE ARE few circumstances among those which make up the present condition of human knowledge, more unlike what might have been expected, or more significant of the backward state in which speculation on the most important subjects still lingers, than the little progress which has been made in the decision of the controversy respecting the criterion of right and wrong. From the dawn of philosophy, the question concerning the *summum bonum*, or, what is the same thing, concerning the foundation of morality, has been accounted the main problem in speculative thought, has occupied the most gifted intellects, and divided them into sects and schools, carrying on a vigorous warfare against one another. And after more than two thousand years the same discussions continue, philosophers are still ranged under the same contending banners, and neither thinkers nor mankind at large seem nearer to being unanimous on the subject, than when the youth Socrates listened to the old Protagoras, and asserted (if Plato's dialogue be grounded on a real conversation) the theory of utilitarianism against the popular morality of the so-called sophist.

It is true that similar confusion and uncertainty, and in some cases similar discordance, exist respecting the first principles of all the sciences, not excepting that which is deemed the most certain of them, mathematics; without much impairing, generally indeed without impairing at all, the trustworthiness of the conclusions of those sciences. An apparent anomaly, the explanation of which is, that the detailed doctrines of a science are not usually deduced from, nor depend for their evidence upon, what are called its first principles. Were it not so, there would be no science more precarious, or whose conclusions were more insufficiently made out, than algebra; which derives none of its certainty from what are commonly taught to learners as its elements, since these, as laid down by some of its most eminent teachers, are as full of fictions as English law, and of mysteries as theology. The truths which are ultimately accepted as the first principles of a science, are really the last results of metaphysical analysis, practised on the elementary notions with which the science is conversant; and their relation to the science is not that of foundations to an edifice, but of roots to a tree, which may perform their office equally well though they be never dug down to and exposed to light. But though in science the particular truths precede the general theory, the contrary might be expected to be the case with a practical art, such as morals or legislation. All action is for the sake of some end, and rules of action, it seems natural to suppose, must take their whole character and colour from the end to which they are subservient. When we engage in a pursuit, a clear and precise conception of what we are pursuing would seem to be the first thing we need, instead of the last we are to look forward to. A test of right and wrong must be the means, one would think, of ascertaining what is right or wrong, and not a consequence of having already ascertained it.

The difficulty is not avoided by having recourse to the popular theory of a natural faculty, a sense or instinct, informing us of right and wrong. For—besides that the existence of such a moral instinct is itself one of the matters in dispute—those believers in it who have any pretensions to philosophy, have been obliged to abandon the idea that it discerns what is right or wrong in the particular case in hand, as our other senses discern the sight or sound actually present. Our moral faculty, according to all those of its interpreters who are entitled to the name of thinkers, supplies us only with the general principles of moral judgments; it is a branch of our reason, not of our sensitive faculty; and must be looked to for the abstract doctrines of morality, not for perception of it in the concrete. The intuitive, no less than what may be termed the inductive, school of ethics, insists on the necessity of general laws. They both agree that the morality of an individual action is not a question of direct perception, but of the application of a law to an individual case. They recognise also, to a great extent, the same moral laws; but differ as to their evidence, and the source from which they derive their authority. According to the one opinion, the principles of morals are evident *à priori,* requiring nothing to command assent, except that the meaning of the terms be understood. According to the other doctrine, right and wrong, as well as truth and falsehood, are questions of observation and experience. But both hold equally that morality must be deduced from principles; and the intuitive school affirm as strongly as the inductive, that there is a science of morals. Yet they seldom attempt to make out a list of the *à priori* principles which are to serve as the premises of the science; still more rarely do they make any effort to reduce those various principles to one first principle, or common ground of obligation. They either assume the ordinary precepts of morals as of *à priori* authority, or they lay down as the common groundwork of those maxims, some generality much less obviously authoritative than the maxims themselves, and which has never succeeded in gaining popular acceptance. Yet to support their pretensions there ought either to be some one fundamental principle or law, at the root of all morality, or if there be several, there should be a determinate order of precedence among them; and the one principle, or the rule for deciding between the various principles when they conflict, ought to be self-evident.

To inquire how far the bad effects of this deficiency have been mitigated in practice, or to what extent the moral beliefs of mankind have been vitiated or made uncertain by the absence of any distinct recognition of an ultimate standard, would imply a complete survey and criticism of past and present ethical doctrine. It would, however, be easy to show that whatever steadiness or consistency these moral beliefs have attained, has been mainly due to the tacit influence of a standard not recognised. Although the non-existence of an acknowledged first principle has made ethics not so much a guide as a consecration of men's actual sentiments, still, as men's sentiments, both of favour and of aversion, are greatly influenced by what they suppose to be the effects of things upon their happiness, the principle of utility, or as Bentham latterly called it, the greatest happiness principle, has had a large share in forming the moral doctrines even of those who most scornfully reject its authority. Nor is there any school of thought which refuses to admit that the influence of actions on happiness is a most material and even predominant consideration in many of the details of morals, however unwilling to acknowledge it as the fundamental principle of morality, and the source of moral obligation. I might go much further, and say that to all those *à priori* moralists who deem it necessary to argue at all, utilitarian arguments are indispensable. It is not my present purpose to criticise these thinkers; but I cannot help referring, for illustration, to a systematic treatise by one of the most illustrious of them, the *Metaphysics of Ethics,* by Kant. This remarkable man, whose system of thought will long remain one of the landmarks in the history of philosophical speculation, does, in the treatise in question, lay down a universal first principle as the origin and ground of moral obligation; it is this:— "So act, that the rule on which thou actest would admit of being adopted as a law by all rational beings." But when he begins to deduce from this precept any of the actual duties of morality, he fails, almost grotesquely, to show that there would be any contradiction, any logical (not to say physical) impossibility, in the adoption by all rational beings of the most outrageously immoral rules of conduct. All he shows is that the *consequences* of their universal adoption would be such as no one would choose to incur.

On the present occasion, I shall, without further discussion of the other theories, attempt to contribute something towards the understanding and appreciation of the Utilitarian or Happiness theory, and towards such proof as it is susceptible of. It is evident that this cannot be proof in the ordinary and popular meaning of the term. Questions of ultimate ends are not amenable to direct proof. Whatever can be proved to be good, must be so by being shown to be a means to something admitted to be good without proof. The medical art is proved to be good by its conducing to health; but how is it possible to prove that health is good? The art of music is good, for the reason, among others, that it produces pleasure; but what proof is it possible to give that pleasure is good? If, then, it is asserted that there is a comprehensive formula, including all things which are in themselves good, and that whatever else is good, is not so as an end, but as a mean, the formula may be accepted or rejected, but is not a subject of what is commonly understood by proof. We are not, however, to infer that its acceptance or rejection must depend on blind impulse, or arbitrary choice. There is a larger meaning of the word proof, in which this question is as amenable to it as any other of the disputed questions of philosophy. The subject is within the cognisance of the rational faculty; and neither does that faculty deal with it solely in the way of intuition. Considerations may be presented capable of determining the intellect either to give or withhold its assent to the doctrine; and this is equivalent to proof.

We shall examine presently of what nature are these considerations; in what manner they apply to the case, and what rational grounds, therefore, can be given for accepting or rejecting the utilitarian formula. But it is a preliminary condition of rational acceptance or rejection, that the formula should be correctly understood. I believe that the very imperfect notion ordinarily formed of its meaning, is the chief obstacle which impedes its reception; and that could it be cleared, even from only the grosser misconceptions, the question would be greatly simplified, and a large proportion of its difficulties removed. Before, therefore, I attempt to enter into the philosophical grounds which can be given for assenting to the utilitarian standard, I shall offer some illustrations of the doctrine itself; with the view of showing more clearly what it is, distinguishing it from what it is not, and disposing of such of the practical objections to it as either originate in, or are closely connected with, mistaken interpretations of its meaning. Having thus prepared the ground, I shall afterwards endeavour to throw such light as I can upon the question, considered as one of philosophical theory.

Chapter 2
What Utilitarianism Is

A PASSING remark is all that needs be given to the ignorant blunder of supposing that those who stand up for utility as the test of right and wrong, use the term in that restricted and merely colloquial sense in which utility is opposed to pleasure. An apology is due to the philosophical opponents of utilitarianism, for even the momentary appearance of confounding them with any one capable of so absurd a misconception; which is the more extraordinary, inasmuch as the contrary accusation, of referring everything to pleasure, and that too in its grossest form, is another of the common charges against utilitarianism: and, as has been pointedly remarked by an able writer, the same sort of persons, and often the very same persons, denounce the theory "as impracticably dry when the word utility precedes the word pleasure, and as too practicably voluptuous when the word pleasure precedes the word utility." Those who know anything about the matter are aware that every writer, from Epicurus to Bentham, who maintained the theory of utility, meant by it, not something to be contradistinguished from pleasure, but pleasure itself, together with exemption from pain; and instead of opposing the useful to the agreeable or the ornamental, have always declared that the useful means these, among other things. Yet the common herd, including the herd of writers, not only in newspapers and periodicals, but in books of weight and pretension, are perpetually falling into this shallow mistake. Having caught up the word utilitarian, while knowing nothing whatever about it but its sound, they habitually express by it the rejection, or the neglect, of pleasure in some of its forms; of beauty, of ornament, or of amusement. Nor is the term thus ignorantly misapplied solely in disparagement, but occasionally in compliment; as though it implied superiority to frivolity and the mere pleasures of the moment. And this perverted use is the only one in which the word is popularly known, and the one from which the new generation are acquiring their sole notion of its meaning. Those who introduced the word, but who had for many years discontinued it as a distinctive appellation, may well feel themselves called upon to resume it, if by doing so they can hope to contribute anything towards rescuing it from this utter degradation.[1]

[1] The author of this essay has reason for believing himself to be the first person who brought the word utilitarian into use. He did not invent it, but adopted it from a passing expression in Mr. Galt's *Annals of the Parish*. After using it as a designation for several years, he and others abandoned it from a growing dislike to anything resembling a badge or watchword of sectarian distinction. But as a name for one single opinion, not

The creed which accepts as the foundation of morals, Utility, or the Greatest Happiness Principle, holds that actions are right in proportion as they tend to promote happiness, wrong as they tend to produce the reverse of happiness. By happiness is intended pleasure, and the absence of pain; by unhappiness, pain, and the privation of pleasure. To give a clear view of the moral standard set up by the theory, much more requires to be said; in particular, what things it includes in the ideas of pain and pleasure; and to what extent this is left an open question. But these supplementary explanations do not affect the theory of life on which this theory of morality is grounded— namely, that pleasure, and freedom from pain, are the only things desirable as ends; and that all desirable things (which are as numerous in the utilitarian as in any other scheme) are desirable either for the pleasure inherent in themselves, or as means to the promotion of pleasure and the prevention of pain.

Now, such a theory of life excites in many minds, and among them in some of the most estimable in feeling and purpose, inveterate dislike. To suppose that life has (as they express it) no higher end than pleasure—no better and nobler object of desire and pursuit—they designate as utterly mean and grovelling; as a doctrine worthy only of swine, to whom the followers of Epicurus were, at a very early period, contemptuously likened; and modern holders of the doctrine are occasionally made the subject of equally polite comparisons by its German, French, and English assailants.

When thus attacked, the Epicureans have always answered, that it is not they, but their accusers, who represent human nature in a degrading light; since the accusation supposes human beings to be capable of no pleasures except those of which swine are capable. If this supposition were true, the charge could not be gainsaid, but would then be no longer an imputation; for if the sources of pleasure were precisely the same to human beings and to swine, the rule of life which is good enough for the one would be good enough for the other. The comparison of the Epicurean life to that of beasts is felt as degrading, precisely because a beast's pleasures do not satisfy a human being's conceptions of happiness. Human beings

have faculties more elevated than the animal appetites, and when once made conscious of them, do not regard anything as happiness which does not include their gratification. I do not, indeed, consider the Epicureans to have been by any means faultless in drawing out their scheme of consequences from the utilitarian principle. To do this in any sufficient manner, many Stoic, as well as Christian elements require to be included. But there is no known Epicurean theory of life which does not assign to the pleasures of the intellect, of the feelings and imagination, and of the moral sentiments, a much higher value as pleasures than to those of mere sensation. It must be admitted, however, that utilitarian writers in general have placed the superiority of mental over bodily pleasures chiefly in the greater permanency, safety, uncostliness, etc., of the former—that is, in their circumstantial advantages rather than in their intrinsic nature. And on all these points utilitarians have fully proved their case; but they might have taken the other, and, as it may be called, higher ground, with entire consistency. It is quite compatible with the principle of utility to recognise the fact, that some *kinds* of pleasure are more desirable and more valuable than others. It would be absurd that while, in estimating all other things, quality is considered as well as quantity, the estimation of pleasures should be supposed to depend on quantity alone.

If I am asked, what I mean by difference of quality in pleasures, or what makes one pleasure more valuable than another, merely as a pleasure, except its being greater in amount, there is but one possible answer. Of two pleasures, if there be one to which all or almost all who have experience of both give a decided preference, irrespective of any feeling of moral obligation to prefer it, that is the more desirable pleasure. If one of the two is, by those who are competently acquainted with both, placed so far above the other that they prefer it, even though knowing it to be attended with a greater amount of discontent, and would not resign it for any quantity of the other pleasure which their nature is capable of, we are justified in ascribing to the preferred enjoyment a superiority in quality, so far outweighing quantity as to render it, in comparison, of small account.

Now it is an unquestionable fact that those who are equally acquainted with, and equally capable of appreciating and enjoying, both,

a set of opinions—to denote the recognition of utility as a standard, not any particular way of applying it—the term supplies a want in the language, and offers, in many cases, a convenient mode of avoiding tiresome circumlocution.

do give a most marked preference to the manner of existence which employs their higher faculties. Few human creatures would consent to be changed into any of the lower animals, for a promise of the fullest allowance of a beast's pleasures; no intelligent human being would consent to be a fool, no instructed person would be an ignoramus, no person of feeling and conscience would be selfish and base, even though they should be persuaded that the fool, the dunce, or the rascal is better satisfied with his lot than they are with theirs. They would not resign what they possess more than he for the most complete satisfaction of all the desires which they have in common with him. If they ever fancy they would, it is only in cases of unhappiness so extreme, that to escape from it they would exchange their lot for almost any other, however undesirable in their own eyes. A being of higher faculties requires more to make him happy, is capable probably of more acute suffering, and certainly accessible to it at more points, than one of an inferior type; but in spite of these liabilities, he can never really wish to sink into what he feels to be a lower grade of existence. We may give what explanation we please of this unwillingness; we may attribute it to pride, a name which is given indiscriminately to some of the most and to some of the least estimable feelings of which mankind are capable: we may refer it to the love of liberty and personal independence, an appeal to which was with the Stoics one of the most effective means for the inculcation of it; to the love of power, or to the love of excitement, both of which do really enter into and contribute to it: but its most appropriate appellation is a sense of dignity, which all human beings possess in one form or other, and in some, though by no means in exact, proportion to their higher faculties, and which is so essential a part of the happiness of those in whom it is strong, that nothing which conflicts with it could be, otherwise than momentarily, an object of desire to them.

Whoever supposes that this preference takes place at a sacrifice of happiness—that the superior being, in anything like equal circumstances, is not happier than the inferior—confounds the two very different ideas, of happiness, and content. It is indisputable that the being whose capacities of enjoyment are low, has the greatest chance of having them fully satisfied; and a highly endowed being will always feel that any happiness which he can look for, as the world is constituted, is imperfect. But he

can learn to bear its imperfections, if they are at all bearable; and they will not make him envy the being who is indeed unconscious of the imperfections, but only because he feels not at all the good which those imperfections qualify. It is better to be a human being dissatisfied than a pig satisfied; better to be Socrates dissatisfied than a fool satisfied. And if the fool, or the pig, are of a different opinion, it is because they only know their own side of the question. The other party to the comparison knows both sides.

It may be objected, that many who are capable of the higher pleasures, occasionally, under the influence of temptation, postpone them to the lower. But this is quite compatible with a full appreciation of the intrinsic superiority of the higher. Men often, from infirmity of character, make their election for the nearer good, though they know it to be the less valuable; and this no less when the choice is between two bodily pleasures, than when it is between bodily and mental. They pursue sensual indulgences to the injury of health, though perfectly aware that health is the greater good.

It may be further objected, that many who begin with youthful enthusiasm for everything noble, as they advance in years sink into indolence and selfishness. But I do not believe that those who undergo this very common change, voluntarily choose the lower description of pleasures in preference to the higher. I believe that before they devote themselves exclusively to the one, they have already become incapable of the other. Capacity for the nobler feelings is in most natures a very tender plant, easily killed, not only by hostile influences, but by mere want of sustenance; and in the majority of young persons it speedily dies away if the occupations to which their position in life has devoted them, and the society into which it has thrown them, are not favourable to keeping that higher capacity in exercise. Men lose their high aspirations as they lose their intellectual tastes, because they have not time or opportunity for indulging them; and they addict themselves to inferior pleasures, not because they deliberately prefer them, but because they are either the only ones to which they have access, or the only ones which they are any longer capable of enjoying. It may be questioned whether any one who has remained equally susceptible to both classes of pleasures, ever knowingly and calmly preferred the lower; though many, in all ages, have broken down in an ineffectual attempt to combine both.

From this verdict of the only competent judges, I apprehend there can be no appeal. On a question which is the best worth having of two pleasures, or which of two modes of existence is the most grateful to the feelings, apart from its moral attributes and from its consequences, the judgment of those who are qualified by knowledge of both, or, if they differ, that of the majority among them, must be admitted as final. And there needs be the less hesitation to accept this judgment respecting the quality of pleasures, since there is no other tribunal to be referred to even on the question of quantity. What means are there of determining which is the acutest of two pains, or the intensest of two pleasurable sensations, except the general suffrage of those who are familiar with both? Neither pains nor pleasures are homogeneous, and pain is always heterogeneous with pleasure. What is there to decide whether a particular pleasure is worth purchasing at the cost of a particular pain, except the feelings and judgment of the experienced? When, therefore, those feelings and judgment declare the pleasures derived from the higher faculties to be preferable *in kind,* apart from the question of intensity, to those of which the animal nature, disjoined from the higher faculties, is susceptible, they are entitled on this subject to the same regard.

I have dwelt on this point, as being a necessary part of a perfectly just conception of Utility or Happiness, considered as the directive rule of human conduct. But it is by no means an indispensable condition to the acceptance of the utilitarian standard; for that standard is not the agent's own greatest happiness, but the greatest amount of happiness altogether; and if it may possibly be doubted whether a noble character is always the happier for its nobleness, there can be no doubt that it makes other people happier, and that the world in general is immensely a gainer by it. Utilitarianism, therefore, could only attain its end by the general cultivation of nobleness of character, even if each individual were only benefited by the nobleness of others, and his own, so far as happiness is concerned, were a sheer deduction from the benefit. But the bare enunciation of such an absurdity as this last, renders refutation superfluous.

According to the Greatest Happiness Principle, as above explained, the ultimate end, with reference to and for the sake of which all other things are desirable (whether we are considering our own good or that of other people), is an existence exempt as far as possible from pain, and as rich as possible in enjoyments, both in point of quantity and quality; the test of quality, and the rule for measuring it against quantity, being the preference felt by those who in their opportunities of experience, to which must be added their habits of self-consciousness and self-observation, are best furnished with the means of comparison. This, being, according to the utilitarian opinion, the end of human action, is necessarily also the standard of morality; which may accordingly be defined, the rules and precepts for human conduct, by the observance of which an existence such as has been described might be, to the greatest extent possible, secured to all mankind; and not to them only, but, so far as the nature of things admits, to the whole sentient creation.

Against this doctrine, however, arises another class of objectors, who say that happiness, in any form, cannot be the rational purpose of human life and action; because, in the first place, it is unattainable: and they contemptuously ask, what right hast thou to be happy? a question which Mr. Carlyle clenches by the addition, What right, a short time ago, hadst thou even *to be?* Next, they say, that men can do *without* happiness; that all noble human beings have felt this, and could not have become noble but by learning the lesson of Entsagen, or renunciation; which lesson, thoroughly learnt and submitted to, they affirm to be the beginning and necessary condition of all virtue.

The first of these objections would go to the root of the matter were it well founded; for if no happiness is to be had at all by human beings, the attainment of it cannot be the end of morality, or of any rational conduct. Though, even in that case, something might still be said for the utilitarian theory; since utility includes not solely the pursuit of happiness, but the prevention or mitigation of unhappiness; and if the former aim be chimerical, there will be all the greater scope and more imperative need for the latter, so long at least as mankind think fit to live, and do not take refuge in the simultaneous act of suicide recommended under certain conditions by Novalis. When, however, it is thus positively asserted to be impossible that human life should be happy, the assertion, if not something like a verbal quibble, is at least an exaggeration. If by happiness be meant a continuity of highly pleasurable excitement, it is evident enough that this is impossible. A state of exalted pleasure lasts only moments, or in some cases, and with some intermissions, hours or days, and is the occasional brilliant flash of enjoyment, not its permanent and steady flame. Of this the philosophers who have taught that happiness is the end of life were as fully aware as those who taunt them. The happiness which they meant was not a life of rapture; but moments of such, in an existence made up of few and transitory pains, many and various pleasures, with a decided predominance of the active over the passive, and having as the foundation of the whole, not to expect more from life than it is capable of bestowing. A life thus composed, to those who have been fortunate enough to obtain it, has always appeared worthy of the name of happiness. And such an existence is even now the lot of many, during some considerable portion of their lives. The present wretched education, and wretched social arrangements, are the only real hindrance to its being attainable by almost all.

The objectors perhaps may doubt whether human beings, if taught to consider happiness as the end of life, would be satisfied with such a moderate share of it. But great numbers of mankind have been satisfied with much less. The main constituents of a satisfied life appear to be two, either of which by itself is often found sufficient for the purpose: tranquillity, and excitement. With much tranquillity, many find that they can be content with very little pleasure: with much excitement, many can reconcile themselves to a considerable quantity of pain. There is assuredly no inherent impossibility in enabling even the mass of mankind to unite both; since the two are so far from being incompatible that they are in natural alliance, the prolongation of either being a preparation for, and exciting a wish for, the other. It is only those in whom indolence amounts to a vice, that do not desire excitement after an interval of repose: it is only those in whom the need of excitement is a disease, that feel the tranquillity which follows excitement dull and insipid, instead of pleasurable in direct proportion to the excitement which preceded it. When people who are tolerably fortunate in their outward lot do not find in life sufficient enjoyment to make it valuable to them, the cause generally is, caring for nobody but themselves. To those who have neither public nor private affections, the excitements of life are much curtailed, and in any case dwindle in value as the time approaches when all selfish interests must be terminated by death: while those who leave after them objects of personal affection, and especially those who have also cultivated a fellow-feeling with the collective interests of mankind, retain as lively an interest in life on the eve of death as in the vigour of youth and health. Next to selfishness, the principal cause which makes life unsatisfactory is want of mental cultivation. A cultivated mind—I do not mean that of a philosopher, but any mind to which the fountains of knowledge have been opened, and which has been taught, in any tolerable degree, to exercise its faculties—finds sources of inexhaustible interest in all that surrounds it; in the objects of nature, the achievements of art, the imaginations of poetry, the incidents of history, the ways of mankind, past and present, and their prospects in the future. It is possible, indeed, to become indifferent to all this, and that too without having exhausted a thousandth part of it; but only when one has had from the beginning no moral or human interest in these things, and has sought in them only the gratification of curiosity.

Now there is absolutely no reason in the nature of things why an amount of mental culture sufficient to give an intelligent interest in these objects of contemplation, should not be the inheritance of every one born in a civilised country. As little is there an inherent necessity that any human being should be a selfish egotist, devoid of every feeling or care but those which centre in his own miserable individuality. Something far superior to this is sufficiently common even now, to give ample earnest of what the human species may be made. Genuine private affections, and a sincere interest in the public good, are possible, though in unequal degrees, to every rightly brought up human being. In a world in which there is so much to interest, so much to enjoy, and so much also to correct and improve, every one who has this moderate amount of moral and intellectual requisites is capable of an existence which may be called enviable; and unless such a person, through bad laws, or subjection to the will of others, is denied the liberty to use the sources of happiness within his reach, he will not fail to find this enviable existence, if he escape the positive evils of life, the great sources of physical and mental suffering—such as indigence, disease, and the unkindness, worthlessness, or premature loss of objects of affection. The main stress of the problem lies, therefore, in the contest with these calamities, from which it is a rare good fortune entirely to escape; which, as things now are, cannot be obviated, and often cannot be in any material degree mitigated. Yet no one whose opinion deserves a moment's consideration can doubt that most of the great positive evils of the world are in themselves removable, and will, if human affairs continue to improve, be in the end reduced within narrow limits. Poverty, in any sense implying suffering, may be completely extinguished by the wisdom of society, combined with the good sense and providence of individuals. Even that most intractable of enemies, disease, may be indefinitely reduced in dimensions by good physical and moral education, and proper control of noxious influences; while the progress of science holds out a promise for the future of still more direct conquests over this detestable foe. And every advance in that direction relieves us from some, not only of the chances which cut short our own lives, but, what concerns us still more, which deprive us of those in whom our happiness is wrapt up. As for vicissitudes of fortune, and other disappointments connected with worldly circumstances, these are principally the effect either of gross imprudence, of ill-regulated desires, or of bad or imperfect social institutions.

All the grand sources, in short, of human suffering are in a great degree, many of them almost entirely, conquerable by human care and effort; and though their removal is grievously slow—though a long succession of generations will perish in the breach before the conquest is completed, and this world becomes all that, if will and knowledge were not wanting, it might easily be made—yet every mind sufficiently intelligent and generous to bear a part, however small and unconspicuous, in the endeavour, will draw a noble enjoyment from the contest itself, which he would not for any bribe in the form of selfish indulgence consent to be without.

And this leads to the true estimation of what is said by the objectors concerning the possibility, and the obligation, of learning to do without happiness. Unquestionably it is possible to do without happiness; it is done involuntarily by nineteen-twentieths of mankind, even in those parts of our present world which are least deep in barbarism; and it often has to be done voluntarily by the hero or the martyr, for the sake of something which he

prizes more than his individual happiness. But this something, what is it, unless the happiness of others, or some of the requisites of happiness? It is noble to be capable of resigning entirely one's own portion of happiness, or chances of it: but, after all, this self-sacrifice must be for some end; it is not its own end; and if we are told that its end is not happiness, but virtue, which is better than happiness, I ask, would the sacrifice be made if the hero or martyr did not believe that it would earn for others immunity from similar sacrifices? Would it be made if he thought that his renunciation of happiness for himself would produce no fruit for any of his fellow creatures, but to make their lot like his, and place them also in the condition of persons who have renounced happiness? All honour to those who can abnegate for themselves the personal enjoyment of life, when by such renunciation they contribute worthily to increase the amount of happiness in the world; but he who does it, or professes to do it, for any other purpose, is no more deserving of admiration than the ascetic mounted on his pillar. He may be an inspiriting proof of what men *can* do, but assuredly not an example of what they *should*.

Though it is only in a very imperfect state of the world's arrangements that any one can best serve the happiness of others by the absolute sacrifice of his own, yet so long as the world is in that imperfect state, I fully acknowledge that the readiness to make such a sacrifice is the highest virtue which can be found in man. I will add, that in this condition of the world, paradoxical as the assertion may be, the conscious ability to do without happiness gives the best prospect of realising such happiness as is attainable. For nothing except that consciousness can raise a person above the chances of life, by making him feel that, let fate and fortune do their worst, they have not power to subdue him: which, once felt, frees him from excess of anxiety concerning the evils of life, and enables him, like many a Stoic in the worst times of the Roman Empire, to cultivate in tranquillity the sources of satisfaction accessible to him, without concerning himself about the uncertainty of their duration, any more than about their inevitable end.

Meanwhile, let utilitarians never cease to claim the morality of self devotion as a possession which belongs by as good a right to them, as either to the Stoic or to the Transcendentalist. The utilitarian morality does recognise in human beings the power of sacrificing their own greatest good for the good of others. It only refuses to admit that the sacrifice is itself a good. A sacrifice which does not increase, or tend to increase, the sum total of happiness, it considers as wasted. The only self-renunciation which it applauds, is devotion to the happiness, or to some of the means of happiness, of others; either of mankind collectively, or of individuals within the limits imposed by the collective interests of mankind.

I must again repeat, what the assailants of utilitarianism seldom have the justice to acknowledge, that the happiness which forms the utilitarian standard of what is right in conduct, is not the agent's own happiness, but that of all concerned. As between his own happiness and that of others, utilitarianism requires him to be as strictly impartial as a disinterested and benevolent spectator. In the golden rule of Jesus of Nazareth, we read the complete spirit of the ethics of utility. To do as you would be done by, and to love your neighbour as yourself, constitute the ideal perfection of utilitarian morality. As the means of making the nearest approach to this ideal, utility would enjoin, first, that laws and social arrangements should place the happiness, or (as speaking practically it may be called) the interest, of every individual, as nearly as possible in harmony with the interest of the whole; and secondly, that education and opinion, which have so vast a power over human character, should so use that power as to establish in the mind of every individual an indissoluble association between his own happiness and the good of the whole; especially between his own happiness and the practice of such modes of conduct, negative and positive, as regard for the universal happiness prescribes; so that not only he may be unable to conceive the possibility of happiness to himself, consistently with conduct opposed to the general good, but also that a direct impulse to promote the general good may be in every individual one of the habitual motives of action, and the sentiments connected therewith may fill a large and prominent place in every human being's sentient existence. If the impugners of the utilitarian morality represented it to their own minds in this its true character, I know not what recommendation possessed by any other morality they could possibly affirm to be wanting to it; what more beautiful or more exalted developments of human nature any other ethical system can be supposed to foster, or what springs of action, not accessible to the utili-

tarian, such systems rely on for giving effect to their mandates.

The objectors to utilitarianism cannot always be charged with representing it in a discreditable light. On the contrary, those among them who entertain anything like a just idea of its disinterested character, sometimes find fault with its standard as being too high for humanity. They say it is exacting too much to require that people shall always act from the inducement of promoting the general interests of society. But this is to mistake the very meaning of a standard of morals, and confound the rule of action with the motive of it. It is the business of ethics to tell us what are our duties, or by what test we may know them; but no system of ethics requires that the sole motive of all we do shall be a feeling of duty; on the contrary, ninety-nine hundredths of all our actions are done from other motives, and rightly so done, if the rule of duty does not condemn them. It is the more unjust to utilitarianism that this particular misapprehension should be made a ground of objection to it, inasmuch as utilitarian moralists have gone beyond almost all others in affirming that the motive has nothing to do with the morality of the action, though much with the worth of the agent. He who saves a fellow creature from drowning does what is morally right, whether his motive be duty, or the hope of being paid for his trouble; he who betrays the friend that trusts him, is guilty of a crime, even if his object be to serve another friend to whom he is under greater obligations. But to speak only of actions done from the motive of duty, and in direct obedience to principle: it is a misapprehension of the utilitarian mode of thought, to conceive it as implying that people should fix their minds upon so wide a generality as the world, or society at large. The great majority of good actions are intended not for the benefit of the world, but for that of individuals, of which the good of the world is made up; and the thoughts of the most virtuous man need not on these occasions travel beyond the particular persons concerned, except so far as is necessary to assure himself that in benefiting them he is not violating the rights, that is, the legitimate and authorised expectations, of any one else. The multiplication of happiness is, according to the utilitarian ethics, the object of virtue: the occasions on which any person (except one in a thousand) has it in his power to do this on an extended scale, in other words to be a public benefactor, are but exceptional; and on these occasions alone is he called on to consider public utility; in every other case, private utility, the interest or happiness of some few persons, is all he has to attend to. Those alone the influence of whose actions extends to society in general, need concern themselves habitually about so large an object. In the case of abstinences indeed—of things which people forbear to do from moral considerations, though the consequences in the particular case might be beneficial—it would be unworthy of an intelligent agent not to be consciously aware that the action is of a class which, if practised generally, would be generally injurious, and that this is the ground of the obligation to abstain from it. The amount of regard for the public interest implied in this recognition, is no greater than is demanded by every system of morals, for they all enjoin to abstain from whatever is manifestly pernicious to society.

The same considerations dispose of another reproach against the doctrine of utility, founded on a still grosser misconception of the purpose of a standard of morality, and of the very meaning of the words right and wrong. It is often affirmed that utilitarianism renders men cold and unsympathising; that it chills their moral feelings towards individuals; that it makes them regard only the dry and hard consideration of the consequences of actions, not taking into their moral estimate the qualities from which those actions emanate. If the assertion means that they do not allow their judgment respecting the rightness or wrongness of an action to be influenced by their opinion of the qualities of the person who does it, this is a complaint not against utilitarianism, but against having any standard of morality at all; for certainly no known ethical standard decides an action to be good or bad because it is done by a good or a bad man, still less because done by an amiable, a brave, or a benevolent man, or the contrary. These considerations are relevant, not to the estimation of actions, but of persons; and there is nothing in the utilitarian theory inconsistent with the fact that there are other things which interest us in persons besides the rightness and wrongness of their actions. The Stoics, indeed, with the paradoxical misuse of language which was part of their system, and by which they strove to raise themselves above all concern about anything but virtue, were fond of saying that he who has that has everything; that he, and only he, is rich, is beautiful, is a king. But no claim of this description is made for the virtuous man by the utilitarian doctrine. Utilitarians are quite aware that there are other desirable possessions and qualities besides virtue, and are perfectly willing to allow to all of them their full worth. They are also aware that a right action does not necessarily indicate a virtuous character, and that actions which are blamable, often proceed from qualities entitled to praise. When this is apparent in any particular case, it modifies their estimation, not certainly of the act, but of the agent. I grant that they are, notwithstanding, of opinion, that in the long run the best proof of a good character is good actions; and resolutely refuse to consider any mental disposition as good, of which the predominant tendency is to produce bad conduct. This makes them unpopular with many people; but it is an unpopularity which they must share with every one who regards the distinction between right and wrong in a serious light; and the reproach is not one which a conscientious utilitarian need be anxious to repel.

If no more be meant by the objection than that many utilitarians look on the morality of actions, as measured by the utilitarian standard, with too exclusive a regard, and do not lay sufficient stress upon the other beauties of character which go towards making a human being lovable or admirable, this may be admitted. Utilitarians who have cultivated their moral feelings, but not their sympathies nor their artistic perceptions, do fall into this mistake; and so do all other moralists under the same conditions. What can be said in excuse for other moralists is equally available for them, namely, that, if there is to be any error, it is better that it should be on that side. As a matter of fact, we may affirm that among utilitarians as among adherents of other systems, there is every imaginable degree of rigidity and of laxity in the application of their standard: some are even puritanically rigorous, while others are as indulgent as can possibly be desired by sinner or by sentimentalist. But on the whole, a doctrine which brings prominently forward the interest that mankind have in the repression and prevention of conduct which violates the moral law, is likely to be inferior to no other in turning the sanctions of opinion again such violations. It is true, the question, What does violate the moral law? is one on which those who recognise different standards of morality are likely now and then to differ. But difference of opinion on moral questions was not first introduced into the world by utilitarianism, while that doctrine does supply, if not always an easy, at all events a tangible and intelligible mode of deciding such differences.

It may not be superfluous to notice a few more of the common misapprehensions of utilitarian ethics, even those which are so obvious and gross that it might appear impossible for any person of candour and intelligence to fall into them; since persons, even of considerable mental endowments, often give themselves so little trouble to understand the bearings of any opinion against which they entertain a prejudice, and men are in general so little conscious of this voluntary ignorance as a defect, that the vulgarest misunderstandings of ethical doctrines are continually met with in the deliberate writings of persons of the greatest pretensions both to high principle and to philosophy. We not uncommonly hear the doctrine of utility inveighed against as a *godless* doctrine. If it be necessary to say anything at all against so mere an assumption, we may say that the question depends upon what idea we have formed of the moral character of the Deity. If it be a true belief that God desires, above all things, the happiness of his creatures, and that this was his purpose in their creation, utility is not only not a godless doctrine, but more profoundly religious than any other. If it be meant that utilitarianism does not recognise the revealed will of God as the supreme law of morals, I answer, that a utilitarian who believes in the perfect goodness and wisdom of God, necessarily believes that whatever God has thought fit to reveal on the subject of morals, must fulfil the requirements of utility in a supreme degree. But others besides utilitarians have been of opinion that the Christian revelation was intended, and is fitted, to inform the hearts and minds of mankind with a spirit which should enable them to find for themselves what is right, and incline them to do it when found, rather than to tell them, except in a very general way, what it is; and that we need a doctrine of ethics, carefully followed out, to *interpret* to us the will of God. Whether this opinion is correct or not, it is superfluous here to discuss; since whatever aid religion, either natural or revealed, can afford to ethical investigation, is as open to the utilitarian moralist as to any other. He can use it as the testimony of God to the usefulness or hurtfulness of any given course of action, by as good a

right as others can use it for the indication of a transcendental law, having no connection with usefulness or with happiness.

Again, Utility is often summarily stigmatised as an immoral doctrine by giving it the name of Expediency, and taking advantage of the popular use of that term to contrast it with Principle. But the Expedient, in the sense in which it is opposed to the Right, generally means that which is expedient for the particular interest of the agent himself; as when a minister sacrifices the interests of his country to keep himself in place. When it means anything better than this, it means that which is expedient for some immediate object, some temporary purpose, but which violates a rule whose observance is expedient in a much higher degree. The Expedient, in this sense, instead of being the same thing with the useful, is a branch of the hurtful. Thus, it would often be expedient, for the purpose of getting over some momentary embarrassment, or attaining some object immediately useful to ourselves or others, to tell a lie. But inasmuch as the cultivation in ourselves of a sensitive feeling on the subject of veracity, is one of the most useful, and the enfeeblement of that feeling one of the most hurtful, things to which our conduct can be instrumental; and inasmuch as any, even unintentional, deviation from truth, does that much towards weakening the trustworthiness of human assertion, which is not only the principal support of all present social well-being, but the insufficiency of which does more than any one thing that can be named to keep back civilisation, virtue, everything on which human happiness on the largest scale depends; we feel that the violation, for a present advantage, of a rule of such transcendant expediency, is not expedient, and that he who, for the sake of a convenience to himself or to some other individual, does what depends on him to deprive mankind of the good, and inflict upon them the evil, involved in the greater or less reliance which they can place in each other's word, acts the part of one of their worst enemies. Yet that even this rule, sacred as it is, admits of possible exceptions, is acknowledged by all moralists; the chief of which is when the withholding of some fact (as of information from a malefactor, or of bad news from a person dangerously ill) would save an individual (especially an individual other than oneself) from great and unmerited evil, and when the withholding can only be effected by denial. But in order that the exception may not extend itself beyond the need, and may have the least possible effect in weakening reliance on veracity, it ought to be recognised, and, if possible, its limits defined; and if the principle of utility is good for anything, it must be good for weighing these conflicting utilities against one another, and marking out the region within which one or the other preponderates.

Again, defenders of utility often find themselves called upon to reply to such objections as this—that there is not time, previous to action, for calculating and weighing the effects of any line of conduct on the general happiness. This is exactly as if any one were to say that it is impossible to guide our conduct by Christianity, because there is not time, on every occasion on which anything has to be done, to read through the Old and New Testaments. The answer to the objection is, that there has been ample time, namely, the whole past duration of the human species. During all that time, mankind have been learning by experience the tendencies of actions; on which experience all the prudence, as well as all the morality of life, are dependent. People talk as if the commencement of this course of experience had hitherto been put off, and as if, at the moment when some man feels tempted to meddle with the property or life of another, he had to begin considering for the first time whether murder and theft are injurious to human happiness. Even then I do not think that he would find the question very puzzling; but, at all events, the matter is now done to his hand.

It is truly a whimsical supposition that, if mankind were agreed in considering utility to be the test of morality, they would remain without any agreement as to what *is* useful, and would take no measures for having their notions on the subject taught to the young, and enforced by law and opinion. There is no difficulty in proving any ethical standard whatever to work ill, if we suppose universal idiocy to be conjoined with it; but on any hypothesis short of that, mankind must by this time have acquired positive beliefs as to the effects of some actions on their happiness; and the beliefs which have thus come down are the rules of morality for the multitude, and for the philosopher until he has succeeded in finding better. That philosophers might easily do this, even now, on many subjects; that the received code of ethics is by no means of divine right; and that mankind have still much to learn as to the effects of actions on the general happi-

ness, I admit, or rather, earnestly maintain. The corollaries from the principle of utility, like the precepts of every practical art, admit of indefinite improvement, and, in a progressive state of the human mind, their improvement is perpetually going on.

But to consider the rules of morality as improvable, is one thing; to pass over the intermediate generalisations entirely, and endeavour to test each individual action directly by the first principle, is another. It is a strange notion that the acknowledgment of a first principle is inconsistent with the admission of secondary ones. To inform a traveller respecting the place of his ultimate destination, is not to forbid the use of landmarks and direction-posts on the way. The proposition that happiness is the end and aim of morality, does not mean that no road ought to be laid down to that goal, or that persons going thither should not be advised to take one direction rather than another. Men really ought to leave off talking a kind of nonsense on this subject, which they would neither talk nor listen to on other matters of practical concernment. Nobody argues that the art of navigation is not founded on astronomy, because sailors cannot wait to calculate the Nautical Almanack. Being rational creatures, they go to sea with it ready calculated; and all rational creatures go out upon the sea of life with their minds made up on the common questions of right and wrong, as well as on many of the far more difficult questions of wise and foolish. And this, as long as foresight is a human quality, it is to be presumed they will continue to do. Whatever we adopt as the fundamental principle of morality, we require subordinate principles to apply it by; the impossibility of doing without them, being common to all systems, can afford no argument against any one in particular; but gravely to argue as if no such secondary principles could be had, and as if mankind had remained till now, and always must remain, without drawing any general conclusions from the experience of human life, is as high a pitch, I think, as absurdity has ever reached in philosophical controversy.

The remainder of the stock arguments against utilitarianism mostly consist in laying to its charge the common infirmities of human nature, and the general difficulties which embarrass conscientious persons in shaping their course through life. We are told that a utilitarian will be apt to make his own particular case an exception to moral rules, and, when under temptation, will see a utility in the breach of a rule, greater than he will see in its observance. But is utility the only creed which is able to furnish us with excuses for evil doing, and means of cheating our own conscience? They are afforded in abundance by all doctrines which recognise as a fact in morals the existence of conflicting considerations; which all doctrines do, that have been believed by sane persons. It is not the fault of any creed, but of the complicated nature of human affairs, that rules of conduct cannot be so framed as to require no exceptions, and that hardly any kind of action can safely be laid down as either always obligatory or always condemnable. There is no ethical creed which does not temper the rigidity of its laws, by giving a certain latitude, under the moral responsibility of the agent, for accommodation to peculiarities of circumstances; and under every creed, at the opening thus made, self-deception and dishonest casuistry get in. There exists no moral system under which there do not arise unequivocal cases of conflicting obligation. These are the real difficulties, the knotty points both in the theory of ethics, and in the conscientious guidance of personal conduct. They are overcome practically, with greater or with less success, according to the intellect and virtue of the individual; but it can hardly be pretended that any one will be the less qualified for dealing with them, from possessing an ultimate standard to which conflicting rights and duties can be referred. If utility is the ultimate source of moral obligations, utility may be invoked to decide between them when their demands are incompatible. Though the application of the standard may be difficult, it is better than none at all: while in other systems, the moral laws all claiming independent authority, there is no common umpire entitled to interfere between them; their claims to precedence one over another rest on little better than sophistry, and unless determined, as they generally are, by the unacknowledged influence of considerations of utility, afford a free scope for the action of personal desires and partialities. We must remember that only in these cases of conflict between secondary principles is it requisite that first principles should be appealed to. There is no case of moral obligation in which some secondary principle is not involved; and if only one, there can seldom be any real doubt which one it is, in the mind of any person by whom the principle itself is recognised.

Chapter 3

Of the Ultimate Sanction of the Principle of Utility

THE QUESTION is often asked, and properly so, in regard to any supposed moral standard—What is its sanction? what are the motives to obey it? or more specifically, what is the source of its obligation? whence does it derive its binding force? It is a necessary part of moral philosophy to provide the answer to this question; which, though frequently assuming the shape of an objection to the utilitarian morality, as if it had some special applicability to that above others, really arises in regard to all standards. It arises, in fact, whenever a person is called on to *adopt* a standard, or refer morality to any basis on which he has not been accustomed to rest it. For the customary morality, that which education and opinion have consecrated, is the only one which presents itself to the mind with the feeling of being *in itself* obligatory; and when a person is asked to believe that this morality *derives* its obligation from some general principle round which custom has not thrown the same halo, the assertion is to him a paradox; the supposed corollaries seem to have a more binding force than the original theorem; the superstructure seems to stand better without, than with, what is represented as its foundation. He says to himself, I feel that I am bound not to rob or murder, betray or deceive; but why am I bound to promote the general happiness? If my own happiness lies in something else, why may I not give that the preference?

If the view adopted by the utilitarian philosophy of the nature of the moral sense be correct, this difficulty will always present itself, until the influences which form moral character have taken the same hold of the principle which they have taken of some of the consequences—until, by the improvement of education, the feeling of unity with our fellow-creatures shall be (what it cannot be denied that Christ intended it to be) as deeply rooted in our character, and to our own consciousness as completely a part of our nature, as the horror of crime is in an ordinarily well brought up young person. In the meantime, however, the difficulty has no peculiar application to the doctrine of utility, but is inherent in every attempt to analyse morality and reduce it to principles; which, unless the principle is already in men's minds invested with as much sacredness as any of its applications, always seems to divest them of a part of their sanctity.

The principle of utility either has, or there is no reason why it might not have, all the sanctions which belong to any other system of morals. Those sanctions are either external or internal. Of the external sanctions it is not necessary to speak at any length. They are, the hope of favour and the fear of displeasure, from our fellow creatures or from the Ruler of the Universe, along with whatever we may have of sympathy or affection for them, or of love and awe of Him, inclining us to do his will independently of selfish consequences. There is evidently no reason why all these motives for observance should not attach themselves to the utilitarian morality, as completely and as powerfully as to any other. Indeed, those of them which refer to our fellow creatures are sure to do so, in proportion to the amount of general intelligence; for whether there be any other ground of moral obligation than the general happiness or not, men do desire happiness; and however imperfect may be their own practice, they desire and commend all conduct in others towards themselves, by which they think their happiness is promoted. With regard to the religious motive, if men believe, as most profess to do, in the goodness of God, those who think that conduciveness to the general happiness is the essence, or even only the criterion of good, must necessarily believe that it is also that which God approves. The whole force therefore of external reward and punishment, whether physical or moral, and whether proceeding from God or from our fellow men, together with all that the capacities of human nature admit of disinterested devotion to either, become available to enforce the utilitarian morality, in proportion as that morality is recognised; and the more powerfully, the more the appliances of education and general cultivation are bent to the purpose.

So far as to external sanctions. The internal sanction of duty, whatever our standard of duty may be, is one and the same—a feeling in our own mind; a pain, more or less intense, attendant on violation of duty, which in properly cultivated moral natures rises, in the more serious cases, into shrinking from it as an impossibility. This feeling, when disinterested, and connecting itself with the pure idea of duty, and not with some particular form of it, or with any of the merely accessory circumstances, is the essence of Conscience; though

in that complex phenomenon as it actually exists, the simple fact is in general all encrusted over with collateral associations, derived from sympathy, from love, and still more from fear; from all the forms of religious feeling; from the recollections of childhood and of all our past life; from self-esteem, desire of the esteem of others, and occasionally even self-abasement. This extreme complication is, I apprehend, the origin of the sort of mystical character which, by a tendency of the human mind of which there are many other examples, is apt to be attributed to the idea of moral obligation, and which leads people to believe that the idea cannot possibly attach itself to any other objects than those which, by a supposed mysterious law, are found in our present experience to excite it. Its binding force, however, consists in the existence of a mass of feeling which must be broken through in order to do what violates our standard of right, and which, if we do nevertheless violate that standard, will probably have to be encountered afterwards in the form of remorse. Whatever theory we have of the nature or origin of conscience, this is what essentially constitutes it.

The ultimate sanction, therefore, of all morality (external motives apart) being a subjective feeling in our own minds, I see nothing embarrassing to those whose standard is utility, in the question, what is the sanction of that particular standard? We may answer, the same as of all other moral standards—the conscientious feelings of mankind. Undoubtedly this sanction has no binding efficacy on those who do not possess the feelings it appeals to; but neither will these persons be more obedient to any other moral principle than to the utilitarian one. On them morality of any kind has no hold but through the external sanctions. Meanwhile the feelings exist, a fact in human nature, the reality of which, and the great power with which they are capable of acting on those in whom they have been duly cultivated, are proved by experience. No reason has ever been shown why they may not be cultivated to as great intensity in connection with the utilitarian, as with any other rule of morals.

There is, I am aware, a disposition to believe that a person who sees in moral obligation a transcendental fact, an objective reality belonging to the province of "Things in themselves," is likely to be more obedient to it than one who believes it to be entirely subjective, having its seat in human consciousness only. But whatever a person's opinion may be on this point of Ontology, the force he is really urged by is his own subjective feeling, and is exactly measured by its strength. No one's belief that duty is an objective reality is stronger than the belief that God is so; yet the belief in God, apart from the expectation of actual reward and punishment, only operates on conduct through, and in proportion to, the subjective religious feeling. The sanction, so far as it is disinterested, is always in the mind itself; and the notion therefore of the transcendental moralists must be, that this sanction will not exist *in* the mind unless it is believed to have its root out of the mind; and that if a person is able to say to himself, This which is restraining me, and which is called my conscience, is only a feeling in my own mind, he may possibly draw the conclusion that when the feeling ceases the obligation ceases, and that if he find the feeling inconvenient, he may disregard it, and endeavour to get rid of it. But is this danger confined to the utilitarian morality? Does the belief that moral obligation has its seat outside the mind make the feeling of it too strong to be got rid of? The fact is so far otherwise, that all moralists admit and lament the ease with which, in the generality of minds, conscience can be silenced or stifled. The question, Need I obey my conscience? is quite as often put to themselves by persons who never heard of the principle of utility, as by its adherents. Those whose conscientious feelings are so weak as to allow of their asking this question, if they answer it affirmatively, will not do so because they believe in the transcendental theory, but because of the external sanctions.

It is not necessary, for the present purpose, to decide whether the feeling of duty is innate or implanted. Assuming it to be innate, it is an open question to what objects it naturally attaches itself; for the philosophic supporters of that theory are now agreed that the intuitive perception is of principles of morality and not of the details. If there be anything innate in the matter, I see no reason why the feeling which is innate should not be that of regard to the pleasures and pains of others. If there is any principle of morals which is intuitively obligatory, I should say it must be that. If so, the intuitive ethics would coincide with the utilitarian, and there would be no further quarrel between them. Even as it is, the intuitive moralists, though they believe that there are other intuitive moral obligations, do already believe this to be one; for they unanimously hold that a large *portion* of morality turns upon the consideration due to the interests of our fellow-creatures. Therefore, if the belief in the transcendental origin of moral obligation gives any additional efficacy to the internal sanction, it appears to me that the utilitarian principle has already the benefit of it.

On the other hand, if, as is my own belief, the moral feelings are not innate, but acquired, they are not for that reason the less natural. It is natural to man to speak, to reason, to build cities, to cultivate the ground, though these are acquired faculties. The moral feelings are not indeed a part of our nature, in the sense of being in any perceptible degree present in all of us; but this, unhappily, is a fact admitted by those who believe the most strenuously in their transcendental origin. Like the other acquired capacities above referred to, the moral faculty, if not a part of our nature, is a natural outgrowth from it; capable, like them, in a certain small degree, of springing up spontaneously; and susceptible of being brought by cultivation to a high degree of development. Unhappily it is also susceptible, by a sufficient use of the external sanctions and of the force of early impressions, of being cultivated in almost any direction: so that there is hardly anything so absurd or so mischievous that it may not, by means of these influences, be made to act on the human mind with all the authority of conscience. To doubt that the same potency might be given by the same means to the principle of utility, even if it had no foundation in human nature, would be flying in the face of all experience.

But moral associations which are wholly of artificial creation, when intellectual culture goes on, yield by degrees to the dissolving force of analysis: and if the feeling of duty, when associated with utility, would appear equally arbitrary; if there were no leading department of our nature, no powerful class of sentiments, with which that association would harmonise, which would make us feel it congenial, and incline us not only to foster it in others (for which we have abundant interested motives), but also to cherish it in ourselves; if there were not, in short, a natural basis of sentiment for utilitarian morality, it might well happen that this association also, even after it had been implanted by education, might be analysed away.

But there *is* this basis of powerful natural sentiment; and this it is which, when once the general happiness is recognised as the ethical standard, will constitute the strength of the utilitarian morality. This firm foundation is that of the social feelings of mankind; the desire to be in unity with our fellow creatures, which is already a powerful principle in human nature, and happily one of those which tend to become stronger, even without express inculcation, from the influences of advancing civilisation. The social state is at once so natural, so necessary, and so habitual to man, that, except in some unusual circumstances or by an effort of voluntary abstraction, he never conceives himself otherwise than as a member of a body; and this association is riveted more and more, as mankind are further removed from the state of savage independence. Any condition, therefore, which is essential to a state of society, becomes more and more an inseparable part of every person's conception of the state of things which he is born into, and which is the destiny of a human being.

Now, society between human beings, except in the relation of master and slave, is manifestly impossible on any other footing than that the interests of all are to be consulted. Society between equals can only exist on the understanding that the interests of all are to be regarded equally. And since in all states of civilisation, every person, except an absolute monarch, has equals, every one is obliged to live on these terms with somebody; and in every age some advance is made towards a state in which it will be impossible to live permanently on other terms with anybody. In this way people grow up unable to conceive as possible to them a state of total disregard of other people's interests. They are under a necessity of conceiving themselves as at least abstaining from all the grosser injuries, and (if only for their own protection) living in a state of constant protest against them. They are also familiar with the fact of co-operating with others and proposing to themselves a collective, not an individual interest as the aim (at least for the time being) of their actions. So long as they are co-operating, their ends are identified with those of others; there is at least a temporary feeling that the interests of others are their own interests. Not only does all strengthening of social ties, and all healthy growth of society, give to each individual a stronger personal interest in practically consulting the welfare of others; it also leads him to identify his *feelings* more and more with their good, or at least with an even greater degree of practical consideration for it. He comes, as though instinctively, to be conscious of himself as a being who *of course* pays regard to others. The good of others becomes to him a thing naturally and necessarily to be attended to, like any of the physical conditions of our existence. Now, whatever amount of this feeling a person has, he is urged by the strongest motives both of interest and of sympathy to demonstrate it, and to the utmost of his power encourage it in others; and even if he has none of it himself, he is as greatly interested as any one else that others should have it. Consequently the smallest germs of the feeling are laid hold of and nourished by the contagion of sympathy and the influences of education; and a complete web of corroborative association is woven round it, by the powerful agency of the external sanctions.

This mode of conceiving ourselves and human life, as civilisation goes on, is felt to be more and more natural. Every step in political improvement renders it more so, by removing the sources of opposition of interest, and levelling those inequalities of legal privilege between individuals or classes, owing to which there are large portions of mankind whose happiness it is still practicable to disregard. In an improving state of the human mind, the influences are constantly on the increase, which tend to generate in each individual a feeling of unity with all the rest; which, if perfect, would make him never think of, or desire, any beneficial condition for himself, in the benefits of which they are not included. If we now suppose this feeling of unity to be taught as a religion, and the whole force of education, of institutions, and of opinion, directed, as it once was in the case of religion, to make every person grow up from infancy surrounded on all sides both by the profession and the practice of it, I think that no one, who can realise this conception, will feel any misgiving about the sufficiency of the ultimate sanction for the Happiness morality. To any ethical student who finds the realisation difficult, I recommend, as a means of facilitating it, the second of M. Comte's two principal works, the *Traité de Politique Positive*. I entertain the strongest objections to the system of politics and morals set forth in that treatise; but I think it has superabundantly shown the possibility of giving to the service of humanity, even without the aid of belief in a Providence, both the psychological power and the social efficacy of a religion; making it take hold of human life, and colour all thought, feeling, and action, in a manner of which the greatest ascendancy ever exercised by any religion may be but a type and foretaste; and of which the danger is, not that it should be insufficient, but that it should be so excessive as to interfere unduly with human freedom and individuality.

Neither is it necessary to the feeling which constitutes the binding force of the utilitarian morality on those who recognise it, to wait for those social influences which would make its obligation felt by mankind at large. In the comparatively early state of human advancement in which we now live, a person cannot indeed feel that entireness of sympathy with all others, which would make any real discordance in the general direction of their conduct in life impossible; but already a person in whom the social feeling is at all developed, cannot bring himself to think of the rest of his fellow creatures as struggling rivals with him for the means of happiness, whom he must desire to see defeated in their object in order that he may succeed in his. The deeply rooted conception which every individual even now has of himself as a social being, tends to make him feel it one of his natural wants that there should be harmony between his feelings and aims and those of his fellow creatures. If differences of opinion and of mental culture make it impossible for him to share many of their actual feelings—perhaps make him denounce and defy those feelings—he still needs to be conscious that his real aim and theirs do not conflict; that he is not opposing himself to what they really wish for, namely their own good, but is, on the contrary, promoting it. This feeling in most individuals is much inferior in strength to their selfish feelings, and is often wanting altogether. But to those who have it, it possesses all the characters of a natural feeling. It does not present itself to their minds as a superstition of education, or a law despotically imposed by the power of society, but as an attribute which it would not be well for them to be without. This conviction is the ultimate sanction of the greatest happiness morality. This it is which makes any mind, of well-developed feelings, work with, and not against, the outward motives to care for others, afforded by what I have called the external sanctions; and when those sanctions are wanting, or act in an opposite direction, constitutes in itself a powerful internal binding force, in proportion to the sensitiveness and thoughtfulness of the character; since few but those whose mind is a moral blank, could bear to lay out their course of life on the plan of paying no regard to others except so far as their own private interest compels.

Chapter 4
Of what sort of Proof the Principle of Utility is Susceptible

IT HAS already been remarked, that questions of ultimate ends do not admit of proof, in the ordinary acceptation of the term. To be incapable of proof by reasoning is common to all first principles; to the first premises of our knowledge, as well as to those of our conduct. But the former, being matters of fact, may be the subject of a direct appeal to the faculties which judge of fact—namely, our senses, and our internal consciousness. Can an appeal be made to the same faculties on questions of practical ends? Or by what other faculty is cognisance taken of them?

Questions about ends are, in other words, questions what things are desirable. The utilitarian doctrine is, that happiness is desirable, and the only thing desirable, as an end; all other things being only desirable as means to that end. What ought to be required of this doctrine—what conditions is it requisite that the doctrine should fulfil—to make good its claim to be believed?

The only proof capable of being given that an object is visible, is that people actually see it. The only proof that a sound is audible, is that people hear it: and so of the other sources of our experience. In like manner, I apprehend, the sole evidence it is possible to produce that anything is desirable, is that people do actually desire it. If the end which the utilitarian doctrine proposes to itself were not, in theory and in practice, acknowledged to be an end, nothing could ever convince any person that it was so. No reason can be given why the general happiness is desirable, except that each person, so far as he believes it to be attainable, desires his own happiness. This, however, being a fact, we have not only all the proof which the case admits of, but all which it is possible to require, that happiness is a good: that each person's happiness is a good to that person, and the general happiness, therefore, a good to the aggregate of all persons. Happiness has made out its title as *one* of the ends of conduct, and consequently one of the criteria of morality.

But it has not, by this alone, proved itself to be the sole criterion. To do that, it would seem, by the same rule, necessary to show, not only that people desire happiness, but that they never desire anything else. Now it is palpable that they do desire things which, in common language, are decidedly distinguished from happiness. They desire, for example, virtue, and the absence of vice, no less really than pleasure and the absence of pain. The desire of virtue is not as universal, but it is as authentic a fact, as the desire of happiness. And hence the opponents of the utilitarian standard deem that they have a right to infer that there are other ends of human action besides happiness, and that happiness is not the standard of approbation and disapprobation.

But does the utilitarian doctrine deny that people desire virtue, or maintain that virtue is not a thing to be desired? The very reverse. It maintains not only that virtue is to be desired, but that it is to be desired disinterestedly, for itself. Whatever may be the opinion of utilitarian moralists as to the original conditions by which virtue is made virtue; however they may believe (as they do) that actions and dispositions are only virtuous because they promote another end than virtue; yet this being granted, and it having been decided, from considerations of this description, what *is* virtuous, they not only place virtue at the very head of the things which are good as means to the ultimate end, but they also recognise as a psychological fact the possibility of its being, to the individual, a good in itself, without looking to any end beyond it; and hold, that the mind is not in a right state, not in a state conformable to Utility, not in the state most conducive to the general happiness, unless it does love virtue in this manner—as a thing desirable in itself, even although, in the individual instance, it should not produce those other desirable consequences which it tends to produce, and on account of which it is held to be virtue. This opinion is not, in the smallest degree, a departure from the Happiness principle. The ingredients of happiness are very various, and each of them is desirable in itself, and not merely when considered as swelling an aggregate. The principle of utility does not mean that any given pleasure, as music, for instance, or any given exemption from pain, as for example health, is to be looked upon as means to a collective something termed happi-

ness, and to be desired on that account. They are desired and desirable in and for themselves; besides being means, they are a part of the end. Virtue, according to the utilitarian doctrine, is not naturally and originally part of the end, but it is capable of becoming so; and in those who love it disinterestedly it has become so, and is desired and cherished, not as a means to happiness, but as a part of their happiness.

To illustrate this farther, we may remember that virtue is not the only thing, originally a means, and which if it were not a means to anything else, would be and remain indifferent, but which by association with what it is a means to, comes to be desired for itself, and that too with the utmost intensity. What, for example, shall we say of the love of money? There is nothing originally more desirable about money than about any heap of glittering pebbles. Its worth is solely that of the things which it will buy; the desires for other things than itself, which it is a means of gratifying. Yet the love of money is not only one of the strongest moving forces of human life, but money is, in many cases, desired in and for itself; the desire to possess it is often stronger than the desire to use it, and goes on increasing when all the desires which point to ends beyond it, to be compassed by it, are falling off. It may, then, be said truly, that money is desired not for the sake of an end, but as part of the end. From being a means to happiness, it has come to be itself a principal ingredient of the individual's conception of happiness. The same may be said of the majority of the great objects of human life—power, for example, or fame; except that to each of these there is a certain amount of immediate pleasure annexed, which has at least the semblance of being naturally inherent in them; a thing which cannot be said of money. Still, however, the strongest natural attraction, both of power and of fame, is the immense aid they give to the attainment of our other wishes; and it is the strong association thus generated between them and all our objects of desire, which gives to the direct desire of them the intensity it often assumes, so as in some characters to surpass in strength all other desires. In these cases the means have become a part of the end, and a more important part of it than any of the things which they are means to. What was once desired as an instrument for the attainment of happiness, has come to be desired for its own sake. In being desired for its own sake it is, however, desired as *part* of happiness. The person is made, or thinks he would be made, happy by its mere possession; and is made unhappy by failure to obtain it. The desire of it is not a different thing from the desire of happiness, any more than the love of music, or the desire of health. They are included in happiness. They are some of the elements of which the desire of happiness is made up. Happiness is not an abstract idea, but a concrete whole; and these are some of its parts. And the utilitarian standard sanctions and approves their being so. Life would be a poor thing, very ill provided with sources of happiness, if there were not this provision of nature, by which things originally indifferent, but conducive to, or otherwise associated with, the satisfaction of our primitive desires, become in themselves sources of pleasure more valuable than the primitive pleasures, both in permanency, in the space of human existence that they are capable of covering, and even in intensity.

Virtue, according to the utilitarian conception, is a good of this description. There was no original desire of it, or motive to it, save its conduciveness to pleasure, and especially to protection from pain. But through the association thus formed, it may be felt a good in itself, and desired as such with as great intensity as any other good; and with this difference between it and the love of money, of power, or of fame, that all of these may, and often do, render the individual noxious to the other members of the society to which he belongs, whereas there is nothing which makes him so much a blessing to them as the cultivation of the disinterested love of virtue. And consequently, the utilitarian standard, while it tolerates and approves those other acquired desires, up to the point beyond which they would be more injurious to the general happiness than promotive of it, enjoins and requires the cultivation of the love of virtue up to the greatest strength possible, as being above all things important to the general happiness.

It results from the preceding considerations, that there is in reality nothing desired except happiness. Whatever is desired otherwise than as a means to some end beyond itself, and ultimately to happiness, is desired as itself a part of happiness, and is not desired for itself until it has become so. Those who desire virtue for its own sake, desire it either because the consciousness of it is a pleasure, or because the consciousness of being without it is a pain, or

for both reasons united; as in truth the pleasure and pain seldom exist separately, but almost always together, the same person feeling pleasure in the degree of virtue attained, and pain in not having attained more. If one of these gave him no pleasure, and the other no pain, he would not love or desire virtue, or would desire it only for the other benefits which it might produce to himself or to persons whom he cared for.

We have now, then, an answer to the question, of what sort of proof the principle of utility is susceptible. If the opinion which I have now stated is psychologically true—if human nature is so constituted as to desire nothing which is not either a part of happiness or a means of happiness, we can have no other proof, and we require no other, that these are the only things desirable. If so, happiness is the sole end of human action, and the promotion of it the test by which to judge of all human conduct; from whence it necessarily follows that it must be the criterion of morality, since a part is included in the whole.

And now to decide whether this is really so; whether mankind do desire nothing for itself but that which is a pleasure to them, or of which the absence is a pain; we have evidently arrived at a question of fact and experience, dependent, like all similar questions, upon evidence. It can only be determined by practised self-consciousness and self-observation, assisted by observation of others. I believe that these sources of evidence, impartially consulted, will declare that desiring a thing and finding it pleasant, aversion to it and thinking of it as painful, are phenomena entirely inseparable, or rather two parts of the same phenomenon; in strictness of language, two different modes of naming the same psychological fact: that to think of an object as desirable (unless for the sake of its consequences), and to think of it as pleasant, are one and the same thing; and that to desire anything, except in proportion as the idea of it is pleasant, is a physical and metaphysical impossibility.

So obvious does this appear to me, that I expect it will hardly be disputed: and the objection made will be, not that desire can possibly be directed to anything ultimately except pleasure and exemption from pain, but that the will is a different thing from desire; that a person of confirmed virtue, or any other person whose purposes are fixed, carries out his purposes without any thought of the pleasure he has in contemplating them, or expects to derive from their fulfilment; and persists in acting on them, even though these pleasures are much diminished, by changes in his character or decay of his passive sensibilities, or are outweighed by the pains which the pursuit of the purposes may bring upon him. All this I fully admit, and have stated it elsewhere, as positively and emphatically as any one. Will, the active phenomenon, is a different thing from desire, the state of passive sensibility, and though originally an offshoot from it, may in time take root and detach itself from the parent stock; so much so, that in the case of an habitual purpose, instead of willing the thing because we desire it, we often desire it only because we will it. This, however, is but an instance of that familiar fact, the power of habit, and is nowise confined to the case of virtuous actions. Many indifferent things, which men originally did from a motive of some sort, they continue to do from habit. Sometimes this is done unconsciously, the consciousness coming only after the action: at other times with conscious volition, but volition which has become habitual, and is put in operation by the force of habit, in opposition perhaps to the deliberate preference, as often happens with those who have contracted habits of vicious or hurtful indulgence.

Third and last comes the case in which the habitual act of will in the individual instance is not in contradiction to the general intention prevailing at other times, but in fulfilment of it; as in the case of the person of confirmed virtue, and of all who pursue deliberately and consistently any determinate end. The distinction between will and desire thus understood is an authentic and highly important psychological fact; but the fact consists solely in this—that will, like all other parts of our constitution, is amenable to habit, and that we may will from habit what we no longer desire for itself, or desire only because we will it. It is not the less true that will, in the beginning, is entirely produced by desire; including in that term the repelling influence of pain as well as the attractive one of pleasure. Let us take into consideration, no longer the person who has a confirmed will to do right, but him in whom that virtuous will is still feeble, conquerable by temptation, and not to be fully relied on; by what means can it be strengthened? How can the will to be virtuous, where it does not exist in sufficient force, be implanted or awakened? Only by making the person *desire* virtue—by making him think of

it in a pleasurable light, or of its absence in a painful one. It is by associating the doing right with pleasure, or the doing wrong with pain, or by eliciting and impressing and bringing home to the person's experience the pleasure naturally involved in the one or the pain in the other, that it is possible to call forth that will to be virtuous, which, when confirmed, acts without any thought of either pleasure or pain. Will is the child of desire, and passes out of the dominion of its parent only to come under that of habit. That which is the result of habit affords no presumption of being intrinsically good; and there would be no reason for wishing that the purpose of virtue should become independent of pleasure and pain, were it not that the influence of the pleasurable and painful associations which prompt to virtue is not sufficiently to be depended on for unerring constancy of action until it has acquired the support of habit. Both in feeling and in conduct, habit is the only thing which imparts certainty; and it is because of the importance to others of being able to rely absolutely on one's feelings and conduct, and to oneself of being able to rely on one's own, that the will to do right ought to be cultivated into this habitual independence. In other words, this state of the will is a means to good, not intrinsically a good; and does not contradict the doctrine that nothing is a good to human beings but in so far as it is either itself pleasurable, or a means of attaining pleasure or averting pain.

But if this doctrine be true, the principle of utility is proved. Whether it is so or not, must now be left to the consideration of the thoughtful reader.

Chapter 5
On the Connection between Justice and Utility

IN ALL ages of speculation, one of the strongest obstacles to the reception of the doctrine that Utility or Happiness is the criterion of right and wrong, has been drawn from the idea of Justice. The powerful sentiment, and apparently clear perception, which that word recalls with a rapidity and certainty resembling an instinct, have seemed to the majority of thinkers to point to an inherent quality in things; to show that the Just must have an existence in Nature as something absolute, generically distinct from every variety of the Expedient, and, in idea, opposed to it, though (as is commonly acknowledged) never, in the long run, disjoined from it in fact.

In the case of this, as of our other moral sentiments, there is no necessary connection between the question of its origin, and that of its binding force. That a feeling is bestowed on us by Nature, does not necessarily legitimate all its promptings. The feeling of justice might be a peculiar instinct, and might yet require, like our other instincts, to be controlled and enlightened by a higher reason. If we have intellectual instincts, leading us to judge in a particular way, as well as animal instincts that prompt us to act in a particular way, there is no necessity that the former should be more infallible in their sphere than the latter in theirs: it may as well happen that wrong judgments are occasionally suggested by those, as wrong actions by these. But though it is one thing to believe that we have natural feelings of justice, and another to acknowledge them as an ultimate criterion of conduct, these two opinions are very closely connected in point of fact. Mankind are always predisposed to believe that any subjective feeling, not otherwise accounted for, is a revelation of some objective reality. Our present object is to determine whether the reality, to which the feeling of justice corresponds, is one which needs any such special revelation; whether the justice or injustice of an action is a thing intrinsically peculiar, and distinct from all its other qualities, or only a combination of certain of those qualities, presented under a peculiar aspect. For the purpose of this inquiry it is practically important to consider whether the feeling itself, of justice and injustice, is *sui generis* like our sensations of colour and taste, or a derivative feeling, formed by a combination of others. And this it is the more essential to examine, as people are in general willing enough to allow, that objectively the dictates of Justice coincide with a part of the field of General Expediency; but inasmuch as the subjective mental feeling of Justice is different from that which commonly attaches to simple expediency, and, except in the extreme cases of the latter, is far more imperative in its demands, people find it difficult to see, in Justice, only a particular kind or branch of general utility, and think that its superior binding force requires a totally different origin.

To throw light upon this question, it is necessary to attempt to ascertain what is the distinguishing character of justice, or of injustice: what is the quality, or whether there is any

quality, attributed in common to all modes of conduct designated as unjust (for justice, like many other moral attributes, is best defined by its opposite), and distinguishing them from such modes of conduct as are disapproved, but without having that particular epithet of disapprobation applied to them. If in everything which men are accustomed to characterise as just or unjust, some one common attribute or collection of attributes is always present, we may judge whether this particular attribute or combination of attributes would be capable of gathering round it a sentiment of that peculiar character and intensity by virtue of the general laws of our emotional constitution, or whether the sentiment is inexplicable, and requires to be regarded as a special provision of Nature. If we find the former to be the case, we shall, in resolving this question, have resolved also the main problem: if the latter, we shall have to seek for some other mode of investigating it.

To find the common attributes of a variety of objects, it is necessary to begin by surveying the objects themselves in the concrete. Let us therefore advert successively to the various modes of action, and arrangements of human affairs, which are classed, by universal or widely spread opinion, as Just or as Unjust. The things well known to excite the sentiments associated with those names are of a very multifarious character. I shall pass them rapidly in review, without studying any particular arrangement.

In the first place, it is mostly considered unjust to deprive any one of his personal liberty, his property, or any other thing which belongs to him by law. Here, therefore, is one instance of the application of the terms just and unjust in a perfectly definite sense, namely, that it is just to respect, unjust to violate, the *legal rights* of any one. But this judgment admits of several exceptions, arising from the other forms in which the notions of justice and injustice present themselves. For example, the person who suffers the deprivation may (as the phrase is) have *forfeited* the rights which he is so deprived of: a case to which we shall return presently. But also,

Secondly; the legal rights of which he is deprived, may be rights which *ought* not to have belonged to him; in other words, the law which confers on him these rights, may be a bad law. When it is so, or when (which is the same thing for our purpose) it is supposed to be so, opinions will differ as to the justice or injustice of infringing it. Some maintain that no law, however bad, ought to be disobeyed by an individual citizen; that his opposition to it, if shown at all, should only be shown in endeavouring to get it altered by competent authority. This opinion (which condemns many of the most illustrious benefactors of mankind, and would often protect pernicious institutions against the only weapons which, in the state of things existing at the time, have any chance of succeeding against them) is defended, by those who hold it, on grounds of expediency; principally on that of the importance, to the common interest of mankind, of maintaining inviolate the sentiment of submission to law. Other persons, again, hold the directly contrary opinion, that any law, judged to be bad, may blamelessly be disobeyed, even though it be not judged to be unjust, but only inexpedient; while others would confine the licence of disobedience to the case of unjust laws: but again, some say, that all laws which are inexpedient are unjust; since every law imposes some restriction on the natural liberty of mankind, which restriction is an injustice, unless legitimated by tending to their good. Among these diversities of opinion, it seems to be universally admitted that there may be unjust laws, and that law, consequently, is not the ultimate criterion of justice, but may give to one person a benefit, or impose on another an evil, which justice condemns. When, however, a law is thought to be unjust, it seems always to be regarded as being so in the same way in which a breach of law is unjust, namely, by infringing somebody's right; which, as it cannot in this case be a legal right, receives a different appellation, and is called a moral right. We may say, therefore, that a second case of injustice consists in taking or withholding from any person that to which he has a *moral right*.

Thirdly, it is universally considered just that each person should obtain that (whether good or evil) which he *deserves;* and unjust that he should obtain a good, or be made to undergo an evil, which he does not deserve. This is, perhaps, the clearest and most emphatic form in which the idea of justice is conceived by the general mind. As it involves the notion of desert, the question arises, what constitutes desert? Speaking in a general way, a person is understood to deserve good if he does right, evil if he does wrong; and in a more particular sense, to deserve good from those to whom he does or has done good, and evil from those to whom he does or has done evil. The precept of returning good for evil has never been regarded as a case of the fulfilment of justice, but as one in which the claims of justice are waived, in obedience to other considerations.

Fourthly, it is confessedly unjust to *break faith* with any one: to violate an engagement, either express or implied, or disappoint expectations raised by our own conduct, at least if we have raised those expectations knowingly and voluntarily. Like the other obligations of justice already spoken of, this one is not regarded as absolute, but as capable of being overruled by a stronger obligation of justice on the other side; or by such conduct on the part of the person concerned as is deemed to absolve us from our obligation to him, and to constitute a *forfeiture* of the benefit which he has been led to expect.

Fifthly, it is, by universal admission, inconsistent with justice to be *partial;* to show favour or preference to one person over another, in matters to which favour and preference do not properly apply. Impartiality, however, does not seem to be regarded as a duty in itself, but rather as instrumental to some other duty; for it is admitted that favour and preference are not always censurable, and indeed the cases in which they are condemned are rather the exception than the rule. A person would be more likely to be blamed than applauded for giving his family or friends no superiority in good offices over strangers, when he could do so without violating any other duty; and no one thinks it unjust to seek one person in preference to another as a friend, connection, or companion. Impartiality where rights are concerned is of course obligatory, but this is involved in the more general obligation of giving to every one his right. A tribunal, for example, must be impartial, because it is bound to award, without regard to any other consideration, a disputed object to the one of two parties who has the right to it. There are other cases in which impartiality means, being solely influenced by desert; as with those who, in the capacity of judges, preceptors, or parents, administer reward and punishment as such. There are cases, again, in which it means, being solely influenced by consideration for the public interest; as in making a selection among candidates for a government employment. Impartiality, in short, as an obligation of justice, may be said to mean, being exclusively influenced by the considerations which it is supposed ought to influence the particular case in hand; and resisting the solicitation of any motives which prompt to conduct different from what those considerations would dictate.

Nearly allied to the idea of impartiality is that of *equality;* which often enters as a component part both into the conception of justice and into the practice of it, and, in the eyes of many persons, constitutes its essence. But in this, still more than in any other case, the notion of justice varies in different persons, and always conforms in its variations to their notion of utility. Each person maintains that equality is the dictate of justice, except where he thinks that expediency requires inequality. The justice of giving equal protection to the rights of all, is maintained by those who support the most outrageous inequality in the rights themselves. Even in slave countries it is theoretically admitted that the rights of the slave, such as they are, ought to be as sacred as those of the master; and that a tribunal which fails to enforce them with equal strictness is wanting in justice; while, at the same time, institutions which leave to the slave scarcely any rights to enforce, are not deemed unjust, because they are not deemed inexpedient. Those who think that utility requires distinctions of rank, do not consider it unjust that riches and social privileges should be unequally dispensed; but those who think this inequality inexpedient, think it unjust also. Whoever thinks that government is necessary, sees no injustice in as much inequality as is constituted by giving to the magistrate powers not granted to other people. Even among those who hold levelling doctrines, there are as many questions of justice as there are differences of opinion about expediency. Some Communists consider it unjust that the produce of the labour of the community should be shared on any other principle than that of exact equality; others think it just that those should receive most whose wants are greatest; while others hold that those who work harder, or who produce more, or whose services are more valuable to the community, may justly claim a larger quota in the division of the produce. And the sense of natural justice may be plausibly appealed to in behalf of every one of these opinions.

Among so many diverse applications of the term Justice, which yet is not regarded as ambiguous, it is a matter of some difficulty to seize the mental link which holds them together, and on which the moral sentiment adhering to the term essentially depends. Perhaps, in this embarrassment, some help may be derived from the history of the word, as indicated by its etymology.

In most, if not in all, languages, the etymology of the word which corresponds to Just, points distinctly to an origin connected with the ordinances of law. *Justum* is a form of *jussum,* that which has been ordered. Δικαιον comes directly from δικη, a suit at law. *Recht,* from which came *right* and *righteous,* is synonymous with law. The courts of justice, the administration of justice, are the courts and the administration of law. *La justice,* in French, is the established term for judicature. I am not committing the fallacy imputed with some show of truth to Horne Tooke, of assuming that a word must still continue to mean what it originally meant. Etymology is slight evidence of what the idea now signified is, but the very best evidence of how it sprang up. There can, I think, be no doubt that the *idée mère,* the primitive element, in the formation of the notion of justice, was conformity to law. It constituted the entire idea among the Hebrews, up to the birth of Christianity; as might be expected in the case of a people whose laws attempted to embrace all subjects on which precepts were required, and who believed those laws to be a direct emanation from the Supreme Being. But other nations, and in particular the Greeks and Romans, who knew that their laws had been made originally, and still continued to be made, by men, were not afraid to admit that those men might make bad laws; might do, by law, the same things, and from the same motives, which if done by individuals without the sanction of law, would be called unjust. And hence the sentiment of injustice came to be attached, not to all violations of law, but only to violations of such laws as *ought* to exist, including such as ought to exist, but do not; and to laws themselves, if supposed to be contrary to what ought to be law. In this manner the idea of law and of its injunctions was still predominant in the notion of justice, even when the laws actually in force ceased to be accepted as the standard of it.

It is true that mankind consider the idea of justice and its obligations as applicable to many things which neither are, nor is it desired that they should be, regulated by law. Nobody desires that laws should interfere with the whole detail of private life; yet every one allows that in all daily conduct a person may and does show himself to be either just or unjust. But even here, the idea of the breach of what ought to be law, still lingers in a modified shape. It would always give us pleasure, and chime in with our feelings of fitness, that acts which we deem unjust should be punished, though we do not always think it expedient that this should be done by the tribunals. We forego that gratification on account of incidental inconveniences. We should be glad to see just conduct enforced and injustice repressed, even in the minutest details, if we were not, with reason, afraid of trusting the magistrate with so unlimited an amount of power over individuals. When we think that a person is bound in justice to do a thing, it is an ordinary form of language to say, that he ought to be compelled to do it. We should be gratified to see the obligation enforced by anybody who had the power. If we see that its enforcement by law would be inexpedient, we lament the impossibility, we consider the impunity given to injustice as an evil, and strive to make amends for it by bringing a strong expression of our own and the public disapprobation to bear upon the offender. Thus the idea of legal constraint is still the generating idea of the notion of justice, though undergoing several transformations before that notion, as it exists in an advanced state of society, becomes complete.

The above is, I think, a true account, as far as it goes, of the origin and progressive growth of the idea of justice. But we must observe, that it contains, as yet, nothing to distinguish that obligation from moral obligation in general. For the truth is, that the idea of penal sanction, which is the essence of law, enters not only into the conception of injustice, but into that of any kind of wrong. We do not call anything wrong, unless we mean to imply that a person ought to be punished in some way or other for doing it; if not by law, by the opinion of his fellowcreatures; if not by opinion, by the reproaches of his own conscience. This seems the real turning point of the distinction between morality and simple expediency. It is a part of the notion of Duty in every one of its forms, that a person may rightfully be compelled to fulfil it. Duty is a thing which may be *exacted* from a person, as one exacts a debt. Unless we think that it may be exacted from him, we do not call it his duty. Reasons of prudence, or the interest of other people, may militate against actually exacting it; but the person himself, it is clearly understood, would not be entitled to complain. There are other things, on the contrary, which we wish that

people should do, which we like or admire them for doing, perhaps dislike or despise them for not doing, but yet admit that they are not bound to do; it is not a case of moral obligation; we do not blame them, that is, we do not think that they are proper objects of punishment. How we come by these ideas of deserving and not deserving punishment, will appear, perhaps, in the sequel; but I think there is no doubt that this distinction lies at the bottom of the notions of right and wrong; that we call any conduct wrong, or employ, instead, some other term of dislike or disparagement, according as we think that the person ought, or ought not, to be punished for it; and we say, it would be right to do so and so, or merely that it would be desirable or laudable, according as we would wish to see the person whom it concerns, compelled, or only persuaded and exhorted, to act in that manner.[1]

This, therefore, being the characteristic difference which marks off, not justice, but morality in general, from the remaining provinces of Expediency and Worthiness; the character is still to be sought which distinguishes justice from other branches of morality. Now it is known that ethical writers divide moral duties into two classes, denoted by the ill-chosen expressions, duties of perfect and of imperfect obligation; the latter being those in which, though the act is obligatory, the particular occasions of performing it are left to our choice; as in the case of charity or beneficence, which we are indeed bound to practise, but not towards any definite person, nor at any prescribed time. In the more precise language of philosophic jurists, duties of perfect obligation are those duties in virtue of which a correlative *right* resides in some person or persons; duties of imperfect obligation are those moral obligations which do not give birth to any right. I think it will be found that this distinction exactly coincides with that which exists between justice and the other obligations of morality. In our survey of the various popular acceptations of justice, the term appeared generally to involve the idea of a personal right—a claim on the part of one or more individuals, like that which the law gives when it confers a proprietary or other legal right. Whether the injustice consists in de-

[1] See this point enforced and illustrated by Professor Bain, in an admirable chapter (entitled "The Ethical Emotions, or the Moral Sense"), of the second of the two treatises composing his elaborate and profound work on the Mind.

priving a person of a possession, or in breaking faith with him, or in treating him worse than he deserves, or worse than other people who have no greater claims, in each case the supposition implies two things—a wrong done, and some assignable person who is wronged. Injustice may also be done by treating a person better than others; but the wrong in this case is to his competitors, who are also assignable persons.

It seems to me that this feature in the case—a right in some person, correlative to the moral obligation—constitutes the specific difference between justice, and generosity or beneficence. Justice implies something which it is not only right to do, and wrong not to do, but which some individual person can claim from us as his moral right. No one has a moral right to our generosity or beneficence, because we are not morally bound to practise those virtues towards any given individual. And it will be found with respect to this as to every correct definition, that the instances which seem to conflict with it are those which most confirm it. For if a moralist attempts, as some have done, to make out that mankind generally, though not any given individual, have a right to all the good we can do them, he at once, by that thesis, includes generosity and beneficence within the category of justice. He is obliged to say, that our utmost exertions are *due* to our fellow creatures, thus assimilating them to a debt; or that nothing less can be a sufficient *return* for what society does for us, thus classing the case as one of gratitude; both of which are acknowledged cases of justice. Wherever there is a right, the case is one of justice, and not of the virtue of beneficence: and whoever does not place the distinction between justice and morality in general, where we have now placed it, will be found to make no distinction between them at all, but to merge all morality in justice.

Having thus endeavoured to determine the distinctive elements which enter into the composition of the idea of justice, we are ready to enter on the inquiry, whether the feeling, which accompanies the idea, is attached to it by a special dispensation of nature, or whether it could have grown up, by any known laws, out of the idea itself; and in particular, whether it can have originated in considerations of general expediency.

I conceive that the sentiment itself does not arise from anything which would commonly, or correctly, be termed an idea of expediency; but that though the sentiment does not, whatever is moral in it does.

We have seen that the two essential ingredients in the sentiment of justice are, the desire to punish a person who has done harm, and the knowledge or belief that there is some definite individual or individuals to whom harm has been done.

Now it appears to me, that the desire to punish a person who has done harm to some individual is a spontaneous outgrowth from two sentiments, both in the highest degree natural, and which either are or resemble instincts; the impulse of self-defence, and the feeling of sympathy.

It is natural to resent, and to repel or retaliate, any harm done or attempted against ourselves, or against those with whom we sympathise. The origin of this sentiment it is not necessary here to discuss. Whether it be an instinct or a result of intelligence, it is, we know, common to all animal nature; for every animal tries to hurt those who have hurt, or who it thinks are about to hurt, itself or its young. Human beings, on this point, only differ from other animals in two particulars. First, in being capable of sympathising, not solely with their offspring, or, like some of the more noble animals, with some superior animal who is kind to them, but with all human, and even with all sentient, beings. Secondly, in having a more developed intelligence, which gives a wider range to the whole of their sentiments, whether self-regarding or sympathetic. By virtue of his superior intelligence, even apart from his superior range of sympathy, a human being is capable of apprehending a community of interest between himself and the human society of which he forms a part, such that any conduct which threatens the security of the society generally, is threatening to his own, and calls forth his instinct (if instinct it be) of self-defence. The same superiority of intelligence, joined to the power of sympathising with human beings generally, enables him to attach himself to the collective idea of his tribe, his country, or mankind, in such a manner that any act hurtful to them, raises his instinct of sympathy, and urges him to resistance.

The sentiment of justice, in that one of its elements which consists of the desire to punish, is thus, I conceive, the natural feeling of retaliation or vengeance, rendered by intellect and sympathy applicable to those injuries, that is, to those hurts, which wound us through, or

in common with, society at large. This sentiment, in itself, has nothing moral in it; what
is moral is, the exclusive subordination of it
to the social sympathies, so as to wait on and
obey their call. For the natural feeling would
make us resent indiscriminately whatever any
one does that is disagreeable to us; but when
moralised by the social feeling, it only acts in
the directions conformable to the general
good: just persons resenting a hurt to society,
though not otherwise a hurt to themselves,
and not resenting a hurt to themselves, however painful, unless it be of the kind which society has a common interest with them in the
repression of.

It is no objection against this doctrine to
say, that when we feel our sentiment of justice
outraged, we are not thinking of society at
large, or of any collective interest, but only of
the individual case. It is common enough certainly, though the reverse of commendable,
to feel resentment merely because we have
suffered pain; but a person whose resentment
is really a moral feeling, that is, who considers
whether an act is blamable before he allows
himself to resent it—such a person, though he
may not say expressly to himself that he is
standing up for the interest of society, certainly
does feel that he is asserting a rule which is
for the benefit of others as well as for his own.
If he is not feeling this—if he is regarding the
act solely as it affects him individually—he is
not consciously just; he is not concerning himself about the justice of his actions. This is
admitted even by anti-utilitarian moralists.
When Kant (as before remarked) propounds
as the fundamental principle of morals, "So
act, that thy rule of conduct might be adopted
as a law by all rational beings," he virtually
acknowledges that the interest of mankind collectively, or at least of mankind indiscriminately, must be in the mind of the agent when
conscientiously deciding on the morality of
the act. Otherwise he uses words without a
meaning: for, that a rule even of utter selfishness could not *possibly* be adopted by all rational beings—that there is any insuperable
obstacle in the nature of things to its adoption—cannot be even plausibly maintained. To
give any meaning to Kant's principle, the sense
put upon it must be, that we ought to shape
our conduct by a rule which all rational beings
might adopt *with benefit to their collective interest.*

To recapitulate: the idea of justice supposes
two things; a rule of conduct, and a sentiment

which sanctions the rule. The first must be
supposed common to all mankind, and intended for their good. The other (the sentiment) is a desire that punishment may be suffered by those who infringe the rule. There is
involved, in addition, the conception of some
definite person who suffers by the infringement; whose rights (to use the expression appropriated to the case) are violated by it. And
the sentiment of justice appears to me to be,
the animal desire to repel or retaliate a hurt
or damage to oneself, or to those with whom
one sympathises, widened so as to include all
persons, by the human capacity of enlarged
sympathy, and the human conception of intelligent self-interest. From the latter elements,
the feeling derives its morality; from the
former, its peculiar impressiveness, and energy
of self-assertion.

I have, throughout, treated the idea of a
right residing in the injured person, and violated by the injury, not as a separate element
in the composition of the idea and sentiment,
but as one of the forms in which the other two
elements clothe themselves. These elements
are, a hurt to some assignable person or persons on the one hand, and a demand for punishment on the other. An examination of our
own minds, I think, will show, that these two
things include all that we mean when we speak
of violation of a right. When we call anything
a person's right, we mean that he has a valid
claim on society to protect him in the possession of it, either by the force of law, or by
that of education and opinion. If he has what
we consider a sufficient claim, on whatever
account, to have something guaranteed to him
by society, we say that he has a right to it. If
we desire to prove that anything does not belong to him by right, we think this done as
soon as it is admitted that society ought not to
take measures for securing it to him, but should
leave him to chance, or to his own exertions.
Thus, a person is said to have a right to what
he can earn in fair professional competition;
because society ought not to allow any other
person to hinder him from endeavouring to
earn in that manner as much as he can. But
he has not a right to three hundred a-year,
though he may happen to be earning it; because society is not called on to provide that
he shall earn that sum. On the contrary, if he
owns ten thousand pounds three per cent.
stock, he *has* a right to three hundred a-year;
because society has come under an obligation
to provide him with an income of that amount.

To have a right, then, is, I conceive, to have something which society ought to defend me in the possession of. If the objector goes on to ask, why it ought? I can give him no other reason than general utility. If that expression does not seem to convey a sufficient feeling of the strength of the obligation, nor to account for the peculiar energy of the feeling, it is because there goes to the composition of the sentiment, not a rational only, but also an animal element, the thirst for retaliation; and this thirst derives its intensity, as well as its moral justification, from the extraordinarily important and impressive kind of utility which is concerned. The interest involved is that of security, to every one's feelings the most vital of all interests. All other earthly benefits are needed by one person, not needed by another; and many of them can, if necessary, be cheerfully foregone, or replaced by something else; but security no human being can possibly do without; on it we depend for all our immunity from evil, and for the whole value of all and every good, beyond the passing moment; since nothing but the gratification of the instant could be of any worth to us, if we could be deprived of anything the next instant by whoever was momentarily stronger than ourselves. Now this most indispensable of all necessaries, after physical nutriment, cannot be had, unless the machinery for providing it is kept unintermittedly in active play. Our notion, therefore, of the claim we have on our fellow-creatures to join in making safe for us the very groundwork of our existence, gathers feelings around it so much more intense than those concerned in any of the more common cases of utility, that the difference in degree (as is often the case in psychology) becomes a real difference in kind. The claim assumes that character of absoluteness, that apparent infinity, and incommensurability with all other considerations, which constitute the distinction between the feeling of right and wrong and that of ordinary expediency and inexpediency. The feelings concerned are so powerful, and we count so positively on finding a responsive feeling in others (all being alike interested), that *ought* and *should* grow into *must,* and recognised indispensability becomes a moral necessity, analogous to physical, and often not inferior to it in binding force.

If the preceding analysis, or something resembling it, be not the correct account of the notion of justice; if justice be totally independent of utility, and be a standard *per se,* which the mind can recognise by simple introspection of itself; it is hard to understand why that internal oracle is so ambiguous, and why so many things appear either just or unjust, according to the light in which they are regarded.

We are continually informed that Utility is an uncertain standard, which every different person interprets differently, and that there is no safety but in the immutable, ineffaceable, and unmistakable dictates of Justice, which carry their evidence in themselves, and are independent of the fluctuations of opinion. One would suppose from this that on questions of justice there could be no controversy; that if we take that for our rule, its application to any given case could leave us in as little doubt as a mathematical demonstration. So far is this from being the fact, that there is as much difference of opinion, and as much discussion, about what is just, as about what is useful to society. Not only have different nations and individuals different notions of justice, but in the mind of one and the same individual, justice is not some one rule, principle, or maxim, but many, which do not always coincide in their dictates, and in choosing between which, he is guided either by some extraneous standard, or by his own personal predilections.

For instance, there are some who say, that it is unjust to punish any one for the sake of example to others; that punishment is just, only when intended for the good of the sufferer himself. Others maintain the extreme reverse, contending that to punish persons who have attained years of discretion, for their own benefit, is despotism and injustice, since if the matter at issue is solely their own good, no one has a right to control their own judgment of it; but that they may justly be punished to prevent evil to others, this being the exercise of the legitimate right of self-defence. Mr. Owen, again, affirms that it is unjust to punish at all; for the criminal did not make his own character; his education, and the circumstances which surrounded him, have made him a criminal, and for these he is not responsible. All these opinions are extremely plausible; and so long as the question is argued as one of justice simply, without going down to the principles which lie under justice and are the source of its authority, I am unable to see how any of these reasoners can be refuted. For in truth every one of the three builds upon rules of justice confessedly true. The first appeals to the acknowledged injustice of singling out an individual, and making him a sacrifice, without his consent, for other people's benefit. The second relies on the acknowledged justice of self-defence, and the admitted injustice of forcing one person to conform to another's notions of what constitutes his good. The Owenite invokes the admitted principle, that it is unjust to punish any one for what he cannot help. Each is triumphant so long as he is not compelled to take into consideration any other maxims of justice than the one he has selected; but as soon as their several maxims are brought face to face, each disputant seems to have exactly as much to say for himself as the others. No one of them can carry out his own notion of justice without trampling upon another equally binding.

These are difficulties; they have always been felt to be such; and many devices have been invented to turn rather than to overcome them. As a refuge from the last of the three, men imagined what they called the freedom of the will; fancying that they could not justify punishing a man whose will is in a thoroughly hateful state, unless it be supposed to have come into that state through no influence of anterior circumstances. To escape from the other difficulties, a favourite contrivance has been the fiction of a contract, whereby at some unknown period all the members of society engaged to obey the laws, and consented to be punished for any disobedience to them; thereby giving to their legislators the right, which it is assumed they would not otherwise have had, of punishing them, either for their own good or for that of society. This happy thought was considered to get rid of the whole difficulty, and to legitimate the infliction of punishment, in virtue of another received maxim of justice, *Volenti non fit injuria;* that is not unjust which is done with the consent of the person who is supposed to be hurt by it. I need hardly remark, that even if the consent were not a mere fiction, this maxim is not superior in authority to the others which it is brought in to supersede. It is, on the contrary, an instructive specimen of the loose and irregular manner in which supposed principles of justice grow up. This particular one evidently came into use as a help to the coarse exigencies of courts of law, which are sometimes obliged to be content with very uncertain presumptions, on account of the greater evils which would often arise from any attempt on their part to cut finer. But even courts of law are not able to adhere consistently to the maxim, for they allow voluntary engagements to be set aside on the ground of fraud, and sometimes on that of mere mistake or misinformation.

Again, when the legitimacy of inflicting punishment is admitted, how many conflicting conceptions of justice come to light in discussing the proper apportionment of punishments to offences. No rule on the subject recommends itself so strongly to the primitive and spontaneous sentiment of justice, as the *lex talionis,* an eye for an eye and a tooth for a tooth. Though this principle of the Jewish and of the Mahometan law has been generally abandoned in Europe as a practical maxim, there is, I suspect, in most minds, a secret hankering after it; and when retribution accidentally falls on an offender in that precise shape, the general feeling of satisfaction evinced bears witness how natural is the sentiment to which this repayment in kind is acceptable. With many, the test of justice in penal infliction is that the punishment should be proportioned to the offence; meaning that it should be exactly measured by the moral guilt of the culprit (whatever be their standard for measuring moral guilt): the consideration, what amount of punishment is necessary to deter from the offence, having nothing to do with the question of justice, in their estimation: while there are others to whom that consideration is all in all; who maintain that it is not just, at least for man, to inflict on a fellow-creature, whatever may be his offences, any amount of suffering beyond the least that will suffice to prevent him from repeating, and others from imitating, his misconduct.

To take another example from a subject already once referred to. In a co-operative industrial association, is it just or not that talent or skill should give a title to superior remuneration? On the negative side of the question it is argued, that whoever does the best he can, deserves equally well, and ought not in justice to be put in a position of inferiority for no fault of his own; that superior abilities have already advantages more than enough, in the admiration they excite, the personal influence they command, and the internal sources of satisfaction attending them, without adding to these a superior share of the world's goods; and that society is bound in justice rather to make compensation to the less favoured, for this unmerited inequality of advantages, than to aggravate it. On the contrary side it is contended, that society receives more from the more efficient labourer; that his services being more useful, society owes him a larger return for them; that a greater share of the joint result is actually his work, and not to allow his claim to it is a kind of robbery; that if he is only to receive as much as others, he can only be justly required to produce as much, and to give a smaller amount of time and exertion, proportioned to his superior efficiency. Who shall decide between these appeals to conflicting principles of justice? Justice has in this case two sides to it, which it is impossible to bring into harmony, and the two disputants have chosen opposite sides; the one looks to what it is just that the individual should receive, the other to what it is just that the community should give. Each, from his own point of view, is unanswerable; and any choice between them, on grounds of justice, must be perfectly arbitrary. Social utility alone can decide the preference.

How many, again, and how irreconcilable, are the standards of justice to which reference is made in discussing the repartition of taxation. One opinion is, that payment to the State should be in numerical proportion to pecuniary means. Others think that justice dictates what they term graduated taxation; taking a higher percentage from those who have more to spare. In point of natural justice a strong case might be made for disregarding means altogether, and taking the same absolute sum (whenever it could be got) from every one: as the subscribers to a mess, or to a club, all pay the same sum for the same privileges, whether they can all equally afford it or not. Since the protection (it might be said) of law and government is afforded to, and is equally required by all, there is no injustice in making all buy it at the same price. It is reckoned justice, not injustice, that a dealer should charge to all customers the same price for the same article, not a price varying according to their means of payment. This doctrine, as applied to taxation, finds no advocates, because it conflicts so strongly with man's feelings of humanity and of social expediency; but the principle of justice which it invokes is as true and as binding as those which can be appealed to against it. Accordingly it exerts a tacit influence on the line of defence employed for other modes of assessing taxation. People feel obliged to argue that the State does more for the rich than for the poor, as a justification for its taking more from them: though this is in reality not true, for the rich would be far better able to protect themselves, in the absence of law or government, than the poor, and indeed would probably be successful in converting the poor into their slaves. Others, again, so far defer to the same conception of justice, as to maintain that all should pay an equal capitation tax for the protection of their persons (these being of equal value to all), and an unequal tax for the protection of their property, which is unequal. To this others reply, that the all of one man is as valuable to him as the all of another. From these confusions there is no other mode of extrication than the utilitarian.

Is, then, the difference between the Just and the Expedient a merely imaginary distinction? Have mankind been under a delusion in thinking that justice is a more sacred thing than policy, and that the latter ought only to be listened to after the former has been satisfied? By no means. The exposition we have given of the nature and origin of the sentiment, recognises a real distinction; and no one of those who profess the most sublime contempt for the consequences of actions as an element in their morality, attaches more importance to the distinction than I do. While I dispute the pretensions of any theory which sets up an imaginary standard of justice not grounded on utility, I account the justice which is grounded on utility to be the chief part, and incomparably the most sacred and binding part, of all morality. Justice is a name for certain classes of moral rules, which concern the essentials of human well-being more nearly, and are therefore of more absolute obligation, than any other rules for the guidance of life; and the notion which we have found to be of the essence of the idea of justice, that of a right residing in an individual, implies and testifies to this more binding obligation.

The moral rules which forbid mankind to hurt one another (in which we must never forget to include wrongful interference with each other's freedom) are more vital to human well-being than any maxims, however important, which only point out the best mode of managing some department of human affairs. They have also the peculiarity, that they are the main element in determining the whole of the social feelings of mankind. It is their observance which alone preserves peace among human beings: if obedience to them were not the rule, and disobedience the exception, every one would see in every one else an enemy, against whom he must be perpetually guarding himself. What is hardly less important, these are the precepts which mankind have the strongest and the most direct inducements for impressing upon one another. By merely giving to each other prudential instruction or exhortation, they may gain, or think they gain, nothing: in inculcating on each other the duty of positive beneficence they have an unmistakable interest, but far less in degree: a person may possibly not need the benefits of others; but he always needs that they should not do him hurt. Thus the moralities which protect every individual from being harmed by others, either directly or by being hindered in his freedom of pursuing his own good, are at once those which he himself has most at heart, and those which he has the strongest interest in publishing and enforcing by word and deed. It is by a person's observance of these that his fitness to exist as one of the fellowship of human beings is tested and decided; for on that depends his being a nuisance or not to those with whom he is in contact. Now it is these moralities primarily which compose the obligations of justice. The most marked cases of injustice, and those which give the tone to the feeling of repugnance which characterises the sentiment, are acts of wrongful aggression, or wrongful exercise of power over some one; the next are those which consist in wrongfully withholding from him something which is his due; in both cases, inflicting on him a positive hurt, either in the form of direct suffering, or of the privation of some good which he had reasonable ground, either of a physical or of a social kind, for counting upon.

The same powerful motives which command the observance of these primary moralities, enjoin the punishment of those who violate them; and as the impulses of self-defence, of defence of others, and of vengeance, are all called forth against such persons, retribution, or evil for evil, becomes closely connected with the sentiment of justice, and is universally included in the idea. Good for good is also one of the dictates of justice; and this, though its social utility is evident, and though it carries with it a natural human feeling, has not at first sight that obvious connection with hurt or injury, which, existing in the most elementary cases of just and unjust, is the source of the characteristic intensity of the sentiment. But the connection, though less obvious, is not less real. He who accepts benefits, and denies a return of them when needed, inflicts a real hurt, by disappointing one of the most natural and reasonable of expectations, and one which he must at least tacitly have encouraged, otherwise the benefits would seldom have been conferred. The important rank, among human evils and wrongs, of the disappointment of expectation, is shown in the fact that it constitutes the principal criminality of two such highly immoral acts as a breach of friendship and a breach of promise. Few hurts which human beings can sustain are greater, and none wound more, than when that on which they habitually and with full assurance relied, fails them in the hour of need; and few wrongs are greater than this mere withholding of good; none excite more resentment, either in the person suffering, or in a sympathising spectator. The principle, therefore, of giving to each what they deserve, that is, good for good as well as evil for evil, is not only included within the idea of Justice as we have defined it, but is a proper object of that intensity of sentiment, which places the Just, in human estimation, above the simply Expedient.

Most of the maxims of justice current in the world, and commonly appealed to in its transactions, are simply instrumental to carrying into effect the principles of justice which we have now spoken of. That a person is only responsible for what he has done voluntarily, or could voluntarily have avoided; that it is unjust to condemn any person unheard; that the punishment ought to be proportioned to the offence, and the like, are maxims intended to prevent the just principle of evil for evil from being perverted to the infliction of evil without that justification. The greater part of these common maxims have come into use from the practice of courts of justice, which have been naturally led to a more complete recognition and elaboration than was likely to suggest itself to others, of the rules necessary to enable them to fulfil their double function, of inflicting punishment when due, and of awarding to each person his right.

That first of judicial virtues, impartiality, is an obligation of justice, partly for the reason last mentioned; as being a necessary condition of the fulfilment of the other obligations of justice. But this is not the only source of the exalted rank, among human obligations, of those maxims of equality and impartiality, which, both in popular estimation and in that of the most enlightened, are included among the precepts of justice. In one point of view, they may be considered as corollaries from the principles already laid down. If it is a duty to do to each according to his deserts, returning good for good as well as repressing evil by evil, it necessarily follows that we should treat all equally well (when no higher duty forbids) who have deserved equally well of *us*, and that society should treat all equally well who have deserved equally well of *it*, that is, who have deserved equally well absolutely. This is the highest abstract standard of social and distributive justice; towards which all institutions, and the efforts of all virtuous citizens, should be made in the utmost possible degree to converge.

But this great moral duty rests upon a still deeper foundation, being a direct emanation from the first principle of morals, and not a mere logical corollary from secondary or derivative doctrines. It is involved in the very meaning of Utility, or the Greatest Happiness Principle. That principle is a mere form of words without rational signification, unless one person's happiness, supposed equal in degree (with the proper allowance made for kind), is counted for exactly as much as another's. Those conditions being supplied, Bentham's dictum, "everybody to count for one, nobody for more than one," might be written under the principle of utility as an explanatory commentary.[1] The equal claim of every-

---

[1] This implication, in the first principle of the utilitarian scheme, of perfect impartiality between persons, is regarded by Mr. Herbert Spencer (in his *Social Statics*) as a disproof of the pretensions of utility to be a sufficient guide to right; since (he says) the principle of utility presupposes the anterior principle, that everybody has an equal right to happiness. It may be more correctly described as supposing that equal amounts of happiness are equally desirable, whether felt by the same or by different persons. This, however, is not a *pre*-supposition; not a premise needful to support the principle of utility, but the very principle itself; for what is the principle of utility, if it be not that "happiness" and "desirable" are synonymous terms? If there is any anterior principle implied, it can be no other than this, that the truths of arithmetic are applicable to the valuation of happiness, as of all other measurable quantities.
[Mr. Herbert Spencer, in a private communication on the subject of the preceding Note, objects to being considered an opponent of utilitarianism, and states that he regards happiness as the ultimate end of morality; but deems that end only partially attainable by empirical generalisations from the observed results of conduct, and completely attainable only by deducing, from the laws of life and the conditions of existence, what kinds of action necessarily tend to produce happiness, and what kinds to produce unhappiness. With the

body to happiness in the estimation of the moralist and of the legislator, involves an equal claim to all the means of happiness, except in so far as the inevitable conditions of human life, and the general interest, in which that of every individual is included, set limits to the maxim; and those limits ought to be strictly construed. As every other maxim of justice, so this is by no means applied or held applicable universally; on the contrary, as I have already remarked, it bends to every person's ideas of social expediency. But in whatever case it is deemed applicable at all, it is held to be the dictate of justice. All persons are deemed to have a *right* to equality of treatment, except when some recognised social expediency requires the reverse. And hence all social inequalities which have ceased to be considered expedient, assume the character not of simple inexpediency, but of injustice, and appear so tyrannical, that people are apt to wonder how they ever could have been tolerated; forgetful that they themselves perhaps tolerate other inequalities under an equally mistaken notion of expediency, the correction of which would make that which they approve seem quite as monstrous as what they have at last learnt to condemn. The entire history of social improvement has been a series of transitions, by which one custom or institution after another, from being a supposed primary necessity of social existence, has passed into the rank of a universally stigmatised injustice and tyranny. So it has been with the distinctions of slaves and freemen, nobles and serfs, patricians and plebeians; and so it will be, and in part already is, with the aristocracies of colour, race, and sex.

---

exception of the word "necessarily," I have no dissent to express from this doctrine; and (omitting that word) I am not aware that any modern advocate of utilitarianism is of a different opinion. Bentham, certainly, to whom in the *Social Statics* Mr. Spencer particularly referred, is, least of all writers, chargeable with unwillingness to deduce the effect of actions on happiness from the laws of human nature and the universal conditions of human life. The common charge against him is of relying too exclusively upon such deductions, and declining altogether to be bound by the generalisations from specific experience which Mr. Spencer thinks that utilitarians generally confine themselves to. My own opinion (and, as I collect, Mr. Spencer's) is, that in ethics, as in all other branches of scientific study, the consilience of the results of both these processes, each corroborating and verifying the other, is requisite to give to any general proposition the kind and degree of evidence which constitutes scientific proof.]

It appears from what has been said, that justice is a name for certain moral requirements, which, regarded collectively, stand higher in the scale of social utility, and are therefore of more paramount obligation, than any others; though particular cases may occur in which some other social duty is so important, as to overrule any one of the general maxims of justice. Thus, to save a life, it may not only be allowable, but a duty, to steal, or take by force, the necessary food or medicine, or to kidnap, and compel to officiate, the only qualified medical practitioner. In such cases, as we do not call anything justice which is not a virtue, we usually say, not that justice must give way to some other moral principle, but that what is just in ordinary cases is, by reason of that other principle, not just in the particular case. By this useful accommodation of language, the character of indefeasibility attributed to justice is kept up, and we are saved from the necessity of maintaining that there can be laudable injustice.

The considerations which have now been adduced resolve, I conceive, the only real difficulty in the utilitarian theory of morals. It has always been evident that all cases of justice are also cases of expediency: the difference is in the peculiar sentiment which attaches to the former, as contradistinguished from the latter. If this characteristic sentiment has been sufficiently accounted for; if there is no necessity to assume for it any peculiarity of origin; if it is simply the natural feeling of resentment, moralised by being made coextensive with the demands of social good; and if this feeling not only does but ought to exist in all the classes of cases to which the idea of justice corresponds; that idea no longer presents itself as a stumbling-block to the utilitarian ethics.

Justice remains the appropriate name for certain social utilities which are vastly more important, and therefore more absolute and imperative, than any others are as a class (though not more so than others may be in particular cases); and which, therefore, ought to be, as well as naturally are, guarded by a sentiment not only different in degree, but also in kind; distinguished from the milder feeling which attaches to the mere idea of promoting human pleasure or convenience, at once by the more definite nature of its commands, and by the sterner character of its sanctions.

THE GREAT IDEAS, *Volumes 2 and 3*